THE CUBAN INSURRECTION, 1952–1959

THE CUBAN INSURRECTION, 1952–1959

RAMÓN L. BONACHEA
AND MARTA SAN MARTIN

Transaction Publishers
New Brunswick (U.S.A.) and London (U.K.)

Library of Congress Catalog Number: 72-94546
ISBN: 978-0-87855-074-6 (hardcover); 978-0-87855-576-5 (paperback)
eBook: 978-1-4128-2090-5
Printed in the United States of America

To the memory of
JOSE ANTONIO ECHEVERRÍA
and
FRANK ISAAC PAIS

Contents

Preface   xi
   Major Historical Events 1868-1952   xiv
   Political Institutions and Insurrectionary Organizations xv

Introduction   1

1   The Moncada Attack   9
   The Road to Action   12
   The Moncada Barracks   15
   The Capture of Fidel Castro   19
   Public Opinion and the Trial   21
   Fidel Castro's Defense   24

2   Elections and Amnesty   33
   The *Forrajeo*   35
   General Amnesty   37
   The Search for a Movement   39
   Frank País   41

3   The Student Movement   47
   Batista and the Students   48
   José Antonio Echeverría   50
   Santa Marta and Lindero   52
   The Directorio Revolucionario   54
   Ideology of the DR   56
   Student Demonstration: A New Escalation   57
   The Sugar Workers' Strike and the DR   60

4   Prologue to Insurrection   69
   The Exiles   72
   Heroes or Martyrs   72
   "Che" Guevara   74
   The Pact of Mexico   76
   Creating the Conditions   79

5	The Making of the Guerrillas	87
	Conditions in Cuba	87
	A Matter of Arms	87
	The Santiago Uprising	90
	Conditions in Havana	93
	Fidel Castro: Disaster and Recovery	94
	Initial Setback and Regrouping	98
	The Assault on La Plata	98
	Treason and a New Beginning	99
	Reinforcements from the Cities	101
	The Battle of El Uvero	104
	Estrada Palma, Bueycito, Pino del Agua	104
	Organization of the Regular Army	105
	Pino del Agua II	106
	Elements of the Mystique	108
6	The Palace Attack	119
	The Strategy	121
	The Attack	125
	Aftermath	131
	The Executive Council Meets	133
	Humboldt 7	138
	Praises to Batista	141
7	Challenge and Repression	149
	The Death of Frank País	152
	The Cienfuegos Uprising	160
8	Ideology and Politics	173
	M-26-7: Its Ideology	173
	The Tampa Declaration	179
	Junta de Liberación Cubana	180
	Castro versus Chomón	183
9	A New Strategy	193
	The DR's Decision to Fight Guerrilla War	195
	The Expedition	196
	The Manifesto of Escambray	198
	The DR Guerrilla Front	200
	Internal Division	203
	The Second Front of Escambray	204
	The Second Front, "Frank País" in Oriente Province	205
	Structural Organization	210

10	The Frustrated Strike: April 9, 1958	221
	Prelude: U.S. Arms Embargo	221
	Genesis of the Strike	223
	The Pérez-Ray Interview	229
	Objections to the Strike	231
	The Call to Strike	233
	The Meeting at Altos de Mompié	236
	The May Report	238
	A New Alignment: The Communists	240
	The New Reality	242
	The Aftermath	243
11	The Summer Offensive	253
	Military Plans	256
	Problems of Command	257
	The Offensive	258
	First Move: The Army	259
	Santo Domingo	261
	Unity of the Insurrectional Sector	262
	The Pact of Caracas	264
	Attack: An Intrepid Maneuver	265
	Confidencial Report	271
	Operation "N"	274
	The Battle of Las Mercedes	275
	Regular Army: Summer Offensive	279
	Progressive Disintegration of the Armed Forces	283
12	The Westward March	293
	Guevara, Chomón and Menoyo	304
	Guevara and Oltusky	307
13	The Last Battle	315
	November Farce	316
	The Strategy	321
	The Battle	321
	The Armored Train	325
	The Fall of Santa Clara	326
14	The Final Decision: Batista Leaves	333
	The Castro-Cantillo Meeting	337
	Batista and Cantillo Meet	338
	Plots and Counterplots	339
	The Last Decision	340

Departure 341
Now What Do We Do, General? 342
The Underground Acts 344

15 The Perils of Counterrevolution 351
Castro Reacts 351
The Mirage of Power 354
The Revolution 360

Appendices 365

1 Leadership Positions Held by Militants of the Insurrection
in the Cuban Revolutionary Government (1972–1973) 365

2 Major Events of the Urban Insurrection 1952–1959 371

3 Guerrilla Actions against the Regular Army, December 2,
1956-December 31, 1958 378

4 Population in Selected Cities 380

5 Density and Distribution of Population by Province
1953–1958 382

Bibliography 383

Index 415

Preface

For several years now, the authors have felt that no meaningful understanding of the Cuban Revolution can be obtained without exhaustive research into the political-military factors that led to the victory of the insurrection. Our interest in the 1952-59 period sprang from intellectual rebelliousness; we wanted to challenge what we felt had become a maze of ill-founded premises about the social, military and political genesis of the Cuban revolutionary process. We believed that a legitimate beginning to any study of this period would require us to unearth the names of men and women whose ideas and actions, oddly fallen into an aura of anonymity, had been central to the nature and direction of the struggle. Thus, this book has been written from the point of view of the Cuban insurrectionists.

Research for this work is based as much as possible on primary sources. Important gaps would have remained had it not been for the enthusiastic cooperation of hundreds of people, many of whom were actors in the struggle. Through the facilities of a community action agency located in the heart of a Cuban exile community, the authors were able to establish fruitful relationships with Cubans from all walks of life. We found that these persons were eager not only to share their part in the events but to supply the authors with letters, documents and names of persons for corroboration of their information. The fact that a good number of the people we interviewed were militants or participants but not leaders of the various struggling sectors adds a satisfactory measure of history from the point of view of the individual insurrectionist, former regular army soldier, rural guard, supporter of Batista, 26 of July member or member of the Directorio Revolucionario (DR).

These data were added to the personal experiences of one of the authors (Ramón L. Bonachea), who was a direct participant in several of the events described, as well as a member of a DR cell. In this capacity, he had the privilege of interviewing most of the leaders of the insurrection while in Cuba, and of visiting the sites of the main events—Sierra Maestra, Sierra Cristal, Escambray, Cienfuegos, Sagua la Grande and others. At the suggestion of Major Ernesto "Che" Guevara, one of us prepared a series of reports analyzing guerrilla warfare in Cuba in February 1959, which also proved useful in preparing this book.

Additionally, the authors have relied on abundant use of secondary sources, including material that the Cuban revolutionary government has published during the last 15 years. This material complemented the data obtained by the authors through personal interviews and letters from former militants. No small amount of rigorous assessment was needed to separate the obvious from the trivial and hagiography from historical facts.

We owe special thanks to the family of José Antonio Echeverría who placed at our disposal the private documents of the DR leader and participated in what amounted to their first public interview. Dora Rosales Westbrook shared many hours reminiscing about the political philosophy of her son. Joe Westbrook, and discussing the participation of many of his *compañeros* in the formation of the DR. Ricardo ("Popi") Corpión was kind enough to review point by point the historical Pact of Mexico between the DR and the 26th of July movement, to which he and Fidel Castro are the only living witnesses. Ricardo Bianchi and Sra. Bianchi shed light on the Auténtico cooperation with the DR, the events surrounding the Humboldt 7 episode, as well as on the preparations for the Palace attack and various other actions. Félix A. Murias, Armando Fleites, Adalberto Mora, Julio Fernández, Roger González and other DR members were extremely kind in revealing important sequences to the authors.

Raúl Chibás, Mario Llerena and Manuel Urrutia Lleó greatly enhanced the sections of the book pertaining to the ideology and formation of the provisional revolutionary government. We were privileged to make special use of Dr. Llerena's candid manuscript without which we would have been unable to reconstruct the internal structure of the Dirección Nacional.

Former members of the 26th of July movement were equally helpful. Of special importance for the authors was their acquaintance with the men and women who fought side by side with Frank País. They were not only helpful but extremely patient and kind in answering our queries about Frank, his movement and role during the insurrection. Above all, the authors feel a special gratitude toward Agustín País, whose courage, candidness and simplicity gave the authors a measure of what Frank, his brother, must have been like.

Thanks are also due to Carlos Prío Socarrás, Carlos Márquez Sterling, Eusebio Mujal Barniol, Manuel Antonio de Varona and Antonio ("Tony") Santiago for clarifying events in which they participated. Enrique Pizzi de Porras, from the staff of *El Tiempo* newspaper, availed the authors of the opportunity to examine Fulgencio Batista's answers to some specific questions concerning the last days of December 1958.

For assistance in formulating our analysis of events in the military sector we must express our appreciation to many guerrilla fighters and soldiers of the regular army. Many front-line guerrilla fighters provided a most objective account of the guerrilla campaign and their names are duly recorded in the text. Among the officers of the regular army, we are indebted to General Eulogio Cantillo who broke his long silence to discuss with us his personal role in the insurrection, and allowed us access to his private documents and correspondence. Colonel Nelson Carrasco Artíles, active in the Sierra Maestra campaign, wounded in battle and prisoner of the Rebel Army until 1959, was very helpful in sharing articles and letters about the regular army. Colonel Fernando Neugart described to us his experiences as the government's negotiator in special talks with Fidel Castro during the summer offensive of 1958. This was also the first interview granted by the colonel since 1959. Captain Abon Ly spent many hours with the authors describing the battle of Yaguajay as well as giving his own impression of guerrilla leader Major Camilo Cienfuegos. Colonel Merob Sosa was interviewed on his role during the early stages of the Sierra Maestra campaign. He corroborated the legitimacy of military communiques published by the Cuban revolutionary government, and gave his version of the government's "preventive" measures against the Oriente peasants.

Rev. Cecilio Arrastía and Rev. Sergio Manejías described the participation of the Protestant churches and members during the struggle. Manuel Ray helped reconstruct the sequences leading to the frustrated April 9, 1958 general revolutionary strike. Luis Chaviano Reyes was instrumental in reviewing for the authors the details surrounding the Santo Domingo expedition. Rural teacher, René M. Romero provided the authors with a map of the Escambray guerrilla fronts that enabled us to locate battle sites, geo-political divisions of the territory and numerical strength of the 26th of July and DR forces.

Finally, we must thank Hugo García Barnet for sharing his artistic talents in drafting the maps accompanying this book. Thanks are also due to the López family for their enthusiastic support in urging the authors not to dismay while researching this work, and for caring for Ramón Jr. while his parents were busy typing, interviewing and travelling back and forth. Mary E. Curtis and Frances Shuman have our heartfelt gratitude for their forbearance and analytical insight. The authors deeply appreciate Professor Irving Louis Horowitz's encouraging and relentless moral support for this book. Any errors of judgment, interpretations or intellectual gaps are solely the responsibility of the authors.

Major Historical Events 1868-1952

1868-78	Ten Year War against Spain.
1895	War of Independence begins.
1898	The United States declares war on Spain; the Treaty of Paris is signed and Cuba remains under U.S. protection.
1901	Platt Amendment is attached to the Cuban Constitution granting the United States the right to intervene.
1906-09	Internal uprising and second U.S. intervention.
1912	Partido Independiente de Color leads an uprising; massacre of Negros by the Rural Guard and the army.
1917	Internal uprising; U.S. troops land to protect the government from rebels protesting against electoral frauds.
1922	University reform movement begins after visit of José Arce, rector of the University of Buenos Aires. The Directorio de la Federación de Estudiantes (FEU) is organized with Felio Marinello, president; Julio Antonio Mella, secretary.
1923	Group of young intellectuals signs the *protesta de los 13,* calling for rejection of fraudulent governments.
1925	Gerardo Machado is elected president. Julio A. Mella forms the Anti-Imperialist League; the Cuban Communist Party (CCP) is organized, and Mella is expelled from Havana University.
1927	Machado attempts reform of the Constitution extending his period: student protest leads to the organization of the Directorio Estudiantil Universitario (DEU).
1929	Mella assassinated while in exile in Mexico.
1930	Bloody student demonstrations; organization of the DEU of 1930.
1931	Expedition led by Sergio Carbó and others land at Gibara, Oriente province: Antonio "Tony" Guiteras supports a frustrated uprising. Organization of the ABC terrorist movement led by Joaquín Martínez Sáenz.
1933	U.S. Ambassador Benjamin Sumner Welles attempts to mediate between dictatorship and revolutionaries; localized strike begins on August 6, spreads into a spontaneous general strike; by August 11, the army demands Machado's resignation, and the dictator abandons power on August 12. On September 4, 1933 Sergeant Fulgencio Batista y Zaldívar leads revolt and is backed by civilian revolutionaries. Revolutionary Government of Dr. Ramón Grau San Martín is not recognized by the United States.
1934	Batista's coup d'etat against the revolutionary government; the deposed revolutionaries form the Partido Revolucionario Cubano-Auténtico.

1934-40	Batista rules the country; attempts at insurrection fail throughout period, and the opposition compromises with the Constitution of 1940 as a result.
1940-44	Batista elected president; Juan Marinello and Carlos Rafael Rodríguez appointed members of Batista's cabinet.
1943	Manolo Castro elected president of the FEU.
1944-48	Ramón Grau San Martín elected president as candidate of the Auténticos.
1948	Jesús Menéndez, labor leader, and Manolo Castro are assassinated. Carlos Prío Socarrás is elected president as candidate of the Auténticos.
1949	In a student meeting, Carlos Rodríguez, a worker, is beaten to death by police lieutenant Rafael Salas Cañizares; Fidel Castro acts as lawyer for Rodríguez's family.
1952	Fulgencio Batista y Zaldivar leads a coup d'etat against President Carlos Prío Socarrás, 81 days before general elections are scheduled. Rafael Salas Cañizares is promoted to the rank of Brigadier General, and appointed chief of police; General Francisco Tabernilla, Sr. is appointed chief of the army. Batista cancels the elections and appoints himself chief of state, prime minister and commander-in-chief of the armed forces.

Political Institutions and Insurrectionary Organizations

AAA (Triple A)	Founded in 1952 by Aureliano Sánchez Arango. A clandestine orga nization against Batista financed by Carlos Prío Socarrás.
ABC	Founded in 1931 by Joaquín Martínez Saénz and Carlos Saladrigas. At first, an anti-Machado terrorist organization that later became a party.
AM	Agrupación Montecristi, Founded in 1952 and led by Justo Carrillo as an underground organization against Batista.
AIE	Ala Izquierda Estudiantil. A Marxist organization led by Aureliano Sánchez Arango in 1930; a splinter group from the DEU.
AL	Accion Libertadora. Founded in 1952 after Batista's coup; as an underground organization most active in Oriente where it was led by Raúl del Mazo.
ANR	Acción Nacional Revolucionaria. ARO became ANR when from 1954–55 it recruited members from other provinces. Also founded by Frank País and Pepito Tey.
ARO	Acción Revolucionaria Oriental. Founded in 1953 by Frank País and Pepito Tey as an underground organization against Batista.
CTC	Confederación de Trabajadores de Cuba. Founded in 1939. In the 1950s it was led by Eusebio Mujal Barniól.

DEU   Directorio Estudiantil Universitario. Founded in 1930; an anti-Machado organization led by Carlos Prío Socarrás, Ramiro Valdés Daussá and Rubén de León.

DR   Directorio Revolucionario. Founded in 1955 by José Antonio Echeverría as the students' insurrectionary instrument to depose Fulgencio Batista.

DR   3-13 Directorio Revolucionario 13 de Marzo. Name adopted by Faure Chomón and Rolando Cubelas to designate the DR guerrillas in the Escambray.

FEAP   Federación de Escuelas y Academias Privadas. Founded in 1955 by Joe Westbrook and Ramón Rodríguez to organize secondary education students under the aegis of the FEU.

FEU   Federación Estudiantil Universitaria. Founded in 1923 by Julio Antonio Mella as the instrument of Havana University's students to channel changes in the educational system. In 1955, it was led by José Antonio Echeverría.

FON   Frente Obrero Nacional. Founded by Frank País in 1957 to mobilize the working class for the general revolutionary strike.

JC   Joven Cuba, Founded in 1934 by Antonio ("Tony") Guiteras; an anti-Batista underground organization that believed in armed insurrection.

JS   Juventud Socialista. The youth section of the PSP led by General-Secretary Raúl Valdés Vivó, Antonio Carcedo, Alfredo Font and Amparo Chaple among others.

M-26-7   Movimiento 26 de Julio. Founded in 1955 by Fidel Castro and members of the ANR, Young Ortodoxos, and MNR groups.

MLR   Movimiento de Liberación Radical. Founded in the mid-1950s by Andrés Valdespino as a political party seeking a peaceful solution to Cuba's problems.

MNR   Movimiento Nacionalista Revolucionario. Founded in 1952 and led by Professor Rafael García Bárcena.

MRS   Movimiento de Resistencia Cívica. Founded in 1957 by Frank País as an instrument of the M-26-7 to mobilize professional sectors. It was led by Angel Santos Buch, Faustino Pérez and Manuel Ray.

MSR   Movimiento Socialista Revolucionario. An anti-Communist terrorist organization led by Rolando Masferrer, veteran of the Spanish Civil War and former member of the Cuban Communist Party.

OA   Organización Auténtica. A clandestine organization founded by Carlos Prío Socarrás in 1934 to wage urban warfare against the puppet governments of Fulgencio Batista. In the 1950s its action and sabotage section was led by Menelao Mora Morales until 1955 and financed by Prío.

PAU   Partido Acción Unitaria. Fulgencio Batista's political party in 1951.
PPC-O   Partido del Pueblo Cubano (Ortodoxo). A splinter party from the
            PRC-A; founded in 1947 by Eduardo R. Chibás.
PSP   Partido Socialista Popular or Communist Party. Founded by Julio
            Antonio Mella in 1925. In the 1950s it was led by Blas Roca, Juan
            Marinello, Aníbal Escalante, Severo Aguirre and others.
PRC-A   Partido Revolucionario Cubano (Auténtico). Founded in 1934 by
            members of JC, DEU, AIE and individuals such as Rubén de León,
            Carlos Prío Socarrás and Manuel Antonio de Varona. Ramón Grau
            San Martín was its president.
SAR   Sociedad de Amigos de la República. Founded in 1954 by Cosme
            de la Torriente, a veteran from the Independence Wars, to seek a
            peaceful solution to the Cuban political situation.
UIR   Unión Insurreccional Revolucionaria. A terrorist organization
            created in the mid-1940s involved in gang warfare and led by
            Emilio Tró.

THE CUBAN INSURRECTION, 1952–1959

Introduction

The coup d'etat was successful. Within mere hours, on March 10, 1952, General Fulgencio Batista y Zaldívar overthrew the constitutional government of President Carlos Prío Socarrás, which had been in power since 1948. Confronted with the military coup, elected officials decided to flee rather than fight, while the national oligarchy rejoiced at the return to power of a tyrant who promised an era of "law and order." Labor leaders hurried to make common cause with the military caudillo; politicians offered him their services hoping to partake in the spoils of power; the Cuban people, unable to resist the emerging dictatorship, stood as mute witnesses to the events; and the nation's political institutions did not challenge what the army decisively supported. Predictably, the United States and the Latin American governments extended recognition to the de facto regime. An era of national complacency had ended. In Cuba, only the students strongly protested the violation of the Constitution of 1940 and the return to a praetorian military government.

The effect of Batista's coup was threefold: First, it demonstrated that as long as the traditional regular army existed, no constitutional order was safe from eventual destruction. The regular army was Batista's army. He had restructured it in 1933, appointed his loyal collaborators to key positions and instilled in the troops a sense of patrimony over the destiny of the nation. The regular troops saw Batista as the *man* who had led them out of anonymity and poverty to the highest political echelons. Second, the political parties, and especially the Partido Revolucionario Cubano-Auténtico (PRC-A), had failed to transform the army into an institution at the service of the constitutionally established order. Complacently, the Auténticos emphasized that there had been continuous electoral processes since 1940, shrugging off the possibility of a military coup. Finally, the Auténtico party structure was inefficient; it failed to aggregate a new generation of Cubans eager to engage in politics. Unlike the Auténticos, the Partido del Pueblo Cubano-Ortodoxo (PPC-O) boasted a dynamic youth section. It was, however, completely powerless; the Ortodoxos were controlled by old politicians primarily concerned with inner-party disputes against the Auténticos, of which they were an offshoot. These political institutions were robbed of whatever political vitality they had by the March 10 coup d'etat.

The challenge posed by Batista was answered by the young people in seven years of unprecedented organized violence. The authors have no quarrel with Major Ernesto "Che" Guevara's apt conceptualization that an insurrection is the period of "armed struggle," and revolution the period of "social, economic and political transformations." Hence, the concept of insurrection is applied throughout the text as the process of violent resistance against what was perceived by the insurrectionists as an illegitimate order. Resistance becomes organized acts of violence through urban and rural warfare, climaxing in a widespread civil war. Thus, the thrust of this study is to survey the political and military aspects of the insurrection that led to the defeat of the regular army, and the extraordinary victory of the insurrectionists on January 1, 1959.

The Cuban insurrection was led by a new generation of Cubans whose ideological tenets seemed to have departed little from the ideals of the frustrated revolution of 1933. The political generation of 1950 was more determined than the previous generation to wage violence until they achieved their ultimate objective: to overthrow Fulgencio Batista by force. Thus, the victory over Batista was a military one in the urban and rural battlefields, and not—as it may seem—a voluntary withdrawal from power by the tyrant. Because of the duration of the struggle, the methods of violence applied by both sides and the political unsophistication of the insurrectionary leaders, no philosophical program emerged that deserves to be called an ideology. Yet the text includes discussions over the relevant manifestos written throughout the struggle. These were not so much blueprints for the future revolutionary government, as they were guidelines fostered by the complexities of the war that was waged.

Inconsistencies aside, by and large the *leit motif* of the insurrection evolved around—and was prompted by—the rupture of the constitutional order. Central to all the manifestos was the issue of restoring the Constitution of 1940, holding general elections after Batista's overthrow, overhauling the country's economy by revising its dependent status, reorganizing the civil service system, carrying out a functional agrarian reform and achieving full political sovereignty at home and abroad. These aspirations were already embodied in the law of the land but had not constituted concrete policies of Cuban governments. They had been ignored or brushed aside, but those who became personally involved in the insurrection unquestionably cherished these goals. Those who remained aloof from the struggle but wanted a return to constitutional order simply expected to have the governing civilian-military elite replaced by another group professing exclusively civilian-oriented goals. This expectation was soon to collide with the objectives of the fighting youth who, as the struggle became radicalized, came to despise the very social, political and economic institutions in which they had grown up.

Cuban insurrectionists borrowed no model from abroad to carry out their fight against the dictatorship. In fact, Cuban history afforded rich experience both in the organization of insurrectionary groups and in the application of violence. The Wars of Independence had been fought in a guerrilla fashion that prompted contempt from British and Spanish officers. The 1933 revolution had provided examples of general strikes, sabotage and terrorism. The ensuing violence of the action groups (1944-1948) had given ample proof of how lives were wasted in the pursuit of internecine disputes. Above all, the action groups had shown how alienated a generation of former revolutionaries had become in a closed-system society such as Cuba's. The lessons drawn from the action groups were many-faceted for those who came in contact with them and later participated in the struggle against Batista. When pertinent, the authors have traced certain political behavior of the insurrection's leaders and/or militants to their previous training with the action groups. To conclude, as unsophisticated *batistiano* sources have, that the struggle against Fulgencio Batista was purely a struggle for power, just as the action groups struggled to control Havana University, is a grotesque oversimplification and quite an unscientific model for the Cuban insurrection. The insurrection was an all-embracing process more powerful than the individual motivations of its leaders—although there were personal motivations, as in every other political struggle.

Equally simplified is the assertion that the experiences of the Sierra Maestra guerrillas as well as those of the Escambray were grounded in their familiarity with the works of Mao Tse-tung or Vo Gnuyen Giap. It raises the question whether such observers, in pursuing their objective account of the events, have fallen prey to the prejudice that a small nation is unable to devise its own means of national liberation. The same historical error is observed concerning the role of the United States in the struggle. The insurrectionists were not disturbed by previous United States-Cuban relations, nor by the proximity of the United States. The absence of a vigorous U.S. presence in determining the direction of the struggle led "Che" Guevara to analyze this feature of the Cuban insurrection "as an exceptional condition . . . difficult to exploit again by other peoples. . . ." Thus, the insurrectionists concentrated their firepower on Batista, knowing that the matter of the United States would come later. Strictly speaking, then, the insurrection was won against, over and despite the United States since at no time did the latter become the prime justification for the struggle.

In terms of stages, the insurrection embraced two overall phases: the organization, growth and equipment of an urban underground; and the formation, development and upkeep of a guerrilla army. Within each stage, there were subsequent stages of development all of which led to increasing political consciousness on the part of militants and leaders.

The first act of overt violence was the attack on the Moncada barracks on July 26, 1953 in Oriente province. The Moncada attack was a departure from traditional opposition tactics in the context of the 1950s. Because it came on the heels of the coup, it was also an act of defiance against the symbol ruling over Cuba, the army. Moncada had a decisive influence over the insurrectionary process. It opened an abyss between the youth who advocated the violent overthrow of the regime, and older Cubans who supported a political solution, that is, an understanding with the dictator, elections and a transition to the *status quo ante*. The radicalization of the youth began with the attack on the Moncada, spread to street demonstrations and localized acts of terrorism against the regime. These actions helped to polarize the political scene, with the insurrectionists on one side, Batista on another. In between were the electoralists, who depended on Batista's willingness to step down and turn the government over to a civilian elite, thus preventing the insurrectionists from reaching power.

In 1955, Cuban youth entered into a new stage in their struggle against Batista. That year the two most important insurrectionary movements were formed: the 26th of July Movement (M-26-7), and the Directorio Revolucionario (DR). The former pursued a strategy of armed uprising leading to a revolutionary general strike, while the latter concentrated on the one-blow method: Batista's assassination. Both of these tactics proved unsuccessful. The M-26-7 was the first to realize that overthrowing the regime would mean a long, protracted struggle against the regular army. The DR insisted on striking at the top, assuming that if Batista were eliminated, the whole regime would crumble. Methodologically, therefore, the M-26-7—and Fidel Castro above all—entered the second stage sooner than any other insurrectionary organization, building an effective apparatus in the form of a guerrilla army in the Sierra Maestra. The opening of this guerrilla front signaled another change in insurrectionary tactics, and paved the way for the second overall stage of the insurrection that ended with the defeat of the regular army, and Batista's downfall by means of combined urban and rural guerrilla warfare.

The urban underground struggle may be viewed in three stages: formative, offensive and support-defensive. The formative stage dated from the creation of Professor Rafael García Bárcena's Movimiento Nacionalista Revolucionario (MNR) and the Moncada attack in 1953, to the founding of the DR and the M-26-7 in 1955. As these movements entered into the offensive stage, they took the initiative of the struggle away from the Triple A and the Organización Auténtica of Aureliano Sánchez Arango and Carlos Prío Socarrás respectively. The politico-military vanguard of the struggle fell into the hands of the new generation, and challenged the Triple A and the OA to perform a supportive role. But, paradoxically, throughout most of the insurrection, the DR and the M-26-7 depended on Prío's purse to carry out their main acts of violence against Batista. The interrelationship of these four movements oscillated between a series of alignments, co-opting of militants, confrontations and commitment to the main objective, the overthrow of the dictatorship.

The offensive stage culminated with the failure of the Palace attack and the frustrated revolutionary general strike of April 9, 1958. The urban undergrounds of both movements were practically depleted by these defeats. These setbacks forced the urban insurrectionists to an all-out support of the guerrillas' role in the Sierra Maestra, Sierra Cristal and Escambray mountains. Action in the cities continued, but priority was given to survival. No major operational risks were undertaken that could have destroyed what remained of both the DR and the M-26-7. The urban underground lost its initiative and independence, and from then on, all strategic plans were issued from the Sierra Maestra.

Guerrilla warfare developed in two main stages. The first was characterized by the action of small groups of guerrilla fighters against a vastly superior regular army. The objectives were simple: exploit to the utmost the advantages of the terrain, maintain initiative over the regular troops—and survive. From the Granma landing on December 2, 1956 and the Uvero attack on May 28, 1957 to the opening of a second guerrilla front in northern Oriente province on March 10, 1958, the guerrillas' strategy centered on quick attacks and quick retreats. Each retreat was followed up by ambushes of pursuing regular troops until the latter adopted a defensive strategy and abandoned "search and destroy" tactics inside the guerrillas' theater of operations. Gradually, small army posts in the mountains were vacated, and the regular troops were concentrated in marginal areas adjacent to the Sierra Maestra. As Guevara candidly admitted, the guerrillas were unable to move down to the plains, and the army could not penetrate the mountains without sustaining a great number of casualties. This stalemate ended with the failure of the 1958 general strike, which opened the way for the regular army's summer offensive of 1958.

The transitional phase from the first to the second stage of the guerrilla campaign began at this point. The guerrilla army conducted strategic withdrawals into the heights of Sierra Maestra, while the regular army overextended its lines to the point where a guerrilla counterattack became feasible. Overestimation of his own guerrilla army's ability to wage a conventional battle against the regular army almost led Fidel Castro to a military defeat toward the end of July 1958. But by the end of the summer offensive, the guerrillas were increasing their encounters with the defeated regular army until the former invaded central Cuba. A considerable amount of large scale warfare took place in late 1958, But, at all times, guerrilla columns maintained a high degree of mobility and were able to exercise tactics of dispersion and concentration of forces. The guerrilla army engaged in offensive warfare toward November-December 1958, and their push into the plains in Oriente and Las Villas provinces was characterized by more conventional war operations.

The development of guerrilla warfare in Cuba was made possible by the support of the urban underground in Oriente province. The first stage, the formation of guerrilla units and establishment of operational guerrilla bases, channels of supplies and communications, rested on the capability of Frank País' organization in Santiago de Cuba. The fact that guerrilla warfare developed from the first directly into the third state—in terms of Mao Tse-tung's discussion of guerrilla warfare phases—is further proof of the uniqueness of the Cuban case. The guerrillas responded to changing needs of the military campaign; moving backwards as the regular army showed the will to fight, forward as the army deteriorated.

Within the insurrectionary movement leadership evolved around three talented leaders: Fidel Castro, Frank País and José A. Echeverría. Each of them was young, deeply committed and possessed his own charismatic style. Each exhibited distinct personality traits that reflected his social and political upbringing. The authors' argument is that of the three, Fidel Castro felt most at ease with the conservative views of the Old World. A generous share of egocentrism and male authoritarianism permeated Fidel's actions. These were largely grounded in his father's experiences as a Spanish immigrant; Angel Castro Argiz was a hard-working landowner who treated his peasants sternly, had fought on the side of Spain against the Cuban creoles, and was quite gracious to American overseers of the United Fruit Company. Fidel's relations with his father were, of course, less than friendly. But this background, and the disciplinarian Jesuit education Fidel received at Belén shaped a powerful political personality.

Several years Fidel's junior, José Antonio Echevarría belonged to a middle-class Catholic family and was nurtured in the Auténtico mainstream. Jovial and candid, José Antonio had none of Fidel's political experience with the action groups—despite what *batistiano* sources have suggested. His secondary education was in the public school system of his native city of Cárdenas, where he assumed leadership roles climaxing with his rise as head of the Cuban student movement. Echeverría was strongly antidictatorship, nationalistic and believed in overthrowing military caudillos throughout Latin America. He was one of the first insurrectionists to embrace the fight against colonialism in Asia and South America. It was no accident that Guevara would recruit many DR members who shared Echeverría's vision of a liberated continent.

Frank País had the most humble origins of the three leaders. Little is known of his writings, although he wrote as many letters and documents as Fidel. He was reared under the influence of the Baptist church, one of the most socially concerned Protestant institutions in Oriente province. País knew first-hand the humiliating conditions of Cuba's sugar workers, some of whom he taught to read and write. Like Echeverría, he strongly repudiated dictatorial regimes in Latin America. Quiet, self-assured and setting himself as an example, Frank País blended his deeply-felt Christian beliefs with revolutionary action. He appears to have been the most visionary of the three, and to have experienced human situations in a dimension unknown either to Fidel Castro or José Antonio Echeverría.

Each man surrounded himself with a group of followers whose loyalty was beyond question, and also far beyond their fealty to the movements of which they were members. Their ability to win militants over to their cause rested on the essentially distinct features of their charismatic styles. Each developed his charisma in different settings and time periods. Echeverría, as president of the University Student Federation, fearlessly headed militant student demonstrations, finally clashing with heavy-set, armed policemen in Havana, Frank País, unassuming and dedicated, moved from city to town throughout Cuba organizing and strengthening the M-26-7. Fidel Castro tirelessly spoke of the people's capacity to make the revolution, and used the mass media to carry forth his message. Neither Echeverría or Frank País enjoyed the luxury of frequent speeches. Urban warfare does not permit such indulgences. Only Fidel Castro had the means, the time and the vision to use Radio Rebelde to reach the most remote villages of the nation. Relationships among the three leaders were not always friendly, but they gave sufficient proof of their courage, audacity and perseverance. A receptive youth was willing to emulate these leaders' behavior.

It was this type of a person who questioned Fulgencio Batista's coup d'etat, and sought redress by means of an insurrectionary struggle. Not only was Batista the symbol of an oppressing praetorian institution, but he himself had been a political institution since 1933 and the movement known as the "sergeants' revolt." In 1952, Cuba's adult population remembered Batista's rise to power as well as the bloody episodes unleashed by his determination to crush any opponents standing in his way. Certain aspects of Batista were profoundly appealing to various sectors of Cuban society. First, his humble origins: Batista had been born in 1901, in the sugar town of Banes, 40 miles from the village of Birán where Fidel was born in 1927. Batista's parents were peasants and descendants of the Bany Indians of northern Oriente province. His father, Belisario, had been a sergeant in the Cuban Army of Liberation serving under General José Maceo. Belisario Batista worked in the early 1900s for the United Fruit Company where Angel Castro Argiz, Fidel's father, was also employed. While Angel Castro managed to acquire some land and build a productive sugar colony, Belisario Batista never left the canefields. Fulgencio Batista learned from his father the rigors of the sun-up, sun-down swing of the *machete.* He was taught how to read and write at night in a public school and ambitiously pronounced English words at Los Amigos, a school run by American Quaker missionaries. Until 1921, Batista worked as a cane-cutter, carpenter, timekeeper, wood-cutter, store attendant, planter and railroad brakeman. From a Marxist perspective, Batista in 1933 was the exemplary revolutionary leader according to his class origins.

Second, his military experience played a large part in his appeal. At age 20, Batista had enrolled in the army in order to move westward to the dynamic city of Havana, to learn and see things he had heard of but did not know from personal experience. He was assigned to the Fourth Infantry Division based at Camp Columbia in Havana. He hoped to become a lawyer but did not know he needed a high school diploma first; so he enrolled in the evening division of the San Mario academy to become a speedtypist and stenographer. In 1923,

Batista faced an examination and won the rank of corporal; in 1926, in a second examination—his last one—he was promoted to sergeant and assigned as reporter to the councils of war. At the War Department, he learned the arts of arm-twisting, backroom politics and class privileges. Knowing as no other man of his time the human conditions of low-ranking officers, peasants and workers, he led soldiers, corporals and sergeants to the revolt of 1933. The Batista of 1933 was a young man turned overnight into a colonel and chief of the Cuban Armed Forces who postulated that a revolution was "an instrument of social change." He held that Cuba had abandoned its colonial status to become a slave of foreign capitalism. The country's fabric needed thoroughgoing reforms so that the revolution could fulfill its destiny. Batista had strongly advocated racial equality and nondiscrimination (of which he had been perpetually a victim himself). He was an idol to the peasantry because he had emerged from the humble; an idol to immigrant groups—mostly Spaniards—who mirrored themselves in Batista, a sort of militaristic version of a Cuban Horatio Alger; and an idol to his troops, whom he had redeemed from squalor by means of swift promotions, improvement of military quarters, salary increases and no small amount of class privilege.

In 1952, Batista knew that his strong-man image would suffice to frighten the weak Auténtico administration and elicit the unconditional allegiance of the regular army. He also guessed correctly that wealthy entrepreneurs, peasants and workers would not feel economically threatened by his coup. The prevailing political parties he dismissed, for neither the Auténticos nor the Ortodoxos were led by able political leaders who were a fair match to his own political seniority. Fulgencio Batista made one mistake though: he underestimated the frame of mind of a generation of young Cubans who were tired of political cynicism and ready for a fresh start on the road to revolution.

1

The Moncada Attack

Fidel Castro Ruz was born on August 13, 1927,[1] on "Manacas," the farm owned by his father, Angel Castro Argiz, in Birán, municipality of Mayarí, Oriente. At age seven he began his primary education in Santiago de Cuba. He completed these early studies at the Jesuit school of Dolores. In 1941 Fidel was accepted at the Colegio Belén in Havana, which was the most exclusive Jesuit educational institution in the country. In 1945 he entered the University of Havana's law school.

Fidel's political career began in that year, with his unsuccessful campaign for the presidency of the law school. In 1947 he ran for secretary to the student assembly but again failed to muster enough support from his fellow students.[2]

Fidel was not unique in attempting to start a political career while still a young man. Cuban youth in general was highly politicized, for Cuba had long been a country of shifting power and alliances. In their university years or even earlier, many Cubans became involved in theorizing, planning and acting to grab whatever share of power was available. Thus many groups formed, worked together, broke up and realigned with slightly different objectives. Fidel Castro was but one of the radical young Cubans who had an early vision of power and took every opportunity to reach his goal.

Fidel's political activism led him to become involved with the "action groups" predominant under the Ramón Grau San Martín (1944-48) administration. Andrés Suárez has described the young revolutionary who joined these groups as "loyal only to his tiny independent group, full of contempt for those he referred to as the ideologists," and "thoroughly convinced that violence alone could decide everything."[3] There were several action groups, but two of the most important were the Revolutionary Socialist Movement (MSR), led by Rolando Masferrer, and the Revolutionary Insurrectional Union (UIR), headed first by Emilio Tró, and later by Jesús Diéguez. These organizations fought each other savagely under the cloak of their particular "revolutionary" program. Leaders like Policarpo Soler, Masferrer, Mario Salabarría and Tró surrounded themselves with young men who became terrorists ready to murder for political leverage, money or personal rivalry. The activities of these groups affected every aspect of Cuba's public life. Havana University was the main headquarters, even though many of the group leaders and members were not registered students. Masferrer and Salabarría provide excellent examples of the widely divergent types of young Cubans who were involved in "revolutionary" activities.

Rolando Masferrer combined student life with political activism. His academic record was outstanding, and he had won almost every major honorary distinction in open competition in the law school. He had at one time belonged to the Communist party, had been a renowned fighter against the Gerardo Machado dictatorship (1925-33) in his youth, and later had enrolled in the International Brigades which fought in the Spanish Civil War (1936-39). After he left the Communist party, he became a notorious gang leader. Mario Salabarría, on the other hand, was a brutal killer with little or no academic background. The Grau administration commissioned Salabarría and Tró as majors, giving one charge of the national police academy and the other control of the national police's investigation department.

At the university the action groups exerted total control over university affairs. Under the influence of "Ojos Bellos" (Pretty Eyes), "El Colorado" (The Reddish) and "El Manco" (The Lamed), they were even able to help determine who would be granted professional degrees, particularly in the school of law. As in most such organizations, recruits had to prove their intentions by participating in "direct action" like shooting an enemy of a rival group or engaging in terrorist activities against their critics.[4]

Public reaction to these activities is suggested by a 1949 editorial demanding government action against the high incidence of daylight shooting in the capital: "Gangsterism—once again—erupted in broad daylight in the downtown area, resulting in two deaths, those of Justo Fuentes, vice-president of the Federation of University Students (FEU) and Miguel Siaez, a bus driver. Both were victims of that somber cloak—Mafia-like—that has taken over a large part of our youth."[5] At the scene of the shooting the police arrested Fidel Castro Ruz, a member of the UIR. He was held briefly at police headquarters and then released. In an interview with the press, young Castro said Fuentes had died because "he had refused protection from the UIR."[6] Two weeks later the UIR's Felipe Salazar ("Wichy") was shot to death by men of the MSR. The only witness to the shooting was Fidel Castro, who testified that the MSR was responsible for the assassination.[7]

Earlier in the summer of 1947 Fidel, despite his association with the UIR, had joined an MSR-sponsored group of Dominican exiles, soldiers of fortune, revolutionary idealists and gangsters who planned to invade the Dominican Republic and depose dictator Rafael L. Trujillo (1930-61). The MSR was to supervise the Cubans who enrolled in the expedition, and to that end it appointed a committee which included among others, Manolo Castro (no relation to Fidel) and Carlos Gutiérrez Menoyo.[8] On July 30 the would-be invaders reached Cayo Confites, off the port of Nuevitas, Camagüey province, where they awaited orders to proceed to the Dominican Republic. In

September the Grau administration decided not to support the invasion, and the Cuban navy arrested the expeditionaries. Fidel returned to Havana after a daring escape from a navy frigate.[9]

The rivalry between the MSR and the UIR continued to escalate. In September 1947, shortly after the Confites episode, the two groups fought a bloody battle in what became known as the "massacre of Orfila." Emilio Tró was killed; Policarpo Soler was arrested but escaped and joined Trujillo as one of the dictator's henchmen; and Jesús Diéguez was promoted to the leadership of the UIR.

Still the terrorism continued. On February 22, 1948, Manolo Castro—president of the FEU—was assassinated. He had been elected to the FEU presidency in 1944, running successfully against Fidel's friend, Luis Conte Agüero. Manolo had been active in organizing the Confederation of Cuban Peasants and in promoting various campaigns against dictators such as Trujillo and Spain's Francisco Franco. Rolando Masferrer charged Fidel with the murder, and two days after the killing. Fidel was arrested, though he was later released for lack of evidence. Fidel responded by accusing Masferrer of attempting to take over the MSR's leadership and of slandering him for not supporting Masferrer's aspirations to control the university.[10] Masferrer pledged to kill Fidel at the first opportunity.[11] At this point Fidel decided that it would be a good idea to leave the country for a while until things cooled off.

He found his opportunity in dictator Juan Perón's attempt to organize "anti-imperialist fronts" throughout Latin America. The Latin American Student Association was the *peronista* instrument for mobilizing public opinion against the United States throughout Latin American universities. Perón's delegate. César Tronconi, gained the support of several students in Havana. Together they organized a congress to denounce imperialist activities throughout the continent. It was agreed that the congress would take place in Bogotá, Colombia, to coincide with the Ninth Inter-American Conference. Among the chief Cuban organizers of this congress was Fidel Castro, Enrique Ovares, Alfredo Guevara, Pedro Mirasón, Armando Gali-Menéndez and Rafael del Pino.[12] Fidel arrived in Bogotá on March 31, 1948, accompanied by del Pino, Ovares and Guevara. On April 9, Jorge Eliecer Gaitán, leader of the Colombian Liberal Party, was assassinated and the *Bogotazo* erupted. The Cubans sought refuge in the Cuban embassy, and returned to their country on April 13, 1948.[13] Fidel was back in Havana by June 6, 1948, when he was charged, at Havana's Fourth District Criminal Court, with the assassination of Oscar Fernández Caral, a campus police sergeant and member of the MSR. Caral had been instrumental in supplying ammunition to the MSR for the massacre of Orfila, and had been sentenced to death by the UIR. The charges were dropped, however, since there was no evidence that Fidel was the assailant.[14]

Four months after this incident Fidel married Mirta Díaz Balart. Mirta, a philosophy student, bore an only son who was Fidel's name-sake. Gang warfare began to subside, finally, toward the end of 1948, and the Partido del Pueblo Cubano-Ortodoxo (also known as PPC-O), led by Eduardo R. Chibás, gained strength in Cuban politics. Fidel withdrew from the action groups, and began to dedicate himself to party politics.

Fidel's experiences throughout his years of involvement in acts of violence convinced him that direct action was the shortest way to political solutions. This conviction would keep him one step ahead of the other young leaders who emerged during the insurrection, for he grasped only too well the role of violence in Cuban politics. He also knew that most politicians had had their share of involvement in graft, corruption and murder through the action groups. In the course of the insurrection, former members of action groups were to play important roles in acts of violence against Batista. Fidel's first-hand knowledge of violence and back-room politics helped him establish his important position in the decisive period of the insurrection.

The Road to Action

Several years later Fidel's insurrectionary career swung into high gear. The FEU of Havana and Oriente issued declarations condemning Fulgencio Batista's 1952 coup d'etat. On March 24, 1952, Fidel Castro filed a suit against Batista. Quoting from the Social Defense Code he asked that Batista be punished for violating the constitution and the laws, thereby challenging the judicial system to act. According to Article 147 of the code, anyone who attempted to change the constitution or the form of government through violent means would be imprisoned for six to ten years. Furthermore, Article 148 stated that "anyone who promotes an armed uprising against the constitutional power of the state will be imprisoned for three to ten years."[15] If the insurrection was carried out, the penalty could be 20 years of imprisonment. Other violations of the code would sentence Batista to a total of 100 years of imprisonment. Fidel Castro argued:

> If, in the face of these flagrant crimes and confessions of treachery and sedition, he is not tried and punished, how will this court later try any citizen for sedition or rebelliousness against this unlawful crime, the result of unpunished treason? That would be absurd, inadmissible, monstrous in the light of the most elementary principles of justice.[16]

Similar suits were introduced by Eduardo Suárez Rivas, of the Partido Revolucionario Cubano-Auténtico (also known as PRC-A), and Pelayo Cuervo Navarro, of the PPC-O; in all of them the courts ruled that "revolution is a lawful source." Batista's coup d'etat was interpreted as a de facto, revolutionary overturn of the constitution. Fidel Castro took careful note of this judicial decision.

Many young people were troubled by the coup. Even many who had not been previously involved in politics started to consider opposing Batista. Among the first to agree on the need to fight the regime were Abel Santamaría

Cuadrado and Jesús Montané Oropesa. Santamaría was an accountant for the Pontiac branch in Havana, and Montané was personnel manager for the General Motors Inter-American Corporation of Havana. On May 20, 1952, Santamaría and Montané put out the first edition of a mimeographed paper entitled *Son los mismos* (They are the same). In this task they were helped by Abel's sister, Haydée, Melba Hernández, a lawyer, Raúl Gómez García, a philosophy student, and Elda Pérez among others.[17]

Since all of them belonged to the youth section of the Ortodoxo party it was inevitable that they would come into contact with other Ortodoxos' ideas, like those of Fidel. At the suggestion of the latter, the title *Son los mismos* was changed to *El Acusador*.[18] The second issue of *El Acusador* included two articles: one signed by the poet Raúl Gómez García entitled "The Origin of a Dwarf"—a sarcastic attack on Alberto Salas Amaro, editor of the *Ataja* newspaper and staunch supporter of Fulgencio Batista; the other signed by Alejandro (Fidel) and entitled "Critical Assessment of the PPC."[19] The latter article argued that only two political alternatives remained open: electoral politics or insurrection. Fidel called for a return to constitutional normalcy while offering his pledge to oppose the regime until it gave up power.[20] This article by Fidel was reprinted in the third issue of *El Acusador*, dated August 16, 1952. The issue also included Fidel's "I Accuse" article, and Gómez García mourned the first anniversary of the death of Eduardo R. Chibás in an article, "A Voice."[21] This third issue of *El Acusador* was distributed at Havana's national cemetery around the tomb of Chibás.

The group editing *El Acusador* included Raúl Gómez García, chief editor, Abel Santamaría Cuadrado, assistant editor, and Juan Martínez Tinguao and Jesús Montané as editorial assistants. The chief source of political orientation was Fidel Castro.[22]

Whether out of a sense of duty or feverish enthusiasm this tiny group began to approach other young people who shared similar ideas about the Cuban situation. In this fashion they looked for students associated with the Ortodoxo party at Havana University. Thus, Pedro Miret, majoring in engineering, Lester Rodríguez, a medical student, and Abelardo Crespo, also in the school of engineering, were recruited into the incipient "movement." Despite their efforts, in mid-1952 the common expectation was that the ousted Auténtico party of Carlos Prío Socarrás (1948-52) would take the lead in returning the country to constitutional normalcy. Aureliano Sánchez Arango, for example, gave the impression that he and his secret Triple A organization would soon lead an insurrection against Batista.

Rumors about the Auténticos' activities led Castro to extend his contacts to the nearby province of Pinar del Río, especially to Artemisa, where a number of young Ortodoxos were persuaded to join the movement. Some of the recruits who came over to Fidel Castro shared high hopes about the "Auténtico's famous revolution."[23] It did appear that of all the groups only the Auténticos had the material resources to equip a force capable of leading a frontal attack against the dictator. Aware of the situation, Fidel began to prepare small commando groups who were expert in handling small weapons as well as accustomed to military discipline.

From August to December 1952, Pedro Miret, Lester Rodríguez, José "Pepe" Suárez and Abelardo Crespo trained young Ortodoxos. Especially important were the Artemiseños, who included, among others, Ramiro Valdés, Ciro Redondo, Julio Díaz and José Suárez Blanco. Target shooting was carried out in the basement of Havana University, the Club de Cazadores del Cerro, and at various farms such as Los Palos, Pijirigua, Capellanía and Porvenir in Havana and Pinar del Río provinces.[24] Target practice at the Club de Cazadores was very expensive, but Castro managed to persuade Oscar Alcalde, owner of Thion Laboratory, to join the movement and help finance some of its costs. Since Alcalde was a public utilities inspector working for Batista's Ministry of Treasury, he was able to secure loans from the Agrícola Industrial Bank and the Nuñez Bank. These funds were used to pay the $30 admission fee to the club as well as to buy shotguns and bullets.[25]

As 1952 came to an end, Castro had over 100 men, most of whom had little knowledge of their exact mission. Castro had overseen the training of these young men every Sunday, and felt optimistic about the future. The would-be insurgents centered their hopes on the aid Fidel was to receive from the Auténticos.[26]

One evening in December 1952, Castro issued orders to his men to meet at several houses in Havana. It was a state of alert, a sort of military mobilization carried out with utmost discipline. At Melba Hernández's home all the men met with a group of Auténticos who reviewed a list of arms which they supposedly would give to Castro's outfit. This meeting raised the expectations of the militants, but as the weeks went by the promise was never fulfilled.[27] It became necessary to change strategy. Castro and Abel Santamaría concluded that the group itself would have to obtain the weapons necessary for an action against Batista. Despite this obvious setback, the group had trained themselves for action, and they were willing to stay on. During the second stage of planning that began after December 1952, the idea of attacking the Moncada military barracks in Oriente province was first discussed.

At about the same time—early 1953—that Castro had prepared his group, another group of enthusiastic young men had gathered around a university professor, Rafael García Bárcena. Bárcena had formed the Movimiento Nacionalista Revolucionario (MNR) in May 1952 with the idea of taking decisive action to overthrow Batista. The MNR recruited university and high school students in Havana and in Santiago de Cuba as well. Active with the MNR at that time were Armando Hart Dávalos, Joe Westbrook Rosales, Eva Jiménez— the only woman in the group—Faustino Pérez, Fernando Sánchez Amaya, Edgardo Buttari, Jr., Silvino Rodríguez and Julián Fernández, among others.[28]

The MNR planned to assault the military camp of Columbia, to arrest Batista at his quarters, and to call friendly army officers to join the movement to oust the unconstitutional government. The organization rented a house close to Columbia where a "school" was set up. Several evenings before the assigned day of the assault, the students became familiar with the Columbia's gates and the shortest routes to Batista's headquarters. On April 5, 1953, all MNR members were ordered to be at certain locations throughout the capital; the attack would take place that day.

Before the group could even begin operations, Chief of Police Salas Cañizares moved in and arrested Professor Bárcena and a group of 70 youths. All were taken to the army's dreaded bureau of intelligence where, after severe mistreatment, the youngest ones were released in their parents' custody. García Bárcena was sentenced to two years' imprisonment, and the government mocked the assault, calling it "the razor blade coup."[29]

Meanwhile, the Auténticos met at Montreal, Canada, in June 1953 with other opponents of the regime to formulate a strategy for the overthrow of Batista. Led by former president Carlos Prío, the Auténticos favored unity among all groups, with the exception of the Communists, who were not admitted to the discussion. The Montreal Pact, signed on this occasion, declared that Batista must be overthrown but had no concrete suggestions about implementing the objective. The group's statements were criticized in Cuba, particularly by university students who referred to the Auténticos as the "heroes from afar."[30]

The Moncada Barracks

The MNR's frustrated attempt and the evident incapacity of the Auténticos to engage in direct action against the regime seemed to ensure Batista some calm half way through 1953. Yet the emerging rebelliousness of the youth had not been totally appeased. Fidel Castro and his group of men continued their contacts, reaching some youths from Santiago de Cuba. Of these, Renato Guitart would play an important role in the coming assault. Guitart had met Fidel in February 1953 at the time of the death of Rubén Batista, the first student martyr of the insurrection. Guitart had been active in an insurrectionary group named Acción Libertadora (AL) along with Otto Parellada, Frank País and Pepito Tey, among others.[31] He, too, had hoped that the Auténticos would provide weapons and men for some sort of action against Batista.

Since the Auténticos had no arms to give to these young revolutionaries, Fidel and Abel Santamaría decided that their first priority was to get weapons. They purchased, one by one, several dozen shot-guns and .22 caliber semi-automatic rifles at various armories. The armament included one Browning submachine gun, one M-l carbine and several Winchester rifles.[32] On the entire operation they spent $16,480 of which $5,000 went for the purchase of arms and $80 for ammunition. The target was selected by Fidel and Abel

Santamaría; Renato Guitart provided a map of the Moncada barracks. The objective was discussed by Fidel's general staff, which included, besides Fidel and Abel, José Luis Tasende, Guitart, Antonio López Fernández ("Ñico") and Pedro Miret. Castro's entire force consisted of approximately 165 men grouped in squads of seven.[33]

The operation was to unfold with a surprise attack against the barracks at Moncada, Santiago de Cuba.[34] Simultaneously, another group would attack the army post at Bayamo in a diversionary move to relieve pressure on Fidel and his men. Overall, it meant a daring, almost suicidal blitz unless the men could take the camp by surprise. However, Fidel's idea was that a small group of men, ill-armed as they were, could take control of the military camp if they could retain the element of surprise. Once they had established control at Moncada and at Bayamo Fidel hoped the regular troops would join the anti-Batista movement.[35] The arms at Moncada were to be distributed to the people, especially to the students who had been active even before Fidel's group was organized and who would probably join the movement. In this fashion, Batista would be confronted with a fait accompli. Fidel must also have thought that his initiative would place the Auténticos and other groups well behind his, and that a successful attack would greatly enhance his national leadership. Previously, Professor García Bárcena had chosen much the same path to leadership except that Fidel's target was Moncada, not Havana.

The fact that the Moncada garrison was on the opposite end of the island from Batista's quarters spoke well of Castro's strategy for two reasons: first, such a victory would give him control over the entire movement. By being far from Havana, the main center of all kinds of conspiracies and the area of operation for old politicians, Castro need fear no immediate challenge, and those who eventually joined him would have to go to Oriente. Second, Oriente traditionally was the cradle of revolutionary movements in the country, and the attack on Moncada plus Castro's surprise victory would spread throughout Oriente province. Castro's capture of the Moncada might also accelerate a rift within the army, perhaps even producing a coup. Should an immediate coup not take place in the capital, Castro could organize an armed resistance, and then march on the city.

In preparation for the attack, Fidel dispatched Ernesto Tizol to Santiago de Cuba. Tizol's mission was to coordinate efforts with Renato Guitart and rent a farm on the outskirts of the city to serve as their headquarters. The farm chosen was called "Siboney." Arms began to be transported, and Abel Santamaría left Havana in mid-June. On July Melba Hernández arrived at the farm carrying a shipment of army uniforms that had been obtained through an army sergeant, Florentino Fernández.[36]

In Bayamo, Guitart had established contact with a former schoolmate from La Progresiva school, Fernando Fernández, who, ignoring the impending assault, helped Guitart rent a farm on July 14. Guitart made at least six trips to Bayamo before the attack took place. On Saturday, July 25, he accompanied Fidel on an inspection tour of the city of Bayamo. Twenty-seven members of the movement were ready for the attack on Bayamo, which was to be led by Mario Martínez Arará, "Nico" López and Hugo Camejo among others. They planned to approach the army post, which was guarded by a small detachment of soldiers, from three different sides. The operation was to coincide with Fidel's attack on Moncada.

Also on Saturday, Fidel and Raúl Gómez García gave the final touches to a manifesto they would present to the nation in the event of victory. The first draft had been written two days earlier and differed little from traditional Cuban revolutionary rhetoric. José Martí's centennial was 1953, and the ideas of the apostle of Cuban independence ran throughout the declaration. Fidel not only claimed an ideological continuity with the ideas of Martí but also with those of Céspedes, Agramonte, Maceo, Julio A. Mella, Antonio Guiteras and Eduardo R. Chibás.[37] The step that Castro's forces had taken, said the manifesto, was actually the continuation of the revolutions of 1895 and 1933. After a lengthy summary of the country's political situation, the declaration set forth nine points. The revolution stemmed from the youth and was free of foreign influence, political mediation or personal ambitions. The revolutionaries were not against the men in uniform, only those who had betrayed the constitution and the laws. Cuba's economy would be developed and the exploitation of economic resources carried out by previous governments without benefit to the nation would stop. The declaration further stated the groups' respect for students and workers, Last, in a sweeping statement, it accepted the political platforms not only of Martí's Partido Revolucionario Cubano, but also the programs issued in the thirties by Jóven Cuba (JC). the ABC-Radical and the PPC-O.[38] The 1940 constitution was to be fully reinstated.

In the early morning hours of Sunday, July 26, Fidel briefed his men a final time. The attack would be carried out by three groups, while two other groups would take over the Saturnino Lora Military Hospital and the Palace of Justice. With ten men, Raúl Castro[39] was to take the palace, while Abel Santamaría and 20 men would establish control over the hospital. Accompanying Abel would be Melba Hernández and Haydée Santamaría as assistants to Dr. Mario Muñoz, the group's physician. All were dressed in army uniforms.[40]

Fidel was in charge of a group of 95 men who were to carry out the actual attack on Moncada. Before leaving Siboney he asked for volunteers for the first car which would have the task of taking over camp gate No. 3. Jesús Montané, Carmelo Noa, José Luis Tasende, Renato Guitart, Ramiro Valdés. José Suárez Blanco and Pedro Marrero volunteered for the advance group. Guitart was appointed chief of the operation, and at five o'clock they headed toward the Moncada. As they approached the gate 15 minutes later, the four guards exchanged salutes with what they thought was a patrol of comrades-in-arms. Guitart's squad disarmed the post, and quickly proceeded into the barracks when the sounds of the alarm were heard. Nearby soldiers opened fire. The other cars arrived just as the shooting started, and Castro's car was fired on by a patrol car. Meanwhile, Montané, Ramiro Valdés and Suárez Blanco entered one of the barracks and exchanged fire with about 50 soldiers. Other attackers became confused and assaulted a group of private officers, homes instead of continuing their initial push toward the arsenal. From the main barracks the troops poured over the camp's assembly grounds. Fidel's support group, some 40 heavily equipped men, lost their way in the unfamiliar Santiago streets, and were unable to join the vanguard in time.[41]

The army, with superior fire power, numerical strength and thorough domination of the terrain, appeared unassailable. Fidel was unable to enter the camp but he managed to send orders from the outside. Realizing that the surprise element had been lost and that the success of the entire operation had depended on it, Fidel called for retreat. At first, the retreat was orderly, with groups of eight and ten men protected by six sharpshooters[42]; but soon everyone began to run for cover. Approximately 87 men, including those at the hospital and the Palace of Justice, had participated.[43]

Montané, Ciro Redondo and Suárez Blanco escaped in a car toward Siboney, where the group had agreed to meet in case of failure. Juan Almeida. Oscar Alcalde, Francisco González. Eduardo Montano. Jaime Costa, Armando Mestre, Israel Tápanes and Reynaldo Benítez (who had been wounded in the leg) also escaped toward the farm.

At the Saturnino Lora Military Hospital, Abel Santamaría was captured by the army and, with Mario Muñoz, was shot to death after savage torture. Raúl Castro was taken prisoner.

In Bayamo the attackers moved in three groups. One stayed at the aqueduct close to the army post, while a second group, led by a dentist, Pedro Aguilera, approached the post from a nearby house.[44] A third group, led by Mario Martínez Arará, moved toward the camp's entrance. Only five soldiers were on duty that morning, but as Aguilera's group moved closer one of the guards spotted them and demanded that they stop and identify themselves. To this the group answered with rounds of fire against the guard; in a matter of seconds machine-gun fire showered the area, causing Aguilera's group to retreat in total disarray.[45]

Army Lieutenant Juan A. Roselló was the chief of the 13th squadron of the rural guards in Bayamo. He led the counterattack. Some of the attackers escaped, but most of them were captured and killed. José Testa Zaragoza was arrested while trying to leave the city in a bus, taken back to the post and immediately assassinated. Others, like Hugo García Camejo, Pedro Vélez and Andrés García, succeeded in reaching the city of Manzanillo. But there they were arrested, and taken to the city's outskirts. With ropes tied around their necks they were dragged along a rugged roadside. Only Andrés García survived when he and the others were left behind by the army as dead. At a place called Ceja de Limones, four other youths were caught and executed on the spot.

Over half of the group of 27 were shot to death after being taken prisoner. The army sustained one dead and two wounded. The attack on the Bayamo military post had met disaster, as had the attempt at Moncada.

In Santiago de Cuba, the army prepared itself for one of the worst massacres since Batista's coup. Colonel Alberto del Río Chaviano, commander of the city, issued a military communique to calm the citizenry, which was beginning to protest arbitrary arrests. The communique read, in part: "We want the people to understand that this decision of our Armed Forces is the only one that guarantees normalcy to the city. Everyone may continue his everyday activities as the government is the first to offer guarantees for commerce, industry, and work."[46] The colonel praised the people for a "serene and responsible behavior."[47]

At the capital, Batista stated that the attempt was incredible and mad, adding that though his government would respect all rights it would also be "inflexible in applying whatever measures are necessary to guarantee the democratic process of the March 10 revolution, and the security of the nation." Batista claimed that the people, the armed forces and the government were fairly united in "the patriotic purpose of maintaining peace and harmony in the Cuban firmly."[48] General Francisco Tabernilla, chief of the Joint Chiefs General Staff, stated that the army was ready to support any measures which would bring amity among Cubans, leaving the door open for a private initiative to convince the fugitives of the Moncada assault to surrender. Monsignor Enrique Pérez Serantes, archbishop of Santiago de Cuba, offered to help bring the fugitives to the authorities. The government accepted. It was the first time that a high prelate of the Catholic church had mediated in the country's political violence since the coup.

"The revolutionaries must not fear," Monsignor Serantes said. "Let me know where you are, and I shall come there to take you to the authorities. Your life is guaranteed."[49] Radio commentators, television and press reporters echoed the monsignor's words throughout the nation.

The Capture of Fidel Castro

Fidel returned to Siboney, where about 38 survivors discussed what to do next. Fidel addressed the group. As one of the survivors, Severino Rosell, recalled the scene, "The leader told us anyone who wanted to could follow him because he was taking to the mountains. There was a discussion over our possibilities—nil at the time—and then the majority decided to disperse."[50] According to Fidel, "Our plans were to follow up the struggle in the mountains in case the attack met failure. I managed to gather a third of our forces but many were already disheartened. Around 20 decided to come along."[51] Only 18 actually accompanied Fidel to the mountain of La Gran Piedra.

The group marched across the "Arroyo Casabe" farm to Granjita hill, where Fidel proposed to stop and wait for the army so that they could fight. The others persuaded him to continue marching, and soon they came to the house of a very old Negro woman, Leocadia García Garzón ("Chicha"). The old woman identified herself to Fidel by showing him an old document signed by the independence hero, General Antonio Maceo, which certified that she had been a guide for the Cuban Army of Liberation in the War of 1895. She told the group the route to La Gran Piedra mountain, and Fidel's men continued their march. They were joined by the old woman's grandson, who led them across the Carpintero river (where they stopped to rest). The peasants of the area received the group well, and the survivors were given food when they reached the hut of a Negro peasant, Pedro Despaigne. At the house of another peasant, Agustín Heredia, Fidel listened to Batista's July 27 speech in which the latter announced that 32 of the attackers had died. For some of the peasants, the group's arrival brought their first knowledge of the attack. Fidel Castro was interested in finding out the strength of the Ortodoxo party in that area.[52]

The last peasant who helped the fugitives was Juan Leizán who gave food to the whole group, and allowed Fidel, Oscar Alcalde and Suárez Blanco to use the small hut at the "Cilindro" farm. On the morning of August 1 the army surrounded the shack. A 17-man army patrol led by Lieutenant Pedro Manuel Sarría captured Fidel, Alcalde and Suárez Blanco as they were lying on the floor of Leizán's hut. As the soldiers were ready to start firing on the three men, Lieutenant Sarría order a halt, saying "one does not kill ideas." The officer had issued this reprieve because he had recognized Fidel from Havana University where, as a young officer, he had studied law at night.[53] Scattered shooting took place not too far away where other fugitives wandered about. Two hours later, the escapees surrendered to the army and joined Fidel, Suárez Blanco, Alcalde, Juan Almeida, Jesús Montané, Francisco González, Armando Mestre and others. Lieutenant Sarría led the group to Manuel Leizán's farm. Leizán drove the prisoners to Santiago in his own truck. On the way Monsignor Serantes caught up with and began to follow the group.[54] However, before reaching Santiago a troop detachment commanded by Major Andrés R. Chaumont Altazurra stopped the caravan. Major Chaumont and Lieutenant Sarría engaged in a heated argument, with Sarría refusing to hand the prisoners over. Monsignor Serantes' presence probably kept Major Chaumont from taking any drastic action. As it was Sarría admitted that Fidel was among the prisoners, and said that they would all be delivered to the appropriate authorities. Taking various detours, Lieutenant Sarría took the prisoners to the Santiago de Cuba prison rather than army headquarters in Moncada where they would have been assassinated at once. When the lieutenant brought his captives and the monsignor to the prison, he was confronted by Colonel Río Chaviano, who could hardly hide his irritation that Sarría had not done away with Castro.[55] Once they had been informed of the charges against them the prisoners were placed at the disposal of the courts.

Public Opinion and the Trial

The government's version of the events was presented in a report issued by Colonel Alberto del Río Chaviano:

> Elements led by Carlos Prío Socarrás, Aureliano Sánchez Arango, Eufemio Fernández, and someone named Fidel Castro—who travels frequently to Havana and Santiago—Juan Marinello, Blas Roca, Emilio Ochoa and other leaders of the Communist, Auténtico and Ortodoxo parties, me; in this city to take the Moncada barracks by assault.

The attack, the colonel claimed, had been carried out without any scruples or regard for customs or laws of war and "lacking pity or respect for the sick at the hospital." The official report was intended to link Fidel Castro's group with the Auténtico meeting at Montreal, Canada. "As has been fully demonstrated," the report argued, "by the war materiel captured (which is at the disposal of the court), almost all the arms came from Montreal, Canada, as the seals of the boxes containing ammunition used in the attack indicate."[56]

The government's charges that former president Prío had been involved in the planning of the attack, and that the attack resulted from the Montreal meeting were completely false. As for the involvement of the Communist party, as alleged by the government, nothing was farther from the truth.[57] But Batista was at that time conducting a campaign against Prío's activities in Miami, Florida, and the attack lent itself to the perfect official charge against the Auténticos.

The Cuban people found it quite difficult to believe that a group of young people could plan and carry out such an attack without having the support of the politicians—whether the Auténticos or the Ortodoxos. Of more interest in the ensuing national debate over the significance of Moncada was the personality of the man whom the government report vaguely referred to as "someone named Fidel Castro."

Public interest steadily increased throughout the month of August, and as the day for the trial neared, students demonstrated to demand justice for the attackers, proclaiming that they were defending the constitution and the laws. Most politicos criticized the episode as an irresponsible act led by dreamers who in the end would be used by political opportunists. Those in favor of a solution through elections—the "electoralists"—maintained that the country's crisis could not be solved through violence, but through a compromise with those government officials who leaned toward a peaceful return to democratic government. A "civic revolution" was foreseen by some electoralists, while Dr. Grau San Martín enigmatically declared that very serious events were developing rapidly for the nation's future.

In the streets, cafes and parks the people argued about Castro's strategy, either questioning or admiring his manliness and courage. What seemed to have impressed the people most was Fidel's decision to take direct action. Suggestions that he was involved with the Auténticos were soon discounted, for most people fell that the old politicians would never risk their well-being on such an action.

The Communists promptly called Castro's attack a "bourgeois putsch" and publicly stated their adherence to a conciliatory course instead of the one followed by the youth of the Centennial.[58] In an attempt to analyze the meaning of the attack, the Communists suggested that those who fought Batista came from "different factions and of these the former Partido del Pueblo Cubano-Ortodoxo founded by Chibás is split," and their leaders were led by the hope of "achieving Batista's defeat through a combination of every type of minority action, counter coups d'etat, putsch, terrorism, etc., with the hope of obtaining the support of Washington." The common denominator of those groups, the Communists claimed, was "sabotage, unity and popular action." It was under those conditions that the attack on Moncada took place. A "little group of young men, well intentioned but influenced by the putschist line, made a frustrated assault against the military barracks in Santiago de Cuba, hoping to take possession of this important position and therefrom launch an attack against Camp Columbia in Havana."[59] For the Communists, such insurrectionary action was "petit bourgeois adventurism." The Communists thought it neither expedient, desirable nor necessary that they be associated with a group which seemingly had embraced a philosophy of violence. Only anti-Communist fanatics took at face value Batista's implication that the Communists were involved in the attack. Cuban Communists were widely considered staunch *batistianos*, and very few persons could imagine Juan Marinello, Blas Roca, Fabio Grobart or other aging theoreticians taking part in a real insurrection. Like their comrades in Latin America, Cuban Communists were as comfortably bourgeois as the members of the oligarchy with whom they were always on the best of terms.

Despite the variety of opinions concerning the attack, there was common agreement that it had inaugurated a new stage in the country's politics, a period of violence in which the country's youth would become deeply involved.

The trial had begun on September 21 and received full press coverage. Presiding were Justices Adolfo Nieto Piñeiro, Juan Francisco Mejías and Ricardo Díaz Oliveira. During the first hearing, Castro and his followers were informed of the charges against them. At this point, Fidel engaged in a heated argument with Attorney General Francisco Mendieta. When the argument threatened to get out of hand, the court ordered a postponement.

Confronted with daily street demonstrations conducted by the students, Batista declared a few days after the trial began that the government was ready to quell any disorders with a strong hand in order to maintain law and order.[60]

On September 24 the trial resumed, but when Fidel was called to the stand, Colonel Río Chaviano stepped forward to tell the court that he did not have enough soldiers to maintain the necessary order in the courtroom, and the court again postponed the proceedings for 24 hours. This second postponement gave way to the rumor that the government was trying to prevent Fidel from making a public statement. A more serious rumor was that Castro was going to be murdered, either in prison or while the authorities were taking him to the courtroom. Thus, when Fidel was called to the stand the following day, and the prison authorities said he was sick and could not attend the trial, the audience reacted with cries and shouts. With the aid of one of the prison guards, Fidel had managed to slip a brief letter to Melba Hernández, and amidst the confusion prevailing in the court, she approached the bench asking the judges to allow her to read the letter to the tribunal and the public as well.

The letter stated that there were very important matters that required immediate attention by the court. These were: that Fidel had been prevented from appearing before the court because of the government's fear of what he might say concerning the death of many of his comrades, that he had been kept incommunicado for 57 days, and that there were plans to eliminate him by poisoning or "other means." Fidel requested the court to order his "immediate physical examination by a competent and prestigious physician, such as the Dean of the School of Medicine of the University of Oriente." He also requested the court to appoint a member of the tribunal to accompany the prisoners when they were taken to and from the court.

Aware of the publicity such letter would receive, Fidel challenged the court to discharge its duties according to law. The significance of the trial, Castro argued, imposed an exceptional obligation on the court. If the trial continued to be conducted under the conditions Castro had unveiled, it would be nothing but a "ridiculous farce, an immorality which will be completely repudiated by the nation." "All of Cuba has its eyes set on this trial," he said. "I do hope this court will uphold with dignity its privileged hierarchy and honor which is at this moment the honor of the judiciary power before the history of Cuba."

Announcing that he would act as his own defense lawyer, Fidel ended his letter with a dramatic quotation from José Martí that elicited shouts from the audience, and the applause of the Moncada veterans: "As to myself, if I have to give up my rights or my honor to remain alive, I prefer to die a thousand times. A just principle from the depths of a cave is stronger than an army."[61]

The trial thereafter was carried out in three stages. The first part of the proceedings was held at the regular court, the second in the Spanish Clinic, and the last part behind closed doors at the Civic Hospital. Fidel Castro was called to the stand only during the last stage of the trial.

Fidel Castro's Defense

On October 16, 1953, Castro appeared before the tribunal at the Civic Hospital, in a small room which was surrounded by troops. There he presented his plea as the trial came to an end. Today Castro's defense is known as "History Will Absolve Me," but the published version is not the exact plea made on that day. Fidel revised the original speech while he was in prison, and eventually covered a number of subjects, ranging from a description of the attack to reflections on himself, criticisms of Batista and a detailed discussion of his revolutionary program. The revised version probably was completed during the early part of 1954. In a letter addressed to Melba Hernández, dated April 17, 1954, Castro mentioned the revised edition, which he suggested be published in the form of a pamphlet.[62] Castro's wife, Mirta Díaz Balart, took the manuscript to Havana, where after some editing, it was published by the underground press.[63] The pamphlet had a limited distribution at the time, and its contents were largely unknown until 1959.

Castro's arguments before the court included his interpretation of the attack, charges of horrible crimes committed by the army against defenseless prisoners, and harsh attacks against the unconstitutionality of Batista's de facto regime. Five revolutionary laws constituted the crux of Castro's political and economic plans. The first law, "would return power to the people and proclaim the 1940 Constitution as the supreme law of the land until such time as the people should decide to modify or change it." To implement the constitution, "the revolutionary movement . . . the only source of legitimate power, would assume all the authority inherent to it except that of modifying the constitution itself: in other words, it would assume the legislative, executive and judicial powers." The second law "would grant property, not mortgageable and non-transferable to all planters, sub-planters, renters, sharecroppers, and squatters holding plots of five or less *caballerías* of land [one *caballería* is about 33.16 acres]: the state would indemnify former owners on the basis of the average income they would have received for these plots over a period of ten years."

The third law would grant workers and employees the right to share 30 percent of the profits of large industries including the sugar mills. The fourth would allow all planters "the right to share 50 percent of the sugar production and be allotted a minimum grinding quota of 500 tons of cane to all small planters who have been growing sugar cane for three or more years." The fifth law "would order the confiscation of all holdings and ill-acquired profits of those who committed frauds during previous administrations, as well as the holdings and ill-acquired profits of all their heirs."

Fidel described his view of Cuba's foreign policy in the Western Hemisphere as one that would align with the democratic governments of the continent, while extending generous asylum to all persecuted people. Cuba "should become the bulwark of freedom, and not a shameful link in the chain of despotism."[64] Six problems demanding the immediate attention of a revolutionary government were land reform, industrialization, housing, unemployment, health and welfare.

A large part of Fidel's argument was devoted to impressing upon the court the right to resist despotism; thus he attempted to justify the attack on Moncada with both historical and moral evidence. His defense was based on Article 40 of the constitution of 1940: "It is legitimate to use adequate resistance to protect previously granted individual rights." The prosecution based its case on Article 148 of the Code of Social Defense, the same one that Castro had used earlier in his suit against Batista.

Fidel quoted several thinkers and political theorists such as John of Salisbury. St. Thomas Aquinas, Martin Luther, Althusius, Milton and Jean Jacques Rousseau. He also cited the American Declaration of Independence and the Declaration of the Rights of Man of the French Revolution. Fidel ended his defense with the dramatic phrase: "Condemn me, it does not matter. History will absolve me."

It took the court only a few minutes of deliberation to sentence Castro to 15 years in prison at the Isle of Pines penitentiary. Sentenced to 13 years were Raúl Castro and Tizol. Ciro Redondo, Ramiro Valdés and Juan Almeida received ten years each. Montané was also sentenced to ten years and Melba Hernández and Haydée Santamaría to seven months each. The condemned were flown to the Isle of Pines penitentiary. For the time being, the leader of the Moncada attack was out of circulation.

Notes

1. Hugh Thomas writes: "Castro was born on 13 August, 1926, despite rumors that he was actually born a year later." See Hugh Thomas, *Cuba: The Pursuit of Freedom* (New York: Harper and Row, 1971), p. 802. Also citing 1926 as the correct year is Herbert Matthews. *Fidel Castro* (New York: Simon and Schuster, 1969), p. 17. However Gerardo Rodríguez Morejón. *Fidel Castro: biografía* (Havana: P. Fernández y Cía., 1959), p. 1. gives the correct date of Castro's birth. This short biography opens with a letter to the author signed by Lina Rúz de Castro certifying the accuracy of Castro's biographical data. Fidel was born after Angela and Ramón. Later came Raúl, Juana, Emilia and Agustina. Lidia and Pedro Emilio were Angel Castro's sons by his first marriage. On Castro's biographical data see also Luis Conte Agüero, *Fidel Castro, vida y obra* (Havana: Editorial Lex, 1959), pp. 5–9; "Síntesis cronológica de la vida de Fidel," *Revolución* (Havana), May 3, 1963. p. 3. Rolando E. Bonachea and Nelson P. Valdés, eds., *Revolutionary Struggle, 1947–1958*, vol. 1 (Cambridge: MIT Press, 1972). p. 4.

2. Ramón Castro held the view that this defeat was a blow to his young brother's ego, and that it furthered his political participation in the university through other ways, that is, the "action groups" (interview with Ramón Castro and Lalo Sardiña, Havana. February 1960). Castro's ambition and "desire to be a figure of importance" was apparently manifested in his early days as a law student, according to his mother. Lina Rúz de Castro, in a conversation at which one of the authors was present near her home in Birán. Oriente.

June 1959. An account of Castro's early life and entry into politics and revolution appears in Jules Dubois, *Fidel Castro: Rebel-Liberator or Dictator?* (Indianapolis: Bobbs-Merrill, 1959). Rather subjective in its anti-Castroism is Charles Malamuth. .028" Biography: Fidel Castro. Messiah Who Needs Help," *Communist Affairs*, vol. 1 (February-March, 1963): 15–26. On his involvement in university politics see Boris Goldenberg. (February-March, 1963): 15–26. On his involvement in university politics see Boris Goldenberg. *The Cuban Revolution and Latin America* (New York: Praeger, 1965), pp. 147–50.

3. Andrés Suárez, *Cuba: Castroism and Communism, 1959–1966* (Cambridge: MIT Press, 1967) p. 11. During the Grau administration many violent incidents were reported in the press, particularly in the "Sección en Cuba" of *Bohemia* (Havana), a weekly magazine.

4. Interviews with Mario Oropesa and José Garrucho Caral, former members of the UIR and MSR respectively (Union City, New Jersey, June 1972).

5. *Bohemia* (Havana), April 10, 1949, p. 63.

6. Ibid. See also *Bohemia* (Havana), April 24, 1949. p. 71.

7. *Bohemia* (Havana), April 24, 1949. p. 71.

8. Rolando Masferrer to one of the authors (Bridgeport, Connecticut, June 1961). See also Bohemia (Havana), April 10, 1949. pp. 62-63 and Bonachea and Valdés, *Revolutionary Struggle*, p. 24.

9. José Maceo (Bridgeport, Connecticut, June 1961) and Rolando Masferrer told one of the authors how Fidel jumped into shark-infested waters and swam ashore, managing to escape. At Cayo Confites, Fidel and Masferrer had a fist fight because Fidel refused to board a ship unless someone sent him a rowboat as the water was full of sharks there, too. Aboard the ship at last, Fidel asked Maceo to jump overboard into the water in a test of manliness. Fidel assured Maceo that his "santo" (saint or religious devotee) would protect them both. Maceo refused. Fidel jumped and Masferrer thought it was the last time they would see him.

10. The MSR newspaper. *Tiempo en Cuba*, covered the event in its issue no. 4, February 27, 1949. pp. 13–14. However *Tiempo en Cuba* was completely partisan in its interpretation of the event: further conflicts with the UIR thus became inevitable.

11. Masferrer to one of the authors. Masferrer asserted that Fidel was plotting his assassination.

12. See Jaime Suchlicki, *University Students and Revolution in Cuba* (Coral Gables, Fla.: University of Miami Press. 1969), p. 53.

13. Evidence of a former Cuban ambassador to Colombia, Guillermo Belt, to one of the authors (Washington, D.C., February 1968). Also see "Llegó de Bogotá un avión conduciendo siete refugiados." *Diario de la Marina* (Havana), April 14, 1948. p. 1. and *Bohemia* (Havana), April 25, 1948, p. 7; also see "Síntesis cronológica de la vida de Fidel." *Revolución* (Havana), May 3, 1963, p. 3.

14. A nephew of the victim, Garrucho Caral, told the authors he had accompanied Dr. Clara Pérez, an attorney, to the Vedado district of Havana where Jesús Jinjaume (UIR) was arraigned for the murder of Sergeant Caral. According to this version, Caral's son had witnessed the shooting, and the family asked protection from Major José Rego Rubido who appointed a police officer, Rafael Salas Cañizares, to the case. After preliminary investigation,

Jinjaume was arrested but soon released for lack of sufficient evidence. Allegedly, Masferrer overheard Caral's last words charging Fidel with the shooting. Caral's nephew refutes this, explaining that when Masferrer arrived at the hospital his uncle was listed as critical, and was not permitted to have any visitors. Caral died before anyone could talk to him (Garrucho Caral to the authors, Union City, June 1972). For a different version see *Tiempo en Cuba* (Havana), October 10, 1948. p. 51, and the UIR newspaper *El Matutino* for countercharges.

15. *Granma* (Havana), July 26, 1966. p. 5. A photostatic copy of the document is found in *Mil Fotos Cuba, territorio libre de América* (Havana: Comite Central del Partido Comunista de Cuba, 1967), p. 141. Fidel's brief consisted of three single-spaced typewritten pages.

16. *Granma* (Havana), July 26, 1966, p. 5.

17. Melba Hernández, "Siempre supimos que el asalto al Moncada culminaría en la victoria," *Verde Olivo* (Havana), July, 28, 1963, p. 29. It must be noted that *Son los mismos* was the "Official bulletin of the Ortodoxo Fraternity." *See A Sketch on the Clandestine and Guerrilla Press Covering the Period 1952–1958* (Havana: Instituto del Libro, 1971), p. 16.

18. Hernández, "Siempre supimos."

19. *The Clandestine and Guerrilla Press*, p. 16. Also see Raúl Castro, "En el VIII Aniversario del 26 de Julio," *Fundamentos* (Havana), no. 175 (June–July 1961), p. 5.

20. See Bonachea and Valdés, *Revolutionary Struggle*, p. 153.

21. *The Clandestine and Guerrilla Press*, p. 19.

22. Jesus Montané, "El Moncada." *La Calle* (Havana), July 26, 1959. p. C–8.

23. Pedro Miret once recalled. "We lost faith in all of those false leaders [the Auténticos] . . . and instead of waiting for what others would not give us, we decided to go into action with our own resources." See *Verde Olivo* (Havana), July 29, 1962, p. 6: and Lisandro Otero. "Entrevista a Haydée Santamaría y Melba Hernández." *Bohemia* Havana), September 9, 1966, p. 10.

24. Major José Ponce Díaz. "Recuerdos del ataque," *Verde Olivo* (Havana), July 28, 1963. p. 15; *Bohemia* (Havana), July 24, 1970, pp. 98–100, and *Revolución* (Havana), July 22, 1963, p. 6.

25. Marta Rojas. "Ochenta pesos de tiros." *Verde Olivo* (Havana), July 29, 1962, p. 36. and *Juventud Rebelde* (Havana), July 20, 1966.

26. Otero, "Entrevista." pp. 10–11.

27. Ibid., p. 11.

28. See "Datos biográficos de García Bárcena," *El Mundo* (Havana), July 8, 1952, p. 8. The MNR socioeconomic composition grouped militants from assorted backgrounds. Edgardo Buttari, Julián Fernández, Armando and Enrique Hart and Humberto Bacallao were sons of wealthy families. Others, like Frank País. Pepito Tey, Otto Parellada. Silvino Rodríguez, Joe Westbrook and Eva Jiménez, belonged to families of modest economic means. Mario Llerena and García Bárcena were professors, and Faustino Pérez was a medical student. Overall the movement was predominantly academic and intellectually oriented (evidence of one of the authors involved in the MNR movement).

29. The expression, *el golpe de la navajita*, was intended as a satirical metaphor depicting the impotence of the young revolutionaries vis à vis Fulgencio Batista's military prowess.

30. See "Acuerdo entre el PRC y el PPC." *El Mundo* (Havana), June 3, 1953, and *El Mundo* (Havana), June 22, 1953. The text of the pact appears, along with other Auténtico documents, in Aracelio Azcuy, *Cuba: campo de concentración* (Mexico: Ediciones Humanismo. March 10, 1954). pp. 308–09. The undersigners were Carlos Prío Socarrás, Emilio Ochoa, Manuel A. de Varona. José Pardo Llada, Guillermo Alonso Pujol. Isidro Figueroa Bontempo, Carlos Hevia. José M. Gutiérrez Planas and Eduardo Suárez Rivas.

31. Mario G. del Cueto, "Trazo biográfico de Renato Guitart," *Bohemia* (Havana), July 21, 1967. p. 7. Renato was a close friend of Otto Parellada, José (Pepín) Naranjo, and José A. Echeverría, who would in time play roles in the insurrection. See also "Renato Guitart," *Cuba Internacional*, no. 63 (Havana), July 1967.

32. Rojas, "Ochenta pesos," p. 36. The ammunition was purchased at the José Marina & Co. armory in Old Havana; each .22 caliber rifle cost $80. An earlier account gives another estimate of the group's military equipment that included one submachine gun .45 caliber with 2,000 rounds of ammunition, one M-l, 30 to 40 pistols, automatic rifles .22 caliber, one hand grenade, .16 caliber automatic shotguns and two Winchesters; Fidel's weapon was a .9 mm. Luger which was obtained through army Sergeant Florentino Fernández. See Miguel Enrique, "Artemisa en el Moncada." *Lunes de Revolución*, no. 19 (Havana), July 26, 1959. p. 8.

33. Raúl Castro has set the number of combatants at 165. See "En el VIII Aniversario," p. 5. Jesús Montané has placed the number at 133. See "El Moncada," p. C–8. But Fidel, in his account of the attack, listed 153 men. See Fidel Castro, *Pensamiento Político, Econòmico y Social de Fidel Castro* (Havana: Editorial Lex. 1959). pp. 29–30.

34. Fidel's scheme was not exactly innovative. Almost two decades earlier, on April 29, 1932. Antonio Guiteras, founder of Joven Cuba, an anti-Machado insurrectionary organization, had led an uprising and simultaneous attack against the barracks of San Luis and Victoria de las Tunas. The uprising was to take control of the Caney, Santiago de Cuba and Moncada army posts. Guiteras had planned to bombard the latter, lead an insurrection from Oriente province and provoke a nationwide general strike to depose dictator General Gerardo Machado (1925–33). See *Pensamiento revolucionario cubano*, vol. 1 (Havana: Instituto del Libro, 1971). p. 385.

35. See Castro, *Pensamiento Político*, p. 32. It must be noted that at the time of Batista's coup in March 1952, the officialdom of the Moncada barracks was reported to have wavered in its support of the coup. See "Trazo biográfico de Renato Guitart," p. 6.

36. Hernández. "Siempre supimos," p. 29. However, Jesús Montané recalls that the army material was purchased at the San Ambrosio barracks by Sergeant Fernández and then made into uniforms at Melba's home. See Montané, "El Moncada," p. C–8.

37. Fidel Castro, "Manifiesto de los revolucionarios del Moncada a la nación." in *13 documentos de la insurrección*. (Havana: Organización Nacional de Bibliotecas Ambulantes. 1959), pp. 19–22. A brief Soviet interpretation of the attack is found in "The Storming of Moncada: How the Cuban Revolution Began." *New Times* (Moscow), July 31, 1963. pp. 4–7. Carlos M. de Céspedes, Ignacio Agramonte and José Martí were leaders of the independence

movement. Julio A. Mella was one of the founders of the Cuban Communist party, and Rafael Trejo was a martyr in the revolution against Machado.

38. This is a reference to the Partido Revolucionario Cubano founded by José Marti in 1892 to organize the war of independence against Spain. The Montecristi Manifesto issued by Martí and General Máximo Gómez declared war on Spain, and was released from the Dominican Republic. Joven Cuba was Antonio Guiteras' underground organization, and ABC-Radical was led by Oscar de la Torre. See *Pensamiento revolucionario cubano*, pp. 128–33 and 192–93; also see Mario Riera Hernández. *Cuba Libre 1895–1958* (Miami: Colonial Press, 1968) and Medardo Vitier, *Las ideas en Cuba*, 2 vols, (Havana: Editorial Trópico, 1938).

39. Raúl had just returned from the International Youth Festival in Vienna. He had visited Rumania and Hungary. The Cuban delegation, whose expenses were paid by the PSP, also included Fabio Grobart. Raúl Valdés Vivó. Alfredo Guevara and Vilma Espín, Raúl was arrested on his arrival in Havana but released soon. See Ramón Calcines. "Reporte al Partido Socialista Popular." *Fundamentos* (Havana), February. 1959, pp. 83-85. Raúl's military target, the Palace of Justice, was by every consideration less dangerous than Abel's since the building was empty on a Sunday morning.

40. See Marta Rojas. "Los testigos del hospital." *Bohemia* (Havana), July 24, 1970, p. 10.

41. The surprise factor had been lost when the second car driven by Fidel unexpectedly collided against the pavement at the entrance of post 3. This incident prompted a guard to sound the alarm system and forced the second group to rush for shelter behind the walls near the post. This is the position which, according to Pedro Miret's account. Fidel occupied while the first group helplessly attempted to gain a foothold in the barracks. Since the reinforcement group never showed up it was common sense it order retreat. See Marta Rojas. *La Generación del Centenario* (Havana: Ediciones R, 1964), pp. 247–248.

42. According to Pedro Miret the sharpshooters held the soldiers back for at least three hours. During this time Fidel had ample time to withdraw himself and his men from the barracks' surroundings. In Miret's own words, "I kept on shooting for at least three hours at post 3, the only place where there was a combat." See Rojas. *La Generación*, pp. 237, 248–49.

43. This computation is based on Fidel's account of the actual distribution of his men before the court in Santiago. See Fidel Castro. *La Historia me absolverá* (Havana: Editorial Lex, 1959), and Castro. *Pensamiento Politico*. pp. 29–30. The actual distribution of fighters does not provide an accurate figure for the amount of actual participants. Marta Rojas' semiofficial coverage of the accounts at the trial shows that some combatants refused to go along with the plan. See *La Generación*, p. 173.

44. Pedro Aguilera ("Aguilerita") was an Ortodoxo dentist working at the Charco Redondo mines near Bayamo. His participation in the overall plan was vital for he was responsible for securing the dynamite with which the bridges over the great Cauto river would be blown up. Guamo. Cauto Cristo and Palmarito were the targets: thus all access lines of reinformcements to Santiago de Cuba would be cut. See Germán Sánchez Otero, "El Moncada: inicio de la Revolución Cubana." *Punto Final* (Santiago de Chile), suplemento no. 162. July 18, 1972. p. 7: and Rojas. *La Generación*, p. 99.

45. See *Revolución* (Havana), July 20, 1962. p. 1: also, Marta Matamoros. "El asalto al cuartel de Bayamo." *Granma* (Havana), July 6, 1967. pp. 4–5.

46. *Diario de la Marina* (Havana), August 5, 1953. Colonel Alberto del Rio Chaviano's statement appears in *Reporte emitido por el Estado Mayor del Ejército sobre el asalto al cuartel Moncada* (Havana: August 2, 1953). 22 pp., an unpublished manuscript of former captain Augusto Morales Santiesteban.

47. *Reporte Oficial*, p. 10.

48. Fulgencio Batista y Zaldívar, "Declaraciones," *Diario de Cuba* (Santiago de Cuba). July 30, 1953. pp. 1, 3.

49. *Bohemia* (Havana), August 9, 1953, p. 67: *El Mundo* (Havana), July 31, 1953, and *Diario de la Marina* (Havana), August 9, 1953.

50. See Alfredo Reyes Trejo, "Del Moncada a las Montañas." *Verde Olivo* (Havana), July 30, 1972, pp. 24–33. July 22, 1963, p. 6. The first article is particularly revealing in that journalist Trejo covered a field trip undertaken by former Moncada combatants Oscar Alcalde and Mario Lazo to recall the peasants and places where they had been helped 19 years earlier. It was the first such trip to the area after so many years. Rosell's account appeared in *Revolución* (Havana), July 22, 1963, p. 6.

51. Castro, *Pensamiento Político*, p. 31.

52. Trejo, "Del Moncada," p. 32. Other peasants who helped the fugitives were Ramón González (Cundingo). Hortensia Salgado. Alfonso Feal and Justino Rigel. Felipe Rigel refused to sell food to Fidel. In 1972 they all were living in the same places as in 1953.

53. Ibid., pp. 32–33: also "Cuando Sarría detuvo a Fidel Castro y a dos de sus compañeros el sábado 1 de agosto de 1953." *Revolución* (Havana), July 26, 1962, p. 15.

54. "*Cuando Sarría,*" p. 15.

55. See Rodolfo Rodríguez Zaldívar. "Por qué Fidel Castro no fué asesinado al capturarlo el Ejército de Oriente," *Bohemia* (Havana), March 8, 1959, pp. 63. 112: and "En la cárcel de Santiago de Cuba 8 fugitivos capturados." *Diario de la Marina* (Havana), August 2, 1953, pp. 1. 39. On August 20, 1957. Lieutenant Sarria was charged with conspiracy and sentenced to one year, one month and one day in prison. He appealed this sentence on December 28, 1958, and two days later the Rebel Army freed him from a cell in the Moncada barracks.

56. *Reporte Oficial*, p. 17.

57. In a letter to Herbert Matthews. Juan Marinello of the PSP stated "with reference to the assaults on barracks and expeditions from abroad taking place without relying on popular support our policy is very clear: we are against these methods." See Herbert L. Matthews. *The Cuban Story* (New York: Braziller, 1961), p. 51.

58. See Alfredo Gómez. "The Political Situation in Cuba." *Political Affairs*, no. 10 (October 1954) 49–59.

59. Ibid., pp. 53–54.

60. *Diario de la Marina* (Havana), July 27, 1953, pp. 1, 3.

61. See Rosa H. Zell, "6 documentos del Moncada." *Bohemia* (Havana), July 27, 1962. p. 67: also see Marta Rojas. *El juicio del Moncada* (Buenos Aires: Ediciones de Ambos Mundos. 1966).

62. Luis Conte Agüero, *Los dos rostros de Fidel Castro* (Mexico: Editorial Jus, 1960), p. 65. "Mirtha [Fidel's wife] will tell you about a pamphlet of great importance because of its ideological content, and tremendous accusations [to] which I would like you to pay the closest attention."

63. Francisco de Armas. "Como se editó en la clandestinidad la primera edición de la Historia me Absolverá." *Hoy* (Havana), July 21, 1963. pp. 2–3; see also Luis Conte Agüero. *Cartas del presidio* (Havana: Editorial Lex, 1959). p. 37.

64. Castro, *La Historia me Absolverá*, pp. 19, 20, 22–24.

2

Elections and Amnesty

In 1954 General Batista apparently felt that the political climate was ripe for the legitimation of his power. Opposition to his regime was weak and ineffective. The insurrectionists had been defeated in their attempts to unseat him, and the electoralists were badly divided.

The PPC-O had split at the end of 1953. Some high-ranking party members would not accept the leadership of Roberto Agramonte, and the party's younger members increasingly favored an insurrectionary line. Competing against Agramonte for the party's leadership was Carlos Márquez Sterling. When the government announced that elections would be held the following year, Márquez Sterling immediately announced his intention to run for the presidency.

The PRC-A also split into two main factions. One followed the insurrectionary approach led by former president Prío, and the other supported former president Grau San Martín, who, like Márquez Sterling, was opposed to a violent solution of the Cuban dilemma. Grau San Martín registered as the candidate of the PRC-A for the elections of 1954. Offices to be filled included the presidency, vice-presidency and the governorships of the six provinces. Also to be elected were 54 senators, 150 representatives, 125 mayors and 2,214 councilmen.

In a move to further weaken the opposition, Batista eliminated the requirement that established a minimum number of registered voters for any party to participate in the election.[1] José Pardo Llada, former senator and radio commentator, was the first to take advantage of this political maneuver; he registered under the auspices of his newly created Partido Nacional Revolucionario and moved to declare his own candidacy. By December 10, 1953, nine parties had registered to participate in the November 1954 elections,[2] but most of them later dropped out of the race. Those which did remain had been organized by politicians hungry for the spoils that the law of minorities offered the defeated. Internal dissent and intense political rivalries among the leaders of the electoralists prevented coordinated opposition to Batista's candidacy. The general had the support of the Coalición Progresista Nacional which was formed by all the political groups involved with the regime. To fulfill a constitutional requirement,

Batista resigned from the presidency, yielding the post to Secretary of State Andrés Doming y Morales del Castillo.

The students clearly did not accept the pledge that the elections would be free and honest. Led by the FEU they continued public demonstrations against the elections and Batista's regime. Clashes between police and students became more frequent during the weeks prior to the elections. Terrorist activities were also intensified, and the students found themselves cooperating with the clandestine Triple A movement organized by former Secretary of Education Aureliano Sánchez Arango.

In July, Márquez Sterling was the victim of a terrorist attempt on his life, but this did not persuade him to withdraw. A second attempt, from which he miraculously escaped, was made in October.[3] Following this incident. Márquez Sterling arranged a meeting with Santiago Rey, Justo Luis del Pozo and Alfredo Jacomino, who represented Batista. Márquez Sterling made several demands on behalf of all candidates: total guarantees of honest elections; reestablishment of the 1943 Electoral Code; freedom for all political prisoners; permission to allow political exiles to return; cancellation of the Public Order Law; and last, *voto directo* (direct vote).[4] Batista's representatives acquiesced to all of these demands except the issue of *voto directo*. Márquez Sterling then ended the meeting, saying, "Under these circumstances we cannot take the Ortodoxos to the elections."[5]

Throughout the campaign, the opposition did not have the same degree of freedom of expression as the government candidates. Many caches of arms were discovered by the police. Some of these had been sent by Prío's clandestine Organización Auténtica (OA), but others evidently had been placed by the authorities to support their accusations that the opposition had already decided to sabotage the election results.

As the election date neared, most Ortodoxo politicians followed Márquez Sterling, and withdrew from the race. Forty-eight hours before voting took place, Grau San Martín announced his withdrawal also. Yet the PRC-A ballots remained in the booths at the electoral precincts, and several Auténtico candidates were elected to Congress. By the law of minorities, 18 of 54 senate seats were alloted to the minority party, the PRC-A.[6]

In a race from which all other candidates had previously withdrawn it was only natural that Batista was "elected" president. He received 1,262,587 votes, or 45.1 percent of the total electoral population of 2,768,186 (which amounted to 47.46 percent of the total population eligible to vote). The government announced that 52.44 percent of the voters had participated in the process. Grau received 188,209 votes, or 6.8 percent of the total.[7]

The election had many irregularities. In some areas more votes were cast than there were registered voters, and therefore most of the districts went to Batista. All electoral precincts were closely guarded by armed soldiers, who allegedly coerced the voters into marking their ballots for Batista. Immediately after the results were announced, charges and countercharges of corruption were made. The electoral tribunal hurriedly rejected all accusations made by the opposition and conceded the election to Batista and his running mate, Rafael Guás Inclán. Certificates of election were rapidly issued, and the electoral tribunal publicly declared its investigation and supervision of the process closed.[8] On February 24, 1955, General Batista assumed the presidency for a four-year term.[9]

For many Cubans the elections were a farce and proof that Batista wished to remain in power regardless of political conditions in the country. The insurrectionists claimed that the elections had been rigged and the only way to get rid of Batista was through violent revolution.

The *Forrajeo*

The national police welcomed Batista's decision to remain in office for another term, for they were enjoying an economic boom through the exploitation of various means of corruption, graft and extortion. Most police officers supported the dictator not for his political beliefs but because they had become involved in a system that permitted them to acquire an economic status they had lacked previously. The system in question, from which the police so benefited, was known as the *forrajeo.*

The *forrajeo* was a well-organized instrument of extortion managed by police officers throughout the country, but especially predominant in the municipal zones of Greater Havana, i.e., Regla, Guanabacoa and Marianao. It was in that zone that most small stores and medium and large business, centers were located. Through the *forrajeo* every business, regardless of its size, had to contribute daily to the police precinct in each locality.

Approximately 3,400 *bodegas* (small grocery stores usually owned by a single family) were located in Greater Havana. Each *bodega* had to pay a "tax" of one to two pesos daily, in addition to whatever consumer goods the police demanded from the owner. This "tax" was collected by the local patrol car every afternoon. Havana's 180 bakeries and all snack bars supplied the police with their products, plus paying three pesos daily to the foot patrol. Nearly 400 service stations paid one peso daily, and serviced free of charge all police officers' private cars. Butcher shops, some 940, had to contribute two to three pounds of meat per day, plus one peso to the local patrol officer. Not even the street vendors escaped the widely instituted practice of supporting their local police officers!

There were about 62 delivery trucks of "La Polar" beer factory; 46 from "Hatuey" and 42 from "La Tropical." Each truck was "taxed" for two pesos daily. Two hundred cigar delivery trucks paid one peso daily, plus products on demand. Milkmen also were assigned a quota of two liters per day, or two pesos in cash. All these transactions were carried out openly, on any corner, in public and whenever the police felt like collecting these special "taxes."

Together with prostitution and drug traffic, gambling was the most profitable business for the police. Around 2,000 small *vidrieras* (booths) were scattered throughout the capital where numbers were played every hour on the hour. The *vidrieras* were "taxed," and their income distributed as follows: the bureau of investigation received $10 from each *vidriera* per day; the district police commander, $10; the captain of the local precinct, $10. Payment was made every day. Additionally, the *vidrieras* had to allow each local police officer $2 daily for his personal gambling. Here the breakdown was as follows: police lieutenants, sergeants and corporals, $2; recruits (depending on time served in the force) from 50 cents to $1.50 daily. The secret police, however, was only assigned $10 weekly from each *vidriera*, probably because it participated very little in persecuting insurrectionists, and its main duties were to investigate common criminals. The *forrajeo* was designed for the lower echelons of the police.

Six banks controlled gambling. All were referred to by their nick-names, i.e., "Castillo y Colon," "Chano," "Juan," "La China," "La Central" and "Campanario." The latter was owned by a consortium of government officials, and thus was exempt from the *forrajeo*. Each bank had to pay an estimated $400 a day to various high-ranking police officers. "La China" paid $1,000 a day in order to be permitted to expand into new areas of the city. In total, the banks' share to the *forrajeo* system and other "taxes" amounted to approximately $1 million a year paid to high-ranking officers.[10] The *vidrieras* represented an income to the police of about $3.8 million a year, which was divided up from the rank of majors, through captains, to regular patrolmen.[11] The *forrajeo* was not exclusive to Havana, but existed in every small town or city of the country, including the Isle of Pines. In the countryside, the rural guard corps obtained easy credit, food and clothes from the towns' small country stores. Estimates of the size of the entire system defy the imagination, and go a long way toward explaining the police's support for Batista (who looked the other way), and their staunch opposition to the insurrectionists.

But of all the commercial transactions carried out by the police one of the most ominous and important was prostitution. In Havana alone, there were approximately 2,000 houses of prostitution, small and large, humble and luxurious. Each casa paid an amount calculated by the local patrolmen after figuring out the number of clients per night, and the fees charged each one. Thus, very humble casas could pay from $50 to $70 per night, while the richest of all—Casa Marina—contributed from $3,000 to $5,000 a night. All payments were due between 12 midnight and 5 AM. Uniformed police officers would arrive at the various casas, and the madam would have the cash on hand. The transaction was made in front of any clients who happened to be present.

Police officers were not excluded from performing as procurers. Some had their own team of girls working on their own time and not affiliated with a casa. The girls sometimes were drug peddlers, and the police officers supplied the drugs. On occasions when there was a scarcity of girls the police procured new recruits for the system. On New Years' Eve, or when a large U.S. Navy vessel paid a call to Havana, new girls appeared. Sometimes they were brought from the countryside, transported to Havana's casas, and initiated into what they referred to as *la vida*. The case of the *guajiritas* (young peasant girls) was particularly infamous. Some had gone into prostitution when, lured by the prospects of big city life, they found themselves unskilled, unfamiliar with city customs, and presented with an offer that a *caballeroso Habanero* (a Havana gentleman) would solve all economic problems. The *guajiritas* had mostly been maids for middle-class families in the countryside towns where they were paid 8 pesos a month and given food and used clothes. Some *guajiritas* had eloped with boyfriends and brought "dishonor" to their homes; for these there was no return home once traditional values were broken, and only life in populous Havana would hide them from the scorn of family and neighbors. At any rate, the casas paid well for new girls, depending on their age. A twelve-to-fifteen year old could bring $1,000 from a very special customer.[12] Once in *la vida*, the girls stayed in the casa, for a return to the countryside was unthinkable.

Drug traffic was just as good an "industry," mostly supplying the rich and American tourists. Not all police officers, even those with high rank, partook in the spoils, for drug traffic on a heavy scale was controlled by organized crime from the United States. But a substantial percentage of the profits probably reached the highest governmental circles.

The importance of the *forrajeo* system to the insurrectionists cannot be underestimated. Police exploitation eventually turned businessmen against the dictatorship. The urban underground gathered much of their intelligence information from prostitutes and then relayed it to the rural areas through such women. Their mission consisted of "debriefing" as much as possible any important customer connected with government agencies, and to contact underground agents. The "bankers," who themselves exploited the people, gave the insurrection almost as much money as they paid the police. Each bloc of vested interests supported the insurrection for different reasons, but in the end only one sector could politically benefit from a system of corruption—the insurrectionists.[13]

General Amnesty

After Batista's inauguration, general amnesty became the goal of the opposition. Granting amnesty to political prisoners was a tradition in Cuban politics; new governments customarily extended a general amnesty as a gesture of conciliation. Yet, this time there was a group of rebels in prison who elicited the hatred of every member of the armed forces.

Throughout his prison term, Fidel Castro had kept up a voluminous correspondence with friends and relatives on the mainland. From the Isle of Pines, he tried to keep the flame of resistance burning by means of letters, secret messages, an occasional manifesto and speeches read by friends to small gatherings. Luis Conte Agüero, a popular radio commentator, and Fidel's long-time friend from the university, received most of Fidel's letters from prison.

Although there is evidence that Fidel held discussion groups with the other Moncada prisoners in an effort to deepen the group's commitment to the struggle,[14] his letters from prison best reveal his concerns during those months of confinement from 1953 to 1955. The first letter was dated December 12, 1953, and in it Castro complained that Ortodoxo politicians had criticized the Moncada assault. Some of the critics were members of the executive council of the PPC-O, and, echoing the Communists, they had referred to Castro's action as a putsch, something Castro deeply resented. Castro defended his membership in the PPC-O, and argued firmly he was a loyal party member and follower of Chibás' postulates.'[15]

At the Isle of Pines, Castro became more convinced than ever that the only way to get rid of Batista was through violent insurrection. Propaganda was to be the main instrument, but the movement behind the insurrection "must have its own style, and must adjust itself to the circumstances."[16] A good revolutionary, in the process of organizing the struggle, should have a lot of "tolerance and be amiable." Later, there would be time "to crush all the cockroaches together." Meantime, the prison was not the place from which to launch an insurrection: "To be imprisoned is to be condemned to forced silence; to listen and to read what is being written and spoken without being able to express any opinions."[17] All efforts, therefore, had to be directed toward forcing the government into granting a general amnesty.

The amnesty campaign, led by Luis Conte Agüero, spread. In May 1955, Senator Arturo Fernández Tellaheche (PRC-A) presented a motion for general amnesty; Congress backed it, and Batista signed it into law.[18] All political prisoners were released, and many exiles returned home, among them Carlos Prío. But the most famous of the released prisoners was Fidel Castro. Indeed, it was Castro, not Prío or any other exiled politician, whom the press wanted to interview. Castro's opinions, which he voiced at every opportunity, received the greatest attention.

The mood in the streets, however, was still hostile to violent revolution, and Castro readily interpreted the feelings of the population in this as well as other matters. Leaders of the PPC-O paid their respects to him not only because he was the most popular figure among the youth of the party, but also because his support represented an asset no politician could easily dismiss. Asked if he would support congressional elections, Castro rejected the idea as a political maneuver by some opportunists wishing to become mayors and congressmen. He pointed out there could be no solution other than holding general elections at the earliest possible time and with constitutional guarantees for all, because under those conditions the defeat of the dictatorship would be an incontrovertible fact. Those wishing to know if Castro planned to lead another revolutionary action were told by the Moncada leader that he supported peaceful change "because we are not agitators by profession," and thus "if a change in circumstances calls for a shift in the factors of the struggle, we will comply out of respect for the nation's highest interests." When asked to define his political ideology, Castro stated that he considered himself a genuine Ortodoxo. Castro declared that while in prison he had studied the programs of the Ortodoxo party as well as the programs of several newly created parties and political movements. "They all agree," Castro said, "on what is important: the need for great political, social, and economic reforms, and the necessity to establish a regime of freedom and justice." But in order to attain those goals, unity was necessary. Castro called for a wide opposition front against Batista: division, he warned, would never result in any positive action against the Batista regime.[19]

Raúl Chibás, brother of the late Eduardo R. Chibás—founder of the Ortodoxo party—and Roberto Agramonte, its acting president, received Castro into the party with open arms. During a visit at Castro's apartment in the suburbs of Havana Raúl Chibás expressed the hope that "the courageous youth of the Moncada will work with us in the same civic spirit which they have displayed to date, and return democratic procedures to Cuba and the full enjoyment of its trampled freedoms."[20] This accommodation was temporarily beneficial for all the parties involved. Fidel needed the Ortodoxos to enhance his own leadership aspirations, and the Ortodoxos needed Fidel so that they could pose as benefactors of the famous rebel. Eventually the benefactors were to take orders from their protegé, with Raúl Chibás and Roberto Agramonte following Castro's directives in the struggle against Batista.

The reality was that Castro still commanded only a small sector of the Ortodoxo youth, courageous as they were. But if any of Cuba's long-established politicians thought they could control or even advise Castro or involve him in their kind of politics, they were soon disappointed. Fidel Castro was not a man to be used. If anything, Castro would use the politicians to gain the leadership of the revolution. This young man, who had gathered experience during his involvement in the "action groups," appears to have anticipated the politicians' intentions to the letter. While he avoided getting involved with them, he did not attack them head on, at least not until he could count on the support of his own movement, or until he was out of reach and in exile, organizing the insurrection.

The Search for a Movement

Castro's top priority when he left the Isle of Pines was to recruit individuals likely to go along with his plans for the formation of a revolutionary movement. He had discussed this matter aboard the ship El Pinero, where he was brought to the city of Havana, with Melba Hernández and Haydée Santamaría, among others.[21] Once the initial excitement of Castro's release had simmered down he began working on *La Calle*, a newspaper sponsored by the Ortodoxo leader Luis Orlando Rodríguez, who welcomed him. In it Castro published articles critical of the government, attempting to arouse readers' enthusiasm for an organization vaguely labeled "the revolutionary movement."[22]

On May 25, 1955, Fidel denounced the arrest of Pedro Miret. Warning the public that "amnesty is becoming a bloody hoax played on the people and the press," he claimed that no guarantees existed for the Moncada veterans, and therefore "we plan to remain in the country in an effort to find a decent solution without bloodshed to the tragic situation of Cuba."[23] Four days later he attacked Colonel Alberto del Río Chaviano for a letter sent to *Bohemia* which used threatening words toward the recently released prisoners. In a challenge to Chaviano's *machismo* Fidel asked, "Had he thought perhaps that, because of his colonel's brass and being used to absolute power when he gave orders in the brave land of Oriente, that we . . . would not know how to reply to him vigorously?" Then he went on to list the crimes committed by the troops against the Moncada prisoners under Chaviano's command, citing places and number of casualties, and comparing these to casualties inflicted during the Wars of Independence. Fidel also denounced Chaviano's vices and connections with smuggling and challenged him to expose his "murky" businesses. Finally, he had words of praise for Batista's soldiers and "all honorable military men even though they might not think as I do." Of the soldiers he wrote, "I defended them more than anyone before March 10 [1952], and there are my articles in the newspaper *Alerta* as irrefutable proof."[24]

On June 11, Fidel assumed an antiterrorist position when in an article entitled "Against Terror and Crime" he argued that "to set off bombs . . . can only be the work of scoundrels without conscience." Fidel declared that such a tactic helped the dictatorship and thus "I would not hesitate to publicly denounce the bunch of savages. . . ."[25]

In spite of the attention he drew with his articles. Fidel still had only a small group of followers. Uppermost in his mind was the creation of an elite insurrectionary movement made up of experienced, determined and disciplined militants. He felt that a mass movement would fail, since the insurrectionists as yet lacked the experience to control a large organization. An elite insurrectionary movement, carefully screening its cadres, exerting rigorous criteria for recruitment and abiding by discipline from above constituted the basic elements of an efficient apparatus as envisioned by Fidel in his discussions with Charles Simeón, founder, with "Tony" Guiteras, of Jóven Cuba.[26]

Haunted by a "putschist" image since the Moncada assault, and needing to erase the notion that only terrorist tactics were applicable to the Cuban problem, Castro sought the aid of Cubans who were esteemed as members of the intelligentsia. He was particularly interested in a recently formed group named Movimiento de Liberación Radical (MLR) which very actively opposed Batista in the city of Havana.[27] The members had an assortment of backgrounds—there were Catholics and Protestants, Auténticos and former Marxists. The MLR boasted a program somewhat radical for the mid-fifties. It supported agrarian reform, a revamping of education and restructuring the electoral system.

Fidel sought a meeting with this group, though MLR secretary-general Amalio Fiallo was ill-disposed to meet with a man who, in his opinion, had a gangster-like reputation. Through Pedro Trigo of the MLR, Fidel established contact with Mario Llerena, who apparently persuaded the MLR leadership to exchange ideas with Castro. A meeting was arranged during June 1955. For hours Fidel and the MLR leaders discussed Cuba's problems, what course to take and what kind of revolution to carry out. Finally Fidel asked the MLR to dissolve and join "his movement." since in his opinion both groups would complement each other.[28] Despite the fact that members of the MLR and a few veterans of the Moncada attack, including Fidel, met again for further discussion, no understanding was ever reached. The intelligentsia was not ready to accept Castro, and Castro found the thinking of the MLR members too fuzzy.

Soon after the MLR discussions, in June, Castro met with a group of Moncada veterans: Lester Rodríguez, Jesús Montané and Pedro Miret; also present at the gathering were María Antonia Figueroa, an Ortodoxo activist from Oriente province, and two former members of García Bárcena's MNR: Faustino Pérez and Armando Hart.[29] María Antonia had been brought to Havana at the invitation of Lester, a native of Oriente, so that she could meet Fidel. At Fidel's request María Antonia accepted the position of provincial treasurer of the revolutionary movement.

Because María Antonia had extensive contacts in Santiago, Fidel asked her to recruit members for his revolutionary group. María Antonia told Fidel about a dynamic group of young people in Oriente led by a young man "of exceptional talent, patriotic commitment and organizational skills."[30] Fidel was interested in this young man, and it was decided that Lester Rodríguez and María Antonia would speak to Frank País, leader of the Oriente activists.

Frank País

Frank Isaac País was born on December 7, 1934, in Santiago de Cuba, Oriente, son of Doña Rosario García, a humble Spanish immigrant, and Francisco País Pesqueira, pastor of Santiago's First Baptist Church. Frank had two younger brothers, Agustín and Josué.[31] País attended the Martí Institute, which was located on the ground floor of his father's church, and then registered at the "Juan Bautista Sagarra" school in Santiago. Because his family lacked the economic means to send him to a private institution. Frank was given free tuition at Santiago's institute of secondary education. Thereafter he entered the National Teachers School of Santiago de Cuba and took English classes at night.[32] For academic year 1952-53 Frank was elected president of the student association at the National Teachers, School.

Frank was versed in the works of José Martí and the Bible. Gifted in many ways, he wrote poetry and composed music, including several hymns he wrote for his father's church.[33] While at the Teachers' School he met such future revolutionaries as José ("Pepito") Tey, René Ramos Latour, Oscar Lucero Moya and Carlos Díaz Fontaina, among others.

At the time of the assault against the Moncada barracks Frank was already the leader of a group of young insurrectionists—Acción Revolucionaria Oriental (ARO).[34] ARO recruited students from all of Santiago's secondary institutes, and used the facilities of the Teachers' School as well as the "Ursula Céspedes" school for meetings and printing revolutionary leaflets. ARO later became Acción Nacional Revolucionaria (ANR) when "Pepito" Tey, as president of the FEU of Oriente University, recruited other students from Camagüey and Las Villas provinces.[35] When the MNR conspiracy in Havana, led by García Bárcena, failed, several MNR militants from Guantánamo joined the ANR, by now the strongest group in Oriente.

The ANR, led by Frank País, was a clandestine organization divided into three fronts or sectors: propaganda, action and sabotage, and finances. It had already compiled an insurrectionary record: an assault against the El Cristo arms depot, numerous bombings, and an assault on the Club de Cazadores in Santiago. In the Charco Redondo mines, ANR militants had managed to secure enough dynamite to carry out sabotage activities.

It was to this solidly established group that Fidel turned in the summer of 1955. On July 7, 1955, Castro left Cuba for Mexico City. On July 10, Pedro Miret and Lester Rodríguez left for Bayamo and Santiago de Cuba, respectively, to begin an arduous search for people willing to become part of a *fidelista* movement.[36] Miret met with the youth section of the Ortodoxo party (Juventud Ortodoxa) in the cities of Bayamo, Manzanillo and Holguín, all of which were in Oriente province.[37] Miret was able to gather enough support so that, on November 15, 1955, at a meeting between Fidel's men and the Ortodoxos, the *fidelista* movement became a reality.[38] Meanwhile, throughout the fall Lester Rodríguez. María Antonia Figueroa and Miret kept trying to persuade Frank País and Pepito Tey to join their movement. Frank was offered the position of chief of action and sabotage for Oriente province if he would bring his group of men under the aegis of what was now being called the 26th of July Movement (M-26-7). País accepted the offer toward the end of 1955.

On February 24, 1956, Frank País arrived in Bayamo, met with members of the Ortodoxo youth and syndicate workers from the tobacco sector. By the time of his departure, he had organized an M-26-7 underground group in Bayamo.[39] Thus began Frank País' preparation of the clandestine apparatus of the M-26-7, that would pave the way for Oriente's courageous defiance of the dictatorship.

Notes

1. See *Gaceta Oficial* (Havana), Decree-Law' No. 1307. February 26, 1954, pp. 1–3.
2. Ibid., p. 2.
3. Authors' interview with Carlos Márquez Sterling (New York, November 25, 1972) According to Márquez Sterling the assailants were Antonio (Ñico) López, a Moncada veteran. Marcelo Sánchez and Manuel López Pérez of the Ortodoxo Youth. Also see Carlos Márquez Sterling. *Historia de Cuba: desde Colón hasta Castro* (New York: Las Américas Publishing Co., 1963), p. 361.
4. Direct vote consisted of splitting the ballot for president and congress. Batista favored voting on a single slate, thus avoiding split voting. The PSP favored the "negative vote." or voting against Batista and for Grau. For the latter's electoral position see Alfredo Gómez. "The Political Situation in Cuba." in *Political Affairs*, vol. 33, no. 19 (October 1954): 56–57.
5. Márquez Sterling, *Historia de Cuba*, p. 574.
6. Though Grau asked everyone elected to resign, only one of the elected senators did so; Dr José Morales Gómez. See José Alvarez Díaz. *A Study of Cuba* (Coral Gables; University of Miami Press, 1965). p. 419, n. 40. For a discussion of these election see Hugh Thomas, *Cuba: The Pursuit of Freedom* (New York: Harper and Row, 1971). pp. 845–62.
7. "Cómputo total de votes sumados para Presidente de la República," *Diario de la Marina* (Havana), December 22, 1954, p. 1.
8. *Diario de la Marina* (Havana), December 21, 1954 and *Prensa Libre* (Havana), December 20, 1954.
9. On February 23, 1955, Batista appointed the following persons to his cabinet: Jorge Garcia Montes, Prime Minister; Carlos Saladrigas, Secretary, of State; Fidel Barreto. Agriculture; Amelia Fernández Concheso, Education: Raúl Menocal, Commerce: Justo Garcia Rayneri, Finance; Armando Coro. Health; José Suárez Rivas, Labor; Santiago Verdeja, Defense; Ramón Vasconcelos; Communications; and Andrés Domingo y Morales del Castillo, Secretary of the Presidency. See *Diario de la Marina* (Havana), February 24, 1955, p. 1.
10. José A. Fernández. "El forrajeo policiaco durante la tiranía. "*Bohemia* (Havana), May 10, 1959. pp. 32–34. 137.
11. Data given to the authors by two former police captains, and corroborated by three former patrol officers whose names are withheld on request (Union City and West New York, New Jersey, September 4–5, and November 3 and 8, 1971).
12. Interviews with two former madams now living in the United States, whose names are withheld at their request (New York, New York, December 1970).
13. The role of the prostitutes in the Cuban insurrection has not been sufficiently explained by the revolutionaries. Their cooperation was very decisive, particularly during the last months of the regime. Some of them were assassinated by the police who traced information leakage to some casas. Several revolutionaries now living in Cuba owe their lives to prostitutes who helped them evade police persecution — José ("El Flaco'") Llanusa, Armando ("Jacinto") Hart Dávalos, Faustino ("Fausto") Pérez and Walfrido ("Baby Face") Suárez, among others (Evidence of one of the authors in conversations held with "El Flaco" Llanusa in February 1959, Havana, Cuba).

14. Jesús Montané, "El Moneada," in *La Calle* (Havana), July 26, 1959. p. C-8, and *Revolución* (Havana), July 23, 1963. The Moneada prisoners spoke of these gatherings as "ideological classes of the 'Abel Santamaría School,'" where Fidel taught philosophy.

15. Castro asked Conte Agüero to edit this letter and release it to the public as a manifesto. The manifesto was named "Mensaje a Cuba que sufre," and published as a pamphlet in January 1954. See Luis Conte Agüero. *Los dos rostros de Fidel Castro* (Mexico: Editorial Jus, 1960), pp. 62–4; Luis Conte Agüero, *Cartas del presidio, anticipo de una biografia de Fidel Castro* (Havana: Editorial Lex, 1959). pp. 7–16; "Manifiesto a la Nación." *Bohemia* (Havana), July 24, 1970. pp. 17–18; Rolando E. Bonachea and Nelson P. Valdés. eds., *Revolutionary Struggle 1947–1958* (Cambridge: MIT Press. 1972), pp. 221–30.

16. Luis Conte Agüero, *Fidel Castro, vida y obra* (Havana: Editorial Lex, 1959). pp. 12–16. and *Los dos rostros*. p. 65.

17. Letter to Luis Conte Agüero dated March 1955, in *Los dos rostros*, p. 84.

18. *Prensa Libre* (Havana), May 15, 1955. pp. 1–2.

19. *Bohemia* (Havana), May 22, 1955. pp. 22, 24, 70, 73.

20. Ibid., p. 70.

21. Lisandro Otero. "Aquél 26 de Julio: Entrevista a Haydée Santamaría y Melba Hernández." *Bohemia* (Havana), September 9, 1966, p. 19. Faustino Pérez, on the other hand, states that on May 19 the first discussion took place regarding the need to create a movement and select a name. See Faustino Pérez, "La lucha contra Batista," *El Mundo* (Havana), December 2, 1964. pp. 1, 7.

22. Otero. "Aquel 26 de Julio." p. 19 .Haydée Santamaría recalls that the young revolutionaries toyed with the idea of naming the future movement Moncada. But Luis Conte Agüero asserts that Fidel had chosen the name "26th of July Movement" at the Isle of Pines. Conte Agüero argued with Fidel that such a choice had regionalistic overtones and none of the national appeal a revolutionary movement should encompass (Authors' interview with Luis Conte Agüero. Miami, Florida, January 18. 1973).

23. Throughout May and June 1955, Fidel openly stated the need to find a peaceful solution though he was already organizing an insurrection. See Melba Hernández's statements in *Bohemia*, pp. 18–19. Fidel's letter on Pedro Miret's arrest appears in Bonachea and Valdés. *Revolutionary Struggle*, p. 243. The original letter was published in *El Mundo* (Havana), May 25, 1955. p. 1.

24. Bonachea and Valdés, *Revolutionary Struggle*, pp. 244–49.

25. This attack had more of a personal overtone than a position of principle since the terrorists in question were the Triple A of Aureliano Sánchez Arango which had let Castro down in December 1952 (see chapter 1). The article is reprinted in Bonachea and Valdés. *Revolutionary Struggle*, pp. 252–53.

26. Interview with Charles Simeón (Union City. July 1972). To Luis Conte Agüero. Fidel had written in the summer of 1954 that "ideology, discipline and leadership . . . were the basic conditions of a true movement . . . but leadership is essential." Agüero, *Los dos rostros*, p. 77.

27. MLR was intellectually oriented though still within the oppositionist mainstream. Its members were Amalio Fiallo, Charles Simeón, Andrés Valdespino, Antonio Maceo, Pedro Trigo, Segundo Ceballos, Carlos de la Torre

and Mario Llerena, among others. Charles Simeón to the authors, July 1972. Of the above. Mario Llerena would become one of the most distinguished thinkers of the M-26-7.

28. In Mario Llerena, "The Unsuspected Revolution," unpublished manuscript, p. 47, and Mario Llerena, "La bilis de los mediocres," *Bohemia* (Havana), March 29, 1959, p. 102.

29. Mario Mencia, "Ahora sí se gana la revolución." *Bohemia* (Havana), December 1, 1972. pp. 62–63, and Minerva Salado. "Esta combatiente," *Vida Universitaria* (Havana), 14. no. 212 (July–August, 1968): 39. At this meeting the M-26-7 of Oriente was established as follows: Gloria Cuadras (Ortodoxo), propaganda; Baudilio Castellanos (Ortodoxo), ideology: Ramón Alvarez (Ortodoxo), workers; Maria Antonia (Ortodoxo), treasury: and Lester Rodríguez, coordinator for Oriente province. Action and sabotage was left open for Frank País (ANR). Faustino Pérez was appointed national treasurer coordinator, and Armando Hart, national coordinator for propaganda.

30. Mencia, "Ahora sí se gana la revolución," p. 63. According to Maria Antonia Fidel had been kept posted on Frank's insurrectionary activities through Lester Rodríguez and Pedro Miret.

31. Luis Rolando Cabrera. "Doña Rosario, la madre de los hermanos País." *Bohemia* (Havana), August 9, 1959. pp. 6–8.

32. Nydia Sarabia, "Y mi honda es la de David." *Bohemia* (Havana), July 28, 1967, p. 4 Also see. "Frank País: en el XV aniversario de su muerte," *Verde Olivo* (Havana), July 30. 1972. p. 17, and "Frank País" *Bohemia* (Havana) July 23, 1965. p. 20.

33. Interview with Sara González, classmate of Frank País at the National Teachers' School (New York, New York, July 1972). After graduation, Frank taught at El Salvador Baptist school until September 1955 when he asked Rev. Agustín González Seisdedos to accept his resignation because "Cuba needs me," See "Frank País," *Bohemia*, p. 20. For a revisionist view of Frank País' moral and revolutionary qualities see Enrique Pineda Barnet, "Frank País: los héroes de tú a tú," *Cuba Internacional* (Havana), 7, no. 78 (October 1968): 117. Barnet is a poet and ethnologist and with the staff of the literary magazine *Union*.

34. José Tey, Félix Pena, Carlos Díaz Fontaina, Oscar Lucero, Otto Parellada, René Ramos Latour, Renato Guitart, "Tony" Alomá and Frank País had earlier been militants of Acción Libertadora, under Raúl del Mazo, and of the MNR. These organizations dissolved, and País and Tey founded ARO, while Guitart died at the Moncada barracks assault. See Vicente Cubillas, Jr., "Los sucesos del 30 de noviembre de 1956," *Bohemia* (Havana), November 29, 1959, p. 42; Mencia, "Ahora sí se gana la revolución," pp. 61–62; and Mario G. del Cueto, "Trazo biográfico de Renato Guitart," *Bohemia* (Havana), July 21, 1967. p. 7.

35. Sarabia. ". . . Y mi honda es la de David," p. 6, and "Frank País, en el XV aniversario de su muerte," p. 17.

36. "Historia de Bayazo," *Revista de la Universidad de la Habana* (Havana), 32, no. 192 (October–December): 57.

37. The *fidelista* group included Pedro Miret, Marcos Bravo, Marcelo Sánchez, Julio Pérez Guitián and Andrés Luján Vázquez (Chibás). Ibid., p. 57.

38. They were Antonio (Ñico) López, Luis Mariano López Pérez, "Machaco" Almeijeiras, Andrés Luján Vázquez (Chibás), Armando Cubrias and Rolando

Rodríguez Acosta. The Ortodoxo Youth was represented by José Yero Rodríguez, Eloy Paneque Blanco, Gilberto Verdecia León, Armando Estrada Gallegos, Enrique Catá Fonseca and Roberto A. Paneque, Ibid., p. 57.

39. Ibid., p. 59. The M-26-7 structure included: Cristóbal Guilarte, municipal coordinator: Roberto A. Paneque, treasurer: Rubén Cuevas, action and sabotage; Roque Vallabriga, propaganda; Elio Rosette, workers' front; and Gilberto Verdecia León, student brigades.

3

The Student Movement

Cuban students have a long tradition of commitment to the struggle for political and human freedom, which has been waged since Cuba was a colony of Spain. The majestic University of Havana had fostered this spirit in the proud young people who traversed the campus, passing between the Greek columns which guarded the schools of arts, philosophy, law, architecture, and business and administration. Below these columns a statue of the alma mater wordlessly witnessed the student political activities that were often held on the 163-step *escalinata*.

The 200-year-old university was a symbol of student resistance against corrupt and dictatorial government. From the university emerged such outstanding revolutionaries of the thirties as Julio Antonio Mella, a founder of the Federation of University Students (FEU) and of the Cuban Communist party in the 1920s; Rafael Trejo, first student martyr in the struggle against Machado (1925-33); and the legendary Antonio ("Tony") Guiteras, mentor of Jóven Cuba. These men, like others before and after them, exchanged their books for weapons, becoming involved in the political violence which was ignited under Machado's regime. Many student leaders eventually went into politics. This group included Carlos Prío Socarrás, former secretary general of the Directorio Estudiantil Universitario (DEU) of 1930; Aureliano Sánchez Arango; Rubén de León; Eduardo R. Chibás, a well-noted populist leader; Joaquín Martínez Sáenz, founder of ABC (an anti-Machado terrorist organization); Pelayo Cuervo Navarro; and many others. Some had pursued literary activities; men like Jorge Mañach, Raúl Roa and Juan Marinello had been outstanding social commentators; Rubén Martínez Villena led a protest in 1923[1] against the corrupt political system and called for a thorough change; the activities of Pablo de la Torriente Brau finally led him to fight on the side of the republic and to die in the Spanish Civil War; Francisco Ichaso, Alejo Carpentier, José Z. Tallet, Félix Lizaso and Martín Casanovas, together with Mañach and Marinello, founded the *Revista de Avance*,[2] the most representative literary and social voice of the "generation of 1930." [3] Together, all had been christened *universitarios del 30.*

Why students become so politicized is open to question, but some generalizations can be made. For a substantial number of students involved in

47

university politics, the university stood as a symbol, as an ideal stepping-stone from anonymity to some public recognition. As such, university education could easily become a means, not an end, and the end would more likely be politics than furthering one's knowledge. Havana, after all, was the mecca of Cuban politics. Considering the university's proximity to the center of political power it was almost inevitable that many students would become politically oriented, regardless of personal motivation.

An interesting case was that of those students who came from the campo. Many were intent upon securing a degree to build their status within the closely knit traditional pueblo (village). Some of these rural students remained in Havana, while others returned disillusioned to the countryside; yet others fought for a congressional seat at the provincial level. But all were exposed at the university to processes that naturally elicited political participation.

Heightening the political climate was the fact that the students could not long resist the enticement of playing their "historical role." Traditionally, Cuba's youth was responsible for carrying the torch of sacrifice, freedom and dignity. Such was the legacy of their forefathers: young people must atone for the wrongs of the past. Thus it was written in the national anthem. José Martí's prose and poems, and political manifestos: *morir por la patria es vivir* (to die for the fatherland is to live). In the end, despite varying motives, every generation produced a substantial number of young people who were called to martyrdom.

Batista and the Students

Many students rejected Batista's coup a few hours before the de facto regime had gained stability,[4] and maintained a stern attitude of condemnation throughout the seven years of his dictatorship. The students' rejection of Batista can be divided into two main phases. During the first phase (from the coup until the creation of the Directorio Revolucionario [DR] in September 1955) the students demonstrated in the streets against Batista. Clashes with the police were customary; isolated shots were occasionally fired against the policy by students on the rooftops of the university buildings, and the latter's violent reaction accentuated the radicalism of some militants. The police's brutality helped increase student resistance to the regime. The second phase came about as a result of the failure of the political parties favoring elections (the electoralists) and of the Batista regime to reach a peaceful solution to the country's dilemma. The students' determination to fight force with force increased as Batista's government continued to countenance police coercion against free speech, and police brutality. After September 1955 the students assumed a decisive insurrectionary position. Isolated events prior to the formation of the DR and the students' involvement in various frustrated attempts at overthrowing Batista's dictatorship allowed their leaders to gain experience in organization, and furthered their dedication to insurrection.

The first phase witnessed constant street demonstrations against Batista. Historic dates and anniversaries became occasions for parading, depositing flowers on a monument, inflammatory speeches against Batista and clashes with the police, who could not resist the temptation of engaging students in open battles with sticks, stones and sometimes bullets. January 28 was José Martí's birthday, and the students always marched to Havana's Central Park, seldom arriving without a violent clash with the police. February 24 and October 10 were remembered in relation to the wars of independence, and on those days the students paraded to various statues of heroes of the war against Spain. There were other important dates for demonstrations: December 7, the death of General Antonio Maceo; January 10, the anniversary of Mella's death; September 30, Rafael Trejo's death; and May 20, when the students denounced the Platt Amendment.

Batista's name was connected with every demonstration. Thus "Tony" Guiteras, the great revolutionary figure of the thirties, who was assassinated by Batista's army in 1935, became one of the first martyrs in the struggle against Batista. Mella's death was related to Batista by comparing Gerardo Machado to the dictator and emphasizing the terroristic methods of both. The symbol of Rafael Trejo as the first student martyr in the anti-Machado struggle was equated with that of Rubén Batista, the first student martyr in the anti-Batista struggle. May 20 and the Platt Amendment recalled Batista's submissiveness before U.S. interests in Cuba and allowed discussion of Batista's protection of various U.S.-owned industries.

During the first phase of student resistance to the regime there were three basic categories of students attending Havana University. The first group (the majority) were reluctant to become involved in antigovernment activities. Their main concern was completing their studies before the government ordered the university shut down.

The second group of students, the so-called professional students, included remnants of the "action groups," those who were expert in agitation, opportunism and conciliatory moves toward the police. Although the "professional" student officially registered every year, his daily activities conformed strictly with the aphorism that "martyrs seldom govern the country." At student demonstrations the "professional student" would be found in the rear guard. More experienced than the rest, his skepticism served to rationalize his lack of participation in antigovernment acts. When student clashes with the police became bloodier, the opportunists drifted away from the university premises.

The third group of students were the idealists. They opposed Batista on principle. Given their adoration for José Martí, the idealist students were Martiano to the core, imitated his prose and verbal style, and some, even his gestures and attire. An excellent *orador de barricada* (barricade speaker), the idealist was instrumental in igniting enthusiasm among other students prior to a demonstration. With outstanding leadership qualities, the idealist's message to his *compañeros* always centered on the idea of martyrdom in defense of the cause. Whatever following the idealist mustered depended to a large extent upon his willingness to assert his *machismo*. The leader, by his own definition, had to be a master of the sword as well as the word. A number of such idealistic student leaders gave theories to the movement which were loyally translated into action.

José Antonio Echeverría

The leader of the student movement, "the voice of the new generation" against Batista's dictatorship, was born in Cárdenas, Matanzas province, on July 16, 1932. José Antonio ("El Gordo" to his *compañeros*) was the son of Antonio J. Echeverría González and Concepción Bianchi, both from Cárdenas.[5] As a child he attended the Colegio Champagnat of the Marista Catholic Brothers in his native city. In 1945 he registered at the Cárdenas Institute to continue his secondary education. During the 1949-50 school year José Antonio was elected president of the institute's students association.[6]

Despite his asthmatic condition José Antonio was adamant about pursuing a university career. He moved to Havana, and in 1950, at age 18, registered as a student of the school of architecture at Havana University. Although he had a jovial personality, a ready smile and an impressive build, José Antonio's main concern was his studies until March 10, 1952. Surprised by Batista's coup in his native city of Cárdenas, he rushed to Havana and joined the students led by Alvaro Barba, president of the FEU, who were waiting to be called by the threatened president. Carlos Prío Soccarrás. But President Prío chose exile in Mexico. Four days after the takeover, the students, including José Antonio, condemned the coup in an angry declaration.[7] Soon they began street protests, and José Antonio, as recently elected delegate of the school of architecture,[8] travelled to the easternmost provinces to contact other students from Las Villas and Oriente universities in an effort to organize the coming student strike. During this trip he met José ("Pepito") Tey, Cuqui Bosch and Renato Guitart, all of whom would in time be drawn into the bloody struggle against the dictator.[9]

The University of Havana opened again in October of 1952, José Antonio Echeverría was elected vice-president and then president of his architecture school's student association, a rank he held until his death. Already well known among the students, Echeverría was becoming the "new voice" of that generation of students influenced by Martí's nationalistic ideas. On January 15, 1953, Rubén Batista became the first student killed in the struggle; he was shot in a street demonstration when police clashed with the students. Echeverría began to address informal as well as formal groups of students, warning of the need to prepare to battle the dictator.

On the day of the Moncada attack Havana University was surrounded by the police. Most of the students censured the police for the massacre at Moncada, but also accused Castro of irresponsibility and cowardice for having left the scene before participating in the events inside the Moncada camp.[10] Publicly, the students made no bones about the viciousness of Batista's repressive retaliation against the defenseless Moncada combatants.

Another school year began in September of 1954, and José Antonio Echeverría temporarily assumed the unofficial presidency of the FEU because the president had resigned and the vice-president had already completed his studies at the university. Seasoned by the beatings and imprisonment of previous street protests, José Antonio openly repudiated the regime. On March 28 he led a group of students to the steps of the capitol building to denounce the elections that Batista had scheduled for November. The police broke up this demonstration by beating the participants indiscriminately. On May 8, as FEU's president, he organized the Third Secondary Schools Congress, and on June 22 he headed a rally supporting Guatemala, which was then being invaded by Colonel Carlos Castillo Armas.[11]

In subsequent meetings and events, the voice of José Antonio Echeverría filled the rooms of the university, cried out at mass rallies and inspired street demonstrations. Time and again he stressed the theme that this was the generation of the "new pines," the generation called on to carry out its historic destiny following Martí's doctrine. In December of 1955 Costa Rica was invaded by dictator Anastasio ("Tacho") Somoza. Heading a group of students from the FEU, Echeverría arrived in San José and, along with his *compañ*eros, joined José Figueres's meager though successful forces.[12] Upon his return to Cuba he was jailed by the police.

Left to right: MNR members Félix Pena, Joe Westbrook, Professor Rafael García Bárcena and Temístocles Fuentes, spring 1953, Havana (Courtesy of Dora Rosales Westbrook).

José Antonio Echeverría (arm raised) speaking on the death of Mario Agostini, an underground fighter. Agostini's widow holds a handkerchief to her face (Havana, 1955).

In new elections at the University of Havana José Antonio was officially elected president of the FEU and vowed to "continue the fight with the people to rescue the wronged freedoms."[13] Echeverría's program as president of the FEU included the creation of the "Rafael Trejo" Popular University, and the "Rubén Batista Rubio" literacy campaign. These measures reflected the students' concern for extending education to all Cubans. With a fine sense of internationalism, Echeverría encouraged the creation of a Latin American student congress to air the issues of tyranny, university autonomy and the rights of students.

On May 15 Fidel Castro and a small number of Moncada veterans were freed. José Antonio invited Castro to address a student rally at the university's Aula Magna in order to celebrate their release from prison. Aware of the rally, the police surrounded the building and Castro was unable to come to the meeting. However, the FEU managed to broadcast the students' talks to the public in Havana.[14] The rally and subsequent speeches were gestures of solidarity toward the veterans of Moncada, and were meant to close ranks for the coming insurrectionary struggle.

Santa Marta and Lindero

Throughout the spring of 1955, Echeverría, Fructuoso Rodríguez, Juan Pedro Carbó Serviá, José Machado and Jorge Valls had trained themselves and others in the underground shooting galleries of the agronomy school located at the Quinta de los Molinos across Havana University. When the police stormed the May 20 student rally the students shot back with pellet rifles. At about this time Menelao Mora Morales contacted Echeverría with a plan for a decisive action against Batista.

Menelao Mora was counting on the support of the deposed president, Carlos Prío Socarrás, and Aureliano Sánchez Arango. A veteran of the revolution against Machado, Mora had been part of the frustrated Cayo Confites expedition, and a former member of cell 7 in the ABC movement of Joaquín Martínez Sáenz.[15] A staunch opponent of Batista since September 4, 1933. he had supported "Tony" Guiteras' proposition to eliminate Batista. Mora was a lawyer by profession, and head of the Allied Bus Cooperative of Havana. He had been elected to Congress with the support of the working class, where he championed the demands of the transporation workers.

After March 10, 1952, Mora returned to his underground activities, cooperating with Aureliano Sánchez Arango's Triple A movement. His task was to smuggle arms and to organize action cells. Mora's background, his record with the workers in Havana and his courage appealed to the student leader. Echeverría met with him, a meeting which had a decisive influence on the future course of the insurrection; for it was Menelao Mora's idea that Echeverría would try to put into practice two years hence: to assassinate Batista, simultaneously attacking the national police's motorized division and the dreaded bureau of investigation.

In pursuit of this plan, Mora had gathered substantial quantities of arms from Carlos Prío through the Triple A movement. Originally Prío and Sánchez Arango were to participate, but it later turned out that some Auténticos torpedoed the idea, provoking Mora's anger. The latter found in Echeverría a congenial and receptive revolutionary willing to support him in due time.

Mora, an experienced urban fighter, had already surrounded himself with a number of interesting people. Daniel Martín Labrandero, born in Spain, was a former Loyalist officer during the Spanish Civil War who had fought bravely against Generalissimo Francisco Franco; and Carlos Gutiérrez Menoyo, also a veteran of the Spanish Civil War, had experience in World War II. Lesser known figures included Angel ("Mitico") Fernández, Domingo Portela, Ernesto Morales and Fernando Amador Silverino, among others.

Mora outlined the details of the plan to Echeverría. The latter agreed to support the operation with at least 150 students. From May to August 4, 1955, the students intensified their training, centering their hopes on the swift end of the dictatorship.

On August 4, Menelao Mora ordered a general mobilization throughout the capital. Nearly 1,000 militants were ready to attack designated sites. Heavy mortars had been placed around the Presidential Palace and the bureau of investigation. At various places in the city, students were waiting for arms to be distributed. Luis Gómez Wangüemert, Faure Chomón, Enrique Rodríguez Loeches, Humberto Castelló and Eduardo Castillo were stationed close to the

Bureau. Echeverría, Fructuoso Rodríguez, Rolando Cubelas, José Machado, Juan Pedro Carbó Serviá and Jorge Valls went to Mora's headquarters at Santa Marta and Lindero streets. There, the group awaited the final orders, but they never came. The police had become suspicious and surrounded the place, an old warehouse containing hundreds of rifles, mortars, shells, grenades, machine guns and thousands of rounds of ammunition. The operation failed to materialize and the police moved in force to arrest as many people as possible.[16]

The results of the frustrated attempt to assassinate Batista (in what became known as the episode of Santa Marta and Lindero) were the arrests of Fructuoso Rodríguez, Daniel Martín Labrandero, and dozens of students and Mora's followers. Echeverría managed to escape the police raid, but the regime was aware of his involvement in the operation. The bureau of investigation opened a new file on José Antonio Echeverría, carrying the same code, No. 20122, under which the police had accumulated data about his activities as student leader. Criminal charges were filed against him under Case No. 359, as "an agitator of the FEU," who had "escaped the police raid" at Santa Marta y Lindero, and who had been pursued since May 25, 1955, for his participation in student demonstrations against the government.[17] Had the episode of Santa Marta and Lindero been successful there probably would have been a coalition government including well-known Auténticos like Prío or Aureliano, and younger ones like Menelao Mora and Labrandero. As for the role of the students, it has been speculated that they would have acted as the "moral conscience" of such a government.[18] In the political context of the mid-fifties, José Antonio and the students took the same steps Castro and his group had followed when they first sought the aid of the Auténticos and then turned to the Ortodoxos. Not until later were the various leaders of the opposition to understand that a break with the old politics was essential to wrest power from Batista and others like him. However, as will be shown, the insurgents never rejected financial aid from the politicians, particularly the Auténticos, if that aid could be translated into purchases of arms and ammunition with which to fight Batista.

The Directorio Revolucionario

Echeverría felt that the students must create their own insurrectionary apparatus, for the FEU, as a student organization chartered by the university, lacked those elements of a clandestine organization and structure necessary to launch violent struggle. In addition, it represented the interests of the student body as a whole, rather than only that small fraction of students involved in the politics of confrontation with the police. Hence, special cells for action and sabotage could develop efficiently only within a structure which could provide secrecy, organization, discipline and leadership.

We do not know whether Echeverría met with Castro prior to the latter's departure for Mexico on July 7, 1955. But at the same time that Fidel was deciding to prepare his group abroad, José Antonio called a meeting at the home of his uncle, Ricardo Bianchi, in the Campo Hill Building in Havana.[19] Attending the meeting were Faure Chomón, Joe Westbrook, René Anillo, Juan Pedro Carbó Serviá, Jorge Valls, Fructuoso Rodríguez and José Antonio Echeverría. José Antonio stressed two points: 1) the students must create "an instrument of equilibrium" between the regular politicians and the insurrectionist line supported by Fidel Castro;[20] 2) the goal of the newly created apparatus would be to dedicate all of its resources and energies toward overthrowing Batista. Because this was a preliminary talk between José Antonio and his closest followers, no mention was made of what kind of ideological program it would adopt. These ideas were to develop gradually through speeches by members of the executive council, manifestoes and interviews in several periodicals. For the moment, Echeverría and his closest associates focused attention on toppling the dictator.

Structurally the DR would be made up of an executive council headed by a secretary general and eight members.[21] José Antonio was unanimously elected secretary general, and the remaining members were Fructuoso Rodríguez, Rolando Cubela, José ("Pepín") Naranjo, Juan Pedro Carbó Serviá, Faure Chomón, Joe Westbrook, René Anillo and Félix Armando Murías. The membership of the DR would remain secret until José Antonio thought it wise to reveal it to the country at large.

Within the organization there soon developed two ideological currents— that of the "thinkers" and that of the "hard-liners." The former were amply represented in the figures of Jorge Valls and Joe Westbrook.[22] Valls was an outstanding philosophy student prone to making thoughtful assessments of the Cuban student movement in light of the country's history. Opposed to formulas imported from abroad—whether from the Soviet Union or the United States—Valls emphatically asserted that all other insurgent groups must be integrated under the aegis of the DR. Jorge Valls criticized the Moncada assault, classifying it as a traditional approach to the solution of a dictatorial situation, for he was convinced that Castro had attempted to precipitate a coup d'etat on July 26, 1953. Within the DR Valls was highly respected both for his intellectual talents and because he was also willing to confront the police in any well-planned insurrectionary operation.

Closely following Valls was Joe Westbrook Rosales, a bright and perceptive youngster who was profoundly idealistic in his thinking. Known as "little Martí," he was a devoted student of Martí's works, and professed an unusual sense of objectivity for his years. With more than enough willingness to fight, young Joe, a talented orator, was made a member of the inner circle of the student movement.

Hard-liners abounded in the DR. Most notable were Fructuoso Rodríguez, Juan Pedro Carbó Serviá, Rolando Cubela and Faure Chomón. Fructuoso and Juan Pedro were both impetuous, aggressive and dangerous; Cubela was less boisterous; and Chomón was taciturn, reserved and shrewd.[23] Each was willing to engage in action but had little patience for spelling out programs or writing manifestos. In the middle was José Antonio Echeverría, the catalyst within the DR. Idealistic, dynamic and frank, Echeverría could also be pragmatic, stern and thoughtful. Envied and worshipped, sought after and despised, Echeverría's foremost charismatic qualities consisted of being candid, unpresumptuous, honest and courageous.

Ideology of the DR

Neither the leaders nor the rank and file of the FEU or the DR ever sat down to elaborate a comprehensive program of government to put into effect if and when they succeeded in overthrowing Batista. They did not envision themselves in a power position; their role was to fight the dictatorship. In pursuit of this the student leaders concentrated on making statements of principle expressing in the clearest possible form what they stood for and against.

On November 19, 1955, the Sociedad de Amigos de la República (SAR) held a meeting at the Muelle de Luz plaza in old Havana. All political parties of the opposition were represented, and the university students were also invited. Feelings ran high among this excitable crowd. Leaders of the political parties advocated a democratic alternative to the Cuban problem that included participation in the congressional elections called by Batista, but the crowd reacted negatively to any proposal.

José Antonio Echeverría rose to speak in the name of the FEU.[24] As he approached the microphone rhythmic voices from the crowd began chanting "Fidel Castro, Fidel Castro!" The FEU leader remained undisturbed and serenely summarized the unfeasibility of a democratic solution to Cuba's problem. Halfway through his speech his voice was drowned by further chants of "Fidel Castro, Fidel Castro!" At this point he vigorously told the people not to let themselves be "provoked by the all-time provocateurs at the service of the tyrant."[25]

As the people calmed down, Echeverría set down the position of the students. He asked the chairmen of the political parties not to participate in the coming electoral farce. Echeverría gave a succinct analysis of why Batista's regime was bad for the nation: first, because it placed itself at the service of reactionary and monopolist interests at the expense of hungry people; second, because it practiced political crimes such as the assassinations of over 100 young people at Moncada; and third, because it suppressed all freedoms.

The FEU stated its "clear and precise" understanding concerning the nation's problems. Echeverría held that only a "deep transformation of Cuba's political, social and economic realities" could free Cuba from its problems. To this end, the immediate task was to overthrow the dictator, establish a democratic form of government, and then carry out a revolutionary program to solve "the problems of landless peasants, exploited workers and young people condemned to economic oblivion." In bold terms Echeverría proclaimed that Cuba "urgently needs a real revolution to remove the hard roots of colonialism." At this point, the crowd cheered wildly, and the FEU leader ended shouting, "Batista, get out! Don't make us wait to throw you out like Gerardo Machado!"

Student Demonstration: A New Escalation

Following this meeting the student leaders discussed the political situation, the role of SAR, the convenience of continuing to support a peaceful solution, and the degree of harm that support would cause the movement's popularity. Since the DR had already been formed around an insurrectionary line, the break with SAR had to be announced by FEU, and it was also necessary to prepare the grounds for the public declaration of the DR's organization. The student leaders concluded that they had to accelerate street protests in what they called the "radicalization of mass actions."[26] The immediate objectives were to provoke police brutality by changing the tactics of student demonstrations; to denounce a political settlement with Batista, proclaiming that the only road open to the people was that of violent struggle; and to increase the momentum of the mass protests to prepare the ground for the public announcement of the creation of the DR.

All student demonstrations had previously been halted by the police without the demonstrators using firearms, but the new approach was to have a plan whereby student snipers would shoot at the police, thus inflicting some casualties and calling forth a brutal reaction on the part of the police force. Street demonstrations should culminate with the closing down of the university, which would aggravate the situation. All these actions were planned to escalate the struggle in the capital and in the provinces.

The date selected to begin a series of mass protests was November 27, the anniversary of the execution of students by the Spanish in 1871. The plan was as follows: Echeverría would lead a student demonstration to the home of Cosme de la Torriente (SAR's president) to hand deliver a letter announcing the students' withdrawal of support to a peaceful solution. All students were notified of the coming demonstration, but only the cadres knew of the strategy that would be developed during the demonstration. Every student organization in every province was alerted to the need to organize mass protests on November 27.

On that date hundreds of students gathered at Havana University. Stones, bottles, pipes and other articles were collected for the coming confrontation with the police. Coeds from the school of nursing contributed to the arsenal with bottles of alcohol; medical students contributed bottles of formol acid; and students from the school of architecture distributed several containers with used oil which burned for a long period of time. There were about 400 student demonstrators who would march down the *escalinata* and towards the police barricades which were some 300 meters from the university and blocked by close to 200 police officers.[27] The latter were commanded by Major Francisco ("Paco") Pérez and Major Oscar Rey Castro.

At 9:00 AM, student cadres received their instructions from Juan Pedro Carbó Serviá and Fructuoso Rodríguez. About 50 students, veterans of many demonstrations, were divided into two 25-man squads, covering the right and left flanks of the demonstration. Once the vanguard approached the police barricade, José Antonio Echeverría would signal the start of the first phase of the student action by throwing himself against the police officers. At that point militants were to throw stones, empty bottles and pipes at the police. It was expected that the police's reaction would be as usual: fall back, reorganize and charge on the demonstrators. The students were ordered not to wait for the police attack after throwing their weapons, but to fall back rapidly in retreat toward the university. Cadres were to be the last to withdraw, and were to make the advance of the police difficult by throwing the oil containers and alcohol bottles against the pavement and then igniting the volatile "bombs." Snipers posted on top of the buildings facing the *escalinata* and the path usually used by the police to chase the students were to wait until police officers were close enough to offer a feasible target. Snipers were to shoot to kill. If everything developed as planned, the police would halt their attack while the bulk of the demonstrators fled from campus and a small group of militants continued to throw stones at the police from within the university's perimeter. All snipers were to leave the campus immediately following the first volley against the police, in order to leave no trace in case the regime dared violate the university's autonomy by pursuing the snipers there. Any bloodshed was to be blamed on the government; thus the capture of even one student sniper would place the student leaders in a difficult situation, since the students could be condemned as provocateurs.

At 10:00 AM José Antonio led the demonstration down the *escalinata* and toward the police. It was an excellent example of discipline and good coordination on the part of the students. As José Antonio approached the police barricade, Major Francisco ("Paco") Pérez ordered the student leader to turn back, but José Antonio pushed his way into the first line of police officers, and the encounter began.

As had been expected, the police fell back under a rain of stones, bottles and pipes thrown by the students. But José Antonio and his brother Alfredo were attacked by a dozen police officers with clubs. The leader fell to the ground, and Alfredo threw himself on top of his brother to protect him from the savage blows of the police. Fulgencio Oroz, a student militant, tried to rescue José Antonio and was wounded; Fructuoso Rodríguez lay unconscious on the pavement. Joe Westbrook and Ramón and Silvino Rodríguez led the demonstrators in the retreat toward the university as planned. When the police force charged, most of the demonstrators had reached the *escalinata*, and the cadres were throwing their "bombs" and burning the pavement. The last cadre members reached the university, and that left the police alone in front of the university and close enough to present a feasible target.

The police, led by Major "Paco" Pérez, approached the university, while another group of police officers, commanded by Major Rey Castro, walked across the small park facing the university. The snipers opened up, and the first to fall was Pérez with a slight wound in the head: Major Castro was hit in the chest: and Sergeant Antonio Martínez was also wounded. Infuriated and at the same time surprised, the police attempted to enter the university grounds, and the snipers wounded two more police officers, Enrique Gutiérrez and Orlando L. García.[28] The rest, some 100 police officers, retreated into the nearby buildings, leaving their leaders bleeding in the street.

José Antonio, his brother, Alfredo, and Fructuoso Rodríguez, Carbó Serviá, Juan Nuiry and a host of students were arrested, charged with inciting to riot and released on bail.

In Santiago de Cuba, Oriente province, FEU's president José ("Pepito") Tey led the students in a massive demonstration. Student protests took place in Bayamo, Holguín, Palma Soriano, Guantánamo and Manzanillo in Oriente province; Morón, Camagüey City, and Ciego de Avila in Camagüey province; Santa Clara and Sancti-Spíritus in Las Villas Province; and violent clashes were reported in Cárdenas and Colón in Matanzas province. In Artemisa and Guanajay in Pinar del Río province, police and students also clashed in bloody confrontations.[29]

The new tactics had been extremely successful, and José Antonio immediately called for a 72-hour student strike throughout the capital in solidarity with the *compañeros* in the provinces. On November 30, José Antonio spoke at a student rally at Havana University and called for more street protests. He led a student demonstration during a ball game in El Cerro Stadium, and thousands of television viewers witnessed the police chasing the students, who carried a large banner reading *Abajo Batista!* (Down with Batista).[30]

On December 7, another massive demonstration took place, and students again marched from the university toward the police barricades. This time, as the student demonstrators approached the police line, Esteban Ventura Novo, who was commanding the police officers, did not wait for what he certainly expected to be a repetition of the November 27 strategy, and opened up against the demonstrators with .45 caliber pistols. Nineteen students were wounded, but, miraculously, no one was killed. This time there were no snipers, but there were dozens of newspaper photographers who reported on the police's clear overreaction to the unarmed students.[31] There was an outcry of protest against police brutality, and most people discarded as false reports that in the previous demonstrations the students had fired upon the police.

In Ciego de Avila, Camagüey province, Raúl Cervantes, a student, was shot to death by the police during a demonstration. Immediately students in Havana planned a symbolic funeral for the dead *compañero* in the *escalinata*.[32]

Echeverría took advantage of the momentum, and on December 12 he issued an appeal to all workers for a five-minute work stoppage in solidarity with the student victims of police brutality. The stoppage was called for December 14, from 10:00 AM to 10:05 AM. It was an astonishing success; the workers showed spontaneous support for the anti-Batista cause and the students. The efforts of the Confederación de Trabajadores de Cuba (Confederation of Cuban Workers, or CTC) to boycott the stoppage failed, thus demonstrating that the workers were not as submissive as some leading pro-Batista labor leaders had assumed. Transport workers stopped their vehicles in the cities; radio announcers ceased to broadcast for five minutes; employees of the Cuban telephone and electric companies joined the demonstration, as did drug stores, hotel and restaurant workers. The workers at the Goodrich Tire Company walked out, and so did textile workers in Havana and Matanzas provinces; several sugar mills were affected when workers left their jobs, and dock workers simply refused to work for the rest of the day, creating confusion in Havana, Santiago de Cuba and other busy ports.

The stoppage represented the first mass mobilization since the Batista coup.[33] It also coincided with preparations for a massive protest and a strike by sugar workers.

The Sugar Workers' Strike and the DR

During the November 27 demonstration, the students had an opportunity to distribute the first manifesto of the DR. In this declaration the DR presented the insurrection as an aggregate of forces struggling against a common enemy, regardless of political allegiance or socioeconomic background. The DR reiterated its opposition to a coup d'etat because such a move would not take the country in the direction of substantial structural changes. The DR felt that Batista had exploited the good intentions of those who had tried to find a peaceful solution. Thus it advocated "revolutionary insurrection," or direct and sharp action against the tyrant. Such an insurrection would pave the way for the creation of a "revolutionary state" which was to be instrumental in the "integral construction of society." The manifesto forcefully called for political freedom, social justice and economic independence. The DR invited average citizens, revolutionary leaders and their followers, workers and students to unite their efforts for "the sake of the oppressed, underprivileged, and the martyrs of the Fatherland."[34]

From a tactical standpoint the November 27, 1955, manifesto conceptualized the national struggle under the aegis of the DR. This had been Jorge Valls's assumption throughout the DR's organizational stage. Valls had also been actively contacting workers and advocating that the DR close ranks with the working class and make common cause with their demands for higher wages and better living conditions. Valls appeared convinced that the experience of siding with the workers would benefit the students and would also open the doors of the DR to the people as a whole.[35] The opportunity to join the workers presented itself with the sugar workers' protest.

The sugar workers rebelled against the submissive altitude of the CTC, under Eusebio Mujal, and against the Federatión Nacional de Trabajadores Azucareros (FENETA), controlled by Mujal's man, José Luis Martínez. Led by Conrado Rodríguez and Conrado Bécquer, the workers demanded payment of the *diferencial.* For years it had been established through wage agreements that if the price of sugar exceeded that of the previous year, bonuses based on the difference *(diferencial)* were to be paid to the workers.

In 1955, however, the government made the decision to limit the sugar harvest to 4,400,000 tons,[36] and to keep 350,000 tons in reserve for export to the United States.[37] Wages were estimated on the basis of the price obtained per pound of sugar; until 1953 that price was 4.96 cents per pound, and it dropped during the same year to 4.70 cents a pound. In 1955, the government fixed the price at 4.40 cents per pound, while the Instituto Cubano del Azúcar (ICEA) calculated the price by including the 350,000 tons in reserve, arriving at a price of 2.77 cents a pound.[38] The result was that wages earned by sugar workers dropped considerably.

The workers demanded that sugar production be declared unlimited, that a fixed price of 5 cents per pound be set by the government, and that the government pay the *diferencial* accumulated for the year 1955. The government refused to negotiate, and Mujal's CTC supported Batista while labor leaders such as Facundo Pomar, Jesús Artigas and José Luis Martínez strongly criticized those workers who were demanding fair treatment.[39]

José Antonio Echeverría, aware that the protesters needed a meeting place to discuss strategy, offered the workers the use of the facilities at the university. The meeting was held at the Hall of Martyrs at Havana University, and it was agreed that the students would participate in all demonstrations led by the workers, as well as a strike which was to be organized by men such as Bécquer, Conrado Rodríguez, Isidoro Salas, Rodrigo Lominchar, Luis Bonito, David Salvador, Diego Alvear and others.[40]

The DR distributed its leaders as follows: Fructuoso Rodríguez, Joe Westbrook, Jorge Valls and Carbó Serviá were assigned to Las Villas province; and Martínez Brito and José Azeff were to travel throughout Camagüey province contacting workers, helping to organize the strike, and then returning to Ciego de Avila to join Echeverría and Faure Chamón for the strike's actions against the police and the Rural Guard.[41]

The 500,000 sugar workers began their strike on December 5, 1955, at 8:30 AM. It was not long before riots broke out and violent confrontations between workers and students against the police and the Rural Guards took place, mainly in Las Villas and Camagüey provinces. Action in other provinces was not lacking, and in Güines, in Havana province, Heriberto Espino, a sugar worker, was shot to death by the police. In Matanzas province, sugar cane fields were burned and six sugar mills were abandoned by the workers: the Coliseo, Cárdenas, Banaguises, Pedro Betancourt, Perico and Alacranes mills.[42]

In Las Villas province, the towns of Santo Domingo, Sancti-Spíritus, Sagua la Grande, Fomento, Cabaiguán and Yaguajay were almost taken over by sugar workers, and there were violent clashes with the Rural Guards. DR leaders built barricades around the local schools and institutes while local students joined the strikers and helped fight the police with stones and Molotov cocktails. Several sugar mills were paralyzed in Las Villas province, including the Trinidad, Amazonas, San José, Tuinicú, Zaza, Santa Isabel, Escambray, Soledad, Unidad, Parque Alto, Resolución, Macagua, Andreíta, Hormiguero and Santa Teresa; and in Sagua la Grande, 14 workers were wounded and railroad cars were overturned by strikers.

In Camagüey, José Antonio Echeverría led the students in Ciego de Avila, while Isidoro Salas led the sugar workers. Between the two groups they established complete control of the city and the Rural Guard had to ask for reinforcements from the "José Ignacio Agramonte" Military Camp in Camagüey City. Eleven sugar mills and towns were declared "dead" by the workers. Two sugar workers were wounded by the Rural Guard in the Vertientes sugar mill, and strikers also overturned railroad cars in Camagüey province.[43]

On December 27, Batista summoned Mujal and José Luis Martínez and told them that the strike had to end immediately. The dictator evidently feared an escalation of the sugar workers' strike into a revolutionary general strike. Batista offered to negotiate with the strikers, and announced that he was willing to grant 4 percent of the total payment of the *diferencial* to the workers.[44] On December 28, Mujal called on the strikers to accept Batista's offer and to go back to work, but the workers refused. Finally, on December 30, Batista announced that the *diferencial* would be paid to the workers. The strike had been a success, although the sugar workers did not collect the promised *diferencial*, and most of them received only a nominal amount of money. The strikers could not maintain the momentum of the strike, however; despite their political victory over the CTC and Batista, other working sectors did not join in solidarity. Any new attempts at challenging Batista's power would have been met with savage repression. The regime had apparently learned not to underestimate the amount of anti-Batista feeling in the working class.

The sugar workers' leaders attempted to organize their own independent FENETA and held a congress which 151 out of 231 unions attended, with a total of over 300 delegates.[45] The CTC expelled the rebel leaders[46] from the official FENETA, while the strikers issued a proclamation, the first article of which was dedicated to expressing the workers' gratitude to the students for their support and decisive participation in the strike, and also for extending to the workers the courtesy of letting them use the premises of the university for their organizing activities.[47]

Following the strike of the sugar workers, the creation of the DR was made public on February 24, 1956, when Echeverría read the November 27 manifesto in a meeting at the university's Aula Magna. On March 9, 1956, the FEU held another meeting at the university, on the topic "Against the Latin American Dictatorships." Among the audience were exiled students from Latin America. José Antonio, as president of the FEU, spoke of the tortuous historical-political development of the American republics.[48] Observing that neither inter-American conferences or Pan Americanism could alleviate the endemic illnesses of the Latin American countries, he told the group that the peoples of the continent must rise together in the struggle against all tyrannies.

Echeverría warned against the danger of "North American expansionism stealing away the Mexican territory, intervening in Cuba through the Platt Amendment, kidnapping Puerto Rico's independence, intervening in Nicaragua and provoking Sandino's death, intervening in Santo Domingo and placing Rafael Leónidas Trujillo in power, and encouraging the repressive forces in Guatemala. . . . It is," he said, "an interventionist policy succeeded by a policy of areas of influence loyally defended by new gendarmes allowing the exploitation and destruction of national resources by foreign enterprises." Again Echeverría lashed out against the forces of colonialism. Asking his listeners to have faith in the destiny of the Americas, Echeverría warned that "revolutions cannot be exported; they are born out of the social reality of each [nation]." But men and women in the American republics must unite against all tyrannies "to plant the seeds of the new Americas."

In March, the DR again set forth its position in an extensive manifesto to the people. Denying the possibility of a coup d'etat in conjunction with civil resistance it reiterated once more its demand for "the integral liberation of the nation, free from foreign interference and domestic exploitation." The DR viewed the revolution as an "integral change in the political, judicial, social, economic system," and "the emergence of a new collective psychological attitude to consolidate and encourage the revolutionary program."[49]

The insurrectionary program was being radicalized. On April 4, 1956, a military conspiracy led by Colonel Ramón Barquín was aborted, and on April 25, Reynold González of the Triple A led an attack on the Goicuría barracks in Matanzas province, leaving dozens of dead victims.[50]

On July 13, 1956, José Antonio was reelected president of the FEU, and the students began to plan a new attempt to kill Batista in Línea Street, in El Vedado, a neighborhood of Havana, with the support of the Organización Auténtica (OA). The plot, however, was never consummated.

In August students from all over Latin America gathered in Santiago de Chile to open the Second Inter-American Student Congress. Echeverría, representing the FEU, arrived in Santiago de Chile accompanied by Ricardo ("Popi") Corpión. The congress tackled the issues of dictatorships in Latin America, the rights of students and the specific situation of Cuba under

Batista. By unanimous acclamation the congress elected Echeverría to its presidency. Echeverría and Corpión left Chile for Lima, Perú, to meet with Peruvian students, and then went on to Panamá, and San José, Costa Rica.[51] Their trip ended with visits to Mexico and Miami.

At the end of September the FEU president left for Ceylon to attend the Sixth International Student Conference held at Peradeniya University. Over 200 delegates heard Echeverría's brief speech denouncing Cuba's dictatorship, lack of university autonomy and the assassinations of students. Unanimously, the conference approved Resolution 78, which demanded "freedom of expression for Cuban students, respect for their lives, and due process of law for those held arbitrarily by the police. José Antonio warned the students at the conference that the "policy of colonialism afflicting underdeveloped nations is nothing but the result of complicity of national dictators with vested interests."[52]

Havana University was forced to close its doors on November 30, leaving the students neither a physical nor a symbolic sanctuary. This was to be a struggle to the death that would test both the insurrectionists and their opponents.

Notes

1. Known as the "protest of the 13" it presented a revisionist critique of the country's political development since 1902, and it was considered an important step toward assuming a revolutionary position on the part of the young intellectuals of that generation. See Félix Lizaso, *Panorama de la cultura cubana* (Mexico: Fondo de Cultura Económica, 1949). p. 23. For a discussion of the intellectual impact of that generation, see Francisco López Segrera, "Psicoanálisis de una generación, III," *Revista de la Biblioteca Nacional José Martí* (Havana) (May–August, 1970), pp. 101–52.

2. Founded in 1927 it lasted until 1930, when Machado's dictatorship increased its repressive methods: the last number was distributed shortly after the death of Rafael Trejo in September 1930. Five of the signers of the "protest of the 13" were also editors of the magazine: Juan Marinello, Jorge Mañach, José Z. Tallet, Francisco Ichaso and Martín Casanovas. See Martín Casanovas. "Prólogo," *Orbita de la Revista de Avance* (Havana: Ediciones Union, 1965), pp. 7–24.

3. Jorge Mañach coined the name by which that generation became known, the *generación de la treintena*. See Carlos Ripoll, *La generación del 23 en Cuba* (New York: Las Américas, 1968). p. 49. For Mañach's interpretation of his own generation, see his *Pasado vigente* (Havana: Editorial Trópico, 1939).

4. The FEU delegation led by Alvaro Barba included José Hidalgo, Agustín Valero, Danilo Baeza and Orestes Robledo, among others. The students asked President Prío for arms, pledging they would offer resistance at the University. See "10 de marzo de 1952: una fecha negra en la historia," *Bohemia* (Havana), March 8, 1959, p. 70.

5. "José Antonio en su ciudad natal," *Juventud Rebelde* (Havana), March 15, 1967. Also see José M. Cusco Gelpi, *Discursos sobre José Antonio Echeverría* (Havana, September 5, 1959), pp. 5–12.

6. Interview with Frank Cruz Alvarez, classmate of José Antonio (December 10, 1970, Union City, New Jersey).

7. Declaración *de la FEU ante el golpe de estado* (Havana), March 14, 1952, mimeo., authors' copy. Also *Bohemia* (Havana), "Sección en Cuba," March 15, 1952.

8. Echeverría's election campaign in the university was always characterized by strong condemnation of members of gangs and undesirable elements within the university. This policy gathered to José Antonio a large croup of young student leaders favoring a FEU independent from the remnants of the "action groups" and other juvenile delinquents. For a background of Echeverría's position see a discussion by José Azeff, Juan Nuiry Sánchez, Zaida Trimino and Mary Pumpido in Javier Rodríguez, "Visión de José Antonio Echeverría," *Bohemia* (Havana), March 8, 1968, pp. 50–57.

9. Rolando Cubelas, "Recuento histórico de la lucha estudiantil universitaria," *Bohemia* (Havana), July 23 1965, p. 101.

10. This claim is further substantiated in evidence given by Pedro Miret to Mario Llerena Mario Llerena's manuscript, "The Unsuspected Revolution."

11. Juan Nuiry Sánchez, "José Antonio Echeverría, pensamiento y acción," *Bohemia* (Havana), March 10, 1967, p. 76.

12. Other FEU members were José Hidalgo Peraza, Juan Pedro Carbó Serviá, "Pepin" Naranjo. Fructuoso Rodríguez and Rolando Cubelas. The Costa Rican flag of Figueres' troops was given to Echeverría and deposited at the Aula Magna (Authors' interview with José M. Figueres, Buffalo, New York, March 23–25, 1968).

13. Nuiry, "José Antonio Echeverría, p. 76.

14. Samuel B. Cherson, "José Antonio Echeverría: héroe y mártir," *Bohemia* (Havana), March 15, 1959, p. 98.

15. Enrique Rodríguez Loeches, "Menelao Mora: el insurrecto," *Bohemia* (Havana), March 15, 1959, p. 78.

16. Evidence of Luis Chaviano Reyes and Ricardo Bianchi to the authors (August 27–29, 1972, San Juan, Puerto Rico). Bianchi was in charge of lodging the insurrectionists while Chaviano was one of the chiefs of the operation.

17. From the private papers of the family of José Antonio Echeverría, August 27–29, 1972. San Juan, Puerto Rico.

18. This claim has been further asserted by former DR members such as Félix Armando Murias and Samuel B. Cherson and Auténtico figures close to the DR's leadership such as Ricardo Bianchi, Luis Chaviano Reyes and Antonio ("Tony") Santiago in interviews cited elsewhere in this book.

19. The meeting took place in June 1955. As such it was a preliminary discussion concerning the creation of a clandestine apparatus led by the students and other militants of an assorted background (Evidence to the authors by Ricardo Bianchi, August 29, 1972, San Juan, Puerto Rico).

20. Bianchi told the authors Echeverría was deeply worried about Fidel's demands for absolute control. A similar impression was recorded by Mario Llerena when Fidel met with the leaders of Movimiento de Liberación Radical in June 1955 (Authors' interview with Bianchi, August 29, 1972, San Juan, Puerto Rico; Llerena manuscript).

21. The executive council used a system of rotation whereby each member would preside at a subsequent meeting. This device would lessen the chances for personality cults (Authors' interview with Félix Armando Murias, September 4, 1972, Miami, Florida).

22. Jorge Valls is now in prison at La Cabaña Fortress, where he was sentenced to 30 years by the Castro government (Evidence of one of the authors: also authors' interview with Julio Fernández, who was very close to Valls throughout the insurrection. February 7, 1972, Union City, New Jersey). On Joe Westbrook Rosales, see "Mártires del 13 de marzo: Joe Westbrook Rosales, estudiante," *Revolución* (Havana), May 7, 1965, p. 3.

23. Faure Chomón had been a member of Rolando Masferrer's MSR and later of Aureliano Sánchez Arango's Triple A Movement. A close friend of Manolo Castro (FEU president in the mid-forties) and avowed enemy of Fidel Castro (UIR) throughout the internicine gangster-like wars of the "action groups," Chomón was invited to join the DR under the assumption that Echeverría's leadership abilities would keep his ambitions checked (Evidence of Félix Armando Murias, September 4, 1972, Miami, Florida; and Samuel B. Cherson and Lucy Echeverría, August 27–29, 1972, San Juan, Puerto Rico).

24. A tape recording of José Antonio's speech at Muelle de Luz has been made available to the authors by courtesy of the Echeverría family.

25. The chanting agitators were led by Gustavo ("Machaco") Ameijeiras, a courageous Ortodoxo militant at this time with Fidel's movement, and brother of Efigenio Ameijeiras. See "Gustavo Ameijeiras: en el XIII aniversario de su desaparición," *Bohemia* (Havana), May 28, 1971, p. 68.

26. Javier Rodríguez, "José Antonio Echeverría y la clase obrera," *Bohemia* (Havana), March 10, 1967, pp. 52–55.

27. Evidence of one of the authors.

28. Enrique Gutiérrez, "El dramático viernes de la semana pasada," *Carteles* (Havana), December 11, 1955, pp. 46–47, 100. For a brief coverage of the demonstration, see Jaime Suchlicki, *University Students and Revolution in Cuba 1920–1968* (Coral Gables, Fla.: University of Miami Press, 1969). p. 68

29. Rodríguez, "José Antonio Echeverría y la clase obrera," pp. 52–53. For a chronology of the demonstrations, see Juan Nuiry Sánchez, "José Antonio Echeverría, pensamiento y acción," *Bohemia* (Havana), March 10, 1967, pp. 76–77; and Javier Rodríguez, "Visión de José Antonio Echeverría," *Bohemia* (Havana), March 8, 1968, p. 55.

30. Rodríguez, "Visión de José Antonio Echeverría," *Bohemia* (Havana), March 8, 1968, pp. 50–56.

31. On this and other demonstrations during November–December, 1955, see "Sección en Cuba," *Bohemia* (Havana), December 11, 1955, pp. 65–67; *Diario de la Marina* (Havana), December 9, 1955; "Sección en Cuba," *Bohemia* (Havana), December 18, 1955, pp. 127–41; and Enrique Gutierrez, "El dramático viernes de la semana pasada," *Carteles* (Havana), December 11, 1955, pp. 46–47, 100.

32. Rodríguez, "José Antonio Echeverría y la clase obrera," p. 53.

33. Ibid., pp. 52–55.

34. *Constitución del Directorio Revolucionario.* Authors' copy. Excerpted passages appear in Cherson, "José Antonio Echeverría," p. 99. The DR constitution was drawn up at Rolando Cubelas' house in September 1955 with the assistance of Félix Armando Murias, Cubelas, René Anillo, Echeverría and Joe Westbrook Rosales (Murias to the authors, September 4, 1972, Miami, Florida).

35. Evidence of Ricardo Bianchi to the authors (August 28, 1972, San Juan, Puerto Rico).

36. José A. Díaz, *Un estudio sobre Cuba* (Miami: University of Miami Press, 1963), p. 977, quoting from Decree no. 125, published in the *Gaceta Oficial*, January 25, 1955.

37. See Hugh Thomas, *Cuba, The Pursuit of Freedom* (New York: Harper and Row, 1971). pp. 871–72.

38. Díaz, *Un estudio sobre Cuba*, p. 979. See also Oscar Pino Santos, "Sobre el convenio de Londres, la rebaja de la cuota y el aprovechamiento de los sub-productos de la caña," *Carteles* (Havana), December 25, 1955, pp. 46–49, 108.

39. See Carlos Franqui, "Zafra de 5 millones, pago del diferencial y ruptura del convenio de Londres piden los obreros azucareros," *Carteles* (Havana), January 1, 1956, pp. 39, 92.

40. Rodríguez, "José Antonio Echeverría y la clase obrera," pp. 52–55. For previous involvement of the university in matters pertaining to the sugar industry, see Jorge Vega, "Incidentes y polémica en el III Forum azucarero," *Carteles* (Havana), December 11, 1955, pp. 48–50, 102.

41. Rodríguez, "José Antonio Echeverría y la clase obrera," p. 55.

42. Ibid.

43. See Carlos Franqui, "La huelga azucarera tuvo el apoyo popular," *Carteles* (Havana), January 8, 1956, pp. 38–39.

44. Carlos Franqui, "Los problemas obreros," *Carteles* (Havana), January 22, 1956, p. 38.

45. Carlos Franqui, "Rechaza la zafra y reclama el 7.3 la nueva FENETA," *Carteles* (Havana), January 22, 1956, p. 31.

46. Carlos Franqui, "Notifica la FENETA oficial la suspensión de los dirigentes separados." *Carteles* (Havana), January 22, 1956, pp. 38, 88.

47. See Rolando F. Pérez. "Mantendremos sin tregua nuestra lucha." *Carteles* (Havana), January 1, 1956, pp. 38-39. 92. See also Luis Navarro Yarce, "Los acontecimientos más destacados del año 1955." *Carteles* (Havana), December 15, 1955, pp. 48–53, 141–42.

48. The speech appears in *Vida Universitaria* (Havana) 20, no. 214 (January–March, 1969): 32–33.

49. *Bases ideológicas del Directorio Revolucionario*. Authors' copy. For a brief passage, see Nuiry, "José Antonio Echeverría," p. 77.

50. Authors' interview with Fernando Reyes Llera (February 12, 1971, Union City, New Jersey) who was one of the survivors of the Goicuría attack.

51. Authors' interview with Ricardo ("Popi") Corpión (September 1972, Miami, Florida).

52. From the personal papers, letters, and documents of José Antonio Echeverría. Courtesy of the Echeverría family to the authors, August 27–29, 1972. San Juan, Puerto Rico.

4

Prologue to Insurrection

In 1955 a group of civic, professional and political figures, led by Don Cosme de la Torriente, a well-known veteran of the War of Independence and former president of the League of Nations, organized the Sociedad de Amigos de la República (SAR). Among the better known figures collaborating closely with Cosme de la Torriente was SAR's secretary, José Miró Cardona,[1] president of the National Bar Association of Cuba. SAR's purpose was to make a final serious attempt to find a peaceful solution to the country's problems. The organization did its best to convince Batista of the need to call elections before his term expired in 1958. Public meetings were organized to explain SAR's objectives, and religious and other institutions were invited to join in the effort for a prompt and peaceful transfer of power.

At first the government adopted a conciliatory attitude toward SAR. But as SAR gradually showed its seriousness of purpose through its demands, Batista's position became one of paternalistic indifference, particularly toward Cosme de la Torriente. Government spokesmen began to insist that elections could not be held until Batista had completed his term in power, and that to call for elections before that date would be an unconstitutional political maneuver. Batista himself seems to have been unwilling to acquiesce to SAR's petitions for early, free and honest general elections. The FEU accused Batista of delaying tactics and challenged the government to offer immediate proof of its good will. Otherwise, it said, revolution would be the answer to Batista's refusal to negotiate.

By this time, Fidel Castro had been convinced of the futility of any peaceful settlement with the government, and had left the island to organize the revolution from Mexico City, where he could move freely and raise the necessary resources. Before leaving Cuba, Fidel had visited Miguel Angel Quevedo, editor of the magazine *Bohemia*, and had asked him to publish a letter in which Fidel unveiled his decision and his plans for the future.[2]

In the fall of 1955 Castro travelled from Mexico to the United States. During a number of political rallies in Miami he maintained that to ensure legitimate general elections, Batista would have to transfer the presidency to Don Cosme de la Torriente so the latter could preside "over the general elections that are demanded. . . . If there is an electoral settlement without Batista's resignation,"

Castro announced, "before those elections are held, the revolution will begin."[3] Government spokesmen reacted by calling Castro a professional agitator and gangster. They always mentioned his former association with an action group as proof that he would not accept any settlement short of the violent overthrow of the regime. The government launched a campaign to discredit the insurrectionists, but were un-willing to offer a concrete solution to the electoralists.

From exile, Castro drew attention to his cause by writing letters to the editors of several Cuban papers. In an article entitled "Against Everybody" ("*Contra todos*"), published in *Bohemia*, Castro made several observations about Cuba's future.[4] First, he commented sarcastically on how he was ignored by Cuba's most powerful politicians until his daring attack against the Moncada barracks in Santiago de Cuba. Then he criticized the values of the politicians who, in his opinion, would have accepted him had he agreed to play into their hands. Claiming he had broken every rule of the game, by remaining rigid about following the forms of traditional politicking and upholding an impeccable rule of conduct, Castro dismissed the thought that he ever had political ambitions. Accordingly,

> I gave up any electoral ambition from the outset. I renounced the presidency of the Municipal Assembly of Havana, which the Ortodoxo Party offered me, a post coveted by all as the second most important position in the Republic. I gave up an appointment in the executive council of the party. At the same time I gave up a salary of $500 per month that an insurance company offered me, because I do not profit from my prestige—a prestige that does not belong to me but to a cause. I declined the salary of an important Havana newspaper and wrote instead for Luis Orlando's newspaper, which could not pay me a cent . . . I . . . rejected silence . . . a comfortable refuge for those who fear defamation and danger.

These reminiscences impressed Castro's readers, reminding them how easy it would have been for him personally, had he decided to abandon the insurrectionary program. Furthermore, Castro emphasized that the people wanted more than a simple change of command, and that they "must be given something more than liberty and democracy in abstract; decent living must be made available to every Cuban." The state should not ignore the fate of its citizens because there was no greater tragedy than "that of a man capable and willing to work but he and his family starve because he lacks a job." Castro insisted that the revolution could not depend on the help of any of the politicians who had stolen the republic's funds. "Money stolen from the republic cannot be used to make revolutions. Revolutions are based on morals. A movement that has to rob banks or accept money from thieves cannot be considered revolutionary." He rejected any possibility of compromise with the government and the politicians, because they would make common cause with injustices and privileges. Accordingly, Castro continued, "the embezzlers are perplexed by the shouts of 'revolution' which occur with increasing force at every large meeting and which sound like bells calling the wicked to final judgment."[5]

Castro was aware that students were using the threat of revolution as an unmistakable challenge to SAR's members, the politicians and the Batista government; he had even ordered many of his followers to attend SAR's meetings to join the chant.

Seemingly, what impressed people most was not Castro's attack on Moncada nor his brief imprisonment, but his refusal to profit monetarily from his increasing popularity. Brave men were not hard to find in Cuba; honest men were. And honesty was determined by what a man did when offered profitable positions. Many leaders in the past had taken the revolutionary path until they had attained enough fame to demand a position within the establishment. Castro had turned down everything, and his insistence on the insurrectionary course, accompanied by his independence from political parties and oldtimers, made the young rebel attractive.

With Castro active in the United States, the political picture was polarized only in an abstract sense. True divisiveness would appear once the insurrection began its work within Cuba: Batista on the one side, the insurrectionists on another. In between was an ineffectual "electoralist" opposition.[6]

However, even before the lines were sharply drawn several conspiratorial attempts developed. Unrest within the armed forces led Colonel Ramón Barquín and a group of officers to plot a rebellion against Batista, later labeled "conspiracy of the pure." But before such a conspiracy could meterialize it was exposed and its leaders tried and sent lo prison. Former president Prío returned to Miami, Florida, shortly thereafter and the SAR soon ceased to exist. Batista exploited the "conspiracy of the pure" to his advantage, refusing to negotiate with the electoralist opposition as long as there were hidden intentions to depose his regime by force. As the SAR withdrew into the background, the road to insurrection was left wide open.

Those who favored insurrection knew it would not be an easy matter, and that most of the initiators would die in the process. With few exceptions—such as Castro—most people wished for a peaceful transition which would have saved much blood. Yet, the government's rejection of every peace formula based on Batista's withdrawal from power eventually closed all channels to compromise. Insurrection appeared to be the only alternative.

The youth, especially, wanted to confront violence with violence. On April 29, 1956, Reynold García, a young revolutionary with Auténtico connections, commanding a group of about 30 men, led an attack against the well-fortified Goicuría barracks in Matanzas province. Armed with old and useless rifles, the attackers planned to take over the military camp and distribute arms to the people. Army General Pilar García—later Chief of National Police—was aware of the group's activities, and the camp's defense was ready. When the attackers entered the camp the troops were waiting for them. There were no survivors.[7] This disaster was particularly significant; for the remaining years of the insurrection no more isolated groups would attempt such Moncada-like attacks.

The Exiles

The exile colony, mostly in Miami, Florida, was divided into several groups. There were young students eager to go back to the island to join the underground struggle; passive exiles hoping for an amnesty, or to go back for a few months until being forced into exile again; and well-known politicians deposed by Batista's coup, the Auténticos or the Ortodoxos. The latter groups carried their old rivalries into exile. Chief among the Auténticos was former president Carlos Prío Socarrás whose rapidly acquired fortune and considerable political legitimacy as the last constitutionally elected president gave him substantial public support.

As in the past there were exiles who thought Cubans capable of liberating themselves from a dictatorship, and those who viewed the situation in terms of what—if anything—the United States would be willing to do against Batista. In between were the *brinca-cercas*, (literally, fence jumpers), willing to accept anything, including U.S. intervention, as long as they could obtain power or share in its spoils.

Since the start, Fidel Castro stood as one of the few independent figures in exile, and the only one who appeared fully convinced of the need for an insurrection—a real insurrection, not an imaginary one which would take place in the comfortable lobbies of Miami hotels. To organize an insurrection, however, he had to raise capital in the United States, the traditional source of economic support in Cuba's struggles for independence. Fidel followed tradition with excellent results. He kept busy visiting American cities and organizing "patriotic clubs" in Bridgeport, Connecticut; Elizabeth and Union City, New Jersey; and in New York City, Chicago, Philadelphia, Tampa and Key West.[8]

Heroes or Martyrs

"From trips such as this," Castro had written, "one does not return, or if one does, it is with the tyranny beheaded at our feel." After his return to Mexico from the United States Castro began to organize his followers while translating the idea of an expedition into practical efforts to launch an invasion force.

Castro's group received financial support from various sources. Money from Florida was diligently supervised by Juan Manuel Márquez, Castro's eyes and ears in that area. Funds also came from Mexico, Venezuela and Cuba. In Mexico, Castro was financially aided by Alfonso Gutiérrez ("Fifo"), a Mexican engineer married to a Cuban singer, Orquídea Pino, and by Manuel

Machado, owner of a large printing shop in Mexico. Rafael Bilbao, a wealthy Cuban long established in Venezuela also contributed. From Cuba, Reverend Cecilio Arrastía once delivered $10,000 to Castro in Mexico—money which was collected from M-26-7 sympathizers.[9]

Castro's men began to train in what were called camp houses. Some of their military education was supervised by Alberto Bayo, a veteran of the Spanish Civil War who was well known to Latin American revolutionaries living in Mexico. At first Castro's men stayed in the suburbs of Mexico City, on a farm called "Santa Fé." When the Mexican police moved in on the group, Castro found suitable quarters on the "Santa Rosa" farm about 20 miles from the capital.[10]

On July 24, 1956, the group was arrested by Mexican authorities, charged with violating the country's neutrality, and put in prison. It was there that Teresa Casuso met Fidel Castro. Teresa ("Teté") was the widow of Pablo de la Torriente Brau, a Cuban intellectual and member of the 1930 generation, who died in the Spanish Civil War. Teté and her husband were well known by young Cubans, who respected and admired their background as revolutionaries. Teté was to become one of Castro's most important allies in Mexico, and her access to Carlos Prío and other members of the 1930 generation would be very useful to Fidel. It was at Teté's home in 1956 that Mario Llerena first discussed with Fidel some of the relevant aspects of a program for the 26th of July movement, and where Fidel kept his favorite guns hidden in a closet—including his famous telescopic rifle.[11] Fidel asked Teté to arrange a meeting with Carlos Prío Although he had previously made the same request of Antonio ("Tony") Santiago and Carlos Vega in Mexico.[12] Teté had direct access to Prío and persuaded the former president to meet Fidel Castro.[13]

In August 1956, Fidel and Prío met at a small motel in McAllen, Texas.[14] They discussed the future of the insurrection for over an hour, and then Fidel introduced Faustino Pérez to Prío Fidel, ever the pragmatic, was not about to abide by his repeated statements that a revolution could not be made with money from the politicians. So, despite his years of opposition to Prío's administration, and his charges that the Auténticos were corrupt, Fidel asked Prío for money to finance his expedition to Cuba. The former president agreed to help. Carlos Prío sent his first contribution of $50,000 to Fidel Castro's movement through Juan Manuel Márquez.[15] Later, Fidel wrote Prío asking for more money—exactly $22,000—and again Prío sent the money. Before the insurrection was over, Prío's aid to Fidel's guerrillas amounted to almost one quarter of a million dollars in arms and money.[16] Associates of Prío also contributed. Justo Carillo, former president of the Bank for Reconstruction and Development under Prío's administration, contributed $5,000 in cash, while Lopez Villaboy, president of Cubana de Aviación and a close friend of Batista, also sent a financial contribution to Fidel.[17]

Soon after funds started coming to the insurrectionaries Fidel met a man who would become indispensable to the movement as an organizer, a strategist and combatant: Ernesto Guevara de la Serna.

"Che" Guevara

Ernesto Guevara de la Serna was born on June 14, 1928, in Rosario de Santa Fé, Argentina, the eldest of five children of a middle-class family.[18] Guevara's life was characterized by constant movement, challenge, adventure and a search for knowledge. In 1945, he was admitted to the school of medicine at Buenos Aires University, where he decided to become an allergist. He was not granted his M.D. degree until March 1953, when he was 25, for Guevara the adventurer held sway over Guevara the medical student.

In 1947, he worked for a month aboard a merchant ship. In 1949, with a motorbike and a knapsack, he began a journey through the northern provinces of Argentina. He left Córdoba, went to the province of Salta, and then moved into Jujuy, Tucumán, Santiago del Estero, Chaco and Formosa. From there he travelled across the Andes and to five other provinces.

On December 29, 1951, Guevara embarked once again on a new journey, this time by motorcycle, reaching Santiago de Chile on foot after the vehicle broke down. From there he went to Macchu Picchu, Perú. At the time of Batista's coup d'etat in 1952, Guevara was working in the leprosarium of San Pablo on the shores of the Amazon.[19]

From the leprosarium, Guevara and his friend Alberto Granados flew to Colombia, and on July 14, 1952, crossed into Venezuela. After Caracas, Guevara moved on, arriving in Miami, Florida, aboard a horse-carrying airplane chartered by one of his uncles who sold horses abroad, on July 25, and going back to Argentina in August.[20] Only then did Guevara finish his studies and obtain his M.D. degree. Afterwards, he moved to La Paz, Bolivia, then in the midst of its national revolution. From Bolivia, Guevara travelled to Perú, Ecuador, and from there to Panamá with a free ticket which he obtained from the Great White Fleet of the United Fruit Sugar Company. From Panamá, Guevara moved on to Costa Rica where, under the sheltering roof of José Figueres' populist government, many a leader from Latin America's democratic left resided. While in Costa Rica, Guevara met Romulo Betancourt, Juan Bosch, and Raúl Leoni and some Cuban exiles.[21]

In December 1953 Guevara arrived in Guatemala City.[22] There he met Hilda Gadea, a Peruvian. An articulate and widely read woman, Hilda was instrumental in searching out a job for the young Argentinian. As a prominent APRA (Alianza Popular Revolucionaria Americana) student leader—who had sought refuge in Guatemala because of her opposition to Manuel Odría's dictatorship—Hilda had sound contacts with exiled Latin Americans of the democratic left. At the time of Guevara's arrival, Hilda, who held a degree in economics from San Marcos University, was working in the Department of Economic Studies of the Instituto de Fomento de la Producción.[23]

Though Ernesto Guevara originally impressed Hilda as "too superficial, egotistic and conceited," she gradually became fond of him. Guevara was to profit, intellectually and politically, from his relationship to Hilda Gadea.

She introduced Guevara to many of the outstanding intellectuals and politicians residing in Guatemala City, at that time the haven of Latin America's revolutionaries. Thus, the Argentinian met Alfonso Bauer Paíz, Guatemala's Minister of Economy, Jaime Díaz Rozzoto, Secretary of the Presidency, Robert J. Alexander and Harry A. Kantor from the United States, and a host of Venezuelan, Guatemalan and Panamanian activists.[24] Finally, Guevara met a group of Cubans, former Moncada combatants also exiled in Guatemala. These were Antonio ("Nico") López, Mario Dalmau, Armando Arencibia and Antonio ("El Gallego") Darío López.

On Hilda's personal recommendation Guevara was hired as a translator, teacher and researcher. He abandoned these pursuits from time to time as opportunities arose for trips to nearby countries like Ecuador or El Salvador, but he spent a great amount of time reading the vast literature that Hilda had placed at his disposal. Through Hilda's tutorial abilities Ernesto Guevara learned about Mao Tse-tung's Chinese Revolution, and read Jose Carlos Mariátegui's *Siete Ensayos sobre la realidad Peruana*, Albert Einstein's works, Walt Whitman and a host of Latin authors.[25]

Guevara's intellectual politicization may have become more defined after Guatemala experienced the invasion of the CIA-supported forces of Colonel Carlos Castillo Armas, although this event by no means turned him into a revolutionary.[26] Hilda suffered persecution and eventually was jailed, and Guevara took asylum in the Argentinian embassy, when the government of Jacobo Arbenz fell from power. As Guevara had confessed to Hilda, he had left Argentina "to walk the world and return to Argentina after 10 years."[27] For the moment, it seemed that Guevara's next stop on his trip around the world would be Mexico City, where he arrived in August 1954.

In Mexico, Guevara worked as a free-lance photographer and occasional book salesman for the Fondo de Cultura Económica. Hilda Gadea soon came to Mexico and, in the late fall of 1954, found Guevara working as an assistant medic at the General Hospital of Mexico City.[28] Guevara also held a moonlight job as news photographer for Alfonso Pérez Vizcaíno, director of the Latin News Agency, financed and operated by the Argentinian dictator Juan Domingo Perón.[29] In this enterprise he was aided by several Cubans of the 26th of July movement who needed an income to survive in Mexico. Although Guevara apparently had not been strongly affected by the Guatemalan revolutionary experience—he was contemplating going into the movie industry or making a trip to China and Africa—his plans changed when he re-encountered the Cubans he had met in Guatemala.

At the beginning of the summer of 1955 Guevara met Raúl Castro, and in July he met Fidel at the house of María Antonia Figueroa, located in the Lomas de Chapultepec.[30] "I spoke with Fidel a whole night," Guevara would later write. "At dawn I was already the physician of the future expedition." Castro made a lasting impression on Guevara: "He [Castro] faced and resolved the impossible. He had an unshakable faith that once he left he would arrive in Cuba, that once he arrived he would fight, that once he began fighting he would win.... I shared his optimism."[31] On hearing Castro's plan, Guevara later remarked: "My almost immediate impression on hearing the first lessons, was of the possibility for victory, which I had seen as very doubtful when I joined the rebel commander. I had been attached to him from the outset, moved by a feeling of romantic adventurous sympathy, and by the conviction that it would be worth dying on an alien beach for such a pure ideal."[32]

Thus, "Che" began his training at the Santa Rita farm to learn the trade of war under the guidance of Alberto Bayo, who in time would select the Argentinian as the best pupil in the group.[33]

The Pact of Mexico

As Castro intensified his preparations for the expedition, José Antonio Echeverría and Ricardo ("Popi") Corpión, representatives of the DR, arrived in Mexico. Echeverría and Corpión met Fidel Castro on the night of August 30, 1956, at approximately 10 PM.[34] Fidel, in a mysteriously conspiratorial manner, speaking almost in a hush, embraced José Antonio with tears in his eyes. The three men went to a house and began a long conversation that lasted until 8 AM. Fidel dwelled at length on the impressive organization he had in Cuba, the readiness of its cadres, military equipment and numerical strength. He asked José Antonio to support the "general uprising" throughout the island when his scheduled landing force touched on Cuban shores. In Fidel's view, the uprising's success depended largely on whatever logistical support the DR could give throughout Havana, Matanzas, Las Villas and Camagüey provinces. Thus, the forces of the DR had to initiate continuous acts of violence in the cities before and after the landing.

Strongly impressed by Fidel's description of the M-26-7 offensive capability, José Antonio readily supported his proposal and asked Fidel if he would like to meet with President José Figuéres in Costa Rica.[35] The latter had agreed to pay Fidel's fare, and Fidel responded enthusiastically since Figuéres was pledging financial support to the struggle. On the same topic, Fidel asked José Antonio to get in touch with Prío in Miami, and to ask him for more financial aid. Then both men began writing the draft of the pact which bound the DR and the M-26-7 to carry out insurrectionary actions together. Once the draft was finished, José Antonio, Corpión and Fidel went to Teté Casuso's home, where Teté typed the original copy of the Pact of Mexico.[36]

The declaration warned that any participation in elections called by the regime would be considered a betrayal to the insurrectionists. Both movements viewed the social and political conditions in the country as favorable, stating that the revolutionary plans were advanced enough to offer the people their liberation in 1956. The insurrection was to be supported by a general strike which, together with popular action, would make victory inevitable.

Batista was accused of being as despotic as Dominican dictator Trujillo, and the latter was charged with attempting to intervene in the internal affairs of Cuba. The Pact of Mexico's attacks on Trujillo's activities resulted from José Antonio's firm insistence that both movements clearly reject any aid from the Dominican caudillo. The declaration charged various Cuban army officers with conspiring with Trujillo to get rid of Batista, among them Alberto del Río Chaviano, Martín Díaz Tamayo, Leopoldo Pérez Cougil, Manuel Ugalde Carrillo, Manuel Larrubia, Juan Rojas and José Rego Rubido. The latter, the declaration charged, had been supported by gunman Policarpo Soler.

But there were also honorable officers, among them Colonel Ramón Barquín and his colleagues from the "conspiracy of the pure." The declaration stated: "Because it was led by prestigious officers, the military would have the respect and admiration of the revolutionaries." Unity was advocated for the insurrectionary groups, the SAR was asked to cease its efforts at finding a peaceful solution with Batista, and all groups in the society were asked to cooperate with the insurrection. Once the insurrectionists rose to power they would carry out a program of social justice, establish freedom and respect the dignity of all men.[37]

Strategically the plans called for simultaneous uprisings in Havana and Oriente provinces. Supportive operations were planned for Matanzas, Las Villas and Camagüey provinces as well. Fidel's landing was to coincide with an uprising in Oriente, and the expeditionary force would join with insurgents waiting in the triangle of Bayamo-Yara-Manzanillo in Oriente. The DR, acting simultaneously with the M-26-7 at Havana, would keep Batista's forces divided. Thus, the insurgent forces in Oriente would presumably be able to consolidate their positions, arm the people and contact other anti-Batista groups. The main thrust against the regime would come from Oriente province, and the decisive phase in the attempt would be the fall of Santiago de Cuba. Castro's men were to move inland, a general strike would be declared, and the city of Manzanillo would fall under Castro's combined attack.

In the event of failure, Fidel contemplated retreat to the mountains of Sierra Maestra.[38] There was no specific date set for the uprising, although the watchword suggested it would be at the end of 1956. José ("Pepito") Tey was to be responsible for letting José Antonio know well in advance Fidel's date of departure from Mexico.[39]

When the news of the pact reached the students in Havana, Fructuoso Rodríguez—acting FEU president—scheduled an urgent session with the presidents of all the schools at the Balneario Universitario.[40] The participants voiced surprise, complaints and suspicion. Fructuoso tried to explain that Echeverría had signed the pact in his position as secretary-general of the DR and president of the FEU, thus binding the DR directly to the pact. Since the presidents of the schools were also members of the DR they presumably fully supported Echeverría's endorsement of the agreement.[41]

Left to right: Fructuoso Rodriguez, Joe Westbrook, Faure Chomón and Juan Nuiry at the signing of the Mexico Pact between the M-26-7 and the DR, Chapultepec Forest, Mexico City, October 1956 (Courtesy Dora Rosales Westbrook).

But even at this point suspicions concerning an alliance with Fidel had not been entirely erased. Upon his return to Cuba, Echeverría held a meeting with the DR executive council. After a heated discussion about the pact it was agreed that several members of the DR would meet with Fidel in Mexico to outline a common strategy of struggle.

Thus, early in October of 1956 Echeverría, Juan Nuiry, Joe Westbrook, Faure Chomón, Juan Pedro Carbó Serviá, José Machado and Fructuoso Rodríguez arrived in Mexico for a second round of talks with Fidel.[42] Several topics were discussed, but the most important, concerning a common method of struggle, produced no agreement among the participants.[43] Each organization pledged to support one another in actions called against Batista. Castro was to give Echeverría 48 to 72 hours notice before landing in Cuba so that the DR and the M-26-7 cells would be able to carry out their insurrectionary plans.[44]

A fairly certain account of what transpired at these talks may be surmised from a speech delivered by Joe Westbrook in October 1956 at the footsteps of Havana University. Some excerpts read:

> It is necessary to destroy the *latifundio* but it would be deadly to follow the path of the *minifundio*. It is essential to recover our natural resources from foreign hands but it would be foolish to close all doors to sound investments. A revolution must not allow its followers to become so fanatical as to thwart economic progress in the name of

an illusory freedom lying ahead, nor must it exploit those issues that ought to be faced rationally—and I refer to American expansionism—for [such revolution] would end up subduing those who today are fighting against oppression. I don't support a revolutionary movement of cynical and frustrated men. I don't support a revolution which hands us emotional freedom but leaves us in rags. I don't go along with that *revolucioncita* promoted by demagogic *caudillos*. I am on the side of that revolution invoked by serious-minded, stable, self-assured Cubans. We have come to pledge ourselves to the attainment of a Cuba with schools in the countryside so the peasant too may share in the free competition for justice; where everyone's rights are respected as our own; where truth is upheld without resorting to gangster-like hysteria; where the economy does not rest on a single product; a progressive Cuba, free of irrrational tantrums, where private property becomes the social function of society; where blacks, mulattoes and whites become more Cuban-like than white, mulattoes or blacks. This and no other is the revolution of the Directorio. If this is our revolution Cuba will be saved or else we will all fall in the battlefield.[45]

Creating the Conditions

In Mexico the DR had been asked to "produce actions," to prepare the conditions for the general uprising that would ensue upon Castro's landing.[46] To fulfill this pledge isolated acts of terrorism spread through Havana, Santa Clara, Camagüey and Oriente. The first action came as a result of a plan to assassinate Santiago Rey Pernas, a member of Batista's cabinet. A group of members of the DR's action cells met at a restaurant close to the university, and had a random drawing to determine who would participate in the execution. Juan Pedro Carbó Serviá. Juan Nuiry, Rolando Cubela, José ("Pepe") Fernández Cossio and Faure Chomón "won" the job of conducting the operation. At the last minute Faure Chomón refused to go, and Fernández Cossío was assigned the task of driving the getaway car.[47]

On October 28 Carbó Serviá, Nuiry and Cubela entered the Montmartre nightclub. Santiago Rey Pernas was not there. As they were leaving, they spotted Colonel Antonio Blanco Rico, chief of the bureau of investigations, and Colonel Marcelo Tabernilla. The DR group opened fire, killing Blanco Rico on the spot while some of the bullets aimed at Colonel Tabernilla wounded Mrs. Marta Poli, his wife. The shooting incident provoked a fiery search by the Havana police.[48]

The resulting political climate, plus participation in other actions, forced a group of revolutionaries to seek political asylum in the Haitian embassy. The morning after Blanco Rico's death, Brigadier General Rafael Salas Cañizares led an assault against the embassy, violating the right of asylum in an unprecedented act. In the process, one of the refugees shot Cañizares, who died almost instantly. In retaliation the police assassinated ten revolutionaries on the premises of the embassy.[49] The incident shocked the nation, and was widely discussed throughout Latin America, as the Inter-American Press Society was then meeting in Havana.

The DR issued a statement to the press society condemning the regime for acts of brutality. The document reported that on September 26. 18 youths had been found dead in Oriente province, and then left in the streets for public exhibition. In addition two girls suspected of membership in the DR had been sexually molested by the police, and then murdered. Their naked bodies had been abandoned in a Havana suburb.[50]

The death of Chief Salas Cañizares threw the police into an unprecedented wave of official terrorism. The DR answered in kind by attacking known collaborators with the regime. Every day students were found shot to death in Havana, Marianao and Guanabacoa. At night action cells of the DR exploded bombs, while the M-26-7 placed phosphorous in movie theaters and buses. Signs appeared on the walls of many Havana buildings and the deaths of insurgents were avenged by the deaths of those suspected of their murders.

Esteban Ventura Novo, police captain of the 9th precinct, became increasingly vicious. In both the 9th and 5th precincts under Ventura's jurisdiction, personal safety was out of the question. This climate of hatred and open warfare molded the character of many underground fighters.

While Batista granted promotions to the worst assassins of his regime the students learned the many complex requirements of urban guerrilla fighting. Experience taught them certain rules had to be obeyed which were never to be violated. Foremost was secrecy about one's connections and whereabouts, if one wished to survive. A minor indiscretion could jeopardize the work of an entire group of people. In the event of capture by the police, a prisoner was morally bound not to give any information for at least 24 hours to allow his *campañeros* time to flee. In cases where prisoners were deeply involved with the underground, suicide was considered the most honorable way out, and the only alternative to a confession. Hesitation could not deter an urban fighter from killing the enemy or being himself killed. One could not permit his emotions to be involved during action, or it ran the risk of failure.

The word "assassination" was not to be used; the death of an adversary was an "execution." Such an "execution" was carried out in the name of the people, justice and one's cause; for justice was always on the side of the fighter and therefore those he opposed had violated justice and the law. The urban fighter could not, therefore, be confused with an ordinary killer. He fought to gain freedom for his people, and everything he did was rationalized in those terms. Each guerrilla fighter in the urban areas underwent a difficult process of psychological adaptation, and not until he was beyond feeling any remorse could he be assigned difficult missions.

The fighter's degree of objectivity, his overt lack of emotionalism and his willingness to carry out any operation determined his promotion within the ranks of the urban guerrillas. A cadre leader, chief of an action cell, had to meet those conditions. He also had to be a good judge of human character, be ready to assign a "final" mission to those appearing *quemados* ("hot" or identified by the police), and who refused to go into exile, and generally keep calm at crucial moments.

The DR at this time was the most active urban organization. It prohibited its members from attacking low-ranking police officers unless they were known and dangerous to the underground. The strategy was to select their objectives carefully, and to plan all operations well ahead of time. Members of the elite were selected for "execution" in order to instill panic among the *batistianos*. The theory held by the DR's action cells was that if they hit at the top, those at the bottom would become "neutral" out of fear; in this respect they, too, were the object of the underground's selective terrorism. The goal was to create a gap between those in power and those who upheld that power from the bottom.

The M-26-7 urban underground maintained that only actions conducted in public places could create a general climate of insurrection, damage the economy, promote chaos and place the regime on the defensive. Thus, the M-26-7 placed bombs in nightclubs, theaters, parks and buses. The strategy was to execute those lower-level officers whose daily acts of brutality sustained the regime. The M-26-7 action cells—just a few at this time—were very efficient. Their attacks on police patrol cars forced the regime to increase the number of police officers driving or occupying each car. The M-26-7's bombs in public places caused innocent casualties but were effective in creating a climate of fear and suspicion which in turn tarnished the government's "law and order" image. All these actions helped foster a certain tension, but not enough turbulence to lead to a nationwide insurrection. As the spring of 1956 approached the country was moving toward increasing political instability and social paralysis provoked by violence. The answer was official terrorism. Its concomitant, insurrection, was just a matter of time, effort and sacrifice. Cuban youth abounded in all three elements. The government did not.

In mid-November, the Mexican press reported Castro and his followers were not to be found in their usual gathering places in Mexico City. At about the same time, the Mexican police raided several training sites, confiscating arms and other war materiel. Sensing immediate danger, Castro had speeded up plans. Although he had first planned to buy a Catalina flying boat with Prío's money, he eventually purchased a 58-foot yacht, the Granma, for $15,000. The expeditionaries quietly moved from Mexico City to Veracruz on November 21. Four days later, on November 25, 1956,[51] Fidel Castro and his men boarded the Granma at Tuxpan, Veracruz, and set their compass for Cuba.

Notes

1. Dr. José Miró Cardona was widely respected by the students and it was mainly his presence along with Cosme, at SAR that led Echeverría to temporarily support its goals. Carlos Márquez Sterling unjustly criticized Miró Cardona, charging that Miró had exerted a negative influence on Cosme de la Torriente, and argued that Miró actually was running SAR. See Carlos Márquez Sterling, *Historia de Cuba: desde Colòn hasta Castro* (New York: Las Americas, 1968). p. 366.

2. See text of this letter in Rolando E. Bonachea and Nelson P. Valdés, eds., *Revolutionary Struggle, 1947–1958*, vol. 1 (Cambridge: MIT Press, 1972), p. 257.

3. See Luis Conte Agüero, *Los dos rostros de Fidel Castro* (Mexico: Editorial Jus, 1960) p. 116, and *Bohemia* (Havana), March 11, 1956, pp. 30–31.

4. See *Bohemia* (Havana), January 8, 1956. The article was dated December 15, 1955.

5. Ibid.

6. Francisco Ichaso, a pro-Batista journalist, wrote: "They [electoralists] now feel displaced by the size which the July 26 movement is acquiring in the battle against *Marzismo*," *Marzismo* refers to the coup d'etat of March 10th; the participants of the coup were also known as *Marzistas*. See *Bohemia* (Havana), December 4, 1956.

7. See *Diario de la Marina* (Havana), April 30, 1956, and *Prensa Libre* (Havana), May 2, 1956. García was an Auténtico, and ex-chauffeur of Aureliano Sánchez Arango, former secretary of education under the Prio administration (1948–52).

8. See "Una carta de Fidel," Revolución (Havana), February 2, 1959, p. 127.

9. According to Rev. Cecilio Arrastía the money was collected among ordinary Cubans, and only José M. Gutiérrez, an Ortodoxo senator, gave 1,000 pesos. Letter of Rev. Cecilio Arrastía to the authors, August 6, 1972.

10. Certain illuminating passages on these training activities are found in Hilda Gadea, *Ernesto: A Memoir of Che Guevara* (New York: Doubleday, 1972) and Teresa Casuso, *Cuba and Castro* (New York: Random House, 1961).

11. Mario Llerena, ms, Authors' interview with Teresa Casuso, September 13, 1972, Miami, Florida. Also see Mario Llerena, "La bilis de los mediocres," *Bohemia* (Havana), March 29, 1959, p. 102, and Casuso, *Cuba and Castro*, p. 114.

12. Antonio "Tony" Santiago acted as Prío's liaison with Fidel Castro following the initial contact established by "Teté" Casuso; Santiago and Carlos Vega arrived in Mexico a day after the sailing of the Granma to discuss ultimate details of the expedition at Prío's request. "Tony" Santiago corroborated the matter of financial aid to Castro, and the amounts issued by Prío to Castro (Authors' interview with Antonio "Tony" Santiago, September 4, 1972, Miami, Florida; and February 24, 1973, Union City, New Jersey).

13. Authors' interview with Carlos Prío Socarrás, August 29, 1972, San Juan, Puerto Rico.

14. Casuso, *Cuba and Castro*, pp. 111–12.

15. Prío to the authors. Also, authors' interview with Francisco Varona, an Auténtico close both to Prío, and later in Mexico with Fidel Castro. September 1972, Miami, Florida.

16. Some of the arms shipments financed by Prío included: one plane loaded with arms that landed in Sierra Maestra in the autumn of 1958; one large arms shipment to Camilo Cienfuegos in the fall of 1958; and an assortment of arms shipments reaching both Raúl Castro's Second Front "Frank País," and Fidel's Column No. 1. Eloy Gutiérrez Menoyo's Second Front at Escambray Mountains also received considerable amounts of arms (Carlos Prío to the authors, August 29, 1972, San Juan. Puerto Rico).

17. See Hugh Thomas, *Cuba: The Pursuit of Freedom* (New York: Harper and Row, 1971), p. 886.

18. "De Rosario a Cuba," *Granma* (Havana), October 29, 1967, p. 6. Guevara's biographical data appear in a number of books and essays. See Dolores Moyano Martín, "The Making of a Revolutionary: A Memoir of the Young Guevara," *New York Times Magazine* (August 18, 1968); John Womack, Jr., "Che Guevara," *The New York Review* (January 28, 1971), pp. 3–6; Fluvio Fuentes, "Ché, niñez, adolescencia, juventud," *Bohemia* (Havana), October 20, 1967, pp. 70–77; José Aguilar, "La niñez del Ché," *Granma (Havana), October 29, 1967, p. 10:* Fernando Barral, "Che, estudiante," *Granma* (Havana), October 29, 1967, p. 11; and Julia Constela, "Cuando Ernesto Guevara aún no era el Ché: una entrevista con doña Cecilia de la Serna de Guevara," *Bohemia* (Havana), August 27, 1961. pp. 32–33. See also "Ché en Guatemala y Mexico," *Granma* (Havana), October 16, 1967, p. 8; and Luis González and Gustavo A. Sánchez Salazar, *The Great Rebel Che Guevara in Bolivia* (New York: Grove Press. 1969), pp. 30–34; John Gerassi, ed., *Venceremos: The Speeches and Writings of Che Guevara* (New York: Macmillan, 1968). pp. 1–10: Hilda Gadea, *Ernesto: A Memoir of Che Guevara* (New York: Doubleday, 1972).

19. For these itineraries see Enrique Salgado, *Radiografía del Ché* (Barcelona: Dopesa, 1970), pp. 56–65: Hugo Gambini, *El Ché Guevara* (Buenos Aires: Editorial Paidos, 1968), pp. 62–70; and Gadea, *Ernesto: A Memoir*, pp. 14–17.

20. Hilda Gadea, *Ernesto: A Memoir*, p. 14.

21. Ibid., p. 4.

22. Hilda Gadea, "Ché en Guatemala y Mexico," *Granma* (Havana), October 29, 1967. p. 6.

23. Gadea, *Ernesto: A Memoir*, p. 1.

24. Ibid., p. 12, 25.

25. Ibid., pp. 29–30.

26. See Richard J. Barnet, *Intervention and Revolution: The United States and the Third World* (New York: World, 1968), pp. 229–36: and Guillermo Toriello, *La batalla de Guatemala* (Buenos Aires: Ediciones Pueblos de America, 1956).

27. Gadea, *Ernesto: A Memoir*, p. 17.

28. Ibid., p. 79; also see *Granma* (Havana), October 29, 1967. Guevara married Hilda Gadea in Mexico on August 18 and Jesús Montané, not Raúl Castro, served as official witness.

29. Guevara's admiration for dictator Juan Domino Perón is illuminating. Hilda Gadea recalls that upon learning of Perón's downfall, Guevara hoped "the people would fight to defend that popular government." Gadea, *Ernesto: A Memoir*, p. 115. According' to Hilda, "For Ernesto the fall of Perón was a heavy blow. . . ." Ibid.

30. *El Mundo* (Havana), October 5, 1965. pp. 1. 8. See also "Esta combatiente." *Vida Universitaria* (Havana), 14, no. 212 (July-August, 1968), 39–40.

31. "Che en Guatemala, de una entrevista del periodista argentino Jorge Ricardo Masetti con Che en la Sierra Maestra," *Granma* (Havana), October 29, 1967, p. 6. This interview was originally held in April 1958.

32. Ernesto "Che" Guevara, "Una revolución que comienza," *Vida Universitaria*, 20, no. 214 (January–February–March, 1969): 12–14.

33. See Alberto Bayo, "El mejor alumno," *El Mundo* (Havana), October 19, 1967, p. 4, and *Mi aporte a la revolución cubana* (Havana: Imprenta del Ejército Rebelde, 1959).

34. Authors' interview with Ricardo ("Popi") Corpión, the only living witness to the Pact of Mexico besides Castro, September 1972, Miami, Florida.

35. Corpión was also present at the Figueres-Echeverría meeting in San José, Costa Rica, August 1956. Corpión told the authors that Figueres suggested that Echeverría wage guerrilla warfare instead of continuing the urban struggle.

36. Teresa Casuso to the authors, September 13, 1972, Miami, Florida. Also see Casuso, *Cuba and Castro*, p. 107.

37. "Carta de Mexico." *Vida Universitaria* (Havana), 14, no. 213 (September-December. 1968): 30–31, Also *Carta de Méjico: pacto entre el Directorio y el 26* (Havana, 1958), mimeo.

38. Simón Torres and Julio Aronde, "Debray and the Cuban Experience," in Leo Huberman and Paul M. Sweezy, eds., *Regis Debray and the Latin American Revolution* (New York: Monthly Review Press, 1968), p. 49. The authors, Cuban revolutionaries, state that guerrilla warfare was an alternative to the Granma's original plan. See also Marta Rojas, "Proa a Cuba!" *Trabajo* (Havana), November 1961, pp. 34–39.

39. The watchword, "in 1956 we will be heroes or martyrs," was launched by Fidel Castro at a speech given in Palm Garden, in New York City. See Vicente Cubillas, "Mitin oposicionista en Nueva York," *Bohemia* (Havana), November 6, 1955, pp. 82–83. On, the issue of the date for Fidel's arrival it must be noted that neither Frank País nor José Antonio Echeverría knew exactly the date or the month when it would take place (Letter of Agustín País to the authors, January 21, 1973, p. 1: and authors' interview with Ricardo "Popi" Corpión, September 1972, Miami, Florida).

40. Jorge Puente Blanco. "Preámbulo al 13 de Marzo," *Bohemia* (Havana), March 8, 1971, p. 89. Echeverría phoned Fructuoso Rodríguez from Mexico to arrange a meeting with the FEU's executive council (Evidence of one of the authors present at the meeting, Havana, September 1956).

41. Present at this meeting were the presidents of several schools. The only dissident voice was that of Jorge Valls who walked out in disapproval of a DR alliance with Fidel. Valls firmly believed the DR was to serve as the revolutionary instrument under which all others were to be integrated (Evidence of one of the authors present at the above meeting, Havana, September 1956).

42. Evidence of Dora Westbrook Rosales to the authors (Union City. September 1972). Also see Juan Nuiry, "José Antonio Echeverría, pensamiento y acción," *Bohemia* (Havana), March 10, 1967, p. 78.

43. One official source has suggested that Fidel Castro proposed that the insurrectionary struggle "must begin by creating guerrillas in the countryside and thereafter organize the clandestine struggle in the cities. . . ." See Fidel Castro and Janette Habel, *Proceso al sectarismo* (Buenos Aires: Editorial Jorge Alvarez, 1965). pp. 12–13.

44. Felix Armando Murias recalls that the message was not received until December 2, 1956, when it reached Julio García Olivera (Authors' interview with Félix Armando Murias, September 1972, Miami, Florida). For a different version see chapter 5 of this book.

45. Speech by Joe Westbrook, (Havana: October 1956), authors' personal copy, Dora (Westbrook) Rosales told the authors that Joe had a bitter argument with Fidel concerning the latter's deprecation of Professor Rafael García Bárcena of the MNR. Some of the issues discussed at the October meeting between the DR members and Castro may be surmised from Joe's speech.

46. According to Lucy Echeverría, sister of José Antonio, Fidel was emphatic in his demands that the Directorio group show its good faith by immediately producing actions against Batista (Evidence of Lucy Echeverría to the authors, August 28, 1972, San Juan, Puerto Rico).

47. According to Ricardo ("Popi") Corpión, Faure Chomón became frightened about the "mission" and refused to even be the chauffeur to the group (Corpión to the authors, September 1972, Miami, Florida). The meeting was held at the "Delicias" restaurant in Havana.

48. The assassination of SIM's chief, Colonel Antonio Blanco Rico was widely criticized throughout the nation since he was not a sinister character, but was that rare breed of officer that all *batistianos* could feel proud of. One of those who joined the criticism was Fidel Castro who condemned the action for its arbitrariness. See "Entrevista con Fidel Castro," *El Mundo* (Havana), November 20, 1956. p. 9.

49. They were Eduardo Crespo, Orlando Hernández, Leonel Cabrera, Felipe Hernández, Carlos Casanova, Israel Escalona, Alfredo Massip, Salvador Ibañez, Secundino Martínez and Gregorio García. Carmen Castro and Nélida Avila, of Mujeres Martianas and the Triple A, respectively, were the liaisons of the urban underground with the refugees (Evidence of Nélida Avila to the authors, Washington, July 1967).

50. Ramón Prendes, *Statements by the Federation of University Students to the Inter-American Press Association* (Havana: October 16, 1957), p. 2. The document listed a number of crimes allegedly perpetrated by the police.

51. Fernando Sánchez Amaya, *Diario del Granma* (Havana: Editorial Tierra Nueva, 1959), p. 52.

5

The Making of the Guerrillas

Conditions in Cuba

In Havana, the DR kept up its pressure on the government through demonstrations and acts of terrorism in coordination with the M-26-7. On November 27, 1956, for example, members of the FEU marched toward the monument which commemorated the students who died at the hands of the Spanish crown in 1871. In the ensuing confrontation, 17 police officers were wounded, several students were arrested, and José Antonio Echeverría suffered a brutal beating.[1]

Meanwhile in Santiago, the M-26-7 increased the tempo of its bombings and isolated attacks on police officers. Students demonstrated against the government, and all public high schools were closed along with the University of Oriente. Students were also arrested in Holguin while attempting to demonstrate against a military parade in that city.

On November 28, Batista's government announced that dictator Rafael Leónidas Trujillo was interfering in the internal affairs of Cuba.[2] The following day, General Tabernilla, Sr., declared that even though an attack upon Batista's regime was imminent, there should be no undue concern since the army was prepared to meet the attackers. Echeverría countered Tabernilla's statement by calling on the students to attend a massive meeting at the Cerro Stadium, a "Protest Day," on December 4. In the same statement, Echeverría pointed out that during the recent confrontation with the police, the students had "thrown Cuban stones which are not Trujillo's."[3] However, the government was right when it charged Trujillo with trying to intervene.

A Matter of Arms

The role of Generalissimo Rafael Leónidas Trujillo and of agents close to the Dominican despot is one of the obscure passages in the history of the insurrection. Trujillo's involvement in acts against Batista may have been related to the competition between the two countries in the sugar market. A state of war in Cuba would have created a sugar deficit from which Trujillo's controlled sugar industry in the Dominican Republic would benefit.[4] There is also the argument that Trujillo was handsomely paid for all his services, just as Nicaraguan dictator Anastasio ("Tacho") Somoza was paid for arms sold to Carlos Prío.[5] Why Trujillo conspired against Batista may be in question, but his involvement in the insurrection is a fact.

In the fall of 1956, Carlos Prío convinced Trujillo to support an operation against Batista, a landing in Oriente province. The invading force would be trained in the Dominican Republic. All expenses were to be paid by Prío, and arms were to be purchased from Dictator Somoza in Nicaragua and transported to the Dominican Republic. Generalissimo Trujillo approved the idea, and issued orders to his army to clear the barracks of Battalion No. 4, close to the capital, to make room for a group of Cuban exiles affiliated with Prío's OA. The training camp had 85 men when Luis Chaviano, who was formerly with Prío's palace guard, arrived to take over command of the expeditionary forces.[6] Chaviano was appointed commander of the group, and arms arrived on schedule from Nicaragua.

Prío's plan had been developed independently, until after his meeting with Fidel in Texas, his subsequent financial support of the Granma expedition, and the agreement between the two to conduct simultaneous operations against Batista.[7] At that point, Chaviano's force had grown to 147 men, and their plans called for a landing near a place called Chivirico, one of the Granma's original landing spots.[8]

While Prío continued to develop his plans, the M-26-7 was kept informed of the events by an agent who had infiltrated the ranks of the OA. David Figueredo was the contact man between the OA militants (commanded by a man named "El Cojo" Parladés) and the group under Chaviano; he was also a secret member of the M-26-7.[9] Figueredo reported to Lester Rodríguez, who had been appointed by Frank País to be in charge of supplies. It was Figueredo who alerted Lester Rodríguez of the arrival of a large shipment of arms which was part of the OA expedition.

The Dominican navy transported eight tons of these weapons to a place close to Chivirico, named Marverde, in Oriente province, where it buried the arms in a sugar cane field. The arms were to be used to reinforce the expeditionary group, and would also be used to arm the OA militants led by Parladés. Cándido de la Torre—Prío's man in Havana—gave representatives of the M-26-7 in Santiago, "Pepito" Tey and Jorge Ibarra, an assortment of weapons including two Maxim machine guns, two Thompsons and three M-1 rifles.[10] Previously, the M-26-7 had obtained 22 rifles from the Club de Cazadores of Santiago, and a few more weapons in a raid against a small army post at El Caney.

País's arsenal still was not large enough to sustain an uprising in the city, which was controlled by the Moncada garrison. He had to persuade Fidel and other leaders of the movement that such an action was not feasible. On August 6 through 8, 1956, Frank met Fidel in Mexico City for the first time. The substance of the conversations may be gathered from a letter Fidel sent to María Antonia Figueroa, the M-26-7 treasurer in Oriente. Fidel described the talks as "very useful," and commented to Maria Antonia that he was impressed with "[Frank's] courage, talents, and organizational skills." Fidel instructed Maria Antonia to divert the funds of the M-26-7 to the action and sabotage section in Santiago: "upon receiving this letter, give to [the action sector] the money allocated to Mexico [Fidel and his men], that is, 80 percent of [our funds]. . . ."[11]

On returning to Cuba, Frank arranged a meeting with the M-26-7 cells in Havana. He again discussed the matter of readiness for the uprising Fidel had proposed to coincide with his landing. The Cotorro meeting indicated to Frank that the M-26-7 cells in Havana were eager to second the uprising as Fidel had scheduled it. Frank's sense of exactness led him to undertake another trip to Mexico around October 23-28 to persuade Fidel to give the M-26-7 underground more time to equip themselves and to strengthen the organizational bases of the operation. País requested an extension of two months during which he could prepare more cadres and raise $20,000 to purchase arms through a contact within the Guantanamo Naval Base.[12] But his efforts were useless. Fidel adamantly refused to entertain any delay in his plans, arguing that the Mexican police were after the M-26-7's arsenal, and he had publicly announced he would be in Cuba before the year ended. The mood among the chiefs of action and sabotage seemed to support Fidel's demands, and Frank País accepted the decision of the majority. Fidel's plan, as approved, consisted of simultaneous uprisings throughout the country which would coincide with the expeditionaries' landing and attack on Manzanillo and Bayamo in western Oriente province. Once Santiago de Cuba was under the control of Frank País' men Fidel's group would move to that city to solidify a general uprising against Batista by taking over the Moncada arsenal and making Santiago the rebel stronghold.[13] If the plan failed, Fidel's group had the alternative of reaching the Sierra Maestra mountains to wage guerrilla warfare against the regular army.[14]

Once Fidel's plan moved into high gear, Figueredo established contact with Lester Rodríguez in Santiago, and the latter met with "El Cojo" Parladés. They agreed to divide the arms shipment in half, while Parladés promised to take his men into the uprising. Trujillo's arms were transported from Marverde to Santiago by Lester in a truck owned by a militant of the M-26-7, Luis Felipe Rosell. The arms were distributed throughout the city, with the largest quantity stored at the M-26-7's headquarters for the operation, the "Carrousell's" store which was the property of Suzette Bueno de Rousseau.[15] There were two obstacles. One was that Fidel Barreto, Secretary of Agriculture, and Batista's personal envoy to Trujillo, succeeded in having Trujillo stop the expedition in exchange for concessions in meat exports to Cuba. Another was that Fidel Castro did not announce his departure to Carlos Prío, who then considered himself betrayed by Fidel. The evidence suggests that Prío was right: Castro planned to abandon Prío once he had received all the financial aid possible from the former president.[16]

The Santiago Uprising

Before leaving Mexico, Fidel sent a cable to Arturo Duque Estrada, the M-26-7 treasurer in Santiago. The cable, dated November 27, read: "Requested book out of print." By previous agreement that meant that the Granma would be landing within the following 48 hours, in time to support the Santiago uprising. The message called the underground organization into frantic activity.

Frank País and "Pepito" Tey were the leaders of the operation. Tey was in charge of action, while Frank was responsible for the overall strategy of the uprising. Frank divided the operation in two phases. The first would consist of attacking police headquarters and the maritime police while keeping the Moncada barracks under bombardment by one of Trujillo's .81mm mortars. Once the headquarters of the police and the maritime police building had been captured, arms were to be distributed to the population, and a full-scale attack could be mounted against the Moncada barracks. Elsewhere, the M-26-7 was to go into action in Guantánamo and Holguín. In Guantánamo, Julio Camacho Aguilera, chief of action of the movement, would attack the army post, while René ("Daniel") Ramos Latour and his brother Freddy were to attack the army camp at Holguin, thus delaying any troop movements towards Santiago from Camagüey province.[17]

The key to the success of the uprising was complete surprise in the first stage. The firing of the .81 mm mortar served two purposes: to signal that the operation had begun, and to keep the troops from reaching the city before the two initial objectives had been secured by the rebels. The mortar was placed in the Vista Alegre suburbs, the firing distance was measured by engineer Rafael Oliver, and Lester Rodríguez was put in charge of that part of the operation. Lester's group included Frank's brother, Josué País, Orlando Regalado, Camilo Fernández, Caleb Quesada and Héctor Delfín.

The attack on the police headquarters was to be carried out by Tey, Ignacio ("Tony") Alomá and Otto Parellada's group. One group, under Jorge Sotús, would lead the assault on the maritime police building.

Lester was to fire the first mortar grenade at exactly 6 AM and an hour later another of Frank's brothers, Agustín País, would take to the streets to procure more arms. Agustín's group included, among others: Enzo Infante, José N. Causse and Reineiro Jiménez.[18] A sixth group, under the command of Félix Pena, would support the attack on police headquarters while placing snipers throughout the city. Three other groups were to intercept patrol cars and to establish control of the streets; they were led by Tin Navarrete. Emiliano ("Nano") Díaz and Enrique Hermo.

Early on Friday, November 30, the militants put on their olive-green uniforms for the first time in the insurrection, and red and black bracelets with a "26" in white. A last-minute checkup by Frank and "Pepito" Tey disclosed that everything was in order. At that point, army Major Nelson Carrasco Artíles, chief investigator of the army in Santiago de Cuba, was completely unaware of any plans for an uprising.[19]

Just before 5:30 AM Lester Rodríguez left to occupy his position at the mortar. On his way, he was recognized by a police officer, stopped and searched. The police found on Lester a copy of a map with a description, "Operation Mortar," Lester was placed under arrest, the police occupied the mortar, and the alarm went out. At about the same time, in another section of the city, Otto Parellada left his headquarters at the Lido Club, in Vista Alegre, to requisition four more automobiles. He was intercepted by a patrol of the regional intelligence service, and shooting broke out. Parellada escaped, but by then the authorities were expecting something unusual. The advantage of surprise, the key to the uprising, had been lost.

Frank País changed plans rapidly. Since the mortar was no longer part of the plans, he sent two groups of snipers to the Moncada barracks to try to hold the army inside the camp. The brothers Jorge and Antonio Niubot were ordered to blow up various Standard Oil gasoline trucks to create confusion. Jorge Sotús, Tey. Parellada and "Tony" Alomá were to attack their targets at 7 AM.

As Tey's group approached police headquarters they found that a heavy machine gun was sweeping the area in front of the building and had blocked both Tey's and "Tony" Alomá's groups. Otto Parellada approached the building from the back, took over the library next to police headquarters, and threw five hand grenades, but only one exploded. Molotov cocktails hit the walls of the building, but the inexperienced insurgents had filled the bottles with gasoline rather than with used oil which would have stuck to the walls until they burned. In a house next to their objective, Tey and Frank País installed the Maxim machine gun—the Auténticos' donation—and concentrated their fire on the windows of the building. The police held the position.

The first assault was led by "Tony" Alomá, and he became the first casualty of the uprising. Tey led the second attempt, reached one of the walls close to the building's entrance and threw his hand grenades. They failed to explode, and Tey was shot to death. His second-in-command, Luis Padrón, was shot in the leg. The third attempt was led by Otto Parellada, who was killed instantly. Five police officers had been killed, and three insurgent leaders lay dead on the ground. The rest continued firing at the building. Trujillo's arms had been buried in a very humid place, and most of the grenades never worked. The rifles were also defective and some of the ammunition was damp.

While the groups at police headquarters were doing poorly, Jorge Sotús had succeeded in taking over the maritime police building. Accompanied by 19 men,[20] Sotús inflicted two casualties on the six-man garrison in charge of the building. The attackers took over almost immediately, and stayed there until approximately 10 AM when the first army patrol approached the area. Sotús ordered a withdrawal, and then went back to headquarters.

The snipers around Moncada kept shooting, but the army remained silent. It was then close to 11 AM. At headquarters in the "Carrousell" store, Frank País, Armando Hart, Vilma Espín, Haydée Santamaría and others began to comprehend that the uprising had failed, and that it was just a matter of time before the army approached the city from the Moncada barracks. The army had not yet entered into battle because the commander of Santiago, General Martín Díaz Tamayo, refused to release the troops, fearing another massacre like that of July 26, 1953.[21]

The streets were under the control of the M-26-7. The police remained inside their quarters, defending it, but refusing to go out to fight the rebels in the streets. Later on in the insurrection this became a pattern that determined the downfall of many army posts, towns and cities.

Frank País ordered the execution of Plan "B." Felix Pena's snipers were deployed with orders to keep shooting at approaching army patrols. Meanwhile, arms were hidden, uniforms exchanged for civilian clothes, and the insurgents "filtered" back into the population. País stayed until the last moment, supervising an orderly retreat. The insurgents had suffered only the three casualties mentioned above: "Pepito" Tey, "Tony" Alomá and Otto Parellada. The police sustained five dead at headquarters, and two at the maritime police building. About ten police officers were wounded.[22]

In Guantánamo, Julio Camacho Aguilera found no resistance to his assault against army post Ermita, where he and his men captured some Springfield rifles. When news arrived that an army patrol was approaching Guantánamo, Camacho ordered his 268 men—organized in cells of ten men each—to disperse. Then he took to the hills. A strike organized by Octavio Louit failed to materialize. Some days later, in mid-December, País would arrive at Guantánamo, dressed as a peasant, to collect all of the underground arms. Some 25 rifles and about 4,000 rounds of ammunition were put on a truck, and were dispatched to the Sierra Maestra and Fidel Castro.[23]

In Holguín and elsewhere the M-26-7 was unable to conduct more than a few isolated acts of terrorism. In Havana, the M-26-7 remained inactive for lack of arms, and was not even aware of the uprising until it was too late to do anything.

The DR had received the message of Fidel's landing plans, but too late to take any effective action. José Antonio Echeverría immediately called for an emergency meeting of the executive council to consider what to do. He was informed by Faure Chomón—chief of action—that the movement lacked sufficient arms for an uprising in Havana. The government was expecting some action; it apparently had been informed of Fidel's departure from Mexico, and was ready to counteract any action in the cities. Julio García Olivera, who received Fidel's message on November 29, proposed that the DR take over the university as a symbol of resistance. Luis Gómez Wangüemert proposed that they place snipers throughout the capital to create chaos and confusion.[24]

During the afternoon of November 29, with news coming from Santiago about the imminent uprising, the DR met with José ("Pepe") Suárez, chief of action of the M-26-7 in Havana. "Pepe" Suárez, a veteran of Moncada and a dedicated fighter, declared that the M-26-7 could not engage the government in battle because they lacked arms. "Pepe" Suárez had not expected Fidel's invasion until later, and was not aware of the impending uprising in Santiago. Next, the DR and the M-26-7 turned to the Auténticos, who had plenty of arms in storage. The Auténticos refused to cooperate because they had not been notified by Prío, and because they felt it was too late to risk their men in a useless action in the streets of Havana. Thus, Echeverría's plan to attack the bureau of investigations, the presidential palace and the police precincts could not be carried out.

The DR met late that day to reconsider the situation. By then, Faure Chomón was strongly against taking any action that would risk the best cadres of the movement in what at that point would be just a gesture. Chomón favored saving whatever resources the DR could muster for a decisive operation against Batista.[25] He argued that there were not enough men on the alert and that the most they could do was to arm about 30 men, half with rifles and half with pistols.[26] This would be equivalent to suicide. Félix Armando Murias agreed with Chomón's estimate of the situation, pointing out that the regime's forces were already out in the streets waiting to crush any move.[27]

José Antonio summed up the situation. He rejected both Wangüemert's and García Olivera's earlier plans as unfeasible. The plan for the M-26-7 and the DR to conduct simultaneous attacks depended upon the cooperation of the Auténticos. "We can not," he said, "sacrifice a group of *compañeros* in a plan without possibilities of success." Rather than risk men in what most members of the executive viewed as adventurism, they supported Echeverría's statement that the DR should concentrate on plans to eliminate Batista altogether. "For that," Echeverría emphasized, "we'll need the *compañeros* who would die in an attempt which now amounts to suicide." For the DR's plan to eliminate Batista, it would be worthwhile to "take any risk and to make any sacrifice, since it can do away with the regime" in a single blow.[28] Thus, the DR abstained from taking any action at that time, in a decision which probably saved the lives of most members of the movement. For while the M-26-7 had suffered only three deaths during the Santiago struggle, an uprising in Havana would have cost them much more. In Havana, once a confrontation was initiated on a massive scale, there was but one way to emerge safely, namely to liquidate the dictatorship. Any uprising would have to contend with Batista's brutal elite corps who were mostly concentrated in the capital.

Conditions in Havana

A cosmopolitan city with a million and a half inhabitants, Havana was the center for the upper class, the bureaucratic machinery and numerous parasitic elements feeding on the system against which the insurrection was directed. By and large, the youth who opposed Batista came from Havana University and public high schools, and an isolated few from private schools and institutions of secondary education. Very few politically involved youths belonged to the upper class. Instead, the *niños bitongos* ("spoiled brats") danced and dined at the clubs of the high society. Their "insurrection" was limited to criticizing Batista—not because he was a despot—but because he was a mulatto. Still, most referred to the dictator as "the president," an apocryphal expression that infuriated the militant youth, who claimed no one had elected Batista to the presidency. Like their families, the *niños bitongos* approved of Batista's "law and order" concept, and were generally delighted at the closing of Havana University, since the "troublemakers" had caused some nightclubs to close earlier than usual. Their main concerns revolved around the latest American hit parade, the regattas and the luxurious fiestas offered by the upper class. They gathered at the lavish private country clubs—the "Miramar Yacht Club," "Havana Yacht Club" or the "Spanish Casino"—and were to be found at the University of Villanova in the exclusive Miramar suburbs. As the insurrection deepened it became necessary to use bomb threats to put an end to the fancy parties of the upper class and to force the "clubs" not to open their elegant halls to honor the dictator's parasites.

The urban underground in the capital had to deal not only with brutal repression, but with a population whose terror of Batista was so profound that it dared not take any action to protect the militants. As in all revolutions, a small portion of the population helped all it could, and to that sector many urban fighters owed everything. But it was not the rich nor the upper-middle-class population who helped the fighters, but the lower-middle class and the working families. The humble made the insurrection in Havana, regardless of the myths fabricated by middle-class professionals after the insurrection succeeded. For each professional involved in positions of leadership—which in the urban struggle implied less risk—there were three times as many humble people who fought in the front lines; and in the front lines, people died. The fighter did not have social relations with Latin American ambassadors and could not seek political asylum. The front-line fighter had no financial means to go into exile or to buy his way out of trouble at a certain point. Certainly he had no "contacts" among pro-Batista individuals, whose personal intervention saved the life of many professionals with friends close of police officer Esteban Ventura Novo, or who could ask Batista to spare the life of a prisoner and to issue a safe-conduct out of Cuba. The front-line fighter was the pillar of the insurrection, and with few exceptions the list of martyrs was made up of previously unknown names. With the exception of the DR and some M-26-7 cell leaders, most chiefs survived the insurrection while the greater number of casualties was sustained by lower rank members of the various movements.

Fidel Castro: Disaster and Recovery

Immediately after the Santiago uprising, the army declared a state of siege, and troops were mobilized by General Tabernilla, Sr., to repel any further attacks against the government.[29] Civil guarantees were suspended in the provinces of Oriente, Camagüey, Las Villas and Pinar del. Tanks were mobilized along the central highway in Oriente, and the army was reinforced at Bayamo and at Holguín.[30] At this point Fidel Castro re-entered Cuba.

The Granma voyage had taken seven days. Rough seas and a navigational error delayed the arrival of the expeditionary forces to Cuba. About 180 miles from the island their radio picked up the news of the uprising.[31] On December 2, 1956, the expedition arrived at a place called Playa Colorada, in Niquero, southern Oriente province. The landing place was the worst possible site, swampy and filled with mangroves. The men reached the shore exhausted, having lost part of their equipment.[32]

Weeks before the expedition was scheduled to arrive, Celia ("Norma") Sánchez, Guillermo García and Manuel Fajardo had scouted the area, examining different sites along the coast. A small group of revolutionaries was also posted near Ojo del Toro, in Niquero, waiting for the expedition with trucks, cars and a few arms.[33] Celia Sánchez had already established contact with peasant guides in the Sierra Maestra mountains.[34]

It is now certain that Batista's army knew details of the expedition five days after the Granma departed from Mexico. On November 30, General Tabernilla, Jr., reported to air force headquarters that the air patrol had been unable to locate a "white 65-foot yacht, no name, Mexican flag with a chain across the bow."[35] On December 1 Brigadier General Pedro Rodríguez Avila issued further orders to the air force and to the army to locate and capture a yacht with the same description of the Granma, and which had departed from "Tuxpán, Veracruz. Mexico, on November 25, and will supposedly land in Oriente."[36] The events of Santiago and rumors of Castro's impending expedition, however, kept the air force busy with search-and-destroy operations.

Upon landing, Castro's men lost no time marching inland. It was then 6 AM on December 2.[37] Within the hour, army Lieutenant Aquiles Chinea, chief of the army post at Niquero—12th Squadron of the Rural Guards—received information on the whereabouts of Castro's group. The army at Bayamo ordered Captain Caridad F. Fernández to move toward the area, while Commodore Mario Rubio Baró dispatched coast guard ship 106 toward the site of the Granma landing.[38] The army embarked on a series of operations which were geared to block Castro's access to the Sierra Maestra.

While Lieutenant Chinea flew over the landing site to try to determine Castro's direction, Captain Gabriel Ulloa Franquis reinforced the post at Niquero. The army mobilized close to 1,000 men in 24 hours, and prepared to move in force into the area. On the evening of December 2, the troops of Lieutenant Chinea and Captain Ulloa returned to Niquero following brief patrols which resulted from rumors of Castro's plans to attack Niquero. The following morning Lieutenant Chinea led a patrol into the area where Castro was assumed to be hiding.

The army marched along Río Nuevo to Alegría de Pío, a small sugar cane village, and from there it moved to a place called El Plátano. Here they camped, and were expecting to cut the "enemy's access to the Sierra Maestra." At nightfall on December 3 Major Juan González, chief of operations, ordered Captain Ulloa and Lieutenant Chinea to move to the village of Pilón, and then to Marión, where they camped for the night.[39]

On December 4 an army detachment moved into the Agua Fina forests and surveyed the area. Unable to detect any traces of Castro's group, the detachment returned to Alegría de Pío. Later, out on patrol again, the army left its vehicles and heavy machine guns with Lieutenant Adolfo A. Aguirre in Río Nuevo. But before re-entering the Agua Fina forests detachments set up ambushes at Alegría de Pío and Esperanza. The latter ambush was commanded by Sergeant Miguel Román y Guerra with 12 men hiding in the bushes. That ambush was of "great importance because [Esperanza] was the only exit from Alegría de Pío to the Sierra Maestra."[40]

On December 5, an army detachment marched into the forest, and after following the trail for some time—while Castro's group advanced through the bushes—they found traces of the expeditionary force. The army realized that the expeditionaries were moving toward Alegría de Pío, so they turned around and followed Castro's men. Meanwhile, for no logical reason the ambush at Esperanza had been ordered moved by the army's chief of operations.[41]

"Che" Guevara later charged a guide who had been released the previous night with informing the army of the group's whereabouts.[42] However, even Batista's Rural Guard was able to follow the march of the expeditionaries. Once the Granma had landed in Playa Colorada the only way to reach the Sierra Maestra was through Alegría de Pío, then to Esperanza, and from there toward the heights of the Sierras. Guevara himself also explained that "due to our inexperience we killed our hunger by eating canes, and leaving the waste pulp by the side of the road."[43]

Castro ordered a rest at Alegría de Pío, a poor choice. Surrounded by cane fields, there were no hills or slopes or rocks from which to maintain watch. Most of the men fell exhausted to the ground. A few engaged in a heated discussion over what to do next. An argument broke out among expeditionaries of Raúl Castro's group.[44] And they were still arguing, when—to use Guevara's phrase—a "hurricane of bullets . . . rained on the heads of 82 men."[45] Some of the men at first answered the army's attack, firing at random, and trying to gain cover as best they could. Others began dispersing, running for their lives. Some were wounded—Guevara received his first wound at Alegría de Pío—and four men died on the spot. One wounded prisoner was executed by the army instantly. The rest fled in all directions. Most were captured later on or, upon surrendering to the army, were shot to death.

Fidel, Universo Sánchez and Juan Manuel Márquez—the leader of the Ortodoxo youth organization—were separated from the rest of the men. Later, Faustino Pérez joined the trio. Retreating from the area, Juan Manuel Márquez became lost, and was later found by the army and assassinated.[46]

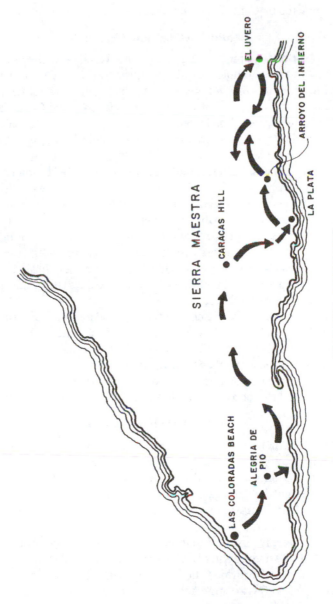

GRANMA LANDING.
DEFEAT AND RECOVERY

SIERRA MAESTRA

LAS COLORADAS BEACH

ALEGRIA DE PIO

CARACAS HILL

EL UVERO

LA PLATA

ARROYO DEL INFIERNO

ORIENTE PROVINCE

After days of hiding in the sugar fields[47] the trio was able to get out of the army's encirclement. Once they had reached the marginal areas of the Sierra Maestra mountains, Crescencio Pérez, the old patriarch of the mountains, was contacted by Celia Sánchez and came to their rescue.

Initial Setback and Regrouping

The expeditionaries remained divided for several days. Those who survived the army's attack continued toward the agreed-upon place, the Sierra Maestra. Two hundred and fifty kilometers long by about 10 kilometers wide, the Sierra Maestra is located between Guantánamo Bay and Cabo Cruz, close to the Gulf of Guacanayabo. Several mountain chains run parallel to the coast, surrounded by dense tropical forests. The Sierra Maestra is one of the most rugged areas of Cuba.[48]

After days of wandering around, a group commanded by Juan Almeida, and including Ramiro Valdés and Ernesto ("Che") Guevara, established contact with the men led by Camilo Cienfuegos. Together—eight men in all—they went to look for peasants who could help them find out whether Fidel Castro was still at large. The peasants led the group to an Adventist minister named Argelio Rosabal, who in turn contacted Crescencio Pérez. The men found their leader at Crescencio's house. Fidel had already established contact with another group of eight expeditionaries, and two days later, four more showed up. The survivors numbered 20.[49]

The men's morale was extremely low. They had lost most of their friends after the first hours of landing. They also had heard more news about the Santiago uprising, and had some idea of the disaster. Their equipment was minimal, and the task ahead loomed larger than ever. The first to realize the extent of the problem was Fidel; he knew that a victory would not only bring the group arms and food, but that would also boost morale. Their opportunity came on January 17, 1957.

The Assault on La Plata

Fidel Castro's first military victory in the insurrection came in an attack on La Plata military post, located at the mouth of the La Plata river. The importance of this operation was twofold. It provided the guerrillas with supplies they desperately needed and, as predicted, it boosted the morale of the group; it also helped set a pattern for future guerrilla operations against isolated government posts in the area.

La Plata's army post was guarded by 15 soldiers. Shortly before the attack began, Castro's men captured a peasant who appeared to be friendly with the soldiers, and who provided the attackers with necessary information about the post. When Castro approached La Plata, he knew the password and the number of soldiers within the camp's perimeter.

Once the first shot had been fired, the guerrillas had to take the post. A retreat would have been disastrous, since they had no ammunition and would be closely followed by army patrols in the area. The attack actually lasted only for a few minutes. Taken by surprise, the troops attempted to resist, but they were faced with an enemy of unexpected aggressiveness. The detachment surrendered: two of its members were dead, and five had been wounded. The guerrillas cared for the wounded soldiers in the humane way that was to become a distinguishing characteristic and an important asset to the future rebel army.[50] The group, on its way to becoming full-fledged guerrilla fighters, had suffered no casualties.

The peasant, who was an informer of the regular army, was executed. During their retreat—orderly this time—Castro's men carried food, eight Springfield rifles, one Thompson submachine gun, a few thousand rounds of ammunition and, most important of all, a new sense of accomplishment.

While the guerrillas hurried to the Sierras, a column under army Lieutenant Angel Sánchez Mosquera—who would also become famous in the Sierra Maestra—set out after them. Aware that they would be followed, the guerrillas prepared an ambush into which the soldier's vanguard fell, sustaining five casualties. The guerrillas then captured more arms and ammunition.[51]

The pattern of attacking an isolated army post, withdrawing immediately, and then preparing an ambush for pursuing troops became the guerrillas' strategy throughout the campaign. One of the main problems the guerrilla command had to confront during the first months was the high rate of desertion. Desertion, insubordination and defeatism were punishable by death,[52] as were treason, rape, theft, lack of discipline and other crimes that could endanger the morale of the guerrillas or create conflicts between them and the rural population.

Treason and a New Beginning

In February 1957 a peasant guide named Eutimio Guerra betrayed the guerrillas. Under pressure from army Major Casillas Lumpuy, active in the mountain zone, Guerra led Castro and his small group of guerrillas into an area where they were to rest for a few days. Guerra then left the group and established contact with the army, which in turned called on the air force to conduct an air raid on Castro's guerrilla camp. This early air raid, like those that followed, was almost completely ineffective: seldom did air attacks cause any casualties among the guerrillas.[53] Guerra, the guide, returned to find out how many guerrillas had been killed, and instead found Castro waiting for an explanation of where he had been. The peasant allegedly confessed to his treason. A revolutionary tribunal was immediately organized; Guerra was sentenced to death and executed within the hour. This was the second guerrilla execution in the mountains. These executions were not hidden from the rural population but were publicized widely by the guerrillas. In a short time the guerrilla's code became the law throughout the area. Most of the time Ramiro Valdés administered the "revolutionary justice."

The guerrillas became the real and effective authority to whom the peasants referred all problems. With the regular troops unwilling to go into the mountain areas to establish or regain their own authority over the population, the Sierras' peasants were aware that their survival and security depended mainly on whether they helped the guerrillas or not. Since in an insurrection there can be no middle ground, the peasants helped the guerrillas not only because they liked them, but also because not to have done so would not have improved their position with the government. Since the regular troops viewed the Sierra peasants as an enemy from the very beginning, the rural population backed the guerrillas so that they could keep the regular army out of the small villages. Reprisals were applied by the guerrillas, as well as by the army. But the guerrillas remained in control of the area where reprisals had been conducted, while the army would execute a few peasants and then withdraw to the plains, allowing the guerrillas to return in a few hours. The political cadres were then able to explain to the peasants that the army had executed innocent civilians. When the guerrillas executed peasants who refused to cooperate, the cadres described them as "traitors to the fatherland," or as agents of some faraway landlord.

When the guerrillas "executed" someone, the victim was forever branded a traitor, but when the army "murdered" someone the victim was elevated to the category of a "martyr" of the insurrection. Before long the army was the mortal enemy of the peasants. Very few army officers tried to establish good relationships with the rural population. Most dealt with them brutally, a behavior the foot soldiers—former peasants themselves—soon imitated. In this sense, the guerrillas had in the army their best ally in winning the support of the rural population throughout Sierra Maestra.

In February 1957 Fidel Castro's survival and existence in the Sierra Maestra was made known to Cuba and to the world. Castro realized that he needed publicity for his campaign in the mountains, and that it was necessary to let those involved in the M-26-7 know that he was still alive and fighting. Thus Faustino Pérez arrived in Havana in late December and established contact with a few people involved in the movement. Pérez contacted Javier Pazos, a militant of the movement, and Mario Llerena. He informed them that Cuban reporters must be sent to the Sierra to cover the Cuatro story. Javier Pazos broached the subject to his father, Felipe Pazos, an economist who was also a friend of Ruby Hart Phillips, the *New York Times* correspondent in Cuba, who in turn contacted Herbert Matthews, the Latin American specialist of the *New York Times*.

The Batista regime had declared that Castro was dead, and that among the other dead insurgents was Faustino Pérez. The government version was so widely accepted in Havana that collections were taken for the widows of the Granma expeditionaries. Even the attack on the La Plata barracks was not proof that Castro was alive.

Herbert Matthews travelled to Cuba and, through a complicated series of contacts in the underground, to the mountains to conduct his now famous interview with Fidel Castro.[54] The interview coincided with the first meeting of M-26-7 leaders in the Sierra Maestra, at which they delineated the future strategy of the movement. The impact of Matthew's articles cannot be underestimated. Batista's government announced that the interview was false; the *Times* responded by publishing Fidel's picture with his telescopic rifle. Thus an American reporter had succeeded where Cuban newsmen had feared to go. Batista lifted press censorship (for he realized that the military chiefs of the provinces had misinformed the general staff). The reports of Castro's death had been so emphatically supported by the general staff that even Batista at first doubted the veracity of the interview. Later Batista wrote that the interview "had in fact taken place, and its publication was of considerable propaganda value to the rebels. Castro was to begin his era as a legendary figure."[55]

Before the publication of Matthews' article, Felipe Pazos met with Mario Llerena, suggesting that it would be a good idea to travel to New York, have the articles reprinted and mail them to Cuba. Llerena thus went to New York, where around 3,000 envelopes were stuffed with Matthews' articles and mailed back to the island. While he was in New York Llerena established contact with CBS correspondent Robert Taber, who later became the war correspondent in the Sierra Maestra.[56]

The militants thought Matthews' attitude not only brave, but an example of what all Americans ought to feel about Batista's military dictatorship. His initial coverage of the Sierra Maestra story encouraged hundreds who were being persecuted. It reached the darkness of Batista's political prisons; it was commented upon by almost everyone who was interested in Cuban affairs; and it was a message of hope for all the militants and sympathizers of the M-26-7. The articles disclosed that the generals had been lying all along, and that Batista, the so-called "great commander," had after all failed to capture Fidel. Throughout the movement, Herbert Matthews was mentioned with respect.[57]

Reinforcements from the Cities

After three months of operations, Castro's guerrillas began to tire. The rate of desertion had increased dramatically after the guerrillas were taken by surprise at Altos de Espinosa. Although it caused no physical damage, the raid was demoralizing. In addition, the army had ventured into the mountains for the first time, and the guerrillas were constantly in retreat. Once they even lost contact with Fidel. When they were reunited, in what "Che" Guevara called the Reunified Revolutionary Army of February 12, 1957, they numbered only 18 men.

At this sad juncture the February meeting was called, and Fidel explained to Frank País the need for supplies. The Santiago leader had already sent a

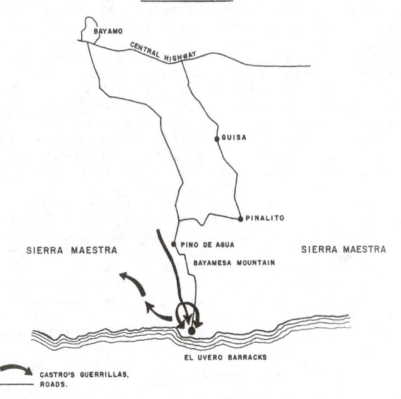

EL UVERO ATTACK

BAYAMO

CENTRAL HIGHWAY

GUISA

PINALITO

SIERRA MAESTRA

PINO DE AGUA

BAYAMESA MOUNTAIN

SIERRA MAESTRA

EL UVERO BARRACKS

CASTRO'S GUERRILLAS.
ROADS.

ORIENTE PROVINCE

shipment of arms to the Sierra Maestra around December 12-14, after learning from Celia Sánchez, on December 4, that Fidel was alive. He had collected these arms from the urban fighters in the Guantánamo underground, and sent them to the Sierra Maestra by truck. País agreed at the February meeting to continue his support of Fidel, promising immediate aid in the form of men, food and ammunition.

Frank País' help was essential for the guerrillas' survival. With only 18 men, lacking reinforcements, with few arms and practically no supplies, Castro would have been limited to small raids on isolated posts. And even these would have been impossible if the army had established a search-and-destroy policy in the mountains. The guerrillas had to remain on the offensive or perish. Lack of activity would increase demoralization—the worst enemy of the guerrilla force—and thus desertion. Without Frank País' support, Castro would have found himself in a position similar to "Ché" Guevara's in the jungles of Bolivia in 1967[58]: easy victims of the regular army, unable to establish their own bases of operation or to patrol their own areas, full of ideals out lacking the arms and the logistics to fight for them.

Upon his return to Santiago, Frank began to enlist a group of the most experienced urban fighters to join Castro. He sent out a call for arms to every cell on the island. From several sources—some not related to the M-26-7—came uniforms, boots, medicines, maps, radio equipment, rifles, pistols, hand grenades; a whole array of war materiel was gathered in a short period of time. The Auténticos contributed arms they had hidden in Oriente province, which were to be distributed among various OA cells in Cuba.

By the end of February, País was already involved in the final stages of pre-paring a group of 52 men, each carrying a substantial amount of food, rifles and ammunition for the other guerrillas. The group was commanded by one of the most valuable urban fighters, the leader of the attack on the maritime police on November 30, Jorge Sotús.[59] Castro assigned Guevara as guide and liaison between the group of urban fighters and the main guerrilla group of 17 men. As Guevara and Sotús exchanged greetings, the radio announced there had been an attack against the presidential palace at Havana.[60] The group immediately left for the mountains. It was March 13, 1957.

Castro's forces now numbered 68. He divided the men into three main guerrilla groups, which from that moment on operated simultaneously. With the Santiago and the Bayamo and Manzanillo undergrounds sending more men and equipment during the following weeks, Castro's guerrillas began to become a small army. In spite of desertions—mostly from young peasants who preferred to go back to their small, unproductive plots of land—there were 80 guerrillas by April of 1957.[61] After four months of operations, then, the group was growing in numbers and equipment. In addition, with the aid of País' reinforcements they had firmly established a resupply area.

The Battle of El Uvero

On May 28, 1957, the guerrillas attacked El Uvero, another small outpost on the edge of the Sierra Maestra. This time the guerrillas outnumbered the regular troops by a margin of 80 to 53. They approached the garrison silently and opened fire, taking the unit by surprise. The exchange lasted only about 20 minutes, but it was quite intensive. Guevara, although exaggerating, considered it the bloodiest encounter of the insurrection.[62] But it was certainly the bloodiest up to then, not counting Alegría de Pío. Six guerrillas were killed, with nine wounded. The army sustained 14 dead and 19 wounded.[63] Surprisingly, despite the attacks on La Plata and El Uvero the army still did not reinforce small outposts.

Following this attack, the Bayamo underground, one of the main channels of aid to the mountains, increased the ranks of the guerrillas with an expedition of approximately two dozen men. The M-26-7 had been organized in Bayamo by Frank País and Jorge Sotús in order to coordinate an uprising with the arrival of the expedition of the Granma. Near Bayamo, at a place called "El Pinalito," a guerrilla school was organized, and a group of young Ortodoxos prepared themselves for the events to come. During the Santiago uprising, Bayamo's militants had not been able to move because the army had been reinforced with about 500 men.[64] Despite the fact that this reinforcement continued,[65] Bayamo became the "gateway" for students from every province on the island who wished to join the guerrillas.

Bayamo's population suffered heavily during the insurrection. Scores of students were killed and some of its most respected elders were assassinated or imprisoned by the Army's regional intelligence service. Here, as in other cities and towns throughout the island, the government's repressive organizations helped turn the people against the authorities until hatred against anything resembling a military uniform became almost universal. In most cases, innocent people were the victims of acts of repression.

Estrada Palma, Bueycito, Pino del Agua

The guerrillas intensified their activities by attacking the army and maintaining the offensive. To commemorate the fourth anniversary of the attack on the Moncada barracks, guerrilla Captain Guillermo García attacked Estrada Palma sugar mill. After burning a few buildings, the guerrillas withdrew toward the mountains as the troops of Colonel Pedro Barreras approached the area.[66]

On July 31, 1957, "Che" Guevara's guerrillas approached the small army post at Bueycito which was guarded by approximately 20 regular troops. The guerrillas surprised the army, wounding six soldiers, but sustaining one dead, Pedro Rivero, and three wounded guerrillas. Some of the guerrillas who participated in the attack later became important figures in the Rebel Army: Lalo Sardiñas; Ramiro Valdés, then a captain; the guerrilla Vilo Acuña; and Ciro Redondo, who died in combat in late 1957. As the guerrillas marched away from Bueycito, a miner joined the group, Cristino Naranjo, later a major in the Rebel Army.[67]

"Che" Guevara and Fidel Castro met on August 29 to plan the takeover of Pino del Agua. There was no military detachment at Pino del Agua, but it was assumed that once the rebels entered that village the army would send reinforcements to the area, and the guerrillas would be able to ambush the incoming troops. On September 10, Fidel and "Che" entered Pino del Agua; "Che" stayed in the village, and Fidel left the following day to prepare the ambush. Meanwhile "Che" organized various ambushes covering the roads into Pino del Agua. Efigenio Almeijeiras, Lalo Sardiñas, Ciro Redondo, Victor Mora, Derminio Escalona and "Che" were posted at selected areas. On September 18 army troops neared the village in five trucks. As the first truck turned a curve in the road guerrilla Ignacio Pérez opened fire.[68] The army lost three soldiers, one was wounded and two were taken prisoner by the guerrillas. One guerrilla was lost and one was wounded. "Che" collected six Garand rifles, one automatic rifle and several individual packs left behind by the troops.

Organization of the Regular Army

The regular army was organized along a chain of command posts in the marginal areas of the Sierra Maestra as early as January 1957. By September, unable to cope with the guerrilla strategy, the army received fresh reinforcements, and General Tabernilla, Sr., effected various changes in command.

The army chief of operations became Colonel Manuel Ugalde Carrillo, and his assistant was Colonel Curbelo del Sol, while Colonel Jesús Cañizares was placed in charge of support operations. The army general staff in the field of operations included Captain Raúl Saenz de Calahorra, Lieutenant Enrique Pérez (Intelligence); Major José Triana y Tarrau (Operations); Lieutenant Fernández Ball-Llovera (Logistics). There was a "special general staff" composed of lieutenants José M. Llinás and Ricardo Montero Duque; majors Nemesio Suárez Hernández (Medical Division) and José Rodríguez, and Captain Leopoldo Ugalde Carrillo. A "personal general staff" reporting directly to the chief of operations, was formed by Colonel Miguel Matamoros, chief of patrol squads; Navy Colonel René Cancio, liaison officer with the army; and Lieutenant Juan J. Blanco, of the First Regiment of the Rural Guards.[69]

Colonel Cándido Curbelo was chief of a sector in Sierra Maestra, and commanded Battalion No. 5. Angel Sánchez Mosquera, already promoted to the rank of major, commanded Battalion No. 1; Major Merob Sosa, later promoted to colonel, led Battalion No. 3; Captain Ricardo L. Grao, later a major, was the chief of the first company of Battalion No. 3, and Major Pedro Castro Rojas, chief of Battalion No. 2 was in charge of sector "B" around the area known as Altos de California in Sierra Maestra.

The total number of troops in Oriente province in early 1958 was 1,195 including officers. Merob Sosa and Sánchez Mosquera were two of those few officers who constantly penetrated the mountains, chasing the guerrillas.[70] Despite repeated ambushes, the army continued to go into the Sierra Maestra, falling into the same ambushes in the same places.

Each company of regular troops was assigned armaments as follows: 13.30 caliber carbines; eight automatic rifles and 68.30 caliber rifles. In addition each company carries 100 hand grenades. 1000.30 caliber capsules for each rifle, and 1,300.30 caliber rounds of ammunition for each carbine.[71] The command post was at Bayamo.

On November 13, 1957, Major Castro Rojas wrote to Colonel Francisco Tabernilla Palmero in the hope that the army's tactics might be changed.[72] Major Castro Rojas went directly to Tabernilla, Jr., because of his loyalty toward "the Maximum Leader, General Batista." Copies of the report were filed with the general staff in Havana, and a copy submitted to Batista for examination. No attention was ever paid to that report, but Castro Rojas was already predicting disaster if the army did not change its strategy throughout the mountains. He proposed that a "demobilization plan" be adopted, cancelling all incursions into the mountains and reinforcing a blockade in the plains. The plan rested on the assumption that Castro, forced to conduct attacks due to the need to maintain the guerrillas united and militant, would have to seek the army on its own, more favorable, terrain. The "demobilization plan" was to be accompanied by a massive propaganda effort by the government to convey the impression that Castro's guerrillas were inactive. Despite its simplification, the report was the first one to signal to the general staff and to Batista that the guerrillas were not so easy to deal with that they could be crushed at the will of the regular troops.

Pino del Agua II

Press censorship had been lifted temporarily and Fidel took the opportunity to create an impact by attacking Pino del Agua for the second time. With a population of about 200 people, the village had been reinforced by the army with a full company under the command of Captain Guerra Ortiz.

In January 1958, Brigadier Fernández Rey, attached to the Third Regiment of the Rural Guards, had received a telephone call from the United States. The caller, a government sympathizer, warned Fernández Rey about an attack that was being planned on Pino del Agua. The guerrilla attack would "take place during the night at any moment" and the guerrillas would be led by "an Argentinian called 'Che,' who is a member of the general staff of Fidel Castro." With "Che," Raúl and Fidel Castro, the informer reported, the guerrillas numbered "1,800 men." The general staff passed the message to the army command post at Bayamo via microwave radio.[73]

Fidel Castro's strategy was to begin the attack with Camilo Cienfuegos' guerrillas advancing from Bayamesa to Pino del Agua to confront the army. Captain Raúl Castro Mercader and his guerrillas were ambushed on the road to Bayamo; Captain Guillermo García and his group took up positions close to the Peladero River, Lalo Sardiñas covered the road to Vega de San Pablo, and Vilo Acuña's guerrillas prepared an ambush around La Virgen hill. Fidel and "Che" Guevara set up headquarters close to El Zapato hill.[74] The main plan was to draw the army stationed in Oro de Guisa toward Pino del Agua to rescue the army garrison. Thus Raúl Castro waited for the army reinforcements between Oro de Guisa and Pino del Agua supported by guerrillas under the command of Captain Francisco "Paco" Cabrera and Eddy Suñol.

On February 16, Camilo Cienfuegos marched on Pino del Agua only to find that the army was prepared and waiting for the attack. In the first exchange of gunfire three guerrillas were killed, Camilo was wounded, and the guerrillas lost a machine gun. When Camilo tried to recover the machine gun he was wounded again. Guerrilla Luis Macías rescued Camilo from the line of fire, was wounded himself, and later died as a result of his wounds.[75] The army held off the rebel attack, and asked for reinforcements at the Oro de Guisa post.

In the evening "Che" Guevara suggested to Fidel that a second attack be mounted with Derminio Escalona and Raúl Castro Mercader's guerrillas. The guerrillas attacked, but were repelled by the army. Next "Che" Guevara insisted on leading a third assault on the army position with the idea of approaching the trenches and throwing Molotov cocktails. In the ensuing confusion, "Che" planned to take the army by assault. Once in position, ready for the attack, "Che" received a message from Fidel, delivered by Juan Almeida, in which the leader asked Guevara not to occupy any dangerous position; the moment called for him to lead his men but not to risk his life.[76] Almeida also voiced his opinion that Guevara should withdraw rather than risking more casualties at the hands of the army. "Che" ordered his men back and the third attack did not take place.

From Oro de Guisa the army mobilized a platoon toward Pino del Agua, commanded by Captain C. Sierra. As the soldiers approached Pino del Agua, guerrilla Captain Francisco "Paco" Cabrera ambushed the troops, killing 16 soldiers and taking five prisoners and 12 rifles. A second army reinforcement approached the area, and Raúl Castro hesitated long enough to allow the army to locate the guerrilla position. In the ensuing encounter, Fidel's brother lost one guerrilla who was killed and another who was wounded. Raúl withdrew under fire.

The army suffered approximately 20 dead, and the guerrillas captured 33 rifles, five machine guns and a large quantity of ammunition. The guerrillas lost 16 men at Pino del Agua and along the road to Oro de Guisa.[77]

Camilo Cienfuegos was undoubtedly the most distinguished guerrilla fighter while army Lieutenant Rodríguez Armesto was mentioned by the regular army as the "bravest officer at Pino del Agua." Twice during the attack Lieutenant Rodríguez Armesto wounded Camilo Cienfuegos. Subsequently, one army prisoner who had escaped the guerrilla camp described the rebels as "armed with rifles, with homemade hand grenades and the majority under 30 years of age."[78] The prisoner who was wounded had been placed by the guerrillas next to the wounded Camilo Cienfuegos, whom he took to be "Che" Guevara. Thus, the army reported "Che" seriously wounded in the encounter at Pino del Agua.[79]

Elements of the Mystique

The mystique that surrounded Castro and his guerrillas and eventually took the young leader to the heights of his charismatic leadership of the Cuban insurrection was sustained by the guerrilla laws and rules of behavior imposed in the mountains. Discipline was usually the main topic of conversation at all guerrilla gatherings. Good behavior toward the peasants was the golden rule of the guerrilla fighters. Anyone who violated that law was brought before Fidel Castro, who would personally apply harsh public punishment to the violator.[80] As the guerrilla movement gained in strength, a more sophisticated code of law was developed by Dr. Humberto Sorí Marín.[81]

Toward the end of the insurrection the rural inhabitants of the Sierra Maestra looked upon Castro's men as the representatives of the law—but a law that was far more just than the one they had known, which generally had been used against them. The peasants—not only those in Sierra Maestra—feared the Rural Guard Corps, were suspicious of the courts of law and were well acquainted with the power of the landowner. Those who were small planters depended mainly upon intermediaries to sell their crops in the city market. The intermediary was, thus, the immediate exploiter of the peasant. The guerrillas banished the intermediaries from the area, and although the peasants could not easily leave the mountains, they felt more satisfied witnessing how the guerrillas avenged them from years of miserable exploitation, than resentful of the fact that they could no longer sell their produce in the city.

As applied by the guerrillas, justice was not blind; rather it granted anything the poorest peasants asked for in the case of a conflict. Castro's image improved not only as a result of propaganda and encounters with the army, but as the direct consequence of his determined good behavior with the peasantry. After the first months of stern application of guerrilla rule—which was necessary if they hoped to survive at all—Castro became the benefactor of the peasants. His mystique, and that of his guerrillas, grew steadily as they confronted the army openly. Whereas the government was known for its false reports on the progress of the campaign, the guerrilla command strictly adhered to the truth.

Sincerity was an element of the mystique. Thus, the guerrillas would reveal to the people the difficulty of their situation, their lack of arms or their losses in an encounter with the army. The result was felt immediately. They were compared to the *mambises* of the wars of independence. If a report was unfavorable for the guerrillas, the people would react in favor of the guerrillas, for they were the underdogs. If an announcement of a government victory came

A Sierra Maestra peasant is being tried by a revolutionary tribunal presided over by Fidel Castro (wearing the rank of colonel). Behind Fidel is Major Ernesto "Che" Guevara, who is smoking a pipe. To Fidel's right, looking over the text of the Rebel Army penal code, is Major Humberto Sori Marin, and at his right, Major Félix Pena. Summer 1957 (Reprinted by permission of Yale University Library.)

A guerrilla firing squad administers revolutionary justice in the Sierra Maestra, fall 1957 (Reprinted by permission of Yale University Library).

from guerrilla sources, people who had refused to give financial aid through the underground in the cities would then offer it voluntarily. When the Radio Rebelde station was in operation, and the guerrillas asked for large quantities of medicine, penicillin, bandages, etc., the people assumed there had been a grave defeat in the ranks of the freedom fighters, and the underground would be so overloaded with contributions that they had to ask the people not to donate so many things in such a brief period of time.

Fidel's image was that of a romantic fighter—a fighter who, due to the many frustrations of the Cuban people, would (in the popular mind) never reach power. But he was a figure who, true to the great tradition of Cuban revolutionaries, would know how to die, fighting to the last minute. Cubans assumed that one day Fidel, out of ammunition, would be encircled with his fighters. Fighting against the superiorly equipped army, they would fall one by one, and Fidel then would die with "valor and with dignity," two very important elements of the mystique. These concepts in Hispanic culture influenced the granting or the withdrawal of support to a political leader. Castro, to most people, was a young idealistic revolutionary trying to destroy tradition and the might of the army. And Cubans had learned from sad experience that such crusaders do not have long lives ahead of them. Those who had something material to lose if the insurrection ever triumphed did not take the programs of the insurrection seriously. After all, Fidel would end his days under a rain of bullets, as had "Tony" Guiteras, Mella and scores of others who tried to change the system.

The guerrillas themselves came to feel that they were changing history, and this increased their capacity for heroic acts. Fidel instilled an absolute surety in the final victory among his men. His messages were never—not even at the worst junctures—pessimistic. For this charismatic leader, victory was always around the corner, and perhaps one final effort would win for them what others refused to admit they could ever attain. Fidel was a leader of men, a convinced insurrectionist, born for action and for command, and definitely not for martyrdom, although twice in the insurrection, during the Moncada attack and at Alegría de Pío, he almost died. A strong sense of loyalty also developed among the guerrillas toward their immediate leaders. Pride in their units led to constant competition—emulation—among the various units. Fidel Castro was the Maximum Leader, to whom they all owed respect and supreme loyalty. But their immediate group leader was their direct and most important chief in the practical sense.

These leaders—none of whom was more loved than "Che" Guevara— imparted justice, not only to the men under their command, but to the population where they happened to be operating. In this respect, the leader had to maintain the same standard for everyone, executing an authority above his own, that of the Rebel Army. Every guerrilla leader obeyed Castro's orders to the letter. Any act of insubordination would be punishable by death. Orders, the maxim went, were to be obeyed, not discussed—a principle which in time converted Castro's guerrillas into a well-organized and disciplined movement in the rural areas of Oriente province.

When possible, the guerrillas received political indoctrination into the reasons for their struggle, the goals of the insurrection and the characteristics of the enemy. By the end of the process each guerrilla fighter felt he was a symbol of the entire movement. The fact that the peasants hung medals of their virgins and saints on the guerrillas' uniforms showed that each fighter was able in some way to communicate his own sense of mission to the rural population.

Some parenthetical comments may be useful at this point. The higher echelons of the Rebel Army were almost entirely devoid of men of peasant background. Contrary to the beliefs popular in some circles after 1959, there were, unfortunately, no peasants among the guerrilla chiefs selected by Castro, with the exception of Guillermo García. An examination of the list of majors—*comandantes*—the highest rank in the Rebel Army, reveals that nearly all were of middle-class background, except for some who could be classified as members of the upper sector of the laboring classes.

Raúl Castro, Fidel's brother, could not be further from a typical Cuban peasant. Hubert Matos was a graduate of the School of Teachers, and had served as a rural teacher in Camagüey province before joining the guerrillas. Juan Almeida, a bricklayer, was born and raised in Havana. Efigenio Ameijeiras was a Havana cab driver until he joined Castro for the Granma expedition. José Ponce, a veteran of previous insurrectionary activities, was born in Artemisa, Pinar del Río province, and owned a print shop. Universo Sánchez was a small businessman from Matanzas province. Camilo Cienfuegos, one of the folk heroes of the revolution, worked as a tailor and as a salesman while a member of the underground in Havana before joining the expeditionary force. Ciro Redondo, killed during the insurrection, was a student. Marcelo Fernández was a medical student. Faustino Pérez was born in Las Villas' capital and was a medical doctor. In the upper echelons of the Rebel Army, Humberto Sorí Marín was a lawyer, as was Armando Hart Dávalos, who was a member of one of the most prestigious families in Havana. Ramiro Valdés was a student and a white-collar worker. Celia Sánchez, perhaps the most important courier (besides Faustino Pérez) in Sierra Maestra, came from a bourgeois Manzanillo family in Oriente province.[82]

Men of peasant origins who were directly involved in the guerrilla campaign and who occupied important positions in the line of command were Crescencio Pérez, Castro's guide and protector in the first days; Manuel Fajardo, who was in charge of supplying cattle to the rebels[83]; and Guillermo García, who fought bravely and was promoted to the highest rank of the Rebel Army. Crescencio Pérez was not an "average" peasant; his background in the Sierra Maestra as a patriarch who controlled crops and some intermediary men was well known. His tremendous knowledge of the terrain was valuable for the guerrillas, and made him acceptable to the leadership.

Disclosure of the socioeconomic composition of Batista's army is also enlightening. The 45,000 regular army men were mostly recruited from among the peasantry. The army, traditionally a haven for poor and unemployed peasants, had a substantial number of high-ranking officers whose background was purely peasant. Batista himself was a former cane-cutter and field laborer, and some of those who surrounded the dictator were also from the countryside. In the army, officers who had been promoted through the ranks and whose first duties were fulfilled with the Rural Guard Corps, included Jesús Sosa Blanco, Merob Sosa, Angel Sánchez Mosquera, Pilar García, Alberto Río Chaviano, Nelson Carrasco Artíles, Caridad F. Fernández, Jacinto Menocal and many others.[84] As for the troops active in the Sierra Maestra they came mostly from the countryside where they had many friends and even their families. Most of these friends they lost as a result of the civil strife and the brutality of a savage minority of officers and troops.

The irony perhaps was best represented by the contrast between Batista and Castro. The former had been a laborer in his youth while the latter was from a landowning family, and later became a lawyer, a profession characteristic of a middle-class bourgeois hoping to become a politician through the Ortodoxo party. But class origin had little to do with political roles in the insurrection. Castro's Rebel Army had many peasants in its lowest echelons but—perhaps unfortunately—that does not mean the insurrection was a peasant uprising. The army's troops ceased to be identified with the class from which they had emerged, behaving as if they had always belonged to an elite that exerted power.

With such attitudes and consequent harsh behavior, the regular army failed to gain the cooperation of the peasants. The next step was to try to purchase information from them. Thus a leaflet was distributed throughout the Sierra Maestra offering $5,000 for "information leading to the capture, dead or alive, of Crescencio Pérez, Raúl Castro and Guillermo González" (actually García). For Fidel Castro's head the price was $100,000 and the army promised that "the name of the informer will never be revealed."[85]

Notes

1. *Información* (Havana), November 30, 1956, p. 1.
2. This sequence of events is discussed in *Diario de Cuba*. (Santiago de Cuba), November 30, 1956, p. 1.
3. Ibid.
4. See Jules Dubois, *Fidel Castro: Rebel, Liberator or Dictator?* (Indianapolis: Bobbs-Merrill, 1959), pp. 104, 122–23; Rolando E. Bonachea and Nelson P. Valdés, eds., *Revolutionary Struggle. 1947–1958*, vol. 1 (Cambridge: MIT Press, 1972) pp. 84–85, n. 244; and Batista, *Respuesta*, (Mexico City: Editorial Botas, 1960) p. 41.
5. Authors' interview with Luis Chaviano Reyes, and Carlos Prío Socarrás (August 28, 29, 1972, San Juan, Puerto Rico). Antonio "Tony" Santiago, leader of the Auténtico Youth rejected Trujillo's coopération as a matter of principle and asked Prío not to embark on that operation, but he was rejected

by Prío (Antonio "Tony" Santiago to the authors, February 24, 1973, Union City, New Jersey).

6. Upon his arrival, Chaviano found that Trujillo's main contact with the expeditionaries was Policarpo Soler, a Cuban gangster who was referred to by the Dominicans as "General." (Chaviano to the authors, August 28, 1972, San Juan, Puerto Rico.)

7. Prío to the authors, quoting from letters from Fidel Castro to that effect, dated in Mexico, November 1956 and addressed to Prío, August 29, 1972, San Juan, Puerto Rico.

8. Chaviano to the authors. Also interview with Antonio ("Tony") Santiago, leader to the Auténtico' Youth (September 1972, Miami, Florida).

9. Lester Rodríguez, "30 de noviembre: 7 AM," *Hoy*, supplement (Havana), December 2, 1963. See also Eduardo Yasells, "Recuerdos sobre Frank y Daniel," *Verde Olivo* (Havana), August 4, 1963, p. 8. Following the uprising in Santiago de Cuba, David Figueredo was involved in an attempt to Chaviano in the Dominican Republic; Chaviano learned of Figueredos affiliation to the M-26-7 in August, 1972 (Chaviano to the authors, August 28, 1972, San Juan, Puerto Rico).

10. Vicente Cubillas, Jr., "Los sucesos del 30 de noviembre," *Bohemia* (Havana), November 29, 1959, p. 42, See also "30 de noviembre de 1956" (interview with Haydée Santamaría, Vilma Espín and Armando Hart), *Hoy* (Havana), November 30, 1965.

11. Mario Mencia, "Ahora sí se gana la Revolución," *Bohemia* (Havana), December 1, 1972, p. 60.

12. Cubillas, "Los sucesos del 30 de noviembre," p. 42.

13. The original plan was to culminate in a general strike as related by Frank País to his brother Agustín País: the first phase of the plan was the takeover of Santiago de Cuba while Castro's expedition attacked the army post at Niquero and proceeded to attack Manzanillo and Bayamo (Evidence of Agustín País in letter to the authors dated January 21, 1973, San Juan, Puerto Rico). The same information is confirmed by Faustino Pérez, "Yo vine en el Granma," *Bohemia* (Havana), January 11, 1959; and Carlos Franqui, *Cuba: el libro de los doce* (Mexico: Colección Ancho Mundo, 1968), pp. 54–55, 75.

14. Rev. Cecilio Arrastía in letter to the authors (August 6, 1972, New York, New York) stated that in a conversation with Fidel and "Che" Guevara in Mexico, 1956, they discussed the possibilities of guerrilla warfare in Cuba. Also Mario Llerena and Castro, in Mexico, in 1956, discussed various topics and Llerena received the impression that Fidel was prepared to wage guerrilla war if the original plan failed (Manuscript by Mario Llerena, "The Unsuspected Revolution"). Evidence that Castro contemplated his escape to the mountains as a contingency plan is the guerrilla training received by the expeditionaries while in Mexico. See Fernando Sánchez Amaya, *Diario del Granma* (Havana: Editorial Tierra Nueva, 1959), p. 52; and Alberto Bayo, *Mi aporte a la Revolución Cubana* (Havana, 1960); Hilda Gadea, *Ernesto: A Memoir of Che Guevara* (New York: Doubleday, 1972), p. 122. Guevara's first wife states that they practiced climbing the Iztaccihuatl and the Porocatrpetl volcanoes in Mexico. G. Rodríguez Morejón, *Fidel Castro, biografía* (Havana: P. Fernández y Cia., 1959), pp. 131–32, 135–36, states that Castro developed his strategy according to the circumstances, that for the attack

on the army the expedition brought to Cuba two anti-tank cannons, four tripod machine guns and other close-range fighting weapons. The authors believe that Castro changed plans when he learned about the failure of the Santiago uprising aboard the *Granma* thus applying his contingency plan (the same plan he had tried after the Moneada attack; see chapter 1). The expedition thus marched toward the mountains and away from Niquero.

15. Cubillas, "Los sucesos del 30 de noviembre," p. 89.

16. Authors' interview with Carlos Prío (August 29, 1972, San Juan, Puerto Rico).

17. Frank País, "La valerosa acción de Santiago de Cuba," *Pensamiento Critico* (Havana), no. 29 (June 1969): 240–41; País' description was first published in the underground edition of *Revolución*—first called *Aldabonazo*—for the issue of February 1957. *Revolución's* interview took place at the *Carteles* magazine office of Mario Llerena in Havana; present at that interview were Félix Pena, and Carlos Franqui. The first committed suicide in 1959, and Franqui is in exile in Paris, France. Also see El Comandante Daniel," *Bohemia* (Havana), July 23, 1965.

18. País, "La valerosa acción," pp. 240–41, See also Vicente Cubillas, Jr., "Los sucesos del 30 de noviembre," *Bohemia* (Havana), December 6, 1959, p. 120; Francisco Pordiero, *La valerosa acción de Santiago de Cuba* (Havana, 1959), pp. 241–42, whose author was trained in Mexico together with Fidel's men; and "Frank, el jefe del levantamiento," *Verde Olivo* (Havana), December 5, 1971, pp. 42–49. First aid centers were attended by medical doctors *Juan* Martorell, Carlos Mirabal and Domingo Q. Armiñán; Ramón and Antonio López, Enrique Fajardo and María Munder as aides, the staff was trained at the School of Nursing in Santiago by Vilma Espín, while medicines were kept at Maria C. Munder's house.

19. Colonel Nelson Carrasco Artiles in letter to the authors, dated December 16, 1972, Miami. Florida.

20. País, "La valerosa acción," pp. 240–41.

21. Cubillas, "Los sucesos del 30 de noviembre," p. 120.

22. País' "La valerosa acción," pp. 240–41.

23. Cubillas, "Los sucesos del 30 de noviembre," p. 120, and *Verde Olivo*, "Frank, el jefe del levantamiento," pp. 42–49.

24. Faure Chomón, "El ataque al palacio presidencial," *Combate*, supplement (Havana), March 13, 1959, pp. 2–3, Also authors' interview with Félix Armando Murias, September 4, 1972, Miami, Florida.

25. Authors' interview with Samuel B. Cherson who was present at the meeting (August 29, 1972, San Juan, Puerto Rico).

26. Julio García Olivera, "13 de marzo," *Combatiente* (edición limitada al Departamento de Instrucción Revolucionaria del Ejército de Oriente) (Santiago de Cuba), no. 6 March 15, 1965: 2–3.

27. Authors' interview with Félix Armando Murias (September 4, 1972, Miami, Florida).

28. Chomón, "El ataque al palacio presidencial," p. 3.

29. Troops had been mobilized toward Bayamo and Manzanillo on November 29, See *Diario de Cuba* (Santiago de Cuba), November 29, 1956, p. 1.

30. Alfredo Trejo. "Los dias que precedieron al desembarco del Granma," *Verde Olivo* (Havana), November 30, 1966, p. 13.

31. Faustino Pérez. "El Granma era invencible como el espíritu de sus combatientes," *Dias de Combate* (Havana: Instituto del Libro, 1970), p. 5.

32. Ibid., p. 6.

33. Carlos Franqui, *Cuba: el libro de los doce* (Mexico: Colección Ancho Mundo, 1968), p. 75. See also "El desembarco," *Cuba Internacional* (Havana, May–June, 1970), pp. 11–12.

34. She left for that area on November 29. See "Crescencio Pérez era el hombre que desde noviembre 30, 1956 aguardaba la llegada de la expedición," *Bohemia* (Havana), February 8, l959. p. 20.

35. Francisco Tabernilla Palmero, JFAE, "Telegrama Oficial al Ayudante General del Ejército" (Cuidad Militar) (November 30, 1956: 10:30 AM: File SO No. 678–956) in *Ché* (Edición limitada de la Dirección Politica del Ministerio de las Fuerzas Armadas) (Havana: instituto del Libro, 1969), p. 141.

36. General Pedro Rodríguez Avila, "Telefonema Oficial Via TT al Jefe de la Marina de Guerra" (File SO No. 698–956), ibid., p. 141.

37. Faustino Pérez, "El Granma era invencible," pp. 6-8; and "Hablando del Granma," *Revolución* (Havana), December 4, 159, p. 2.

38. Authors' interview with Corporal Luis Siam, 13th Squadron of the Rural Guards (June, 1970, Union City), Also letter from Colonel Nelson Carrasco Artiles so the authors, (November 12, 1972, Miami, Florida).

39. "Reporte Confidencial: al Regimiento No. 1 de la Guardia Rural," *Chè.* pp. 142–43

40. José C. Tandrón, "Escuadrón No 13: Confidencial, No. 956." ibid., p. 145.

41. Ibild., pp. 144–45, Also authors' interview with Private José Diéguez Chenán of the 12th Squadron of the Rural Guard, (June 12, 1970, Union City).

42. *Ché*, p. 142.

43. Guevara, *Dias de Combate* (Havana Instituto del Libro, 1970), p, 16.

44. Fernando Sánchez Amaya, *Diario del Granma* (Havana: Editorial Tierra Nueva, 1959), p. 52.

45. "Relato del comandante Guevara." *Dias de Combate* (Havana: Instituto del Libro, 1970). pp. 15-70.

46. Franqui, *Cuba: el libro de los doce*, pp. 47–53.

47. Joaquin Oramas, "The Landing and the First Encounter," *Granma,* English edition (Havana), December 11, 1966, p. 9, claims that they were hiding in the sugar cane fields for about 15 days.

48. The highest peak in Cuba is the Turquino, 1,960 meters above sea level. For details about the island's geographical features, see James E. Preston, *Latin America* (New York: Odyssey Press, 1959), pp. 753–68; Juan Pérez de la Riva, "Introducción a Cuba: Geografía," *Bohemia* (Havana), December 11, 1964, pp. 26–27; Irving Rouse, *Archeology of the Maniabon Hills, Cuba* (New Haven, Conn.: Yale University Press, 1942); and William Seifriz, "The Plant Life in Cuba," *Ecological Monographs*, 13 (October 1943): 375–426. For an idea of Cuba's tropical forests, see Earl E. Smith, *The Forests of Cuba* (Cambridge, Mass.: Maria Moor Cabot Foundation, 1954).

49. The likely number of survivors is 20, and this figure was mentioned to one of the authors by Ernesto "Che" Guevara who sarcastically remarked that the "exact number of pilgrims" was unimportant, and that people who spend their time counting heads "ended up by losing theirs" (Remarks to a question asked by one of the authors at a lecture offered by Guevara to instructors of

the National Revolutionary Militia of the Metropolitan area of Havana, at the Federation of Bank Employees in 1960). Lieutenant Armando Rodríguez Moya, a Granma expeditionary who was a trainer of the expeditionaries while in Mexico, joined the original group of survivors at Ramón Pérez's house in Sierra Maestra. On April 22, 1973, during an interview at Union City. New Jersey, Rodríguez Moya listed 20 survivors: Rodríguez Moya, Fidel and Raúl Castro, "Che" Guevara, Faustino Pérez, Ramiro Valdés., Universo Sánchez, Efigenio Amejeiras, René Rodríguez, Camilo Cienfuegos, Juan Almeida, Calixto Garcia, Calixto Morales. Benítez, Julio Días, Chao, Ciro Redondo, Morán, Bermúdez and Pancho González; César Gómez was wounded and left behind, and was captured by the army, but not killed, and Pablo Hurtado was also left behind sick. Later, Rodríguez Moya testified, four more joined the original group: Crescencio and Sergio Pérez, Guillermo García and Manuel Fajardo. The "12 survivors" version was for propaganda purposes. Raúl Castro mentioned 16 survivors; sec Luis Suárez, "Entrevista al Ministro de las Fuerzas Armadas Revolucionarias, Raúl Castro," *Bohemia* (Havana), February 19, 1971, p. 60, and Universo Sánchez, "De Alegría de Pío al Purial de Vicana," *Bohemia* (Havana), December 25, 1972, pp. 24–25. The "12" version appears in Franqui, *Cuba: el libro de los doce*. In 1966, Fidel Castro stated that there were seven, and a few lines later, that the survivors numbered 19. See Fidel Castro, "Decimocuarto aniversario del asalto al Cuartel Moncada," *Documentos Politicos*, no. 2 (Havana, 1966), p. 220. For a discussion on the survivors, see Hugh Thomas, *Cuba. The Pursuit of Freedom* (New York: Harper and Row, 1971), pp. 897–901.

50. See *Ché*, p. 59 and Ernesto "Che" Guevara, *Relatos del Che*, Obras completas, vol. I (Montevideo, Uruguay: Editorial Sandino, 1966), pp. 10–15. Towards the end of the insurrection the Rebel Army counted on a well-organized medical corps; the chief surgeon was Dr. Julio Martínez Páez attached to Fidel's Column No. 1; others in charge of small field hospitals were Sergio del Valle, Vicente de la O, Manuel Fajardo Rivera. José Ramón Machado, René C. Vallejo, Oscar Fernández Mell, Ivieta Torremendia, Eduardo B. Ordaz, Raúl Trillo, Eduardo Sarria Vidal and Enrique Creahg. Some of the most important field hospitals were at La Plata, Pozo Azul, Cabezas de Plata and Charco Redondo. See Julio Martínez Páez, *Médicos en la Sierra Maestra* (Havana: Ministerio de Salubridad y Asistencia Social, 1959). pp. 41–60.

51. Guevara, *Relatos del Che*, pp. 15–18.

52. Ibid., p. 19.

53. Ernesto "Che" Guevara, "Una revolución que comienza," *Vida Universitaria*, no. 214 (Havana, 1969): 22; and "Ataque aéreo; "Sorpresa en Altos de Espinosa"; "Fin de un traidor," in *Relatos del Che*, pp. 18–22; 22–27; and 28–31.

54. Herbert L. Matthews, *Fidel Castro* (New York: Simon and Schuster. 1970), pp. 105–10. See also Herbert L. Matthews, "Cuban Rebel is Visited in Hideout," *New York Times*, February 24, 1957. pp. 1, 34.

55. Batista, *Respuesta*, p. 49.

56. Llerena, manuscript.

57. In gratitude for his services to the insurrection, Matthews was decorated by Castro, a committee with Manolo Iglesias, chairman, was formed to raise funds among workers, and a relief map of Cuba was presented to

Matthews who later donated it to Columbia University (Authors' interview with Manolo Iglesias, March 15, 1972, Union City).

58. Guevara lacked the support of an urban organization such as the Bolivian Communist party to fulfill the role of the urban branch of the M-26-7 during the 1950s.

59. After the victory of the insurrection, Sotús abandoned the country, charging Castro with betraying the original goals of the struggle, and leading commando raids from abroad; he died in an accident in Miami, Florida.

60. Guevara. *Relatos del Ché*, pp. 36–38.

61. Ibid., p. 39. See also Guevara. "Una revolución que comienza." pp. 12–15.

62. Ernesto "Ché" Guevara, *Apuntes de la guerra revolucionaria cubana* (Montevideo, Uruguay, 1966), p. 115. Fidel Castro directed the operation, and he opened fire prematurely while the guerrillas were still approaching from an open field. Former army Colonel Pedro Barrera, who was on operations in the area later stated that the regular troops were drunk from a party the night before. See *Bohemia Libre* (Caracas), August 20, 1961. A description of the battle appears in *Verde Olivo*, (Havana), June 2, 1963; the first description of this battle appeared in the clandestine *Revolución* (Organo oficial del M-26-7), June 1957, pp. 1–2.

63. Carlos Tabernilla Palmero, "Confidencial: Operaciones Zona Uvero," in *Ché*, pp. 146–147. Colonel Nelson Carrasco, chief army investigator of the Uvero attack, described the encounter to the authors (Letter dated January 18, 1973, Miami, Florida).

64. Alberto Río Chaviano, "Informe sobre las operaciones hasta septiembre 28, 1957: Director de Operaciones G-3, Estado Mayor del Ejército," in *Ché*, pp. 153–55.

65. For information about Bayamo's role, see Rubén C. Ramos, "Choque estudiantil contra la policia en Bayamo," *Nosotros* (Santiago de Cuba), December 1956.

66. Regino Martín, "¿Está Fidel Castro en la Sierra Maestra?" *Carteles* (Havana), April 21, 1957, p. 21; and Rubén Castillo Ramos, "Misión a Estrada Palma," *Bohemia* (Havana), July 14, 1957, pp. 74–75, 92.

67. Guevara, "El ataque a Bueycito," in *Relatos del Che*, pp. 81–87.

68. "Pino del Agua I." Ibid., pp. 93–101; and Jorge Le Santé, "Resultado de investigación practicada acción Pino del Agua, Zona de Operaciones," and Curbelo del Sol, "Al Director de Operaciones G-3," in *Ché*, pp. 147–48. 149–151.

69. Colonel Manuel Ugalde Carrillo. "Organización de las Fuerzas de la Zona" de Operaciones, Oriente: S-3." in Ché, pp. 251-53.

70. General Francisco Tabernilla Dolz, "Secreto: Plan de Operaciones R," in *Ché*, pp. 247–48.

71. Ibid., p. 249.

72. J. de Castro Rojas, "Resümen de operaciones," in *Che*, pp. 155–65.

73. Fernández Rey, "Confidencial: via microondas, 13:55 hrs.," in *Ché*, p. 172.

74. Guevara, *Ché*, pp. 126–28.

75. Guevara, "Pino del Agua II," in *Ché*, pp. 83–92.

76. The letter was dated February 16, 1958: see *Verde Olivo* (Havana), January 12, 1964. pp. 7-8. For a translation, see Bonachea and Valdés. *Revolutionary Struggle*, p. 372.

77. *Chè*, pp. 89–92.
78. Colonel Manuel Ugalde Carrillo, "Al Director de Operaciones G-3, Estado Mayor del Ejército." *Ché*. p. 173.
79. "Numerosas bajas de los rebeldes en Pino del Agua," *Tiempo en Cuba* (Havana), February 18, 1958, pp. 1, 8; and R. Dole Alba. "Declaraciones de heridos en la zona de operaciones," *Ché*, pp. 174–75.
80. In July-August, 1957, at a place called Altos del Negro, close to the village of Camaroncito, Raúl Castro executed three peasants as informers for the army, which at this time was infiltrating their own agents into the mountains (Evidence to the authors from Ernesto Lara, a peasant living at the time in Camaroncito, Sierra Maestra, October 3, 1972, Union City).
81. See Arnaldo Rivero, "La disciplina revolucionaria en la Sierra Maestra," *Humanismo* (Mexico), 7, no. 53–54 (January–April, 1959): 369–82.
82. Celia Sánchez, herself an accountant, was the daughter of a doctor and a member of the Auténtico party from Manzanillo, Oriente province. See K. S. Karol, *Guerrillas in Power. The Course of the Cuban Revolution* (New York: Hill and Wang, 1972), p. 142, no. 85; and Eusebio Mujal Barniol, Secretary General of the C.T.C., in letter to the authors dated June 7, 1967, Washington, D.C.
83. A brief biography of 12 of the participants appears in Franqui, *Cuba: el libro de los doce*, pp. 10–13.
84. Nelson Carrasco Artilles was born in Pinar Del Río province, and he enlisted at age 16 in the Revolutionary Guard organized by Batista during the 1933 revolution (Letter to the authors from Nelson Carrasco dated December 16, 1972, Miami, Florida).
85. Authors' private collection of documents.

6

The Palace Attack

The decision of the Directorio Revolucionario to wait to conduct a "decisive" operation against the Batista regime had been based on solid ground, since it took into account the condition of the insurrectionary sector.

The Santiago uprising had failed, suggesting that Frank País had been correct in assessing the lack of organization of the M-26-7 urban movement. That group could not conduct, much less sustain a nation-wide insurrection, and the DR was also unable to do so. It would take many months before Batista would be confronted with a well-organized insurrectionary movement that could topple his dictatorship.

The landing and subsequent disaster at Alegría de Pío, plus the guerrillas' rate of desertion following the Altos de Espinosa incident, had left Fidel with only a handful of men willing to continue the fight in the mountains. The leaders of the DR were aware that Fidel had less than 20 men in February 1957, and they knew that the group would take a long time to develop into a force capable of posing a threat to the regular army. Not even Frank País believed that rural guerrilla warfare alone could overthrow Batista; and he went to the Sierra Maestra in early 1957 to convince Fidel to go into exile in order to reorganize the movement. País' argument was that Fidel was more valuable in exile than in the mountains where he could be killed.[1]

Actually, the M-26-7 strategy had always been based upon increasing terrorist activities in the urban areas, organizing cells within the labor movement, and executing a final revolutionary general strike coupled with widespread insurrectionary acts. Fidel was to have timed his landing to coincide with the Santiago uprising and other acts of rebellion throughout Cuba, since the expeditionary force was supposed to support the internal insurrection. The move into the mountains was the only alternative to disaster, once the other actions failed. Fidel's contingency plan, to seek refuge in the mountains, had worked, but the DR could not see the revolutionary potential of Fidel's rural troops and concluded that the insurrection was at a point of stagnation.

The idea of conducting an all-out attack on Batista developed before the Granma landing. On November 29, 1956, José Antonio Echeverría had spoken of a decisive action for which any risk would be worthwhile. The subsequent disaster of the Santiago uprising and Castro's landing simply reinforced the idea of conducting one final action against the dictatorship. Then, too, relations between Castro and Echeverría were worsening.

In December, Faustino Pérez delivered a letter from Fidel Castro to Echeverría. Faustino contacted José ("Pepe") Llanusa, who in turn asked Ricardo ("Popi") Corpión to arrange a meeting with José Antonio Echeverría. Present at that meeting were Llanusa, Faustino, Corpión and Julio García Olivera. Faustino delivered the letter to Echeverría, who read it aloud. Fidel Castro charged the DR with treason. "Especially you, José Antonio," he wrote, "who promised me you would join in the uprising." The men of the DR, Castro charged, were "assassins because you cut down the life of Blanco Rico who was a decent person."[2] The letter ended by repeating charges of treason, and calling all the members of the DR cowards. Echeverría physically attacked Faustino Pérez, while everyone else tried to bring some calm into the situation.

Echeverría wrote a note to Fidel strongly rejecting all of the charges and written in terms that left no doubt as to the student leader's bitterness toward Fidel. He handed the note to Faustino, and then told Fidel's envoy that he did not ever want to see him again. As Llanusa and Faustino left, Corpión, García Olivera and Echeverría discussed the situation. Echeverría was furious and Corpión tried to calm him. García Olivera sided with his *compañeros,* agreeing that Fidel did not "deserve too much attention." Echeverría declared that regardless of what happened to him, no member of the DR should ever join the Sierra Maestra guerrillas.

It appears certain that Fidel's letter deeply hurt Echeverría, and the relations between the two leaders of the insurrection, had Echeverría survived, would have never been friendly after those charges and countercharges. The immediate effect of the letter seems to have been to persuade the student leader of the need for prompt, decisive action against Batista.

On December 30, 1956, the DR conducted a commando operation which was to be a prologue for an attack on the presidential palace. Osvaldo Díaz Puentes. Abelardo Rodríguez and Martín Labrandero had been imprisoned at Príncipe Castle since 1955, for having participated in the frustrated attack on Batista in the summer of 1955. To rescue the trio a two-phase operation was planned.

The author of the plan was Abelardo Rodríguez, and the success of "Operation Rescue" depended upon the exact timing of each step. Arms were passed to the prisoners, whose task was to reach the main gate while an outside group attacked the castle's garrison, pinning the troops down until everyone was safely away from the immediate area. The outside group included José Briñas, driver of the getaway car, and Julio García Olivera, Luis Gómez Wangüemert, Faure Chomón and the driver of the second car, Julio Garcerán. They were armed with one M-2 rifle, one M-1 rifle, a .45 caliber pistol, and a "Mauser" pistol. The signal for action was shooting inside the castle by the prisoners. The operation began at 8 PM and it was carried out with perfect timing and only one casualty, Martín Labrandero, who fell and broke his back and was later shot to death by the police. The operation demonstrated that a small group of people acting in perfect coordination and with the advantage of surprise could perform a significant action.[3]

The palace attack on March 13, 1957, followed the axiom *golpear arriba* (hit at the top) as had Menelao Mora's 1955 plan to kill Batista in which several DR leaders had participated.[4] While Menelao Mora and his followers continued to plan another attempt, Carlos Gutiérrez Menoyo was developing his own plan of get rid of Batista. Carlos had been born in 1922 in Castille, Spain. His older brother, José Antonio, died fighting for the Republic in 1937. Before he was 20, Carlos joined the troops of French General Philippe Leclerc and saw action in North Africa. On June 6, 1944, as a lieutenant in the French army, Carlos landed in Normandy, reaching Paris with General Leclerc's troops and taking part in the battle of the Ardennes in December 1944. In 1947, Carlos joined his family in Cuba, where they had moved after the Spanish Civil War, and shortly thereafter he joined the Confites expedition against dictator Trujillo. He went into exile in Mexico, returning to Cuba accompanied by Daniel Martín Labrandero to organize actions against Batista. It was through Labrandero that Carlos met Menelao Mora. Eventually, the DR and Mora's people decided to work together on an attack on the presidential palace. Carlos Gutiérrez Menoyo joined the group on the assumption that once Batista had been "executed" his entire regime would crumble.[5]

The group was heterogeneous in age as well as in political background and activities. It included some of Fidel's former colleagues in the "action groups" from the UIR, the MSR and Joven Cuba—Ignacio González, Enrique Rodríguez Loeches, José L. Gómez Wangüemert, Humberto Castelló and Evelio Prieto Guillaume, among others. Also in the group was Eduardo Domínguez, who had accompanied Fidel in the Confites expedition in 1948.

Other small groups were involved in the overall plan. Jorge Valls, who led a group of students, was initially contacted by Mora,[6] who asked him to visit José Antonio Echeverría to discuss a role in the attack. Valls' group included, among others, Tirso Urdanivia, Silvino ("El Chivo") Rodríguez and Julio Fernández, all students.[7] Calixto Sánchez, a leader of the airport workers, was also asked to join the operation, as was Ignacio González, who had been involved with both the action groups and the Auténticos. Other groups were commanded by Ramón Rodríguez Milián, a union leader, and Osvaldo Révola, who was related to Menelao Mora's family.

The Strategy

During January of 1957 there were several meetings in which the strategy for the attack was developed. A first meeting was attended by Faure Chomón, Eduardo García Lavandero and Mora. José Antonio Echeverría, Mora, Chomón and Lavandero met for a second time before a meeting at Alturas del Vedado, in Havana. That meeting was attended by leaders from various groups: Mora, Enrique Rodríguez Loeches, Carlos Gutiérrez Menoyo, Gerardo Medina and Ignacio González. It was decided at that meeting that a "military committee" should be organized to supervise and coordinate the action. The committee included Chomón, Armando Pérez Pintó and Carlos Gutiérrez Menoyo. The plan was also discussed on several occasions by José Antonio Echeverría and Menelao Mora in private meetings at the home of Ricardo Bianchi in Havana.[8]

This plan called for a commando operation directed at the physical elimination of Batista. It called for three simultaneous operations, led by three main groups. One group of 50 men was to lead the assault on the Presidential Palace, supported by another group of over 100 men, while a third group, led by José Antonio, would take over the CMQ radio station to announce the death of Batista and call the people to revolt. The headquarters for the operation was Havana University.[9] The assault group would be armed with automatic weapons. The support group was to have ten .30 caliber machine guns, ten automatic rifles, one .50 caliber machine gun mounted on a truck for greater mobility and rifles for snipers, whose task was to protect the machine gunnests. The support group, led by Ignacio González, was to occupy the tallest buildings around the Presidential Palace, the Arts Building, "La Tabaquería" factory, the Sevilla-Biltmore Hotel, and the Reporter's Association Building. Machine guns were to be placed on the rooftops to concentrate their fire on the palace's third floor, where the palace guards were garrisoned.

Carlos Gutiérrez Menoyo would lead the assault group, which in turn was divided into two smaller groups. Arriving in two cars and a truck, eight commandos were to secure the gate, while Faure Chomón gained entrance to the second floor. He was to wait for Gutiérrez Menoyo's group and then proceed with it towards Batista's executive offices. Others were to attack the third floor to keep most of the palace guard from reaching the second floor. The communications room, the palace switchboard and the electric plant, all located on the ground floor, were to be destroyed by Ricardo Olmedo's group. In the event of failure to locate Batista, the commandos were to burn the buildings by blowing up the gasoline tanks in the palace's guard cellar.

Calixto Sánchez was assigned to take over the airport and stop all flights, while Valls', Urdanivia's, Rodríguez Milián's and Arévola's groups were to go to the palace to reinforce the attack and participate in subsequent operations. José Antonio Echeverría was to announce the attack and then proceed to the university, where several dozen students would be waiting with arms to organize the resistance. A group of students was to secure the bridge connecting Havana with Camp Columbia, while snipers would be posted on top of the tallest buildings around the university. All the avenues connecting Columbia with Havana were to be occupied by the student snipers, and the bureau of investigations, police precincts and selected government strongholds were to be attacked by José Antonio's group. Once Batista had been eliminated, Havana University would serve as the rallying point to arm other people.[10]

On February 20 another meeting took place and was attended by Mora, Rodríguez Loeches, Gutiérrez Menoyo, Ignacio González, Gerardo Medina, Chomón and Armando Pérez Pintó. The latter had been assigned the task of checking on Batista's daily moves. As an employee of the collection department of the "Centro de Dependientes," Pérez enjoyed great mobility and contacts. He organized a network consisting of three checking points along the route used by Batista to travel from Columbia to the Presidential Palace. Headquarters was located at the apartment of Eulalia Porto at 163 Malecón Avenue in Havana. Pérez's team included Fernando Pita Iglesias. Jesús Cordero, Pedro Martínez, Carmen Barreto and Fernando Cortina. A former secret service agent during the Prío administration, Manuel Vilarino was consulted by Pérez every time unusual changes in Batista's schedule took place. After January 28, a 24-hour vigil on Batista's schedule went into effect.[11] At the February 20 meeting, Pérez rendered a full report on the dictator's schedule, state visits, usual habits, number of guards at the palace gates, timing for the changing of the guard, and activities around the palace and buildings surrounding the palace where men of the military intelligence service were usually located while guarding the area. The proposal was made that the attack be postponed until a group of police officers sympathetic to the insurrection was able to join the operation. This suggestion was rejected on the grounds that the plans were to be solely in the hands of the inner group, and that if any informer succeeded in penetrating the group it would mean sure disaster for the entire operation. It was also decided that the M-26-7 should be informed of the plans and asked to join.[12] During another meeting which Evelio Prieto Guillaume attended. Mora moved that the Auténticos be given the wrong information. Apparently, Prío's men were suspicious that an impending operation was being planned, and the group decided to inform them that there would be an attack on Batista some place near Puentes Grandes, close to Havana. In order to create confusion among the intelligence services of the regime another version of the plan was to suggest that the area of attack was to be the Cattle Exposition in Rancho Boyeros. Although Menelao Mora had been one of Prío's men in Havana until 1955, he no longer thought Prío was interested in overthrowing Batista through an attack on the Presidential Palace. The experience of 1955, when Prío had apparently hesitated and some of his men had obstructed the operation, seems to have influenced Mora's decision not to confide in the Auténticos.[13]

Meanwhile, José Antonio called for a meeting of the executive council of the DR to discuss overall strategy. Samuel B. Cherson, secretary of propaganda, voted against the whole project, considering it "unfeasible." He also expressed the opinion that, in the event of failure, the DR would be totally destroyed, with little possibility of recovering from the blow.[14] But the majority favored

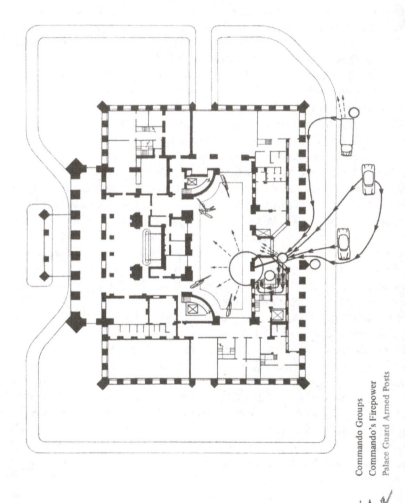

Commando Groups

Commando's Firepower

Palace Guard Armed Posts

The Palace Assault, March 13, 1957, first floor operation. This blueprint and those following are based upon the original architectural plan.

the plan, and José Antonio went over every detail, announcing that there would be plenty of arms waiting at the university.[15]

The last meeting took place on March 10, the fifth anniversary of Batista's coup d'etat. Batista's celebrations were to be followed by a series of meetings between the dictator and representatives of the Cuban Telephone Company, a subsidiary of ITT; the meetings were to last until March 13.[16] It was expected that Batista would stay at the Presidential Palace, and the leaders issued orders for all the participants to report to various houses and to remain there until the final order of attack was issued. The initial date was set for March 12, but it was postponed at the last minute to March 13.

The DR established its headquarters in the Vedado section of Havana in two houses. José Antonio, José Azzef, Pedro Martínez Brito, Nestor Bombino, Joe Westbrook and Otto Hernández occupied one house, while the other was occupied by Fructuoso Rodríguez, Mario Reguera, Antonio Guevara, Héctor Rosales, Carlos Figueredo, Armando Hernández, Juan Nuiry, Enrique Rodríguez Loeches and Humberto Castelló.[17]

The commando group, led by Carlos Gutiérrez Menoyo, appointed Faure Chomón as second in command. Other members of the group included Ormani Arenado, Gerardo Medina, Wangüemert, José Castellanos, Luis Almeida, Luis Goicochea, Menelao Mora, Evelio Prieto Guillaume, Ubaldo Díaz, Carlos Castellanos, Juan Briñas, Adolfo Delgado, Abelardo Rodríguez, Juan Pedro Carbó Serviá and José Machado.[18]

The Attack

At exactly 3 PM on March 13, Carlos Gutiérrez Menoyo directed the commando group into two cars and a red panel truck with the words "Fast Delivery" painted on its sides. The palace attack was about to begin.

José Antonio's men left for the CMQ radio station in three cars. Travelling in the first car were Azzef, Pedro Martínez Brito, Rodríguez Loeches, Humberto Castelló and Nestor Bombino; the men reached the radio station at 3:14 PM. Azzef and Martínez Brito took the elevator to the third floor of the building, where Radio Reloj transmitted 24 hours a day, issuing the time between announcements. Samuel B. Cherson had prepared for this moment by timing the various announcements, measuring the traffic of people across the halls, and becoming thoroughly familiar with the third floor of Station CMQ.

José Antonio drove in the second car, accompanied by Joe Westbrook, Fructuoso Rodríguez, Otto Hernández and Carlos Figueredo. The first three marched into the building and went to the third floor. The third car, with Juan Nuiry, Mario Reguera, Héctor Rosales and Julio García Olivera, arrived on schedule to guard the main entrance to the radio station.[19]

Almost at the same time—3:22 PM—Carlos Gutiérrez Menoyo stopped his car at the palace entrance and was the first to reach the main gate, firing bursts at the palace guards. Carlos was followed by eight men who also fired

against the guards.[20] From a second car emerged Chomón, Abelardo Rodríguez, Wangüemert and Osvaldo Díaz, who together wich Luis Goicochea
ran towards the palace. Chomón was wounded before reaching the palace
and crawled out of the area, winning the dubious honor of being the first to
escape while his *compañeros* stayed behind to continue the attack. From the
"Fast Delivery" truck the group commanded by Mora hurried toward the
palace: Machado, Mora, Evelio Prieto Guillaume, Antonio ("Tony") Castell,
Reinaldo León Llera, Briñas, and Carbó Serviá, among others. Carbó Serviá
was wounded as he left the truck, and bullets destroyed his submachine gun,
leaving gun powder traces on his face. In the process, Carbó Serviá lost his
eyeglasses, but wounded, unarmed and with his vision considerably impaired,
he reached the palace gate, picked up a machine gun and ran upstairs to join
the commando group.[21]

Inside the building on the ground floor, there was a delay of seconds, and
an army sergeant answered the fire from behind a marble column. Before he
was shot to death the palace guard closed the doors to the communications
room. Throughout the building, the palace guard reacted rapidly to the sound
of shooting, and ran to the balconies, which gave them access to the interior
of the building. The commandos continued their advance upstairs towards
the second floor.

The Presidential Palce is a three-story building.[22] The executive office was
located on the second floor but, apparently unknown to the attackers, Batista
also worked in a small private office located on the third floor, close to his
private quarters. On this particular day, Batista was working on the third floor,
although he had been on the second floor just minutes before, drinking a cup
of coffee in the palace kitchen. He heard the shots. "I rang for the adjutant on
duty," he wrote later, "and ordered him to investigate immediately. He came
back to report that after killing members of the guard at the gate, one group
shooting and throwing hand grenades had penetrated the lower floor of the
building."[23]

Outside the palace the streets were being swept by machine gun fire from
the palace guard from the third floor. There was a machine gun emplacement
in the Church of Santo Angel across the palace opening fire against anything
that moved around the palace. Ignacio González's group had not yet engaged
the army.

Inside the palace, Gutiérrez Menoyo, Mora, José Machado, Luis Almeida,
Luis Goicochea, José Castellanos, Prieto Guillaume, Wangüemert and others
reached the top of the stairs, and ran onto the second floor seeking Batista's
office. They turned left and ran along the corridor into the Hall of Mirrors.
Another group reached the top of the stairs and turned to the right. In this
group were Carbó Serviá, Briñas, Adolfo Delgado, Osvaldo Díaz and Abelardo
Rodríguez, among others. The commandos led by Gutiérrez Menoyo raced
to Batista's office at the end of the Hall of Mirrors. Goicochea, Wangüemert

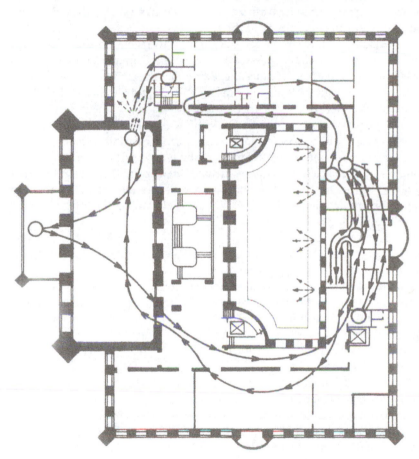

The Palace Assault, March 13, 1957, second floor operation.

and Gutiérrez Menoyo heard voices inside, and threw three Brazilian-made hand grenades which failed to explode. The fourth one did fire, however, and the commandos entered the office, shooting in all directions. Two men were dead, but Batista was not among the victims.[24]

The commandos crossed the Hall of Mirrors once more, went to the North Terrace, and fired a few shots at the police who were already moving towards the palace. They ran back to the stairs and regrouped. They tried again to find Batista, going through several offices on the right-hand side of the palace, but failed, and returned once more to the stairs.[25]

José Machado and Carbó Serviá attempted to reach the third floor, but Major Alfredo Rams, commander of the palace guard, fought the commandos bravely and stopped their advance. Realizing that the attack had failed, Gutiérrez Menoyo ordered his men to prepare to retreat. By then the third floor garrison was concentrating its fire on the stairs leading to the ground floor.

José Castellanos attempted to leave; he was killed instantly. Close by, Menelao Mora, who was suffering from an asthma attack, and had also been critically wounded, made an effort to cover the retreat, but to no avail. He died along with Evelio Prieto Guillaume, Briñas, Delgado and Esperón. Gutiérrez Menoyo was the second to try to escape via the stairs and he, too, was shot to death.[26] Then José Machado covered the retreat, throwing sticks of dynamite, and the remaining men rushed for the stairs at the same time and managed to reach the ground floor. Machado was then able to escape, but once outside the palace he could not find Carbó Serviá. He reentered the palace to look for him, and then had to escape a second time.

Outside the palace, Ignacio González had failed to perform as expected. The machine gun emplacements were not operating, and only student snipers kept the army and the police in line. The navy had been ordered to reinforce the palace, and troops were already cautiously moving towards the area.

From the microphones of Station CMQ, radio announcers Héctor de Soto and Floreal Chomón (Faure's brother) read from a script prepared by Samuel B. Cherson and García Olivera. At 3:21 PM the attack was announced to be in progress by a "group of unidentified men." There were "numerous civilian and military casualties." and "fresh contingents of civilians have arrived and are shooting against the palace." At 3:22 PM, Floreal Chomón read an "official communique" which he reported had been issued by the general staff: officers and troops had established control over Columbia, and General Tabernilla. Sr., had been placed under arrest, together with high-ranking army officers and supporters of Batista. The same communique was repeated at 3:23 PM, and the next minute was used to read commercials. The people were told to buy Norwegian cod, Cuban cigarettes, shoes and chocolate, to smoke an American brand of cigarettes and to learn the English language at a private Havana academy. At 3:25 PM it was announced that "due to the trascendental events taking place, the President of the Federation of University Students" would address the people. José Antonio read his message: "The dictator, Fulgencio Batista, has just met revolutionary justice. The gunfire that extinguished the bloody life of the tyrant may still be heard around the presidential palace. It is we, the Directorio Revolucionario, the armed hand of the Cuban Revolution who have accomplished the final blow against this shameful regime still twisting in its own agony."[27]

At the palace Batista kept in constant touch with the chiefs of the army, navy and police, keeping them informed of the situation inside the building.[28] José Antonio had reported that the head of the army, General Tabernilla, Sr., was under arrest, and this caused great concern among the *batistianos.* Batista kept busy answering telephone calls from close friends who wanted to know what was really happening.[29] By then the commandos were in full and desperate retreat.

Around the palace building, government reinforcements were pouring into the area from La Punta fortress, less than two miles away, Student sharpshooters took a heavy toll of the dazed soldiers and marines who realized the magnitude of the attack only upon their arrival. Snipers fired against a police precinct less than 100 yards away from the Palace of Arts, which lay directly across from the Presidential Palace, and about 100 police officers remained inside the building, unable to reach the streets.[30]

Confusion was general. The commandos coming out of the palace did not know whether support groups were engaging the government forces, or whether the battle was being conducted by isolated snipers. Actually, Ignacio González's planned initial force of 100 men had been reduced to only 50, since most had failed to show up at the last minute. González had hesitated long enough to allow the garrison to react, and the lack of machine gun fire covering the terrain lead to the death of many attackers. Some students who had been told to be around the palace at that time did not know what was happening, but they took up arms and fought. From the third floor of the palace, several .50 caliber machine guns continued sweeping the area.

Carbó Serviá, Goicochea, Wangüemert, José Machado and Luis Almeida had succeeded in reaching the palace's gardens. Almeida was shot to death while trying to reach the opposite side of the street. Wangüemert was shot to death while running across the park. Goicochea and Machado ran across the same park and out of the area. There were dead and wounded soldiers, students and civilians everywhere.

The battle continued, with snipers blocking the army's advance, and some civilians taking up arms and supporting the attackers. Snipers continued shooting from the Palace of Arts, "La Tabaquería" factory and the Sevilla-Biltmore Hotel. Some distance away from the palace grounds, General Tabernilla, Sr., was kept up to date on the operations. Other army and police officers decided to remain a safe distance from the shooting.[31]

Meanwhile, Echeverría had left the radio station to go to the university. Less than a block away from his Alma Mater, a police patrol car came in the

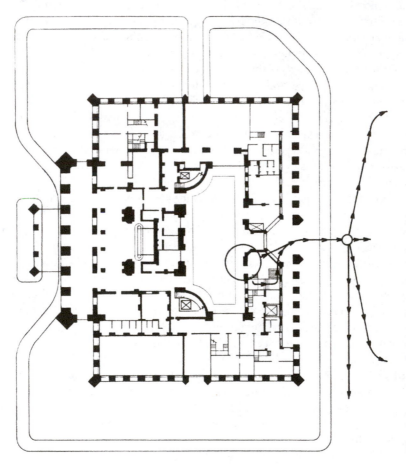

The Palace Assault, March 13, 1957, third floor operation.

opposite direction, and Carlos Figueredo opened fire against it. In the ensuing exchange, José Antonio was wounded. Instead of remaining by his side to fight the police, his companions fled towards the university. Only Joe Westbrook stayed momentarily, firing a few shots at the police.[32] José Antonio Echeverría, the student leader, died approximately an hour after being wounded.[33] The student movement and the DR would never recover from his death. The Cuban insurrection had lost a genuine, democratic leader.

At the university, Armando and Lorenzo Hernández, Lorenzo Pérez, León Lleras, Juan Nuiry, Rodríguez Loeches and others prepared to fight. There were three .30 caliber machine guns: one on top of the school of architecture firing against the Principe Castle, one overlooking the main entrance to the campus, and a third one covering a side entrance. Several police cars arrived at the area and rapidly left when they realized the students were well armed. Meanwhile, Fructuoso Rodríguez had arrived with the news about José Antonio; he reported that the leader had been wounded. Shortly, Faure Chomón arrived, and although he had not entered the Presidential Palace, he carried the news that the attack had failed. At 5:30 PM most students left the university, although some stayed behind to fight the police to the end. Those who did, like the student leader from Pinar del Río university, Pedro Saibén Rivera, were shot to death. Mario F. Morejón, a university guard who attempted to stop the police from entering the campus, was also shot to death. The police took over the university and captured all the arms.[34]

Around the palace the shooting did not stop until about six in the afternoon. At approximately 4 PM the last snipers at the Palace of Arts were silenced by the army after a bloody struggle. Other snipers continued to resist from the Sevilla-Biltmore Hotel. A column of tanks from the March 10th tank division arrived on the scene and succeeded in silencing some isolated snipers. Soldiers posted at the Santo Angel Church across from the palace were wounded by an isolated sniper who was firing from the rooftop of the Reporter's Association Building.[35]

The army thus regained absolute control of the area. Police officers fired isolated shots at wounded students who lay on the ground around the palace building. Some 200 people—mostly innocent bystanders—were being treated by the Cuban Red Cross in spite of the police's refusal to let that organization care for the wounded for fear that some could have been involved with the attack. Throughout Havana, people hid behind closed doors. Rumors spread, predicting that the police would take unprecedented vengeance that night upon known members of the opposition.

Aftermath

For various reasons the groups comanded by Jorge Valls, Calixto Sánchez and Ramón Rodríguez Milián were not contacted prior to the attack and therefore did not occupy their planned positions in the operation. Ignacio González's group did not perform as expected by the commando group, and it appears that González's main fault was indecision at the last moment. There were machine guns which were not placed according to plan; and the truck carrying the heaviest machine gun for the attack was left standing at a nearby corner. About half of González's men never showed up, and those who did were not sufficiently trained to handle anything but rifles and pistols. As the shooting started some panicked and fled from the area, while others remained and fought as best they could.

In accordance with the regulations governing the DR, Fructuoso Rodríguez assumed the leadership of the movement. With most action cells destroyed during the attack, the situation was more than precarious.

José Machado had left the palace grounds with a bullet in his thigh. He sought refuge in a Catholic church and was refused entry, but finally María Cobiellas welcomed the fugitive and cared for his wound; he was then transferred to a DR house in the Vedado section of Havana. Fructuoso Rodríguez was helped by Javier Pazos—of the M-26-7—and then went to the house where Machado was staying.[36] Joe Westbrook, with his cousins Héctor Rosales and Carlos Figueredo, at first hid in a rooming house, but Westbrook later went to stay with Dr. Primitivo Lima in the Vedado section.[37] There he was able to associate with his *compañeros* Machado and Rodríguez. Juan Pedro Carbó Serviá, who also was wounded, was taken by the Red Cross to a first aid station where he was interrogated by the police and gave his name as Juan Faife. He was transferred to the Emergency Hospital where some medical students treated him. He fled from the Emergency Hospital just as Rolando Masferrer was arriving to arrest him.[38] Carbó Serviá also went to the DR house. "Tony" Castell, who escaped from the attack, succeeded in reaching the hideout. Faure Chomón, also wounded, was helped by Mrs. Felipe Pazos. Others were not so fortunate, and radio stations reported their deaths. Some of those who were unable to find a hiding place were arrested and assassinated by the police during the evening of March 13-14; They included Pedro N. Monzón and Enrique Echeverría, transport workers; Angel S. González and Eduardo Domínguez Aguiar, construction workers; and store employees Pedro Zaydén and Celestino P. Medina. An accountant and member of the DR, Pedro Téllez Valdés, was also shot to death by the police, as were students Ramón Betancourt, Mario Casañas. Salvador Alfaro and Carlos M. Pérez. José M. Hernández, a student leader from Pinar del Río University, escaped from the university grounds, but was captured that night and shot to death. Pedro Martínez Brito, who participated in the takeover of Station CMQ, escaped, only to be assassinated by police officer Esteban Ventura Novo on July 10, 1958, together with Ramón Rodríguez Vedo. Mario ("Reguerita") Reguera succeeded in averting police capture until he was finally arrested and assassinated on April 20, 1958, while Carlos Figueredo escaped on that occasion.[39]

The Executive Council Meets

On March 24, 1957, the survivors of the executive council of the DR met to discuss the palace disaster. Attending were Joe Westbrook, Julio García Olivera, Fructuoso Rodríguez, Chomón and Enrique Rodríguez Loeches.[40] Samuel B. Cherson was not present.[41] Four decisions were made at the meeting: to publish a declaration to the nation; to promote Machado and Carbó Serviá to membership on the executive council; to send Faure Chomón into exile with the task of procuring arms; and to promote the distribution of José Antonio's political testament.

Written the night before the palace attack, José Antonio's testament[42] was a continuing promise of insurrection. "We trust that our noble intentions," he wrote, "meet God's approval so as to enable us to achieve a kingdom of justice in our country." But should they fail in the attempt, their blood would pave the way to ultimate freedom. Echeverría stated that whether or not the palace attack was successful it would "produce such an impact as to make us go forward on the road to victory." If the leaders perished, the militants of the DR were asked to maintain the faith in the "ultimate victory of the insurrection. For there shall not be want of capable leaders to replace ourselves, and as the Apostle [Martí] once said, 'When there are no more men left others will rise out of the stones to fight for the liberty of our country.'" José Antonio's last message asked the students to organize themselves better than ever and to be the "vanguard of the struggle." He asked the armed forces not to defend the dictatorship, but to fulfill their function—that of protecting the freedom of the country.

José Antonio had correctly foreseen one of the possible consequences of the attack. After this event—despite its failure—Batista's aura of invincibility suffered a serious setback. To the people at large, the attack showed that the dictator was safe nowhere in Cuba. The suicidal aspect of the operation indicated that the young were determined to fight the regime without compromise, and that only complete victory would be acceptable. Older Cubans who had regarded Batista with awe and fear since the thirties felt that the attack was a defiant gesture without precedent which had taken the general by surprise. To many this was a sign of weakness on the part of the dictator: he had underestimated the students' decision to fight and their determination to challenge their parents' belief that Batista was invulnerable. Only luck, the man in the street commented, had saved Batista's life.

The DR did not need to start rumors to make Batista seem a coward in the face of danger. The people themselves said that Batista's cowardice was a fact, and as partial revenge against the dictator made a point of downgrading his aura of *machismo*. Stories of the attackers' heroism were maximized, and new acts of sacrifice by participants were rapidly developed in the people's imagination. Such tales were compared with stories of the cowardice of the authorities.

133

On April 2 the executive council met again, and Joe Westbrook read a declaration entitled "From the Directorio Revolucionario to the People of Cuba: The Attack on the Presidential Palace."[43] The declaration was preceded by a one-page description of the martyrs who fell during the palace attack. It explained that the failure was caused by those who had not met their responsibilities to issue orders for trucks full of arms to approach the palace for the supportive operation. "Those gentlemen," the statement continued, "did not issue the order for the trucks, and this detail prompted the failure of the most carefully planned attack to overthrow the dictatorship in the five years during which Cuba has become the Hungary of America." The plan had been put into effect on the assumption that "once the dictator had been eliminated the best sectors of the armed forces would second our blow." The DR charged the following men with treason for failing to support the strategy: Norberto Martínez, former director of the Mazorra General Hospital, Calixto Sánchez, Jimmy Morales, Roberto Valladares and Alfredo Flores.

The pact between the M-26-7 and the DR had signaled the path to be followed by the new generation. "On that occasion [the statement read] we altered our criteria on the methods to overthrow the regime. We posited that it was at the top, and not at the bottom, where the regime's weakness resided in a centralized government under one strongman, and we said that upon that man all the blows should be concentrated so that the government would crumble."

The statement specified that the signers of the Pact of Mexico between the DR and Fidel Castro's M-26-7 had agreed on "the ultimate objective, but we also agreed to continue following our own strategy." The M-26-7's plans were "developed, and we did not intervene decisively, in spite of the fact that we participated in various actions throughout the capital." The DR considered its tactical agreements with Castro as "fulfilled," although the principles which inspired the Pact of Mexico would still be valid as the guiding light for the whole new generation as "long as the dictatorship is not overthrown." This statement probably resulted from the DR's frustration at the M-26-7's lack of support in the palace attack. Although Faustino Pérez had been advised of the attack and had been asked to join, the M-26-7 abstained from participating. Since any accusations concerning this refusal to cooperate might cause hard feelings, the DR preferred to withdraw from the partnership on the understanding that the terms of the pact had been satisfied. Thereafter the student movement would pursue its own course, a strategy of hitting at the top, and would refrain from criticizing Fidel's strategy of keeping a sanctuary in the Sierra Maestra.

The statement's explanation for the failure of the attack appears at best a rationalization, with charges that several of the plotters were traitors more a product of the emotionalism of the survivors than an analysis of what had really happened. Ignacio González's group—brought into the plans by Menelao Mora—had failed to act in time; the commando raid had faltered the moment Major Rams of the palace guard blocked the way to the third floor. Batista's absence from his executive office was a decisive factor in the failure. Also, the executive council of the DR charged people who were expected to support the operation but did not explain why the commando group had not burned the palace building to the ground. In retrospect it appears that the most experienced leaders of the attack have to be blamed for their omission of plans to blow up the entire building in the event that attempts to capture the dictator were unsuccessful.

The hand grenades and some of the arms were defective, and this was the responsibility of the leaders, rather than of support groups. In that sense, the former members of UIR, MSR and the veterans of the Spanish Civil War could be blamed for careless preparation of the equipment. Some of the arms had been purchased by former president Prío for the attack on Batista in 1955.[44] Some of the hand grenades had been buried for over two years, and most failed to explode. There were dozens of snipers who did not know how to use or how to handle heavy weapons, and no one had trained them to serve in the place of those who fell wounded or dead.

The entire operation was based upon the assumption that Batista was at his office on the second floor, that he would be caught by surprise, and that the communication center on the ground floor would be destroyed before any messages could be issued to the nearby army and navy garrisons.

In actuality, of course, Batista was on the third floor; the surprise factor was lost with the attack on the palace guard at the gate; and the communication center was not destroyed. The palace's switchboard was destroyed, but not the main center from which the army and navy were alerted. Planners knew that the attack would succeed or fail within the first ten to 15 minutes. They knew that if Batista had not been killed by then, government reinforcements would reach the area from various army and navy strongholds less than two miles away from the palace.

But if the military plans failed because of a few mishandled details—always decisive in this kind of operation—the political plans of the attackers left even more to be desired. The DR had no plans for replacing Batista in the event the attack was victorious. It assumed that any government would have to count on heavy representation from the students and Mora's group. José Antonio Echeverría mentioned only once or twice a possible head of the provisional government, and the only thing that appears to have been thoroughly discussed between José Antonio and Mora was that general elections would be held within six months after the successful palace attack.[45]

Although José Antonio's plan called for a general uprising, and arms had been stored at the university for use by the populace, the palace attack had all the characteristics of a putsch, as had the Moncada attack in 1953, for in each case a small group of brave men attempted a "decisive operation" against the government, and claimed that an insurrection would follow. Leaders of both groups were vague about plans to create a provisional government and about the future in general.

The DR declaration was drafted by Joe Westbrook and signed by Fructuoso Rodríguez, Faure Chomón. Carbó Servia, Westbrook, José B. Alemán, José Machado, Eduardo García Lavandero, Rolando Cubela, "Víctor" Bravo" and "Luis Gordillo." ("Víctor Bravo" and "Luis Gordillo" were the wartime pseudonyms used by Julio García Olivera and Rodríguez Loeches.)[46]

A few days later, at the insistence of Faure Chomón and Fructuoso Rodríguez,[47] Jorge Valls and Tirso Urdanivia were expelled from the DR and also charged with abandoning the plan at the very last moment. Chomón and Rodríguez ignored the fact that Valls and Urdanivia had progressively but quietly withdrawn from the organization long before the attack. Rather than engage in a useless clash with the leaders of the DR, Valls chose to retreat from his role gradually, since he had been one of the founders of the organization and was viewed as the brains behind the entire set-up. Tirso Urdanivia was close to Valls, as was Joe Westbrook. Valls expressed the view on various occasions that the DR should not develop as one more organization, but should serve as a united front against the dictatorship, directing the struggle in all its aspects. As the DR increased in membership, and as its action cells engaged in insurrectionary activities, others—especially Chomón and Fructuoso Rodríguez—began to view Valls as a "man of words," not a "man of action." In the fall of 1956, Valls, together with René Anillo and Samuel B. Cherson, were the ideologues of the DR.[48] Anillo and Cherson appeared to have translated what the leaders of the movement wanted said, while Valls retained his autonomy and expressed his own ideas on certain subjects quite strongly.

Valls felt that the DR could not really carry out a thorough revolution if it attained power without the participation of the workers. Thus, for a time he was the coordinator of the movement's activities within the labor sector.[49] On several occasions he also refuted statements made by members whose main ideas of the insurrection was that violence would decide the entire issue. It was the traditional conflict between men of action and intellectuals in insurrection. The latter did not have to wait long before they gained the disdain of the men of action and were ostracized from the inner group.[50] While Joe Westbrook was a young man who had ideas in addition to the ability to engage in acts which were viewed as insurrectionary by the men of action, Valls concentrated more and more on the realm of ideas, plans for the future and philosophical debates over the principles of an insurrectionary process. With the exception of Anillo, Cherson and Westbrook, the intellectuals within the organization gathered around Valls.[51] But the radicalization and the progressive influence of the men of action soon isolated Valls. He finally left the movement voluntarily, maintaining excellent relations with José Antonio Echeverría but, clearly, gaining only displeasure from Fructuoso Rodríguez and Faure Chomón. Tirso Urdanivia had also clashed with Fructuoso Rodríguez. The latter were intelligent, ready for action, brave and willing to make any sacrifice for the insurrection, but they were also jealous of each other, and competed in acts of heroism against Batista.

Just before the attack on the palace, in February, Valls and Urdanivia had gone to see José Antonio, who asked Valls to join Fructuoso and Chomón for the operation, leaving his own men under the comand of someone of his own choosing. In order to participate in the attack, Valls and Urdanivia agreed to place themselves under the direct orders of Fructuoso and Chomón, and shortly before the attack they reported to the apartment where their *compañeros* awaited orders to proceed with the attack. Almost immediately, a heated argument began between Urdanivia and Fructuoso over an irrelevant issue. Valls and Chomón agreed that in order to avert a more serious confrontation, Valls would join his men and wait there for Chomón's envoy, who would inform him of the exact time of the attack. However, Chomón sent an envoy to Valls early on March 13 notifying him that the attack had been postponed for some days. Rather than demobilize his men, who were quartered at Cifré No. 8 in Havana, Valls chose to wait for a few hours; in the meantime he went to pick up a machine gun. While he was returning to his men, Valls learned of the attack by radio. Even though it was too late to do anything, Valls ordered his group to proceed to Havana University in the hope of joining José Antonio in the resistance.[52] Faure Chomón has never explained why he gave Valls the wrong date.

At both the March 24 and April 2 meetings of the executive council, Joe Westbrook appears to have refused to charge Valls and Tirso Urdanivia with treason. Only after Westbrook left on April 2, did Fructuoso Rodríguez and Faure Chomón issue a supplementary notice with Valls' and Tirso Urdanivia's names and addresses on it.[53]

This incident is described in detail because it influenced many students not to support the DR after Faure Chomón assumed its leadership. A public denunciation such as the one issued by the executive council was viewed by most underground fighters as unfair. The code of the urban underground was to hold an extremely secret meeting with any people who had apparently betrayed the organization, and to refrain from issuing charges without being absolutely sure that the accused party was guilty. In the event that the accused was found guilty there were two alternatives: to execute the traitor, and make it look as if Batista's police had committed another murder, or to assign him an almost impossible task. The first alternative would create another "martyr" for the insurrection, while the second allowed the traitor to vindicate himself before his *compañeros* and before history. If he was killed, he would be a martyr, but if he emerged from the operation alive then he had proved that he was willing to risk everything to continue serving the cause. But hearsay accusation was neither allowed nor accepted by those charged. In that case, the accused party had the right to save his honor by doing away with the accusing individual. Chomón failed to follow these precedents in denouncing Valls and Tirso Urdanivia, and the DR suffered from his action.[54]

Humboldt 7

Joe Westbrook, José Machado, Juan Pedro Carbó Serviá and Fructuoso Rodríguez—the new leader of the DR—left their hideout soon afterwards. Machado, Carbó Serviá and Fructuoso wandered from place to place until Chomón told them to meet with him at the home of Ricardo Bianchi.[55] At Bianchi's the group discussed what to do next. The police were searching every possible hideout, seeking the students, and the young men feared that it was just a matter of time before Esteban Ventura Novo caught up with the entire group.

Ricardo Bianchi, a benefactor of the DR, never failed the students. He drove Chomón to Enrique Rodríguez Loeches' home, and Mrs. Bianchi fed the hungry fugitives and tended their still-fresh wounds. Machado, Carbó Serviá and Fructuoso Rodríguez left for Humboldt No. 7, an apartment that had been rented by Eugenio Pérez Cowley, a friend of Marcos ("Marquitos") Rodríguez who told Joe Westbrook of the place. Westbrook passed the news on to his *compañeros*, and after meeting at Bianchi's all but Chomón decided to move to the new apartment, while Chomón stayed with Rodríguez Loeches. They arrived at Humboldt No. 7 on the morning of April 20, 1957.[56]

"Marquitos" Rodríguez was a drama student at the University Theater. He was also a member of the Juventud Socialista, the youth organization of the Partido Socialista Popular—Communist. At the university, "Marquitos" was assigned by the party to the "very delicate task of informing" on the activities of the DR. Working closely with other members of the Juventud Socialista, "Marquitos" observed "every action planned, every agreement or compromise" of the student movement, and then "dutifully informed the party."[57]

From the very beginning of the struggle against Batista, the Communists had worked hard to establish their hegemony over the student movement. But the party could not compete against leaders like José Antonio. Westbrook or Valls, who were known to share democratic ideas and who were opposed to communism because it was considered by most students a traditional front used by Batista. The Communists' cooperation with the dictator from his assumption of power in the 1930s to 1944 was not easily forgotten.

Rejected by the student body, and with the doors to the DR closed to them, the Communists reverted to their traditional policy of creating a clandestine apparatus to destroy that which they had been unable to control—in this case the DR.

The Communists' organization consisted of the University Bureau or, in Communist parlance, the Central Directorate. The secretary general of the Central Directorate was Raúl Valdés Vivó. Branching out of the Central Directorate were three secretariats: organization, propaganda and finance, whose respective secretaries were Antonio Caicedo, Alfredo Font and César Gómez. There were three "roving" members specifically responsible to Valdés Vivó: Amparo Chaple. Hirán Prats and Marcos Zorrilla.

Chaple's task was to maintain control over a number of informers who had infiltrated the student movement, und "Marquitos" was one of her most important charges. "Marquitos" had worked as a part-time janitor in the editorial house "Nuestro Tiempo," a party propaganda front. At the university he received a weekly allowance from the party, and in time he succeeded in establishing excellent contacts within the DR. "Marquitos" was at first directly responsible to Chaple, but as his importance and contacts grew with his participation in the DR's activities, he became responsible only and directly to Valdés Vivó.[58]

The informer knew that the students were planning an important operation. When news of the attack broke, "Marquitos" did his best to establish contact with the survivors. He knew of the apartment rented by his friend, Eugenio Pérez Cowley, and went about frantically trying to get in touch with members of the movement. Finally, "Marquitos" was able to get in touch with Westbrook, offered the apartment at Humboldt No. 7 to the fugitives, and Westbrook passed on the news to the fugitives at Ricardo Bianchi's home.

As mentioned earlier, Fructuoso, Machado and Carbó Serviá moved to Humboldt No. 7, while Westbrook remained hidden close by. Several people knew of the hideout, among them Chomón. Westbrook, García Olivera, Disis Güira (Westbrook's girlfriend), Rodríguez Loeches. Tirso Urdanivia and Héctor Rosales.[59]

The treachery of "Marquitos" was soon apparent. He visited the apartment on April 19, in the evening, and the following day he called on Esteban Ventura Novo and supplied the police officer with the address of the hideout. Shortly before the police arrived at the building, Joe Westbrook came to see his friends. The police surrounded the area, and as several police officers climbed the stairs the students realized they were in the building. Joe Westbrook escaped to the apartment below and asked the tenant to remain quiet while he sat on a sofa trying to pass as a visitor. However, the police broke into the apartment, took Westbrook to the stairs and assassinated him. Carbó Serviá was machine gunned while running through the halls, while Fructuoso and Machado jumped to the floor below through a window and then onto the pavement behind the Sante Motors Company. Fructuoso hit the pavement and passed out, and Machado, too, was stunned by the impact. But their escape attempt was useless. The building was completely surrounded by the police, and they stopped firing into the bodies of Machado and Fructuoso only when the neighbors' protests became too loud.[60] The police even fired a few shots into nearby buildings. With one blow the DR had lost four of its most dedicated militants, and within a month it had suffered the death of two secretary generals.

"Marquitos" Rodríguez sought political asylum in the Brazilian embassy, and from there he was allowed to leave Cuba for Costa Rica; he went on to Argentina and finally to Mexico. Once in Mexico, Edith García Buchaca and Joaquín Ordoqui, veteran members of the party, took care of him. The informer was recommended by Ordoqui for admission to the party, and was immediately accepted, a considerable promotion.[61]

This was not the only betrayal suffered by the DR and other underground organizations such as the OA and the Triple A. From January 1957 to about June 1958, approximately 50 to 60 presumably secure underground headquarters were raided by the police. There were other surprising "victories" for Batista's intelligence agencies which functioned mainly on the basis of reports from informers.[62] On April 1, 1958, Batista's police captured a large cache of arms sent to Havana by former president Prío to his Auténticos. Following the unsuccessful strike of April 9, 1958, there were also numerous arrests of people whose cover as underground members had seemed almost impossible to break. All these were great setbacks for the underground movement and retarded the insurrectionary process, and they all occurred during the period in which the Communists considered the insurrection to be a petit bourgeois maneuver against Batista.[63]

After the summer of 1958, following the Communists' agreement with Fidel Castro to cooperate with the insurrection (see Chapter 10), no more great and mysterious raids were conducted by the police. Those militants who died during the remainder of the insurrection did so while engaged in battle, not at some underground hideout. Once the party decided that support for the insurrection was beneficial to its political objectives, Batista's police and intelligence services returned to their previous inefficiency and lack of professionalism. There is little evidence, however, that party members regularly acted as informers against the insurrectionists. The only case that has been officially substantiated is that of "Marquitos" Rodríguez.[64] But since no Communists were ever captured by Batista's police in any of the raids conducted in the cities, and since in this instance the party was clearly involved in delivering to the police four of the most outstanding leaders of the urban insurrection, they were probably involved in other betrayals.

With the death of Fructuoso Rodríguez, Faure Chomón[65] was next in line to occupy the post of secretary general of the DR. The repression that followed the attack on the palace was swift, and left an undetermined number of casualties throughout the country, especially in Havana. In the wake of this violence, former senator Pelayo Cuervo Navarro was murdered by Batista's henchmen on March 13. The death of this prestigious politician caused great unrest in the nation. Cuervo Navarro's death showed that not even those of Batista's opponents who rejected violence were safe.

The attack on the Presidential Palace marked a turning point in the insurrection. After the attack a process of internal elimination was initiated within the insurrectionist sector. The death of Echeverría was an irreparable blow, and the events which followed left Fidel Castro virtually the sole representative of the insurrection. From the Sierra Maestra, Fidel condemned the attack on the Presidential Palace, arguing that it had been futile bloodshed and that the dictator's life did not really matter. He also said that the insurrectionists had to fight the regime in the Sierra Maestra. He condemned terrorism, saying that it would solve nothing.[66]

At best, the students viewed Castro's statements as hypocritical, especially in view of previous involvement with the terrorist "action groups," and the increasing terrorism in Santiago de Cuba. Oriente province, being developed by the excellent organizer, Frank País. But Fidel's advice that all insurrectionists should go to the Sierra Maestra to fight Batista was not yet taken seriously.

Praises to Batista

In reaction to the palace attack, Batista pressed for a public demonstration of support to his regime. Consequently, all government-controlled organizations answered the call for a mass mobilization to show Batista the "people's" rejection of violent attacks on the regime. Intellectuals, lawyers, socialites, politicians, entrepreneurs, religious representatives and labor leaders answering to Eusebio Mujal's Confederation of Cuban Workers, and a host of opportunistic individuals, civic associations, boards and bankers went to the Presidential Palace to pay homage to the dictator. For the hacienda owners it was "evident" that public opinion supported Batista rather than the insurrection.[67]

The *Diario de la Marina*, the voice of the conservatives, directed editorials against the insurrectionists, whom it compared to common criminals and gangsters.[68] *Prensa Libre*, considered more liberal, also editoralized against the attack on the palace. *Prensa Libre* rejected violence, and lamented the death of Senator Pelayo Cuervo Navarro, although it did not mention that the attackers of the palace had also been assassinated without mercy, even after some of them were captured wounded.[69] Abel Mestre, representing Station CMQ, paid his respects to the dictator as did the Association of Veterans of the Wars of Independence, through its president, Daniel Gispert García, who rendered tribute to the dictator and called the students a group of "perfidious men."[70]

A mass demonstration was organized, and thousands of peasants were brought from the countryside to participate in it. The machete-carrying peasants joined government employees, who were required to attend or be dismissed from their jobs. Workers were also mobilized through the various unions.[71]

There were also spontaneous rallies of support for Batista. Peasants in Oriente province organized their own meetings, and carried their own signs condemning "terrorists" and "gangsters." In the sugar areas of Camagüey province, canecutters demonstrated for Batista with little or no pressure from the authorities. To many, Batista was still a charismatic caudillo to be admired and respected.[72] Batista appeared at various rallies and always referred to the students as "Communists."

In those areas where *santería*, the Cuban variety of voodoo, was most entrenched, support for Batista needed no encouragement from the authorities. Hundreds of hand-carved wooden heads depicting Batista arrived at the palace with special "blessings" for the general.[73] At Guanabacoa, across the bay from Havana, a traditional source of *santería*, special masses were held for the general's protection. The Negro population also supported the caudillo in most rallies.

It would be a grave illusion to think that the "masses" were universally opposed to the dictatorship, or even that a majority of the Cuban people participated in the insurrection against Batista. If the thousands of peasants, workers and middle-class people who demonstrated in favor of the dictator had cooperated even marginally with the insurrectionists, the regime would have crumbled immediately. But this was not the case. On the contrary, hundreds of thousands of Cubans, like the thousand upon thousands of Dominicans who sincerely admired Trujillo, felt respect and awe in Batista's presence. Yet, despite this popular support, the attack on the presidential palace shook the confidence of pro-Batista people. That a group of men had dared attack the caudillo was something beyond their comprehension. For the practitioners of *santería* or other varieties of Cuban folklore religions, the event was especially significant.

Batista was supposed to be infallible. His "mission" was to rule the country, but only as long as he had the protection of the saints, and no longer. The very fact that the caudillo had been ignorant of the plans for the attack, that he had emerged safely almost by chance, could mean that the saints were no longer ready to protect him. The attack itself could be interpreted as a message for the caudillo to withdraw from politics and to abandon power.

Some sectors of the urban underground in Havana tried to use this approach towards part of the population of "believers." Rumors were started by some anthropology students to the effect that, indeed, the saints were abandoning Batista, whom they had protected for over two decades. The attack on the palace was just a signal. While it was true that Batista had been assassinating youths, he did so against his own will and under the spell of bad spirits. Were he to continue on that path of total condemnation, all *santeros* (high priests) and spiritualists would have to withdraw their support from the dictator and recommend that their clients do the same.

In due time, masses were also celebrated for the spiritual elevation of students murdered by Batista. Some *santeros* even decided that the caudillo's "mission" was about to end, and changed their loyalties to the insurgents. There were many "believers" in the ranks of the insurgents—men who visited the "spiritual centers," to be blessed and protected by their respective saints and by the good spirits. Dozens of red, white and blue beaded collars previously blessed by *santeros* were sent to the Sierra Maestra. For, despite the militancy of the revolutionaries, the Afro-Cuban religious heritage did not recognize political frontiers.[74]

As the insurrection gained momentum, more and more people turned against Batista. By late 1958 the majority of the population despised the regime. Fidel began to emerge as the new caudillo whose "mission," the *santeros* assured, would be fulfilled. Fidel's face appeared on was figurines in public places, and "blessed" Cuban cigars were sent to the Sierra Maestra for the leader of the Rebel Army. Most *santeros* were satisfied to learn that Fidel himself carried a scapulary around his neck, two small bits of flannel with an image of Santa Bárbara—the goddess of war—embroidered on it.[75] This very Catholic custom allowed each individual to draw his own conclusions, all favorable to the insurrectionist leader.

Notes

1. Carlos Franqui, *Cuba: el libro de los doce* (Mexico: Ediciones ERA, 1966), p. 64

2. Authors' interview with Ricardo ("Popi") Corpión (September 13, 1972, Miami, Florida).

3. Faure Chomón, "El ataque al palacio presidencial," *Combate* (Havana), March 13, 1959, pp. 3–4.

4. José Antonio Echeverría, Juan Pedro Carbó Serviá, Juan Nuiry, Jorge Valls, Julio Fernández, among others. Fructuoso Rodríguez was arrested at Santa Marta and Lindero, in Havana, after being recognized by Juan Castellanos, a government agent (Authors' interview with Francisco [Pancho] Varona, September 2, 1972. Miami, Florida). See also Enrique Rodríguez Loeches, "Menelao Mora: el insurrecto," *Bohemia* (Havana), March 15, 1959, pp. 78–79.

5. Enrique Rodríguez Loeches, "Biografía de Carlos Gutiérrez Menoyo," in Faure Chomón, ed., *El ataque al palacio presidencial* (Havana, 1965), pp. 119–22.

6. Carlos Manuel Pellecier, *Utiles después de muertos* (Mexico: B. Costa-Amic, 1966), p. 107.

7. Evidence of one of the authors with names and details corroborated in interview with Julio Fernández (January 10, 1973, Union City).

8. Authors' interview with Ricardo Bianchi (August 27–28, 1972, San Juan, Puerto Rico).

9. The strategy for the CMQ radio station appears in Julio Garcia Olivera, "La operación Radio Reloj," *Bohemia* (Havana), March 15, 1959, pp. 10–12; Julio García Olivera, "Asalto a Radio Reloj," in Chomón, *El ataque al palacio presidencial*, pp. 45–47. The palace attack is discussed in a serialized article by Faure Chomón in "El ataque al palacio presidencial el 13 de marzo de 1957," *Bohemia* (Havana), March 15, 1959; March 22, 1959, and April 5, 1959.

10. Chomón, "El ataque al palacio presidencial," *Combate*, pp. 5–6.

11. Armando Pérez Pintó, "El chequeo a Batista," in Chomón, *El ataque al palacio presidencial*, pp. 49–50.

12. Chomón, "El ataque al palacio presidencial," *Combate*, p. 6.
13. Ibid., pp. 6–7.
14. Authors' interview with Samuel B. Cherson (August 29, 1972, San Juan, Puerto Rico).
15. Author' interview with Ricardo Bianchi. Also authors' interview with Julio Fernández (September 1, 1972, Union City).
16. On the morning of March 14, U.S. Ambassador Arthur Gardner visited Batista's Presidential Palace with officers of the economic staff of the embassy to witness Batista's signing of a new contract providing for a rate increase with the Cuban Telephone Company. See Robert Taber, *M-26, the Biography of a Revolution* (New York: Lyle Stuart, 1961), p. 125; Jules Dubois, *Fidel Castro: Rebel, Liberator or Dictator?* (Indianapolis, Ind.: Bobbs-Merrill, 1959). pp. 155–56, and Leland Johnson, *U.S. Business Interests in Cuba and the Rise of Castro* (Santa Monica, Calif.: The RAND Corporation, 1964), pp. 14–16.
17. Chomón, "El ataque al palacio presidencial." *Combate*, p. 5.
18. Ibid., p. 6.
19. Julio García Olivera, "La operación de Radio Reloj," *Bohemia* (Havana), March 15, 1959, pp. 10–12.
20. Faure Chomón, "El viaje hasta palacio," in *El ataque al palacio presidencial*, pp. 53–56. See also Taber, *M-26*, pp. 114–15.
21. Faure Chomón, "Semejaba un cíclope," in *El ataque al palacio presidencial*, pp. 63–64.
22. The exhibit included in this book is a copy of the original blueprint used by the attackers to study the building. It was published in "13 tiempos del asalto a palacio," *Bohemia* (Havana), March 12, 1971, pp. 5–9.
23. Fulgencio Batista, *Cuba Betrayed* (New York: Vantage Press, 1962), p. 62.
24. The struggle inside the building was described by Juan Pedro Carbó Serviá to Chomón and appears in "Lucha desesperada," in Chomón, *El ataque al palacio presidencial*, pp. 65–67. Luis Goicochea, one of the attackers, also mentioned two dead men inside Batista's office. See Taber, *M-26*, pp. 114–15.
25. *Bohemia* (Havana), March 12, 1971, p. 7.
26. Ibid., pp. 7–8. See also, Chomón. *El ataque al palacio presidencial*, p. 66.
27. José Antonio Echeverría, "Acción Radio Reloj," *Combate* (Havana), supplement, March 13, 1959, p. 15, and *Bohemia*, (Havana), March 24, 1957, pp. 72–73. For the sequence and text of the script, see Julio García Olivera "Asalto a Radio Reloj," in Chomón. *El ataque al palacio presidencial*, pp. 45–47. Echeverría was unable to read the entire document, for a special mechanism regulating the pitch of the voice ended the transmission. Upon leaving, Fructuoso Rodríguez opened fire against the control room in the belief that the transmission had been cut off there, but it was at the Televilla Center, miles from the station.
28. Batista, *Cuba Betrayed*, p. 620.
29. Ibid., pp. 620–21. See also "Frustrado el asalto al palacio presidencial por un grupo de 40 hombres con numerosas armas," *Diario de la Marina* (Havana), March 14, 1957, p. 12–A; and "Rebel Suicide Squad Wiped Out," *The Times of Havana*, March 14, 1957. p. 1.
30. Authors' interview with former police officer Carlos Fontanar (June 25, 1972. West New York, New Jersey).
31. Ibid.

32. Dora (Westbrook) Rosales in letter to the authors (July 15, 1972, Miami, Florida).

33. Julio García Olivera, "La muerte de José Antonio Echeverría," in Chomón, *El ataque al palacio presidencial*, pp. 49–51. His death is still surrounded by controversy: wounds inflicted by the police would not have caused death had he received medical attention: he was shot twice in the face at very close range, and there is no reasonable explanation as to why the car stopped so suddenly, although an accident was claimed with the police car. Lucy Echeverría attested to José Antonio's wounds in the face, and traces of gunpowder on his right cheek from shots fired two or three feet away; Ricardo ("Popi") Corpión stated that he was abandoned and bled to death; and the authors believe that there are some obscure details which only two persons can solve, Carlos ("Chino") Figueredo, and Julio Garcia Olivera, both with the Castro regime in Cuba as of 1973.

34. Ibid., p. 51.

35. Silvino ("El Chivo") Rodríguez to one of the authors (March 1957, Havana).

36. Rodríguez Loeches, "E1 crimen de Humboldt No. 7" *Bohemia* (Havana), April 26, 1959, p. 68.

37. Dora (Westbrook) Rosales in letter to the authors (August 1, 1972, Miami, Florida).

38. Rodríguez Loeches, "El crimen de Humboldt No. 7," pp. 68–69.

39. Chomón, *El ataque al palacio presidencial*, pp. 77–78. The following were also captured and shot to death by the police and the army; Gerardo Medina, Eduardo Panizo, Abelardo Rodríguez, León Llera and Osmani Arenado, among others; José Muleón and Ramón González and Aestor Bombino escaped wounded.

40. Rodríguez Loeches, "El crimen de Humboldt No. 7," p. 68.

41. Authors' interview with Samuel B. Cherson.

42. From the personal papers of the family of José Antonio Echeverría.

43. *Del Directorio Revolucionario al Pueblo de Cuba: Ataque al Palacio Presidencial* (Havana), 2 pp., mimeo, authors' private collection of documents. Excerpts appear in "13 de marzo: Manifiesto Póstumo," *Baraguá* (Union City), March 13, 1970, pp. 1–2, and a summary was published in "La capital el sábado de dolor," *Bohemia* (Havana), April 28, 1957, pp. 81–84.

44. Authors' interview with Carlos Prío Socarrás (August 29, 1972, San Juan, Puerto Rico).

45. Ricardo Bianchi told the authors that Mora and Echeverría mentioned six months as sufficient time to call for general elections. The names of possible candidates for the provisional government in the event Batista was assassinated were not discussed, with the exception of that of Roberto Chomat, dean of the school of architecture at Havana University; Mora and Echeverría met at Bianchi's house on at least three occasions (Authors' interview with Ricardo Bianchi).

46. Rodríguez Loeches, "El crimen de Humboldt No. 7," pp. 68–69.

47. Sufficient evidence has been accumulated by the authors through personal interviews to lead to that assertion. Joe Westbrook told his mother that he had not participated in that decision nor was he present when it was made. Dora (Westbrook) Rosales to the authors in interview (December 4, 1972, Miami, Florida).

48. Valls' task was to review all philosophical aspects while Anillo wrote incendiary leaflets (Evidence of one of the authors). Samuel B. Cherson edited the documents and later wrote important pieces, i.e., the first part of the script used on March 13, 1957 on Radio Reloj (Cherson to the authors).

49. Ricardo Bianchi to the authors, Félix Armando Murias, a member of the DR respected by both men of action and of ideas, contends that after the attack the men of action gained the upper hand within the DR until the end of the insurrection (Interview with Félix Armando Murias, September 4, 1972, Miami, Florida).

50. One of the authors was present at meetings for the organization of DR cells in the Institute of El Vedado, Havana (November–December, 1955) during which Valls stressed the point that violence was a part and not the whole of an insurrection, while Fructuoso Rodríguez, Faure Chomón, and Carbó Serviá, among others, posited that only action could make an insurrection.

51. Valls' dedication to serious theoretical studies on revolution, his knowledge of foreign works and authors, and his generally superior culture were not entirely welcomed by members of the inner circle with the exception of Joe Westbrook, who, despite his youth, was considered one of the most brilliant students in the university (Ricardo ["Popi"] Corpión and Samuel B. Cherson concur in interviews with the authors).

52. Interview with Julio Fernández, one of Valls' bravest cadre members, who was the leader of a commando group in Lawton, Havana, where he was notified by Valls that the attack had failed (January 13, 1973, Union City).

53. Authors' private collection of documents.

54. Félix Armando Murias condemned the charges as unfair, and had a serious confrontation with Faure Chomón in Miami, Florida. These charges appear to have caused a rift within the DR that did not become evident immediately, but that emerged with the Chomón-Gutiérrez Menoyo confrontation in the mountains of Escambray, Las Villas province, in 1958 (Authors' interview with Félix Armando Murias, September 4, 1972, Miami, Florida).

55. Ricardo Bianchi to the authors.

56. Rodríguez Loeches, "El crimen de Humboldt No. 7," pp. 68–69; 94–95.

57. *Bohemia* (Havana), March 27, 1964, p. 40, quoted from a letter written by Marcos ("Marquitos") Rodríguez to Joaquín Ordoqui describing his mission at the university.

58. *Bohemia* (Havana), April 3, 1964, p. 29.

59. Rodríguez Loeches, "El crimen de Humboldt No. 7," pp. 69; 94–95.

60. Ibid.

61. *Bohemia* (Havana), March 27, 1964, and April 3, 1964.

62. Esteban Ventura Novo, *Memorias* (Mexico, 1961), pp. 295–99.

63. At this time the Communists maintained that armed action was an "inadequate and incorrect" tactic which did not take into account the country's condition. See José Barbeito, *Realidad y Masificación* (Caracas: Ediciones Nuevo Orden, 1965), pp. 46–47.

64. Marcos Rodríguez returned to Cuba in 1959, was appointed to the Department of the Cultural Division of the Rebel Army by Major Raúl Castro. Marta Jiménez, Fructuoso Rodríguez's widow, and Jorge Valls demanded an immediate investigation to establish the activities of Marcos Rodríguez at the time of Humboldt No. 7; Major Camilo Cienfuegos ordered his

immediate arrest and the investigation was left in the hands of Ramiro Valdés (G-2). Three key witnesses to the meeting between the informer and Colonel Esteban Ventura Novo who were still in prison at La Cabaña Military Fortress — then under the command of "Ché" Guevara — were to be confronted by "Marquitos" Rodríguez the morning after two of them were executed; the third one, Felipe Mirabal, failed to recognize "Marquitos" as the informer and the latter was released for lack of evidence. Joaquín Ordoqui asked the party to send "Marquitos" to Czechoslovakia as a student, and in 1963–1964 Castro opened his attacks on sectarianism against the party's old guard, whereupon "Marquitos" was arrested by the Czechoslovakian secret police and sent to Cuba. Upon arriving in Havana, "Marquitos" signed a confession involving Ordoqui and Edith García Buchaca and describing his and the party's role as informers within the university. "Marquitos" was found guilty, sentenced to death and executed; the old guard members were purged and morally sanctioned. See *Bohemia* (Havana), April 3, 1964, pp. 29–30. Castro's statement during the trial appears in Janette Habel, *Proceso al sectarismo* (Buenos Aires, 1965), pp. 69–70.

65.   Esteban Ventura Novo, *Memorias*, pp. 251–59, although not a serious source, claims that the informer was Faure Chomón who, together with Raúl Díaz Argüelles, received $3,500 for delivering the student leaders to the police; Ventura claims that Chomón betrayed his friends so that he would become the secretary general of the DR; he also claims Chomón was issued a safe conduct out of Cuba. The authors were unable to establish Chomón's whereabouts on April 20. However, Chomón, Westbrook, Fructuoso Rodríguez, Carbó Serviá and Machado met on April 19 at Bianchi's house to discuss the move to Humboldt No. 7, and the only one who refused to hide at that apartment building was Chomón, who was driven by Bianchi on April 20, in the morning, to the house of Rodríguez Loeches (Authors' interview with Ricardo Bianchi). The authors were also unable to establish how Chomón managed to escape in a Mexican merchant ship from the bay of Havana, how he was able to establish the contacts, or further details concerning the episode.

66.   "En Cuba," *Bohemia* (Havana), May 26, 1957, p. 97.

67.   *Bohemia* (Havana), May 28, 1957. See also Pedro M. Rodríguez, *El segundo asalto al palacio presidencial* (Havana, 1960), pp. 226–7.

68.   *Diario de la Marina* (Havana), March 15, 1957, p. 1.

69.   See *Prensa Libre* (Havana), March 15, 1957, p. 1, and March 19, 1957, pp. 1–2. Senator Pelayo Cuervo Navarro was assassinated by Batista's police on March 13, 1957, not long after he had declared that he would file a brief in the courts against Batista, and in 1956 the senator had filed a suit to block a proposal to increase the rates for the American-owned Cuban Telephone Company. The rates were increased a day after the senator's assassination.

70.   Rodríguez Loeches, "El crimen de Humboldt No. 7," p. 227.

71.   Rolando Masferrer's newspaper, *Tiempo en Cuba* (Havana), March 26, 1957, called for a general mass mobilization in support of Batista: the Movimiento Sindicalista Radical, a small pro-Batista labor organization, announced its National Anti-Communist Congress also in *Tiempo en Cuba*. See also "Mensaje de Anticomunistas," *Prensa Libre* (Havana), March 26, 1957, p. 2.

72.   For these demonstrations and other pro-Batista accounts, see Ramiro Boza Valdés. "Escrutando," *El Crisol* (Havana), April 9, 1957; Mario Barreras,

"Nota Breve," *Prensa Libre* (Havana), April 9, 1957, p. 3; and Masferrer's editorial in *Tiempo en Cuba* (Havana), April 9, 1957. Advocating a political solution as opposed to insurrection was Francisco Ichaso, "Buenos augurios," *Diario de la Marina* (Havana), April 9, 1957, and "Lo político solo puede arreglarse políticamente." *Diario de la Marina* (Havana), April 9, 1957.

73.   Studies on Cuban folklore religion, its social impact and the Afro-Cuban religion appear in the works of Cuban ethnologist Fernando Ortíz. See *La Decadencia Cubana* (Havana: Imprenta La Universal, 1924), and "El movimiento Africanista en la música cubana," *Estudios Afro-cubanos*, 2, no. 1, (1938), (Havana); Raimundo Cabrera, *Cuba and the Cubans* (Philadelphia: Levytype, 1896); Alejo Carpentier, *La música en Cuba* (Mexico: Fondo de Cultura Económica, 1946); José E. Entralgo, "El carácter cubano," *Revista Bimestre Cubana* (Havana) (March–April, 1931), pp. 267–94; Carlos T. Echánove, "La santería cubana," *Revista Bimestre Cubana* (Havana) (June–July, 1934). pp. 135–67; Rómulo Lachatañere. "Las religiones negras y el folklore cubano," *Revista Hispánica Moderna* (New York) (January–April, 1943). pp. 138–43. On the black population see David W. Ames, "Negro Family Types in a Cuban Solar," *Phylon*, 11, no. 2 (1960); Alberto Arredondo, *El negro en Cuba* (Havana: Editorial Alfa, 1939); and David D. Saez, *El problema del negro en Cuba* (Havana, 1953); Fernando Ortíz. *Los bailes y el teatro de los negros en el folklore de Cuba* (Havana: Ediciones Cárdenas y Cía, 1951).

74.   Actually the Rebel Army guerrillas marched into Havana wearing necklaces that most people assumed were Catholic symbols. For the influence of *santería*, see Major Joel Iglesias, "En la guerra revolucionaria junto al Che," *Verde Olivo* (Havana), October 13, 1968, pp. 39–40; Norberto Fuentes, *Cazabandido* (Montevideo, Uruguay: Impresora Cordón, 1970), which includes a collection of articles, interviews with Castro's rebel soldiers and descriptions of counter-guerrilla warfare as carried out by the LCB (Lucha Contra Bandidos) battalions in the early 1960s: they were all originally published in *Hoy*, *Granma* and *Semanario Mella* in 1963, 1964 and 1967.

75.   As explained to one of the authors by a Catholic priest in Guanabacoa, Havana province, in 1958, and further researched by the authors with *santeros* in the area of Union City.

7

Challenge and Repression

In early 1957, Luis Chaviano's 147 men trained at Trujillo's Dominican Republic returned to Miami, Florida. The Dominican dictator and Batista had apparently agreed to follow a policy of nonaggression toward one another. Whatever the reason behind Trujillo's decision to clear the Dominican army barracks of Battalion No. 4 of Cuban exiles, Carlos Prío was left with a large group of well-trained Cubans ready to join an invasion of the island.

Prío decided to prepare an expedition to land on the northern coast of Oriente, near Baracoa, where more OA militants would join the expeditionary forces. The task of this force would be to open a second guerrilla front in the Sierra Cristal. This was an idea that dated back to conversations between Prío and Castro in 1956 in Texas, and had been mentioned in subsequent letters exchanged between the two. Prío had agreed to support all of Castro's actions with some of his own people, and Fidel for his part had told Prío that "no decision will be made without your consent and approval."[1] Following Castro's landing in Cuba and the failure of the Dominican expedition (see Chapter 5), Prío decided to open his own front in northern Oriente province.

Coinciding with the preparations for the expedition, Calixto Sánchez arrived in Miami, went to see Prío, and asked to be placed at the head of the expedition. Tirso Urdanivia also accompanied Calixto Sánchez. Carlos Prío called upon Luis Chaviano, and asked that he relinquish the command of the expedition since Sánchez's name was already known in labor circles and could attrack some support in that sector. Alberto Bayo was paid to prepare small infiltration teams for Cuba, and to give the expeditionaries briefings on the art of guerrilla warfare.[2] Twenty-six men were to serve as cadre members for the organizational stage of guerrilla warfare in northern Oriente.[3] The expedition was named after its 80-foot yacht, the Corinthia.

On May 19 Sánchez and his men were bid farewell by former president Prío, and a few hours later the Corinthia sailed towards Cuba. It sailed without the captain of the vessel who had fractured an arm and had to be hospitalized. Without informing Prío about that detail, Sánchez took over control of the Corinthia and over the protests of Luis Chaviano, directed the yacht toward northern Oriente province and Baracoa.[4] Meeting heavy waves, the boat lost its bearings, and on May 23, it crashed near a place called Carenerito, in a small inlet. The expeditionaries salvaged the equipment and reached shore at Dos Bahias, close to the town of Cabonico and the Nickel Processing Corporation there. Already exhausted, the group marched inland, trying to reach the mountains. It was a slow, difficult march, not only because of the group's fatigue, but also because they did not know the terrain. Two hours after they began marching, the group stopped to rest, and there the first internal clash took place. Lieutenants Fernando Mirelles and José Raufull, Corporals Lázaro Guerra Calderón and Mario Rodríguez Arena, and Antonio M. Cáceres, a recruit, refused to continue marching. Shortly thereafter, two other expeditionaries, Aníbal Celso Stakerman and Frank Pujol, left the main group. The rest continued to march towards the mountains.

A navy gunboat, the SB-5, patrolling the fourth coastal sector of Oriente, alerted the army to the presence of an abandoned yacht. At 6 AM. Captain Miguel A. Pino, chief of the 84th Squadron of the Rural Guards based in Mayarí, radioed the 8th Regiment in Holguín. The latter was commanded by Colonel Fermín Cowley Gallegos, who was not known for having a soft hand with insurgents. Under Colonel Cowley's command, the army was immediately mobilized. The colonel himself flew to the area to make doubly sure that it was an expedition.

Cowley's reaction reflected the experience which the army had gained from the Granma expedition. He knew the expeditionary force must be intercepted before it could reach the Sierra Cristal, or Castro's example could be repeated. Cowley landed at the Preston army post in his private plane to find that two of the expeditionaries, Mario Rodríguez Arenas and Lázaro Guerra Calderón, had been captured. From them, Cowley learned the leader's name and the numerical strength of the group. On his way back to the 8th Regiment, Cowley issued orders to local military units to block all access to the mountains.[5]

Cowley developed his strategy assisted by Lieutenant Colonel Julio Diez Díaz (chief of operations), Major Miguel Alvarez de la Noval and Captain Rosendo Abreu Jiménez. It consisted of forming a semicircle between the coast and the mountains while combing the area in between with small guerrilla-like patrols. Meanwhile, Cowley was to march from the east towards the Levisa river, attempting to cut the expeditionaries' advance in the event that they succeeded in breaking the encirclement. Consequently, patrols were dispatched to secure specific places: Marea hill, Brazo Grande, Poza Redonda, Prado hill, and the small village of Levisa along the Levisa River, and the area between the town of Mayarí and the Nickel Processing Corporation. These patrols were led by Captains Eliseo Cárdenas Taylor and Angel Sánchez Mosquera, who was temporarily assigned to northern Oriente province after the Arroyo del Infierno encounter. Other patrols were led by Lieutenants Félix Aispurúa Miñoso, José M. Fernández, Ramiro C. González, Zamora Varona, Guillermo Herrera, Raúl Poyedo, Martín Horta, Orlando Enrizo and José Castillo. Cowley was accompanied by Captain Pino of Mayari, 80 men from the 8th Regiment

Left to right: Young guerrilla recruit, Major Calixto Garcia and Major Ernesto "Che" Guevara (smoking a cigar) during a rest period in the Sierra Maestra, spring 1957 (Reprinted by permission of Yale University Library).

The architect of the M-26-7, Frank Isaac País, at the trial held on May 20, 1957, for his participation in the Santiago uprising of November 30, 1956 (Courtesy of Agustin País).

and 50 selected guards from the 2nd Regiment "Ignacio Agramonte." This group reached the Prado hill on May 27.

On that day Calixto Sánchez's men halted their march to attend their leader, who had fainted from exhaustion. They drank their last three cans of condensed milk and decided to camp for the night. Luis Valdéz Roque read the 23rd Psalm to the demoralized expeditionaries.[6] Close to their temporary camp was the Brazo Grande river. Unknown to them, an army patrol was searching the area. Early next morning, the expeditionaries came across two peasants who agreed to give them food and guide them to the mountains. Instead, they were led to an ambush, the Corinthia's "Alegría de Pío"; after a brief exchange of gunfire the group had no alternative but to surrender. Of the 16 left in the original force, only two escaped, Héctor Cornillot and José Aguirre.

When Captain Cárdenas Taylor reached the town of Levisa he called his regiment in Holguín and notified Captain Rosendo Abreu Jiménez of the capture of the expeditionaries. Captain Abreu ordered the prisoners executed. Captain Cárdenas Taylor refused, but Colonel Cowley personally endorsed the order. On the night of May 28, Captain Cárdenas Taylor left his patrol, and apparently drove to Mayarí to explain his situation. When he returned to Levisa, all the prisoners were dead.[7]

Colonel Cowley officially explained the murders by saying he had received a message from Captain Cárdenas Taylor to the effect that a fight had taken place "between our troops . . . and a group of rebels lead by Calixto Sánchez at a place called Brazo Grande, resulting in the deaths of 15 rebels."[8] The army had no casualties. Cowley also claimed he was camped far from Brazo Grande and quite far from the area where the fight took place. However, the evidence suggests there was no combat at all and that the expeditionaries were assassinated by the army.

From Havana, the army general staff issued the report of a combat in which all the rebels had been killed. Cowley returned to his quarters in Holguín where, shortly before holding a press conference, he received a coded cable from Brigadier General Luis Robainas Piedra, dated May 29, 1957: "On issuing the news to the press regarding Sierra Cristal action: do not state surprise, but battle."[9]

An essential difference between the insurrectionists and Batista's army, as this incident illustrates, was the way each dealt with its prisoners. The regular troops would in time be profoundly affected psychologically by the difference in human values between their commanders and their enemies, the guerrillas.

The Death of Frank País

The year 1957 had been tragic for the insurrectionists. The unsuccessful palace attack, the subsequent death of Menelao Mora, José Antonio Echeverría, Joe Westbrook, Fructuoso Rodríguez, Carbó Serviá and José Machado, and the assassination of Pelayo Cuervo Navarro and a host of other activists had left the opposition to Batista stunned. Then came the Corinthia disaster and, that summer, the death of Frank País.

As the national chief of action of the M-26-7,[10] Frank País was desperately sought by Batista's forces in Santiago. País had slowly built up an urban movement in the cities of Manzanillo, Bayamo, Palma Soriano, Guantánamo, Baire, Mayarí, Nicaro. Charco Redondo, Jiguaní and Holguín. Even remote villages in Oriente were showing the influence of his tremendous organizational abilities. Yet Frank's activities were not confined only to Oriente province. Secretly he traveled back and forth to Las Villas and Havana provinces extending the branches of the M-26-7 underground. The unsuccessful November 30 uprising had called for renewed efforts to increase terrorism in Santiago. Bombs, assassination attempts against police officers and wide distribution of insurrectionary leaflets created momentum in Santiago. To counter Fidel Castro in the Sierra Maestra, and the growing resistance movement, the government turned to brutal acts of official terrorism. The terror-counterterror cycle was well established in Santiago.

País' immediate objective was the opening of a second guerrilla front in the Sierra Cristal. The reasons behind this move were twofold: first, a second front would ease the pressure on Fidel's guerrillas, and second. País seemingly concluded that in due time he had to leave Santiago or risk certain capture by the police or the army.[11] In the meantime he still had important matters to deal with, and he gave himself entirely to eradicating some of the problems affecting the movement.

These problems were varied. In 1957, Fidel's guerrillas literally depended on País' urban organization for survival. Arms, men, ammunition, uniforms and medical supplies came from Santiago. Wounded guerrillas would sometimes be taken to Santiago under the care of medical doctors working for País movement. Intelligence reports on army maneuvers were gathered in the city, for Castro's guerrillas had not yet created a communications network in the mountains.[12] Propaganda activity was also supervised by País. All urban action chiefs—one per province and city—worked under País' diligent and strict apparatus. He was concerned with the need for better coordination in the movement.[13] He hoped to create a united front against Batista and to organize a revolutionary general strike—although he had not thought a strike feasible in late 1956. To this end, he paid considerable attention to the role that the working class would play. Finally, he was involved in the structural reorganization of the M-26-7, and the creation of the second guerrilla front.

The latter task gained momentum after the remnants of the weapons used by the DR during the palace assault were "confiscated" by Faustino Pérez.[14] The DR arms were transported to Santiago de Cuba towards the end of April though their final destination was to be the Sierra Maestra. There were 10 machine guns, 11 Johnson rifles, 6 shotguns and an assortment of hand weapons.[15] On April 23, Carlos ("Nicaragua") Iglesias, an M-26-7 member of the Santiago underground, informed Fidel Castro of the shipment's safe arrival and of País' intention to use them to open a second front. Castro's reaction to this news was swift. He relayed to the Santiago underground his opposition to the idea of using those weapons to open the second front, and "issued orders that all weapons must go to reinforce our front."[16]

Castro's arguments evidently led País to acquiesce to his demands for on May 18, the bulk of the weapons were taken to the Sierra Maestra leaving the Santiago underground with only a few.[17] Despite this unexpected turn in his plans, País remained determined to open a second front. He assigned this task to René ("Daniel") Ramos Latour, promoting him to major of the Rebel Army. "Daniel" had been second-in-command of the first reinforcements sent to Fidel, and after his return to Santiago, had been appointed chief of action and sabotage in Oriente province by País.[18] The creation of the second front now depended upon a successful attack against the army post at the Miranda sugar mill. With the arms captured at that post, "Daniel" was to go into the mountains of the Sierra Cristal.[19] For the operation to succeed, "Daniel" counted on logistical support from a guerrilla detachment sent by Fidel.[20] The attack was carried out on June 30, and the group succeeded in capturing some weapons though it had to withdraw rapidly under the pursuit of Major Ceferino Rodríguez. Castro's guerrillas had not shown up and "Daniel" and his men were totally surrounded. He ordered all arms buried, and after 15 days of siege, broke the encirclement and escaped along with Oscar Lucero, Raúl Perozo, Taras Domitro, Miguel A. Manals and César Lara.[21] The operation had failed to materialize.

That same day, in Santiago, Rolando Masferrer had organized a pro-Batista political rally. Frank País used a clandestine radio to cut into Masferrer's speech, issuing a call for revolution and blasting Batista while praising the M-26-7 and Fidel Castro. In a subsequent encounter with Masferrer's "tigers," Frank's brother. Josué, was shot to death, together with Floro Vistal and Salvador P. Salcedo.[22]

These events intensified the search for País, and Santiago's chief of police. Colonel José María Salas Cañizares (nicknamed "Massacre" by the urban guerrillas), issued orders to get him at any cost.[23] País hurried to complete his unfinished tasks.

In a letter to Fidel, dated July 5, 1957, País discussed the events leading to "Daniel's" frustrated attempt at organizing a second guerrilla front. He wrote of the Masferrer meeting in Santiago and the death of some *compañeros*: "My pen shakes all over when I have to recall that terrible week . . . everything failed." He alerted Fidel to certain army movements near the town of Palma, giving the number of troops and tanks involved. He complained to Fidel that "Norma" (Celia Sánchez) gave only vague answers to his queries about how much materiel could be sent to the mountains in a single trip. He told Fidel a sewing pattern would be sent to Sierra Maestra, so that all Rebel Army uniforms would be alike, and asked specific information on what kind of arms, ammunitions and boot sizes Castro needed. He mentioned that "Che" had requested a similar list of items which País had sent promptly.

Frank also rebuked Fidel for failing to send guerrillas to "Daniel's" 95 men so that a second front could be opened.[24] Frank said that the 95 men waited for nearly 15 days, "lost, neither hearing from you or knowing if you were coming, and surrounded by the army." Admonishing Fidel for an obvious lack of responsibility, Frank wrote: "I hardly envy the moments they lived through, especially when I always think of men as normal human beings, not as supermen or superheroes . . . The latter [qualities] can be demonstrated in due time, but meanwhile all of us are normal beings subject to the same defects as everyone else. It is not nice to let people down [*embarcar*] in spite of one's deep convictions."

País criticized the disorganization in the rural guerrilla sector that led to Fidel's failure to contact the group and help them reach the mountains. "It is one thing," he wrote, "when things turn out wrong after careful preparations, and quite another when one sees everything wrong from the start." The rest of the letter concerned the mortars País planned to send Fidel, in addition to grenades, machine guns and ammunitions, some of which País said were destined for the second and third fronts. In addition he mentioned he was in touch with "Jacinto" (Armando Hart) on the issue of restructuring the movement. As customary, he signed with his nom de guerre, "David."[25]

A second letter dated July 7 dealt with the decisive steps País had undertaken to reorganize the whole structure of the M-26-7 in Cuba. First, País reminded Fidel that "when we last spoke in Mexico[26] I told you I had doubts about the [M-26-7] organization, the workers' readiness for the general strike and the efficacy of the action cadres who were helpless, uncoordinated and lacking readiness. The events of the 30 [November 30, 1956], when we were able to measure the results we had feared, left our organization very damaged, disoriented, and almost out of the fight . . ."

Prior to the Santiago uprising, Frank argued, an excess of democratic procedures with too many individuals making decisions had led to chaos. But the same situation had persisted after the uprising. "After the 30th," he went on, "I saw, disgusted, how [the movement] turned back again to appointing national and provincial leaderships exceeded by too many members of low caliber. Too many leaders, too little coordination, and too little conscientious work.[27] País had discussed the situation with "Jacinto," in Frank's opinion, "one of the most profound and politically committed revolutionaries as well as a tireless organizer" and both, Frank and Armando Hart, had "audaciously decided to overhaul the entire movement."

In this letter, Frank informed Fidel of the steps he had taken, supported by Hart. The movement's leadership was being centralized, and all responsibilities clearly assigned. País' restructuring of the M-26-7 rested on stern discipline and issuance of firm orders. His decision to build a homogeneous, disciplined and controlled urban underground was not welcomed by the rural guerrilla leadership. The conflict between the urban and rural branches of the M-26-7 was at present undeveloped, but Fidel's seemingly unconquerable situation in the Sierra was leading him to conclude that guerrilla warfare could, after all, topple Batista. However, until April 9, 1958, Fidel's official position was that the guerrillas were to be a supportive force, and that the main blow against the government would come through a general revolutionary strike. Now Frank País was accelerating the process. At the least, the emergence of a unified, independent and strong urban guerrilla movement within the M-26-7 would mean a balance of power vis- à-vis the Sierra Maestra group, and at most, a gradual decrease in the importance of the rural guerrilla movement.

The new structures País had created in the M-26-7 contemplated implementing plans for the future general strike. He had organized a *Dirección Provincial Obrera* (Workers' Provincial Leadership), and subsequent *Direcciones Municipales* (Municipal Leaderships) each of which was economically independent and free to exercise its own propaganda. Thus, each municipal leadership would posit issues related to important problems of the local people, and was not to be forced to carry on an ideological struggle around issues the local people either did not care about or were ignorant of.

At the head of the workers' organization Frank País instituted a Dirección Nacional Obrera (National Workers' Leadership) which would serve as the main instrument for orientation as well as for setting the date of the general strike once the workers considered it feasible. The responsibility for such structural changes fell on an executive committee then engaged in visiting various provinces seeking endorsement from labor leaders. In addition the committee was organizing cells in the labor movement. País' deadline for the cadres' preparation within the labor sector had been set for October 1957, giving them three months. As he explained to Fidel, the labor movement could aid the insurrectionary sector substantially in the final push against Batista. Delegates were to be chosen from the various levels of the Dirección Nacional Obrera to form a strike committee. The M-26-7 would work with known figures from civic organizations and commercial, labor and religious groups in this committee. To meet the conditions for País' National Action Plan—as he called it—militias were being organized throughout the island to coordinate all acts of terrorism in order to attain the maximum psychological impact.

País remarked to Fidel that "you ought to take into account that the above organizations are of the M-26-7 . . . but there are a number of groups and organizations . . . that despite their allegiance to other movements . . . are agreed to bringing the nation to a halt." País' deadline for the labor movement cadres essentially meant that he was aiming at a general strike around October-November 1957, even though Fidel's envoys to Havana were still announcing a protracted struggle in the mountains.[28]

In addition País informed Fidel that as of July 7 the leadership of the movement would include six members in the executive council: the national treasurer, the propaganda coordinator, the national workers' coordinator, a delegate from the resistance, a delegate from the military section (at the national level) and the national coordinator for the movement. The Dirección Nacional would also include six provincial coordinators. País would no longer act as sole executive of the M-26-7 on the island.

As national coordinator for military affairs, Fidel Castro was granted one delegate to the executive council of the Dirección Nacional, and Frank decided that "Norma" would best fulfill this post because of her contacts and courier abilities. País told Fidel that the movement's military plans included continuous reinforcements to the Sierra Maestra guerrillas and creation of new guerrilla fronts, without diminishing activities in areas already controlled by the M-26-7.

Aware of the need for an ideological program to give substance and credibility to the struggle of the M-26-7, Frank País informed Fidel that:

> A program is being drafted with serious, precise, clear and attainable positions. We now are intensely working on it and it will be attached to our economic program, thus developing a revolutionary program for the movement. The work is being done by various parts, in different sectors and provinces. If you have any suggestions or work of your own send them to me. At any rate, when the project is completed stating what the program will be like I will send it to you to review it and give your opinion.[29]

In País' view, the M-26-7 had been vague about defining exactly the aim of the revolution. País argued that the lack of announced plans and projects had made many people question the capacity of the M-26-7 leadership to bring about the expected revolution.

> For it is now a fact that the Cuban people does not only want to overthrow a dictatorship or change a regime for another, but they want to bring about deep changes in the structures of the nation. So it is everyone's concern as well as a concern of this, country's interests to know the true capacity our leaders have to exert changes, and to know if we deserve their trust for such ends. Nobody doubts any longer the fall of the regime, but they [the people] are concerned about the quality of the M-26-7 engineers to reconstruct the building.[30]

This letter revealed not only that País was a meticulous man with great organizational and programmatic skills, but also it pointed out the real focus of political leadership within the M-26-7 in the summer of 1957, País, not Fidel, really controlled the movement. For all practical purposes, Fidel was isolated from the mainstream of events, while País was on the forefront organizing, planning, moving from province to towns and vice versa in a frenzied race to lay the ground for the prompt overthrow of the dictatorship.

On the question of subordinating military affairs to the civilian leadership. País was merely observing a traditional precept dating back to the wars of independence. Thus in the new M-26-7 Frank País remained the top leader— *coordinador general del movimiento*—while Fidel represented the *coordinador nacional bélico.* País must have presumed that if military affairs were to pre-empt civilian affairs the new military apparatus (Rebel Army) would merely substitute for Batista's organization.

Fidel was to have one delegate of the six representatives controlling decisions in the executive committee. País' arrangements pointed towards reducing chaos, duplication of tasks, lack of discipline and, possibly, Fidel's power within the movement. País' attempts to open up new guerrilla fronts, his use of power to grant ranks up to major, and his increasing popularity threatened to atomize Fidel's guerrilla front. Fidel's forces, in País' view, were to be just one of a number of guerrilla foci the M-26-7 would set up throughout the Sierras of Oriente.

Fidel Castro's reaction was swift. Felipe Pazos and Raúl Chibás were urgently contacted and brought to the Sierra Maestra. In a matter of hours they drafted the "Sierra Maestra Manifesto."[31] On July 12, the manifesto was signed by Pazos, Chibás and Fidel without previous consultation with the Dirección Nacional. This move was a coup aimed at discouraging the political and economic programs that were being drafted under Frank País' instructions, and seemingly with the support of Armando Hart and Faustino Pérez, among others. In another sense, it also meant that Fidel considered the Dirección Nacional second to his command, and subject to whatever decisions he made, not only in military but also in political, social and economic matters.

The July 12 manifesto called for a "democratic regime." and a "constitutional government." and for "truly free, democratic and impartial elections." It proposed the creation of a civic-revolutionary front with a common strategy of struggle, the designation of a person to preside over the provisional government, opposition to mediation or intervention in the internal affairs of Cuba, and it called on the United States to cancel all arm shipments to Batista. It also stated that no military junta would be accepted, and that the apolitical nature of the armed forces was guaranteed. The provisional government would grant freedom to all political prisoners; guarantee freedom of information and of individual and civil rights; establish a civil service; democratize the labor unions; eradicate illiteracy; establish the basis for an agrarian reform with prior indemnification to landowners; accelerate the process of industrialization; and create new jobs.

The provisional president would be selected by all civic institutions, because "those organizations are apolitical, and their support would free the provisional president of partisan compromises thus leading to absolutely clean and impartial elections". To create the civic front it was not "necessary for political parties and civic institutions to declare themselves in favor of the insurrectional thesis or to come to the Sierra Maestra."[32] The meeting could be held at any place, and the M-26-7 could be represented in Havana, Mexico or Miami.

The "Sierra Maestra Manifesto" was not made known to the public until July 28, 1957. In the meantime, Frank País moved from house to house trying to evade the frantic search that had been launched after him. On July 21, two letters were written to Frank. The first came from the Rebel Army in the Sierra, and it was a note of condolence on the death of his brother Josué.[33] The second, dated the same day as the first, was written by Fidel, but only some paragraphs have been made public.[34] In premonitory terms Fidel wrote, "I am overcome by a feeling of suspense every time I listen to the radio and hear that some young man was found murdered in the streets of Santiago. Just today they announced they had found the unidentified body of a young man, about 24 years old, with a mustache, etc., etc. This worry will remain with me for hours until I know the identity of the man."[35] Apparently Fidel concluded that his Sierra Maestra Manifesto, which included a formal proposal for the future provisional government of Cuba, would not interest Frank País, for he did not mention it.

Frank País answered both letters on July 26.[36] He told Fidel of a "fantastic and absurd wave of arrests" and expressed concern about the situation in Santiago, and his persecution by Colonel Salas Cañizares. Frank also wrote: "1 am very happy that at last you have written me on the issues I asked you to. I will take note of everything, and will try to do them [meaning unclear] as soon as possible. From this month on we will be responsible for all the aid coming to you."[37] He ended his letter with good news for Fidel. More sophisticated weaponry and men were to reach the Sierra Maestra guerrillas. In the last two lines Frank expressed his gratitude for the letter of condolence he received from the "officers and the rest of our *compañeros*."[38]

Frank País' last letter was addressed to "Aly," Celia Sanchez's last nom de guerre. He told her there were "14 *muchachos* up in the air [waiting] ... when the way is ready let me know." He stressed how difficult the situation was in Santiago and that Colonel Salas Cañizares "was out of his senses" though in his insanity, "he has made me jump from four houses until today. We have been very lucky, but don't know how long my luck will last. I hope it lasts long enough for me to do something I must do. Do not forget the rest of the compañeros who are living like in a rat hole. We must try to get them out."[39]

País hurried his plans to leave Santiago. Since the attempt to create a second guerrilla front had been frustrated, he could not move to the Sierra Cristal mountains. Two alternatives remained: exile or Sierra Maestra. The first was forbidden as a rule of revolutionary conduct. The second was the most likely possibility open to País, and he made plans to go to Fidel's sanctuary at the earliest possible time.[40]

At the very end of July, Frank moved into Raúl Pujol's house which, despite recent official Cuban descriptions, was the safest hideout in Santiago de Cuba at that time.[41] Colonel Salas Cañizares conducted several random raids during the first 15 days of July, and then all raids stopped. But in the last week of the month, the raids were again renewed. País' whereabouts were known to only four persons—his fiancee, América Domitro. Raúl Pujol, Reverend Agustín G. Seis-dedos and Vilma Espín.[42] Despite this secrecy, Colonel Salas Cañizares was led directly to País' hideout. Because his physical features were not familiar to the Santiago police, Colonel Salas Cañizares enlisted the aid of Mariano Randish, one of País former colleagues at the National Teachers' School, who waited in Salas' car to identify the leader. On July 30, 1957, the police surrounded the building where Frank and Raúl Pujol were hiding. Aware that something was going on, País and Pujol walked out of the building only to confront shots fired at them from nearby police cars. Frank País' body was deposited on the Callejón del Muro, where it was picked up by the women's section of Santiago's civic resistance.[43]

País' death prompted a general demonstration of public indignation.[44] All stores in Santiago de Cuba closed in protest. Thousands defied the regime and accompanied the cortege to the cemetery. The death of Frank País marked a turning point in the internal development of the M-26-7. His elimination decisively weakened the Dirección Nacional. That organization ceased to exert a major influence in the insurrectionary process. Leadership gradually turned to the Sierra Maestra, as the urban underground of the M-26-7 was assigned one specific role: to sustain Fidel Castro's guerrillas. The sole remaining challenge to Fidel's hegemony would not come until 1958, with the growth of the urban branch of the M-26-7 in Havana. The murders of José Antonio Echeverría and Frank Isaac País had eliminated two of the three genuine leaders of the Cuban insurrection. Only Fidel survived.

The Cienfuegos Uprising

The next critical event occurred on September 5, 1957, with the uprising at the Cayo Loco Naval Base. Long a cradle of opposition to the government Cienfuegos, overlooking the Jagua Bay, had one of the largest maritime facilities on the southern coast. Its importance justified the existence of the naval base which monitored naval patrols along the southern coast and served as a refueling station for the coast guard. To the north lay the capital of Las Villas province, Santa Clara.

The uprising at Cienfuegos was a serious blow to the monolithic armed forces' support of the regime, since it was a combined movement between the navy and M-26-7 activists, with OA militants involved. The navy was traditionally not as pro-Batista as the army. A substantial number of naval officers felt frustrated at Batista's appointments of men who had not graduated from the Mariel Naval Academy to the highest ranks in the service. Rear Admiral Rodríguez Calderón was such an officer. A former carpenter attached to the navy's shipyards, but a pro-Batista activist, "Rear Admiral" Calderón was ridiculed by graduate officers. Short, obese and with a protuberant chest full of medals depicting imaginary combats, the chief of the navy was thoroughly objectionable to young naval officers. Such officers had studied for four years at the Mariel Naval Academy, in Pinar del Rio province, after which the more advanced cadets were sent to the U.S. Naval Academy at Annapolis, Maryland; naval air force cadets received further training at the air force base in Pensacola, Florida. Upon their return to Cuba they were placed under the command of nonprofessional officers, and this practice led to their disaffection with the Batista regime.

Immediately after the palace attack, anti-Batista naval officers met secretly with several Auténtico militants and with Faustino Pérez in Havana. They developed a plan, initially to consist of two phases. In the first phase, as the signal for the revolt, a frigate would shell the Presidential Palace, less than half a mile from the northern coast of Havana. Simultaneously, navy pilots were to attack the air force's camp at Columbia, and the navy headquarters would also be bombed. The M-26-7 urban cadres would take over radio station CMQ, trying, as Echeverría did on March 13, to call for a general strike and an uprising. The second phase would be the uprising of all naval posts, but mainly the Cayo Loco Base at Cienfuegos. The Mariel Academy would join the revolt, commanded by Colonel Guillermo Driggs and Lieutenants José Pírz and José Monteagudo. Across from the naval academy and the Bay of Mariel lay the naval air force base of Mariel. Men from the base would also join the uprising. Some forces from Mariel would march on Guanajay, a town along the Central Highway. The town of Mariel, with a small Rural Guard garrison of less than 40, would pose no obstacle to the rebels. The M-26-7, the OA and other small opposition groups would take over the arsenal of the army post and distribute arms to the people.[45]

Cienfuegos was the crucial point in the plan. In the event of failure, a contingency plan called for a retreat from the city towards the Escambray Mountains, where a new guerrilla front would be established.

The national uprising was initially set for May 28, then postponed. The M-26-7 had mobilized 35 cadres members in the city of Cienfuegos, but an informer delivered the group to the authorities. After customary interrogation they were released.

The next date for the uprising was selected for a practical reason. September 4 was Batista's most important anniversary, and the armed forces would celebrate the "sergeants' revolt" until late hours of the night. The troops were traditionally allowed to indulge themselves with alcohol, and all received a special bonus as a gift from the caudillo. The troops' state of euphoria and their assumed relaxation presented optimal conditions for the conspirators. Immediately after the formal celebrations most key officers of the intelligence services held private parties until early the following morning. All indications were that a revolt on September 5 would take Batista and the army completely by surprise.

On September 3, Julio Camacho, then M-26-7 coordinator for Las Villas province, and Miguel Merino, chief of action in Cienfuegos, were called to Havana by Faustino Pérez. The following day, Pérez informed them of the plans for the uprising, and told them to establish contact in Cienfuegos with Lieutenant Dionisio Pérez San Román, chief of artillery of the naval base at Cayo Loco. San Román would be in charge of all operations conducted in the city of Cienfuegos. On their return to Cienfuegos, Camacho and Merino met San Román, and agreed to proceed with the plan at exactly 6 AM on the morning of September 5. Elsewhere, naval officers were also told to go ahead with the plans at the same hour.[46]

While the "sergeants' revolt" festivities were well underway, members of the M-26-7 moved in small groups toward Cienfuegos from various towns throughout Las Villas province. Accompanied by Merino, Lieutenant San Román travelled through the city checking on various groups of the M-26-7 militants. At 6 AM two cars left for the Cayo Loco base; Lieutenant San Román and Merino drove the first car, followed by Camacho, Raúl Col and Osvaldo Acosta. The contact inside the base was Sergeant Santiago Rios Gutiérrez. The machine gun emplacement at the base's gate would have to point upwards as the signal of free access into the base. Everything went as planned: the insurgents entered the base's perimeter, went directly to headquarters, and placed the chief of the naval district, Colonel Enrique Comesañas, under arrest. Lieutenant San Román ordered the unit to form outside headquarters, spoke to the sailors and invited all to join in the uprising. Half of the approximately 200 men in the base joined the revolt, including some who were on leave at the moment when they heard the news. Anchored outside the base were Coast Guards 101 and 41, whose officers joined San Román. Acting with exact coordination, about 40 M-26-7 insurgents arrived at the base by truck, and the sailors taught some of them to handle a rifle before moving toward the city.[47]

Both uniformed personnel and M-26-7 civilians drove from the base to Cienfuegos in navy trucks. Insurgents in the trucks were thus able to identify themselves as allies to M-26-7 snipers along the way. Such was the beginning of one of the bloodiest episodes in the insurrection.

In the first action, the house of the military chief of the Rural Guard Corps, Major Eugenio Fernández, was surrounded; he escaped amidst a crossfire of bullets. A police car and its four occupants were cut to pieces by a platoon of sailors. They were the first casualties of the uprising. As the shooting spread out the population took to the streets asking for arms.

There were three battles in progress.[48] Surrounded at police headquarters, Major Ruiz Beltrón refused to surrender, and asked to parley with the rebels. Heavy fighting was also taking place at the municipal building, and around the Rural Guard barracks. As the fighting progressed it became evident that resistance was dwindling. Merino fired a heavy machine gun in answer to Major Ruiz Beltrón's request for a parley; he finally surrendered and was placed under arrest at Cayo Loco. Shortly before 10 AM Cienfuegos was liberated, and only sporadic shooting continued in a small section of the city were Major Eugenio Fernández of the Rural Guard was still holding a building. The rebels readied for the government's counterattack.

Meanwhile, San Román tried to establish contact with Havana to learn what was taking place in other naval bases. But nothing was happening in that city. The M-26-7 had not attempted to take over Station CMQ as planned, and Colonel Guillermo Driggs remained quiet at the naval academy in Mariel. In Santa Clara, Las Villas' capital, the M-26-7 was also inactive. There were no indications that the Presidential Palace, or the navy's headquarters in Havana, or Camp Columbia were under attack by the naval air force. San Román could not locate Faustino Pérez, and the lieutenant probably concluded that the operation had failed.[49]

The rebels' strongholds were the police headquarters, the San Lorenzo School, and the municipal building around Cienfuegos' main square. San Román positioned snipers all along the rooftops and placed an advance guard at the entrance of the city with orders to alert the insurgents of any army reinforcements.

The army mobilized its best tactical unit in Las Villas, under the command of Lieutenant Colonel Cándido "Chino" Hernández, stationed at the Leoncio Vidal Camp in Santa Clara. His troops were to move to Cienfuegos escorted by tanks. From Havana, Batista ordered Captain Caridad Fernández to reinforce the operation with men from the 1st Regiment attached to La Cabaña Military Fortress, plus ten tanks which were transported to Cienfuegos by trucks.[50]

With Cienfuegos having been siezed by the rebels and with army reinforcements rapidly moving on the city, other groups offered their support to the insurgents. Lawyers asked for weapons to fight alongside their sons and neighbors; medical doctors offered their services and prepared for a bloody afternoon; and mechanics, radio operators and cab drivers asked to be put to some use.[51] The people's euphoria was not lessened by news that the rest of the island was peaceful, even though it meant that the isolated uprising would be mercilessly crushed.

Some groups rejected the rebels. The Cienfuegos Yacht Club—whose commodore was Osvaldo Dorticós Torrado—asked the insurgents not to come closer for fear of damage to their building. Osvaldo Dorticós Torrado and other members of the Partido Socialista Popular abstained from participating in any acts against the government. Osvaldo Dorticós had been appointed by

Batista "consultant to the Cienfuegos aqueduct," and "officer of administration, fifth class," on August 15, 1955.[52] As a loyal *batistiano*, he remained neutral during the events.

As the first troops approached the city, the rebel command ordered the people out of the streets. Lieutenant Colonel Hernández arrived at Cienfuegos shortly after noon. During their baptism of fire the civilians handled themselves as professionals. The orders of the rebel command were brief: maintain complete silence throughout the city, and do not open fire until a heavy machine gun emplacement at the police headquarters signals the beginning of the battle.[53] The rebels hoped the army would march right into the middle of the square, falling into the trap. Only Batista's own officers would have been capable of developing such a sophisticated strategy.

The first government troops arrived in trucks and stopped a short distance from the square. Some 100 men entered the square, running and shouting "Viva Batista!" Encountering no resistance, the troops gathered in the middle of the square, looking toward the buildings around them for some reaction. When it came, it was the end for some 40 of Batista's troops. The rest fled. A second wave of army supporters was dispersed from the police headquarters, and a third assault group was trapped between two buildings from which students threw Molotov cocktails.

The army regrouped.[54] The next attack was also repelled by the insurgents, and then the battle spread throughout the city. From windows and doorways civilians fired at the army, and the soldiers fired back at anything that moved. The air force strafed the city, though some planes dropped their lethal cargo at sea, rather than bombard the Cayo Loco base.

At police headquarters the rebels held off the concentrated attack of a full company of soldiers and two tanks for hours. The army's casualties mounted rapidly. In the main square, the rebels stood their ground, although ammunition began to run out faster than expected. At the municipal building, the M-26-7, led by Luis Pérez Lozano, Galo T. Delgado and Tomás Toledo, turned back the attackers twice, but sustained heavy casualties. The San Lorenzo School was defended by M-26-7 civilians and sailors commanded by Lieutenant Dímas Martínez, who died in the battle, and Professor Gilberto González.[55]

San Román, Merino and Camacho were aware that it was only a matter of time before their resistance crumbled. Ammunition was running low, and civilian casualties were mounting rapidly. San Román left for Coast Guard 101 to establish radio contact with a frigate, and that was the last time the rebels saw him. Upon arrival at the ship he was placed under arrest as the officers tried to change sides at the last minute. Camacho, Merino and Raúl Col, the leaders of the M-26-7, abandoned their positions and fled in a small boat, trying to reach a powerful motorboat belonging to the Lora family. Finding that the motorboat was not in condition to sail, they returned to Cienfuegos, where they were hidden by some fishermen until they managed to escape. They had panicked at the possibility of death, and had abandoned their *compañeros* who were still engaged with the army. They could have retreated from the city *en force*, attempting to reach the mountains of Escambray as planned, but they decided not to delay their departure from the area of combat.

Resistance lasted until September 6. The last bastion of the rebels was the San Lorenzo School, where the insurgents fought the army, and withstood artillery tank fire barrages. Once they ran out of ammunition they surrendered. Most were assassinated as they marched out of the building. At the municipal building, Luis Pérez Lozano, Galo T. Delgado and Tomás Toledo surrendered, and were shot to death immediately.[56] The number of civilian casualties is unknown. The number of prisoners later murdered is also unknown.[57]

San Román, Captain Alejandro González and José María Pérez, a labor leader, were taken to Major Jesús Blanco, the naval chief of La Chorrera Fortress in Havana. The prisoners underwent interrogation at the hands of police officer Esteban Ventura Novo and Captain Julio Laurent of the naval intelligence service. José María Pérez was strangled to death aboard the motorboat "September 4." and dumped at sea with weights attached to his feet. San Román and Brito were savagely tortured and also disposed of at sea. Other prisoners were treated in similar ways. At Mariel, several officers, including Colonel Guillermo Driggs, were charged with conspiring to overthrow the government; they were tried and sentenced to six years imprisonment at the Isle of Pines Penitentiary.[58]

Batista's vengeance had been brutal and his message clear. Any dissidents within the armed forces would be treated without compassion. The Cienfuegos uprising would be remembered as the most serious attempt undertaken by a branch of the armed services to depose the military dictatorship.

Notes

1. Authors' interview with Carlos Prío, who quoted from Castro's letter, dated November 1956 (August 29, 1972, San Juan, Puerto Rico).
2. K. S. Karol, *Guerrillas in Power: The Course of the Cuban Revolution* (New York: Hill and Wang, 1970), p. 144, and authors' interview with Luis Chaviano Reyes (August 28–29, 1972, San Juan, Puerto Rico), who described Bayo's classes to the authors as "extremely theoretical in content."
3. Authors' interview with Carlos Prío and Luis Chaviano. The expeditionaries were Calixto Sánchez White, Héctor Cornillot, Fernando Mirelles, José Raufull, Juan J. Fornes, José Suezcun, Gustavo, Joaquín and Humberto de Blanck, Roberto Martínez, Osvaldo Agüero, Sergio Sierra, Mario Rodríguez Arena, Jorge Prieto Ibarra, Cleto R. Collado, Luis V. Roque, Ernesto Ceballos, José M. Iglesias, Saúl Delgado, José Aguirre, Manolo Roque, Lázaro Guerra, Frank Pujol, Antonio M. Casares, Pedro González Mir, Aníbal C. Stakerman. David Figueredo stayed in the Dominican Republic when the bulk of the group left for Miami.
4. Chaviano to the authors. Also, authors' interview with Francisco ("Pancho") Varona (September 1972, Miami, Florida).

5. Colonel Fermín Cowley Gallegos, "Resúmen de operaciones militares efectuadas en el Regimiento 8 de la Guardia Rural 'Calixto García,'" Ché (Havana: Instituto del Libro, 1969), pp. 217–21.

6   "La gesta del Corinthia," *Bohemia* (Havana), May 24, 1959, pp. 74–75, 96.

7. The consensus of all the interviewed was that the officer who carried out Colonel Cowley's order was Lieutenant Fernandez Chirino. Chaviano told the authors that one of the survivors, Cornillot, charged that officer with the crime.

8. "Nota de prensa," *Parte oficial del Estado Mayor del Ejército* (Havana: Campamento Militar de Columbia, May 29, 1957), p. 1.

9. General Luis Robainas Piedra, "Radiograma cifrado al Coronel Fermín Cowley Gallegos, Jefe Regimiento 8 GR, Holguín." in *Ché*. p. 217.

10. His appointment by the M-26-7 Dirección Nacional to national chief of action and sabotage came after the November 30 uprising, during which he demonstrated outstanding qualities of leadership, discipline and coordination. See Nydia Sarabia, ". . . Ymi honda es la de David," *Bohemia* (Havana), July 28, 1967, p. 7; Fidel Castro Ruz, "Speech at Krakow's Frank País School," *Granma Weekly Review* (Havana), June 18, 1972, p. 7; and Faustino Pérez, "Carta de Faustino Pérez a los compañeros y compañeras de Santiago. Sierra Maestra, August 12, 1958," in *Lunes de Revolución* (Havana), no. 19, July 26, 1959, p. 29.

11. The available evidence indicates Frank País did plan to move to Sierra Cristal or Sierra Maestra sometime during the summer of 1957, but not later than the fall of 1957, to join the guerrillas (Authors' interview with Silvia Alvarez, telephone operator in Santiago de Cuba and member of the M-26-7, New York, New York, June 25, 1972). On this point, the official position given after 1959 was that Frank País always remained reluctant to go to the Sierra despite many such suggestions. See "Frank País: sus últimos días," *Bohemia* (Havana), July 31, 1970, p. 6; Enrique Pineda Barnet, "Frank País: los héroes de tú a tú," Cuba *Internacional* (Havana), October 1968, p. 117; "Frank País," *Bohemia* (Havana), July 23, 1965, p. 21. Agustín País, brother of the late Frank, and for a period of time chief of action and sabotage at both city and provincial level in Santiago de Cuba, asserts that "Fidel Castro blocked Frank from joining him in the Sierra despite knowing that if (Frank) stayed in Santiago, his end was very near" (Letter from Agustín País to the authors, November 14, 1972, p. 2).

12. The Santiago de Cuba intelligence section of the M-26-7 was most powerful at the Central Telephone Company, where M-26-7 telephone operators, under Vilma Espín y Guillois, leader of the women's sector, gathered data on Santiago's police and army movements by monitoring telephone or microwave transmittals. Evidence of Zoraida Jiménez, M-26-7 operator (June 26, 1972, West New York, New Jersey), corroborated by Silvia Alvarez in interview with the authors. Also see "Vilma Espín," in Carlos Franqui, *Cuba: el libro de los doce* (Mexico: Ediciones Era, 1966), p. 157.

13. According to Frank País, before and after the November uprising there were 25 members with executive ranking in the M-26-7 in Cuba as well as abroad. See "Carta de Frank País a Fidel Castro, July 7, 1957," *Pensamiento Crítico* (Havana), no. 29, July 1969, p. 253. The authors offer the following list of members for the period of mid-1956 to mid-1957; Fidel Castro, Frank País,

Armando Hart Dávalos, Haydée Santamaría Cuadrado, Vilma Espín, Celia Sánchez, Faustino Pérez, Enrique Oltusky, Lester Rodríguez, Pedro Miret, Gustavo Arcos, Enrique Hart Dávalos, Carlos Franqui, David Salvador, Jesús Montané, Maria Antonia Figueroa, René de los Santos, José ("Pepe") Suárez, Gloria Guadras, Melba Hernández, Luis Benito, Antonio ("Ñico") López, Gustavo ("Machaco") Ameijeiras, Mario Hidalgo, Marcelo Fernández Font and a host of couriers travelling among the provinces and abroad. See Ernesto "Che" Guevara, "Un año de lucha armada," Ché (Havana: Instituto del Libro, 1969), pp. 106–7; Marta Rojas, "Los días que precedieron a la expedición del Granma," *Bohemia* (Havana), December 27, 1959, pp. 10–13; 139–40; Gregorio Ortega, "Frank País," *Lunes de Revolución* (Havana), no. 19, July 26, 1959, pp. 16–18; and *Revolución* (Havana), July 26, 1959, p. 7.

14. The arms in question were those belonging to the group of Ignacio González. These were loaded on two trucks and taken from a warehouse at Amparanes Street by Faustino Pérez and Luis ("Gallego") Fernández, Ricardo Bianchi, whose task was to rent places to hide DR members and arms stockpiles told the authors that when he arrived at the warehouse to rescue the weapons these were gone, Later, Julio García Oliveras told Bianchi he had promised those weapons to the M-26-7 (Evidence of Ricardo Bianchi to the authors, August 29, 1972, San Juan, Puerto Rico), See also Robert Taber. M-26: *The Biography of a Revolution* (New York: Lyle Stuart, 1961), pp. 137–39. Taber, a CBS cameraman, interviewed Fidel Castro at the Sierra Maestra in April 1957.

15. Ernesto "Che" Guevara, *Obra revolucionaria* (Mexico: Ediciones Era, 1967), p. 154.

16. Ibid.

17. Guevara, *Obra revolucionaria*, pp. 161–62. The arms were transported by boats belonging to the Babún brothers, wealthy lumbermen who helped Fidel often, and delivered in Manzanillo, or about 200 miles from the Sierra Maestra. According to Bob Taber, the arms consisted of "six heavy machine guns, a bazooka and rockets for it, ten light guns, a dozen U.S. Army M-l semi-automatic rifles, and thousands of rounds of ammunition. . . ." See Robert Taber, *M-26: Biography of a Revolution*, pp. 139–40; Guevara gives a somewhat different list of weapons: "3 tripod machine guns, 3 Madzen machine gun rifles, 9 M-l, 10 Johnson rifles, and 6,000 rounds of ammunition." See Guevara, *Obra revolucionaria*, p. 162. It is with these weapons that Castro's 127 men attacked the El Uvero army post on May 28, and presumably it was this military action conceived by Fidel that led País to turn most of the DR weapons over to Fidel.

18. René Ramos Latour had been appointed by Frank País chief of Oriente's northern zone, i.e., the Sierra Cristal area and adjacent towns like Nicaro, Mayarí, Banes, Antilla and Preston. Latour had also organized the M-26-7 militias throughout the island; he was País' closest *compañero*. See Humberto Hernández, "Daniel: un comandante del pueblo," *Lunes de Revolución* (Havana), no. 19. July 26, 1959, pp. 26–27.

19. See "El Comandante Daniel," *Bohemia* (Havana), July 30, 1965, pp. 46–47.

20. See "Carta de Frank País Fidel Castro, July 5, 1957," *Pensamiento Critico* (Havana, 1968), p. 43, Guevara, referring to the attack on the Miranda sugar mill, later remarked that "Field was opposed to splitting up the forces but he

acquiesced because of the *llano* insistence." As the evidence demonstrates, at no time did Fidel support the Miranda attack thus rendering Guevara's statement as untrue. See Guevara, *Obra revolucionaria*, p. 185.

21. "El Comandante Daniel," p. 47.

22. See "Frank País," *Bohemia* (Havana), July 23, 1965, p. 21; "Frank País: sus últimos días," *Bohemia* (Havana), July 31, 1970, p. 6. That Santiago's police and army officers were ready for "the kill" is proven in a series of articles by Lieutenant Colonel Nelson Carrasco Artiles, on supervisory duties for the regular army in Santiago. See Nelson Carrasco Artíles, "El que mal anda, mal acaba: muerte de Frank País," *América Libre* (Miami), September 24, 1971, p. 13, and October 1, 1971; and "El que a hierro mata no puede morir a sombrerazos," *América Libre* (Miami), September 17, 1971, p. 13.

23. See note 11 in this chapter.

24. "Carta de Frank País a Fidel Castro, July 5, 1957." *Pensamiento Crítico* (Havana), (1968), pp. 40–43.

25. Frank País had three noms de guerre throughout his involvement in the insurrection: first, "Salvador," then "David," and at the very end of July 1957, Vilma Espín suggested the name "Cristian," with which he signed his last letter. All three of these intentionally had Biblical connotations (Evidence of Mayra Rodríguez, member of Santiago's First Baptist Church, who sang in the choir with Frank País, New York, N.Y., July 1972).

26. País' last trip to Mexico was in October 1956.

27. País was critical of Fidel's practice of assigning tasks and appointments without consulting with the rest of the members of the national leadership. Mario Llerena was one of those who also felt at a loss and annoyed at the multiplicity of orders and appointees emanating from Fidel, Armando Hart, Lester Rodríguez and Frank País all at once. Agustín País, in letter to the authors dated January 21, 1973, states, "Fidel Castro was never very mindful of those organizations (national and provincial leaderships) preferring instead to work with his own individual choices." It seems that Armando Hart and País had the burdensome task of clarifying some of the confusion of members of the M-26-7 in this respect. See Mario Llerena, "La bilis de los mediocres," *Bohemia* (Havana), March 29, 1959, p. 103, 125; and Mario Llerena, "The Unsuspected Revolution," unpublished manuscript, p. 156.

28. Armando Hart, Haydée Santamaría and Faustino Pérez, among others, emphasized in their contacts with other groups in Havana, that they expected a long period of struggle at the Sierra Maestra.

29. Frank País had sought the aid of Regino Boti, professor of economics at Oriente University, Baudilio Castellanos, in charge of the propaganda sector of Santiago, and Carlos Olivares, who would discuss the race issue. Raúl Chibás, who spoke with Frank País in Santiago, before reaching Sierra Maestra, was aware that this program was under preparation (Authors' interview with Raúl Chibás, December 1972, New York, New York).

30. "Carta de Frank País a Fidel Castro, July 7, 1957," *Pensamiento Crítico* (Havana), no. 29, June 1969, pp. 252–57.

31. See Rolando Bonachea and Nelson P. Valdés, *Revolutionary Struggle, 1947–1958: Volume I of the Selected Works of Fidel Castro* (Cambridge, Mass.: MIT Press, 1972), for the text of the Sierra Maestra Manifesto,

pp. 343–48. Though this manifesto was formally signed on July 12, 1957, it was not released to the press until it appeared in the July 28 issue of *Bohemia* (Havana), pp. 69, and 96–97, under the heading of "To the People of Cuba." On this issue the authors asked Raúl Chibás if Frank País had knowledge of the reasons why he and Pazos had been asked to the Sierra Maestra. Chibás stated, "I presume that Frank País knew we would make some *pronuncia-miento* once we got to the Sierra" (Chibás to the authors, December 1972, New York, New York).

32. Bonachea and Valdés, *Revolutionary Struggle*, pp. 348–49.

33. "Carta del Estado Mayor del Ejército Rebelde a Frank País," *Vida Universitaria* (Havana), 19, no. 213 (September–December 1968): 40; and Bonachea and Valdés, *Revolutionary Struggle*, pp. 349–50.

34. See "Letter to Frank País," in Bonachea and Valdés, *Revolutionary Struggle*, pp. 348–49. This letter has been translated in its entirety from the original which appeared in *Granma* (Havana), July 7, 1968, p. 9. But the original letter has been excerpted for unknown reasons, since Fidel wrote in the last paragraph "I have covered the questions that interest you the most." There is no doubt, given Frank's answer to Fidel's July 21 letter, that Fidel discussed the revamping of the national leadership as envisioned by País and other M-26-7 members in his letter of July 7, 1957 to Castro. Other excerpts of this letter are found in Regis Debray, *Revolution in the Revolution?* (New York: Grove Press, 1967), pp. 85, 112–13.

35. This descriptive reference to the dead "young man's" physical features and age match those of Frank País at the time.

36. "La última carta de Frank a Fidel," *Pensamiento Crítico* (Havana), no. 29, June 1969, pp. 258–59.

37. See note 34 above.

38. A reference to the July 21 letter written to Frank by the Rebel Army.

39. Lázaro Torres Hernández, "Ambito de Frank País," *Bohemia* (Havana), July 30, 1971. pp. 64–69.

40. Authors' interviews with people working under País at the time (Zoraida Trimiño, San Juan, Puerto Rico, August 27, 1972; Carlos Coll, New York, New York, June 1972). These interviews were further corroborated by those with Silvia Alvarez, Zoraida Jiménez and Mayra Rodríguez. According to these interviewees Vilma Espín, one of Frank's closest collaborators in the underground, was in charge of the eastern passageway to Sierra Maestra via El Cobre; Celia Sánchez, on the other hand, was in charge of the western passageway to Sierra Maestra via the Purial de Jibacoa to Pilón.

41. Evidence given to the authors by four former members of the M-26-7 Santiago underground (Alberto Chaples Alonso, New York, New York, September 9, 1972; Mario A. Garrigó, New York, New York, September 10, 1972; Luis P. Justo, New York, New York, September 9, 1972, and Norberto R. Palacios, New York, New York, September 10, 1972).

42. Agustín País, in a letter to the authors (January 21, 1973) confirms that these persons knew of Frank's hideout, and adds that probably the chief of the civic resistance, at Santiago—charged with selecting certain houses for hideouts—also knew. Vilma Espin's version is that Raúl Pujol's house had been vetoed as a hideout because it did not have a back door. See Franqui, *Cuba: el libro de los doce*, p. 157.

43. Vilma Espin's indirect participation in the events leading to Frank País' death is open to question. Reminiscing, she said, "I spoke to Frank over the phone eight or ten minutes before he was killed." Two days earlier, on the 28th, she had indulged in the same practice. It was common knowledge that an underground fighter did not make calls from private phones, or receive them except in an emergency. According to Vilma, she called Frank in order to find out "Why you have not called me? What is it that has happened'?" Nothing could have been more trivial at this moment in País' life than to explain to Vilma the obvious reasons for his silence, particularly when the police, like the M-26-7 telephone operators, had all private conversations wiretapped. Vilma, in her explanation of the events, says Frank called her twice, something which Frank's excellent conspiratorial habits leave open to debate, then she adds, "But he talked in a hurry. . . . I hung up the phone. . . . I hung up the phone, and in about ten minutes I heard shooting in Santiago. . . ." Since the police were almost on his footsteps during his last 48 hours, it was possible that Vilma's call gave "Massacre" the lead to País' hideout. A former telephone operator from Santiago has asserted to the authors that after Vilma made this call, Colonel Cañizares gave a microwave-relayed order to surround the entire block around Pujol's house (Silvia Alvarez to the authors). For Vilma's version see Carlos Franqui, *Cuba: el libro de los doce*, pp. 157–58.

44. The news of Frank País' death reached Fidel Castro at the Sierra Maestra via radio on the same day. According to Raúl Chibás, who was at Fidel's campsite, there was a baptism that day for a peasant child for whom Fidel was to be godfather. Despite the loss of Santiago's "most courageous, useful, and extraordinary of all our fighters," Fidel went on partaking from a huge "barbecued roast pig, with beer and all to the embarrassment of some at the camp, including myself, who felt deeply Frank País' death" (Raúl Chibás to the authors).

45. Navy sergeant Elpidio Sosa to one of the authors, December 1957, Guanajay, Pinar del Río.

46. Roberto Pavón Tamayo, "Cienfuegos: el 5 de septiembre," *Bohemia* (Havana), September 9, 1966, p. 53. See also Faustino Pérez, "Antecedentes del alzamiento de Cienfuegos," *Revolución* (Havana), September 4, 1962, p. 10; and Aldo Isidrón del Valle. "Movimiento armado del pueblo contra la tiranía," *Revolución* (Havana), September 5, 1963, pp. 2–3.

47. Pavón Tamayo, "Cienfuegos," p. 54.

48. For an account of the events, see Julio Camacho, "El alzamiento de Cienfuegos," *Revolución* (Havana) for the issues of September 5, 6, 7 and 10, 1962.

49. Pavón Tamayo, "Cienfuegos," p. 56.

50. Fulgencio Batista, *Respuesta* (Mexico: Editorial Botas, 1960), pp. 67–68.

51. One of the authors visited the city of Cienfuegos in 1960 and was given a tour of the focal points of the uprising and several accounts of popular participation.

52. Decree no. 2739 was dated September 13, 1955, and signed by Jorge García Montes, prime minister, and Fulgencio Batista, president. See *Gaceta Oficial de la República de Cuba*, no. 215 (September 13, 1955), p. 16014.

53. Interview by one of the authors with a participant in the uprising, Ernesto Mir (Cienfuegos, Las Villas province, March 1960).

54. Colonel Cándido Hernández had already been wounded, and his son and Lieutenant Gregorio Moya Aguila shot to death. See Batista. *Respuesta*, p. 67.

55. Attacking the San Lorenzo School, Captain Sergio Seijas, supervisor of Cienfuegos' Maritime Police, Lieutenant Santos Navarro, and Lieutenant Carlos Cuagra Garrote were killed by the rebels. See Batista, *Respuesta*, p. 68.

56. These and other insurgents were buried in the same grave by Eduardo Soto Galindo and José Canellas. See *Bohemia* (Havana), March 29, 1959, pp. 74–75, 92–93.

57. Some of the rebels killed during and after the uprising included: Lieutenant Dimas Martínez Padilla, Lieutenant Angel Jardín Suárez. Carmelo Rodríguez Leiva, Julián C. González. Juan F. Cárdenas, Heriberto M. Soto, Osvaldo Bosch Arias, Miguel G. Yeras, Pedro González, Francisco Curbelo Molina, Alberto Ríos, René G. Cartaya, Gregorio Hernández, Ernestino C. Rodríguez, Adolfo R. Barrientos, Rubén G. Aguiar, José T. Alonso, Rafael Q. Lorié, Galo M. Soto, Francisco Martínez Martell and Héctor Pérez Llosa. See *Bohemia* (Havana), April 5, 1967. pp. 46–87.

58. In 1959, navy Sergeant Pedro Rodríguez Torres, based at the Chorrera Fortress stated that he had been on board the "September 4" motorboat, and had witnessed large packages resembling human bodies carried into the boat; the boat's attendant, Corporal Alberto Rodríguez Hernández, described the death of José María Pérez, adding that "in one month we made more than eight trips. I believe that over 20 corpses were thrown overboard." See *Bohemia* (Havana), March 29, 1959, pp. 74–75, 92–93.

8

Ideology and Politics

On May 1, 1957, in Santiago de Cuba, the trial of another group of insurrectionists came to an end—a trial that was to have a deep and lasting impact. On that date survivors of the Granma expedition and followers of Frank País in the Santiago uprising were sentenced for rebellion against the state, with one of the court magistrates expressing a dissenting opinion. Judge Manuel Urrutia Lleó absolved the accused for what they had done and attempted to do,[1] for, he said, "the sacred right of resistance against oppression is consecrated by Article 40 of the Constitution of 1940."

Article 40 of the constitution read in part: "The legal dispositions, gubernatorial, or of any other order which regulate the exercise of the rights which this Constitution guarantees, will be null if diminished, restricted, or adulterated. The adequate resistance for the protection of the individual rights heretofore guaranteed is legitimate." Dr. Urrutia held that "armed resistance by the accused is legitimate because it was an attempt to end oppression in Cuba."[2]

In his defense at the trial of the men who attacked the Moncada barracks, Castro had argued for the right to resist despotism. Now a magistrate was supporting Castro and refuting the stand of his colleagues and of the government. Such a gesture was impressive, since it came amidst a climate of repression in which no one opposing the regime was exempt, and from a member of a judiciary branch that had undergone the same moral deterioration as other Cuban institutions.[3] Dr. Urrutia was highly praised by all opposition forces and viciously attacked in official circles. To the opposition, Dr. Urrutia's ruling was evidence of the personal courage and conviction of a judge whose conscience took precedence over his own personal safety. Dr. Urrutia acquired national prestige; in time, he would be the candidate of the M-26-7 for the provisional presidency of the republic, and so recognized by all militant insurrectionary organizations.

M-26-7: Its Ideology

In its formative stages, the M-26-7 was closely identified with the Ortodoxo party. As a political institution, the Ortodoxo party had advocated an electoralist approach to the Cuban dilemma, but unrest in the youth section of the party was signaling the disintegration of a cohesive policy. It was to the young Ortodoxos that Fidel had addressed himself and his ideas since early 1952. Fidel's claim that the M-26-7 was "the revolutionary apparatus of Chibasismo rooted in its masses," and that it had never abandoned [Chibás'] ideals,[4] added further substance to the belief of many Cubans that the M-26-7 was the insurrectionary branch of the Ortodoxos.

During the Moncada phase—from December 1952 to July 1953—there was a total absence of ideological programming concerning Cuba's future in the event that the dictatorship was actually overthrown. This period was solely concerned with engineering an action-oriented attack along the lines of a *coup de force* like Batista's or like García Bárcena's frustrated April 4, 1953 attempt. Thus, it was not until the fall of 1956, with Castro and the future Granma expeditioners in Mexico, that arrangements were made to begin working out the ideological basis of a program, to clarify the vagueness of previous statements.

A special commission was created to carry out the task of outlining to the public the central ideas of the M-26-7. The *Comisión de Programa del M-26-7* was headed by Enrique Oltusky, Carlos Franqui and Armando Hart. One of the early manifestos written by this commission was entitled *"Filosofía revolucionaria,"*[5] but involved a series of generalities that left no doubt as to the intellectual inmaturity and lack of sophistication of the commission's members. This manifesto's only noteworthy statement referred to the concept of idealism versus materialism: "We refute the idealist philosophy because it enslaves man to a divinity, and [we refute] materialism because it enslaves [man] to his own deeds. We uphold the principle that 'Man means freedom in possession of its own destiny.'"[6]

This manifesto was followed by another drafted by Armando Hart and entitled, *"Justificación de la revolución y estrategia frente a la dictadura."*[7] Basically, this manifesto outlined the major differences between the approaches of two generations—the 1930 and the 1950— towards confronting dictatorship. This declaration is, as its title indicates, an attempt to justify the use of violent action against Batista, since "the greatest experience drawn by the new generation from that process [the 1933 revolution] was that the revolution, for every moment and under any circumstances, must be prepared for direct action."

Accordingly, the "counterrevolutionary government of March 10," was confronted with the lack of a civilian instrument capable of meeting the challenge posed by Batista. To Hart, Cuba needed a "civilian instrument with the capability for swift action. . . . Thus the M-26-7 emerged in the public scenario, and supported the direct struggle."

The manifesto went on describing life conditions in Cuba, and the negative characteristics of the regime that "openly incited revolutionary violence." It also analyzed briefly the Mexican and French revolutions and the Cuban struggle of 1933, Welles' intervention and the struggle of the proletariat. The manifesto raised this question: What Cuban government has been able to hold power under total convulsion by the direct action of the masses and the general strike?

Hart dismissed the notion that the Batista government would fight until the last soldier, or that Batista would entrench himself in power through terror.

Last, Hart strongly emphasized the civilian character of the M-26-7 "on which Cuban democracy will rest. Especially during the first months of reorganization, restructuring, and implementation of several changes . . . this apparatus, well equipped and skillful, professing a clear democratic consciousness, will be the guarantee for the revolutionary order. . . ."[8]

These and other "position papers" of the ideological commission of the M-26-7 obviously could not explain to the Cuban people what the M-26-7 would be able to offer them once Batista had been overthrown.[9] As these manifestos stood they were nothing more than barricade tirades conceived amidst preparation for the impending struggle.

Nevertheless, the ideological commission had earlier sought the help of Mario Llerena, a gifted and thoughtful intellectual educated in Cuba and the United States. Armando Hart, Faustino Pérez, Carlos Franqui and Enrique Oltusky had approached Llerena in the summer of 1956, almost a year after Llerena had met with Fidel and the MLR group in Havana.[10] These members of the M-26-7 national leadership asked Llerena to work out an ideological program for the movement, using as guidelines some of the papers that the members of the ideological commission had previously written. According to Llerena, from the meetings at Oltusky's apartment in Havana "the idea of the booklet *Nuestra Razón* (Our Cause) came out."[11]

In September 1956, Llerena made a trip to Mexico, and had an opportunity to meet with Fidel Castro at Teté Casuso's home. There, Castro showed him an economic program that had been drafted by Felipe Pazos and other members of the faculty of Oriente University.[12] Llerena returned to Cuba and devoted himself to the task of writing the ideological program for the movement. In March 1957 the first draft was finished, and Llerena showed it to Faustino Pérez and Marcelo Fernández, who showed no great enthusiasm and, indeed, voiced criticism of certain aspects.[13] In late spring, Llerena was forced to seek asylum in Mexico and there he met Pedro Miret—Fidel's representative. Both discussed at length the ideological contents of the first draft of the program. After some corrections, the draft was sent to Cuba to be studied further by the leadership of the movement. On June 21, 1957, Frank País appointed Llerena as delegate in charge of public relations for the movement abroad, the first official appointment Llerena had received from the Dirección Nacional in Cuba. With the appointment went words of praise, and Llerena was told of "our trust in your capacity and discipline so many times demonstrated in Cuba." At the same time Pedro Miret was assigned the position of "representative of the movement outside Cuba."[14]

Llerena's 32-page manifesto was finally published in Mexico, in June 1957, under the title *Nuestra Razón*.[15] The program was dated "November 1956, Cuba," possibly for two reasons: first, to show that it was the result of discussions in Cuba, and second, because Llerena himself felt it was necessary to show that the movement's actions since 1956 were based upon and responded to a definite political philosophy.

The ideas advanced in *Nuestra Razón* reflected, at the time, the thought of the majority within the M-26-7 Dirección Nacional, and it also identified the organization as a true revolutionary movement with democratic aspirations. The significance of the program lay in the fact that it was the first cohesive discussion of the revolution as envisioned by the fighters of the 1950 generation.

The program-manifesto stated clearly that what the M-26-7 had in mind for Cuba was a "true revolution." The struggle involved more than simply ousting from power those who illegally seized it, and the insurgents would not "be satisfied with a mere substitution of rulers." The manifesto viewed Batista's regime as the result of a series of social conditions which had to be removed before the country could consider itself safe from a return to the praetorian situation. In addition, it announced the movement was working on a "program of serious political, economic, agrarian and educational reforms." the revolution would go to the very roots of Cuba's problems: "an effective reorganization of the democratic system . . . an efficient nationalization of public utilities; an intensive policy of agricultural and industrial development, and a new policy concerning foreign trade."

Two forces were at work in the country's ongoing crisis: one side was represented by Batista and the false oppositionists willing to play the political game; the other side was the insurgents. This simplification of the situation enabled the people to "know, without possibility of confusion," who was on the side of the people. Therefore, the "line has been drawn: on one side the negative forces of colonialist regression, and on the other, the positive forces of revolution."

The still-unfulfilled conditions for independence of the Cuban nation were territorial sovereignty, political organization, an independent economy and a distinctive culture. The program described the country's historical process, including an analysis of U.S. hegemony and interventionist policies in Cuba. The political parties had failed after the 1933 revolution; the Auténticos were discredited, and the Ortodoxos turned out to be "nothing but a curious phenomenon of political philosophy lacking ideological content and a true program of its own."

The features of Cuba's economy were: a policy of concessions and great monopoly in the area of public utilities; gigantic concessions to foreign interests; unconditional grants to foreign companies of the most important mineral deposits in the country (nickel, manganese, iron, oil); and a policy of privilege and laissez-faire for the benefit of large foreign investors. Furthermore, the social laws that supposedly protected the workers were being abrogated. The situation could be changed only through the concerted action of a new generation, under the banner of a "national doctrine, and with a firm, patriotic conviction." The revolution could not be one of restoration or punitive action "solely committed to the overthrow of the brigands who usurped power." It was to go beyond that. For such a pursuit, the Sierra Maestra symbolized the "logical antecedent to the revolutionary program." The struggle would consist of two phases: first, the insurrection, a destructive process through which the regime would be reduced to ashes; second, the revolution, the rebuilding of the republic and the realization of its full "integration," i.e., political sovereignty, economic independence and a national culture. The movement was to avoid "abstract formulas and imported solutions"; its ideology would emerge from the very "flesh of Cuba." The political thinking of the M-26-7 was specifically "democratic, nationalist, and for social justice." Accordingly, the M-26-7 democratic concepts were rooted on the Jeffersonian and Lincolnian assertions of "the government of the people, for the people, and by the people." Based upon the principle of respect for the dignity of the human being, the M-26-7 claimed it was inspired by José Martí's deeply humanistic philosophy.

One of the paramount objectives of the revolution would be the affirmation of the complete and total sovereignty of Cuba, and sovereignty would apply to political as well as economic relations with other nations. The principle of economic independence would take form only when the "greater percentage of the net profit of the national product reverts to the country itself." Education was to be another priority for the future revolutionary government. Education was viewed as the "deliberate, organized process of didactical and environmental factors which, aside from providing knowledge and vocational guidance, will seek to develop the fundamental qualities of citizenship and patriotism in the individual."

The movement considered that all political parties in Cuba lacked true ideological content, and it pointed out that the main problems of Cuban society were "corrupt politicians, personality cults, a low degree of civic alertness [political consciousness] in the masses, and political neutrality [political alienation]." As a result of these there were "electoral mercantilism, vote mockery, police abuse and military predominance, messianism and dictatorship." The M-26-7 program upheld the predominance of civilian leadership over military leadership, quoting Martí's phrase: "A nation cannot be established as a military camp is run." To secure a democratic future, the M-26-7 pledged that there would be full freedom of individual rights, a principle rooted in the "political foundation on which Western democracies stand."

The Cuban revolutionary government would advocate the integration of all the American republics. The government would favor a policy of rapprochement rather than isolation, and of friendship rather than enmity toward all the American republics. Cuba's relations with Latin America would have priority over any kind of "non-hemispheric international relations." On U.S.-Cuban relations, the M-26-7 proposed its own doctrine of "constructive friendship," an attitude primarily understood as calling for an ethical approach to all issues arising from the relationship, especially in the areas of economy and culture. The M-26-7 considered that the term "imperialism is no longer rightly applicable to the American realities," although there were still conditions of economic penetration, accompanied by political influence, which caused "great harm, moral as well as material to the affected countries." The doctrine of "constructive friendship" would enable Cuba to be an ally of the United States, and at the same time maintain its sovereign right to guide its own national destiny. By means of new, just agreements, it would be possible "without undue sacrifices, or humiliating submission to increase the natural advantages of proximity."

Viewed as a whole, *Nuestra Razón* was a major effort to provide the M-26-7 with a doctrinal structure it had previously lacked. But many of its tenets had been exhibited earlier in Antonio ("Tony") Guiteras' Joven Cuba program in 1934.[16] *Nuestra Razón* left no doubt as to the major thrust of the M-26-7 struggle: the development of sound political institutions that answered the needs of society and abided by the statutes of the 1940 constitution, a strong economy that responded to national rather than foreign interests, and a viable educational system that enabled Cuba to prepare her infrastructure for rapid development. What was sadly lacking in *Nuestra Razón*, and for that matter, in the Sierra Maestra Manifesto and subsequent statements from Fidel Castro, was a candid discussion on the subject of social integration. In neither of these declarations was the Negro issue ever spelled out clearly or at all, even though Fidel Castro had in 1949 been a member of the University Committee Against Racial Discrimination led by Juan René Betancourt in the city of Havana.[17]

Nuestra Razón reached Cuba, and was the subject of a letter from Marcelo ("Zoilo") Fernández, dated July 22, 1957. In that letter Marcelo reported that he had shown the manifesto to Armando Hart ("Jacinto" and later "Darío"), Haydée Santamaría ("María") and Enrique Oltusky ("Sierra"). They all agreed with the principles advocated in the manifesto, and Marcelo suggested that the booklet's cover be changed and that it be specifically pointed out that the program was the work of the "Propaganda Secretariat" of the M-26-7.[18] Then, a few lines later, Marcelo told Llerena that "the programmatic manifesto of the movement" was being written "in its definitive form right now in the Sierra, and we would not like to give the impression of there being two programmatic manifestos."[19] On October 15, 1957, Armando Hart commented on the manifesto, and hoped it could be "widely distributed." He noticed that it was not "a final document" but that it provided the basis for further work. He suggested that Carlos Franqui join Llerena, Miret and others in writing a new manifesto that conveyed "certain aspects of the political thinking of our leaders."[20]

On July 28, 1957, the Sierra Maestra Manifesto was issued to the people of Cuba in the pages of *Bohemia*.[21] In neither of these revolutionary manifestos or programs was any reference made to Castro's "History Will Absolve Me," or his previous "Manifiesto a la Nación." The Sierra Maestra Manifesto, however, posited an important point for all movements and parties involved in the opposition to Batista: it called for unity, which at the time was one of the main considerations of the public.

The Tampa Declaration

The call for unity was endorsed in October 1957, when a committee was formed by representatives of the M-26-7, the DR and the Auténticos. This committee published a declaration known as the "Tampa Declaration" because its signatories had met in Tampa, Florida.[22] The significance of the declaration resided in the fact that those who pressed for it were militants of the various groups involved in insurrectionary activities. It further expressed the front-line fighters' desire that their leaders would respond to the need for unity in the struggle against Batista. For, despite all the growing opposition, the dictatorship continued in power, and victory was nowhere near. Therefore, it was necessary for the militants to declare that all groups must unite behind one single organization—putting aside individualism and sectarianism—so that the insurgents could confront the regime on equal terms.

After listing the efforts that the opposition had carried out against Batista, the declaration decried "these mass immolations and heroic acts (which) have not crystallized into a true revolutionary unity, but [which] have always been carried out by isolated parties or groups, without the aid, knowledge or support of other similar organizations." As the signatories of the declaration saw it, the lack of revolutionary cohesiveness, both in terms of strategy and tactics, had not made a dent on the regime. No doubt, "had there been a central organization . . . with authorative and coordinated power, able to lay out the revolutionary strategy to produce simultaneous attacks against barracks and in the cities. Batista would no longer be discharging his role of despot . . . nor so many men would be dead, or so much effort wasted."

The committee expressed the opinion that the insurrection was not being fought for any one leader or organization in particular but for the freedom of Cuba. Thus, "it is an undeniable fact that the Cuban cause is above *personalismo* [the cult of personality] or *sectarianismo* [loyalty to a particular organization], and it is beyond understanding why Cubans have not finally realized that only through unity, not through atomization, will victory be achieved." An insurrection, the committee stated, "cannot be the work of wild men who, like wild horses, run blindly through an abyss, nor can a revolution be the outcome of anarchy and unpremeditation. Above all, it cannot be the work of isolated groups without linkages among them."

The committee contended that too many lessons had been learned only through the defeats of the various groups involved in the struggle. It was imperative, then, to create common resources, in terms of ideals and also of war materiel, because such a step would shorten the insurrectionary process. "We," said the declaration, "must be practical. We must direct our behavior with logic. We cannot reveal ourselves simply as *Quijotes*, but we must step down from the rosy clouds of our dreams to the earthly realities and from time to time become *Sanchos*. Idealism must not make us blind. Group spirit and *caudillismo* must not override our deserving condition as Cubans. For Cuba is above all caudillos and personalities, and above all political creeds."

Through this little-known episode of the insurrection, the committee tried to unite the militants so that the leaders would have no alternative but to support the will of the majority, who were dying while their leaders argued with one another. It was the committee's rationale that "upon realizing the union of the revolutionary masses, the leaders will follow, joining their activities in a well-defined and thought-out program forming one single front, powerful and capable with one single blow of crushing the despicable dictatorship."

Junta de Liberación Cubana

With both the militants and Castro calling for a united revolutionary front, unity seemed inevitable. From September to October, representatives of the different movements held a series of discussions in Miami, and everyone agreed that a common front should be created as soon as possible. In the spirit of both the Tampa Declaration, which reflected the consensus of public opinion in Cuba, and the Sierra Maestra Manifesto, several political figures began conversations aimed at creating an organization through which unity would become feasible. The results of these explorative talks was the establishment of the Junta de Liberación Cubana.

The junta was controlled by former president Carlos Prío. With the exception of the DR and the FEU, the participants were all representatives of the old politics: the PRC-Auténticos, represented by Carlos Prío and Manuel ("Tony") Varona; the Ortodoxos, represented by Roberto Agramonte and Manuel Bisbé; the OA, by Carlos Maristani; and the Revolutionary Labor Directorate, by Angel Cofiño and Marcos Irigoyen. The DR was represented by Faure Chomón; and Ramón Prendes, Juan Nuiry and Omar Fernández represented the FEU.

The background of some of the individuals of the junta demonstrated beyond doubt the Prío really made the junta's decisions. In addition to his own PRC-A, Prío controlled the OA, the insurrectionary instrument of the Auténticos. Its representative to the junta, Carlos Maristani, had been Prío's secretary of communications (1948-52), while "Tony" Varona had been Prío's prime minister during that period. Angel Cofiño and Irigoyen were labor leaders closely associated with the Auténticos, and had been completely dependent on the party for control of their respective unions in Cuba before Batista's coup d'etat. The FEU was financed by Carlos Prío. Even Faure Chomón, of the DR, had been initiated into his insurrectionary activities by Aureliano Sánchez Arango's Triple A, an organization also financed by Prío. Other political figures present at the discussions were José R. Andreu, former secretary of health under Prío, and José M. Gutiérrez, an Ortodoxo who had signed the Pact of Montreal in 1953 to unite the Ortodoxos with the Auténticos.

In Miami, Lester Rodríguez (who was in charge of war materiel for the M-26-7) and Felipe Pazos had made their own decision to represent the M-26-7 in the junta.[23] However, on October 20, Pazos wrote to the Dirección Nacional in Cuba, telling them that he would submit to them the junta's basic tenets for their approval. Only with that approval would he continue to represent Castro's movement in the junta.

Felipe Pazos' presence in the junta was welcomed by the politicians. Not only was Pazos associated with Fidel Castro, but he had signed the Sierra Maestra Manifesto after travelling to the Sierra Maestra, something no other participant had done. Pazos' recent travels in the mountains of Oriente gave him a certain romantic aura. But he was a conservative economist who owed his job as president of the National Bank of Cuba to Carlos Prío. He also belonged to the generation of 1930, and was not a radical *bombista* (bomb thrower), an appellation given by old and corrupt politicians to some members of the new generation.

The basic assumptions of the junta were quite flexible. The group totally rejected the electoralist approach, a fact that placed some undecided politicians on the side of the insurrection with no further political opportunity in Batista's Cuba. The council's declaration called for a provisional government, the restoration of the 1940 constitution and general elections within 18 months of the overthrow of the regime, during which time a minimum program of reform would be enforced. The council set forth the following objectives of such revolutionary programs:[24]

1. Immediate freedom for all political prisoners, civilian and military, and the reestablishment of civil rights.
2. Introduction of a penal system to end graft.
3. A civil service law.
4. Establishment of an improved educational system, scientific research, technical training and programs for the preservation of the country's national resources.
5. Improvement of government agencies and institutions destroyed by the dictatorship.
6. Financial stability, and fostering financial credit for the country.
7. Free elections in every labor union.
8. A higher standard of living for workers and peasants by means of the creation of new industries, and the development of agriculture and mining.

The document requested that "until such time when peace prevails in Cuba, the government of the United States must suspend all arms shipments to the regime . . . since the dictatorship is using them against the Cuban people, and not for the defense of the continent." The armed forces were to be completely set apart from politics, while the armed institutions would be reorganized to guarantee the role of the military under a democratic system of government.

Five days after the release of these points, Armando Hart, on behalf of the Dirección Nacional of the M-26-7, addressed a letter to Lester Rodríguez and Felipe Pazos, stating the position of the movement. The M-26-7, Hart asserted, "is an organization that has come of age." Even though some politicians saw it as a branch of the Ortodoxos, Hart made clear that it could not be "taken as a part or branch of any other political group in the country. The fact that some of our leaders, Fidel Castro in particular, have come from the Ortodoxo party does not mean that [the movement] is to be considered a branch of that party."[25] Hart noted the distinction between the political parties before the coup d'etat and the M-26-7, holding the former responsible for the tragedy that confronted the new generation. It was a choice between "revolutionary insurrection" and "politics."

That letter was followed by a communique, dated October 26, addressed also to Lester and Pazos, protesting the way in which the basic principles of the junta had been published "before the members of the Dirección Nacional have had a chance to approve or disapprove of them."[26] In the face of a fait accompli, however, the M-26-7 had no alternative but to extend to Pazos credentials to officially represent the movement in the junta. The document made it clear, however, that the junta's doctrine appeared to be "clever political trickery of certain discredited leaders of the opposition who are simply trying . . . to stop the growing strength shown by civic groups in Cuba."[27] Instructions to Pazos followed: no executive official of the junta was to be a candidate for the ensuing elections; the junta should proceed to organize a government in exile, and to ask the civic institutions to select a provisional president and various officers of the provisional government; the M-26-7 would not participate in the exile government. Four days later, Fidel Castro wrote a letter to Mario Llerena announcing the creation of a committee in exile to represent the M-26-7. The committee in exile was to be represented by: Llerena as secretary of propaganda and public relations; Carlos Franqui, organization; Lester Rodríguez, arms and supplies; and Raúl Chibás, finances. Because Llerena had "expressed with perfect clarity the position that the M-26-7 should maintain despite the chaotic confusion prevailing among the political parties,"[28] Castro recommended that he be nominated as chairman.

Felipe Pazos' reaction was to withdraw from the junta altogether. Mario Llerena then assumed official representation at the junta, and the discussions centered around "Tony" Varona's proposal that a similar junta be created in Cuba to coordinate the strategy for the insurrection. Llerena rejected the move, for it would have reduced the M-26-7 to a subordinate position. This conflict led to an impasse, and the junta's meetings were postponed for further discussions.

If confusion was predominant among the junta members, likewise there was confusion within the ranks of the M-26-7. Fidel's objective was not to become involved in the exiles' machinations, but to conduct a guerrilla war against a regular army. Speaking on behalf of Castro and the Dirección Nacional, Armando Hart asked Llerena to propose that the junta dissolve in favor of a more representative group which would include those Cuban civic institutions which the M-26-7 controlled. Hart's main concern was with making a good impression on all entrenched interest groups in the country, and with conveying the idea that the insurrectionists were engaged in forming an apolitical provisional government. He wrote that "such interests are the military, the banks, big business, big sugar cane planters, etc. They are just the social elements on whom we want to impress our determination to form a government free of political partisanship."[29] A list of five candidates for the provisional presidency arrived from Santiago de Cuba: José Miró Cardona, Raúl de Velasco, Manuel Urrutia Lleó. Felipe Pazos and Justo Carrillo. Of the five, Pazos had the support of the majority of the delegates, excluding only the M-26-7 and the Ortodoxos. Llerena recommended that the Dirección Nacional give its support to Judge Urrutia, and the politicking in exile raged on.[30]

Beneath the charges and countercharges, there actually was a "secret deal" between Carlos Prío, Lester Rodríguez and Jorge Sotús, representing the M-26-7. Prío was to finance a $90,000 operation, of which $30,000 was to be contributed by the M-26-7. When Llerena proposed Urrutia for president, only the Ortodoxos backed his candidacy. The DR and the FEU strongly objected to it, since they were also hoping to receive some financial aid from Carlos Prío. And Prío's candidate was Felipe Pazos.[31]

Thus, Llerena reported to Cuba, "when the turn came for designating the fifth candidate. Urrutia in this case, the junta fell into another impasse, each delegation requesting time for consultation."[32] A few days later, Llerena asked to be relieved of his post, since it was his feeling that more important things could be accomplished elsewhere for the insurrection instead of engaging in the useless game of politicking.

On December 9, Hart again wrote on behalf of the Dirección Nacional. Hart explained to Llerena that the civic institutions had requested that a new article be added to the junta's provisions allowing them to support a president for the provisional government. That changed the situation, and now Hart informed Llerena that he was submitting the entire matter to Fidel for his decision. The decision soon came.

Castro versus Chomón

In a letter addressed to the junta dated December 14, 1957,[33] Fidel stated that the M-26-7 had not authorized any of its overseas representatives to participate in discussions. Lester Rodríguez, a Moncada veteran and Castro's delegate in Miami, could only act as the military delegate abroad. He wrote that it was only natural that any "agreement of unity should be well received by national and world opinion, because, among other reasons, the real situation of the political and revolutionary forces opposing Batista is not known abroad. And in Cuba the word 'unity' had much prestige when the coalition of forces was quite different from what it is today. Finally, it is always positive to join all efforts, from the most enthusiastic to the most timid." For Castro the crucial point was not unity itself but the basis for such unity, "the form in which it is made possible and the patriotic intentions that inspire it." Castro called the Pact of Miami a fraudulent maneuver to force his movement to explain to the public why it could not accept such an agreement. He cited a number of complaints against the other insurrectionary organizations. One of them infuriated the leaders of the DR. Castro wrote that "while the leaders of other organizations are living abroad carrying on imaginary revolutions, the leaders of the M-26-7 are in Cuba, making a real revolution."

Then he advanced his reasons for rejecting the resolutions of the junta, the so-called Pact of Miami: "To delete from the unity document the evident declaration refusing any kind of foreign intervention in the internal affairs of Cuba is evidence of the most lukewarm patriotism and one of self-manifested cowardice."

Castro asserted that even with Batista's overthrow the threat of a military takeover would remain very serious. He attacked the old politicians who lacked faith in the people's will to fight for, "if you do not have faith in the people, if you do not count on their great reserves of energy and combativeness, you do not have the right to lay hold of their destiny."

What Castro was really rejecting was a unity pact that would place his movement on an equal footing with the rest. Up to then, two organizations, the M-26-7 and the DR, had carried the full weight of the insurrection. Under the Pact of Miami, all other movements ascribed to themselves the same stature as these two organizations. The DR was ready to accept this; Castro was not. Castro continued to impress his own military power upon the organizations represented at the council. He claimed that his men were no longer fighting a guerrilla war but a war of confrontation. This was simply not true. Guevara, for example, wrote at about the same period that the guerrillas were "in a state of armed truce with Batista; his men did not go up into the Sierra and ours hardly ever went down."[34] Castro claimed that his movement was ready for an offensive against Batista, and that because the M-26-7 had an "excellent organization" throughout the island, a general strike would soon be called. The workers' section of the M-26-7 was organizing strike committees "in every labor and industrial center . . ." to prepare the Cuban proletariat for the revolutionary general strike. Actually, the "excellent organization" to which Castro referred was just then extending into the western provinces, mainly through the efforts of René Ramos Latour, Manuel Ray and other professionals involved in the underground movement.[35] Early in 1958, the M-26-7 was concentrating on organizing strike committees in every labor center, but the workers generally refused to get involved. If the M-26-7 had had the organization Castro claimed it had in December 1957, the general strike of April 9, 1958, would not have been a disaster.

The war, Castro declared, was going very well for his movement, although in the next paragraph he complained of lack of arms, stating that "the heart bleeds and the spirit is afflicted at the thought that no one has sent these people a gun."[36] But in spite of the lack of arms, Fidel argued, his movement was ready to initiate an offensive against the army. The letter stated that there was a condition of revolt throughout Cuba, which was the sole responsibility of the M-26-7. "It was the M-26-7, and no one else," he claimed, "which brought the revolt from the rugged mountains of Oriente to the western provinces."

In his letter, Fidel presented a distorted picture of the organizational process and the progress made by his movement. "Che" Guevara did not agree with Fidel's evaluation of the situation. At that time, "Che" wrote, the M-26-7 had organizationally "developed sufficiently to have by the year's end [1957] an elementary organization . . . and other minimal services."[37] Fidel stated that they were ready for an offensive, but Guevara wrote that "our ammunition was limited in quantity and lacking the necessary assortment." While Castro was claiming that the revolt had been pushed all the way to the western provinces, Guevara was attempting to create a network of communications to "cope with our difficulties."

Castro went on to describe his demands to the council and to other organizations engaged in the struggle.

> The Revolutionary Movement of the 26th of July claims for itself the functions of maintaining public order and of reorganizing the armed institutions of the Republic, for the following reasons:
>
> 1. Because the M-26-7 is the only organization that has a disciplined and organized militia in the entire territory, and an army waging a campaign with 20 victories over the enemy.
> 2. Because our combatants have shown a spirit of chivalry and an absence of hatred toward the enemy, always respecting the lives of prisoners, healing their battle wounds, never torturing an adversary . . . and maintaining this behavior with unprecedented serenity.
> 3. Because it is necessary to instill in the armed forces this spirit of justice and gallantry which the M-26-7 has instilled in its own soldiers.
> 4. Because the objectivity with which we have proceeded in this struggle is the best guarantee that honorable military persons have nothing to fear from the revolution, nor do they have to pay for the errors of those who by their deeds and crimes have stained the uniform with dishonor.[38]

The government Castro supported would be guided by the constitution of 1940 and its main duty would be,

> to bring general elections to the country in accordance with the Electoral Code of 1943 . . . and to develop a minimum program of 10 points set forth in the Sierra Maestra declaration.

The Supreme Court will be declared null and dissolved because it was helpless in solving the *de facto* situation created by the *coup d'état*... [exempting] some of its members since they have defended the constitutional principles, or upheld a firm attitude before crime, arbitrary acts and abuses during these years of tyranny.... The president of the Republic will devise the method for the reorganization of the Supreme Court and the latter will in turn proceed to reorganize all courts and autonomous institutions, while at the same time removing from office all those whom they consider as having had manifest complicity with the dictatorship.

Castro then stated that instead of accepting a nominee appointed by several organizations—as called for by the Sierra Maestra Manifesto—he was nominating his own man for the post of president—Dr. Manuel Urrutia Lleó. Urrutia, Castro said, had raised the stature of the constitution when he declared in the courtroom during the trial of the Granma expeditionaries, that to organize an armed force against the regime was not a crime, but perfectly in agreement with the spirit and the letter of the constitution and the laws. This was an unprecedented stand on the part of a magistrate in the history of Cuba's struggles for liberty. Urrutia's life, Castro said, had been dedicated to the administration of justice, and this was a guarantee that he would serve all legitimate interests once the Batista regime had been deposed. Castro argued that only Urrutia "could remain impartial to partisan politics, since he does not belong to any political group for reasons of his judicial functions. And no other citizen has as much prestige outside the military by virtue of his deep identification with the revolutionary cause."

Castro's dramatic denunciation of the Pact of Miami was a stunning surprise to everyone involved.[39] Among the first to withdraw from the council were the Ortodoxos, followed by the M-26-7 representatives, who did not challenge Castro's decision. Only the DR answered Castro in a letter sent directly to the Sierra Maestra.[40] Written by Faure Chomón, the letter began by saying that "it was with genuine surprise and deep pain as Cubans and revolutionaries, and sharing a legitimate fear as citizens . . . that we have listened to the reading of Dr. Fidel Castro's letter in the name of the M-26-7, which has been sent to the various organizations which make up the Council of Cuban Liberation." The students thought the council by itself could not make the real revolution, a revolution "capable of transforming our rotten economic, political, social and educational systems . . . that will enable Cuba to become a politically free nation, economically independent, and socially just, liquidating once and for all the corrupt policies that have subdued all honest initiatives."

"Unquestionably," the letter continued, "the *Fidelista* decision to withdraw from the council resulted in a coup de grace against the revolutionary unity achieved in Miami." Since Castro had said no representatives of his movement were authorized to enter in such negotiations, the DR asked Lester Rodríguez,

Mario Llerena, Felipe Pazos, Raúl Chibás and Lucas Morán—all of whom had acted as official representatives of the M-26-7—to clarify their position, and to explain what Castro meant when he said that they were not empowered with authority to discuss a unity agreement. "According to his [Castro's] letter," Chomón wrote, "Sr. Lester Rodríguez has authority only as military delegate abroad. Yet, Llerena and Chibás replaced Rodríguez as Fidel Castro's representatives before the council. On more than one occasion, they consulted with the M-26-7 Dirección Nacional in Cuba over matters left resting at the council, to find out if they were of any relevance [to the movement]." Thus it appeared, as the letter argued, that indeed the M-26-7 had authorized the above persons to represent the movement before the council; except that "at the time of choosing a candidate for the provisional presidency of the Republic," an impasse emerged over the question of whether such a candidate should be elected from among the members of the council. On this matter, the first reaction by the Fidelistas, Chomón argued, was not to endorse such proposal, but to check back with the Dirección Nacional and wait for new orders. This, in itself, was enough evidence that the Dirección Nacional was in full knowledge and agreement with the participation of its members in the council that had been established in Miami.

The DR was also unhappy with some of the council's discussions and conclusions. Thus, it was "with evident displeasure that upon learning of numerous programmatic and doctrinal initiatives largely reflecting those of our own organization . . . [they were being] discarded with the acquiescence and approval of the M-26-7 delegation." The DR set forth four points essential to any unity agreement it was to take part in:

1. That all political sectors were to recognize that the correct solution to Cuba's problems was insurrection.
2. That a unity declaration was to make clear that in no way would national sovereignty be minimized.
3. That the council was to be the sole organization charged with selecting the president for the provisional government.
4. That such government was to be committed to a full program of revolutionary change before scheduling elections.

These four points were unanimously accepted by the council, although the M-26-7 delegates rejected the Directorio's proposals with the assistance of older politicians "who have nothing to offer to the Cuban people, much less to those who day after day struggle, fight, and die for the cause of the Cuban revolution."

The DR was opposed to nominating Manuel Urrutia Lleó as president of the nation because the latter had remained passive to the insurrectionary struggle against Fulgencio Batista. The appointment was flatly rejected because no organization "can or should claim for itself the exclusive representation demanded by Dr. Castro of a revolution that belongs to all of Cuba." Faure Chomón argued:

> Here we have the case where Fidel Castro, struggling as we are against a single unipersonal dictatorship, despotic and cruel, is opposed . . . to having the council integrated by varying sectors, or to exercising the right to appoint the president and his assistants. . . . He [Castro] leaves this function to the president himself, as it is done during constitutional normalcy. . . . Later, he indicates that the executive power will assume legislative functions, and in another paragraph of his letter, he points out that the executive "will decide the organization of the Supreme Court," and the latter will then proceed to reorganize all the courts and autonomous institutions. . . . This means that under a single person, all three powers will be gathered: the executive, the legislative and the judiciary. . . . Conspicuously absent is the classic division of powers postulated by Montesquieu, the cornerstone of every modern democratic state . . . thus envisioned by the *lawyer* Fidel Castro.

Obviously these demands were unacceptable to any insurrectionary movement fighting for democratic principles. If the DR agreed to Castro's demands, there would be no transition toward a democratic system, but there would be the great possibility of falling back to praetorian rule. The concentration of all powers under a single person would make a dictator of Urrutia. But Urrutia was not regarded as a potential dictator, although Castro was beginning to exert that impression on many student militants.

Castro's demand for control of the armed forces was totally unacceptable to the DR. If, in addition to appointing the president, Castro was allowed to control the armed forces, another military regime could become possible, To Castro's complaint that no organization had helped his movement, Faure Chomón retorted that on many occasions they had helped the M-26-7. To Castro's poignant remark that no other organizations were involved in insurrectionary activities. Chomón replied that:

> the Cuban people know very well the criminal persecution the Directorio underwent after the attack on the presidential palace on March 13, and a month later, with the sinister blow that cost the lives of four of our main leaders at Humboldt No. 7. Few organizations have gone through such a crisis . . . its best men torn to pieces, and its resources dwindling. Despite this fact, we have never publicly complained when the M-26-7 did not come to our assistance, though we previously advised Faustino Pérez of our intentions [the Palace attack] . . . so that he would provide us arms for the university. . . . There is also the famous interview where Dr. Castro had such deplorable

words for our March 13 action, when he said the attack on the palace was a "useless bloodshed." How much it would have meant for us to hear a word of comradeship in those uncertain moments! We did not hear such words from the Sierra Maestra hero.

In response to Castro's criticism of revolutionaries overseas, Chomón answered:

> Dr. Castro ought to remember that while he was in Mexico and the United States, we continued the struggle, with José Antonio Echeverría always at the vanguard in the streets of Havana; that he [Castro] had not yet arrived on Cuban shores when our Rubén Aldama had been assassinated in May 1956. . . . Dr. Castro should remember that he still had not landed in Oriente when the Directorio was dealing with Blanco Rico and Tabernilla, while he, from Mexico, decried the death of the first.

Chomón continued: "Castro also should remember that while he was in the lofty mountains of Oriente, we in Havana had stormed the Castillo del Príncipe . . . and we were shooting Colonel Orlando Piedra, burning 15 police cars . . . and with courage we went out into the capital itself to meet the despot in his own hideout." Chomón ended by attacking political opportunists and pledging that one by one all the DR men would fall with their chests "covered with bullets" until revolution attained victory.

Faure Chomón's answer was seemingly devastating, but its impact was limited to politics in exile. In Cuba, Fidel had demonstrated within his own M-26-7 that he would not be an instrument of the politicians. Fidel's decision to denounce the junta, and with it all of the politicians in the opposition, had a lasting effect. The M-26-7 had affirmed its independent position, and no further confusion could exist between the M-26-7 and the Ortodoxos. Besides, the former had a power base in Cuba, where it was carrying out an insurrection, a guerrilla war in the mountains, and this in itself, based on revolutionary ethics, asserted Fidel's leadership over the politicians.

Fidel's decision was also important within the Dirección Nacional. It hinted that in the future, no steps were to be taken prior to consultation with Fidel. Armando Hart learned to follow his leader, who was not about to deliver to a group of strategists in exile the movement he had gradually consolidated under his own leadership.

In the remaining months of the insurrection, the politicians' inactivity would demonstrate their inability to carry out decisive actions against the dictatorship. Soon they would go to Fidel. When they did, they would find a flexible insurrectionary leader who needed all the support he could muster to confront the army's "summer offensive."

Notes

1. Manuel Urrutia Lleó. *Fidel Castro & Co.* (New York: Praeger, 1964), pp. 7–10.
2. Ibid.
3. Throughout his 31 years of service in the judiciary, Urrutia was very familiar with the *clasismo* and *caciquismo* pervading the armed forces, especially in the Rural Guards corps which openly abused the *campesinos*. According to him, Cuba had reached such a degree of political and social disintegration as to make an insurrection not only possible but legally justifiable (Authors' interviews with Dr. Manuel Urrutia Lleó, New York, New York, December 1972 and January 1973).
4. See "El Movimiento 26 de Julio," *Bohemia* (Havana), April 1, 1956, pp. 20_23.
5. Enrique Oltusky, Carlos Franqui and Armando Hart, "Filosofía revolucionaria," Comisión de Programa del M-26-7, November, 1956. *Lunes de Revolución* (Havana), no. 19 (July 26, 1959), pp. 6–8.
6. Ibid., p. 6.
7. Armando Hart, "Justificación de la revolución y estrategia frente a la dictadura," M-26-7, November 1956. *Lunes de Revolución* (Havana), no. 19 (July 26, 1959) p. 40.
8. Ibid.
9. Carlos Franqui, for instance, unsuccessfully attempted to conceptualize the basic theoretical differences between "the caudillo and the leader." Evidence from Mario Llerena's manuscript, "The Unsuspected Revolution." p. 72.
10. Mario Llerena, "La bilis de los mediocres," *Bohemia* (Havana), March 29, 1959, p. 102.
11. Ibid.
12. Ibid. See also, "Tesis económica del Movimiento 26 de Julio, de Felipe Pazos y Regino Boti," *Lunes de Revolución* (Havana), no. 138 (May 18, 1959), pp. 40–47. A somewhat revised version is found in Fidel Castro, *Pensamiento político, económico y social* (Havana: Editorial Lex, 1959), pp. 77–105.
13. The criticisms referred to the emphasis given in the text of the manuscript to the M- 26-7 rejection of "Communist totalitarianism," and the lack of a more radical wording. Llerena manuscript, pp. 109–10.
14. Llerena, "La bilis de los mediocres," p. 49.
15. See Mario Llerena, "El Manifiesto Ideológico del 'Movimiento 26 de Julio,'" *Humanismo* (Mexico), 7, no. 44 (July–August 1957); 88-103. For the complete text see "Manifiesto-Programa del Movimiento 26 de Julio," *Humanismo* (Mexico), 7, no. 52. (November–December 1958), 9–40.
16. For a discussion of Antonio ("Tony") Guiteras" program see *Pensamiento revolucionario cubano* (Havana: Instituto del Libro, 1972), pp. 192–98.
17. Betancourt was chairman of the committee; Fidel Castro and Calixto Morales held positions within the committee. Betancourt recalled that the Sierra Maestra Manifesto was a disappointment that caused "unhappiness among the Negro masses because they were not included in such an important document." See Juan René Betancourt, "Fidel Castro y la integración nacional," *Bohemia* (Havana), February 15, 1959, pp. 66, 122–23.
18. Llerena manuscript, p. 157. Marcelo Fernández had at this time been appointed propaganda coordinator of the M-26-7, and thus he was leaving no doubt as to the proper sponsorship of *Nuestra Razón*.

19. This is a reference to the Sierra Maestra Manifesto that, judging from Marcelo's letter, further illustrates how certain members of the M-26-7 Dirección Nacional like Armando Hart, Oltusky, Faustino Pérez and Marcelo himself, knew well in advance of the manifesto's impending release. Only Frank País, national chief of action and sabotage, was kept in the dark about this important document.

20. Llerena manuscript, p. 159. Hart felt very confident that he and Carlos Franqui were far more intellectually qualified to write a theoretical work discussing leadership concepts than Llerena. But the available insurrectionary literature hardly bears him out on this point.

21. For a discussion of the Sierra Maestra document see chapter 6.

22. *Manifiesto del Comité Pro-Unidad Revolucionaria* (Tampa, Fla., October 1957), pp. 1–15 (authors' copy). This manifesto was signed by militants of the Triple A, OA, the M-26-7, DR and the Federación de Mujeres Martianas.

23. Of Felipe Pazos, "Che" Guevara later wrote that some leaders "signed a declaration with the guerrilla chief, a prisoner in the Sierra Maestra, and then went out with freedom of action to play such trump card in Miami." See Ernesto "Che" Guevara, *Apuntes de la guerra revolucionaria cubana* (Montevideo, 1966), pp. 100–06.

24. *Junta de Liberación Cubana: Nota de Prensa* (Miami, Fla., October 15, 1957), 5 pp. mimeo. (authors' copy).

25. Letter of Armando Hart to Mario Llerena, dated December 17, 1957. Llerena manuscript, pp. 160–61.

26. Ibid., p. 176.

27. Ibid., pp. 177–78.

28. Fidel Castro's letters to Mario Llerena was dated October 30, 1957. In it he praised Llerena for his patriotism and dedication, assuring him of the people's full support for his work as chairman of the Committee in Exile, Castro made no comment on *Nuestra Razón*, except to say it would make a good title for an M-26-7 newspaper in Venezuela.

29. Llerena manuscript, p. 187. The letter was dated November 19, 1957.

30. Mario Llerena's letter to Armando Hart, dated November 26, 1957.

31. Evidence of one of the authors present when Faure Chomón, in a briefing to DR members, observed that Prío's candidate was Pazos, since Prío himself could not be chosen or accepted by the insurrectionists (University of Havana, January 1959).

32. From a letter of Llerena to the Dirección Nacional, dated November 29, 1957, Miami, Florida (Llerena manuscript).

33. See Gregorio Selser, *La revolución cubana* (Buenos Aires: Editorial Palestra, 1960), pp. 127–40. The letter was released in Cuba on December 27, 1957. An English translation is found in Rolando Bonachea and Nelson P. Valdés, *Revolutionary Struggle, 1947–1958*: vol. 1, (Cambridge, Mass.: MIT Press, 1972), pp. 351–63.

34. See Ernesto ("Che") Guevara. *Reminiscences of the Cuban Revolutionary War* (New York: Grove Press, 1968), pp. 202–03.

35. In addition to Agustín Capó, an engineer, Berta Fernández Cuervo, María Taquechel, Heredio Govín, a student, Carmen Castro del Valle, a novelist, José P. Matos, a pilot in charge of arms contraband from abroad. See "Cómo se

trabajaba en la lucha clandestina," *Bohemia* (Havana), February 15, 1959, pp. 20–21, 131.

36. Selser, *La revolución cubana*, pp. 359–60.

37. Guevara, *Reminiscences*, pp. 204–06.

38. Selser, *La revolución cubana*, pp. 358, 362–63.

39. Ernesto ("Che") Guevara in a letter to Fidel Castro dated December 15, 1957, stated: "I confess . . . I feel greatly relieved and glad . . . that step, breaking with the Miami Pact, means so much for the Revolution. Unfortunately, we will have to confront Uncle Sam sooner than later. But, one thing is evident: the 26th of July, the Sierra Maestra and you are three persons and only one true God." See Carlos Franqui, "Textos inéditos o poco conocidos de Ernesto Che Guevara," *Libre* (Paris), no. 1 (September–November 1971): 10.

40. Letter by Faure Chomón to Fidel Castro, December 1957 (authors' copy).

9

A New Strategy

Fidel Castro had survived with a small force of guerrilla fighters in the Sierra Maestra for over a year. Isolated from the rest of the island, sustaining few casualties and supported by the urban underground of the M-26-7, Fidel was creating a well-disciplined group of guerrillas and gaining the backing of the area's population. His mere presence in the Sierra Maestra contributed to his popularity with the people. Urban underground fighters were unknown precisely because of the secret nature of their activities, and after the deaths of Frank País and José Antonio Echeverría, Fidel was the only important insurrectionary leader, urban or otherwise, left in Cuba. Militarily, he had demonstrated that one could wage guerrilla warfare in the mountains against a regular army; and in so doing he had created a sanctuary for the urban cadres, a place where they could continue the struggle rather than perish in the cities.

The DR's insistence upon conducting urban operations in accordance with the theory of "hitting at the top" did not altogether disappear from the minds of some of the leaders, especially Faure Chomón. But it was evident by late 1957 that a change in approach was urgently needed. The organization had probably suffered more than any other in the urban struggle. It was the only movement to have lost all its leaders in a period of one month—the tragic weeks of March and April 1957. The long preparatory period before the attack on the Presidential Palace, the street demonstrations, acts of terrorism and direct confrontations with the police—all of which helped to develop a group of hard-core militants—also damaged the organization. The police had learned many of the cadre members" names and sought them out with pictures after the palace attack. The DR had to initiate a campaign for new recruits and to try to reinstitute the cell structure of the organization.

After the attack on the palace and the Humboldt No. 7 killings, the executive council was reorganized. The new group included Primitivo Lima, Andrés Silva, Osmel Francis and Mary Pumpido among the young professionals. The workers were represented by Pedro Martínez. Orlando Blanco and Jorge Martín, who were leaders of action and sabotage cells and also organizers within the labor movement. The council also included a women's section represented by Fructuoso Rodríguez's widow. Marta Jiménez.[1]

Eloy Gutiérrez Menoyo—the brother of Carlos, who had led the commando group in the palace attack—was appointed chief of action in Havana. Under Eloy's leadership a new group of urban cadre members emerged to replace their dead compañeros, among them: Guillermo Jiménez, Angel Quevedo, Julio Fernández, Héctor Terry, Enrique Zamorano, Domingo Pérez, Jorge ("Mago") Robreño, and Mario ("Reguerita") Reguera.[2]

In Las Villas province, Ramón Pando, president of the Student Federation of the School of Commerce at Las Villas University, became the provincial secretary general of the DR. With Enrique Villegas and Piro Abreu active throughout the province, the DR movement acquired a new impetus in central Cuba. Meanwhile, in Camagüey other militants emerged as important members of the urban organization, among them: Antonio ("Tony") Bastida, Florencio González, Adolfo Mora and Sergio Valle.

The DR recovered rapidly from its defeat and extended its cells into the various sectors of the population reaching even well-to-do students at the Catholic University of Villanova, where Jesús "Paulino" Barreiro represented the DR. Although few of these students were willing to cooperate, those who did help were instrumental in creating the Fourth Guerrilla Front in Pinar del Rio province, west of Havana, in late 1958.[3]

The movement also organized overseas. With funds raised among exiles in Miami and other cities in the United States, the DR sent delegates to various Latin American countries. Venezuelan leader, Rómulo Betancourt, José Figueres of Costa Rica and Juan José Arévalo of Guatemala aided the DR by publicly supporting the insurrection. Results of this support were impressive, opening new contacts throughout the area and helping in the formation of delegations in Chile and in Caracas, Venezuela, following the fall of dictator Pérez Jiménez in early 1958. Delegations also existed in Buenos Aires, Argentina; Montevideo, Uruguay; Lima, Peru; Bogotá, Colombia; San Cosé, Costa Rica; and in Panama, El Salvador and Mexico. In the United States there were delegations in New York, Chicago, New Orleans, Tampa, Jacksonville and Miami.[4] The Nassau delegation was able to extend its contacts throughout the Bahamas and, through the members of this important delegation. The DR developed its system for infiltrating people into Cuba, for conveying contraband arms, and for receiving information on the activities of the urban underground.[5]

One of the important tasks of the delegations was to conduct public campaigns to discredit Batista's regime and to present the case for the insurrection. As the tempo of these activities increased, U.S. authorities began to pay more attention to Cuban exiles in the Florida area. Federal authorities sometimes succeeded in blocking arms shipments to Cuba; more often they were unsuccessful.

Under the leadership of Luis Blanca, Héctor Rosales, Carlos "Chino" Figueredo and Armando Fleites, the DR created a chain of arms depots that extended from New York City to New Orleans and from there to Miami. Arms were never concentrated in a specific place, and sites where arms were gathered were usually outside the Spanish-speaking colonies. When a shipment left, several cars and trucks were used along the route, and deliveries were seldom made at the same place twice. False reports circulated throughout the exile colony to confuse the authorities. However, the general feeling among DR militants was that U.S. authorities were simply looking the other way as much as they possibly could.[6]

The DR's Decision to Fight Guerrilla War

In September, Eloy Gutiérrez Menoyo, the DR's chief of action in Havana, arrived in Miami to discuss future strategy with Chomón, Cubela and Armando Fleites. The latter, a young physician and DR leader in Las Villas province, agreed with Gutiérrez Menoyo on the need to adopt a guerrilla strategy counter to the "hit at the top" tactic. Chomón still favored the direct action tactic, but agreed that the DR should change its approach and open a guerrilla front in Cuba.[7] Eloy Gutiérrez Menoyo returned to Havana and left the capital for the Escambray Mountains, reaching that area in mid-October. Menoyo's task was to inspect the area and to set up a guerrilla group; establish the necessary contacts with DR leaders in the surrounding towns and cities, and prepare the ground for the arrival of a larger group of DR militants. On November 10, 1957[8] the guerrillas issued their first internal order declaring that a second national guerrilla front had been created and instructing the guerrillas to be loyal to the country, to keep all secrets of war, never to abandon their weapons, and to denounce deserters and traitors. In January 1958, various small arms shipments arrived in Cuba and were rapidly distributed throughout the various action cells, and some were transported to the Escambray Mountains.[9] César Páez and Juan Figueroa, students who were born in Las Villas province, arrived in Havana and went to their native province to make contacts for future guerrilla actions. Pedro Martínez Brito, veteran of the Radio Reloj operation in 1957, infiltrated to Havana from Miami to acquaint DR cells of forthcoming operations against Batista. Meanwhile, Enrique Villegas, DR leader in the city of Sancti-Spiritus, in Las Villas, was shot to death by the army while he was taking supplies to Menoyo's guerrilla group. The movement rapidly gathered military information on government troops in Las Villas province, and on forces concentrated in posts close to the mountains.

On January 28, 1958, José Martí's birthday, the DR held a mass rally at Miami's Bayfront Park, scene of many such gatherings by Cuban exiles. At that meeting, it was announced that Cuba would soon be in flames, and other pledges of future action were issued. Rumors of an impending invasion of Cuba circulated throughout the exile colony. During the first week of February, the DR underground was placed on the alert, and various cells prepared to go into diversionary actions against the government.

In the final hours before the expedition, reports circulated in the exile colony about an encounter between an army patrol and guerrillas at Escambray.

Fearing that these guerrillas were Menoyo's, and that Batista would mobilize the army to stop another Castro-like invasion, the DR gave the plan for an expedition its final touches.

The Expedition

In Miami, the students had established contact with an American named Alton Sweeting, captain of a pleasure yacht, the "Thor II," licensed in New York. Captain Sweeting agreed to take the expedition to a point near the northern coast of Cuba. From there a rendezvous ship was to transport the expeditionaries to the mainland, while Captain Sweeting's yacht would be refueled for the trip back to Miami.[10]

A few hours before departure, the authorities raided several places where students usually gathered around Miami. They failed to make any arrests, but they did succeed in letting everyone know that they had to move immediately. To confuse the authorities, the expeditionaries selected the most conspicuous place of departure, the Miami River. There, very close to the MacArthur Causeway which links Miami with Miami Beach, the Cubans gathered and boarded the "Thor II," renamed "Escapade." The decision was made to carry five tons of arms, thus reducing the number of expeditionaries to 15 men and one woman (Esther Martín). With its cargo the "Escapade" quietly cruised out of Miami.

The expedition was a complete success, and coordination between the exiles and the urban cadres was excellent. Captain Sweeting's cruiser anchored at Raccoon Cay off the northern coast of Cuba, and the expeditionaries were transported further by a fishing boat, the "San Rafael." From the moment "Escapade" touched Raccoon Cay, Gustavo ("Tavo") Machín[11] was responsible

Left to right: Eduardo and Luis Blanca, William Morgan, seated, and other DR guerrillas, Escambray Mountains, spring 1958 (Courtesy of Ada Azcarreta).

School No. 1 of the DR: Dr. Humberto Castello is on the left, and Gilberto Mediavilla has a book in his hand (Courtesy of Ada Azcarreta).

for the operation. Close to the coast they boarded a third small craft, the "Yaloven," which carried men and supplies to the fishing village of Santa Rita, close to the port of Nuevitas, in Camagüey province. On February 8, 1958,[12] the DR's small expeditionary force landed and rapidly moved inland toward the capital of Camagüey province where they remained hidden for a day, in groups of two and three at various underground headquarters.

The expedition's cargo was at this point divided between arms to be transported to the DR's underground in Havana, and arms suitable for mountain fighting. Antonio ("Tony") Bastida, manager of a transport fleet of trucks, was in charge of delivering the arms in Havana. The urban underground received 33 Thompsons, a .50 caliber machine gun, two .55 caliber anti-tank rifles, one shotgun, two .30 caliber machine guns, one M-3, two M-ls, a Winchester rifle, one Browning automatic rifle, 300 rounds of ammunition for the anti-tank rifles, 2,000 capsules (30.06mm) and ammunition for .45 caliber pistols, and hand grenades. The would-be guerrilla fighters carried 50 Italian carbines, two "Stern" submachine guns, one Thompson, two M-3s, two Spring-field rifles, one Garand rifle, one M-l, five semi-automatic Remington rifles with telescopic sights, and 20,000 rounds of ammunition of various calibers.[13]

The route leading from Camagüey to the Banao area in the Escambray Mountains (190 kilometers) had been traced by urban cadres. All along the way cadre members met the expeditionaries to render reports on the area they were still to cover, and to pinpoint army positions. The urban cadre members—among them Ramón Pando and Piro Abreu, student leaders in Las

Villas province—took supplies to the expeditionaries and sometimes added men to the group. Dr. Manuel Sorí Marín was also very helpful in finding means of transportation for the expeditionaries.[14]

On February 13, the expeditionaries reached the Banao area in the subregion of the Trinidad-Sancti-Spiritus mountains, to the southeast of Santa Clara, Las Villas' capital, and the next day the group reached the Cangalito hills. At 7 AM on February 15, they arrived at Cacahual, a small guerrilla camp flanked by two hills, where Gutiérrez Menoyo, William Morgan and other guerrillas awaited the group.[15] With Castro's experience at Alegría de Pío in mind, the expeditionaries place two observers on the hills surrounding Cacahual. Two days later, the observers alerted the camp to five army scouts approaching Cacahual; an ambush disposed of three of the five soldiers, but the rest escaped. Fearing the arrival of army reinforcements the expeditionaries broke camp.

At this point there were 29 guerrillas marching in two separate groups. Fourteen guerrillas followed an old peasant guide named Cadenas, among them were Rolando Cubela, Gustavo ("Tavo") Machín, Darío Pedrosa, Alberto Mora and Efrén Mur. The other group included, among others, Eduardo García Lavandero, Rodríguez Loeches, Chomón. Luis Blanca, Armando Fleites, Alberto Blanco, Menoyo, Iván Rodríguez, Ramón Pando, Oscar Ruiz and William Morgan.[16]

The second group of guerrillas marched toward the west and into the mountain chain called Guamuhaya. On February 19, the guerrillas camped at a place where they were to meet the rest of the expeditionaries. Some of the DR men were to separate from the main group and return to the cities to wage urban guerrilla warfare. Ramón Pando and Alberto Blanco decided not to wait for the rest and were led out of the mountains by Leonardo Bombino and a guide named Faustinito. They were intercepted by an army patrol, and Ramón Pando was captured, but the others managed to escape. Pando was later assassinated by order of army Lieutenant Froilán Pérez.[17]

The two groups reunited at the Michelena forests, and the remaining 27 men tried to escape the area and the pursuing army. They marched until 4 PM on February 19, when they camped at the forest of "La Diana." Soon army troops approached along a path in the forest; at 4:45 PM the DR combatants ambushed them, in a 15-minute encounter killing 14 and wounding 16 soldiers.[18] For the next 13 hours the guerrillas, led by Leonardo Bombino, marched along ravines until they managed to escape from the army. On February 24, safe from the army's pursuit, the DR leaders wrote a manifesto which they signed on the 25th.

The Manifesto of Escambray

The DR's manifesto[19] set forth the objectives of the struggle by announcing that its strategy would be to conduct simultaneous urban and rural guerrilla warfare against Batista. The DR would fight for the re-establishment of the

Constitution of 1940, and to open the way for a social revolution. Revolutionary unity was essential for the victory of the insurrection, and the DR proposed that a "party of the revolution" be organized after Batista's overthrow. That party would gather "the real fighters who daily risk their lives fighting the dictatorship," and would guarantee that the constitution and the laws were fulfilled. The need for violence was reaffirmed, for peace could only come through the waging of war. The pillars of the future revolution were to be education, administrative honesty, agrarian reform and industrialization. Internationally, the DR supported the formation of a federation of Caribbean republics, an initial step toward the organization of a confederation of American republics.

The insurrectionary struggle against Batista, maintained the DR, was but the continuation of the country's historical struggle for independence since the nineteenth century. the DR viewed the insurrection as inspired by José Martí's ideas, the nationalism of Antonio ("Tony") Guiteras and the democratic principles of José Antonio Echeverría. The DR's fight was not only against Batista's regime, but also against "those who only a few years ago supported the Nazis on conquered land of Europe." a direct reference to the Communists, who "today are playing Batista's game as vulgar puppets." The caste of old and young politicians would be swept away by the insurrection as a fundamental requisite of social therapy.

On February 27, the guerrillas reached the mountains to the south of Santa Clara, close to the cities of Placetas, Cabaiguán, Santa Clara and Güayos.[20] At a peak called Tres Cruces, Chomón, Alberto Blanco, Rosendo Yero, Rodríguez Loeches, García Lavandero and Luis Blanca began their journey back into the urban struggle. They were led by the peasant guide Bombino and another peasant named Raúl Rosa.

Although the DR had suffered severe casualties in the urban struggle, the theory of "hitting at the top" had not been discarded completely. Faure Chomón, Rodríguez Loeches and Eduardo García Lavandero continued to urge the DR to strike at the dictator. These men had been molded in the urban insurrection, men from the cities, whose insurrectionary outlook was directly connected with struggle in the center of power, Havana.

Consequently, when Rodríguez Loeches left his *compañeros* to seek help in the cities close to the Escambray Mountains, he felt "a sense of relief and security," since as an urban fighter he felt "secure in my own environment."[21] In Sancti-Spiritus, Loeches established contact with Piro Abreu through a lawyer, Emilio Morata. Abreu provided the insurrectionists with a car and with an experienced driver, Carlos Brunet. On the evening of March 3, the group met at Fomentos with plans to reach the city of Placetas, and then move by bus to Havana.

As their car approached the city of Placetas on the Central Highway, an army jeep and a car from the Servicio de Inteligencia Militar (SIM) closed the road to check on all cars. The DR militants sped through the SIM's barricade as the army's car sped after them. Suddenly, Brunet stopped the car; as the soldiers stepped out of theirs, Brunet started the car again and the SIM agents opened fire. The men succeeded in escaping Placetas, heading east toward the city of Cabaiguan. Along the way, the driver refused to continue what he viewed as a suicide mission; the car was stopped and Brunet and Rosendo Yero stayed behind while Alberto Blanco took the driver's seat.

In minutes, the car approached the city of Cabaiguán where an army patrol was waiting, signaling for them to stop. The soldiers "had all kind of weapons," and as Blanco sped through the army's barricade "shots rang out," and "pieces of glasses flew all over."[22] García Lavandero fired his M-3 rifle behind the driver while Chomón fired from the other window as the car went through the army's blockade and into the city. Miraculously, they escaped with García Lavandero suffering only a minor wound in the shoulder. After a daring escape from Cabaiguán and several days of hiding with peasants, the group established contact with the urban underground again and reached Havana. Despite their brush with death they "decidedly felt more secure in the *llano* (plain)."[23] Once in Havana, Chomón met with Faustino Pérez to discuss the feasibility of a general strike.

The DR Guerrilla Front

As the student manifesto circulated throughout the island, the new guerrilla front gained importance. The Escambray Mountains were an excellent location for guerrilla warfare. The Trinidad-Sancti-Spiritus subregion of the mountain range was the second largest coffee-producing area on the island. The valleys surrounding Escambray produced good crops of rice, beans and vegetables, guaranteeing the guerrillas a constant supply of food. The large coffee plantations and cattle ranches also guaranteed a steady income through revolutionary taxes imposed during the campaign. The central Cuba location guaranteed that many urban fighters could reach the Escambray Mountains and participate in rural guerrilla warfare. To the southwest was the city of Cienfuegos, long a bastion of resistance to Batista. From Cienfuegos many young men joined the guerrillas, and intelligence reports about army movements were gathered there and sent to the Escambray. The various sugar mills in the province, the DR's previous involvement with the sugar workers in Las Villas province, and the militancy of DR urban cadres in cities and towns close to the mountains was a factor of great importance in the stabilization of the DR's guerrilla front.

The number of DR guerrillas increased steadily. Many experienced urban fighters who had been identified by the regime's forces went to the mountains for the duration of the insurrection. Others went to the mountains but returned to the cities, some because the life of a rural guerrilla was too devoid of "excitement," others because they could not work well in groups of 20 or 30 and their individualism was too great a risk to the discipline which must exist in a guerrilla unit. Many of these fighters died in encounters with Batista's police. The DR's chief of action, Eduardo García Lavandero, was killed together with Pedro Martínez Brito during the summer of 1958[24]; José Rodríguez Vedo, Raúl González Sánchez, Ramón González Coro and Mario ("Reguerita") Reguera also died fighting the dictatorship in the cities.

In the Escambray Mountains, the students received their baptism of fire in encounters with the army at Fomento, Saltillo, Hanabanilla, Güinía de Miranda and the two battles of Pedrero, during the spring and summer of 1958. They also learned to walk in jungles, to get their bearings in the area and to prepare ambushes, where their collective effort was paramount. The guerrilla's skills eventually led the army to follow the example of their comrades in the Sierra Maestra. The regular soldiers simply refused to enter the mountains.

By the beginning of the summer, the DR controlled the Escambray Mountains. As their power over the area grew, their responsibilities increased and the DR organized a civil administration. A *comisón campesina* led by Juan Miranda, a peasant, was created and enlisted the support of most peasants in the mountains. Under the direction of Pedro Martínez Larrinaga, a sugar worker, a population census was taken in the area for the first time in the country's history. More than 50 schools were built, and all were functioning regularly by the end of the year. An educational unit administered by Professor Gilberto Mediavilla was formed—Unidad Educacional Joe Westbrook—with graduate students in charge of programming and student teachers at all levels of instruction in the system. There was a department of Justice—División Legal Menelao Mora—under the supervision of Dr. Humberto J. Gómez, a criminal lawyer and an officer in the DR guerrilla army. By the end of the insurrection the DR had created a department of public works and was building roads throughout the marginal areas of the Sierra del Escambray. Workers' brigades were organized to help in such endeavors as the maintenance of the three gun factories, and the schools, roads and hospitals.

The activities of the committee of the census and that of the *campesinos* were coordinated to create a system of cattle distribution among the inhabitants of Escambray and adjacent territories under the DR's control. A cattle-breeding center was formed under the direction of professional veterinarians and students of the veterinary school from Havana University. The insurgents built two peasant homes for the elderly and named them after Juan Pedro Carbó Serviá. The Pepe Wangüemert Medical Division at the town of Güinía de Miranda extended medical aid throughout the mountains. Towards December 1958 the service had 15 field hospitals and ten ambulances, and treated more than 400 cases a month.[25] Special attention was given to children's diseases, from intestinal parasites to leprosy.[26] Cases of malnutrition were common; it was estimated that three out of five infants died before reaching the age of two. Before these rather primitive facilities were established, pregnant women received no prenatal care, but instead went to the local "nurse," who was a sort of witchdoctor. Dentists at field hospitals worked without respite in eight-hour shifts, 24 hours a day. Although many of the peasant families had brothers, cousins and other relatives in the Rural Guards, the location of the guerrilla hospitals were never revealed to the army. There were even times when regular soldiers, dressed in civilian clothes and accompanied by friends of the guerrillas, went to these medical centers for aid. There seems to be no doubt that through these activities the guerrillas established an excellent relationship with the rural population, and that the harsh realization of the poverty of the peasants served to radicalize the students further.[27]

There were also problems. The guerrillas tried to organize two agricultural cooperatives, but the plan failed because the peasants refused to abandon their own plots of land or even to discuss collective farming. The DR distributed land to peasants in the marginal areas of the Escambray Mountains, granting immediate title to peasants who requested land and who showed a desire to work. A department of agricultural affairs supervised the DR's agrarian reform and also offered technical advice in an attempt to teach the new proprietors methods of irrigation and the use of fertilizers. However, very seldom did the new owners follow the suggestions of the technicians, and generally they made fun of those who tried to teach them how to plant certain crops.[28] Some students tried to conduct study groups to improve family relations, in an attempt to decrease the *machista* attitude of the peasant men towards their women. The project was discarded when no men attended the study groups, and one of the volunteers for the project alerted his *compañeros* that the peasants were taking their advice as an insult.[29] The new generation of Cuban insurrectionists was learning the social values of the peasants and their religious dogmas; not only were they being confronted with all their problems at once, but also with the realization that the peasants were quite a conservative group. The students learned to differentiate theory from practice, and to understand the complexity of problems involved in a seemingly easy family project which the students conceived as beneficial to the peasants, but which the latter viewed as prejudicial to their own traditions.

The DR established a good communication system. It was based upon a telephone network which covered about 20 square kilometers, linking advance posts with headquarters. Maintenance was handled by a group of technicians of the Cuban Telephone Company, who left the urban underground to join the guerrillas in Escambray. The DR had two radio stations, and by the fall of 1958 these were linked with mobile units that reported the campaign leading to the battle of Santa Clara.

By mid-August 1958 the regular army would not even approach the marginal areas of the Escambray Mountains. However, during the fall of 1958, the army made an attempt to cut the guerrilla front in half by advancing simultaneously from the city of Cienfuegos towards the north, and from Santa Clara to the south. The army's sudden decision to fight the guerrillas was probably due to the arrival of Battalion No. 11, whose chief, Colonel Angel Sánchez Mosquera, was transferred from Oriente to Las Villas province. In theory the main objective was to isolate the guerrillas who had been operating in the western sector of the mountains and had attacked various army posts in the area, moving too close to the city of Cienfuegos. However, after two weeks of futile marching the army withdrew, leaving a few dead, some wounded, and plenty of arms and ammunition. This brief and useless operation allowed the guerrillas to capture dozens of automatic rifles, substantial amounts of ammunition, secret codes and even a tank.

In September 1958 approximately 800 guerrillas were operating in Escambray, with about 150 recruits in training and 50 messengers taken from among the youth in the area.[30] As government persecution increased in the cities more urban militants went to the mountains. It was difficult to get to the Sierra Maestra or to the Sierra Cristal, but it was relatively easy to reach the Escambray Mountains. Some activists of the M-26-7 also took refuge there because the rebel army in the Sierra Maestra would accept only a select number into the ranks of the guerrillas. The Escambray forces were larger, but Castro's 300 fighters had the advantage of being united under one command, his. Castro would not allow any violation of the guerrilla code to threaten the group's unity. His policy was to limit the guerrilla fighters to a manageable number.

Internal Division

In July 1958 Faure Chomón returned to the Escambray Mountains to find a conflict between Rolando Cubela and Eloy Gutiérrez Menoyo over the right of leadership. Menoyo refused to accept Cubela as head of the guerrilla fighters, and he also rejected Chomón's insistence on "hitting at the top," as a useless spilling of blood. Menoyo protested sending arms to the urban underground, claiming that all the arms were needed by the rural guerrillas.[31]

The leadership conflict in the mountains had a number of roots. One was that Menoyo's membership in the DR dated back to 1957, and although he had done a tremendous amount of organizational work as chief of action in Havana, Cubela was a founding member of the organization, and within the DR's tradition he, not Menoyo, had the right to the top position in the Escambray Mountains. Menoyo's claim to leadership was based on the fact that he had been the first DR guerrilla to reach the mountains. The organization found by the DR expeditionaries upon their arrival in central Cuba had been created by Menoyo.[32] The conditions for the establishment of a guerrilla front, the contacts with the peasantry, the selection of sites for guerrilla camps, the knowledge of the terrain, and the contacts with the DR cadres in surrounding urban areas were all the product of Menoyo's dedicated work. Menoyo's claim clashed with Cubela's long standing as a DR leader, and with Chomón's leadership as the secretary general of the movement. But if experience as a guerrilla fighter had been considered as the prerequisite for leadership, then Menoyo, not Chomón, had the right to lead the DR's new phase of struggle.

The solution was simple: Faure Chomón stayed in the mountains as the secretary general of the DR, and Rolando Cubela was recognized as the military leader of the DR. The executive committee of the DR supported Chomón's position, and Menoyo announced that he was leaving the organization to create his own group of guerrilla fighters. Chomón then repeated the same charge that had been passed down after the palace attack, when Jorge Valls and Tirso Urdanivia, among others, were expelled as traitors. Chomón charged Menoyo with treason, proclaimed his expulsion from the DR, and settled down to direct the guerrilla campaign with Cubela.[33]

The division within the DR guerrilla army reflected the absence of the charismatic leadership of José Antonio Echeverría. Echeverría had maintained the control of the organization from its inception to the palace attack and his death; second-level leaders like Chomón and Menoyo appear to have inspired less respect on the part of the militants, and were more subject to criticism. The surviving leaders of the DR appear to have completely lacked the unique qualities which characterized Fidel Castro and made him not only an excellent insurgent, but also an astute politician.

The DR had suffered two serious setbacks: the palace attack and the Chomón-Menoyo split. It may be that the palace attack was the product of amateurish planning; but the Chomón-Menoyo split was the result of the mediocrity of the surviving members of the DR.

The Second Front of Escambray

Because of the conflict between leaders, Eloy Gutiérrez Menoyo formed the Segundo Frente Nacional del Escambray.[34] At this point he attained the rank of major. William Morgan,[35] a former U.S. Marine, was also a commander and close to Gutiérrez Menoyo. Also backing the Second Front was Max Lesnik, a radio commentator and politician who disliked Chomón and Castro. Other guerrilla fighters, most of whom had an Auténtico background, joined the Second Front of Escambray. The main financial backing came from former president Prío, whose contact with Gutiérrez Menoyo was Lázaro Artola, an Auténtico and an admirer of the former president.[36]

This guerrilla group was characterized by its lack of bureaucracy and by its highly mobile units. Its general staff included Majors Armando Fleites, William Morgan, Lázaro Artola, Alfredo Peña, Genaro Arroyo, Jesús Carrera and Gutiérrez Menoyo as chief.[37]

The guerrilla army of the Second Front performed quite well during the remaining months of the insurrection. It had various encounters with the regular army, inflicting 37 casualties at La Diana. At Charco Azul, 30 soldiers were killed, and in the Rio Negro commando raid, 40 Rural Guards were shot to death and over 100 wounded.[38] The encounters of Guanayara, Manantiales.

Dos Bocas, Jibacoa, San Blás, Hanabanilla, the second attack against the Rio Negro army post, and the encounters of Soledad, Guaos and La Moza helped to raise the prestige of the organization, and to consolidate its territory.[39]

Towards the end of the insurrection, while "Che" Guevara and the DR encircled Santa Clara, Major Gutiérrez Menoyo's army attacked the regular toops at Topes de Collantes, and fought the regular army at Camanayagua, Manicaragua, Barajagua, San Fernando de los Camarones, Guaos, Hormiguero and El Hoyo until the army sought refuge inside the city of Cienfuegos. But the approximately 300 guerrillas under his command did not have a definite ideology, nor was the group a disciplined political organization.[40] Its sole purpose was to overthrow Batista.

The division within the ranks of the DR had come at a critical time. Eight hundred guerrillas united under a single command could have created havoc with the regular army; instead, the divisiveness weakened the DR. The guerrilla movement remained divided in the Escambray Mountains, and was not to unite even after "Che" Guevara's arrival in Las Villas province in October 1958. Gutiérrez Menoyo did not change his position toward Chomón; Chomón continued to charge Menoyo with treason; and "Che" took Chomón's side but paid attention to his main task: to defeat the regular army.

Castro did not need to worry about internal divisions over military and political strategy. Although the M-26-7 militants complained of Castro's dictatorial attitude, harsh discipline in its ranks and absolute centralization of command, the M-26-7 was monolithic by the end of 1958. This was the most important factor in the future course of the insurrection; for in insurrections, discipline is of paramount importance.

The Second Front, "Frank País" in Oriente Province

At about the time the DR opened a new guerrilla front at the Escambray Mountains in Las Villas, Raúl Castro was appointed major by his brother Fidel. Raúl was commissioned as chief of guerrilla Column No. 6, which would "operate in northern Oriente Province, from the Municipal term of Mayarí to that of Baracoa."[41] All rebel groups operating in that area were to be under his command. Raúl could appoint officers up to the rank of captain, but had to have the ratification of general headquarters (Fidel) when commissioning chiefs of columns with the rank of majors. Raúl was authorized to maintain strict order, applying the precepts of the rebel army penal code, and to receive and to invest all voluntary economic aid offered the guerrillas.

On the evening of March 10, 1958, Raúl Castro's column approached San Lorenzo, district of Jiguaní. The rebel convoy included three jeeps, three trucks and three automobiles, and close to 70 seasoned guerrilla fighters. The convoy travelled for 20 minutes along the Central Highway and reached a point north of San Luis a few minutes after midnight, March 11 found Raúl's men moving rapidly to the northwest.[42]

The column reached the town of Los Cedros, a small village with an army post guarded by four soldiers who were intelligent enough to stay inside their barracks. The rebels forced a foreman to guide them through the wide savannas known as Vío, through the sugar cane fields of the Palma mill, the village of Uvera and on to the historically famous Mangos de Baraguá.[43] At this point Raúl intercepted an old milkman who led the guerrillas to Cayo Rey, and there a truck driver led them in the direction of Gimbambay.

The column abandoned their transportation at Gimbambay and continued on foot. Shortly before reaching Gimbambay they stopped at a country store, and to the astonishment of a group of cane-cutters who were seeing guerrillas for the first time, purchased $80 worth of groceries. After that they were on favorable terrain. The march took only ten hours.

On March 12 the air force bombed Gimbambay, and a second raid caught up with the rebels who were marching along the open space of Pinares, north of the town of Miranda. There were no casualties, and the column reached the mine of Ramón Castro (the oldest of the Castro brothers) at Piloto Arriba where they took all the dynamite available. At about four that afternoon, Raúl Castro's men arrived at Piloto El Medio, north of San Luis. The following day, Raúl began to organize the area of Majaguabo, which included three sectors: Piloto El Medio, Piloto Arriba and Piloto Abajo. Here Raúl first tried the idea of creating "committees of revolutionary peasants of the M-26-7," including a secretary as chief, a civilian delegate and a military delegate.[44] The task of these committees was to collect supplies for the guerrillas and to prepare a communication system so that the rebels could detect regular troops in the area. The military delegate was to organize ten-man patrols who would maintain order in the area when the regular army withdrew.

By March 14, Raúl camped at the intersection of the roads from Mayarí-Sagua-Songo-Santiago de Cuba, where his force organized a second peasant committee. Here Raúl first found out about other groups of guerrillas who had been operating in those mountains independently of the M-26-7. Before leaving there, Raúl also organized a rebel army's intelligence service. A third peasant's committee was formed in the village of Bayate, close to Calabazas de Sagua, where the guerrillas spent some time in operations. Raúl was moving into the mountains, but leaving behind a well-organized network of support in the rural population.

In Bayate, Raúl met Captain Demetrio ("Villa") Montseny, who had been ordered by René ("Daniel") Ramos Latour to place himself under Raúl's command. Raúl was favorably impressed by the discipline of Montseny's guerrillas and by their armament.[45] Through "Daniel" Raúl also established contact with Lt. Raúl Menéndez Tomassevich who was leading approximately 100 guerrillas.[46] Under Raúl's command Tomassevich was promoted to captain and appointed commander of Company "A," and his guerrilla unit was reduced to about 50. Tomassevich's area of operation was the Alto Songo territory. Montseny was placed under the command of Efigenio Ameijeiras, who led Company "B" in the Guantánamo area.

Realizing that Sierra Cristal was not suitable for an extended guerrilla campaign, because of its sparse animal life and lack of forests, Raúl turned toward the Guantánamo mountains. On the march he continued organizing committees among peasants, establishing contact with the Guantánamo urban underground, and setting up channels to receive men, materiel and intelligence data from urban cadres through couriers. Raúl even found time to help Ameijeiras organize a peasant committee in the area of the Rus Mountains, where he also learned of the activities of small groups of bandits disguised as M-26-7 guerrillas.

Filiberto Torres, a peasant guerrilla leader heading a group of 23 other peasants, contacted Raúl. Torres claimed that he was not to be taken as a bandit, since he had attacked an army patrol and had refused to join a group of bandits who were pillaging small peasant villages. Torres was ready to place himself under Raúl's command. Raúl issued his first order, and the peasant left with the task of capturing the three most notable bandits in the area and bringing

Major Raúl Castro blindfolds a guerrilla convicted of violating the rebel code prior to his execution. Father Guillermo Sardinas administers last rites, while another guerrilla ties the victim's hands. Sierra Cristal, 1958 (Reprinted by permission of Yale University Library).

them back to Raúl. Even before Torres had time to return, Raúl captured three other bandits, executed one and released the other two under "probation."

When Torres finally returned with his catch, Raúl held a quick trial, sentenced three more captured bandits to execution by a firing squad, and carried out the sentence on the spot.[47] In a related incident, the column of Antonio E. Lussón captured a *masferrerista* (a member of Rolando Masferrer's bands acting with the acquiescence of Batista) and sentenced him to death. The act was carried out before the peasants of the area, by a six-member firing squad chosen from "among those who precisely were adamant to carry out this mission. . . ." Lieutenant Alex Struch, of Lusson's column, refused to carry out the coup d'grace and was demoted of his guerrilla rank.[48]

Whether to Masferreristas or to peasants given to looting stores and stealing herds, Raúl Castro's men were implacable in exerting revolutionary justice. The banditry situation on the slopes of Sierra Cristal was compounded by hundreds of men from adjacent towns who had fled to the nearby hills seeking some shelter from the repressive measures adopted by the regular army in Oriente. These *alzamientos en masa*—some 800 to 1000[49]—prompted by the presence of the Second Front "Frank País," posed problems in terms of food supplies, security and discipline. Raúl dealt sternly with the situation and very likely was indiscriminate in chasing them out of his territorial domain. News travelled fast in the mountains, and soon Raúl was seen as a protector of peasants who had lived under fear of the *Masferreristas,* but also as an inflexible young guerrilla leader.

Oriente's Second Front, named "Frank País" in honor of the great martyr of the insurrection, became one of the most efficient guerrilla fronts, and the best organized. It was superior in organization to the Sierra Maestra, where "Che" Guevara had built factories and small airstrips, and had developed an excellent communications network.

By the end of 1958, Raúl Castro commanded six guerrillas columns (Columns Nos. 6, 16, 17, 18, 19 and 20), and had established firm control over the entire Sierra Cristal region, throughout the mountains of Guantánamo, the Sierra de Nipe and the Sierra de Toa. As with the development of the Sierra Maestra guerrillas, the Second Front in Oriente was largely the result of the urban underground efforts of Mayarí, Guantánamo and Santiago de Cuba. Men such as Julio and Senén Casas Regueiro, sons of a wealthy landowner in Soledad de Mayarí Arriba, enrolled; Luis ("Toto") Lara, action and sabotage chief of the M-26-7 in Guantánamo; René ("Daniel") Ramos Latour, national chief of action and sabotage of the M-26-7; Belarmino ("Aníbal") Castilla Más. action and sabotage chief of Santiago; Captain Félix Pena, a business and administration student from Santiago and courageous leader of a guerrilla column. Others who enrolled were Taras Domitro, brother of Frank País' fiancée, and liaison officer between the Dirección Nacional members of Havana and

Santiago; and from Holguín, Augusto Martínez Sánchez, a lawyer, Benjamin Zayas, a dentist and González Mechero, a medical doctor.

The guerrilla columns, named after dead combatants, were commanded thus:

— Column No. 6, "Juan Manuel Ameijeiras," led by Major Efigenio Ameijeiras.
— Column No. 16, "Enrique Hart," led by Major Carlos ("Nicaragua") Iglesias.
— Column No. 17, "Abel Santamaría," led by Major Antonio Lussón Battle.
— Column No. 18, "Antonio López Rodríguez," led by Major Félix Pena Díaz.
— Column No. 19, "José Tey," led by Major Belarmino ("Aníbal") Castilla Más.
— Column No. 20, "Gustavo Fraga," led by Captain Demetrio ("Villa") Montseny.[50]

The performance of the Second Front, "Frank País" during the nine-month period from March 1 to December 31, 1958, was impressive. These guerrilla columns encountered the regular army over 247 times; captured six airplanes; intercepted five ships carrying supplies; captured 12 trains, conducted 36 commando operations; burned, destroyed or captured 31 army posts; shot down three air force fighter planes; and led 11 raids against naval patrol boats.

The "Frank País" front sustained over 160 casualties and killed 1,979 men in the regular army.[51] The various columns welcomed 45 regular soliders who deserted the army, and took 1,216 arms and thousands of rounds of ammunition. The guerrillas also constructed over 400 schools and built 20 field hospitals. The rebel air force had 12 planes and conducted three air raids.[52]

Raúl Castro's front had the best communications network of all the guerrilla fronts in Oriente province. Raúl was able to build 14 airstrips, six of which were capable of supporting relatively heavy cargo planes. Toward December 1958, Raúl Castro's air force included two P-51s, two DC-3 transport planes, three Cessnas used for reconnaisance flights and one T-28. In addition, there were three old planes which were seldom used.

The headquarters of the Second Front and the rebel air force were at Mayarí Arriba, an excellent location, since the topography allowed for the construction of an airstrip near headquarters. The Second Front's Chief of Staff was headed by Raúl, with rank of major; Captains Reinerio Jiménez Lage, Lester Rodríguez and Raúl ("Maro") Guerro Bermejo, who formed Raúl's personal escort; Manuel ("Barba Roja") Piñeiro, an M-26-7 member from Matanzas province, who headed the intelligence section of the rebel army, and Arturo Lince and Armando ("El Francés") Torres, who performed various duties on behalf of the Chief of Staff.[53]

Structural Organization

The structural organization of the Second Front in Oriente deserves a descriptive portrait since it was quite sophisticated. Raúl was a far better organizer than his brother Fidel. The youngest Castro was interested in administrative efficiency and he ran the rebel army under his command with diligence and skill. Moreover, the regular army, under the command of General Jesús Sosa Blanco, did not venture beyond the limits imposed by the paved road from the town of Mayarí, a few miles from the coast, to the Nickel Processing Corporation. Between these two points lay the small village of Levisa. In the fall of 1958, General Sosa Blanco performed one of his "massive attacks" against the village of Levisa, burning the *bohíos* and executing nine young peasants who happened to be walking along the road.[54] The military stupidity demonstrated in the "battle of Levisa," as it was called by the regular army, let Raúl Castro know that he could afford to spend time in organization.

On October 10, 1958, 105 regular troops under the command of General Sosa Blanco approached the town of Levisa for the second time in a few weeks and were sighted by three guerrillas who were on their way to a guerrilla camp at El Jobal. The first guerrilla, Melquiades González, ordered his comrade, Hugo Faubel, to try to establish contact with the guerrilla group of Francisco ("Pancho") Fernández (Melquiades's half brother) which was encamped some six miles from Levisa. Melquiades and Hugo Consuegra, the third man, prepared an ambush.[55]

As the regular army approached, Melquiades opened fire, but Consuegra's rifle jammed. Changing positions, and firing against the troops, Melquiades instilled chaos in General Sosa Blanco's column. After over two hours of shooting, during which the army refused to advance, the troops withdrew. One man, Melquiades González, had captured an army truck, a few hundred rounds of ammunition and a rifle. The army lost a lieutenant. After this "battle," the army remained on the safe side of the Mayarí River, while on the other side, the rebels hung a sign reading, "Welcome to Rebel Territory."[56]

In the south Raúl had no worries, for the army would not go into the mountains under any circumstances. From Sosa Blanco's territory on the north to the Central Highway on the south, and without opposition to the west or to the east, Raúl Castro controlled the entire area.

One further reason for the sophistication of Raúl Castro's guerrilla front was that the rebels employed facilities (such as tractors, jeeps, telephone lines, radio transmitters, office equipment, medicine, food, money and information) placed at their disposal by North Americans and Cubans working for the Moa Bay Mining Company[57] and by wealthy landowners in the surrounding areas.

Exhibit 1 depicts the structural organization of the front. Personnel at the *sección* (section) level were responsible for every member of the guerrilla front, including civilians living within its territory. Identity cards were issued here, and each *sección*, department or rebel column was required to send a periodic report to the personnel department accounting for new persons in its respective area of operation. The territorial inspection department supervised the functioning of all the dependencies of the Second Front "Frank País," an area of about 20,000 square kilometers.

The idea of a rebel police force originated in the early peasant committees created by Raúl Castro to perform as vigilantes; these became the Servicio de Observación Campesina (Peasants' Surveillance Service or SOC). This section worked under the direction of the Rebel Army Intelligence Sector headed by Captain Manuel ("Barba Roja") Piñeiro. As the guerrillas established their position and control, these vigilantes became the police force of the rebel army.[58]

The department of justice resolved all legal matters under the jurisdiction of the Second Front. The penalties for violation of military codes and rules and regulations ranged from death before a firing squad, to imprisonment, to moral sanctions. This department was headed by Augusto Martínez Sánchez, and each column was supposed to have a lawyer to discharge the laws and regulations of the Second Front. By the end of April, Raúl had enlisted the aid of three lawyers, and he contemplated the possibility of having the Dirección Nacional in Santiago send him one for each company.

In the codification and cartography section, military maps and the secret code system of the rebel army were arranged to facilitate communication between headquarters and every guerrilla column. In the maps section, three students, one an architecture student, were responsible for mapping the area from the Sierra Cristal to the Guantánamo Mountains.[59]

The propaganda section was initially under the direction of a law student, Captain Jorge ("Papito") Serguera, and later fell under the leadership of Captain José Nivaldo Causse, director of the Second Front's Tumbasiete Political School.[60] Its task was to distribute leaflets and other propaganda material throughout the zone. The communications section maintained daily contact with the rebel radio station, reporting to the nation on the progress of the campaign in the northern sector of the province.

The department of health administered over 25 hospitals and small first aid centers, headed by a group of physicians. Among them were M.D. Captain José R. Machado Ventura, Dr. Gilberto González, Dr. Julián Rizzo, Dr. González Menchero, Dr. Enrique Creahg and nurse Luis Albistur Soto among others.[61]

Under the supervision of the interdepartmental division were the ministerial-level departments of justice, health, finance, public works, agrarian bureau, propaganda and education.

The finance department collected taxes from landowners, sugar and mining companies in the area, and from the people at large. Raúl Castro issued orders to set up a supply committee in Guantánamo to equip company B, under Captain Ameijeiras, company D, under M.D. Captain Manuel ("Piti") Fajardo, and company E under Captain Félix Pena. In addition, Raúl requested of the Dirección Nacional a monthly budget to allocate expenditures for these companies, the burden of which fell on the urban underground of Guantánamo and Santiago de Cuba.[62] The administrative costs of the northern guerrilla organization, during the month of December 1958, were $150,000 or $5,000 per day. This money was used in a variety of projects that Raúl Castro carried out in the mountain area.[63]

The department of public works opened new dirt roads over an area of 15,000 kilometers, allowing the guerrillas to move rapidly from one sector of the front to another in jeeps and trucks. By the end of the year, the guerrillas were able to move comfortably from Sierra Cristal to Northern Guantánamo in one or two days, a distance that a few months before could not have been covered on foot in less than a week.

The department of education performed very well under the guidance of professional teachers. There were a series of intensive study groups for the guerrillas, and most recruits passed through a crash program of political instruction before being incorporated into a guerrilla unit. The legendary Tumbasiete School was the main source of political instructors of the Second Front,[64] whose twin sister in the Sierra Maestra was the Cuba School at Minas del Frío, founded by Ernesto "Che" Guevara.[65] Education also reached the peasants' children, and it was here, not in the Sierra Maestra, that the first anti-illiteracy campaign was begun in Cuba.

The agrarian bureau came about as the result of Raúl Castro's attempts to incorporate the peasants into the rebel army in the Second Front. The bureau was to be the mechanism through which mediation, punitive actions and distribution of land would be carried out in the zones adjacent to the Second Front. Thus, toward the end of September, the First Peasant Congress met at Lameli, in the zone of Monte Rus, scarcely an hour from the city of Guantánamo. It was attended by 400 peasants at the initiative of the Peasants' Association of that region led by José ("Pepe") Ramírez, who until then had served the interests of Batista's policies toward the peasantry.[66] Accompanying Raúl Castro were Vilma Espín, Jorge Risquet, Manuel Piñeiro, Antonio ("Tony") Pérez Herrero, Arturo Lince, Lester Rodríguez and Raúl ("Maro") Guerra Bermejo.[67] Aside from Pepe Ramírez, other peasant leaders attending the congress were Teodoro Pereira, Juan Frometa, Miguel Betancourt and Vergelino Zaldívar.

Raúl Castro assured the peasants that the rebel army was their friend despite knowing that the peasants distrusted Raúl's policies regarding the "alzamientos en masa," i.e., fleeing to the mountains of Sierra Cristal searching for security from Batista's repressive rural guards. He warned the peasants that their duty was "to fight against the reactionary forces that would attempt to halt the revolutionary process."[68] Above all, the peasants were told that the first revolutionary law of the victorious revolution would be an agrarian reform that would redress the inequitable land situation of the Cuban peasantry. According to an eyewitness, the peasant organizers of the congress had their own opinions, and presumably these were not those of the leadership of the

Second Front.[69] The agrarian bureau never became a fixed department of the Second Front.

During a nine-month period in 1958, from April 24 to December 20, Raúl Castro issued 53 military orders dealing with various aspects of the guerrilla front's organization. Military Order No. 1 (April 24) dealt with the peasant associations as sources of supplies for the rebel army;[70] Order No. 5 dealt with the organization of the medical corps on April 26; and Order No. 34 (July 2) established penalties for guerrillas who misused their rifles. Through Military Order No. 40 (August 3) the guerrilla front was officially recognized as the "Frank País Front." Order No. 41 (August 3) was the rebel penal code; No. 42, an addendum to the law of the rebel civil code; No. 43 (September 18), an organic law for the justice department of the guerrilla front; and No. 44 was the revolutionary penal code. Order No. 46 (September 19) established a law of arbitration in labor conflicts throughout the area, and Order No. 49 issued the organic law of the Second Front on October 28, 1958. The administration of municipalities under rebel control was regulated by the issuance of Military Order No. 53 (December 16) which created the post of local commissioner while the structure of the rebel police force was the subject of Order No. 54 (December 20).

Raúl Castro seems to have been more aware of the importance of the peasants than either Guevara or the leader of the M-26-7 himself. Fidel used the peasantry in his political propaganda, but he usually took a distant or paternalistic attitude toward them. Positions of leadership within Fidel's inner circle were reserved for those who had followed his mandates from the start, and these were men from the cities. Guevara had no real confidence in the peasants, whom he saw as a symbol of revolutionary possibilities rather than as a real insurrectionary force. After the victory of the insurrection, both guerrilla leaders went to great lengths to exalt the peasants as a revolutionary class, but while the insurrection lasted, both Fidel and Guevara kept the peasants in lower-level positions, generally as simple guerrillas, guides and messengers.

Raúl Castro, however, established an excellent relationship with the peasants,[71] and not just those who lived in the Sierra Cristal. As in Sierra Maestra, the peasants living in the mountains were few in number and were not representative of the Cuban peasantry as a whole. But Raúl was able to extend the influence of the insurrectionists far beyond the mountains and into the surrounding valleys and towns. Under his specific orders, peasants were treated with respect and dignity, something they seemed to have appreciated tremendously, for they were used to the derision of Cubans from the cities.

The area surrounding the Sierra Cristal was under the economic control of the United Fruit Sugar Company, the Nickel Processing Corporation and the Moa Bay Mining Company, and thousands of residents were agricultural workers and cane-cutters and miners— wage earners and union members who had a different outlook from the very poor, isolated peasants in the forests and mountains of northern Oriente province.

Raúl Castro managed to reach these workers, too. He was able to convince them to help, to feel free to visit the guerrillas, to walk through the area without fear of attack. Soon agricultural workers began joining Raúl's guerrilla units. Raúl's policy was that if one was a good fighter, disciplined and ready to die for the cause, sooner or later he would be promoted to officer rank, even if he was a peasant. Thus, Raúl Castro's guerrilla force included many peasants and agricultural workers and miners as officers, advisors and leaders of the various territorial zones throughout the liberated territory. The presence of people from the zone of operations and from the marginal towns contributed to the welcome reception that residents gave Raúl's forces. The inhabitants of the area and of the surrounding towns helped in many ways, sending the guerrillas medicine, food and reports on army movements. They also contributed to spreading all news issued by the rebels throughout the entire area of northern Oriente province, which was an important factor in waging psychological warfare.

Raúl took a personal interest in seeing that the peasants were taught different tasks in the small production lines of the rebel factories. War materiel was produced in considerable quantities, and its quality was the highest of any guerrilla front on the island. Many peasants learned techniques they were later to use in peace. No wonder that when Raúl Castro's men left the Sierra Cristal they were able to advance without trouble through the valleys, with the backing of an enthusiastic people.

Within the guerrilla front itself, Raúl Castro demanded absolute discipline. Any serious mistake on the part of a guerrilla was punishable by death. Rape, if proven against a guerrilla, allowed for little after-the-fact discussion. Execution was immediate; Raúl Castro personally executed several men for this violation of the guerrillas' code of ethics.[72]

Raúl Castro actually appears to have enjoyed executions. In this he was very different from his brother Fidel. More a politician, Fidel would not execute anyone himself, but would try to act as moderator, letting others do the dirty work. Raúl would go out of his way to be present when an execution was announced and usually fired the last shot himself. Fidel treated prisoners in a humane way. Raúl did not. While complete companies of regular troops joined Fidel's guerrillas, only 45 regular soldiers ever joined Raúl's.[73] Prisoners were considered spies by Raúl; Military Order No. 15 (May 2, 1958), for example, referred to the revolutionary courts' decision after trials of "a great number of spies."[74] Spies were shot to death. If attacked by Raúl Castro's guerrillas the army had only two alternatives: fight or escape. Surrender was impossible. Since the troops usually decided not to fight, they fled before the guerrillas.

Raúl Castro could be gentle to the peasants, and unmentionably cruel to the enemy or violators of the guerrilla code of conduct. Fidel's younger brother was by any description a dangerous man.[75]

Notes

1. Authors' interview with Adalberto Mora, a member of the DR (October 19, 1972, New York, New York). See Enrique Rodríguez Loeches, *Rumbo al Escambray* (Havana: Editorial Lex, 1959). pp. 16–17.
2. Rodríguez Loeches, *Rumbo al Escambray*, p. 23.
3. Actually named Universidad de Santo Tomas de Villanueva, its administration and faculty acquired a pro-Batista image when it refused to cancel classes in an act of solidarity with Havana University on November 30, 1956. Upper-class students who could afford that private, expensive university continued to make progress in their studies while students from Havana University, Las Villas and Oriente universities fought the military dictatorship. Consequently, on January 11, 1959 the Revolutionary Government passed Law No. 11 nullifying all credits and diplomas extended by Villanova since 1956. See, "Ley No. 11," *Gaceta Oficial de la República de Cuba*, no. 3 (January 14, 1959), pp. 1–3. Also José R. Alvarez Diaz, *Un Estudio sobre Cuba* (Miami, Fla.: Miami University Press, 1963), pp. 1525–26 for the viewpoint of the upper class on this issue.
4. Authors' interview with Reinaldo Puentes Corzo, former courier of the DR (September 5–6, 1971, Brooklyn, New York).
5. Authors' interview with Reinaldo Santiesteban Lorié, active in arms contraband (November 2, 1972, Miami, Florida).
6. Interviewees Puentes and Santiesteban stated that U.S. surveillance of student clandestine trips to and from Cuba was usually less than of other groups, for example the Auténticos, Antonio "Tony" Santiago, leader of the Auténtico Youth, told the authors in an interview that U.S. surveillance of the Auténticos was about the same as that of other groups (April 14, 1973, Union City, New Jersey).
7. Interview with Dr. Armando Fleites, who was present at the meeting and quite active in the preparations for future actions (April 16, 1973, Miami, Florida). Also, Armando Fleites in letter to the authors (May 1, 1973, Miami, Florida).
8. Max Lesnik Menéndez, "Por qué se disuelve el II Frente Nacional del Escambray." *Bohemia* (Havana), March 6, 1960, p. 56.
9. Evidence of Juan M. Toro (DR) to one of the authors (May 1960, Oriente, Cuba). Corroborated with information received from Armando Fleites.
10. Enrique Rodríguez Loeches, "La expedición de Nuevitas," *Bohemia* (Havana), February 22, 1959, p. 98, A vivid description of the expedition appears in Rodríguez Loeches, *Rumbo al Escambray*, pp. 1–59. The complete list of names was Armando Fleites, Eduardo García Lavandero, Julio García, Carlos Montiel, Faure Chomón, Alberto Mora, Alberto Blanco, Raúl Díaz Argüelles, Antonio ("Tony") Castell, Rolando Cubelo, Carlos ("Chino") Figueredo, Guillermo Jimnénez, Julio G. Olivera, Luis Blanco and Rodríguez Loeches, who, in *Rumbo al Escambray*, did not mention Armando Fleites as an expeditionary: the woman was Esther Martin. See also, Hugh Thomas, *Cuba, The Pursuit of Freedom* (New York: Harper and Row, 1971), p. 979. For the activities of the students prior to the expedition, see *Diario de las Américas* (Miami, Florida), January 29, 1958. Data on the activities of the movement in Cuba come from personal notes and recollections; on exile activities at that time information was received from Miguel A. Roché who

was in charge of delivering arms and supplies to Cuba's underground (Fall 1969, Washington, D.C.).

11. Gustavo ("Tavo") Machín is not, as claimed by Thomas, in charge of a factory in Cuba. See Thomas, *Cuba, The Pursuit of Freedom*, p. 979. Machín, born in 1936 in Havana, fought in the Escambray Mountains under the command of Rolando Cubela. After 1959, Machín was under-secretary of the treasury, and later joined the Revolutionary Armed Forces of the Western Army; completed technical and military studies in the Soviet Union before entering Bolivia, on December 9, 1966, via Chile on an Ecuadorian passport, No. 49836, under the name of Alejandro Estrada Puig. "Che" Guevara appointed Machín chief of operations of the guerrilla movement in Bolivia. "Tavo" died fighting on August 31, 1967, at Vado del Yeso, Bolivia.

12. Rodríguez Loeches, "La expedición de Nuevitas," p. 100.

13. Rodríguez Loeches, *Rumbo al Escambray*, p. 64.

14. Other people who lent aid to the expeditionary group in Camagüey province were Jorge Marrero, a medical doctor; Guillermo Fernández Montiel, student; Ignacio Garrido, from a well-to-do family in Camagüey; Guillermo Fernández, a sugar worker; and Eduardo Castillo, a lawyer. See Rodríguez Loeches, *Rumbo al Escambray*, pp. 63–64.

15. Authors' interview with Armando Fleites.

16. Rodríguez Loeches, *Rumbo al Escambray*, p. 69.

17. Ibid., pp. 73–74.

18. Ibid.

19. *El Manifiesto del Escambray* (Las Villas) (February 24, 1958), mimeographed and distributed, dated March 13, 1958, 2 pp. (authors' copy).

20. Rodríguez Loeches, *Rumbo al Escambray*, p. 77.

21. Ibid., p. 89.

22. Ibid., pp. 90–92.

23. Ibid.

24. Eduardo García Lavandero was shot to death in an encounter with the police in Havana, on June 23, 1958; Pedro Martinez Brito and José ("Reguerita") Reguera and José Rodríguez Vedo were shot to death by Colonel Esteban Ventura Novo's men in Havana, on July 10, 1958; Raúl González Sánchez was killed in an encounter with the police on September 2, 1958; Ramón González Coro was shot to death on December 15, 1958. See Rodríguez Loeches, *Rumbo al Escambray*, p. 5.

25. See Humberto Castelló. "Prólogo," in Rodríguez Loeches, *Rumbo al Escambray*, pp. 11–14.

26. Evidence of Arturo Virelles, medical student attached to the DR field hospitals (January 2, 1973, New York, New York).

27. Conversations between one of the authors and DR guerrillas Armando Cabrera and Julio ("Cueto") Fernández (Fall 1959, Havana).

28. In an informal discussion in January 1959 al Havana University, Faure Chomón, Rolando Cubela, Gustavo ("Tavo") Machín and others recalled these experiences (Evidence of one of the authors).

29. Evidence of Manuel Ledón (DR) to one of the authors (July, 1959, Güinia de Miranda, Las Villas province).

30. Authors' estimate of guerrillas operating in the area following various interviews with guerrillas and guerrilla leaders, among them: Captain Armando

Moya, DR (April 22, 1973, Union City); and Armando Fleites, Second Front (April 16, 1973, Miami, Florida).

31. Evidence of Armando Fleites in interview with the authors, and in letter to the authors cited above.

32. Eloy Gutiérrez Menoyo, "El II Frente Nacional del Escambray," *Combate*, no. 7 (Costa Rica), July–August 1959, pp. 48–49, See also Antonio Santiago Ruíz. "La acción revolucionaria del Partido Auténtico." *Combate*, no. 9 (Costa Rica), March–April 1960, pp. 36 –40. Armando Fleites told the authors that the strongest reason remained the matter of strategic differences between supporters of guerrilla warfare and those who insisted in the application of the "hit at the top" tactic.

33. This appears to be the most acceptable explanation after careful review of all the details, disregarding subjective judgements by partisans of either Gutiérrez Menoyo, Chomón or Cubela.

34. See Gutiérrez Menoyo, "El II Frente Nacional del Escambray," p. 49.

35. Nathaniel Weyl, *Red Star Over Cuba* (New York: Hillman Books, 1961, pp. 186–87) quoting from Headquarters 25th Infantry Division, APO 25 (Osaka, Japan), General Court Martial Order No. 8, writes that Morgan had served in the U.S. Army of occupation in Japan; in November 1947 he was in confinement in Kyoto, Japan, but escaped, was captured and tried and convicted of armed robbery and escape; Morgan was dishonorably discharged and confined to hard labor for five years in the Chillicothe Federal Reformatory. See also Thomas, *Cuba, The Pursuit of Freedom*, p. 1030.

36. Authors' interview with Carlos Prío Socarrás (August 29, 1972, San Juan, Puerto Rico). Authors' interview with Antonio "Tony" Santiago (February 24, 1972, Union City).

37. Lesnik Menéndez, "Por qué se disuelve el II Frente Nacional del Escambray," p. 56.

38. Ibid.

39. Gutiérrez Menoyo, "El II Frente Nacional del Escambray," p. 49.

40. Ibid.

41. Fidel Castro, "Comunicado de la Comandancia General del Ejército Rebelde," *Bohemia* (Havana), June 19, 1959, pp. 42–46.

42. Raúl Castro, "Diario de campaña," in Edmundo Desnoes, *La sierra y el llano* (Havana: Casa de las Américas, 1961), p. 206. Originally a letter to Fidel Castro entitled "Informe No. 1" (April 20, 1958). Raúl signed the letter as "Juan Carlos," See Marta Rojas, "Antes de la retención de los norteamericanos," *Bohemia* (Havana), June 28, 1959, p. 99.

43. General Antonio Maceo issued a protest by that name against the Pact of Zanjón ending the war with Spain (1868–1878). See also Eddy Suñol Ricardo, "De la Sierrá Maestra a los llanos del norte de Oriente." *Días de combate* (Havana: Instituto del Libro, 1970), pp. 161–78.

44. Raúl Castro, "Diario de campaña," p. 213.

45. Ibid. The guerrillas were armed with seven Garand rifles, four Springfield rifles, two submachineguns, three Winchester rifles and small firearms.

46. Ibid. See also "Segundo Frente Oriental 'Frank País.'" *Verde Olivo* (Havana), March 12, 1972.

47. Raúl Castro, "Diario de campaña," pp. 218–19.

48. Antonio E. Lussón, "El paso de la columna 9 al Segundo Frente Oriental," in *Dias de combate*, p. 83.
49. Raúl Castro, "Diario de campaña," p. 222, 229, 256–57.
50. "Segundo Frente Oriental."
51. "Graduación en el Segundo Frente 'Frank País,'" *Bohemia* (Havana), September 16, 1966. pp. 68–73.
52. Ibid.
53. Antonio E. Lussón, "El paso de la columna 9," p. 88; Euclides Vázquez Candela, "Recuerdos del II Frente, una concentración," *Combatiente* (Organo del Ejército de Oriente) (Santiago de Cuba), March 15, 1965, pp. 1, 4 and "Graduación en el Segundo Frente." p. 73.
54. They were workers of the United Fruit Company and the Nickel Processing Corporation on their way to the city of Mayarí along the only road connecting this city to the U.S.-owned mines and United Fruit offices (Evidence of one of the authors who visited the village of Levisa and examined the area in the summer of 1958).
55. Melquiades González, "El combate de Levisa," in *Días de combate*, pp. 179–83. One of the authors met Melquíades González in January 1959, in Oriente province; the people viewed Melquiades as a hero who was humble, illiterate, a former canecutter for the United Fruit Company promoted by Raúl Castro to the rank of captain of the rebel army; Melquiades learned to read and write after the insurrection.
56. Evidence by one of the authors who crossed the Mayarí River into rebel territory in the summer of 1958.
57. Evidence by one of the authors related by Renán Pérez, an employee of the Moa Bay Mining Company, and the contact used by the rebels to approach American employees for aid (February 1959, Havana, Cuba).
58. Marta Rojas, "Un Estado Rebelde Modelo," *Bohemia* (Havana), July 19, 1959, p. 45.
59. Raúl Castro, "Diario de campaña," p. 252.
60. Euclides Vázquez Candela, "Recuerdos del II Frente," p. l.
61. Julio Martínez Páez, *Médicos en la Sierra Maestra* (Havana: Ministerio de Salubridad, 1959), p. 40 and Antonio E. Lussón, "Primer ataque al cuartel de la Mina de Ocujal," in *Días de combate*, p. 96.
62. Raúl Castro, "Diario de campaña," p. 251.
63. Marta Rojas, "Un Estado Rebelde Modelo," p. 43.
64. Héctor de Arturo, "Desde el 56," *Verde Olivo* (Havana), December 5, 1971, p. 69.
65. González Tosca, "Escuclas," *Verde Olivo* (Havana), December 5, 1971, p. 84.
66. "Congreso Campesino del Segundo Frente," *Bohemia* (Havana), September 25, 1970.
67. Euclides Vázquez Candela, "Recuerdos del II Frente," p. 1.
68. Ibid., p. 4.
69. Ibid.
70. For a list of the military orders, see Marta Rojas, "Un Estado Rebelde Modelo," p. 45. All military orders were later published in the official gazette of the guerrilla front, *Surco*, at which time military orders acquired the title of "decrees."

71. Based on the impressions of one of the authors who spent some time in the area of Mayarí Arriba, Mayarí, Guaro, Levisa and Calabazas. Of the three Castro brothers, Raúl had a greater rapport with the peasants. Ramón Castro told one of us, "Fidel was considered by our *guajiros* as the 'lawyer from Havana,' or as 'the politician.'" In addition, Ramón remarked that Fidel remained aloof from the peasants whom he considered "lazy" (Conversation with Ramón Castro, March 10, 1960, Havana, Cuba). The same author was present at a luncheon for Lina Ruz de Castro given by her family in the town of Guaro, close to the Castro sugar colony. Fidel's mother expressed her deep concern that her son was trying to carry out an agrarian reform without "knowing how the peasants think, what they want," and commented that Fidel's attitude toward the peasants was "arrogant" (June 1960, Guaro, Oriente province).

72. Ramón Castro to one of the authors, March 10, 1960, Havana, Cuba (Evidence of Emilio Pantoja, a member of Column No. 17, to one of the authors, July 1959, Havana, Cuba).

73. Marta Rojas, "Un Estado Rebelde Modelo," pp. 42–46, 114–15.

74. Ibid., p. 46.

75. Raúl was perceived as so radical, that his extremist behavior was often mentioned by Fidel Castro after 1959, apparently as a deterrent to counterrevolutionaries hoping to unseat Fidel from power.

10

The Frustrated Strike:
April 9, 1958

Prelude: U.S. Arms Embargo

A military assistance pact between the governments of Cuba and the United States had been signed 72 hours before Batista's coup d'etat on March 10, 1952. Article 2 of the pact[1] stated that the United States would supply the Cuban government with arms for the purpose of "implementing defense plans under which the two governments will participate in missions important to the defense of the Western Hemisphere." What kind of "missions" the Cuban government was to conduct that could be important to the defense of the Western Hemisphere was never explained. The fact was that the military equipment which was received under the military assistance pact was being used to fight a civil war, and the pact provisions clearly stated that such military assistance was not to be used for "purposes other than those for which it was furnished," without prior consent of the U.S. government. Thus U.S. support of the Batista regime was clearly implied.

The Committee in Exile took up this argument, contending that the Cuban armed forces would continue to fight as long as arms continued to arrive from the United States. The chairman of the committee, Mario Llerena, frequently explained that the Batista regime was using American-made arms to counter the activities of those Cubans who wanted to restore freedom and justice in their own country. Once the Batista regime had been overthrown, he argued, the people of Cuba would feel that the United States had been Batista's partner in the murder of thousands of Cuba's young people.

The Committee in Exile had its main opponent in Batista's private propaganda agency, Universal Research and Consultants. Inc. With offices in Washington, D.C., these "geopolitical consultants" published a newsletter, "Cuban News," which was distributed among those persons who could help maintain Batista's image as that of a benevolent democrat. The president of Universal Research and Consultants, Colonel John E. Kieffer, USAF, retired, was considered by Cuban exiles in Washington as the eyes and ears of the dictatorship.[2] The main thrust of such a firm—duly registered with the Department of Justice—was to charge that the insurrectionists were thoroughly infiltrated with Communists. But the Committee in Exile did not invest too much energy in challenging the information put out by Colonel Kieffer's machinery. Instead it concentrated on seeking to influence U.S. public opinion against all arms shipments to Cuba, and to mobilize influential members of Congress to take the message to the White House.

The matter of arms had been a concern of the rebels for some time. The Sierra Maestra Manifesto demanded that the United States stop all shipments to Batista, as did the Junta de Liberación Cubana in Miami. Dr. José Miró Cardona, secretary of the civic institutions,[3] lost no opportunity to demand the cancellation of all contracts with Batista's army. Dr. Urrutia conducted his own campaign throughout Latin America, while Ernesto Betancourt, the M-26-7 delegate in Washington, succeeded in establishing contact with a key member of the Cuban embassy in Washington,[4] Sergeant Angel Saavedra. Sergeant Saavedra had been appointed assistant to the Cuban military attaché because of his humble origins and because he had been educated in Batista's civic-military institutes. Although the sergeant had won the trust of the dictator, Saavedra had previously served under Captain Ernesto Despaigne, one of the officers sent to prison for participating in the "conspiracy of the pure." According to Ernesto Betancourte, Saavedra's "personal loyalty to Captain Despaigne" led him to cooperate with the intelligence network of the M-26-7 in Washington.[5] Sergeant Saavedra was instrumental in producing photocopies of documents that proved beyond doubt that U.S. arms were being shipped to Cuba. These documents were given to Llerena, who showed them to Congressman Adam Clayton Powell, who in turn promised to take the issue to the floor of the House of Representatives.

Most of the documents were signed by the Cuban attaché. Colonel José Ferrer Guerra, and were copies of original contracts between the Cuban and the U.S. governments. These documents included a September 1957 request from Batista for the acquisition of eight tanks. This order was still under consideration by higher echelons of the government. In early 1957, the Cuban air force had purchased bombs for an approximate value of $330,000, and had also acquired 300 five-inch rockets. In December 1957, two contracts were approved for the sale of 50 Browning machine guns, and ten radio receivers.[6]

The most important document, however, was a list of arms received by Batista's regime since 1952. The document demonstrated that Cuba had received at least 4,000 M-l rifles, 1,500 .75mm grenades, 1,500 3.5mm rockets, 1,000 .60mm mortar grendades, and seven tanks with 76mm guns, among a large assortment of other weapons and spare parts.[7] Congressman Charles O. Porter joined Congressman Powell in demanding that this type of arms shipment be stopped.

The congressmen's demands were met, for despite the protests of U.S. ambassador to Cuba, Earl T. Smith,[8] the U.S. secretary of state, John Foster Dulles, announced an arms embargo. This decision to declare an arms embargo apparently was made because the Cuban embassy had proven itself unable to maintain strict control over secret documents. The United States could not afford to risk irritating public opinion by continuing this kind of transaction. Batista protested this move, more because of the political implications of the decision than because of the reduction of the military hardware, for arms could still be bought in Europe or in the Dominican Republic.[9]

In answer to Batista, Secretary Dulles announced that Washington's guideline in supplying arms to the American republics would be "the need of a country to have defense against possible aggression from without [and the need for] a normal police force, and the forces required to maintain internal order against subversive activities and the like would be of great proportions, and not stimulated from abroad." He also stated, in response to a question during a press conference, that the action "is taken in accord with the broad policy I have indicated. . . . We don't like to have a large shipment of arms, particularly of a large caliber . . . go where the purpose is to conduct a civil war."[10] That statement was the first recognition on the part of a high administration official that a state of civil war indeed existed in Cuba. Batista was greatly annoyed by this declaration, certainly not what he needed at that stage of the struggle.

Dulles' statement also caused unrest among military officers who tended to interpret the U.S. position as Batista had. To the dictator the arms embargo meant that the United States had assumed a "neutral" position vis-à-vis the Cuban conflict. And within the Cuban political context, such "neutrality" was equivalent to U.S. withdrawal of support for Batista. But actually, aside from an order for 1,950 Garand rifles from the United States which was confiscated, arms seem to have continued arriving aboard unmarked planes. Only the initiative of the rebels finally forced the hand of the United States, and led to an arms embargo on Batista.[11] Even though it was not effective at first, the arms embargo had great psychological impact in favor of the insurrection, and it came less than a month before the attempt at a general strike on April 9, 1958.

Genesis of the Strike

The idea of the general strike preceded by direct action from the masses[12] was a central tenet of the M-26-7 insurrectionary strategy. In August and October of 1956, Fidel Castro had attempted to persuade Frank País of the feasibility of a general strike once the Granma landed in Cuba, but País had realized that launching a general strike would first require patient work among the Cuban proletariat.[13] País' efforts in this task had been cut short when he was assassinated. The M-26-7 Dirección Nacional fell into an impasse.

Ironically, the death of País sent Oriente into a spontaneous strike that could have picked up strength in Havana. On August 5, 1957 the Dirección Nacional called for a general strike in the aftermath of País' death, but according to eyewitness, Vilma Espín "though it could have been something definitive it was not so because of Havana. . . . However, I believe in one week we achieved almost two months of [work] in the insurrectionary process. It was a surprise to find out how ripe were the other provinces."[14]

But before laying the grounds for the next revolutionary strike, leadership within the M-26-7 Dirección Nacional had to be redefined. País' death had provoked a sudden appetite for the position of national chief of action and sabotage. Among the contenders were Ernesto ("Che") Guevara who, assessing the value of the insurrectionary forces in the cities, felt he was qualified to be País' substitute.[15] Yet "Che," in his genuine desire to be of service in the perilous cities, did not know that Faustino Pérez, coordinator between the Sierra and the cities, also coveted the post. According to Faustino Pérez, most of the members of the Dirección Nacional favored his nomination. His only competition was René Ramos Latour, who was favored by Oriente's M-26-7 militants for the position.[16]

René Ramos Latour (also known as "Daniel") belonged to Frank País' initial group, ANR, and was chief of the M-26-7 militias.[17] The Oriente militants argued that if anyone was qualified to carry on Frank País' work it was "Daniel," for "he was very close to [Frank], and was abreast in all the plans . . . he is a great and very talented person."[18] On August 15, 1957, "Daniel" arrived in Havana and held a meeting with Haydée Santamaría. Armando Hart and Faustino Pérez "to brief them on Frank's plans."[19] The meeting was intense and covered the most important problems "affecting the movement and the insurrection." It also afforded "Daniel" an opportunity to impress upon his compañeros his own qualifications for conducting the insurrectionary strategy of the M-26-7 in the cities. "We readily understood," wrote Faustino Pérez, "that he was the best person to substitute for Frank País, as Oriente's thoughtful *compañeros* had suggested."[20]

There was no question that "Daniel" was the man for the job. Not only had he proven to be a courageous and valuable insurrectionist under Frank País,[21] but after País' death, he lost no time in getting the movement back into action. Having been accepted by the Dirección Nacional, "Daniel" went to the Sierra Maestra on October 10, 1957. The evidence available suggests that "Daniel's" trip was in the nature of fact-finding, of attaining as complete a picture as possible of the military strength of the Sierra Maestra guerrillas. Of this meeting, Castro wrote, "'Daniel' is here . . . to discuss all the affairs of the movement . . . 'Daniel' has had a wonderful impression of all that we have achieved here at the Sierra. The whole territory is practically under our control."[22] Indeed, in the fall of 1957 the guerrillas had finally established a solid foothold in the heights of Sierra Maestra. For the first time since Frank País' death, the future looked bright.

After this meeting, Castro left no doubt as to the next form of struggle to be waged by the M-26-7. From El Hombrito, the first free rebel territory, Major Ernesto "Che" Guevara printed the first issue of *El Cubano Libre* at the end of November.[23] Its front page editorial, written by Guevara, disclosed the next strategy of the Sierra Maestra leadership:

> The Sierra Maestra is arriving at the end of its historical commitment (to become) the unassailable fortress against the mercenary army; it is getting ready to launch its legions of combatants over the plains. . . .
> The triumph of the *llanura* (plains) will be based on two of the people's greatest weapons: the systematic burning of canefields—thus weakening the regime's economic grassroots—and the general revolutionary strike which will be the final blow, and the victory over the repressive forces. . . .
> The revolutionary general strike is the definitive weapon, the intercontinental rocket of the peoples; no repressive organization can defeat it when it is carried out in an organized and enthusiastic (way).
> Doubtless, it is the cities' and towns' duty to work from now on; to organize the strike in every detail. . . . The action strike committees must get organized to break any attempt at undermining the strike. The sabotage groups (must become organized) to totally destroy the enemy's lines of communications. . . ."[24]

In the spirit of this editorial, Fidel Castro wrote on December 14, 1957,[25] that "the general strike will be carried out" with the support of "the Civic Resistance Movement, the National Labor Front, and any other labor sector . . . in close contact with the 26th of July Movement." On December 27, "Daniel" met with Faustino Pérez, Arnold Rodríguez, Marcelo Salado, Oscar Lucero and other action cadres to discuss the call to strike.[26] Towards the end of December, or in the first days of January 1958, Armando Hart was caught by the police, and Marcelo Fernández (code named "Zoilo") was appointed national coordinator of the Dirección Nacional.[27]

Towards the last days of January 1958, Batista lifted press censorship, and newsmen at home and abroad were making arrangements to interview Fidel Castro in the Sierra Maestra. In February, Homer Bigart of the *New York Times*, Enrique Meneses of *Paris-Match*, and Andrew St. George of the *Time-Life* publishing company interviewed the guerrillas, particularly Castro. At the same time, a delegation of the Liberal party headed by Congressman Manuel de Jesús León Ramírez and a Manzanillo councilman, all from Batista's government coalition, met with Fidel.[28] In an interview with Homer Bigart, and as a result of talks held with Batista's representatives, Castro declared that "upon withdrawal of the government forces [from Oriente province] . . . we would agree to general elections under President Batista."[29]

The effect of this declaration by the staunch guerrilla rebel was stunning. Dr. Manuel Urrutia Lleó, who had arrived in Venezuela to seek the support of Wolfgang Larrazabal for the M-26-7 struggle, heard the news with deep shock.[30] Similar feelings were shared by Mario Llerena and Raúl Chibás of the Committee in Exile. Immediately, the members of the Dirección Nacional scheduled an urgent meeting in the Sierra Maestra to demand of Fidel an explanation for such an about-face.[31] At the end of February 1958, "Daniel" and Vilma Espín (code named "Déborah") arrived at Pata de la Mesa (nom de guerre for Altos del Conrado).[32] A few days later, they were joined by Marcelo Fernández, Faustino Pérez and Haydée Santamaría at La Plata, Castro's military headquarters.

The meeting of the Dirección Nacional began on March 7 and lasted until March 10.[33] Castro explained that "at no time had the line of the movement been changed," and that his proposals to Batista's representatives were a tactical maneuver since "it put the regime in the position of having to consider unacceptable conditions." Then both Castro and Guevara dwelled at length on the war conditions at the Sierra, the situation of the country at large and the work accomplished by the movement. Based on the favorable impression caused by these analyses, "the strategy of the general strike and the insurrection was ratified," and plans were laid out to increase the "radicalization of the country with a view toward a national revolutionary uprising."

The Sierra leadership was trying to repeat the events that led to the disaster of November 30, 1956—an uprising followed by a general strike. Again, the members of the Dirección Nacional did not unanimously support a general strike. "Daniel" pointed to "general weaknesses within the movement throughout the island, excepting Oriente."[34] He felt that the general strike was a type of struggle "that would cause tremendous loss of lives in the cities." Despite "Daniel's" reservations and concern for the reasonable safety of the M-26-7 militants, the Sierra Maestra optimism concerning the feasibility of radicalizing the struggle prevailed.

On March 5, a team of Cuban newspapermen from the *Bohemia* magazine departed for the Sierra Maestra to interview the guerrillas. At La Plata,[35] Agustín Alles Soberón interviewed Castro on the coming general strike, and the general characteristics of the guerrilla struggle. Castro showed Alles Soberón the March 12, 1958 manifesto calling for a general strike—a declaration which "he had dictated to Celia Sánchez, and whose wording admitted no possibility for failure."[36] The manifesto called for "total war" and announced the revolutionary strike.[37]

In the declaration, the M-26-7 reaffirmed its support of Dr. Manuel Urrutia Lleó for the presidency of the republic. The manifesto clearly stated that "the strategy of the decisive blow is based on the general revolutionary strike supported by armed struggle." To create the desirable conditions, "from this moment on there must be an intensification of revolutionary action ending with the strike which will be called at the climactic moment." It further appealed to all conscientious citizens to cooperate in the struggle, and it bid for the support of army officers who had not been involved in criminal acts, since "to have fought against us does not impair soldiers from serving the fatherland in these decisive moments." Finally, the manifesto specified that the "total war against the tyranny was in effect as of the date of its declaration [March 12] until April." Out of this timetable, one day was to be selected by the Sierra to order the strike. The declaration was broadcast through the rebel radio station and through all available underground channels. It was signed by Fidel Castro and Faustino Pérez (who was not at La Plata).[38]

The revolutionary strike was initially set for March 31, a Monday.[39] On that date the Sierra Maestra would initiate "the campaign of extermination against anyone who serves the tyranny." The insurrectionists assumed that the people would cooperate by liquidating all known Batista followers when the time came.

Castro's decision to call a general strike confirmed his earlier thesis that as guerrillas in the rural areas reached the stage when they could wage offensive warfare against the regular army, a strike in the cities would be needed to paralyze the nation, increase the insurrection's pace and bring about the regime's collapse.[40]

Castro appointed Faustino Pérez as coordinator for the strike in Havana. This was a move that the urban M-26-7 should have never approved. Of middle-class background, a medical doctor by profession, Faustino was one of the most trusted followers of the Sierra Maestra leader. Castro's confidence in Faustino was evidently reciprocated by the latter's unswerving loyalty. But loyalty is not the most important qualification for leadership of an urban movement as complicated as a general strike's organization could be.

Nevertheless, within the clandestine network of the M-26-7, Faustino had excellent ties with the pastors, social workers and teachers of Presbyterian churches and schools throughout Las Villas, Matanzas and Havana.[41] He was acquainted with Reverend Francisco García, executive of the Presbytery of Cuba, and was a close friend of Reverend Raúl Fernández Ceballos, secretary-general of the National Council of Evangelical Churches, and pastor of Havana's First Presbyterian Church. Reverend Raúl Fernández, in particular, was very active in the urban underground resistance in Havana. At the Dispensario Clínico of his church, bombs were manufactured, manifestos written, and enormous quantities of medicine made available to M-26-7 cells and later to the Escambray guerrillas.[42] The facilities of La Progresiva Presbyterian School in Cárdenas, Matanzas province, as well as the Presbyterian schools of Cabaiguán and Sancti-Spiritus were, from time to time, at the disposal of many members of the M-26-7 underground.[43] This sort of contact with religious institutions and leaders would be significant in strike preparations and in caring for and hiding militants throughout the major insurrectionary events. But during 1957 Faustino had mainly been a courier between the Sierra and the cities, concentrating on organizing professionals, supplies and channels of communication rather than engaging the authorities. His previous activities had not really prepared him for his new role, as events were to demonstrate.

The guerrillas' main problem continued to be lack of arms, which were badly needed by both the urban and rural forces. On March 31, President José Figueres of Costa Rica came to the aid of the insurrectionists with a C-46 transport plane loaded with assorted weaponry. Piloted by Manuel Rojo, a Spaniard, the shipment included 250 Bereta machine guns, 250 automatic rifles, one million rounds of ammunition, 225 .60 mm mortars, bazookas, .50 cal. tripod machine gunes, dynamite and hand grendades,[44] enough weapons to arm nearly the entire M-26-7 urban underground in Havana. News of the shipment reached the Havana M-26-7 during the first days of April, and most cadres expected the arms would be forthcoming at any moment through the underground communication channels from the Sierra Maestra.

As preparations for the strike proceeded, Batista readied the government machinery to meet the challenge. The dictator declared a state of national emergency,[45] assuming absolute powers over all phases and spheres of government. A decree was passed allowing the Council of Ministers to assume congressional powers to enact legislation, reorganize the armed forces and supervise the newly created paramilitary units. The council was also empowered to allocate funds to meet expenses under the state of emergency and to manage communications, and air, sea and land transportation to ensure that military operations would run smoothly. This sweeping decree also allowed the council to overhaul the judiciary, since a clause of the emergency law empowered the ministers to define punishable acts and set sanctions for crimes committed against the government in violation of public order. The national police was authorized to handle dissidents according to the judgment of its officers in any given situation. They were thus given a free hand to use the most barbarous methods of terrorism.

The national emergency abolished the remnants of "constitutionality" of which Batista had boasted. With all powers invested in the Council of Ministers headed by Batista, the caudillo felt secure enough to meet the insurrectionists. If thus far political repression had been selective, after the first days of April persecution became open and arbitrary, with personal vengeance being taken throughout the nation regardless of the act committed. Violence increased as the strike approached.

On March 21, the CTC issued a public statement announcing its support of the regime.[46] The CTC rejected all attempts to conduct a political and "adventurous strike." Cautioning that any worker supporting the strike would "play into the hands of an abnormal and counterrevolutionary trick," the CTC warned that participants would lose their jobs immediately and that the labor unions would not support them. The statement rejected violence and terror, pleading for respect for the laws and for the government. The youth were asked to abandon sabotage and terrorism; unity within the electoralist opposition was the declaration's suggestion for effecting a peaceful transition of government. The CTC's declaration closed with the phrase: "It must not be anyone's ambition to destroy the republic in order to govern it."[47]

The Pérez-Ray Interview

Meanwhile, shortly after the meeting in the Sierra Maestra, Faustino Pérez arrived in Havana to meet with Manuel Ray, an active and increasingly able leader of the M-26-7 Civic Resistance Movement, of which he had been secretary-general since August 1957.[48] Middle-class in background, and an engineer by profession, Ray was a resourceful and dedicated organizer. He was also one of the most wanted men on Batista's police lists and was constantly sought by the government's secret organizations.

Pérez and Ray met to discuss the strategy of the general strike. The two were to agree on a date, arrange for various actions in consultation with the cadres and, in general, review the details concerning the operation throughout the island. The leaders assumed they could count on about 300 hard-core fighters from the M-26-7, about 1,000 students from Havana University and from the Federación de Escuelas y Academias Privadas (Federation of Private Schools and Academies or FEAP), and other small groups as reinforcements. There were also some auxiliary units staffed by women. At that time the M-26-7 claimed a membership of about 2,000 in Havana. These people would have a primary role in the struggle, for the outcome in the capital city would be decisive. Throughout the rest of the island, the M-26-7 urban organization could count on approximately 5,000 to 6,000 people. In Santiago de Cuba, there were but a handful of experienced urban guerrillas, and about 200 militants were led by ten or 11 hard-core fighters.

The M-26-7 in Havana had the use of 40 to 50 houses for communication, arms depots and hideaways. The Miramar section of Havana, an upper-class neighborhood, was to be the general headquarters of the underground for this operation. Other bases of operation were set up in the Vedado sector, a middle-class neighborhood also in Havana. As the date for the strike approached, Pérez, Ray, David Salvador and Marcelo Fernández were to issue direct orders from the Vedado neighborhood since it was close to the center of Havana's business section. The proposed date of the strike, March 31, was to be known only to the top leaders, and the cadres would be informed just a few hours before the action was to begin.

The discussions continued to center on strategy. Marcelo Salado,[49] M-26-7 chief of action and sabotage in Havana, was to be in charge of revolutionary action along with Oscar Lucero at their headquarters on the Chibás building located on G and 25th streets. Propaganda headquarters were to found at the residence of Mrs. Piedad Ferrer, where José Luis Boitel,[50] a student, was responsible for communications between the cities of Santiago de Cuba, Havana and Santa Clara in Las Villas province.

The Frente Obrero Nacional (FON), created by Frank País in 1957 as the insurrectionary proletarian arm of the M-26-7, was responsible for mobilizing workers throughout the island. The FON had served as a source of supplies for the Sierra Maestra. It had very few organized cells within the labor movement and, until the strike, Castro used it mainly as a propaganda channel to the labor movement, not as an arm of revolutionary action and organization within the working class. In Oriente, FON was headed by Antonio Torres and Octavio Louit; David Salvador[51] and Arquímedes Caballero were the FON leaders in Camagüey. In Las Villas province, the FON was under the experienced Conrado Bécquer and Raúl Camacho: and Havana's FON included Jesús Soto, José Pellón, José María de la Aguilera and Odón Alvarez de la Campa among others.[52]

Overall, FON could count on various individuals working in the labor movement who were also responsible to their own insurrectionary groups, often helping other movements when requested to do so. FON's lack of thorough organization raised serious doubts as to its performance in the operation. Nevertheless, FON threw its support behind the strike, and began organizing communication centers and supporting intelligence networks while recruiting various women as messenger-carriers between headquarters and the working centers.

The capital was divided into six operational zones. The Youth Brigade of the M-26-7 was assigned the business sector known as Old Havana. Operations in that area were under Captains Marcelo Plá, Mario Gil, Aldo Rivero, Miguel Brugueras and Julio Travieso.[53] Old Havana was the most difficult area of all, for like other Spanish colonial cities, its streets were narrow and twisting, making it difficult for cars to maneuver. Any encounter with Batista's police would be at very close range, which would mean a high number of casualties on both sides. The police, perhaps, could afford this: the Youth Brigade could not.

The remaining zones were placed under the responsibility of various M-26-7 militiamen such as Captains Roberto Rodríguez, in charge of the downtown section; Angel Luis Guí, Manuel Uziel Ramírez, responsible for blowing up the electrical lines; Cecilio Vázquez, José Ferrer and René de los Santos were to operate in Regla and Guanabacoa, two towns adjacent to Havana City. Marcelo Salado and Oscar Lucero, in addition to heading actions in the Vedado sector, were to have supervisory powers over the entire city as chiefs of the action and sabotage section of the M-26-7.[54]

The main objective of the revolutionary action was to create general confusion and chaos, in order to prevent the workers from returning to their jobs. Violence was to give the workers the perfect alibi for staying at home after lunch. While work stoppages and street fighting were effected throughout the island, Castro and his guerrillas would move into the valleys, engage the regular troops, and occupy towns and cities in Oriente province. Once this was accomplished, the general uprising was assured, as thousands would join the revolutionaries through the country. At least this was the sort of revolutionary outcome envisioned by the M-26-7 strategists from Castro on down to Pérez and Manuel Ray. And it was this expectation that the urban M-26-7 leadership impressed upon the minds of its underground fighters.

Though the original strike date was March 31, Faustino Pérez postponed the move, and the guerrillas spent the first week of April waiting for arms to be delivered. Feelings of mistrust began to spread among the rank and file of the M-26-7 urban structure when the cadres reasoned that Castro had had sufficient time to send some of his arms to the cities. Some of Figueres' arms should have arrived shortly after March 31, if not in Havana, then at least in Santiago de Cuba, which was closer to the Sierra.[55] The urban cadres began to suspect that Castro would keep the entire shipment for his guerrillas, and they were, with good reason, resentful; for many months they had collected money, ammunition, arms, food and medical supplies to be shipped to the Sierra Maestra to sustain Castro's guerrillas. Now that they were charged with a very difficult operation, they had no supplies of their own. Nevertheless, it was decided that the strike would proceed on schedule and at any cost.

To meet this critical situation, the underground devised a double-edged contingency plan. Two acts of sabotage were to take place: the first was to blow up the electric company in Havana. Without electricity, great areas of the capital could be brought to a standstill. Captain Sergio ("El Curita") González was put in charge of this operation, but González was soon intercepted by Batista's police and killed. He was succeeded by Captain Arístides Vega, who had knowledge of demolition procedures and access to the electric company plant in Havana. Mysteriously enough, Vega was also caught in a police ambush and killed on the spot.

The second act of sabotage would be almost suicidal. The Youth Brigade was to attack an armory in Old Havana where arms were stocked in unknown amounts. Some of these arms would be given to the cadres, and the rest would be distributed at prearranged points throughout the capital. The success of this attack would depend on the performance of the sharpshooters and the street fighters. With these problems in mind, and with the knowledge that two of the best cadre leaders—González and Vega—had been shot to death, a meeting was called to review the situation.

Objections to the Strike

The meeting was held on the morning of April 8. Faustino Pérez presided over the discussion, which was attended by Manuel Ray, Marcelo Salado, José María de la Aguilera, Odón Alvarez de la Campa, Oscar Lucero, and David Salvador among others.[56] The participants were unanimous in their concern about the lack of arms. Faustino made it clear that the entire machinery of the M-26-7 had already been set in motion, and the strike had to be carried out the following day. In addition, he argued convincingly that Fidel's guerrillas were descending to the *llanos* (plains), "and there was no way to turn back the 'clock of history.'" Faustino posed a challenge to the urban cadres to fulfill their duty to the fatherland, and to offer support to the Sierra guerrillas who presemably were to confront the regular army at any moment.

That very night, some of those who had attended the morning meeting held separate briefing sessions with cadre members from several of the organizations that were to take part in the street fighting. If the strike was to be successful everyone had to know what to do and how to do it. One discussion included representatives of the FON, the action and sabotage cells of the M-26-7, a delegate from the Triple A movement, a delegate from Prío's OA, local organizers of the Union of Bank Employees and a representative of the DR.[57] The meeting raged until the early morning hours of April 9. After each cadre and organizer had presented his point of view, the following consensus emerged from the men who would suffer most if the strike failed:

1. There were not sufficient arms to carry out the tasks assigned to the various groups.
2. The only weapons available were Molotov cocktails, and there were not enough of these, since Faustino Pérez had forbidden the looting of service stations.
3. There seemed to be no alternative plans in the event that the strike failed.
4. The strike was no secret, and Eusebio Mujal's men were on the alert. The experience of his men in handling labor crises could not be underestimated.
5. Without heavy demolition charges, the fight in downtown Havana, and in Matanzas, Camagüey, Santiago de Cuba and Pinar del Río provinces would be extremely perilous. The capital would be open to the army's armored division coming from the Columbia military camp, since the bridges linking the capital with the Columbia camp could not be blown up. Therefore, army tanks could be expected to crush street barricades and inflict heavy damage because of the lack of enough Molotov cocktails to stop them.
6. Cadres were responsible for the lives of their men. To them, the entire operation was useless. Even though Castro and Pérez, with the acquiescence of Marcelo Fernández Font, had planned the undertaking, they were ignorant of the capabilities and needs of the urban branch of the M-26-7.
7. Faustino Pérez was wholly oblivious to the true conditions in the cities.
8. Cadres complained bitterly that Castro had not sent arms long before the strike. Manuel Ray was accused of sheer irresponsibility, for he, if anyone, knew the real situation of the M-26-7 in the cities at that point. At best, the entire situation looked like a potentially Dantesque massacre promoted by the Sierra's wild notions of success.

Before the meeting ended, news arrived that no arms would be available unless the Youth Brigade succeeded in taking over the armory in Old Havana.

At this point, representatives of the Triple A movement and of Prío's OA announced their withdrawal from the operation. It was common for urban movements to help one another in a time of danger in terms of materiel, intelligence and manpower, but this operation seemed too dangerous and too senseless for veteran urban fighters to risk their entire resources and the lives of their *compañeros.*

With only a few hours remaining before the strike, the cadres of the M-26-7 decided to remain with the operation and to do their best for its success. Students of the DR also pledged their aid, and the meeting broke up amidst promises of an effort that would show the *batistianos* that the youth were ready to die fighting face to face. Patriotism, idealism, emotional feelings and a dangerous share of *machismo* prevailed over reason and objectivity, and everyone paid dearly for it.

The Call to Strike

It had been previously agreed that all cadres would start the agitation at noon on April 9. This hour was selected in order to get maximum advantage from siesta time, when the workers went to their homes, and were not back at their jobs until 2 PM. During these two hours, the Youth Brigade would attack the armory, arms would be distributed, and street fighting would create panic and confusion. Urban transportation would be stopped, and people would be unable to return to their jobs even if they wished to do so. Banks would remain closed, stores would not reopen, and the streets would be empty of people, thus allowing sharpshooters to take the initiative without worrying about killing innocent bystanders.

With no prior warning, Pérez changed the strike time. At 11 AM the strike order rang loud and clear through clandestine radios and from headquarters to the Youth Brigade.[58] Dismay, outcry and frustration permeated the ranks of the M-26-7 underground when they were forced to move the entire schedule one hour ahead.

Government forces were waiting for the strike to begin. The Servicio de Inteligencia Militar (SIM), Rolando Masferrer's feared "tigers" and the police patrolled the streets, four men to a car, submachine guns at bay, looking for agitators or signs of revolutionaries.

The first operation of the strike was disastrous and foretold the outcome of the entire action. The Youth Brigade attacked the armory, but found only a few arms which they loaded onto a truck, only to collide with Masferrer's "tigers" in one of the narrow streets of Old Havana. In the ensuing shootout, all the students were killed. Corpses covered the streets and sidewalks of the area. Several blocks away, FON delegates ordered the bank employees to leave their jobs and join the strike. The great majority of the employees refused on the grounds that there was heavy fighting going on in the streets and that to go out meant certain death at the hands of the regime's forces. The police had taken the initiative away from the urban underground, and it was the regime that was firing at random in the streets, instilling panic among the workers and forcing that tiny minority who wanted to join from going out.

Within half an hour, FON delegates were already trying to escape from the working centers. Meanwhile, various sharpshooters took up positions in buildings around the city, usually after disarming policemen in the streets. Within an hour the police had killed most of them, and the rest fled. Students performed incredibly bravely, firing from windows, houses, open doors and roofs. Their arms were mostly .22 caliber rifles. Molotov cocktails were thrown at several intersections in the capital. Fragmentary operations were evident in the electric and transport sectors. Federico Bell Lloch, an engineer, blew up an important register of the electric company, and all commercial activities around Central Park were impaired. Some transport workers abandoned their buses, creating tremendous traffic jams and slowing down the speeding police cars. Other M-26-7 militiamen shot at those buses still running in the streets.

In the city of Guanabacoa, across Havana Bay, underground members—mostly high school students—briefly succeeded in seizing the most important sections of the city. But the population did not second the students' call to help build barricades against the incoming Batista forces. The regime's forces arrived within two hours; the area was placed under military occupation, and most of the underground fighters were killed while trying to escape the encirclement.[59]

Batista's police, Masferrer's "tigers" and the SIM went about the city efficiently, perhaps the first time that Batista's men had so effectively defended the dictatorship. About two hours after the first shots rang out, underground headquarters issued orders to retreat: "Every man for himself," was the message from the leadership. Those who had called for the strike had but minutes to get out of the sight of pro-Batista workers, who were already telephoning the police to deliver known agitators into their hands. The whole M-26-7 underground apparatus in Havana was caught off balance, and the results were catastrophic. Marcelo Salado, chief of action and sabotage, was shot to death while trying to warn some of his men that the strike had failed and that they had to escape. He was just one in a long list of victims and casualties, the exact number of which will probably never be known.

Many of the so-called leaders of the M-26-7 showed extreme cowardice. Jesús Soto, one of Faustino Pérez's closest aides, fled to safety. José María de la Aguilera also abandoned his men from the National Federation of Bank Employees, and was not seen again until Batista's downfall.[60] The supreme architect of the strike, Faustino Pérez, hurriedly disappeared from view, escaping to the Sierra Maestra, closely followed by cadre members who vowed to execute him for treason. Manuel Ray, Reynold González and David Salvador were left to attempt an orderly retreat in order to save as many men as possible.

From Santiago de Cuba, Las Villas, Camagüey and Matanzas provinces came news of complete failure and total disaster. For all practical purposes, the M-26-7 underground movement was decimated in most cities throughout the country. The strike in Sagua la Grande, in Las Villas province, was led by 14 students who were able to blow up sections of the MacFarland Metal Company, burn the Linares lumberyard, portions of the railway between Sagua and La Isabela port, on the north, and perpetrate several sabotage actions in the Santa Teresa and Resulta sugar mills.[61] In Santiago, the M-26-7 militias carried out sabotage actions against gasoline stations while answering the fire of the army from house to house. The Boniato rural post was hit by the militiamen, and the Cuban-Air airlines of Santiago was heavily damaged by a bomb.[62] The toll of known dead in Sagua was estimated at 14; and Santiago, by the evening of April 9, had suffered 23 dead. The total number of casualties, however, was far greater than confirmed.[63] For three days, reports poured through the remaining underground communication channels describing the situation throughout the island.

News of Castro's promised attack on the plains never reached the underground. Though several isolated skirmishes took place, the bulk of Fidel's, "Che's" and Raúl Castro's troops never moved from their positions in the Sierra Maestra and Sierra Cristal, nor had the DR's guerrillas.[64] The urban underground bore the brunt of Fidel Castro's decision to call for a general strike. No explanations were ever forthcoming.

A considerable mythology, on one hand, and a stony silence, on the other, have surrounded the events of April 9, 1958. It can be stated unequivocally that Fidel Castro was responsible for the conception of the strike and for its failure. Manuel Ray did not have the firmness, the courage or the sense to reject the strike idea or even the strike planning imposed by the Sierra delegate, Faustino Pérez. In later years, Castro was to argue that the failure of the strike resulted from "fundamental conflicts of strategy"[65] between the urban and rural branches of the M-26-7. And, at the beginning of the struggle against Batista "it was not clear which was the role of the guerrilla movement, and which was the role of the clandestine struggle."[66] Ernesto "Che" Guevara elaborated that the Sierra position was to win the struggle against Batista "with the Rebel Army as its base," while "the *llano* [urban underground] favored generalized armed struggle throughout the country, culminating in a revolutionary general strike that would drive out the Batista dictatorship and establish a government of 'civilians'; the new army [Rebel army] would then become 'apolitical.'"[67]

These post facto assertions by the Sierra leadership seriously reflect on the intentions of the rural M-2-67 leaders in pressing the urban underground to carry out a strike in the spring of 1958. Such assertions seem to illustrate Castro's consciousness of the growing strength of his M-26-7 movement in the cities, and of the real challenge posed by the urban branch as a future contender for power. The Dirección Nacional of the M-26-7 was—until May

1958—in the hands of a civilian-oriented elite based largely in Havana. To Castro, the M-26-7 in the cities seemed likely to try to strike a compromise with disaffected officers of Batista's armed forces.[68] In this respect, Castro's official position was "to warn . . . that the revolutionary movement would not accept a military coup as the outcome [of the struggle]. . . ."[69] Or "The revolutionary thing is not the coup d'etat but the incorporation of the military into the armed struggle."[70]

The political rationale behind Castro's public and private statements on the issue of a military coup was that any co-opting of the military by the urban branch of the M-26-7 would wrest the leadership of the insurrection away from Fidel Castro, and would render the Rebel Army powerless, or as Guevara aptly defined it, apolitical.

The Meeting at Altos de Mompié

On May 3, 1938, at a place known as Altos de Mompié, the Sierra Maestra leadership met with the leaders of the M-26-7 Dirección Nacional.[71] Present at this meeting and representing the Dirección Nacional—which never wielded any real power over Fidel Castro—were René Ramos Latour, Vilma Espín, Luis Busch, Celia Sánchez, Haydée Santamaría, Marcelo Fernández Font, David Salvador, Enso ("Bruno") Infante, Ñico Torres, Faustino Pérez, and Fidel Castro and Ernesto "Che" Guevara. According to Guevara, he was invited to participate in the discussion at the requests of Faustino Pérez and René Ramos Latour, despite the fact that Guevara had harshly criticized them earlier. Guevara termed the meeting "tense" because the Sierra was to challenge the behavior of the urban combatants "who until that moment, in practice, had run the business of the 26th of July." It was about this "decisive meeting" that Guevara wrote: "The guerrilla concept would emerge triumphant; Fidel's prestige and authority was consolidated, and he was named Commander in Chief of all the forces, including the militia—which until the time had been under the llano leadership—as well as secretary-general of the movement."[72]

The discussions were very heated, especially when the role of the workers' representatives was assessed. "Che" Guevara held that David Salvador of the FON, and René Ramos Latour held the greatest responsibility for the disaster. Guevara argued that "the strike analysis was saturated of subjectivism and putschist conceptions," thus Salvador was accused "of conceiving a sectarian strike forcing other movements to follow behind ours." Faustino Pérez was admonished for lack of perspective in believing there was a "possibility to take over the capital with his militias, without duly appraising the forces of reaction in its main bastion," and Ramos Latour was blamed for lack of vision in expecting that his militias, turned into guerrilla troops for the strike, would perform as those of the Sierra.

For Guevara, who privately assigned great value to the urban struggle,[73] the "weaknesses" of the urban combatants merely demonstrated their moral and combat inferiority in comparison to the Sierra guerrillas. "Che" disdainfully observed that Ramos Latour's militias lacked "training and combat morale, and had not gone through the rigorous process of warfare selectiveness." In addition, "the guerrilla struggle had achieved a great degree of maturity," while the *compañeros* from the cities wore "professionally deformed, i.e., considering the *llano* as more important than the Sierra." Guevara's remarks concerning the city fighter entirely lacked validity. The very nature of urban guerrilla warfare in Cuba made it highly selective in its membership. The "process" to which Guevara referred was even more discriminating than that in the rural areas, for urban guerrillas knew their chances of survival were minimal. Rural fighters had time to learn to avoid the army, and to expand their territory, thus acquiring their own sanctuary. In the urban areas, however, the time factor worked against the city fighters. There the guerrillas were under relentless persecution by the police, the secret services, the SIM and a host of government armed bands. While the rural guerrillas could extend their territory through action, the urban combatants would find themselves more and more surrounded as their faces were recognized, their names posted, and their friends and contacts slowly but surely identified.[74] Had the urban fighters lacked morale there would not have been a Sierra Maestra or a Sierra Cristal, nor so many idealists dead before, during and after the strike.

The outcome of these discussions was not what many underground militants had hoped. René Ramos Latour was retained at the Sierra Maestra by assigning him to a guerrilla group. This in itself was a demotion that came very opportunely in the Sierra strategy. Scarcely two months earlier, "Daniel" had opened up a front to the southeast of Sierra Maestra and to the east of Santiago de Cuba that was to be a link between the Sierra and Raúl Castro's Second Front, "Frank País."[75] In addition, "Daniel" had planned to engage the army at the Boniato rural post on April 9. The strategy had failed, but his men were still positioned between La Gran Piedra and El Cobre, when Belarmino ("Anibal") Castilla, chief of action and sabotage of Orient, broke the news of the strike failure. Furthermore, "Aníbal" conveyed to "Daniel" the "suggestion" that he had to leave his group of men and return to clandestine operations, something which "Daniel" refused to do. "Aníbal" went back to Santiago, then returned to "Daniel's" camp, this time accompanied by Marcelo Fernández, Agustín Navarrete and Vilma Espín. The efforts of this commission to take "Daniel" away from his zone of operation were unsuccessful. Still one more meeting came a week later, when Marcelo Fernández simply appointed "Aníbal" chief of the guerrilla group over and against the opposition of "Daniel."[76] The last vestige of a front independent from the Sierra Maestra "line" disappeared with his removal from the zone of Oriente. At Altos de Mompié, "Daniel's" fate was sealed when he was put in charge of a small column under Castro's close supervision. "Daniel" would die later in what amounted to "a place on the selective list of the Revolution's martyrs."[77]

As for David Salvador, he also was to stay in the Sierra, serving as a delegate of FON. Fidel Castro promoted Faustino Pérez to the post of coordinator of the Civilian and Military Administration of the Free Territory of the Sierra Maestra, although "Che" Guevara considered this a demotion. Actually, to have demoted Faustino Pérez would have been equivalent to casting doubt over Castro's leadership, suggesting that there was something extremely odd about the entire strike operation. Moreover, had Pérez been condemned for ineptitude, Castro would have had to explain—which he never did—why he had not supported the urban operation with the guerrilla attacks he had assured Faustino Pérez would be carried out against the towns and cities of Oriente province. Pérez's promotion indicated to many militants that Castro was above criticism, that no one, no matter how many lives were lost, could question Fidel.

Other changes effected in the 26th of July Movement at Altos de Mompié concerned the appointment of Ñico Torres as leader of FON. In addition, Haydée Santamaría was to take over the movement's finances in exile, and Manuel Urrutia was ratified as candidate for the presidency by the M-26-7. Carlos Franqui, in turn, was ordered back to Sierra Maestra to take charge of Radio Rebelde.

But of all the significant changes resulting from the meeting at Altos de Mompié, Guevara stressed, then and later, the shift of power within the M-26-7 overall structure. First of all, "the war was to be carried out militarily and politically by Fidel, as both Commander in Chief of all the forces and secretary-general of the organization." The "line of the Sierra" was to be followed by all M-26-7 militants, and all decision-making was to emanate from Fidel "thus eliminating certain practical problems . . . that had not enabled Fidel to really exercise the authority he deserved." For "Che," the Sierra's absolute control of the M-26-7 was justified on the basis of "the correctness of our doubts, when we thought of the possibility of failure by the forces of [the] movement attempting a revolutionary strike . . . at a meeting held before April 9." If anything, Altos de Mompié illustrated that not much had changed since the Dirección Nacional lost its only truly independent leader, Frank País.

The May Report

After the Sierra indictment of the M-26-7 urban underground, the latter availed itself of an opportunity to answer and challenge Castro's accusations. On May 11, 1958, Luis Simón, one of the M-26-7 workers' coordinators, hand-delivered a report to Fidel Castro, only excerpts of which have been published.[78] The document, known as the May Report, was signed by Luis Simón, Jorge Ignarra, Enrique Cardoso, Carlos de las Pozas and others numbering up to 15 workers' coordinators that participated in the strike. In addition, the May Report was endorsed by militia captains Aldo Rivero, Marcelo Plá, Mario Gil, Miguel Brugueras and Cecilio Vázquez, all of them members of the Youth Brigade.

"Perhaps, it is not beside the point . . . to point out that many of the under-signed, as well as those who support the enclosed assertions have nothing else to lose but their lives. . . . To think that we are engaged in a race to monopolize on truth or sacrifices . . . is evil-thinking." On the issue of the workers' partic-ipation in the strike, the signers of the May report argued that there was no other way to press the workers to join the strike but through revolutionary action. "It must be said," the report admitted, "that the mass of the workers would have understood no other language . . . since they evidently seem to have a sort of mental disposition that demands 'revolutionary action' as an 'excuse' to 'vacate their jobs, as well as the [backing] of a strong organization as further guarantees." Thus, the M-26-7 workers' section argued that the "basis of the strike did not, therefore, rest on the workers' willingness to [join the strike] but in their cooperation and support to vacate their working centers upon notification." Understandably, the Cuban working class wanted assurances and guarantees that a strong labor organization existed in order to make the strike more forceful. To commit itself to the strike without a well-organized labor movement that answered to the interests of the insurrectionary sector would be sheer suicide and adventurism.

The strike organizers assumed that "sabotage actions against vital industries and a handful of hard-core militants were to guarantee the success of the revo-lutionary strike." To the Sierra Maestra charges that the workers' section of the M-26-7 had remained passive during the strike, the report retorted that "FON's steps were oriented toward the creation of a strong workers' movement," and that in the opinion of its leaders it did fulfill its obligations. On another subject, the report remarked that the Youth Brigade "met failure because of insufficient armament, lack of experience, and poor communication between strike organizers and cadres." The report included the same objections that the cadre members had raised the day before the strike: "Absence of [conditions] and revolutionary morale for lack of enough previous [revolutionary] activi-ties. Of five sabotage actions that were planned, only three took place because of the chaos created by the unexpected orders." Their failure to complete all actions—11 alone were planned for the telephone company—was due to the 11 AM call that took everyone by surprise.

"From the above analysis," the report went on, "it can be ascertained that we have been the victims of the agitation and propaganda apparatus set up to cut the regime to pieces, and lost sight of the real strength of our forces under the optical aggrandizement of our leaders.' In a spirit of self-criticism, the signers of the report realized that "we have fallen into the prejudice of supposing the regime weaker than it really is—and it is very weak. And our leaders, far from being representatives, further distorted the situation and the information that surrounded them."

Clearly, the M-26-7 underground was challenging Castro's lack of activity Prior to the strike, the mounting propaganda that distorted the underground's assessment of Batista's forces, and his judgment in appointing Pérez as coordinator of the urban operation. Since Pérez had been the principal decision-maker during the April strike, he shared most of the guilt. In reality, Faustino Pérez was partially guilty. For the urban resistance leaders who acquiesced to Pérez's decisions were also attempting to cover up their own lack of vision. Urban leaders of the M-26-7 had accepted Castro's view that a general strike was feasible at that time, and that "orders are to be obeyed and not to be discussed."

Feelings of mistrust, disappointment and anger deepened between Havana and Sierra Maestra, and this pointed up the two sectors' differences in methodology, resources and objectives. For Ray, less secrecy, direct contact with the workers well ahead of time, and proper armaments were essential for a successful strike. FON delegates could have counted on effective support from the workers had there been an organization to convert the strike into a truly mass movement backed by revolutionary action (Frank País' thesis).

Faustino Pérez, however, officially argued that surprise was the most significant factor in deciding the outcome of the operation.[79] The need for secrecy was justified on the basis that street fighting, sabotage and terrorism must precede the strike order. Should the date and hour be decided beforehand, Pérez argued, the underground fighters would be left to face a well-prepared government counteroffensive. In this sense, Pérez's thinking reflected his Sierra Maestra training, where ambushes against the army had depended on surprise. Such thinking was undisputably correct for the rural areas, but in the cities, it implied a complete disregard for psychological warfare and seemed to depart from the tenets of the "action groups," which held that action mobilized the masses, and that action alone determined the revolutionary process. Cuban workers knew that the M-26-7 was poorly organized within the labor movement. Most of all they were aware of their lack of experience in handling labor strikes. Even the cadres began to realize this in the meetings prior to the calling of the strike.

The May Report reflected the views of those who had been accused by the Sierra Maestra leadership of promoting the strike, imposing it on the Sierra itself, and committing tremendous blunders based on mistaken assumptions and erroneous orders. The report (at least what is known of it) did not address itself to the question of who was responsible for the corpses that Batista's police threw all over the cities and towns of the country as an example.

A New Alignment: The Communists

Ñico Torres was assigned David Salvador's post, and at the same time ordered to work with the Communists in preparation for a future general strike. Fidel was already waiting for a representative of the PSP to visit the mountains to discuss future cooperation. Guevara wrote that Torres accepted the order reluctantly, but said that he would cooperate with the "Stalinists."[80]

The Communists had openly opposed the strike. There were Communist labor organizers who strongly objected to the strike on the morning of April 9, even before the order had been issued from headquarters. There were instances when the Communists called upon the police—who were patrolling the streets—to arrest strike organizers of the M-26-7. A Communist labor organizer by the name of Alberto Puig—also known in Old Havana as "Papi"—went out even before the strike order was issued to point out active militants of FON to Masferrer's "tigers." Paying for his betrayal, Puig was shot to death by a strike organizer on the corner of Aguiar and Obrapia at exactly 2 PM. Near the same place three other Communist saboteurs stopped Roberto René de los Santos and Cruz Sanabria, strike organizers of the OA movement who were cooperating with the M-26-7. The Communists delivered the two men to the authorities, and their bodies were found on April 14, 1958, in the Nuevo Vedado section of Havana. There were other instances of the Communists' active and militant opposition to the general strike. At the Royal Bank of Canada's main office in Old Havana, two known members of the PSP left the employees' area and sought refuge in the executive office. They needed the protection of Canadian bank officials in the event that strike organizers decided to shoot them to death for sabotage. At the Bank of Nova Scotia a Communist militant delivered to the police a list of names of people who had supported the strike in any way. The man in charge of serving as an informer in the banking unions was Pedro Ruíz, called "El Mejicano." Throughout the capital, there were instances which repeatedly pointed to the Communists as traitors rather than as "neutrals" to the strike. While young insurgents were persecuted in the capital, particularly after the strike, Juan Marinello took his daily walks in the Central Park of Havana, accompanied at all times by two SIM agents who protected his life against possible attempts to avenge some *compañeros* whom the Communists delivered to Batista's police.[81] It is not surprising that urban militants felt strongly anti-Communist. It was not so much a matter of ideological differences—the Communists being far more to the right than Batista—for very few urban fighters knew much about Marxism, Leninism, the PSP or the theory of the class struggle. They were fighters who viewed everything in black and white. The Communists were *batistianos*, for there is no middle ground in an insurrectionary process. No official literature, no dialectical explanation, justified to the fighters any cooperation with enemies of the people. While the Communist position would change immediately after the strike attempt, their well-established record of collaboration with Batista's henchmen would not be easily forgotten.

In May 1958, Carlos Rafael Rodríguez and Osvaldo Sánchez of the PSP went to Sierra Maestra. Aníbal Escalante, secretary general of the Communist party, and in charge of its strategy, briefed Rodríguez on the line to take with Fidel. Escalante wrote a memorandum with instructions for Fidel, containing advice on the best means of conducting the war, on running the country, on the correct attitude Castro should adopt toward other political groups and on international politics.[82] Rather than presenting these instructions to Castro, Carlos Rafael Rodríguez told Osvaldo Sánchez: "I am going to the Sierra to listen to him, to hear what he expects of us, and not ram our policy down his throat."[83]

To date, no evidence is available as to what transpired between Castro and the PSP envoy. It is certain, however, that after Rodríguez' visit to the Sierra Maestra leader, the PSP allowed its militants to support the M-26-7. Members of the PSP began to arrive at Raúl Castro's Second Front, "Frank País," and a small guerrilla group commanded by Félix Torres was organized in the Yaguajay area, Las Villas province.

The New Reality

The April strike and its failure had served Fidel Castro well. After April 9, 1958, the political and military foci of the insurrection became the Sierra Maestra, the Sierra Cristal and the Escambray Mountains.[84] Guevara discussed the new situation in clear terms: "An ideological struggle developed within the M-26-7 which brought about a radical change in the analysis of the country's realities and in its activist sectors. . . . Precisely at this time the rebel army took its first steps to develop the theory and doctrine of the Revolution; this demonstrated that the insurrectionary movement had grown and achieved political maturity. We moved from an experimental stage to a constructive one, from trials to definite deeds."[85] Unfortunately, Castro's "trial" and "experiment" was paid for with the death of scores of men in the cities.

Other urban movements not under Castro's control, but with more experience and contacts in the labor movement than Castro's youthful militants, were also affected by the failure of the strike. For months the OA, the Triple A of Aureliano Sánchez Arango, plus elements close to various independent labor groups, had been working on secret plans for an effective general strike. But when Castro took the initiative away from them all, further efforts at organizing a general strike were futile. The workers would not easily forget the terrible impact of defeat and the official terrorism that followed the strike; the memory of Batista's men killing anyone who was walking in the streets terrified men and women throughout the island. More and more, with no real possibility of overthrowing Batista through a general strike, urban insurrectionists from every movement turned to the Sierra Maestra, the only focus of organized and disciplined resistance that remained untouched by the dictatorship. Castro was not opposed to receiving the aid of various urban groups, including the Communists, as long as he played the decisive role in the leadership of the insurrection. To that end, he would negotiate with anyone who could contribute something to his victory.[86]

The government maneuvers and measures which met the strike revealed to Castro the preparation of Batista's military, the regime's intelligence information and its capabilities in general. Castro also learned Batista's resourcefulness and experience in dealing with strikes and maneuvers to precipitate panic among the workers.[87] He had gained considerable knowledge about the regime's organization.

Internationally, the April defeat enhanced Castro's prestige.[88] Few people knew the realities of the operation and Castro's role in its failure. As mentioned earlier, activity prior to the strike precipitated the U.S. announcement that it was placing an arms embargo on Batista's regime because the situation inside Cuba was recognized as a civil war in which a foreign government theoretically could not intervene.

Interpreting the lack of popular response to the strike as a sign of support for Batista, many army officers concluded that Batista should take the initiative and liquidate the remnants of insurrection in Cuba, the Sierra Maestra guerrillas. Batista was placed in a position where he was forced to proceed against Castro's Sierra Maestra, Reluctantly, Batista responded as Castro had expected him to.

The next few months were decisive. A government attack against the Sierra Maestra would result in the defeat either of the rebels or, in the event of failure, the crumbling of the Batista regime. In a very real sense, Castro had accelerated a final confrontation between his guerrillas and the regular army. Fully aware that the army had been unable, for over a year, to crush the guerrillas in the mountains, Castro's best opportunity to finally demoralize Batista's forces was by defeating a large military offensive. Precipitating a conclusion to the struggle was necessary, for although the army was unable to liquidate the guerrillas, it was also true that the guerrillas were unable to sustain themselves for a long period of time in the valleys. The guerrilla movement was at this time clearly in its second stage of development; that is, quite capable of maintaining a core territory, but not yet strong enough to make the transition from a guerrilla to a more conventional army. If the regular army failed to crush the rebel army, Fidel Castro could turn that failure into the biggest, most serious political victory of the forces of the insurrection. Such an outcome would not only destroy the regular army's will to fight, but would also bring into question the regime's capability for survival among those close to Batista. It would also, presumably, open up great opportunities for maneuvers of a conspiratorial nature with military officers, and in conspiracies Fidel always excelled.

The Aftermath

The declaration of a state of national emergency was followed, on April 16, 1958, by a new presidential decree which suspended constitutional guarantees. For the remaining nine months, until the collapse of the Batista regime, constitutional guarantees were suspended every 45 days. A lame congress ratified every suspension without debate.[89]

As a mere formality, the congress received a report listing the special laws passed during the state of emergency—laws destined to cleanse the government of non-Batista supporters and to eliminate every source of resistance. Some of these laws showed that there were antigovernment elements in areas previously viewed by sympathizers of the insurrection as entrenched defenders of the regime. This, Law No. 3[90] implemented measures against employees and functionaries of the state, the provinces and the municipalities, and corporations as well as persons in "official institutions of retirement or social security, who promoted and incited the violation of the powers of the State or the resistance to the Constitution and the laws." The same law stated that the measures were directed against anyone who at any time during the crisis called in any way for support of the political strike, exerted pressure upon management or raised money for the revolutionaries. Another decree gave Batista the right to draft into the armed forces, as members of the military or naval reserves, employees of public enterprises in case of grave alteration or suspension of constitutional guarantees.[91]

Student protests led to Batista's sweeping decree in which all local boards of education were dissolved throughout the country. Hundreds of teachers were expelled from their jobs, regardless of their involvement in the demonstrations. Any educator who had in his record any sign of not being a *batistiano* was summarily dismissed. Those who had influence with the politicos close to Batista were left untouched, however, even if they had demonstrated against the regime.

Apparently feeling more secure in the cities, Batista raised all local taxes, a measure directed at augmenting the ranks of the police. The sum of $15 million was designated for the construction of military works.[92] Public contracts for these works were given to firms that had sided firmly with the government during the crisis.

Mujal's CTC won Batista's approval for its behavior during the attempted strike. Mujal had been approached by various people claiming to represent the M-26-7 who suggested a possible understanding with the insurrectionists. The Communists, Mujal's former comrades, also approached him through Francisco Calderío (Blas Roca) for a possible pact of mutual cooperation.[93]

Mujal, a veteran politician, a former Communist and a shrewd strategist, was aware that Batista's days were numbered. When Serafino Romualdi, American Federation of Labor representative to Latin America and director of the Institute for Free Labor Development, visited Cuba in March of 1958, Mujal told him that eventually the CTC would have to disengage itself from Batista.[94] Following the frustrated April strike, Mujal attempted to contact former president Prío with an offer for support in a general strike against Batista. However, Prío refused to negotiate with Mujal,[95] a former Auténtico, on the grounds that the insurrection was well on the march to victory without the need of Mujal's cooperation. Although he tried to move his peons favorably in the Cuban political chess game, it was too late for Mujal to turn back.[96] The insurrectionists saw him as a dangerous enemy, a factor in the backwardness and lack of revolutionary cohesion of the working class.

Notes

1. See U.S. Department of State, *Bulletin*, 26, no. 662 (March 3, 1952): 337.

2. Charles Shaw, "La actitud de los Estados Unidos hacia Cuba," *Bohemia* (Havana), February 22, 1959, pp. 4–6, 172–73.

3. Unlike the Committee in Exile, an M-26-7 organization, the civic institutions were a conglomerate of religious and professional groups that included the Cuban Council of Evangelical Churches, the Masonic Lodge, the Cuban Association of Lawyers, Dentists and Doctors, and others as well.

4. See Mario Llerena, "La bilis de los mediocres," *Bohemia* (Havana), March 29, 1959, p. 49.

5. Letter of Ernesto Betancourt to the authors (December 6, 1972).

6. Mario Llerena, manuscript, "The Unsuspected Revolution," pp. 234–35.

7. U.S. Congressional Record (House of Representatives), March 28, 1958, pp. 4407–08.

8. Earl T. Smith, *The Fourth Floor* (New York: Random House, 1962), p. 102.

9. Fulgencio Batista, *Cuba Betrayed* (New York: Vantage Press, 1962), p. 94.

10. U.S. Department of State, *Bulletin*, 26, no. 662 (March 3, 1952): 684–85.

11. See *Sierra Maestra* (Organo Oficial del Movimiento 26 de Julio en el Exilio), vol. I (July 1958): also see chapter 11 in this book.

12. Armando Hart, "Justificación de la revolución y estrategia frente a la dictadura," *Lunes de Revolución* (Havana), no. 19, July 26, 1959, p. 40.

13. "Carta de Frank País a Fidel Castro, July 7, 1957," *Pensamiento Crítico* (Havana), no. 29 (June 1969), p. 252.

14. Letter by Vilma Espín to an exiled revolutionary dated August 14, 1957. See *Mil Fotos Cuba, territorio libre de América* (Havana: Comité Central del Partido Comunista de Cuba, 1967), p. 206. Faustino Pérez also referred to this strike as further proof of the possibility for the future general strike. See Faustino Pérez, "La sierra, el llano: eslabones de un mismo combate," *Pensamiento Crítico* (Havana), no. 31 (1969), p. 73.

15. In a letter to Fidel Castro dated August 1957, "Che" wrote: "I believe you will have to make a strong decision and send, as chief of Santiago, a man with qualities as a good organizer who shares the Sierra strategy. To my knowledge, that man can be Raúl or Almeida, or on the contrary Ramirito (Ramiro Valdés) or myself. . ." See Carlos Franqui, "Che Guevara, textos inéditos y poco conocidos," *Libre* (Paris), no. 1 (September–November, 1971), p. 7. Franqui remarks that "this letter shows how important for Che was the struggle in the cities, and the existence of the Movement." Ibid.

16. Faustino Pérez, "Carta de Faustino Pérez a los compañeros y compañeras de Santiago, Sierra Maestra, August 12, 1958," *Lunes de Revolución* (Havana), no. 19, July 26, 1959, p. 29. This letter was broadcast by the rebel radio station two weeks after Major René Ramos Latour died at the battle of "El Jobal" on July 30, 1958.

17. See Humberto Hernández, "Daniel: un comandante del pueblo," *Lunes de Revolución* (Havana), no. 19, July 26, 1959, pp. 26–28.

18. Espín, *Mil Fotos*, p. 206.

19. Ibid.

20. Pérez, "Carta de Faustino Pérez," p. 29.

21. "Daniel" had been second-in-command of the first reinforcements sent to the guerrillas in the Sierra on March 1957. In June, he had been assigned

to open a second guerrilla front by Frank País in the area of Mayarí Arriba, Sierra Cristal, where he lived and worked as an accountant for the Nickel Processing Corporation. In addition, he was chief of action and sabotage of Oriente province at the time of País' death, and chief of the M-26-7 militias throughout the country. See "El Comandante Daniel," *Bohemia* (Havana), July 23, 1965, pp. 46–49.

22. Letter by Fidel Castro to Mario Llerena, October 1957, Llerena manuscript, p. 181.

23. *El Cubano Libre* became a reality when "Daniel" sent Guevara an old mimeograph machine, ink, paper and various supplies. From excerpted correspondence between "Daniel" and Guevara it seems that the Santiago underground did not think the paper serious, due to its limited circulation (at the most 600) and readers (mostly the rebel troops and neighboring peasants). It can be safely suggested that the relations between these two insurrectionists were not especially friendly. See Nydia Sarabia, "Ernesto 'Che' Guevara, fundador de *El Cubano Libre,*" *Bohemia* (Havana), October 20, 1967, pp. 78–81; *A Sketch on the Clandestine and Guerrilla Press Covering the Period 1952–1958* (Havana: Instituto Cubano del Libro, 1971), pp. 67–73.

24. Ernesto "Che" Guevara, "Editorial," *El Cubano Libre* (Sierra Maestra), Organo del Ejército Revolucionario Nueva Era 1, pp. 1, 3, as quoted in *A Sketch on the Clandestine and Guerrilla Press*, pp. 68–69, and in "*El Cubano Libre* por toda la Sierra," *Cuba Internacional* (Havana), (May–June 1970), p. 112.

25. Fidel Castro, "Carta a la Junta de Liberación Cubana," in *Che* (Havana: Instituto Cubano del Libro, 1969), p. 117. See also Rolando E. Bonachea and Nelson P. Valdés, eds., *Revolutionary Struggle: 1947–1958, vol. I* (Cambridge: MIT Press, 1972), pp. 360–61.

26. Carlos Manuel Rubiera, "Traían en las sayas desde Miami armas y balas las muchachas de resistencia cívica," *Bohemia* (Havana), February 15, 1959, p. 21.

27. Armando Hart was arrested by the Havana police when he was found with a letter he had written to "Che" Guevara in which Hart was critical of the guerrilla leader for an incident in which Guevara harshly criticized "Daniel." Guevara described Hart's letter to him as "controversial." This episode sheds further light on the relations between Guevara and Daniel, and suggests that Hart had sided with "Daniel." For a description of this quarrel see *Che*, p. 84, and Humberto Hernández, "Daniel, un Comandante del pueblo," *Lunes de Revolución* (Havana), July 26, 1959, pp. 26–8. Hart was not set free until the overthrow of the dictatorship, and Marcelo ("Zoilo") Fernández Font immediately occupied Hart's position in the Dirección Nacional on January 1958, and not in May 1958 as Guevara has elsewhere stated (see *Che*, p. 107).

28. *Che*, p. 107. The Manzanillo councilman was Lalo Roca.

29. Homer Bigart's coverage of this interview appeared in the *New York Times*, February 26, 1958, pp. 1, 3.

30. Evidence of Dr. Manuel Urrutia Lleó to the authors, New York, New York, January 1973.

31. About this crucial meeting, Faustino Pérez stated in 1967: "we [the M-26-7 Dirección Nacional] believed the conditions were ripe to call the strike, and so we went to the Sierra Maestra to discuss this problem." See Pérez,

"La sierra, el llano," p. 74. This is simply not true. The Dirección Nacional's meeting at the Sierra was prompted by Castro's astonishing declarations to Homer Bigart of the *New York Times* (note 29). While there, it was Fidel Castro, not "the *llano* (a Guevara word for the M-26-7 in the cities), who pressed for the idea of the strike as evidenced in a document drafted by Marcelo Fernández, dated March 18, 1958, entitled "Circular de Organización CO-2," sent to M-26-7 members abroad. A slightly excerpted copy of this memorandum appears in Llerena's manuscript, pp. 250–53. On the genesis of the strike, K. S. Karol's *Guerrillas in Power: The Course of the Cuban Revolution* (New York: Hill and Wang, 1970) observes: "a whole series of documents, including letters by Fidel to Faustino Pérez before and after the strike, prove quite clearly that the strike was not the result of a unilateral decision by the *Llano* group, but was demanded by the Sierra." Manuel Ray, member of the M-26-7 Strike Committee, told the authors that though "the idea of the strike was always the central strategy of the M-26-7, the time and the plan for the strike came from the Sierra" (authors' interview with Manuel Ray, Union City, New Jersey, February 1973).

32.   Captain José Lupiañez, "Segundo Frente Oriental 'Frank País,'" *Verde Olivo* (Havana), March 9, 1969, pp. 9–10.

33.   Llerena, "Circular de Organización CO-2," pp. 250–53.

34.   Captain Carlos Chaín recalls that "Daniel" suggested that wherever possible, "allow for the movement to join the guerrilla struggle," meaning coordinated actions in the cities as well as against rural posts. "El Comandante Daniel," p. 47.

35.   At La Plata, Fidel had set up his headquarters (in the spring of 1958) in a rundown hut fully supplied with "bags of rice, beans, canned food, cigars, several knapsacks, the archives of the Revolution; in addition there were all types of arms, ammunition boxes of every caliber, medicines, radio amplifiers, an electric plant, a TV set, four battery radios and books—Niccolo Machiavelli's *The Prince*, and José Martí's *Obras completas.*" Agustín Alles Soberón, "Los primeros periodistas cubanos en la Sierra Maestra," *Bohemia* (Havana), February 22, 1959, p. 135. This interview was held in March 1958, but due to censorship it was not published until the triumph of the Cuban insurrection.

36.   Ibid. According to Alles Soberón, Castro "was vividly interested in learning how things looked for the general strike."

37.   See *Proclama-Manifiesto a la Nación*, Estado Mayor de la Comandancia del Ejército Rebelde (March 12, 1958), p. 1, and "Manifiesto del 26 de Julio al Pueblo," *Pensamiento Crítico* (Havana), no. 28 (May 1969), pp. 122–27.

38.   Castro inserted Faustino's name on the document *pro forma*. Had Faustino Pérez been at La Plata when Alles Soberón was shown the manifesto, and listened to its reading by Fidel himself, most likely the *Bohemia* newsman would have recorded it. The available evidence suggests that the only well-known person around Castro that moment was Celia Sánchez who transcribed the dictation.

39.   Tony Delahoza, "El 9 de Abril de 1958," *Bohemia* (Havana), April 19, 1959, p. 59. This is the only comprehensive written account of the April 9, 1958 strike compiled by Tony Delahoza, M-26-7 member of the Civic Resistance Movement, and editor of the *Bohemia's* "Sección en Cuba."

40. See Fidel Castro "Carta a la Junta de Liberación Cubana."
41. The role played by the Protestant churches in the course of the Cuban insurrection has received little or no attention. It appears that at various stages during the struggle, the M-26-7 urban leadership was in the hands of Protestant-affiliated militants, such as Frank, Josué, and Agustín País, Marcelo Salado, Oscar Lucero, Manuel and René Ray, Rolando Cubelas, José ("Pepín") Naranjo, Dr. Mario Llerena, Faustino Pérez, Dr. Julio Martínez Páez, Dr. Eliodoro Martínez Junco, Esteban Hernández, Rev. Agustín González Seisdedos. Félix Pena and many others. See Charles C. Shaw, "The Price of Freedom," *Presbyterian Life* (February 15, 1959), pp. 24–25. For the role of the Catholic church see Leslie Dewart, *Christianity and Revolution: The Lesson of Cuba* (New York: Herder and Herder, 1963), pp. 92–137.
42. The Dispensario Clínico was located in a building annexed to the church, and attended by Faustino Pérez, Dr. Julio Martínez Páez, Armenia Jiménez and the missionary, Felina Llanez (Evidence of Armenia Jiménez, teacher of La Progresiva, to one of the authors, February 1959, Cárdenas, Matanzas).
43. M-26-7 bonds were sold to the students of La Progresiva and given to professor Esteban Hernández (assassinated during the April strike of 1958 after heavy torture). M-26-7 treasurer in the city of Cárdenas. Also medicines, paper, mimeograph machines and a medical mobile unit were made available to M-26-7 militants and rebels (Evidence of one of the authors attending La Progresiva at the time). Also see Louis C. Krochler, "An American Teacher Views Days of Terror . . . and Victory," *Presbyterian Life* (February 15, 1959), pp. 27–9. Miss Krochler belonged to La Progresiva faculty.
44. Authors' interview with President José Figueres (Buffalo, New York, March 23–25, 1968).
45. "Ley No. 2 del 1ro. de Abril: Estado de Emergencia Nacional," *Gaceta Oficial* (Havana), 7, no. 15 (April 1, 1958): 1–4.
46. The CTC labor leadership had struck a compromise of "nonaggression" with the dictator on March 11, 1952, despite the fact that 24 hours earlier it had called for a strike in support of President Carlos Prío. The pact between labor leaders and Batista "assured the workers of their rights," but in fact it was a step in the direction of accommodating labor to the *de facto* regime (Letter of Eusebio Mujal, former CTC secretary general, to one of the authors, July 8, 1968). Also see *Hoy* (Havana), March 19, 1952, p. 1, and *Prensa Libre* (Havana), March 13, 1952.
47. See *El País* (Havana), March 31, 1958, p. 13.
48. See Tony Delahoza, "Entrevista a Manuel Ray," *Bohemia* (Havana), February 15, 1959, p. 34.
49. Alberto Acosta, "Una vida ejemplar: Marcelo Salado," *Bohemia* (Havana), April 9, 1971, pp. 4–6.
50. José Luis Boitel was a candidate for the presidency of the FEU against Rolando Cubelas in 1959–60. Cubelas was backed by Raúl Castro, and Boitel was literally forced to withdraw his candidacy at the last minute; later charged with treason. Boitel was sentenced to La Cabaña prison, and died holding a hunger strike in protest for conditions prevalent in Cuban prisons in 1972. See Theodore A. Ediger, "Cuban Freedom Fighter Dies in Jail," *The Times of the Americas* (July 12, 1972).

51. David Salvador, formerly a Communist, an Auténtico, an Ortodoxo and then member of the labor section of the M-26-7, became secretary-general of the CTC after 1959. In 1960 he was sentenced to prison for conspiring against the revolutionary government. See Hugh Thomas, *Cuba: The Pursuit of Freedom* (New York: Harper and Row, 1971), pp. 872, 1348.

52. "El 9 de Abril de 1958," p. 59.

53. Ibid., p. 60.

54. Ibid., p. 59.

55. On March 31 the arms arrived and were transported to Sierra Maestra by rural teacher Hubert Matos, who had accompanied Manuel Rojo on the flight from Costa Rica to Cuba (Evidence of Captain Dionisio Suárez, personal adjutant of Major Hubert Matos. Union City), February 1973. Another group that had been promised weapons was Raúl Castro's "Second Front 'Frank País.'" who in his diary campaign records: "'Daniel' told me [of] a shipment acquired abroad [part of which] is to be sent over this zone . . . it was supposed to arrive a day before our interview [March 29] but they suspended the shipment as they could not get in touch with me on time." A few lines later, Raúl says: "'Daniel' tells me [the shipment] was sent entirely to you [that is, to Fidel Castro], and seemingly it arrived well." See "Diario de Campaña de Raúl Castro," in Edmundo Desnoes, ed., *La sierra y el llano* (Havana: Casa de las Américas, 1961). pp. 222–23, 225. This is further evidence of how the Sierra Maestra leadership demanded (and always obtained) what Castro, in an August 11, 1957 letter to "Aly" (Celia Sánchez) characterized as 'The most fitting slogan of the day ought to be, *All guns, all bullets, and all Resources to the Sierra'.* See Regis Debray, *Revolution in the Revolution?* (New York: Grove Press, 1967), p. 76.

56. Evidence of Allan López to one of the authors, April 8, 1958. Allan López was member of the Asociación de Jóvenes Estúdiantes Católicos (Association of Catholic Youth Students) and in late 1959, he disclosed to one of the authors, he in fact was a member of the PSP ordered to infiltrate the Catholic youth movement.

57. Evidence of one of the authors, present at this meeting (April 8, 1958, Havana).

58. One of the authors was at the time in the temporary quarters of the Union of Bank Employees in Havana, and along with members of the Youth Brigade heard this order repeated several times.

59. Manuel Pérez Dávila to one of the authors on April 9, 1958, Guanabacoa, Havana. Also see "La huelga del 9 de abril," *Bohemia* (Havana), April 4, 1968, pp. 52–54.

60. In 1959, Aguilera told one of the authors that he had left Havana "only when it was all over, and any resistance was useless. . . ." Others who fled even before the strike had been declared a disaster were Carlos Lechuga and Eladio Blanco. The Youth Brigade, and the militants of several action cells were helplessly abandoned by the cowardice of most of their leaders at the top echelons of the M-26-7.

61. Luis Rolando Cabrera, "Sagua la Grande escribió su nombre en la historia, el nueve de abril," *Bohemia* (Havana), April 5, 1959, pp. 36–38.

62. "La huelga del 9 de abril," p. 54.

63. The death toll in Havana by a conservative estimate has been set at 300 (Evidence of Manuel Ray to the authors, Union City, New Jersey, February 1973).

64. This is evidenced in Castro's military orders at the time amounting to "ambushes" against patrolling army units or isolated rural posts. See Luis Pavón, ed., *Días de combate* (Havana: Instituto del Libro, 1970), pp. 55–76. Raúl Castro wrote: "Faced with a general strike movement there was little we could do militarily except to offer moral support in a given zone." See "Diario de Campaña de Raúl Castro," p. 220. Guevara later asserted the Sierra Maestra guerrillas gave logistical support to the urban underground by sending Major Camilo Cienfuegos to "the Bayamo area," See "Che" Guevara, Preface to *El Partido marxista-leninista* in Regis Debray, *Revolution in the Revolution?*, p. 78. The fact is that Major Camilo Cienfuegos moved on Bayamo to take over the control of M-26-7 guerrillas sponsored by the Bayamo underground that was led by Orlando Lara. Cienfuegos' arrival was on March 28, 1958. A recent source states: "some of the combatants interviewed recall several differences of opinion among the 26 of July (rural and urban) commands ... Orlando Lara was opposed to accepting the leadership of Camilo Cienfuegos who was sent ... by the Sierra leaders." See "Historia de Bayamo," *Revista de la Universidad de La Habana* (Havana), vol. 32, no. 192 (1968), pp. 68, 73.

65. Debray, *Revolution in the Revolution?*, p. 78.

66. Fidel Castro Ruz, "Speech at Sagua la Grande, April 9, 1968," in *Política Internacional* (Havana), nos. 22–24 (1968): 75.

67. Debray, *Revolution in the Revolution?*, p. 78.

68. It is known that in late 1957, Agustín Capó, an engineer and active M-26-7 member with the Civic Resistance Movement in Havana, made a trip to Bayamo accompanied by a representative of a group of military officers who held conversations with Fidel Castro in the Sierra Maestra. See Carlos Manuel Rubiera, "Traían en las sayas. . . ." p. 21. Point 5 of Castro's "Manifiesto del 26 de Julio al Pueblo," *Pensamiento Crítico*, p. 125, observes that "The general strike and the armed struggle will relentlessly continue if a military junta attempted to take over the government. . . ." Regis Debray who researched Castro's private letters and documents, asserts that: "At the beginning, when the rebels were weak, Fidel strongly discouraged attempts to stage coups d'etat and contacts with the military. . . . Later when the Sierra ... acquired sufficient strength ... Fidel lost no opportunity to make contact with the military. . . ." Regis Debray, *Revolution in the Revolution?*, p. 84. Fidel Castro stated in Sagua la Grande: "There were *compañeros* among the revolutionary ranks who believed ... the struggle would end with a type of military uprising." Fidel Castro, "Speech in Sagua la Grande, April 9, 1968," *Política Internacional* (Havana), nos. 22–24 (1968): 75.

69. Fidel Castro, "Speech in Sagua la Grande, April 9, 1968," p. 75.

70. Letter of Fidel Castro to Julio Camacho, M-26-7 action and sabotage cadre in Guantánamo, and participant in the Cienfuegos military uprising, as quoted by Regis Debray, *Revolution in the Revolution?*, p. 85. The letter was dated October 10, 1958.

71. The "Altos de Mompié Meeting," otherwise known as "Una reunión decisiva," was first disclosed in an article by Ernesto ("Che") (Guevara that appeared

in *Verde Olivo* (Havana), November 22, 1964. See also Ernesto ("Che") Guevara. *Pasajes de la guerra revolucionaria cubana* (Mexico: Ediciones Era, S.A., 1969), pp. 208–14.

72. Guevara, *Pasajes*, pp. 208–09.

73. See footnote 15 of this chapter.

74. An insightful analysis of the clandestine struggle vis-à-vis the struggle in the mountains is found in Euclídes Vázquez, "En torno al Movimiento 26 de Julio," *Lunes de Revolución* (Havana), no. 19, July 26, 1959, pp. 4–5.

75. Major Antonio E. Lussón. "El ataque al cuartel de Ramón de Las Yaguas," *Días de combate*, p. 58, and "El Comandante Daniel," p. 47.

76. Ibid. These meetings were held the last two weeks of April 1958.

77. Guevara, *Pasajes*, p. 211.

78. Luis Simón was the M-26-7 workers' coordinator of the electrical sector in Havana, Simón had been appointed by the Havana underground to take the May Report to Castro along with "some propositions about an agrarian reform, and a proposal for institutional reforms. . . ." See Luis Simón, "Mis relaciones con el 'Ché' Guevara," *Cuadernos* (Paris), no. 60, (May, 1962): 36–37. For excerpts of the May Report see "El 9 de Abril de 1958," Bohemia (Havana), April 19, 1959, p. 112.

79. See Faustino Pérez, "La sierra, el llano: eslabones de un mismo combate," *Pensamiento Critico* (Havana), no. 31, (1969), p. 75, and "El 9 de Abril de 1958," p. 112.

80. Guevara, *Pasajes*, p. 210.

81. One of the authors recalls clearly how the PSP weekly *Frontera*—copies of which could not be found in this research—just before the strike was announced by the M-26-7 cells, openly supported Eusebio Mujal's position against agitation! In 1959, several Communist informers during the strike — who had fearfully stayed away from their jobs under threats of reprisals — reemerged in public life dressed in olive green fatigues and newly grown beards. At the Federation of Bank Employees, one of the authors petitioned its executive council to immediately investigate the role of such Communist informers, but was told that "revolutionary unity" demanded a postponement of complaints against these persons. This position was defended by Odón Alvarez de la Campa — now exiled in Orlando, Florida.

82. K.S. Karol, *Guerrillas in Power*, p. 153.

83. Ibid.

84. After the strike it was virtually impossible to persuade the workers to cooperate with the insurrection against Batista, and the militants had to force them to give money for guns and bullets at gun point. Working centers in Havana, Matanzas, Las Villas and Camagüey were permeated by fears. In spite of these "subjective conditions" Castro was determined as ever to call for another general strike as he disclosed to Karl Meyer of the *Washington Post*. See *Hispanic American Report*, 11, no. 9 (September 1958): 495. This is further supported in evidence of Manuel Ray to the authors (Union City, New Jersey, February 1973).

85. See Rolando E. Bonachea and Nelson P. Valdés, eds., *Che: Selected Works of Ernesto Guevara* (Cambridge: MIT Press, 1969), p. 198.

86. See Luis Simón, "Mis relaciones con el 'Che' Guevara," p. 35. Simón had been one of the M-26-7 contacts who set up Castro's interview with General

Eulogio Cantillo. In addition, see chapter on the summer offensive for negotiations with Batista's generals.

87. Guevara would write: "The experience taught us a lesson." Bonachea and Valdés. *Che: Selected Works*, p. 198.

88. Hugh Thomas concluded that the failure of the strike reduced Castro's prestige considerably. Yet, unaware of the inner-decisions and responsibilities for the strike, the people reacted favorably toward the Sierra Maestra leadership, and Castro's prestige grew immensely inside Cuba where the insurrection would be won or lost by the efforts of the last standing resistance. "Che" Guevara was well aware that the strike failure strengthened the M-26-7 considerably. See Thomas, *Cuba: The Pursuit of Freedom*, p. 990.

89. An example of these "automatic decrees" appears in the *Gaceta Oficial de la República de Cuba* (Havana), June 9, 1958. In chronological order: Decree No. 2418, July 23, 1958; Decree No. 10318, September 7, 1958; Decree No. 3548, October 22, 1958; Decree No. 1450, December 7, 1958; All decrees were automatically ratified by Congress following 48 hours of their issuance.

90. *Gaceta Oficial* (Havana), no. 10 (May 26, 1958), p. 926.

91. Ibid., p. 930.

92. Ibid.

93. Decree No. 2418, p. 439.

94. Eusebio Mujal in a letter to one of the authors (July 8, 1968, Washington, D.C.).

95. Eusebio Mujal in a letter to the authors (February 14, 1970, Washington, D.C.).

96. Evidence of Serafino Romualdi to one of the authors (November 1968, Washington, D.C.).

11

The Summer Offensive

Government sympathizers now took the initiative in demanding a final coup de grace against the guerrillas at Sierra Maestra. It was clear that it was the government's turn to act, for its forces were showing signs of recovering their battered morale; the people had been impressed by the regime's ability to crush the strike in the cities; and the urban underground appeared to have foundered under the wave of repression that followed the strike.

The underground had two alternatives: to remain inactive, "dead" in underground parlance, and try to survive police persecution, or to come out fighting in order to throw the government into confusion while raising the morale of the insurrectionists. In a unanimous decision the urban cadres agreed to launch an all-out united offensive against the regime.

The remnants of the M-26-7 and cadres from the OA, the DR and the Triple A began operations. Their objective was to demoralize the authorities through psychological warfare. "Operation Rescue" was their first action. It called for "rescuing" as many arms as possible from the hands of the authorities. Policemen were ambushed in lonely alleys, disarmed, undressed and then turned loose. When the police began to patrol the streets in groups of two and three, "Operation Pep- Rallies" was initiated. Underground agitators would attack the government in public places for a few minutes. Their retreat was covered by other underground fighters who were posted at intersections where they could divert the attention of the authorities by throwing Molotov cocktails or a handful of revolutionary leaflets. The government countered these campaigns by increasing its secret police forces. Eventually the streets of the main cities were filled with blind beggars who were not blind, street vendors with no merchandise and a whole array of clumsy government spies. When it was no longer possible to conduct either "Operation Rescue" or "Operation Pep-Rallies," the urban fighters reached the people by radio. Radio stations were taken over, brief manifestos read to the nation, and news about the progress of the insurrection circulated before the police arrived.

Cuban urban guerrillas incidentally followed maxims applied in Palestine during the 1940s and Algeria during the 1950s. In mountains and jungles, the guerrilla can take physical and emotional rest simply by moving away from the enemy without losing psychological advantage over the regular troops in the area. In the cities, however, guerrillas must attack daily to create a climate in which government forces are kept off balance. In city fighting, a statemate is reached when outbursts of violence force the authorities to call a halt in order to reassess the situation, draw new plans and outline new areas of activities. If the authorities hesitate for even a short period of time, the underground gains precious time to heal its wounds and to recruit new people for its apparatus. Throughout the struggle official repression is the underground's best ally.

Although the M-26-7 underground never fully recovered from the events of April, the Triple A, the OA, urban cells of the DR and a score of small terrorist groups were once again on the offensive. The police, the SIM and Ventura's elite corps reacted in the most brutal possible manner, indiscriminately imprisoning or killing people thought to be involved in the underground. For every real participant affected, many innocent individuals were victimized by the regime's persecution and brutality. The regime's techniques were mostly crude demonstrations of terror. Lacking expertise in urban counterinsurgency, men like Ventura gained many enemies for the government while the revolutionaries gained sympathizers.

The objectives of the underground, however, were carefully selected. Public places were not bombed, although policemen were killed and police cars blown up when possible. But in some isolated cases bombs did explode in theaters, nightclubs and restaurants, killing innocent people. These unauthorized actions were usually carried out by extremists belonging to the M-26-7 and the DR.

As terrorism continued in the cities, the government's ability to put an end to the insurrection in both the urban and the rural areas increasingly came into question. Since 1956, military efforts to capture Fidel Castro's guerrillas had been reduced to token operations in marginal areas of Sierra Maestra. A full-scale assault on Castro's hideout had not been attempted since the Granma landing. The dictator's apparent refusal to take decisive action against the guerrillas was having a negative effect on his troops, who began to ask if Batista was really interested in defeating Castro. The troops were convinced they could annihilate Castro's guerrillas. Junior officers were also highly confident that their men could destroy Castro if a general attack were ordered. Army detachments around the Sierra Maestra had had no contacts with the guerrillas for some time, and most officers interpreted this lack of action as a sign that the guerrillas could be easily defeated.

This was far from true. Castro had concentrated on training his men for what he knew would be a decisive battle with the dictatorship. Avoiding all contact with regular troops, but leaving small guerrilla outposts around the mountains, Castro moved the bulk of his guerrillas to the heights of the mountain chain. There new recruits were briefed and taught to shoot at long range and to walk great distances through the mountains and ravines of Sierra Maestra. Advanced groups were sent scouting daily, mapping the area, learning shortcuts, making indentification marks to check distances, and setting arms depots at various spots throughout the mountains. Castro, Guevara, Cienfuegos and Raúl Castro continued their daily routine of training men. They simply had to wait.

The government prepared for a large military operation, and Fidel, too, was active. In a letter dated April 28, 1958, Fidel wrote to Mario Llerena and Raúl Chibás, as leaders of the Committee in Exile, complaining that "the movement has failed completely in its duty of keeping us supplied." To the selfishness of other organizations toward the M-26-7 Castro felt must be added "the incapacity, the negligence, even the disloyalty of some of our *compañeros*." Castro pointed out that the rebels exerted control over a large territory where planes could land with arms for the insurrection, and he asked, "How [can you] explain the fact that our organization abroad has not been capable of sending us that kind of help?" Castro envisioned that Batista was developing some sort of plan in the hope that "with a correct strategy" the government would "surely try to crush us down." That did not worry Castro, for he defined himself as belonging "to that kind of men who feel far more spirited in the difficult times than when victory seems to be around the corner." But to solve the situation, Castro was appointing Ricardo Lorié and Haydée Santamaría to take charge of matters connected with the shipment of armaments to the guerrillas. Castro's delegates would receive funds from Cuba which Castro expected would be over "$100,000 in two months."

Castro announced the decision to organize a revolutionary government in the Sierra Maestra, and asked Chibás and Llerena to approach Dr. Urrutia on that subject, but to let it rest if the latter had any objections to the idea. As Castro viewed the organization of that government, Dr. Urrutia could arrive in Sierra Maestra, "be proclaimed President, set up a Council of Ministers, and proceed to designate diplomatic representatives abroad."[1] That idea, Castro announced, had the support of the Dirección Nacional of the M-26-7. The project, however, was not put into effect due to the events leading to the summer offensive.

The first sign that a military operation was being seriously planned came when Batista ordered a recruitment campaign. The dictator's desire to increase the number of infantry soldiers boosted the army's morale. All over the island thousands of young peasants joined the armed forces. Most answered the government call for recruits because they were better off in the barracks than cutting cane three or four months a year and being unemployed the rest, while others applied out of genuine support for Fulgencio Batista. Hundreds came from Oriente province, where the insurrection was supposed to have the greatest support among the rural population.

Revolutionaries who had idealized the peasantry were frustrated at the sight of trains loaded with chanting and machete-carrying peasants with their menacing pro-Batista slogans. To counter this show of support, the underground developed a campaign to terrorize the recruits before they left the cities.

Even after the April Fiasco, Batista was not entirely sure of his ability to stop the insurrection. In his own words, "it was indispensable to give the impression that the days of the Sierra were numbered."[2] To rid himself of Castro, Batista had to defeat him militarily, for the Sierra Maestra leader would not accept any solution other than total victory over the regime. One of the two caudillos was going to have to suffer complete defeat. Any doubts about this were clarified by a message from Castro to a peace committee which had been organized on the initiative of the Catholic Church. The peace committee issued a declaration calling for peace and stating that the only way to find a solution was to have an agreement between the government and the insurrectionists. The committee was prepared to travel to the Sierra Maestra and talk directly with Castro. But Castro rejected all contact with the committee, stating that as far as he was concerned there would be no end to the fighting short of complete victory.[3]

Military Plans

In early May, General Eulogio Cantillo discussed a plan of attack with Batista and the general staff. General Cantillo's plan called for 24 infantry battalions, 14 of which were to penetrate the Sierra Maestra while ten would remain in reserve for a final and crushing operation against Castro's guerrillas.

Batista refused to mobilize 24 battalions, and although Cantillo's plan was approved, the operation was to be carried out with 14 infantry battalions. Batista claimed that he could not afford to shift troops who were guarding private farms and sugar mills, and even serving as private escorts for pro-Batista sympathizers. Though Cantillo vigorously argued that a large number of troops would be required to ensure a victorious operation, Batista denied his request—then appointed him chief of operations for the summer offensive.[4] As chief of operations, General Cantillo occupied the position previously filled by two officers who had been removed from the post for ineptitude and bad conduct, Colonel Manuel Ugalde Carrillo and General Alberto del Río Chaviano.[5]

General Cantillo's plan called for the establishment of a blockade around the Sierra Maestra to stop supplies and men from reaching the guerrillas. The blockade was to be effected from Niquero to the west to Maffo and Santiago de Cuba to the east of Sierra Maestra. The strategy would be to attack the guerrillas from the north and from the northeast, thus forcing Castro to move westwards into the plains between Pilón and Cape Cruz. At that point, troops based at Bayamo and Manzanillo were to engage the guerrillas in the final phase of the operation. The operation would be carried out with 12,000 regular troops, of whom about 7,000 were new peasant recruits, known as *casquitos* (little helmets). The latter were poorly trained, however, and had been exposed to tremendous amounts of propaganda from every insurrectionary movement on the island.

General headquarters was established at Bayamo. Two other command posts, at Manzanillo and Yara, linked the area of operations for the summer coordinated offensive against Sierra Maestra.

Meanwhile, the urban underground members were carefully analyzing troop movements, command appointments and the gathering of military supplies at certain points. The urban apparatus concentrated on collecting medicines, bandages, food and other items to be sent to the Sierra Maestra. By the time the government troops reached Bayamo, the urban movement had transported substantial supplies to the Sierra Maestra. Agents were also dispatched to Costa Rica and Venezuela to collect arms.

At the moment of truth the entire underground movement, the Triple A, the OA, the students and individuals acting as contributors on an individual basis, joined in an all-out effort to help Castro's guerrilla army overcome the regular army's attack. In the Sierra Maestra, Fidel accepted all aid with open arms. At such a time revolutionary unity was essential, and Castro was not one to criticize how much aid he received or where it came from.

Problems of Command

The military offensive was still in the planning stages when Batista made his first error. The dictator had personally ordered the removal of General Alberto del Río Chaviano from his command post at Oriente province. But he reappointed Chaviano after General Tabernilla, Sr., the chief of staff, asked the dictator for a second chance for his son-in-law. In order to reappoint Chaviano, Batista divided the province into two combat areas. The Central Highway divided the province in half, and General Chaviano was to be in charge of the eastern sector of the province, which included Santiago de Cuba, while General Cantillo was commander in chief in the west. Chaviano's reappointment caused deep resentment among the troops, and General Cantillo also resented Chaviano's reappointment because it represented a political, rather than a military decision. In the course of events, Chaviano interfered with operations in the entire province and with orders issued by Cantillo in the western area.[6] General Chaviano was in charge of the area where Raúl Castro's guerrillas operated, but he made no attempt to engage the rebels, who continued their operations unhampered between Mayarí and Sagua de Tánamo. On the western front, Cantillo's slow progress soon led to rumors that General Tabernilla, Sr., was not extending the needed logistical support.[7]

All of this revealed Batista's inability to handle a real military operation. Throughout his years in power, Batista had played one officer off against another, dividing and conquering, thus creating an attitude among the officers which was not conducive to any kind of serious military undertaking. The troops were aware of these conflicts, and they were highly demoralizing. Discipline among the enlisted men was at a low ebb even before the first encounter with the guerrillas. These and other problems increased as the attack against the Sierra Maestra gained impetus.

The Offensive

As the army took up positions to launch the attack in May, popular opinion was divided. Some thought that Batista should take direct command of the offensive. If Batista led the army into combat, they said, the troops would fight with determination, and if they fought seriously, the guerrillas did not stand a chance. There was even talk that Batista had called upon his old comrades in arms, veterans of the 1930s like former general José Eleuterio Pedraza, to lead part of the offensive. The image of the caudillo once more at the head of his men impressed the people deeply. In the slums the "believers" hung up posters with Batista's picture on them. In the countryside, especially in northern Oriente province, near where Batista was born, and around Birán, where Castro was born, the peasants were outspokenly pessimistic about the fate of the guerrillas. In the provinces of Camagüey, Las Villas and Matanzas, it was felt that no one could defeat the army if it was really determined to fight, especially if Batista himself directed the campaign.[8]

Some people, however, still hoped for a miracle and thought that the guerrillas might not be altogether destroyed. Even among those who had been loyal to the insurrection from the start, there were many who maintained that the rebels would die fighting, one by one, before surrendering to the army. There was a feeling of the "inevitable," of the need and duty to face the last moment honorably, heroically. And Castro was the man who would do just that. He was expected to die fighting. Had not Martí fallen during the War of Independence? And the great warrior Maceo in the last stage of the war against the Spanish Empire? And Guiteras, Mella, Trejo, Echeverría and many others? Men like Castro were destined to lead the people part of the way, to show the path to be followed and then succumb to the forces of evil. That was the Cuban historical experience.

It was perhaps this conviction—that one must meet defeat with dignity and with honor—that threw the underground into frantic efforts to aid the guerrillas. The youth, more than any other Cubans, were now openly in favor of Castro's guerrillas, and ready to do whatever was necessary to support the insurrectionists. Radio Rebelde addressed the nation every night, stressing the decision to be "martyrs or heroes" to die to the last man in the struggle for freedom.

Castro's charisma increased tremendously, for his decision to remain in Sierra Maestra was for most people an act of incredible courage, one more proof of his *machismo*. The Sierra Maestra stood as a symbol of resistance, where the leader of anti-Batista forces stood fast waiting for his destiny, for his "star" to guide him to death or to victory and unprecedented acclaim.

As the time for the offensive neared, the "believers" seemed to be divided, some now favoring Castro. Fiestas and masses were celebrated for the protection of both caudillos. Excitement was general. It was the first time that Cubans would see the two *jefes* (chiefs) engaged in a deadly struggle for power and supremacy.

First Move: The Army

General Batista did not take command of the attack. Instead the old caudillo remained a safe distance from all military engagements. Pro-Batista elements tried not to discuss the issue further, while sympathizers with the insurrection fully exploited Batista's lack of courage.

By the middle of June, the army began moving in earnest after conducting a few exploratory moves during May. On June 28, two army battalions left the Estrada Palma sugar mill tor the Sierra Maestra. The battle had officially begun: 12,000 regular troops against 300 guerrillas.[9]

"Che" Guevara had done a first-rate job in organizing a communications system throughout the Sierra Maestra. As the first two battalions marched toward the mountains, Guevara's communications network reported every move of the advancing troops. The peasants played a decisive role as observers and messengers. By day they were mere planters, by night, guerrillas.[10] As the troops moved without meeting any resistance, confidence permeated the infantry. The guerrillas, commanded by Guevara, allowed the army's first battalion to move further into the mountain territory.[11] But Guevara did not wait too long. Less than four miles from the Estrada Palma mill, the vanguard battalion was attacked. The first volley came from the darkness of the surrounding forests. As the first soldier fell, the rest disbanded, trying to take cover from an invisible army.[12] The guerrillas stopped firing. Soon the battalion's armored vehicles advanced to cover the flanks. But here they ran into field mines which had been placed by the guerrillas. A few vehicles were blown to pieces. As the soldiers panicked and attempted to retreat, the deadly sharpshooters of the guerrillas' *fusileros* squad felled three or four soldiers. Firing stopped once again. Guevara handled his men with utmost efficiency, for each period of silence threw the regular troops into further confusion.

When the second arms battalion failed to support their comrades, the officers ordered a retreat to Estrada Palma. The guerrillas moved forward. Within minutes they had covered half of the road back to Estrada Palma. Sharpshooters now had a field day. While retreating, the army sustained heavy casualties. Most of the new recruits simply ran wild through the forests, some never to return to Estrada Palma. The rebels reported 86 regular troops killed against three guerrillas dead.[13] The regular army's headquarters ignored the encounter.

Castro's strategy was to bleed the army, to exhaust the troops until the time when it became possible for the guerrillas to counterattack. In a message to his field commanders, Castro said that his fundamental objective was to maintain a basic area where hospitals, the organization and shops would be able to function without interruption; to maintain the radio station on the air,

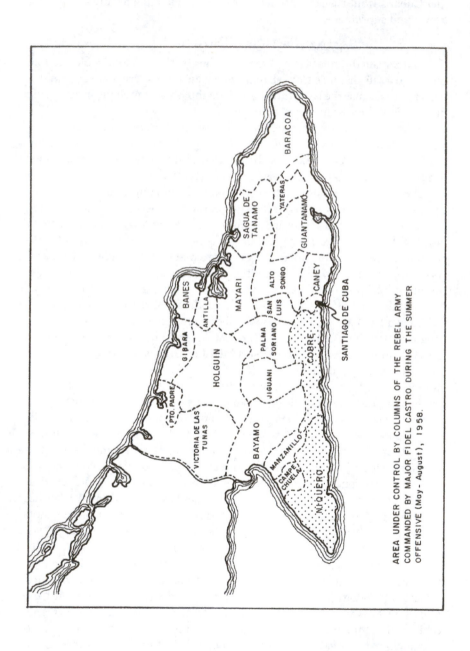

AREA UNDER CONTROL BY COLUMNS OF THE REBEL ARMY
COMMANDED BY MAJOR FIDEL CASTRO DURING THE SUMMER
OFFENSIVE (May - August), 1958.

which Castro considered as a "factor of utmost importance"; and to offer the army greater resistance each time it moved against guerrilla territory. Guerrilla resistance would be accomplished "to the degree that they [the army] lengthen their lines and we fall back toward strategic positions."[14]

Fidel Castro waited until General Cantillo positioned his troops and then secretly moved all guerrilla columns into new positions to avert any leakage of information that would have benefited Cantillo. Before Castro's move, Column No. 3, commanded by Juan Almeida, was operating in El Cobre; Column No. 2, led by Camilo Cienfuegos, operated in the center of Sierra Maestra; Column No. 7, with Crescencio Pérez as the leader, had been operating in the westernmost sector of the mountains; and Ramiro Valdés' Column No. 4 had been active to the east of the Turquino Peak. All these columns were moved west of the Turquino Peak, to join Guevara's Column No. 8 and Fidel's Column No. 1. Thus, the rebel army formed a front of approximately 30 square kilometers with about 300 veteran guerrilla fighters.

The main strategy was to let the army move forward, to extend its lines, to make them feel sure of the terrain. Then the guerrillas would hit the advanced platoons and units and fall back again. The operation was repeated as many times as necessary. If an opportunity arose to ambush the army, the guerrillas would split into two groups: one group would attack and the other would wait for the soldiers' retreat and then shoot isolated soldiers trying to escape.[15]

Since the guerrillas could not afford to sustain many casualties, each engagement with the army had to be planned ahead of time and was not carried out unless the guerrillas held total superiority in terrain and the initiative in the attack. It was better to withdraw than to face the army without the advantages of terrain and surprise. The exception was the battle of Las Mercedes which is described later in this chapter.

The rebel army moved deeper and deeper into the forests, while leaving behind an organized ring of ambushes. Guevara commanded the first defense line of the Sierra Maestra. From his advance post, the Argentinian Could direct Castro's men if there was any need for a prompt mobilization of the second and third lines of defense deeper in the mountains. Without Guevara directing the initial operations, bleeding the army, attacking and retreating in lightning thrusts, Castro would have had little chance of survival, for it was this first series of encounters with the army that destroyed the main thrust of the offensive, never permitting the army to penetrate more than a few miles into the Sierra Maestra.

Santo Domingo

On June 28, when the Estrada Palma mill encounter tool place, another troop movement was unfolding near Santo Domingo. Colonel Angel Sánchez Mosquera was encamped at Santo Domingo, where he awaited the arrival of Major J. Villavicencio, who was commanding Infantry Battalion No. 22. The two battalions were to march together into the mountains to seek the guerrillas. As Major Villavicencio's battalion marched toward Santo Domingo, the rebels followed closely behind. On arriving at Santo Domingo, Colonel Mosquera ordered Major Villavicencio to continue toward a town called Pueblo Nuevo, half a mile into the mountains from Santo Domingo. Two days before, some of Colonel Mosquera's men had been ambushed in that area, and the same rebel unit ambushed the army about 500 meters from the first ambush. As the army's vanguard moved into the mountains, a field mine was detonated while the guerrillas opened fire. Major Villavicencio ordered two companies to move forward and engage the rebels; however the guerrillas managed to isolate Company "N" from the rest of the battalion with a .50 caliber machine gun and a .60 caliber mortar.[16]

At nightfall the guerrillas recovered all arms left behind by the army. With these arms, they attacked the following morning at 8 AM. Company "N" surrendered immediately. Castro reported: "There were 26 enemy soldiers killed and 27 taken prisoner." The following arms were captured by the rebels: one .30 caliber machine gun with ten boxes of ammunition, 38 Garand rifles, seven San Cristóbal submachine guns (made in the Dominican Republic), 15,000 rounds of ammunition, five M-1 carbines, three Springfield rifles, two Thompson submachine guns with 15,000 rounds of ammunition, plus 60 packs full of equipment, blankets, uniforms, tents, belts, canned food and new microwave radio equipment.[17]

By 8:30 AM the army was facing the rebels from three directions, and many soldiers had begun to retreat without awaiting orders from their officers. When Colonel Mosquera sent an army squad to seek reinforcements from Estrada Palma, the rebels blew them apart with field mines. Ten soldiers died, one was wounded, and one was taken prisoner by the rebels. Three San Cristóbal submachine guns were captured, along with various rifles and 3,000 rounds of ammunition. Castro reported only two casualties—one guerrilla killed and another wounded slightly. He reported another ambush in which 36 soldiers were killed, 28 taken prisoner and 50 wounded. The army lost 65 arms of various calibers and about 18,000 rounds of ammunition.[18]

This pattern was followed for the rest of the summer. Attack, counterattack and then disorganized retreat by the army, the demoralized soldiers leaving behind arms and equipment that the rebles immediately seized. Often the army abandoned not only its equipment but its own wounded personnel along the roads.

Unity of the Insurrectional Sector

While the summer offensive proceeded, the urban underground was involved in terrorism. Bombs exploded every night, police cars were machined-gunned, policemen were hunted down, and printed propaganda almost tripled.

The preparations of the urban underground in the weeks prior to the beginning of the offensive began to pay off toward the end of June. Arms were shipped to the underground from Miami and through secret communications channels to the Sierra Maestra and the Escambray Mountains. War materiel arrived from Costa Rica, where José Figueres was helping the insurrectionists, while substantial economic aid was gathered from among the Cuban exiles in Venezuela, Mexico and the United States.

Most arms shipments reached the urban underground from Miami. The shipments were transported by speedboats, usually travelling from Miami to the Bahama Islands, and from there to the northern coast of Pinar del Río province. Close to the bays of Cabañas and Bahia Honda, members of the M-26-7, the DR and the OA would receive the various shipments and in an excellent demonstration of cooperation transport the materiel to the cities for distribution. The movement that financed the arms held the right to divide the materiel in terms of operations planned by each organization. There was no previous pact or written accord that established rules and regulations for this distribution system. One of the most courageous gun runners was Captain Miguel ("El Cojo") Roché, a veteran of many underground missions and a member of the urban M-26-7. Silvino ("El Chivo") Rodríguez, a lieutenant in the OA, was also very active in delivering arms to the underground and led several incursions into Cuba. By and large, the government failed to intercept the arms shipments and the flow of materiel was constant throughout the summer months. However, most of these arms stayed in the cities and did not reach the mountains. Captain Roché claimed that following the experience of April 9, 1958, when the M-26-7 lacked sufficient arms to fight in the streets of Havana, the cadres began to store arms and ammunition for a future battle in Havana.[19]

The people were kept well informed about the progress of the fighting in Sierra Maestra through clandestine radio broadcasts, through Radio Caracas, which transmitted every night by shortwave, and from radio stations based in San José, Costa Rica and Miami.

In 1957, Fidel Castro had rejected unity, but by the summer of 1958, it was convenient to have as much support as possible. Now Castro welcomed the uniting of his insurrectionary sector with the same organizations he had criticized in 1957. Rómulo Betancourt of Venezuela and José Figureres of Costa Rica, as well as figures like Juan Bosch, the exiled Dominican leader, were instrumental in convincing Cuban exile leaders and representatives of the anti-Batista forces to go to Caracas, Venezuela, in July 1958 for a general discussion in order to arrive at a unity pact all insurrectionary forces. Antonio "Tony" Varona, prime minister of Cuba during the Auténtico administration of President Prío, talked to Castro in the Sierra Maestra by radio.[20] Castro agreed to reach a unity pact, and dictated to Varona a text which became known as the Pact of Caracas.[21]

This pact, which united all movements and all resources behind a common insurrectionary strategy, was a historic step on the road to the overthrow of the dictatorship. More important, by dictating the terms of the Pact of Caracas, Castro emerged as the one leader of the entire anti-Batista movement remaining in Cuban territory. Any other well-known figure who might compete for leadership (such as Prío or Varona) remained in exile most of the time.

The Pact of Caracas

In the pact, Castro recognized the efforts against Batista conducted by the military in 1956 and in the Cienfuegos uprising. Castro praised the insurrection in the cities where "sabotage, armed attacks and other revolutionary tactics have been used to show the indomitable spirit of the new generation." Throughout the island resistance was increasing and after reviewing the activities of the M-26-7 rebel army, Castro pointed out that the DR had been "bravely fighting at Escambray and nearby areas for several months."

Not long before, in a 1957 letter to the Cuban Council of Miami Castro had written that the insurrection was being exclusively conducted by his movement. Now other movements and groups were given credit for their efforts. Even the Auténticos were mentioned as battling the army in Las Villas province.

The "imaginary revolution" that the exiles were conducting in 1957 had evidently ended. For now Castro viewed the exiles as Cubans who were making "every effort to free the oppressed Fatherland." Carefully, Castro gave credit to everyone, those who had participated in insurrectionary activities and those who had not, but could help with financial support at that point in the struggle.

Castro emphasized that only a united front of the civic, political and insurrectionary sectors of the opposition could overthrow the dictatorship. Whereas in 1957 the movement toward unity was under the political control of the Auténticos, the Pact of Caracas was the result of Castro's effectiveness in surviving within Cuba, where he had raised the banner of rebellion. Castro now dictated the terms, and since they were within the scope of the demands repeated by various movements throughout the years, every group agreed to unite for the last stage of the insurrection. The pact rested upon three foundations: the adoption of a common strategy to defeat the regime by means of armed insurrection, through the popular mobilization of all labor, civic, professional and economic forces "culminating in a great general strike on the civilian front while on the military front, action will be coordinated throughout the country"; the establishment of a short-term provisional government to lead the country "toward full constitutional and democratic procedures"; and the enactment of a "minimum program that would guarantee punishment guilty of individuals, the rights of the workers, the fulfillment of international commitments, public order, peace, freedom and economic, social and political progress for the people."

The Pact of Caracas reaffirmed Castro's contention that a revolutionary general strike, accompanied by armed action, was to be the instrument for the final overthrow of the regime. Coordinated military action was to be under Castro's guidance.

The second point, calling for a "brief provisional government" and "democratic procedures," seems to have been very well received by the politicians, particularly the Auténticos. The latter hoped to reorganize the party and participate in the first democratic elections in the country after Batista's overthrow. Most people at the leadership level in the OA, the Triple A and other small groups generally agreed that the provisional government would enact a "minimum" program of social reforms in the true sense of the word.[22]

The document ended with a request to the United States to cease all military and other assistance to the regime. The declaration further stressed the insurrectionists' intent to defend the nation's sovereignty and the "nonmilitary tradition of Cuba." The document also called on the military to lay down their arms, stating that Batista, not the army, was the insurrection's main enemy. The dictator was "the only obstacle" to that peace so "desired and needed by all Cubans."

Following the Pact of Caracas, Carlos Prío placed all his economic resources at the disposal of the insurrectionists, and planes bearing arms and men were chartered and flown from landing strips through-out Central América and the Caribbean to the Sierra Maestra and Escambray Mountains. By this time, Castro and his guerrillas were more than ready to confront the final wave of Batista's offensive.

Attack: An Intrepid Maneuver

General Eulogio Cantillo's plan to force the guerrillas onto the western slopes and plains was not working. Castro's stronghold was still west of the Turquino Peak, and the army had been unable to penetrate the mountains in addition to sustaining a heavy number of casualties in most encounters with the advance guerrilla units. Thus, General Cantillo decided to put into effect an intrepid maneuver consisting of an amphibious landing south of the Turquino Peak and troop movements from the north in an attempt to surprise Castro.

Cantillo's plan called for Battalion No. 17, commanded by Colonel Corzo Izaguirre, to land at La Plata in an Operation that was to last for 15 days. The army was to march inland in a lightning move and engage Castro's guerrillas east of the Turquino. The guerrillas would then be caught between the spearhead battalion and the Turquino Peak to the east; and at that point a second landing was to take place west of the Turquino. Two full companies were to land and to rapidly move into position for the final kill while Castro engaged Battalion No. 17. Cantillo's plan was further reinforced with a battalion advancing from the north to cut Castro's retreat and to support the operation. Theoretically, Cantillo assumed that Castro would either be forced to fight or to move westward, in which case army troops based in Purial de Jibacoa, and Campechuela would enter the operation and engage Castro on the slopes of Sierra Maestra. Even if Castro were able to escape the army's persecution, the guerrilla leader would have to abandon his field hospitals, arms factories and even his army prisoners, rebel radio station and the communications center.[23]

As the plan unfolded, the general staff ordered General Cantillo not to use Battalion No. 17 as the landing force and to select another battalion. There was no plausible military reason given to Cantillo and the decision was taken by General Tabernilla, Sr. This order eliminated the opportunity for Cantillo to use Colonel Corzo Izaguirre's veteran troops, some of whom had been serving in the area for nearly 15 months. Cantillo hesitated, but the chief of operations finally decided to take the risk and selected another battalion, leaving Battalion No. 17 for the march southward into the Sierra Maestra. Cantillo chose Battalion No. 18, commanded by Major José Quevedo Pérez, a former student colleague of Fidel Castro's at Havana University.

Supported by a navy frigate and two gunboats, Major Quevedo's troops, most of whom had never participated in actual combat, landed about ten kilometers southeast of the Turquino Peak, at the mouth of La Plata river. The battalion rapidly moved toward the north along the river, and as it approached a subsidiary of La Plata, El Jigüe river, the troops slowed down, apparently fearful of an ambush. In order to instill some courage into the troops, General Cantillo, who was flying in his helicopter over the field, issued orders for the vanguard to fire mortar shells as the battalion advanced. When the battalion reached El Jigüe, the guerrillas were waiting for the troops. Fidel Castro assumed command of the operation. The guerrillas' objective as usual was to inflict as many casualties as possible on the army, and to attract it further into the ravine at El Jigüe.[24] Other rebel units took up positions around Battalion No. 18.

On July 11, at 9 AM, two army platoons marched toward the beach, evidently to bring back supplies to the encircled troops. An ambush forced them to retreat, inflicting five casualties. The rebels took two San Cristóbals, one Thompson, three Springfield rifles, around 1,000 rounds of ammunition and 12 hand grenades. For the next 72 hours, there was complete silence. No one moved. The guerrillas remained in their positions, and the troops waited for the next attack. At the end of three days, the troops were out of food. On July 14, Major Quevedo attempted to break the guerrilla encirclement by moving a full company forward.

The results were about the same. The guerrillas isolated one platoon, while another dispersed into the jungle and into the hands of the guerrillas. The other two platoons withdrew rapidly. Five soldiers were killed, and 21 were taken prisoner.[25] "In this encounter," Castro reported, "the enemy lost ten Springfield rifles, eight Garand rifles, two San Crisfóbals, one Browning automatic, 39 mules with assorted equipment and 2,000 rounds of ammunition."

General Cantillo reexamined the situation. His original plan had failed, but while it was true that the army had been had been surrounded by Castro, the guerrilla leader had committed the bulk of his guerrilla Column No. 1

to the developing battle at El Jigüe. To Cantillo that meant that the guerrilla headquarters could be an easy target, and that Castro could be surprised by fresh troops attacking the guerrillas from their rearguard. If everything went as planned, Battalion No. 17 would have time to get to the area and engage Castro's rebels. General Cantillo decided to go ahead with the second landing, and also made the decision to land fresh troops at La Plata to reinforce Battalion No. 18. Meanwhile, the air force conducted an intensive bombing north of El Jigüe, over the eastern wall of the Turquino and all along La Plata river to clear the way for the reinforcements. General Cantillo's hope was to encircle Castro using troops coming from La Plata and from the landing, together with action by Battalion No. 18, all of which would place Castro in a difficult situation. Cantillo fully realized the tremendous hazards in the plan, but he gambled that it would succeed.

On July 15, the air force conducted a heavy raid while two army companies landed at La Plata. Meanwhile, General Cantillo led the attempt to complete the second landing but was surprised when the navy gunboats and the landing barges were bombarded by intensive firing from two .50 caliber machine guns emplaced on top of the rocks facing the sea. The guerrillas waited for the landing barges to approach the coast. Then, General Cantillo recalls, "the rebels opened up with an amazing coordination and success." The machine gun fire did not kill any soldiers because Cantillo had ordered the barges protected with packs of hay and cement bags, and because he called for an immediate withdrawal from the area. The chief of operations attempted another landing a short distance away, but there, too, received heavy fire from the coast. In spite of intensive bombardment by the air force, Cantillo admits that "the rebels sustained the raid and kept on shooting."[26] Thus, Cantillo decided to land two more companies at La Plata while he flew northward to lead Battalion No. 17 into battle.

When Cantillo's landing failed, Castro asked Quevedo for his surrender. The latter refused, and firing resumed. This time the regular troops were a little more spirited, since they were hoping for prompt reinforcements and knew that new troops had already arrived at La Plata.

"At 6 AM on the 17th," Castro said. "Infantry Company G-4 began its penetration inland. It was moving very slowly and exploring the area with great care. At 2:30 PM 50 automatic rifles and two .30 caliber machine guns opened up on them. In 15 minutes, the first two platoons were decimated, and the remaining troops hastily withdrew. We took 24 prisoners. Twelve soldiers were killed."[27] This time the guerrillas were able to capture 18,000 rounds of ammunition. On July 19, a full battalion advanced from the beach supported by naval bombardment. Although three guerrillas were killed, the reinforcement action was stopped; the army lost 19 soldiers and 21 prisoners to the guerrillas, plus a substantial amount of arms, ammunition and mules with food supplies.

"After this reinforcement was defeated, our troops moved within 50 meters of the enemy trenches, thus cutting its water supply. The same day, a prisoner was sent to the enemy with our conditions for surrender," Castro reported. A truce was called. The humanitarian treatment of the prisoners by the guerrillas (particularly in comparison to guerrilla treatment by army chiefs) had a tremendous psychological impact upon the soldiers of the regular army. After the long encirclement the soldiers knew that they would not be murdered and preferred to surrender rather than continue fighting a war that very few of them cared about by that time.

Later Castro reported that during the truce those soldiers "who were able to walk approached us, asking for water, food and cigarettes. We gave them what they asked. Amazed by this gesture, the soldiers embraced our men, crying with emotion." But Major Quevedo would not surrender to Castro, and the fighting resumed once more. The army troops obeyed the chief and fought as well as they could under extremely difficult circumstances.

On July 20, the guerrillas stopped firing for a while and Castro offered Quevedo a second opportunity for an honorable surrender. But Quevedo was still hoping for reinforcements to arrive, and would not give up. From above, flying in his helicopter, General Cantillo, accompanied by Colonel Leopoldo pérez Cougil, asked Quevedo to come out fighting and to force his way back to La Plata. Major Quevedo talked to Cantillo by radio and stated that if by 6 PM (July 20) he had not received reinforcements, the physical and emotional deterioration of his troops would force him to consider surrender.[28] Major José Quevedo's Battalion No. 18 surrendered on July 21 at 1 PM.

"The terms were humane and dignified," Castro reported. Officers were allowed to keep their arms, food was distributed among the troops, and 170 prisoners were told that they were soon to be released. The rebels captured 91 Springfield rifles, 46 San Cristóbals, 15 Garands, four automatic rifles and two heavy machine guns, one bazooka with 60 rockets, one .81mm mortar with .60 shells, one 60 mm mortar with 65 shells, and 31,000 rounds of ammunition and 126 hand grenades. In total, the guerrillas had taken 249 weapons and 241 prisoners. Thirty soldiers had been wounded and 41 killed. The guerrillas had suffered three deaths.[29]

Meanwhile, Battalion No.17 with Colonel Corzo Izaguirre at the head was unable to reach the area after penetrating the ravines of Sierra Maestra. Elsewhere, Camilo Cienfuegos, Juan Almeida and "Che" Guevara fought the army, whose most aggressive officers were Colonels Angel Sánchez Mosquera, Merob Sosa and Nelson Carrasco Artíles.

On June 26, Raúl Castro's guerrillas had marched on the Moa Bay Mining Company and, simultaneously with the issuance of Military Order No. 30 by Raúl Castro, 12 American and Canadian employees of that U.S.-owned mining concern were kidnapped by the rebels. The kidnappings were in retaliation for the U.S. delivery of 300 rockets to Batista's army via the Guantánamo Naval

Base. The following day the rebels intercepted and took into custody a group of 27 U.S. sailors and marines on their way back to the naval base. The manager of the Isabel sugar mill, a Canadian, was also taken as a hostage. Three days later the rebels kidnapped two other American citizens and six employees of the United Fruit Company. Batista's offensive was not going well, and Raúl Castro's actions further embarrassed the dictator. News of the kidnappings caused the expected impact throughout the United States and Latin America.

On June 30, Raúl Castro wrote a letter to U.S. Ambassador Earl T. Smith stating that the 48 hostages would be released on condition that the United States cease shipment of all equipment, including spare parts, to Batista; that Batista's planes receive no more fuel at the Guantánamo Naval Base; and the United States not permit Batista to use U.S. military hardware to fight the rebels.[30]

On July 1, Secretary of State John Foster Dulles informed the American people of the kidnappings and presented his own distorted interpretation of the events. Secretary Dulles could only infer from the action taken by the guerrillas that they wished to force the U.S. into intervention in Cuba.[31] Dulles added that the accusation that the Guantánamo Naval Base was being used by Cuban military aircraft was totally unfounded.

On July 2, President Eisenhower discussed the subject, saying that it was, indeed, "a delicate question." The President stated that we are not disposed to do anything reckless," that his main concern was to get the Americans back alive. The president denied that his administration was giving "improper" support to the Batista dictatorship. Concerning the kidnappings, President Eisenhower said that they were unjustifiable, and assured the American people that his administration was trying to "convince these people of the errors they have made and to release our people instantly."[32]

The word "instantly," which charged the president's statement with a flair of omnipotence, was certainly not used in the negotiations between Raúl Castro and the U.S. consul in Santiago de Cuba, Parks Wollam. The hostages were not released instantly by Raúl Castro. Rather it took two weeks of discussions—during which time there was a ceasefire in the area of the Sierra Cristals—between the U.S. consul and the rebel leader, with the first chasing the second in helicopters throughout the sierras asking for the opportunity to discuss the problem. Meanwhile, Raúl Castro took advantage of the ceasefire to visit various areas, reorganize one or two weak spots, and give his men a well-earned rest period. It was not until a direct order came from Fidel Castro to release all hostages that Raúl complied.[33]

At that point Ernesto Betancourt, the M-26-7 representative in Washington, received a copy of an original requisition form which had been removed from the Cuban Embassy in Washington, D.C., by an inside agent. Sergeant Angel Saavedra.[34] The photocopy was published in the *Sierra Maestra* newspaper. The requisition form was dated May 28, 1958. Order No. 32-5263-58, and authorized by one W.P. Swain. The order was for 570 Rocket Head Mk-6 and rocket fuses Mk-149. The shipment, the original read, was to "correct materiel shipped in error on Requisition 32-0018-58."[35] The order to the chief of ordinance at Guantánamo Naval Base was to insure "return from the Cuban navy to Guantánamo's stocks of 300, 5" .0 rocket heads inert before release of the new items."

The U.S. State Department recognized that a month before the kidnappings the 300 rocket heads had been delivered to Batista's transport planes, and that these transport planes had indeed landed at the Guantánamo Naval Base. The department also stated that the rocket heads in question were exchanged for another type "erroneously delivered by the U.S. Government in October, 1957 in compliance with a Cuban government purchase order of December 1956." The State Department did admit that one plane had been furnished with sufficient fuel to return to its base.[36]

Batista's prestige was undermined by the kidnappings. In addition to feeling the effects of the tightened arms embargo, the dictator also realized that he could no longer extend guarantees to foreign investors and technicians. Moreover, Batista had been obliged to permit representatives of a foreign government to conduct negotiations within the republic's territory with the enemies of his government. The dictator had no choice but to remain silent while the insurrectionists gained in international stature and in belligerence.

The struggle continued in the Sierra Maestra, with the army moving from the Estrada Palma sugar mill to the town of Las Vegas de Jibacoa which was to be used as a springboard for further operations into Sierra Maestra. The attempt to encircle Castro and to isolate his forces was continued. Beginning with the landing at La Plata, the army moved to secure an offensive line, forming a wide circle around the Turquino Peak.[37]

Moving south from Estrada Palma, the advance army battalion suffered numerous casualties from guerrilla snipers. The usual land mines exploded, blocking the path with useless army vehicles and demoralizing the troops. When the advance battalion reached Las Vegas de Jibacoa, it was already surrounded by "Che" Guevara's fighters. To convey the impression that there were several guerrilla units, Guevara ordered his men to move from one flank to another, firing with weapons of various calibers. Meanwhile, Guevara shouted orders to imaginary columns of guerrillas, further misleading the soldiers who were unable to see their attackers. The three rearguard battalions had advanced with tanks and armored vehicles and were looking for a chance to break the encirclement.

Mobility was the key to success, and Guevara moved constantly, imparting orders to his lieutenants, shouting to the imaginary units for the benefit of the army, and running back and forth between the front line and the guerrillas' communications center. The firing, the voices, the orders and counter-orders, gave the appearance that three or four guerrilla columns were operating in the vicinity.

One of the support battalions stopped within half a kilometer of Las Vegas de Jibacoa. Major Armando González Finalés, commanding an army company, proceeded to inspect the terrain. Then Major Gonzalez Finals carefully moved forward, avoiding any engagement with Guevara's guerrillas. As the major approached the area, coming from a line of trees, three guerrillas ran into him and four of his advance scouts. One of the guerrillas was "Che" Guevara, who is said to have stood without making a motion or a gesture. Major González Finalés turned around first; no fire was exchanged; and "Che" Guevara quickly joined his guerrillas in the forest. Major González Finalés withdrew his forces and returned to the battalion.

After the government offensive came to an end, this episode became known, and González Finalés was charged with cowardice and negligence of duty, and charges of treason were prepared by the prosecutor general of the army, Colonel Fernando Neugart.[38] The major was still at La Cabaña Fortress, in prison, when "Che" Guevara arrived there on January 2, 1959. Guevara released González Finalés, and subsequently appointed him to a committee to purge the regular army.[39]

As soon as contact was established between the support troops and the battalion at Vegas de Jibacoa, the two battalions began an orderly retreat, the armored vehicles followed by well-spread-out companies of troops with heavy machine guns covering the flanks. Major Guevara had moved out of the area, down the mountains, preparing ambushes and waiting patiently until the troops neared a small creek. As soon as the first guerrilla shots were fired the vanguard of the army disbanded, discipline breaking down completely, each soldier trying to reach safety on his own. Only the quick thinking of Colonel Merob Sosa prevented the retreat from ending in complete catastrophe. An experienced officer, Colonel Sosa led his men in a counterattack, and "Che" Guevara's guerrillas rapidly withdrew. But all along the way back to Estrada Palma guerrilla snipers kept firing at will at the soldiers, taking a heavy toll of the army troops, who left behind arms, food, mule packs, radio equipment and even secret codes. A tank was abandoned. Heavy machine guns were left behind by their crews. Soldiers simply threw boxes of ammunition into the bushes. Regular army men even left their wounded colleagues on the road, and the rebel forces took care of the injured men.

"Che" Guevara reappeared, but Colonel Merob Sosa again con-fronted the guerrilla leader. One guerrilla was killed, and the unit withdrew again. Guevara was a good guerrilla leader, not engaging the army unnecessarily, and withdrawing at the correct time.

Confidential Report

On July 26, General Eulogio Cantillo, chief of operations, sent a detailed report to the general staff on the army's operations, its condition and a new plan for a counterattack.[40] The report included Cantillo's own estimate of

Castro's guerrillas. The general said that Castro could count on "very well trained troops for this type of operation [guerrilla warfare], since most of the fighters are natives of the region, and after a long period in the area, the leaders are very knowledgeable of the terrain." Because he was warned prior to the offensive, Fidel Castro was able to gather around him his best officers plus selected troops.

Castro's guerrillas, Cantillo wrongly estimated, could be numbered "between 1,000 and 2,000 first-rate combatants who are also very well armed, plus almost every inhabitant of the mountains controlled by the rebels and who act as informers and as messengers (men, women or children)."

The guerrillas' armament was good before the army's attack, but after the troops commanded by Major Quevedo surrendered at El Jigüe, Castro was able to increase the firing power of his troops considerably. General Cantillo reported that these arms plus those left behind by the soldiers had prepared Castro for the next army operation.

The rebels' physical condition was bad, but the guerrillas, Cantillo said, "can tolerate staying for days at the same place, without moving, eating or drinking water." As far as the rebels' morale, their recent victories "had made them more daring." The army, however, was in a far different situation. More than 75 percent of the regular soldiers, regardless of rank, were second rate. They were incapable of participating in an antiguerrilla operation which requires "great physical resistance, great initiative through the ranks, and the will to chase and defeat the enemy."

General Cantillo complained that his arms, although acceptable in general terms, were insufficient in quality as well as in quantity: "There is a lack of mortars and of automatic rifles. The carbines continue to fail, and there are no more hand grenades." The army's morale was "extremely low." One of the main problems affecting morale was the troops' "awareness that there is no strong penalty against those who surrender or betray their unit, and that falling prisoner to the enemy ends all their problems, has sapped the will to fight through the ranks. . . . The number of self-inflicted wounds is extraordinarily high. It is necessary to punish troops refusing to advance and to occupy their positions."

The topology of the theater of operations was also favorable to the guerrillas. Formed by a series of ravines through the mountains, the elevations gently descend until reaching the plains with a few isolated hills at the level of Estrada Palma sugar mill. The main mountain passes were along the rivers, and it was extremely difficult for regular troops marching at a higher altitude to maintain visual contact with those marching below. The columns frequently lost touch with one another, and it was just a matter of time before the guerrillas ambushed the army at will, while risking very little themselves.

A look at the total picture reveals that General Cantillo suffered from much more than a deficit of mortars and hand grenades. The regular army lacked tactical knowledge of antiguerrilla operations, and the division of command and the refusal to fight among certain officers certainly contributed to the low morale of the troops.

Cantillo was aware of the fact that Fidel Castro was doing his best to concentrate guerrillas "around Battalion No. 11 with definite orders to capture Colonel Sánchez Mosquera." The positions of the regular army still indicated that Cantillo could attempt to develop a new plan. Cantillo suggested that the regular troops should be withdrawn and placed closer to their lines of supply and support, thus increasing the army's maneuverability.

The army held Santo Domingo where Colonel Sánchez Mosquera commanded Battalion No. 11. The army was in control of Providencia where two companies Battalion No. 22 were camped. Battalion No. 19 held Las Vegas de Jibacoa with a company of men holding Gabiro and a position close to Las Mercedes. Battalion No. 17 had reached Minas del Frío in its support operation to Major Quevedo's Battalion No. 18. There was also a company belonging to the same battalion in San Lorenzo, and a second one in a point between Minas del Frío and San Lorenzo. Battalion No. 23 was distributed with one company close to Las Mercedes, another at Arroyón and a third in Cerro Pelado.

General Cantillo informed the general staff of his next maneuver, which was to trap Castro into pursuing Battalion No. 17—which had penetrated into the mountains and had been stranded there after Major Quevedo's surrender at El Jigüe—and thereby lead the guerrillas into an ambush. If that happened, Cantillo stated, "we can finish the campaign." If the rebels felt that the regular army was undertaking a general retreat, they might gain enough land to allow the army to counterattack on more favorable terrain.

Cantillo's plan consisted of developing a triangular perimeter around Las Mercedes in the hope that Castro would pursue Battalion No. 17 retreating from the mountains until it became impossible for the guerrillas to escape the army's encirclement. Cantillo issued immediate orders to put his plan into effect: Battalion No. 11 was to move toward Providencia where it would dig trenches and wait; Battalion No. 22 would move close to Providencia in support of Colonel Sánchez Mosquera; while Battalion No. 17 was to retreat from Minas del Frío to San Lorenzo and then proceed toward Las Mercedes. Las Vegas de Jibacoa was to be reinforced by Company 93 whose men were to retreat from Gabiro, while Company 91 withdrew from Las Vegas de Jibacoa to Las Mercedes to occupy a position at a place called Sao Grande. All the units evacuated from La Plata were to assemble at the command post at Bayamo and be assigned to cover the area between Las Mercedes and Estrada Palma. According to his plan, General Cantillo issued orders to Colonel Corzo Izaquirre, commander of Battalion No. 17, to retreat toward Las Mercedes, while ordering Colonel Sánchez Mosquera to initiate a simulation maneuver from Providencia destined to make the guerrillas conclude that Battalion No. 17 was lost in Sierra Maestra. Cantillo's tactic depended upon Fidel Castro's probable ambition to capture a second army battalion in less than a month, taking advantage of his newly acquired weapons from Battalion No. 18 and the assumed demoralization of the troops in retreat under Colonel Corzo Izaguirre. Meanwhile, Cantillo accumulated arms and tanks at Estrada Palma to be used at the last minute if Castro fell for the trap.[41]

Operation "N"

General Cantillo's new plan was based on his experience in the field. He advised against the army going into the passes after the rebels. Objectively, he recognized that most of the population was on Castro's side, making it doubly difficult for the army to move very far without the peasants informing the guerrillas of any suspicious activities. But on July 30, 1958, the general staff developed Operation "N,"[42] which consisted of a repetition of Cantillo's original plan even though that was already a proven failure.

The general staff's proposal was to encircle the guerrillas' strong-holds around the Turquino Peak by moving the troops from several approaches, while keeping strong forces around the mountains in close contact with their lines of support. The general staff called for the gradual clearing of roads in order to allow the troops to advance, thus making the march extremely slow and paying no attention to Cantillo's report concerning the population's support of Castro which made possible an excellent communications system throughout the mountains that could detect any army movements. The operation called for a defensive-offensive tactic through the establishment of a well-entrenched ring of army units around the mountains. The assumption was that Castro would thus be forced to attack solidly based forces and would be prevented from inflicting further surprise ambushes on moving troops.

The strategy advanced by the generals in Havana contemplated reorganization of all battalions, maintenance of occupied positions, and convergent movement of troops toward the guerrillas' strongholds with support from the air force, artillery and armored units preceded by clearing equipment. The plan was completely unrealistic, since it did not take into account the army's last experiences when it tried to move on Castro's emplacements; it demonstrated the low capability of the Batista-appointed officers of the Cuban army.

Signed by Admiral José E. Rodríguez Calderón. Operation "N" was a compendium of misinformation. It included five sections: General Analysis, Mission, Concept of the Operation, Transportation, and Communications and Effectives. The "General Analysis" section was a descriptive history of the guerrilla operation which included "detailed" information on Castro's army. The latter did not—as Cantillo had stated in his report—number 1,000 or 2,000; rather, the report said, there were "exactly 800 guerrillas." Neither Cantillo nor the general staff was correct, for at that time the guerrillas numbered only about 300 men. The general staff described the area of operations to Cantillo, naming towns, places and giving directions on how to reach certain locations.

"Column No. 2 is commanded," the plan stated, "by Lorenzo (sic) Guevara, known as 'El Che', and is also located in the Sierra Meastra, to the west of Column 1." Then, with an amazing lack of realism, the document assessed the rebels' situation and, despite all reports to the contrary, stated that the rebels had had a "tremendous consumption of ammunition due mainly to the violent attacks of the army to which [rebels] have had to counterattack, and therefore they must be running short of ammunition."

Castro, the report went on, had failed to defeat the army at Vegas de Jibacoa due to the "lightning withdrawal of the regular troops." The guerrilla leader had also failed in his attempt to capture Colonel Sánchez Mosquera "because the latter withdrew with great skill and velocity."

At a time when the guerrillas were demonstrating one of their main advantages—the ability to move rapidly and thereby repel all of the army's maneuvers—the confidential report of the general staff maintained that "fortunately" Castro had been forced by "our strategic plans and our army to establish himself in a fixed area within the Sierra Maestra."

Operation "N" was to include 15 battalions, 11 of which would occupy "positions facing the enemy, while three battalions will occupy rearguard positions to act as supportive forces." One battalion close to Bayamo would be ready to be launched against the guerrillas in the any break along the army lines. A force of 25 planes would "devastate the area with day and night bombardments that will break the nervous system of his [Castro's] men, forcing a constant loss of supplies and of cattle that will cause his military force to crumble at any moment."

Once the Sierra Maestra had been surrounded for the second time in the summer, there would be landings on the southern coast, and the troops would again penetrate the mountains until the guerrillas were liquidated. Operation "N" simply dismissed the events of the past few weeks, the landing on the southern coast, the defeat of Battalion No. 18 and. evidently, most of General Cantillo's reports from the field of operations. Operation "N" was never put into effect since General Cantillo was already involved in his own plan to produce a quick, surprising victory over Fidel Castro.

The Battle of Las Mercedes

Claimed as a victory for the rebel army by Fidel Castro,[43] the battle of Las Mercedes almost resulted in a disaster for the guerrillas and in Castro's capture by Cantillo. The engagement at Las Mercedes signaled the end of the army's offensive, and the beginning of contact between Fidel Castro, General Cantillo and Batista.

General Cantillo's order to Colonel Corzo Izaquirre's Battalion No. 17 initiated the latter's retreat toward Las Mercedes.[44] At the same time, as previously planned, Cantillo ordered Colonel Sánchez Mosquera to lead a force in a mancuver to convince the guerrillas that Battalion No. 17 was in dire need of help, and that the army was trying to rescue it from the mountains. Also, the presence of Colonel Sánchez Mosquera attracted the best guerrilla forces in an attempt to intercept and capture him.

On July 26, 1958, two guerrilla commanders met at Casa de Piedra to ambush the advance unit commanded by Colonel Sánchez Mosquera.

Major René ("Daniel") Ramos Latour (1932-58) had a long history of involvement in the insurrectionary movement.[45] An accountant who was married and father of seven children, "Daniel" was one of the founding members of the M-26-7 in Santiago de Cuba. Together with María Antonia Figueroa, treasurer of the M-26-7 in Oriente, he had organized the movement's cells in the city of Mayarí and the towns of Cueto, Antilla and Nicaro. He had been in charge of a small group that had unsuccessfully attacked an army post at the Preston sugar mill in December 1956. On March 13, 1957, Frank País had ordered "Daniel" to join the first group of reinforcements sent by the urban underground to Castro. Upon País' death, "Daniel" was appointed in his place and performed brilliantly, organizing channels of communications throughout the island. Following the April strike, "Daniel" joined the guerrillas and was appointed commander of Column No. 10.

Major Ramón Paz Barroto was a miner before he joined the urban underground, then commanded by Frank País.[46] On August 15, 1957, Paz left for the Sierra Maestra, where he participated in several encounters, ambushes and combats prior to the army's summer offen-sive. "Daniel" and Paz met at Casa de Piedra to ambush the colonel.

On July 27, the combined guerrillas at Casa de Piedra stopped one company of Colonel Sánchez Mosquera's Battalion No. 11 and inflicted heavy casualties on the army. "Daniel," who led 43 guerrillas, and Paz, with about 60 men, killed 47 army troops, captured 17 men and took possession of 54 rifles, pistols and a bazooka. But the shooting had alerted Colonel Sánchez Mosquera, who was then able to take advantage of his position.

As hoped by General Cantillo, Fidel Castro was interested enough in capturing one of the archenemies of the guerrillas to order a complete mobilization toward the area of combat. Guerrillas led by Camilo Cienfuegos, Félix Duque, Eddy Suñol, Pedro Miret, Vilo Acuña and Guillermo García attempted to encircle the army between San Lorenzo and Las Mercedes. Castro would do his best to capture Battalion No. 17 and close every avenue of escape to Colonel Sánchez Mosquera.

The colonel, alerted to the presence of the guerrillas in the immediate area, moved slowly toward the hills of Providencia. Rather than retreating into Providencia, he took a good offensive position on top of a hill. There, with close to 200 men, he waited for the rebels, while ordering a small convoy to take the road leading out of Providencia. Colonel sánchez Mosquera divided his men into various groups and moved only when the guerrillas approached.

The encounter began on July 28 as Major Paz's guerrillas approached the small hill close to the Yara River and tried to decide whether to march along the river or set ambushes around the hill for Colonel Sánchez Mosquera's troops.[47] At that point Fidel Castro sent a message ordering Paz to move toward the hill, under the assumption that Eddy Suñol's guerrrillas would be awaiting the regular troops there. As Major Paz moved ahead with his column, Colonel Sánchez Mosquera moved downhill with his men. The army troops fired at very close range, the colonel leading the attack, and two guerrillas were instantly killed. Major Paz was also shot to death and the guerrillas panicked at the sight of regular troops coming downhill firing and chasing them. Only Major René Ramos Latour's supportive force saved Paz's guerrillas from extermination. The unusual bravery of the regular troops reflected Colonel Sánchez Mosquera's power to inspire his men in combat, a rare virtue among Batista's officers.

The news of Paz's death and the subsequent defeat of the guerrillas reached Fidel Castro, who caught up with "Daniel" and discussed the situation in Casa de Piedra.[48] With the knowledge that Battalion No. 17 was moving toward Las Mercedes, and that the attempt to capture Sánchez Mosquera had failed, Fidel regrouped the guerrillas and dispatched messengers to Commanders Guillermo García and Lalo Sardiñas, ordering them to join the main group as it marched rapidly towards the foot of the Sierra Maestra in a desperate attempt to ambush Battalion No. 17 as it approached Las Mercedes. When Fidel stopped close to Vegas de Jibacoa, he had almost 200 guerrillas with him.

Some 80 guerrillas took up positions between Las Mercedes and Sao Grande, thus falling into the ring established by General Cantillo, with their backs toward army Company 91 commanded by Captain Aispurúa Miñoso based at Sao Grande. At the same time other guerrilla units closed the army's retreat toward Estrada Palma by positioning men along the roads east and west of Las Mercedes. Thus, these were also within Cantillo's ring between Estrada Palma and Las Mercedes and at the mercy of army reinforcements based by Cantillo at Estrada Palma.[49]

On July 29, the guerrillas positioned between Las Mercedes and Sao Grande ambushed Battalion No. 17 as it moved toward the area. For the next 24 hours, Castro's men used his "war of nerves" tactic and did not fire a shot. Meanwhile Captain Aispurúa Miñoso was moving his company toward the guerrillas' position. On July 30, Battalion No. 17 attempted to break through the encirclement and the battle began. Fidel ordered "Daniel" to move with 100 men to a place called "El Jobal," while he stayed behind, close to Arroyones Pass.[50]

"Daniel" had his troops construct ambushes. At about 11:30 AM, the rebels opened up and all 32 men of the army's advance unit were killed.[51] But the army regrouped; only then did the rebels discover that there was a Sherman tank in the army's column. The army engaged in a fierce struggle with the guerrillas while "Daniel" asked Castro for immediate reinforcements. "Daniel" had also been caught in General Cantillo's trap. The army gained ground over the guerrillas, who bravely withstood several mortar barrages. "Daniel" was wounded, and several of his guerrillas withdrew from the field; the news that their leader had been wounded had the same effect as Paz's death had upon his troops.

Despite the number of casualties they had inflicted on the army, the guerrillas fell back in utter confusion. But "Daniel" was rescued quickly, and a messenger left to ask "Che" Guevara to attend the wounded commander. At about 3 PM Captain Fernando Vecino led the guerrillas out of the area, leaving behind some arms and ammunitions. Fidel did not send reinforcements, and "Che" Guevara did not arrive until after Major René "Daniel" Ramos Latour had died. In three days the rebel army and the insurrection had lost two of its best fighters.[52]

Close by, other guerrilla groups engaged the army and two prisoners were taken. The guerrillas learned that some 370 soldiers were supported by three tanks, 12 heavy machine guns, a bazooka squad and a mortar squad. In spite of everything, Castro settled for what he thought would be a long encirclement while Cantillo moved to take the unique opportunity of engaging the guerrillas on the plains. Castro's error was exactly what Cantillo had hoped for all along. Three army battalions rapidly moved into position from the Estrada Palma post, and Cantillo increased his forces by adding 1,500 troops from Bayamo and Manzanillo.[53]

Fidel Castro finally seems to have become aware of Cantillo's maneuver, for the SIM attached to Cantillo's staff reported that Castro was sending messengers to "Che" Guevara with news of his difficult situation.[54] "Che" Guevara, the ablest of all guerrilla leaders, ap-parently saved Fidel Castro from complete disaster. "Che" had the ability to project himself over the entire field of operations, and without hesitation his guerrillas attacked the army at a place called Cubanacao, inflicting serious casualties and capturing 150 prisoners. Camilo Cienfuegos also managed to inflict heavy casualties on the troops of the corps of engineers, taking all the food and ammunitions which they were transporting in their convoy.[55]

There was a brief impasse in the fighting, then on August 5, the army advanced towards Las Mercedes along the Sao Grande road supported by a tank and an armored car formation. At the same time, Captain Aispurúa Miñoso advanced from Sao Grande toward the guerrillas' position in a pincer movement.

"Firing from our flanks our sharpshooters liquidated the enemy's vanguard,"[56] Castro was to announce later. The guerrrillas held the tanks and the infantry forces for about four hours, until Captain Aispurúa Miñoso's Company 91 reached the area. At the same time, Battalion No. 17 advanced to Las Mercedes, and immediately turned toward Sao Grande in support of Captain Miñoso. Battalion No. 17 moved forward backed by seven Sherman tanks and 1,500 troops.

Captain Miñoso's men caught the guerrillas by surprise. The battle took place at very close range, with the guerrillas holding ground and then falling back, trying to gain security inside the forests. But Captain Miñoso pursued the guerrillas until the latter disbanded, leaving behind a large quantity of arms and ammunition. Captain Miñoso pursued the guerrillas over a small hill close to Sao Grande, capturing an arms depot where many of the arms captured from Battalion No. 18 at El Jigüe had been placed in preparation for more guerrilla attacks.[57]

At El Cerro, a small hill about four kilometers from Estrada Palma, guerrillas under the command of Camilo Cienfuegos ambushed an army patrol. The latter fought back and the guerrillas sustained seven dead and 17 wounded.

Although Castro usually reported the exact number of casualties, this time he did not describe the entire encounter, nor report the true number of dead guerrillas. He had to cover up the fact that his men had been caught by the army as a result of the useless confrontation that he had ordered.[58] In addition, the guerrillas were unable to collect arms and ammunition in quantities large enough to merit the highest number of casualties sustained by the rebel army in the entire summer offensive. It is estimated that the rebel army lost about 40 guerrillas to Captain Aispurúa Miñoso, immediately promoted to major by Cantillo; and approximately 30 guerrillas were killed around Las Mercedes and Providencia.[59] The number of wounded guerrillas was high. The army captured at least two guerrillas and, contrary to their usual practice, even picked up their own wounded personnel.[60]

Regular Army: Summer Offensive

General Staff

Major General Eulogio Cantillo Porras, Chief of Operations
Brigadier General Alberto del Rio Chaviano
Brigadier Démaso Sogo Hernández
Colonel José Manuel Ugalde Carrillo
Lieutenant Colonel Merob Sosa
Majors Raúl de Talahorra
      Juan Arias Cruz
      Bernardo Perdomo Granela
      J. Ferrer Casilda
      Timoteo Morales Villazón
      Raúl M. Trujillo

Operational Forces Unit	*Commander*
Battalion No. 10	Major Nelson Carrasco Artiles
Battalion No. 11	Colonel Angel Sánchez Mosquera
Battalion No. 12	Captain Pedraja Padrón

Battalion No. 13	Major J Triana Tarrao
Battalion No. 14	Major Bernardo Guerrero Padrón
Battalion No. 15	Major Martínez Morejón
Battalion No. 16	Captain Figueroa Lora
Battalion No. 17	Major Corzo Izaguirre
Battalion No. 18	Major José Quevedo Pérez
Battalion No. 19	Major Suárez Zoulet
Battalion No. 20	Major Caridad Fernández
Battalion No. 21	Major Franco Lliteras
Battalion No. 22	Major Eugenio Menéndez Martínez
Battalion No. 23	Major Armando González Finalés
Company No. 1	Captain Modesto Díaz Fernández
Company K	Major Roberto Triana Tarrao
Company L	Captain Noelio Montero Díaz
Second Company, Fifth Regiment	Lieutenant Miguel Pérez
First Company, Third Regiment	Captain Luis Vega Hernández
Second Company, Third Regiment	Lieutenant Adriano Pérez
Tank Company C, "March 10th Regiment"	Captain Victorino Gómez Oquendo
Air Force	Colonel Armando Coto Rodríguez
Naval Task Force	Captain J. Lopez Campos
Rural Guards	Colonel Arcadio Casillas Lumpuy

Despite "Che" Guevara's brilliant action, Fidel Castro's men were still within the army's trap. Fidel could have escaped, but at the cost of sacrificing most of his guerrilla army with the exception of Camilo Cienfuegos' and "Che" Guevara's columns. His guerrillas were caught between Las Mercedes, Sao Grande and Arroyones, and Fidel knew he was in trouble. Castro sent a messenger to General Cantillo's post with the request that a ceasefire be declared and talks be held someplace in the area before the bloodshed continued.[61] Fidel, the politician, would try to save what he almost lost as a guerrilla leader—his guerrilla army.

General Cantillo acquiesced to Fidel Castro's petition. Cantillo's information as to Castro's whereabouts was so accurate that when he ordered Lieutenant Carlos Pina to visit Castro. Lieutenant Orlando Izquierdo, the helicopter pilot, knew exactly where to land.[62]

Castro welcomed Lieutenants Pina and Izquierdo. The guerrilla leader was accompanied by Celia Sánchez and some tired-looking guerrillas.[63] Fidel asked Lieutenant Pina for medicines to cure some guerrillas who could not be moved. He also requested permission and a safe conduct to send some of his own men to the Cuban Red Cross post at Sao Grande. Lieutenant Pina reports that Castro asked him about General Cantillo's attitude toward an "understanding to end the war," and whether he would deliver a letter to Cantillo. Lieutenant Pina agreed to deliver the letter, and Castro wrote in a page from his personal notebook that it was necessary to end the bloody civil strife, and that a meeting would solve many problems and eliminate many obstacles. "It is necessaary to open a dialogue," Castro's letter read, "so that we can put an end to the conflict."[64]

Upon receipt of Castro's letter, General Cantillo questioned Lieutenant Pina and Lieutenant Izquierdo, and both men agreed that Castro "appeared ready to negotiate a settlement, and that his attitude was that of a deeply worried man." Lieutenant Pina interpreted Castro's conversation and behavior as indicating his willingness to reach an understanding with General Cantillo before the army completed its encirclement and attacked. General Cantillo showed that letter to Colonel Nelson Carrasco Artiles,[65] commander of Battalion No.10, and the four men where in accord that the event was important enough to merit the attention Batista.

Batista, who was at the time Varadero Beach, Matanzas province, asked Cantillo to report the situation personally. General Cantillo look Lieutenant Carlos Pina along with him to the meeting, and reported on the letter and Castro's military position to Batista and General Rodríguez Avila.[66] Batista stated that he could not sec how the rebel leader would be willing to negotiate an end to a campaign in which he had the upper hand. In spite of his casualties at Las Mercedes, Castro could, in Batista's estimate, sustain the guerrilla campaign for quite some time. It appeared to Batista that Castro was maneuvering for time, but on Cantillo's insistence that a dialogue be established with the guerrilla leader, Batista appointed the army's prosecutor general, Lieutenant Colonel Fernando Neugart as the government's negotiator and Batista's personal representative. Colonel Neugart was contacted by General Tabernilla, Sr., and Neugart returned with Cantillo and Lieutenant Pina to Bayamo.[67]

Upon arrival at Bayamo's headquarters, Lieutenant Pina received a note from Fidel reading, "I have been expecting your news throughout the morning [August 6] and can only think that you lack transportation. If you so wished I can go directly to your battalion and discuss the matter there."[68] Within hours, Colonel Neugart was flown to Castro's headquarters by Lieutenant Izquierdo. General Cantillo's helicopter carried $10,000 worth of medicines in compliance with Fidel's request. Castro welcomed Colonel Neugart with some suprise, stating that he had hoped to sec General Cantillo.[69] When Neugart offered to leave, Castro said that there were urgent matters to discuss, and that the army had sent an able negotiator. Castro led him into an old brick house belonging to the coffee plantation of Las Mercedes. There they held discussions for three consecutive days.

Castro had one immediate request to make of Colonel Neugart: that a ceasefire be declared throughout the immediate area. Colonel Neugart agreed, and he radioed the air force to stop flying above the meeting grounds. From his command post General Cantillo had ordered all army units to remain at their places without engaging the guerrillas unless fired upon. Colonel Neugart reports that during the first meeting. Castro launched into an "endless speech against the government." Present at that meeting were Celia Sánchez, several guerrillas and, sitting in a far corner, not participating in the conversation, was "Che" Guevara. It was impossible to discuss anything with Castro in front of so many people, so Neugart returned to report to General Cantillo while promising Castro to be back the following day, August 7, at 7 AM. Castro expressed his hope to Colonel Neugart that "we can discuss various important details alone." The second meeting lasted until 5 PM; during this session Fidel launched into a new attack on Batista's regime. He also reviewed the history of the insurrection, the injustice of Cuba's court system, and criticized graft administrative corruption. "Che" Guevara also attended the meeting, as did Camilo Cienfuegos, Celia Sánchez and Humberto Sorí Marín. No one would interrupt Fidel, except Colonel Neugart, who kept "trying to press Castro for serious negotiations."[70]

At 5 PM, Colonel Neugart walked out of the house and toward his helicopter. Castro followed the colonel, who stated that he saw no purpose in continuing a discussion which was actually a monologue. He was there to represent Batista and to ask Castro what he wanted to put an end to the conflict. As they walked back to the helicopter, Castro announced to Neugart that he was ordering the release of some army prisoners to the Red Cross, while Neugart pointed out that his mission had not been accomplished, and that they had not discussed Castro's letter to General Cantillo.

Upon his return to Bayamo, Colonel Neugart reported to General Cantillo that he would meet Castro for the last time early the following morning. He also told Cantillo that since Castro appeared undecided as to whether or not to discuss the real purpose of the meeting, he would take the initiative and advance a plan. Colonel Neugart assumed that Castro would thus be placed in a position whereby he would have to discuss the future end of the civil war. General Cantillo was non-committal.

At the end of the third meeting, Colonel Neugart took Castro away from the other guerrillas and presented his own proposal for the end of the conflict. Neugart's proposal to Castro was the cessation of the government through the formation of a military junta; a ceasefire across Sierra Maestra and the prompt holding of general elections. Fidel asked Neugart to present that proposal to Batista, warning the colonel, however, that the caudillo would never accept that solution. On August 8, Colonel Neugart returned to Bayamo to report to Cantillo, and then to Havana to report personally to Batista.

Fidel's strategy in calling for the meetings soon became clear. He had won time and opportunity to remove his men from General Cantillo's ring of regular troops while at the same time caring for the wounded guerrillas, and receiving a large quantity of medicines. He also rid his guerrilla army of prisoners taken from the regular army, thus gaining stature in the field of propaganda. The fact that the army was willing to negotiate with Castro planted further seeds of discontent among those officers who had fought for so long in the Sierra Maestra and who were not willing to compromise with the guerrillas. Most of all, Castro's master maneuver came at the precise time when the army had performed professionally for the first time the campaign and had all the advantage.

Later Batista charge Colonel Neugart with abusing his power to negotiate with Fidel Castro, and pointed out that the colonel's mission was strictly to listen to what Castro had to say.[71] General Cantillo apparently ageed with Batista's interpretation, for he lost no time in reporting to General Tabernilla, Sr., about his conversation with Neugart and the latter's proposal to Castro. For his part, Colonel Neugart refuted Batista's interpretation, of his mission, pointing out that any recruit could have been sent to Castro if his mission, was "only to listen." In Neugart's case, his mission was to discuss with Castro, if possible, an end to the civil strife and the conditions leading to that objective.[72]

Progressive Disintegration of the Armed Forces

Despite all the false reports issued by army headquarters at Havana, the people knew that the government offensive had ended without the army succeeding either in capturing Castro or destroying his guerrilla movement. The offensive failed not only because the troops had generally refused to engage in earnest fighting, but because of the lack of professionalism of most regular army officers. Like most Latin American regular armies, the Cuban military was not accustomed to real war. Confronted by irregular, guerrilla warfare, Cuban officers demonstrated their lack of technical preparation. The bitter encounter with reality, with death, the long marches through jungles and mountains, the surprise ambushes, were all far removed from the quiet, comfortable life in the city barracks. It was the first time the Cuban military had been really challenged by an armed, well-organized group of young men, and the challenge was too much for the political generals of dictator Batista.

Ernesto "Che" Guevara's communications system,[73] plus his careful preparation throughout the campaign of arms factories, field hospitals, arms depots, trenches, maps, codes and a myriad of important details making guerrilla warfare possible, had enabled the rebel army to confront the regular troops on numerous instances in the summer offensive. It was "Che" Guevara who first confronted the army when the offensive began, and he was also present in the last confrontation, managing to rescue the rebel army from the follies of Fidel Castro. The guerrillas fought well in every instance and bravely defended the ideals which prompted their presence in the mountains in the first place.

The general staff in Havana underestimated the guerrillas' capacity to move through great distances in a short time. The generals never engaged the guerrillas in combat, and Batista did not even visit the area of operations.[74] General Chaviano, who led the troops in northern Oriente province, simply refused to fight Raúl Castro's guerrillas, although from time to time he would order an attack against a village in an isolated region where only innocent peasants were killed.

The final outcome of the summer offensive seemed hard to believe at first. Fidel Castro's official report showed that 25 guerrillas had been killed, among them seven officers,[75] and 48 men had been wounded, for a grand total of 73 casualties. To that figure should be added approximately 70 guerrillas killed in and around Las Mercedes; and about twice that number wounded throughout the summer.[76] The army suffered 231 deaths, and 422 men taken prisoner. The guerrillas captured more than 500 arms, two tanks, bazookas, mortars, one cannon, one anti-aircraft gun, 11 .50 caliber machine guns and approximately 100 submachine guns. Besides, they took hundreds of individual packs, radio transmitters, military codes, maps and over a million and a half rounds of ammunition of all calibers.

Fidel Castro, as commander in chief of the rebel army, addressed the people through the rebel radio and presented a full report of the operation on August

A typical *casamata* (bunker) used by the Sierra Maestra guerrillas in the summer offensive of 1958 (Reprinted by permission of Yale University Library).

Two regular army soldiers under custody of guerrillas in the Sierra Maestra, summer 1958 (Reprinted by permission of Yale University Library).

18 and 19, 1958.[77] Castro charged the army with acts of brutality against the rural population, but said if justice was to prevail the guerrillas could not treat the army in the same way. Prisoners had been well treated. Knowing that they would not be killed if they were captured, the great majority of soldiers refused to fight. Castro stressed the fact that the soldiers were fighting the generals' war, while the latter enriched themselves through graft and fraud.

Castro issued his conditions for the immediate end to the civil war.[78] They were: the arrest and delivery of the dictator to the tribunals of justice; the arrest and delivery of all political leaders who were responsible for the dictatorship, who in any way had helped the regime to function, or who had enriched themselves with the republic's resources: the arrest and delivery of all military personnel who had engaged in crimes of war in the cities and in the country-side, and of those officers who had enriched themselves through gambling, extortion, smuggling and all illicit means, whatever their rank; delivery of the presidency to that man appointed by all sectors fighting the dictatorship, in order that general elections might be held in the shortest time possible.

Castro also stressed the need for a nonpolitical army, so that "the army would never become again the instrument of any caudillo or political party." The army, said Castro, should dedicate itself to defending the nation's sovereignty and to maintaining "the constitution and the laws and the rights of all citizens." "No one more than ourselves," Castro added, "has the right to demand something for the good of the country, because no one else has renounced from the beginning any personal ambition. We await the answer on the march."

285

The impact of the summer offensive marked the turning point of the insurrection and Batista's eventual demise. After Batista proved that he was unable to control the situation, many members of the upper class withdrew their support from the government and tried to establish contact with the insurrectionists. From among the rich substantial amounts of money were accumulated in the treasuries of the insurrectionary movement.[79]

The attitude of the workers also began to change after the summer of 1958. They gained confidence in the young labor militants of the insurrectionist sector, and became more willing to cooperate with the various underground cells in the working centers. Talk about another attempt at a revolutionary general strike became more common, the recent insurrectionist victory over the army somehow erasing the memories of the frustrated strike of April 9, 1958. An idea of the extent to which contributions increased may be measured from a comparison of cash contributions made by bank employees before and after the summer of 1958. Employees of three American and Canadian-owned banks in Havana contributed $172 during March 1958. But during October 1958, the same employees increased their contributions to over $1,200 plus medicines, clothing and canned foods.[80]

Participation of workers in the urban underground also increased. In May 1958 there was only one three-member cell of the M-26-7 in The Royal Bank of Canada of Havana. Six months later, in November, there were ten cells with five employees each. In early 1958 only one militant represented the DR underground in the Goodyear Tire Company on the outskirts of the capital. By mid-October that factory was a main source of tires, spare parts and other services for the movement. From only one militant, the company membership in the movement had increased to a cell of porters, one of foremen and another cell of salesmen.[81] The urban movement, mostly the M-26-7, succeeded, organizing cells in various associations after the summer: the Association of Press Reporters, the cattlemen's association, vegetable growers' association and several landlords' associations. Underground cells were formed by hotel employees to check on visitors from foreign countries, and to maintain vigilance over people invited to Cuba by the government. The Copacabana Hotel, the Chateau-Miramar, Colina, Lido, Rosita de Hornedo, Capri and Havana Riviera, all ill the capital, were mostly under the control of the DR underground. The M-26-7 was stronger in the Hotel Cacique in Santa Clara, Las Villas province; Rancho Club, Santiago de Cuba, Oriente province; the Royal, also in Santiago de Cuba; and in Havana, the Havana-Hilton, St. John's, Flamingo and the Emperador hotels. Cells from the DR and the M-26-7 operated in all Cuban airline companies: Cubana de Aviación, Aerovias "Q" and Expreso Aereo Interamericano.

There were also DR urban cells among the workers in the ports of Cabañas, Bahía Honda and Mariel, Pinar del Río privince; Matanzas Bay, Matanzas province; and a group of cells formed by workers at the Bay of Havana. The

DR also had cells in the Bay of Nipe in Oriente province, and in Santiago de Cuba's bay. The M-26-7 established urban cells in the ports of Antilla, Banes. Baracoa and the Bay of Santiago de Cuba, all in Oriente province.[82]

The urban movement had approximately 10,000 members throughout the country before the summer of 1958. By the end of the year, it counted no less than 30,000 people who contributed cash on a regular basis. From about 1,500 hard-core fighters in the cities— including all movements active in the urban areas—the ranks of the militants increased to 5,000 or 6,000 youths ready to engage in terrorism. During November of 1958, for example, 12 new cells were added to the M-26-7 in the city of Marianao, Havana province.[83] Most of the newcomers were easy victims of the police, for their inexperience worked against them at a time when terrorism had reached a peak on both sides. During the first 15 days of December, 1958, 45 guerrillas were shot to death in Marianao, and about the same number in Guanabacoa City.[84] In one week—November 7-14, 1958—nearly 30 recently recruited guerrillas who were trying to get some supplies to guerrillas in the Sierra de los Organos were captured by Colonel Jacinto Menocal in Pinar del Río province and executed on the spot.[85] From November 1 to December 31, 1958, an estimated 300 bombs exploded throughout the greater metropolitan area of Havana. In Cienfuegos City, Las Villas province, approximately 20 potent bombs exploded during Christmas week, 1958.[86] In Matanzas at least ten policemen were shot to death, and five major bombings took place close to the refineries near the Bay of Matanzas.[87] In the capitals of Camagüey and Oriente provinces the urban underground remained comparatively quiet due to the large numbers of army troops in maneuvers or based in the cities.

After the summer offensive, the Communists mobilized their cadres, and the party's relations with FON rapidly improved. Carlos Rafael Rodríguez left the Sierra Maestra for Havana, where he held discussions with local representatives of the Caracas Pact who did not exactly like Castro's cooperation with the PSP. With veteran labor leader Ursinio Rojas, also a party member, Rodríguez returned to the mountains of Oriente. At about this time, Castro authorized PSP members to join the ranks of the rebel army.[88] The PSP's new attitude in favor of the insurrection was viewed by many militants of the insurrection as the traditional opportunistic approach of the party. But as far as the urban fighters were concerned it did not mean much, for the militants of the party continued to avoid the dangerous aspects of urban guerrilla warfare.

By September, there was an atmosphere of impending crisis which was furthered by the underground movement's increased sabotage operations against police and army precincts and barracks. Fourteen such operations took place during September and October of 1958. The urban underground suffered heavy casualties, and it was usually estimated that each operation that included ten or 12 urban guerrillas would cost five or six deaths. Batista's police killed all wounded men, taking no prisoners. There were approximately

32 guerrilla operations during November, mainly shootings at police precincts in Havana.[89] Public utilities were constantly attacked; there were seven such attacks on the night of November 25.[90] Bombs exploded every night, and on the evening of December 7 over 100 bombs exploded in the capital. No policeman could feel safe in the streets of any town.

Within the army the impact of the summer offensive resulted in at least six separate plots among officers from the ranks of captains to colonels. Other officers criticized the regime and voiced their opposition to the continuation of the civil strife. All such critics were prosecuted by the army's prosecutor general, Colonel Fernando Neugart.[91]

The insurrection was on the march from Sierra Maestra to Pinar del Río, and in every town and city of the country the people began joining the ranks of the insurgents. But more terrain was to be covered and many deaths to be added before Batista's regime would fall.

Notes

1. Letter from Fidel Castro to Mario Llerena and Raúl Chibás, dated April 28, 1958, which appears in Llerena's manuscript, "The Unsuspected Rvolution."
2. Fulgencio Batista, *Respuesta* (Mexico City: Editorial Botas, 1960), p. 84.
3. The committee was organized by Víctor Pedroso, a banker: Gustavo Cuervo Rubio, a physician: and by Reverend Father Pastor González. A copy of the letter was shown to one of the authors by R. P. González in the Escolapios de Guanabacoa (Guanabacoa, Havana, August, 1958).
4. Interview with General Eulogio Cantillo Porras (December 4 and 5, 1972, Miami, Florida).
5. Batista, *Respuesta*, p. 84.
6. Fulgencio Batista, *Cuba Betrayed* (New York: Vantage, 1962), p. 82.
7. Ibid., p. 83.
8. Questionnaire submitted to a sample of 200 Cuban exiles formerly from towns in these provinces at a Community Action Program in Union City, New Jersey.
9. Army estimates given by General Eulogio Cantillo in an interview.
10. Interview with Colonel Merob Sosa (July 1972, Union City), corroborated by an interview with General Cantillo.
11. For Castro's tactics, see Merle Kling, "Cuba: A Case Study of Unconventional Warfare," *Military Review*, 42, no. 12 (December 1962): 11–12. Also Robert Taber, *M-26: The Biography of a Revolution* (New York: Lyle Stuart, 1961), p. 249; R. Aaron, "Guerra de guerrillas en Cuba," *Military Review* (May 1955), and "Why Batista Lost," *Military Review* (September 1965).
12. Interview with Captain Jaime Bacallao, November 10, 1970. New York, New York, Corroborated by participating guerrillas José Villavicencio, Mario García Falla and Benito Rodríguez Provenzano in interviews held during May–June, 1970 in Union City, New Jersey. For Fidel Castro's account of the rebel army's fighting capability at this point, see *Revolución* (Havana), January 10, 1959, and *Obra Revolucionaria*, no. 46 (1961): 12.
13. Fidel Castro, "La batalla de Santo Domingo: Reporte oficial de la comandancia del Ejército Rebelde," Radio Rebelde Broadcast, June 29, 1958, 10 PM.

For the translation see, Rolando E, Bonachea and Nelson P. Valdés, *Revolutionary Struggle, 1947–1958, vol. 1 (Cambridge, Mass; MIT Press, 1972),* pp. 382–83.

14. Fidel Castro, "Instrucciones," *El Cubano Libre* (Sierra Maestra), no. 6 (September 1958): 6.

15. Conversation of one of the authors with Major Juan Almeida, (February 1959, Havana).

16. Castro, "Instrucciones."

17. Some of Castro's descriptions were corroborated in various conversations with guerrilla fighters who participated in this encounter, the most important of whom was Juan ("Belao") Acosta in the Zapata Swamps, Las Villas province, June 1960.

18. Castro, "Instrucciones," It was at this time that "Che" Guevara claimed General Cantillo wrote a letter to Fidel Castro stating that although the offensive would proceed, Castro's life would be spared. See Ernesto "Che" Guevara, "Una Revolución que comienza," *Vida Universitaria,* no. 214 (January–March 1969): 18. General Cantillo categorically denies Guevara's assertion, stating that he wrote to Castro for the first time on December 30, 1958. A copy of the alleged letter has never been published by the Cuban government.

19. Interviews with Miguel Roché (July 20, 1969 and January 15, 1970, Washington, D.C.).

20. Evidence of former prime minister Manuel Antonio ("Tony") de Varona to the authors (August 1970, Passaic, New Jersey, and June 15, 1971, New York, New York).

21. See Juan Acuña, *Revolución traicionada* (Montevideo: Editorial Goes, n.d.), pp. 156–60. For a translation of this and other documents, see Jules Dubois, *Fidel Castro, Rebel-Liberator or Dictator?* (Indianapolis: Bobbs-Merrill, 1959), pp. 280–83.

22. Numerous interviews with Auténtico politicians and militants of the OA and the Triple A lead the authors to conclude that to most the struggle ended with Batista's downfall.

23. Interview with General Cantillo.

24. This information and subsequent details of the operations are reported in Fidel Castro, *La batalla del Jigüe y la rendición del Comandante Quevedo, Reporte de la Comandancia General del Ejército Rebelde,* July 26, 1958, mimeo., 17 pp. See also Bonachea and Valdés *Revolutionary Struggle,* pp. 393–96; and Edmundo Desnoes, ed., *La Sierre y el llano* (Havana: Casa de las Americas, 1961), pp. 189–94; also, José Quevedo Pérez, *La batalla del Jigue* (Havana: Instituto Cubano del Libro, 1971), p. 20.

25. One of these men, former corporal Adolfo Ruíz Fernández, told the authors that the guerrillas fired from the forest and that he and his comrades were never able to see them (January 1970, West New York, New Jersey).

26. Cantillo to the authors.

27. Fidel Castro, *La batalla del* Jigüe, pp. 4–5.

28. Cantillo to the authors.

29. Fidel Castro, *La batalla del Jigüe,* pp. 4–6.

30. *Sierra Maestra,* Organo oficial del M-26-7, en el exilio (Miami, Florida) July 1958, pp. 2–3, See also Earl T. Smith, *The Fourth Floor* (New York: Random House, 1962), p. 142: José L. Cuza, "Combate del centro industrial de Moa,"

Verde Olivo (Havana), July 14, 1963, pp. 18–24; and Marta Rojas, "El Segundo Frente Oriental Frank País: operación antiaerea," *Bohemia* (Havana), July 5, 1955, pp. 50–51.

31. "U.S. Non-Intervention Policy with Respect to the Cuban Situation: Replies Made by the Secretary of State to Questions Asked at a News Conference, July 1, 1958," *U.S. Current Documents: 1958* (New York, 1959), p. 349.

32. U.S. Department of State, *Bulletin* (July 21, 1958), pp. 110–11.

33. Fidel Castro, "Mensaje del comandante en Jefe a las columnas rebeldes," *La Voz de la Sierra Maestra*, Radio Rebelde, July 3, 1958. mimeo. 15 pp. See also *Historia de Cuba* (Havana: Instituto del Libro, 1971), pp. 231–32.

34. Ernesto Betancourt in letter to the authors dated December 15, 1972, Washington, D.C.

35. *Sierra Maestra*, July 1958, p. 3.

36. U.S. Department of State, *Publication Release No. 7322* (Washington, D.C.: Historical Office, July 3, 1958).

37. Colonel Nelson Carrasco Artíles in letter to the authors (December 5, 1972, Miami, Florida).

38. Interview with Lieutenant Colonel Fernando Neugart (January 8, 1973, New York, New York).

39. Batista, *Respuesta*, p. 91, quotes from a letter written by a former captain Olivera about the incident. Three rebel soldiers who were asked about this story during May 1960 in Havana reported that for about half an hour they did not know the whereabouts of Guevara, but that "Che" had left one of the flanks, ordering them to keep firing, and then went to contact another squad about 60 ms. away. Asked about the incident, army Colonel Merob Sosa said he vaguely recalled a discussion among other officers to this effect, and he could offer no further data in an interview with the authors (February 20, 1972, Union City).

40. General Eulogio Cantillo, "Plan de operaciones: Puesto de Mando de Bayamo" (July 26, 1958), in *Che* (Havana: Instituto del Libro, 1969), pp. 254–57.

41. Colonel Nelson Carrasco Artíles, "La operación verano," *América Libre* (Miami, Florida), February 18, 1972, pp. 2, 8.

42. Admiral José Rodríguez Calderón, "Asunto: Nuevo plan de operaciones, Zona Bayamo-Manzanillo-Niquero," in *Ché*, pp. 258–64.

43. Fidel Castro, "Reporte militar: la batalla de Las Mercedes, final de la ofensiva del verano," in René Ray. *Libertad y Revolución: Moncada, Granma, Sierra Maestra* (February 1959), pp. 56–58.

44. Cantillo to the authors.

45. "El comandante Daniel," *Bohemia* (Havana), July 30, 1965, pp. 46–49.

46. "Ramón Paz, de minero a comandante heróico," *Bohemia* (Havana), July 23, 1965, pp. 72–81.

47. Ibid., pp. 80–81.

48. "El comandante Daniel," p. 48.

49. Interview with General Cantillo. Corroborated in letter to the authors by Colonel Nelson Carrasco Artíles (January 10, 1973, Miami, Florida). See also Nelson Carrasco Artíles, "Análisis de la situación militar de ambos bandos," *América Libre* (Miami, Florida), May 12, 1972, pp. 2, 4.

50. "Anexo 66," in *Che*, p. 260.

51. Fernando Vecino, "El combate de El Jobal," *Días de combate* (Havana: Instituto Cubano del Libro, 1970), p. 132. "El Jobal" was between Arroyones and Cerro Pelado.
52. Ibid., p. 141.
53. Cantillo to the authors.
54. Lieutenant Benjamin Cadillo Luzón to the authors in interview held on January 18, 1971, Union City, New Jersey.
55. Fernando Vecino, "El combate de El Jobal," p. 131.
56. Fidel Castro, "Reporte militar," pp. 56–58.
57. Cantillo to the authors.
58. Interview with former guerrilla lieutenant Luis Jorges Veitía, March 23, 1969, Washington, D.C.
59. Estimate of General Cantillo. The army recovered 315 rifles of various calibers, one bazooka and one mortar. See Gervasio G. Ruiz, "La dictadura que cayó derrotada por sus victorias: antología de partes oficiales," *Carteles* (Havana), January 4, 1959, pp. 26–28, 134.
60. Vecino, "El combate de El Jobal," pp. 129–44. See also, "Ramón Paz: de minero a comandante heróico," *Bohemia* (Havana), July 30, 1965, pp. 72–81, and *Bohemia* (Havana), July 23, 1965, pp. 46–51.
61. The original copy, written on a loose page from his notebook, was signed by Fidel Castro and shown to the authors by Cantillo.
62. Orlando Izquierdo to the authors (April 10, 1973, Miami, Florida).
63. Letter to the authors from Lieutenant Carlos Pina (January 17, 1973, Hyattsville, Maryland).
64. Letter of Fidel Castro to Cantillo, see note 61.
65. Nelson Carrasco Artíles in letter to the authors (January 8, 1973, Miami, Florida).
66. Cantillo to the authors.
67. Batista, *Respuesta*, pp. 127–28.
68. Fidel Castro's letter to Lieutenant Carlos Pina was read to the authors by Cantillo. It was also corroborated by Lieutenant Carlos Pina in letter to the authors (January 17, 1973, Hyattsville. Maryland).
69. Interview with Colonel Fernando Neugart (January 8, 1973, Brooklyn, New York).
70. Ibid.
71. Ibid.
72. Neugart to the authors. At this point Batista was told repeatedly to change his approach and to look for a way out before his regime would be thoroughly defeated, and that it would be "too late to find a solution without Castro." Eusebio Mujal Barniol in letter to the authors (July 14, 1970, Washington, D.C.).
73. Ernesto "Che" Guevara, *Pasajes de la guerra revolucionaria cubana* (Mexico City: Serie Popular Era, 1969), p. 214.
74. Ernesto "Che" Guevara, "Una revolución que comienza," *Vida Universitaria* (January–March 1969), pp. 16–17.
75. They were Major René ("Daniel") Ramos Latour at "El Jobal" in Vegas de Jibacoa; Major Ramón Paz at Providencia; Captain Angel Verdecia at Merino; Captain Leonel Rodríguez at Santo Domingo; Captain Andrés Cuevas at El

Jigüe; Lieutenant Carlos Más at Santo Domingo; and Lieutenant A. Cordumy at Las Mercedes.

76. These are the authors estimates based on careful accounting of personal reports of casualties through the interviews with guerrillas and regular army troops, plus official sources cited.

77. Fidel Castro, "Report on the Tyranny's Last Offensive, August 18–19, 1958, *Granma* (Supplement) (Havana), March 18, 1973, pp. 12–19. See also, Bonachea and Valdés, *Revolutionary Struggle*, "Report on the Offensive: Part I (August 18, 1958)," pp. 399–408: "Report on the Offensive: Part II (August 19, 1958)," pp. 408–14.

78. Ibid., pp. 12–19.

79. Raúl Chibás, Rufo López Fresquet and Ignacio Mendoza succeeded in collecting substantial sums of money from industrialists and professionals.

80. Personal notes and records of one of the authors who had access to the fiscal report rendered by the M-26-7, and the FON in the National Federation of Bank Employees, January–February, 1959.

81. Interview with Carlos Fontanal, M-26-7 cadre member (June 10, 1972, Brooklyn, New York).

82. Interview with Ramón Días Mayoz, DR cadre member (January 2, 1971, New York, New York).

83. Interview with Daniel ("Caralinda") Feliu, M-26-7 cadre member (February 1971, New York, New York).

84. Figures are based on estimates offered by various militants of the urban underground, and balanced with estimates offered by police officers from Marianao and Guanabacoa cities respectively.

85. Interview with Carmen del Valle (January 1971, New York, New York).

86. Estimates calculated by police officers based at the time in Cienfuegos, Las Villas province.

87. Interview with Ramiro Sánchez Porduy, a guard in the refineries of Matanzas province (November 5, 1972, Union City, New Jersey).

88. Evidence of Carlos Rafael Rodríguez in Hugh Thomas, *Cuba, The Pursuit of Freedom* (New York: Harper and Row, 1971), p. 1006. See also Blas Roca, "VIII Congress Speech," *Hoy* (Havana), January 11, 1959, p. 38; and K. S. Karol, *Guerrillas in Power, The Course of the Cuban Revolution* (New York: Hill and Wang, 1970), pp. 151–54.

89. Interview with Israel Romero, M-26-7 cadre member (October 5, 1972, Union City).

90. Interview with Israel Romero (October 7, 1972, Union City).

91. Fernando Neugart to the authors, January 8, 1973, New York, New York.

12

The Westward March

Immediately after his victory in the Sierra Maestra, Fidel Castro assigned Major Camilo Cienfuegos a major mission—leading a rebel army column from the Sierra Maestra to Pinar del Río province. Column No. 2, known as "Antonio Maceo," was to leave from El Salto on Wednesday, August 20, 1958. Cienfuegos was granted powers to organize rebel units throughout the territory: to apply the rebel penal code and the agrarian measures of the rebel army; to collect established contributions; and to combine operations with other forces operating against the dictatorship. He was also to establish a permanent guerrilla front in Pinar del Río province and to appoint officers up to the rank of major. The invasion column was to fight the enemy at every opportunity, although its main objective was to reach the westernmost province of Cuba. All weapons captured during engagements with the army were to be used to arm new guerrilla units.[1]

"Che" Guevara was ordered to lead his guerrillas to Las Villas province and to conduct operations in that area in accord with Castro's plan to cut the island in half. Guevara was appointed chief of all M-26-7 rebel units operating in Las Villas province, in rural as well as in the urban areas. He was also authorized to collect taxes, and coordinate administrative and military matters and operations with insurrectionary forces in the area. Guevara was also authorized to appoint officers up to the rank of major. Column No. 8, known as "Ciro Redondo," was to conduct constant attacks on the army throughout the province, and to concentrate all its resources and efforts on paralyzing the army's east-west movement.[2]

Guevara's Column No. 8 departed from Las Mercedes on August 31, 1958. Camilo Cienfuegos' "Antonio Maceo" Column No. 2 led the rebel army's westward march. Travelling the first four days by truck and continuing on foot, the guerrillas stayed close to the southern coast and away from the roads. According to "Che" Guevara's description of the expedition, the guerrillas were confronted with great difficulties, escaping various encirclements, making a few kidnappings and losing guerrillas in encounters with the army on two different occasions. Their most serious situation was in Baraguá, where "we found ourselves totally surrounded, and in very bad physical condition; but we overcame that obstacle crossing Ciego de Avila and the Jatibonico River."[3]

When the guerrillas entered Camagüey province, Captain Alfonso Acosta of the 25th Squadron of the Rural Guards reported to the army's chief of operations, Colonel Suárez Suquet, that "information received at 2100 hours states that a group of 80 well-armed bandits in green fatigues were transported into the area in three trucks which they left eight kilometers from the Lugareño sugar mill, continuing then in an unknown direction. Further investigations to establish their where-abouts continue."[4] During this investigation, the army found a large stock of arms and supplies probably left there by local members of the M-26-7.[5]

To stop the rebels from advancing further into Camagüey province, the army mobilized its forces and carefully laid a series of ambushes and blockades. Regular troops were deployed in a wide circle, closing the ring to the north and to the south, from the military post of Elia to the Santa Rosalía plantation, which lay near Camagüey's border with Oriente province.

The army's positions were as follows: Company 96, Battalion 11, was placed in an ambush at Cuatro Compañeros; Company B, Battalion 22, commanded by Captain Abón Ly, lay in an ambush around the Vertientes area; in addition, seven other ambushes had been set up towards the south; Companies O and N, Battalion 22 were positioned around the Aguilera rice plantation; and Company A and Company 97 were placed in a blockade around La Federal.[6]

Meanwhile, Majors Cienfuegos and Guevara had reached the Tana River, where they separated. Moving with caution through this dangerous terrain Guevara's column marched towards the hacienda La Federal, and Cienfuegos headed to the left. The two leaders agreed to meet at the Bartes rice farm.

On September 8 Guevara stopped for a rest at the Bartes farm and took the opportunity to write the first of at least eight progress reports to Fidel Castro:

> Camilo is nearby, and I was waiting for him here at Bartes but he didn't come. The *llano* [plain] is formidable; there are not as many mosquitoes, and we have not seen one *casquito* [little helmet—or new regular army recruits] and the airplanes look like harmless doves.... Everything indicates that the troops don't want war and neither do we; I confess to you that I fear a retreat with 150 inexperienced recruits in these unknown areas.

As to his immediate plans, he could not inform Castro "because I don't know myself; it all depends upon special circumstances."[7]

After a short rest period the guerrillas continued marching to-wards La Federal, which was at that point being inspected by Colonel Suárez Suquet and a small group of soldiers. Lieutenant Serafín Suárez of Company 97 commanded the regular troops of the hacienda.

On September 9, as the rebel vanguard, formed by Ramiro Valdés, Manuel Hernández, Marcos Borrero and Herman Marck, an American, approached the army's position, a soldier spotted the column and firing broke out.

Captain Marco Borrero was the first to die, and Herman Marck was wounded. "Che" Guevara reacted quickly, or-dering his men to run for cover into a nearby forest.

Colonel Suárez Suquet's regular troops attempted to cut Guevara's del-retreat into the forest, but failed and sustained an undetermined number of casualties. The rebels' forest position forced the army either to advance from an open field or wait for more reinforcements or the arrival of the air force. Evidently determined to capture or kill as many guerrillas as possible, Colonel Suárez Suquet ordered an all-out charge against the well-entrenched rebels. Shooting was heavy, but the guerrillas stood their ground, and only one of Guevara's men was killed. The soldiers retreated after a final effort, forced to leave some of their wounded on the field. Two of Guevara's guerrillas were wounded in the second assault by the army, and "Che" himself took care of their wounds.

The guerrillas kept the army at bay by firing from the fringes of the forest every time a soldier moved. Colonel Suárez Suquet radioed an "urgent mes-sage" requesting more ammunition from the Second Regiment of the Rural Guards. Obviously the colonel was hoping that Guevara would remain in place while Company 97 attempted to encircle the forest. Once the army's maneuver was completed according to the plan, the air force would soften the guerrilla position, and the troops would be able to attack with an outstanding chance of success.

"Send immediately to La Federal," the message read, "two scout cars fully equipped with .30 caliber and .50 caliber machine guns, and an additional vehicle with plenty of ammunition. Send 1,000 bullets for .30 caliber Domin-ican carbines and 500 capsules for American carbines. Also send me a new Browning machine gun with plenty of ammunition." The message pointed out that "the enemy has very good weapons, including bazookas. It is now inside the forest of La Federal. . . . We need an airplane to bombard the zone. It is assumed that there are various rebels dead and some wounded"[8]

But while the army decided to await supplies, Major Cienfuegos sent his own urgent message to "Che" Guevara, advising him to retreat immediately. Without hesitation, Guevara divided his column into two groups and rapidly withdrew from the forest. By the time the army began its attack on the forest, the guerrillas were on the other side of the Tana River, leaving the area as fast as they could.

Five days later, on the night of September 14, Colonel Suárez Suquet and "Che" Guevara clashed again, this time at a place known as Cuatro Com-pañeros. The army had placed an ambush near a small bridge, and when the guerrillas approached the soldiers opened up on them.[9] This time the guerrillas were caught by surprise, and they were saved only because the regular troops had fired prematurely, warning most of Guevara's men. Two guerrillas were killed instantly, but the rest were able to flee into the bushes. Firing was general,

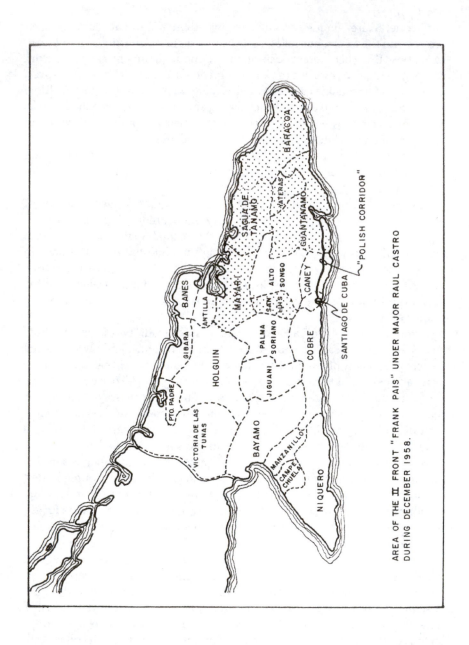

AREA OF THE II FRONT "FRANK PAIS" UNDER MAJOR RAUL CASTRO
DURING DECEMBER 1958.

with the soldiers showing esprit de corps and enthusiasm. Once more Colonel Suárez Suquet led the soldiers, risking his life in open combat. Realizing that Guevara would try to reach a nearby forest, and probably recalling the guerrilla's strategy at La Federal, Colonel Suárez Suquet ordered his men to move forward rabidly to block the guerrilla's way into the forest. The regular troops attempted to cut Guevara's guerrillas from two directions, and a battle ensued all along the railroad line bordering on the forest. Guevara reported to Castro that he was totally unfamiliar with the terrain, and that it had been necessary "to put up a fight to allow the *compañeros* who had stayed behind time enough to pass" the railway lines. The guerrillas held the regular troops for about "two and a half hours, until 9 AM, when I ordered retreat."[10]

The army had failed again and the guerrillas faded into the Forestal Forest. At this point Colonel Suárez Suquet called on the air force, which arrived in minutes, to bombard the forest and the surrounding area. The airplanes succeeded in destroying a small village, killing 20 peasants and wounding several others. Their air attack also helped to create enough confusion for Guevara and his men to leave the area before army reinforcements arrived.[11] One guerrilla was shot to death; a second died as a result of wounds from the air attack; and a third was critically wounded.[12] The retreat was so hasty that the guerrillas abandoned their food, medical supplies and kitchen utensils. They did not, however, leave their arms behind.

On September 15, Guevara's "Ciro Redondo" Column entered the area of Squadron 26 of the Rural Guards. The military chief of this squadron, Captain Manuel Barreiro Suárez, received a curt communique from the army's command post with orders to prepare ambushes around "Gálvez," and on the roads leading to "La Deseada" and "Miradero" hills, and "at such places you may deem necessary to stop the bandits from penetrating your zone. We advise you to give good and plenty of food to the personnel. You will be held accountable for the results."[13]

Meanwhile the guerrillas, though physically exhausted, continued their march, engaging in skirmishes at Loma de Cubitas, Minas, Dibirián, San Francisco de Altamira and Guano Ripiado. The gurrrillas attacked a small post at San Jerónimo and prepared ambushes near Jagua and Monte Grande, inflicting unknown casualties on the army.

The guerrillas emerged unscathed from encounters at San Miguel and Sao Grande and eventually reached the San Jerónimo area. Store owners, especially in the area of the Macareño sugar mill,[14] gave aid to Guevara's men, but rice growers denied help to the marching guerrillas. Guevara wrote a fifth report to Fidel Castro from the Macareño area, noting that "the social conscience of Camagüey's peasantry in the cattle zones is minimal, and we must pay the consequences of numerous betrayals."[15]

Unable to encircle Guevara's column, Colonel Suárez Suquet asked for reinforcements. "I continue to insist that more troops are needed if we are to liquidate the bandits in the province and stop the enemy from entering into Las Villas where they are evidently heading," the colonel radioed his headquarters. He reminded the general staff of the army that it was imperative that all ambushes be placed "exactly where they are ordered so as to block the further penetration which some informers predict, is being planned by Raúl Castro, who plans to join the guerrillas now in this province."[16] Actually, at that time Raúl Castro had no plans to move from the Sierra Cristal.

On September 21, still unable to cope with the guerrillas, the chief of operations rendered a full report to army headquarters at the Agramonte Military Camp in Camagüey. In this report,[17] Colonel Suárez Suquet blamed the success of the guerrillas on the behavior of certain officers, and he offered specific examples of what he called negligence and cowardice. The report mentioned that Lieutenant Jorge Martínez y Chaviano and personnel under his command found a 12-year-old boy who stated that there was a group of guerrillas at a nearby place, and that he could lead the troops to their camp. But Lieutenant Martinez y Chaviano "did not answer. He neither attacked nor reported the incident to the chief of operations." Captain Manuel Barreiro also refused to fight, even after he was informed "by a corporal that there was a group of rebels at a certain location. In response, the captain in question asked the corporal not to create more problems for him, and told him that if he wished he could report this information to headquarters himself." The complaints went on: "Lieutenant Eugenio D.H. González, who was commanding an ambush, returned to headquarters, where he was ordered to return immediately to reinforce Lieutenant Lázaro Castellón, who was fighting the rebels with scarce ammunition and men." However, the lieutenant returned within 20 minutes, "claiming complete physical exhaustion, and abandoning his men, who could have easily walked into a trap." In summary, the presence of "bandits in the territory of this military district is due to the manifest negligence of some officers of Squadron 26 of the Rural Guards who, despite having been told to guard certain locations, did not take any action." Whether these official charges were ever pressed, or whether they were simply brushed aside, no one knows. There is, however, no record of any courts martial against negligent officers and soldiers.

Guevara and Cienfuegos continued to evade the army, and Colonel Suárez Suquet, under increasing pressure from his superior officers, became increasingly frantic, and began ordering measures which resulted in the further alienation of the civilian population. He concentrated his efforts, however, on the urban areas, for he seems to have assumed that the guerrillas were succeeding in escaping the army with the aid of the urban underground. All evidence indicates that the guerrrillas advanced without great support from the urban apparatus of the M-26-7.

"The time to act is now," the confidential set of instructions read.[18] "Therefore conduct house-to-house searches throughout the province, check hotels, rooming houses, etc., and watch all strangers in towns and villages." Soldiers should be extremely careful when performing arrests. "Each case must be solved separately, because they [the rebels] may dress as beggars, and they can take over our arms by surprise, get the personnel inside the barracks into the prison, and take over the precinct." In this rambling series of orders, the colonel stated that it was time "to eliminate every focus of sympathizers or persons who were known to have been imprisoned or in any way connected with the M-26-7, and who are now free on probation." All these acts of repression should be carried out "without causing unnecessary problems to persons who we know have nothing to do with these things, because the displeasure caused by unwarranted arrests would benefit the rebels." The troops should not allow themselves to be impressed by what "Fidel Castro's radio station and his propaganda organs—or the ill-born Cubans who propagate rumors—may say, for such rumors reach Havana and make us appear as if we were paralyzed by some atomic ray inflicted on us by the *guajiritos escopeteros* [foolish little peasant musketeers] of the Sierra Maestra." The army's byword was to be: 'They shall not pass! We shall serve the corpses of their chiefs on a silver platter, because they have had the audacity to think that they can conduct a military parade throughout Camagüey."

The army followed Colonel Suárez Suquet's orders to the letter in towns and villages, thus turning even more civilians against the regime, making it easier for the M-26-7 urban movement to increase its revenues and to recruit new members.

Meanwhile, on September 28 Camilo Cienfuegos' column camped in a sugar cane field close to the city of Ciego de Avila. Cienfuegos sent Sergio del Valle to ask the urban branch of the M-26-7 in the city for aid in the form of trucks, food and guides. The guerrillas waited but the promised help did not arrive and Cienfuegos set out again, this time managing to get two trucks owned by Ramiro Ortiz and Enriqueta Quesada and the help of the drivers, Raúl Hernández and Agustín Rivero.

On September 30, the guerrillas entered the village of Jacinta, taking four prisoners, soldiers Alberto Valle Ríos, Prudencio Nodarse, Mario Lima Olazábal and Pedro Nodal Loyola. The latter two asked to join the guerrillas and were accepted by Cienfuegos. The guerrillas also kidnapped a 62-year-old *batistiano* named Ramón Hernández, and forced him to lead the guerrillas behind enemy lines to the Lituabo River. Once Ramón Hernández was of no further use to the guerrillas they let him go, and the forced guide lost no time in reporting to the army his experiences with the rebels.

Captain Luis Cantón, commanding the 24th Squadron of the Rural Guards, reported to his superiors that Major Cienfuegos and his guerrillas had succeeded in advancing over a great stretch of territory.[19] "Camilo Cienfuegos' column," he reported, "carries rifles and a few shotguns and scarce ammunition." The informer reported that "Guevara is coming with a column of about

200 men marching through the southern sector with bazookas and very good arms, and that further back, and to the north, there is another column and that still others have already reached Las Villas." Further, the informant said, "Fidel Castro is coming out of the Sierra Maestra with about 1,500 men to join these guerrillas and to continue marching all the way to the presidential palace." As to the informer's veracity, the captain made it very clear that Ramón Hernández was a good *batistiano*, and that he had numerous photographs of General Batista on the walls of his home. To further legitimate the informer's condition as a good *batistiano*, Captain Cantón stated: "I can attest for the informer and for his family, for these were the ones who told the army that inside their home there was a bandit, thus enabling us to kill one of them."

Once near the Lituabo river, which the guerrillas reached on September 26, Cienfuegos realized that the army had prepared excellent ambushes all around, and that the way was blocked, making it extremely difficult to reach the other side of the river. Cienfuegos decided to set up his camp, to examine the situation and to explore the terrain.

On September 27, an advance guerrillas patrol detained three men who appeared to be peasants. After intensive questioning, their contradictions, plus the fact that two of them were wearing infantry boots, aroused the curiosity of the guerrillas.

In a letter to Fidel Castro, dated October a 1958, Cienfuegos explained how the "Antonio Maceo" Column evaded the army through the heaviest set of ambushes prepared in Camagüey province during the insurrection. At first, he noted, the three captured "peasants" denied any connection with the army, but when they were told that they would have "to guide us across the bridge [of the Lituabo River] with the three of them marching at the front, they talked." They were, in fact, Corporal Juan Trujillo Medina, soldiers Jesús Pino Barrios and Enrique Navarro Herrera, all attached to Squadron 22, Regiment No. 2 of the Rural Guards. Corporal Trujillo described all the hiding places to the guerrillas, since he himself had planned all the ambushes, making full use of his 30 years of service in the Rural Guards in that area. The ambushes were placed along 27 kilometers, and were manned by five companies with approximately 500 soldiers.[20] The first line of ambushes extended from the southern coast to the Baraguá sugar mill, and from there to the Central Highway. There was a second line covering the area from the Stewart sugar mill to the town of Júcaro, plus platoons throughout the area linking the two army lines. The whole system of army ambushes established army posts linking the following points: from Vertientes to San Carlos, Santa Marta, Santa Cruz del Sur, Macareño sugar mill and, finally, to the town of Júcaro; from Faldigueras del Diablo to Guaicanamar, La Caridad hill, Cascorro, Sibanicú, La Deseada, El Miradero and to the town of Cascorro; from the town of Reynoso to Cayo Confites, Vigil, Montes Grande, San Miguel coffee plantation, Redención and Minas to the town of Nuevitas; from Senado sugar mill to Lugareño sugar mill and then to Caobillas, Limones, Sola, Lombillo, Jaronú, Esmeralda, Jiquí, Chambas, Florida and, finally, to the city of Ciego de Avila, and all around the mountains of the Sierra de Cubitas. The total number of regular troops consisted of seven infantry battalions with approximately 2,800 soldiers.[21] Corporal Trujillo said that the only way to bypass that complex network of army ambushes was to go between the villages of Gaspar and Colorado, close to the city of Ciego de Avila, and then move to the north. Trujillo was told "that the only way to save his life was to guide us out of the area without us firing a single shot." Marching north across the Central Highway, which they crossed on September 28 at 8 PM, Cienfuegos' guerrillas evaded the army through "innumerable ambushes, and even through the area of the Baraguá headquarters where the army had around 200 soldiers."[22]

On September 29, "Che" Guevara arrived in the zone but he did not meet with the kind of good fortune that Cienfuegos had. "Day by day," Guevara wrote later, "our physical condition deteriorated and our mealsone day, yes, another day, no, the third day, perhaps— were not such as to improve our condition." Guevara found that the army had completely blocked the area. Furthermore, a small army patrol discovered the guerrillas. After the guerrills rear guard repulsed those men, Guevara felt that his troops had already penetrated the army's defenses and ordered his column to retire for the night, "sure that we could pass."[23]

But Guevara had made the wrong decision—one that could have been decisive to the outcome of his march on Las Villas had it not been for the army's refusal to fight. "When 1 realized the significance of the skirmish," Guevara reported to Castro, "that the enemy had full knowledge of our position, it was too late to attempt crossing the line, for it was a dark and rainy night and we had no idea of the well-rein-forced position ahead."[24]

Guevara immediately ordered the guerrillas to retreat into a swamp to avoid being pounded by the air force, which in fact arrived shortly and bombed a nearby forest. These were the hardest days for Guevara's column—days spent under siege, "near the Baraguá sugar mill, in pestilential swamps, without a drop of potable water, harassed by planes, without a single horse to aid the weaker among us to cross that unfriendly slough." The guerrillas's shoes were "completely rotted" by the "brackish, muddy water full of vegetation that lacerated our feet."[25]

After almost a week, Guevara penetrated the army's line after walking about two kilometers and crossing the lines scarcely 100 meters from the army post. The splashing of the 140 guerrillas could not be completely avoided; that and a bright moon made Guevara think "with almost certainty that the enemy realized our presence, but that due to their low level of combativeness . . . they were deaf to all suspicious sounds."[26]

Guevara moved at the head of his guerrillas, forcing the pace of the group, and all the time they saw in "each peasant a potential *chivato* [informer]."[27]

Their psychic state resembled that of the rebels who participated in the earliest stages of the Sierra Maestra action.

Guevara's column reached the Jatibonico River on October 7, and the very same night they crossed into Las Villas province. The guerrillas were then in very bad physical condition, which in turn affected their emotional behavior. At that point, Guevara reported "we were truly in a disastrous situation." They had no time to recover, because the weather and the army forced the guerrillas to resume the march. The guerrillas became "more and more exhausted and disheartened." However, "at the most critical moment, when insults, entreaties and tongue lashings were the only way to get the weary men to advance, a distant vision sufficed to restore their courage . . . a blue spot on the horizon toward the west, the blue of the Las Villas mountain range, glimpsed for the first time by our men."[28]

By this time, Colonel Suárez Suquet had reached a state of almost hysterical frustration. In a public exhortation to his troops,[29] Colonel Suárez Suquet called the guerrillas "cowards who attack from the rear, and don't confront our troops face to face." The army had the duty of pursuing the rebels for the prestige of "our Maximum Leader, Supreme General in Chief, and Honorable President of the Republic, Major General Fulgencio Batista y Zaldívar!" Colonel Suárez Suquet assured his soldiers that the "rats," as he called the guerrillas, would not be able to leave Camagüey.

On October 6, when "Che" Guevara's guerrillas were out of the army's reach and on their way to Las Villas' Escambray Mountains, the army reported an encounter with "guerrillas." Colonel Leopoldo Pérez Cougil, chief of the Second Military District, reportedly encircled a "group of guerrillas" near the city of Ciego de Avila and during the "battle" which followed, his troops emerged "victorious," killing five "guerrillas."[30] It is obvious that Colonel Pérez Cougil's "guerrillas" were peasants who had nothing to do with "Che" Guevara or with Camilo Cienfuegos. Four days after Guevara had left the province Colonel Pérez Cougil was still searching the area for him. From his safe refuge in the Agramonte Military Camp in Camagüey City, Colonel Pérez Cougil issued directives to the personnel under his command. The army's mission was "clearly and specifically to capture 'Che' Guevara, dead or alive, and all the bandits who accompany him." Under no circumstances could the guerrillas be allowed to evade the army's encirclement and, if it became necessary, the entire district must join the search." Colonel Pérez Cougil reminded his troops that "now we have to back General Batista as he deserves." The army could do "the job in 24 hours," but the troops had to work "hard and without sentiment," for "the Second District covers itself with glory now, or we show that we are good for nothing."[31] The Second District did not cover itself with glory, for Guevara had succeeded in marching through Squadrons 21, 22, 25 and 26 of the Rural Guards.

Some of the messages exchanged between Colonel Pérez Cougil, Suárez Suquet and other army officers at this time surest their inability to understand how the guerrillas were able to evade the regular troops. "Inform me about operations in Zone 1. I have no news of encounters with the rats from Squadrons 21, 22, 25 and 26."[32] radioed Colonel Pérez Cougil to officers on the field during this period. Then, on October 12, Lieutenant Dubet del Llano reported to Colonel Suárez Suquet that the "rats" had crossed the Jatibonico River, but that he was investigating further. His chief, in utter dismay, replied: "After the rats succeed in crossing the Jatibonico River, we have no need for further reports; we would have to send them to the 3rd District."[33] While Colonels Suárez Suquet and Pérez Cougil sent messages to one another and to the officers throughout the province, "Che" Guevara had arrived at the Escambray Mountains on October 15.[34]

On October 6, Cienfuegos" guerrillas established contact with two advance guides who were members of Félix Torres' guerrillas. The next day, Cienfuegos' column arrived at Torres' camp at Jobo Rosado.[35]

On October 14, Fidel Castro wrote a letter[36] to Camilo Cienfuegos ordering him not to continue advancing toward Pinar del Río province, but to wait for "Che" Guevara in Las Villas province. In Las Villas, Fidel Castro wrote, "the political-revolutionary situation . . . is difficult; thus your presence in the province is indispensable to help ("Che"] establish himself solidly." Cienfuegos was not to advance westwards until the guerrillas had been able to recover physically, and until the struggle intensified in the provinces of Oriente, Camagüey, Las Villas and Pinar del Río. The increase in insurrectionary activities would force the army to deploy its forces and thus prevent the regime from concentrating the bulk of the army against the guerrillas moving westwards. When Cienfuegos received orders to proceed with the invasion, the plan was to be kept rigourously secret. Castro wrote that "the enemy must be led into believing that you have given up the project so that he can be taken completely by surprise." These instructions turned out to be superfluous, for Cienfuegos stayed in Las Villas province for the duration of the insurrection. There would be no invasion of Pinar del Río, for events moved even faster than the rebel leaders expected.

Upon his arrival, Cienfuegos found that Félix Torres' PSP group "did not have the armament to be characterized as [guerrillas]."[37] Cienfuegos established his headquarters in the forest of San Francisco together with the guerrillas commanded by Sergio del Valle and Nené López. Besides these two men, Cienfuegos' general staff included William Gálvez, Aroldo Cantalló, Pablo Cabrera and Roberto "Lawton" Berthelemy. Antonio S. Pinares' guerrillas were to operate in the area of Camajuaní, while William Gálvez's men in the neighborhood of Jobo Rosado. Besides these guerrillas, at this point Column No. 2 also included guerrillas groups led by Major Orestes Guerra, Major Walfrido Pérez, Captain Regino Machado, Major Ramón Parra, Captains Galán and Carbonell, chief of militias Berthelemy, and Gerardo Nogueras, who was in charge of labor matters.[38]

In a very short time, Cienfuegos' presence influenced organization and insurrectionary momentum throughout the northern area of Las Villas province. In late October, Cienfuegos' guerrillas ambushed an army patrol capturing three trucks and 40 rifles. With those arms, Cienfuegos equipped Félix Torres' guerrilla group of about 50 men.[39] Next, Cienfuegos moved to organize the sugar workers in the surrounding sugar mills of Nela, Victoria, Narcisa, Adela, Fé, San Agustín and San Pablo. Cienfuegos appointed Gerardo Nogueras, a PSP member, to organize the workers in coordination with the M-26-7's FON, led by Tito Igualada. A *comisión obrera* (workers' committee) was formed and affiliated with Column No. 2. Its objectives were to eliminate the official pro-Mujal leadership in the sugar mills; hold free elections in the unions; and to draw up a list of demands and supervise their fulfillment with the support of the rebel army. By November, Cienfuegos was able to preside over a meeting attended by about 800 sugar workers from the San Agustín and the Adela sugar mills. On November 28, Major William Gálvez presided over a meeting of 500 delegates representing workers from seven sugar mills in the region. The following day, a peasant congress attracted over 300 participants, and the *asociación campesina* (peasant association) was organized. The main purpose of the "Guillermo Moncada" peasant association was to support the rebel army by blocking access to liberated areas through constructing trenches and destroying bridges. The militias maintained a system of vigilance on the regular army, notifying rebel headquarters of any military maneuvers. Members of the peasant association appointed Ramón Simanca to represent them in the *comisión obrera* of Column No. 2.

The peak of the organizing activities among the workers was the Congress of Sugar Workers at the town of Carrillo during December 15-20, 1958, which was attended by approximately 600 workers. The veteran labor organizers of the PSP, such as Nogueras and Ursinio Rojas, greatly contributed to the efficient organization of the sugar workers under the protection of the rebel army. As Cienfuegos' guerrilla troops dedicated their time and energies to the military defeat of the regular army, PSP cadres increased their control over the emerging revolutionary unions.[40]

Guevara, Chomón and Menoyo

"Che" Guevara and Faure Chomón met on October 22, 1958. At this first meeting, Chomón impressed upon Guevara the fact that any agreement with Eloy Gutiérrez Menoyo's Second Front of Escambray was out of the question. Guevara remained aloof and uncompromising, refusing to take sides or to get involved in the dispute between Chomón and Menoyo. Scarcely a month had elapsed when Guevara's and Menoyo's groups clashed. As a result of this incident Guevara wrote to Chomón on November 7, opening the way for an understanding between the M-26-7 and the DR.[41]

Guevara expressed his opinion that the two movements should "start concrete conversations on points of mutual interest for our organizations." Guevara let it be known that he had established contact with the Communists, who were now willing to help the insurrectionists. "In official conversations held with members of the Partido Socialista Popular," wrote Guevara, "they have shown a frank attitude toward unity, and have placed at our disposal their organization in the valleys and their guerrillas in the Yaguajay front." The Yaguajay "front" did not number over 50 guerrillas, but the important factor in the PSP's cooperation was their cadre members, who were experts in communication, propaganda and infiltration. This kind of aid Guevara would find useful during the attack on Las Villas' capital, the decisive battle of the final stage of the insurrection.

In his answering letter, Faure Chomón did not mention Guevara's meeting with the Communists, but concentrated on the "divisionist" position of Menoyo's guerrilla group, and on the impossibility of reaching any unity pact with them. "We are the first," wrote Chomón, "to be conscious that unity among all those who are fighting the tyranny would be the most effective base on which to achieve the victory"[42] of the insurrection. However, Chomón stressed that he was also "aware that unity cannot be accomplished with elements who are a serious threat to the purposes which inspire our struggle. Among these elements are those who have usurped the name of Second Front of Escambray." These other "elements" were the guerrillas of the OA sponsored by former president Prío, and members of the Triple A of Aureliano Sánchez Arango, who were also active in the Escambray Mountains toward the end of the insurrection.[43]

Unity in strategic matters was finally achieved between the M-26-7 and the DR with the Pact of Pedrero, signed in November 1958, in the village of Pedrero, by Ernesto ("Che") Guevara for the M-26-7 and Rolando Cubela as commander in chief of the DR guerrillas. The Pact of Pedrero read in part: "Wanting to make fully known the close identification that exists between the M-26-7 and the [DR] in their struggle against the dictatorship, both organizations at the Escambray Mountains are addressing themselves to the people of Las Villas, where their forces are fighting for the freedom of Cuba."[44] The pact stated that the two organizations would coordinate their military actions until they could join forces in an all-out attack against the regime. Both organizations would share all means of communications and supplies. Administratively, the territory under control of the two organizations was divided into two zones so that each movement could collect taxes for the war.[45] An agrarian policy and administration of justice was to be studied by both organizations. The Pedrero pact called upon all organizations to coordinate their actions for the good of the nation.

The PSP of Las Villas province seized the opportunity and issued an official communique addressed to the M-26-7 and the DR. Dated December 9,

A lieutenant is drilling a platoon of new recruits on a long march, fall 1958 (Reprinted by permission of Yale University Library).

1958, the document welcomed the call to unity issued by the guerrillas. "For more than six years," it stated, "we have maintained that one of the contributing factors to the dictatorship's survival has been the lack of unity of the opposition and the lack of coordination of the democratic and revolutionary forces."[46] Dialectically, the Communists attempted to erase almost seven years of struggle during which two individually defined approaches had developed vis-á-vis Batista's dictatorship. The "democratic" forces to which the Communists referred were but the same corrupt politicians who had attempted to reach an understanding with Batista as early as 1954. Within the opposition, from the very beginning, there were those who favored an understanding with the dictator, and those who proclaimed the insurrectionist line. The "democratic" forces of the opposition were viewed by the insurrectionists as collaborators with the Batista regime, and there could be no unity between revolutionaries and figures who represented the worst in Cuban politics. Unity was feasible only when the politicians, the opportunists and all those who called themselves the "democratic" forces of the opposition came to accept without hesitation the terms imposed by the insurrectionists. Thus, the Communists accepted the military strategy of the M-26-7 and the DR. Adopting a patronizing attitude, the party let it be known that the Pedrero pact had to be "reinforced with certain ideas and program demands reflecting the hopes of the people." The party appeared to ignore the history of the M-26-7 and of the DR; manifestos, statements of principle, declarations pertaining to future economic, social and political changes issued since 1953 were all seemingly ignored by the Communists, who had recently discovered the road to insurrection in Cuba. The party advanced the suggestion that all insurrectionary forces should unite in a single army under a single command in Las Villas as well as throughout the country. The party did not specify whose command, or what army, although we can assume that they meant Fidel's, but it is clear that the Communists ignored not only the wording of the Pedrero pact but also the problems that such a proposal could create at that difficult point in the history of the insurrection. The Pedrero pact already, in effect, united the M-26-7 and the DR behind a coordinated military strategy in which armed actions would be used to obtain definite military objectives. The party issued all the necessary directives to fulfill the Pedrero pact and contribute to victory.

Guevara and Oltusky

Major "Che" Guevara, however, confronted a problem of a more serious nature with the leader of the urban underground of the M-26-7. On September 20, Fidel Castro had written to the provincial coordinator in Las Villas, Enrique Oltusky (known as "Sierra"), warning him of the arrival of rebel troops in Las Villas. In this letter, which was also addressed to Víctor ("Diego") Manuel Paneque, chief of action and sabotage of the movement in that province, Castro said that the urban movement's position would be significantly strengthened with the addition of Guevara's guerrillas and that the guerrillas needed the urban fighters, too. "Las Villas," Castro wrote, "is very important to our strategic plans. All efforts are worthwhile."[47]

Upon Guevara's arrival in the mountains Oltusky went to meet the already famous guerrilla leader. In their first meeting, while Ramiro Valdés. "Che's" second in command, fell asleep, Guevara and Oltusky engaged in a long discussion over agrarian reform, since Oltusky had written an agrarian reform proposal for the movement. Oltusky suggested imposing high taxes on the landowners and then using that money to buy up the land from them; the land would then be sold to the peasants on credit. Guevara argued that such an approach was reactionary and unjust to the peasants who were the ones who worked the land.

Another point of immediate disagreement was over the United States and the possible effect of imperialism after the insurrection had been won. Oltusky maintained that the future revolutionary government would be forced by its proximity to the United States to moderate the speed of whatever revolutionary changes were to be effected. "Che" Guevara rejected that thesis, pointing out that it was representative of the lukewarm attitude of the *llano* people. Furthermore, "Che" claimed that a real revolution could not be made behind the back of the United States, and that the revolution, because of its geopolitical situation, would have to engage in a deadly struggle against imperialism from the very first moment. "A true revolution cannot be concealed,"[48] said "Che." These were but the first of various ideological clashes between Guevara and Oltusky.

In mid-October, on Guevara's initiative, Victor Paneque and "Che" discussed and approved a plan of conducting a series of bank robberies to augment the organization's funds. "Diego" informed Oltusky of the plan, but the provincial coordinator rejected the idea, warning Guevara that if he insisted on conducting bank robberies the entire movement would be divided. The urban cadres considered this method contrary to the ideals for which they were fighting. Oltusky called Guevara's attention to the fact that Fidel Castro, even in moments of great pressure had never proposed such a scheme, for robbery was completely alien to the conscience of the Cuban people. The insurrection, Oltusky argued (as Castro had years before), could not be made with stolen money. Oltusky claimed that the M-26-7's treasury held $50,000 at that point and that it was not necessary to rob banks.[49] He went a step further and demanded that Guevara sign all receipts for money and materiel sent to the guerrillas by the urban movement, and this demand touched a very sensitive nerve in "Che."

But besides showing his lack of confidence in Guevara, Oltusky was trying to set the record straight regarding the cooperation of the urban and rural guerrillas. During their first meeting, Guevara had complained that the only help his men had received up to that point had come from the PSP. Oltusky angrily replied that the arms that "Che" had received were the result of weeks of efforts on the part of the M-26-7 urban movement and not a gift of the PSP, that the latter had not even contributed a single gun, although now they were trying to take credit for everything.

"Che" Guevara's answer to Oltusky was in a letter dated November 3 and written at Santa Lucía. Among other things this letter proves that Guevara's contempt for the *llano* people did not develop after the revolution was on the march, but resulted from his own interpretation of events during the insurrection. "Che" Guevara started by saying that "Diego" agreed with him when the bank robberies were discussed, but that Oltusky claimed "Diego" now was against conducting such tactics; thus "'Diego' is dishonest or simply has no ideas about the most important problems" of the insurrection. As for Fidel's refusing to engage in bank robberies, "Che's" opinion was that "when he didn't have anything to eat, he didn't have the strength to carry out such an action." "Che" expressed his resentment toward those classes, such as the rice growers of Camagüey province, who had refused to come to the aid of the guerrillas. These classes would be the only ones affected by a tactic of bank robberies.

"Che" was notified by the messenger who brought Oltusky's letter to him that urban leaders of the M-26-7 in various towns were threatening to resign. "I agree," he let it be known," that they should." In fact, Guevara stated, "I even demand their resignations since no deliberate foreclosure can be permitted against a measure so advantageous to the interests of the revolution." Guevara reminded Oltusky that he had been appointed commander in chief to unify the command and do things better within the movement. Therefore, "whether there are resignations or not I will, by the authority vested in me, sweep off all the weak-minded persons from the neighboring towns in the Sierra."

In one of the most revealing paragraphs, "Che" stated, "I never thought I would be boycotted by my own *compañeros.* I now realize that the old antagonism which I thought had been overcome lives again in the word *llano,* and that leaders who are divorced from the mass of the people advance opinions on the people's reaction." Guevara defended his proposed tactic of bank assaults saying that "not a single peasant has objected to our thesis that the land is for the man who works it. Isn't it related to the fact that the fighting masses support robbing banks because they don't have a penny in them?" He asked Oltusky if he had ever stopped to think "about the economic roots of such respect toward one of the most arbitrary financial institutions." "Che" stated that "those who make money through lending and speculating on someone else's money have no right to special considerations. While the poor were bled to death by the economically powerful, people suffered because of the betrayal of their false leaders." Guevara stated that if the policy of bank robberies destroyed the M-26-7's organization, then "as a revolutionary, I accept such responsibility, and I am willing to make myself accountable for my behavior before any revolutionary court whenever that is the wish of the Dirección Nacional of the movement."

In the matter of money spent, "Che" promised to "itemize every cent given to the Sierra combatants as well as any other monies acquired in any way." But "Che" would "also request an itemized statement for every one of the $50,000 you claim to have, since I am letting you know that by Fidel's resolution, in a letter I will show you when you come, the . . . treasury must be here [in the mountains]." Incensed at Oltusky's demand for receipts, "Che" answered that the practice of signed receipts was not used among *compañeros.* "I am, alone, absolutely responsible for my actions, and my word is worthier than all the signatures in the world. If I demand signatures from others, it is because I am not convinced of their honesty." "Che" would not demand a signature from Oltusky, although "I would demand a hundred from Gutiérrez Menoyo." "Che" ended his letter "with a revolutionary embrace." and said that he expected to see Oltusky and "Diego" in the mountains to continue the discussion.[50]

Fortunately, the rift between the two leaders of the M-26-7, the urban Oltusky and the rural "Che," was solved through the quick intervention of the national coordinator of the M-26-7, Marcelo ("Zoilo") Fernández Font.[51] Guevara's plans to rob banks were called off; no urban cadre member resigned; "Che" withdrew his demand; and Oltusky promised to continue aiding the guerrillas. But Guevara and Oltusky never did become very close friends.[52]

Throughout the insurrectionary process, "Che" Guevara succeeded in winning the respect and friendship of the peasants as well as those who fought under him. Towards the peasants Guevara was kind and extremely patient, though he never showed them deep trust. At the same time he was contemptuous of others who held important positions in the movement.[53]

The Escambray guerrilla movement continued to grow during the remaining months of the insurrection. "Che" moved constantly, operating mainly from the Sierra de Gavilanes, while the DR maintained its headquarters at the Dos Arroyos hacienda, near the town of Condado in the Trinidad Mountains. In addition an advance camp was based at the village of Algarruba, one mile from Güinia de Miranda, the scene of one of Guevara's first combats in the Escambray Mountains. Eloy Gutiérrez, Menoyo kept his guerrillas within the area of the Siguanea Mountains, concentrating on actions near and around the cities of Cienfuegos and Tope de Collantes. Soon the guerrillas would initiate their general offensive against the army, and Batista's forces would fall back, step by step, until the final battle for control of the capital of Las Villas province, Santa Clara, the final objective of the insurrection.

Notes

1. *El Mundo* (Havana), October 28, 1965, p. 8. This order was issued on August 18, 1958, at 9PM from the Sierra Maestra.
2. "Orden Militar," *Che* (Havana: Editorial de Ciencias Sociales, Instituto del Libro, 1969), p. 121. This order was issued on August 21, 1958, at 9 PM, from the Sierra Maestra.
3. Interview with Guevara broadcast by Radio Rebelde in December 1958, and by Radio 6BF in Escambray Mountains, Las Villas province. For a translation, see Rolando E. Bonachea and Nelson P. Valdés, *Che: Selected Works of Ernesto Guevara* (Cambridge: MIT Press, 1970), pp. 366–67, as translated from "Cuba, Diciembre 1958," *Verde Olivo* (Havana), December 31, 1966, pp. 23–24. See also Oscar Fernández Mell, "De Las Mercedes a Gavilanes," *Verde Olivo* (Havana), August 25, 1963, p. 15.
4. Alfonso Acosta, "Radiograma 25-1700" (July 1958), in *Ché*, p. 178.
5. "Radiograma No. 2517," p. 181.
6. Ibid., p. 182.
7. Ernesto "Che" Guevara, "A Fidel Castro (sobre la invasión)," *Relatos del Che* (Montevideo: Sandino, n.d.), pp. 148–52. This report was completed on September 13, 1958, at 9:50 PM. See also Ernesto "Che" Guevara, *Pasajes de la guerra revolucionaria* (Mexico: Serie Popular Era, 1961), pp. 251–52; and Roberto Fernández Retamar, ed., *Ernesto "Che" Guevara, Obra revolucionaria* (Mexico: Ediciones Era, S.A., 1967), pp. 255–58.
8. Armando Suárez Suquet, "Radiograma urgente," *Ché*, p. 179.
9. Authors' interview with army Corporal Julián Solaín (June 4, 1970, Washington, D.C.).
10. Ernesto "Che" Guevara, "Diario de la invasión," *Chè* pp. 11–13. Also see Ernesto "Che" Guevara, "Marcha sobre Las Villas," in Retamar, *Ernesto "Ché" Guevara*, pp. 257–58. Colonel Suárez Suquet's troops suffered two wounded and one dead and captured one bazooka grenade and two land mines from the rebels. When Guevara approached the bridge his guerrillas had already evaded four ambushes commanded respectively by Lieutenant Lázaro Castellón Martínez, Lieutenant Eugenio González Pérez, Lieutenant

Sergio Díaz Bello; Captain Tomás Rosado Gil supported Colonel Suárez Suquet in the encounter with the guerrillas. See *Chè*, p. 203. In this and subsequent encounters the following regular army officers and privates were cited for valor: Major Domingo Piñero Carnow, Captain Tomás A. Acosta, Lieutenant Lázaro Castellón Martínez, Lieutenant Humberto Palacios Estévez, Lieutenant Manuel M. Castillo, Lieutenant Blanco E. Corzo Alemán, Lieutenant José de Armas, Corporal Francisco L. Tano, Sergeant Francisco Batista and Privates Augusto Morrillo. Jesús Figueroa, Roberto Puig, Benigno Pérez, Gregorio García and Luis Colás Bell. See *Ché*, p. 183.

11. As during La Federal, Colonel Suárez Suquet depended upon the air force to liquidate the guerrillas rather than attempting to penetrate into the forest.

12. Roberto Dueñas, "Operaciones del Sector G-3. Cuartel Agramonte, Comandancia de las Fuerzas Armadas," September 14, 1958, *Ché*, p. 181.

13. J. Nápoles Rodríguez, "Instrucción: persecución de rebeldes," September 15, 1958, *Ché*, p. 181.

14. In 1958, one of the authors followed the route covered by the guerrillas from the Elia to the Macareño sugar mill, and had the opportunity to talk with small merchants who helped Guervara's column at Pino del Agua 1, 2, 3 and 6 (small villages) by providing vegetables and boots to the guerrillas. Guevara's guerrillas received some help from the PSP in Camagüey province in the form of a few pair of shoes, medicines and often a guide. For Guevara's comments, see "De las jornadas de la invasión," *Ché*, p. 129. See also K. S. Karol, *Guerrillas in Power: The Course of the Cuban Revolution* (New York: Hill and Wang, 1970), p. 180.

15. Guevara, "De las jornadas de la invasión," *Ché*, p. 128.

16. A. Suárez Suquet, "Interesando tropas de refuerzo: al ayudante S-1 Regimiento 2, Guardia Rural," *Ché*, p. 181.

17. A. Suárez Suquet, "Reporte confidencial 41–958." September 21, 1958, *Ché*, pp. 183–84.

18. A. Suárez Suquet, "Confidencial: instrucciones a los jefes de mando," October 6, 1958, *Ché*, pp. 189–90.

19. Luis Cantón, "Operaciones: 10-4-58," *Ché*, p. 201. In Cuban National Archives under the Code 209-C-958.

20. Camilo Cienfuegos, *Diario de campaña* (Havana: Municipio de la Habana, 1961), pp. 7–8. See also Camilo Cienfuegos, "Diario de campaña," *Revolución* (Havana), November 16, 1959, pp. 28, 31–32.

21. A. Suárez Suquet, "Informando de operaciones Segundo Distrito Militar al Coronel Leopoldo Pérez Coujil," October 16, 1958, *Ché*, pp. 197–98.

22. Cienfuegos, *Diario de campaña*, pp. 7–8.

23. Guevara, "A Fidel Castro," pp. 256–57.

24. Ibid.

25. Ernesto "Che" Guevara, *Reminiscences of the Cuban Revolutionary War* (New York: Grove Press, 1968), pp. 247–48.

26. Retamar, *Ernesto "Ché" Guevara*, pp. 256–57.

27. Ibid., p. 257.

28. Guevara, *Reminiscences*, p. 248. At this point Guevara allowed those who so wished to abandon the group. Seven guerrillas departed from the column: Víctor Sarduy, Juan Noguera, Ernesto Magara, Rigoberto Solis, Oscar Macias, Teodoro Reyes and Rigoberto Alarcón. For a comparison between

Guevara and Antonio Maceo's marches, see Loló de la Torriente "Una fecha para dos hombres gloriosos," *Bohemia* (Havana), June 11, 1971, pp. 98–100. For a chronology of Maceo's invasion route during the War of Independence, see *Bohemia* (Havana), June 11, 1971, pp. 4–7. During an interview General Eulogio Cantillo stated that in August 1958 his troops captured a rebel camp and discovered documents showing the approximate route which would be followed by a future invasion westwards; Cantillo reports that he sent the documents to the general staff in Havana. Since he had followed the same exercise march in the early fifties, he was able to attach a description of the entire route (Cantillo to the authors, December 4, 1972, Miami, Florida).

29. A. Suárez Suquet, "Exhortación: a los jefes de unidades que operan en Zona del 2do. Distrito Militar y a todo el mando," September 21, 1958, *Ché*, p. 225.

30. Leopoldo Pérez Coujil, "Reporte al Director de Operaciones G-3, Cuartel Cabo Parrado," October 7, 1958, *Ché*, pp. 225–26.

31. Leopoldo Pérez Coujil, "Comunicado de operaciones en Camagüey," October 11, 1958, *Ché*, p. 226.

32. Leopoldo Pérez Coujil, "Radiograma No. 1640," October 12, 1958, *Ché*, pp. 226–27.

33. A. Suárez Suquet, "Radiograma," October 12, 1958, *Ché*, pp. 226–27.

34. See *Revolución* (Havana), January 15, 1959, and *Verde Olivo* (Havana), October 26, 1961.

35. Camilo Cienfuegos, "La invasión de Las Villas: diario de campaña," in *Cuba: una revolución en marcha* (París: Ruedo Ibérico, 1967), pp. 69–75. Cienfuegos and Torres met on October 14, and the latter placed himself under Cienfuegos's command. See *Cruzeiro Internacional* (Río de Janeiro), July 16, 1964; Carlos Franqui, *Cuba: el libro de los doce* (Mexico: Colección Ancho Mundo, 1966), p. 134; *Hoy* (Havana), October 8, 1963; *Revolución* (Havana), January 3, 1959; and Orestes Guerra, "De El Salto a Jobo Rosado," *Días de combate*, pp. 305–06.

36. Jaime Sarusky, "Camilo, el guerrillero y el politico," *Bohemia* (Havana), October 27, 1972, p. 59.

37. William Gálvez, "Camilo en Las Villas," *Verde Olivo* (Havana), January 7, 1965, pp. 4–7.

38. William Gálvez, "Rasgos de la campaña de Camilo en Las Villas," *Bohemia* (Havana), July 23, 1965, pp. 44–50.

39. Sarusky, "Camilo," pp. 59–65.

40. Ibid.

41. *Bohemia* (Havana), December 10, 1965, p. 56. When "Che" Guevara arrived in the Escambray, Jésus Carreras of Menoyo's group demanded the guerrilla leader's plans in exchange for permission to continue marching into the mountains. Later, Carreras attempted again to stop Guevara from attacking Güinia de Miranda, thus creating unnecessary problems.

42. Faure Chomón, "Cuando el 'Che' llegó al Escambray," *Bohemia* (Havana), May 15, 1960, pp. 17–19.

43. Former president Prío planned to join OA, Triple A and Gutiérrez Menoyo's guerrilla force and attack the city of Cienfuegos, and then move along the southern coast toward Havana. Prío changed his mind, concluding that he was "too old," and physically unable to do "things which were more for the youth" (Prío to the authors, August 29, 1972, San Juan, Puerto Rico).

44. René Ray, ed., *Libertad y Revolución* (Havana, 1959), pp. 63–64.

45. Each bag of coffee in the area was taxed $1, and each bale of tobacco from one to two pesos depending on the grower. Evidence of René Romero, former rural school teacher in Escambray Mountains, and treasurer for the DR, in interview with the authors (July 2, 1971, Union City, New Jersey).

46. "A los dirigentes del movimiento 26 de julio y del Directorio Revolucionario," *Las Villas* (Havana: Ediciones Venceremos, n.d.), p. 29. K. S. Karol mentioned that the PSP also supported the Pedrero pact but failed to discuss the party's position. See Karol, *Guerrillas in Power*, pp. 571–72.

47. See *Cuba: una revolución en marcha*, p. 80.

48. Enrique Oltusky, "Gente del llano," *Cuba: una revolución en marcha*, p. 83.

49. Ibid., pp. 83–84.

50. K. S. Karol posits that Guevara's conflict with the urban branch of the movement makes too much of the disagreement between the *llano* and the mountain fighters. See Karol, *Guerrillas in Power*, pp. 161–80.

51. Oltusky, *Gente del llano*, p. 84. After the revolution, Marcelo Fernández Font substituted for "Che" Guevara as president of the Cuban National Bank, and was later appointed secretary of foreign trade (MINCEX).

52. Oltusky was appointed secretary of communications in 1959; later he was transferred to the Institute of Agrarian Reform whence he was outcast to date.

53. Guevara's treatment of the enemy was inflexible; he taught his guerrillas to hate everything connected with Batista, for "Che" understood that hate was a praiseworthy emotion, making man an effective, selective, cold killing machine. See Ernesto "Che" Guevara, "Mensaje a la Tricontinental," *Granma* (Havana), April 17, 1967.

13

The Last Battle

General Francisco Tabernilla, Sr., has described the military situation which signaled the downfall of the Batista regime as follows: "Oriente with the whole countryside and many towns in the hands of the rebels. . . . Santiago de Cuba, Bayamo and Holguín seriously threatened. . . . Las Villas with many towns in the hands of the enemy after the surrender of the garrisons without a single shot being fired." Each day the island was more isolated from the capital; the main bridges blown up; transportation practically paralyzed; fuel and provisions in low supply in the towns; the sugar cane ready to be harvested with very little chance that the job could be done, and with taxes previously imposed by the insurrectionists. The regular army was tired and decimated by "two years of a prolonged campaign. It had completely lost its combat power. Desertions to the enemy increased daily."[1]

The rebel army was making tremendous gains at the expense of a military without the will to fight, totally demoralized after months of operations and defeats. To forestall desertions the army issued Order No. 196 providing for the immediate execution of any soldier or officer deserting to the rebels. Rebel headquarters then issued a proclamation inviting any soldier, noncommissioned officer or officer of the armed forces who did not want to fight any longer to move into rebel territory. Fidel's terms were quite generous: they were under no obligation to fight, they would continue to receive their salaries, and could be accompanied by their families (food and lodging would be made available). There was only one requisite: the refugees must take their weapons to the Sierra Maestra.

On September 27, Major Juan Almeida's guerrillas ambushed troops under the command of Colonel Nelson Carrasco at a place called "La Torcaza" shortly after Colonel Carrasco had been transferred to the area of Maffo.[2] The encounter was brief but fierce, with Colonel Carrasco leading his men in combat and exposing himself to the guerrillas' fire. The army sustained 25 casualties; Colonel Nelson Carrasco fell wounded by machine gun fire[3] could not be rescued by his troops and was taken prisoner by Juan Almeida. Nelson Carrasco was the highest ranking officer to fall prisoner to the guerrillas throughout the Sierra Maestra campaign.

On the same day, September 27, Major Eduardo Sardiñas, commanding Column No. 12, "Simón Bolívar," successfully attacked an army camp at El Cerro inflicting 67 casualties on the army. The rebels lost Lieutenants Raúl Verdecia and Arturo Vásquez, and three guerrillas. On October 23, the regular army suddenly withdrew its troops guarding the Nicaro nickel company in northern Oriente province; Raúl Castro's rebels moved into the plant, and two days later Colonel Ugalde Carrillo ordered the army to return to Nicaro. On October 25, Fidel Castro denounced the maneuver as one inspired by U. S. Ambassador Earl T. Smith and Batista and geared to provoke the intervention of the United States in Cuba. Castro's broadcast over the rebel radio charged that the American ambassador and Batista were "setting the scene for a battle in the same area where the U. S. Government's nickel plants are located so the installations will suffer material damage and there will be an excuse to send in U. S. troops." Castro pointed out that the rebel command was not moved by feelings of dislike or hostility toward the United States. However, Cubans fighting to regain their freedoms should not be blamed for the insurrection; the guilty party was Batista who had the support of U. S. Ambassadors Arthur Gardner and Smith. Castro observed that Cuba was a "free and sovereign nation," adding that the insurrectionists wanted to maintain the best relations of friendship with the United States. In the event of intervention, the insurrectionists would fight; no threats were to be made against the Cuban people, for "while threats are effective with cowardly and abject people they will never work with men who are willing to die in the defense of their homeland."[4] Fortunately, there was as no incident and the guerrillas withdrew to avert a possible confrontation which could have escalated into a large-scale battle between the regular and the rebel armies, thus damaging the U.S.-owned nickel installations.

General Tabernilla's view of the military situation coincided with that of Castro, who reported that each day "the tactical strategic superiority of the rebels over the decadent and demoralized forces of the tyranny is more clear." Fidel stated that the army continued to lose more territory, more men and more weapons every day.[5]

November Farce

U. S. Ambassador Smith, though politically unsophisticated and openly against the insurrection, worked very hard to find a "solution" that would frustrate the efforts of this new generation of Cuban revolutionaries. As a result of U. S. pressure Batista scheduled general elections to be held on November 3.[6]

The candidates for the opposition were Carlos Márquez Sterling for the Partido del Pueblo Libre; Alberto Salas Amaro, a journalist, for a new group called Unión Cubana; and Ramón Grau San Martín, despite the protests of former president Prío, as the candidate of the PRC-Auténticos.[7] Batista's close friend. Andrés Rivero Agüero, was nominated by the government coalition.

The "election formula" assumed that Batista would invite U. N. observers to guarantee that the elections were honest and free; allow foreign journalists to be present to serve as guarantors of the election process[8]; and fulfill his promise to Ambassador Smith that the elections would not be weighted toward the government candidate.[9]

Ambassador Smith's favored candidate during this electoral farce appears to have been Carlos Márquez Sterling, the Ortodoxo politician who never ceased aspiring to the presidential chair. The election plan apparently consisted of having Carlos Márquez Sterling "win" the elections. Immediately thereafter Batista would leave the country. The new president would then restore constitutional guarantees, and would call upon Fidel Castro to abandon the struggle, leaving Castro a rebel without a cause. With Batista and his henchmen out of Cuba and a president promising a general amnesty, law and order, and above all, peace, the "solution" could have had substantial popular support.

Sensing some kind of change, Eusebio Mujal, the secretary general of the CTC, approached Mario Lazo to ask if the United States was withdrawing its support from Batista. If this were the case, Mujal stated, he would announce the withdrawal of labor's support to the government and would leave the country. Ambassador Smith "thought it best to tell Mujal that the attitude of the United States had not changed." Smith assured Mujal that the United States "did not change its relations with a friendly government simply because that government was facing a serious crisis."[10]

With Mujal quiet, Smith was able to continue to pursue his own extraordinary "solution" to the Cuban problem. The ambassador reasoned that with Carlos Márquez Sterling in the presidential chair, Castro would have no reason to continue his struggle because most of the objectives of the insurrection would have been achieved.[11] This ludicrous solution to the dilemma clearly demonstrated that neither Ambassador Smith nor the government he represented had the vaguest notion of the momentum of the insurrection, nor the extent to which the regular army was incapable of holding off the advance of the rebel army.

From the Sierra Maestra, Fidel Castro promptly reacted to this political maneuver by proclaiming Law No. 2, which had these main points: candidates in the elections were to be barred from participation in politics for 30 years; candidates were asked to demonstrate their rejection of the elections by going into exile, joining the rebel territory or reporting their withdrawal to the foreign press; in the event of capture by the rebels a candidate in the elections would be tried and sentenced with from ten years in prison to death by a firing squad; all political agents caught by the rebels were to be executed on the spot.[12]

While the U. S. ambassador, Batista and the candidates organized the farce, the rebel army moved closer to Santiago de Cuba. Less than 72 hours before the "elections" took place, Major Hubert Matos, commanding Column No. 9,

"Antonio ('Tony') Guiteras," battled regular troops who were attempting to avert an encirclement of the city by the guerrillas. In their two-hour battle, Major Matos' guerrillas captured six prisoners, killed 12 soldiers and lost three of their own men.[13] Major Raúl Castro's guerrillas supported the siege of Oriente's capital, Cuba's second largest city, and by November 3, Major Matos had moved closer to the city and had almost taken over control of the refineries southwest of Santiago.[14]

Elections were held on the appointed date, but voters found that going to the polls was risky. Voting was very light in the capital, and nonexistent in Oriente and Las Villas provinces, the areas where the guerrrillas operated. In Camagüey and Pinar del Río provinces, the people voted only under orders from the army and the Rural Guards.

It would be fruitless to enter into an analysis of this election, for it has been recorded as one of the most corrupt and fraudulent of the republic's history. Batista's candidate was announced to be the winner, while Carlos Márquez Sterling furiously claimed fraud.[15] Batista's decision not to fulfill his pledge to the U. S. ambassador and his preferred candidate[16] must have been based on the assumption that the army could hold off the rebels at least until February 1959, when the new president would be inaugurated. Batista hoped that with a new president, the United States would resume the sale of arms, and with new arms the army could hold the country.[17]

On November 13, in a message to his field commanders in Oriente, Camagüey, Las Villas and Pinar del Río provinces, Fidel Castro displayed complete confidence in victory. Castro announced that regular army officers were changing sides and joining the rebels with their men and their weapons. Castro stated that the event demonstrated "the complete revolutionary support to the insurrection within the ranks of the armed forces." The rebel leader further stated that it was still necessary to fight very hard, but that everything seemed to indicate that the defeat of the government was imminent, "desperate though its final resistance may be."

Castro ordered all traffic to stop in Oriente province, and told the rebel troops to close all roads leading to and from the cities of that province. In a final blow against Santiago de Cuba, Raúl Castro was ordered to "advance, surrounding and attacking all military garrisons in the Mayarí-San Luis-Guantánamo triangle."

Castro's strategy developed around two capital cities, Santiago de Cuba and Santa Clara. The fall of Santa Clara to the rebels would cut the island in half, thus leaving the field open for Castro's attack on Santiago de Cuba. The next objective on the agenda would be Camagüey. The fall of Santiago de Cuba, which also included the fall of the Moncada military camp, would mean the capture of the army's arsenal. With plenty of arms at their disposal, including tanks and artillery, the rebels could move toward Camagücy's Agramonte military camp. It was therefore imperative that the rebel army moving toward

Santiago de Cuba protect their rear guard against a surprise attack from Camagüey. This meant that "the rebel troops operating in the center and west, guarding the entrance to the province of Oriente, must fight tenaciously against all troops which the government may send to the province."[18]

As the insurrectionists gained both strength and new territory, order in the urban areas became one of Castro's top priorities. To help keep the peace, the rebel radio stressed Castro's words to the effect that the people were the chief force in maintaining order in the cities; the people should prevent pillaging, destruction of property and bloodshed.

On several occasions Castro promised that criminals would be arrested and tried by revolutionary tribunals. Personal vengeance was to be avoided at all costs, or chaos and anarchy would make it even more difficult for the insurrection to secure the total defeat of the regime. He appealed to the people to exhibit patriotism, civility and a sense of order, for the revolution could not and should not suffer from any dishonorable acts.

By mid-November, the rebel army controlled rail and bus transportation throughout Oriente province. Food and supplies could be brought in only three days a week, and had to be carried into the cities in small vehicles. Any soldier carrying a rifle would be shot on sight, and civilians were alerted that to travel in government vehicles was to risk being attacked by the insurrectionists.

As the final confrontation approached, Raúl Castro's men engaged in an enormous amount of military activity. On December 2, Column No. 17 attacked the army posts at La Maya, Songo and Alto Cedro; Column No. 6 attacked the posts at San Luis and Ermita. The next day, the guerrillas attacked the posts of Miranda, Alto Cedro, Marcané, Palmarito, Borgitas and Baltony. Major Hubert Matos' guerrillas attacked and defeated the army at Algodonal, while Column No. 19 attacked Mayarí. On December 4, Alto Songo was attacked for the third time, and its fall also determined the army's surrender at the army post of Santa Ana. Further to the east, Baracoa fell to the rebel army on the same day, and the next day the rebels encircled the army at Sagua de Tánamo.[19]

The army had been resisting the rebels' attack at the Soledad sugar mill since December 2, and five days later surrendered. On December 8, Raúl Castro's guerrillas advanced from Mayarí towards the small town of Guaro, causing the men from Guaro's army post to flee and take refuge in Cueto. The rebels pursued the regular troops, and late that day the army abandoned Cueto, moving towards the city of Holguín, burning houses and killing peasants en route.[20] Sagua de Tánamo fell to the rebels on December 16. Four days later, Major Delio Gómez Ochoa, commander of the Fourth Guerrilla Front in Oriente province, attacked Puerto Padre.

The regular army was crumbling on all fronts, and Fidel Castro prepared for the final push. In an official communique, the rebel army announced that Batista's army continued to surrender throughout Oriente province. Fidel Castro stated that the army's resistance was crumbling in the face of the powerful offensive unleashed by the Second Front, under the command of Raúl Castro, while the main body of the rebel army, the First, Third and Fourth Fronts, continued their attacks leaving the army only two alternatives—surrender or annihilation.[21]

The battle of Santa Clara was the decisive military operation of the Cuban insurrection, and the rebel army was well prepared. "Che" Guevara enumerated his munitions on the eve of battle: "By the time of the attack we had increased our weapons considerably. We had gained some heavy weapons but without ammunition. We had a bazooka, but no rockets, and we were fighting against ten or more tanks."[22] What the guerrillas lacked in armament they made up in enthusiasm for, after the summer offensive, the morale of the ragged fighters soared to new heights. During the final phases of the battle of Santa Clara, "Che" would capture enough armament to vastly multiply the guerrillas' firing power. The attackers were greatly outnumbered by the regular troops, but they had the support of the population. In addition, the regular army troops were demoralized, and simply refused to engage the rebels. Had the army decided to put up a fight, the insurrectionists would have had a very difficult time getting to the suburbs of Santa Clara.

The army had approximately 6,000 men quartered at the Leoncio Vidal Camp in Santa Clara.[23] Tanks, cannons and assorted heavy weaponry with sufficient ammunition were at their disposal. The police force, with several hundred men and fresh reinforcements from all over the province, was also available. Troops had been built up in the fall of 1958, when it became clear that all isolated posts were easy targets for the Escambray guerrillas. All military personnel had been ordered to move to Santa Clara to prepare the city's defense. The order to abandon the countryside to confront the guerrillas on the outskirts of the cities and in the valleys was the army's only alternative, considering the guerrillas' strategy and the fact that the troops refused to fight in the mountains. However the army's strategy also meant surrendering a large territory to the rebels without a fight, and assuming a defensive strategy inside a city which could be easily encircled by the rebel troops.

To direct the city's resistance, Batista had appointed General Chaviano. One thousand men were sent from Havana to dislodge the guerrillas who were operating along the Central Highway and in the marginal areas of the Escambray Mountains. These troops were supported by three battalions, for a total of 1,200 men. To secure free access to the highways around the city, the highway patrol was reorganized during September, and a new fleet of cars was put into operation.[24] But General Chaviano was unable to stop the guerrillas in any sector of the province. As in Oriente province, Chaviano had spent most of his time organizing an efficient system for collecting tributes and receiving his share in the productive industry of graft. Against an army commanded by men such as Chaviano, the guerrillas now moved in earnest.

The Strategy

Santa Clara, with its quarter of a million inhabitants, sprawls along the Central Highway in the middle of the province. The capital of Las Villas is surrounded by four important towns, to the north is Encrucijada; to the south, the city of Manicaragua; to the southeast. Fomento; and on the northeast, Remedios. "Che's" strategy was to attack all four towns simultaneously, or at least within the same week, while the guerrillas converged on the capital. Two important sites were also to be taken over before a final assault against Santa Clara—the ports of Caibarién on the north coast and Cienfuegos on the south coast.[25] Any fresh troops would be landed at these ports, which were both defended by large garrisons and supported by the navy.

According to the joint strategy agreed upon at a meeting headed by Guevara and Rolando Cubela, Camilo Cienfuegos and his guerrillas were to operate to the north of Santa Clara, while the forces of Guevara and the DR would cover all areas south of the city. The main objective was to isolate Santa Clara from the rest of the province, and to establish a complete blockade of the city. With the capture of the most important towns and garrisons outside the city, the guerrillas could get down to the task of attacking Santa Clara.

Shortly before the insurrectionists moved, Batista Fired General Chaviano from his post and appointed Colonel Casillas Lumpuy, but the change in command was useless. By then it was too late to prepare for the insurrectionary offensive.

The Battle

On December 14, the guerrillas attacked Fomentos, and on December 17 the city's garrison surrendered. The guerrillas then moved on to the towns of Guayos and Cabaiguán.[26] On December 21, a simultaneous attack was conducted against these two strategic points on the Central Highway. The garrison at Cabaiguán surrendered as soon as troops of the DR approached. At Guayos, Captain Pelayo González put up token resistance to Guevara's guerrillas, but surrendered his 90 men within the first two hours of fighting.

That night, Guevara planned his assault on the city of Placetas, the next in line in a chain leading along the Central Highway into Santa Clara. The following day, Guevara's troops advanced, leaving a number of men behind at strongholds that could counter any attack coming from the province of Camagüey. In Placetas, the army abandoned the streets and took refuge in the barracks. The guerrillas infiltrated the city of 30,000 inhabitants, and after a few shots the army surrendered. The capital was now 35 kilometers away.[27]

Army officers expected that the rebels would move en masse to-ward Santa Clara.[28] Instead, Guevara ordered his forces to spread out and to march toward the towns of Remedios and Caibarién. Meanwhile, the guerrillas captured a locomotive which carried them part of the way, and then crashed against a bridge in Madrigal, close to Sancti-Spíritus.[29] In the course of this march the city of Sancti-Spíritus surrendered, and by December 23 the rebels held authority over 150,000 inhabitants in the province.[30] The same day, the M-26-7 and the DR declared Fomentos and Báez as open cities since, according to humanitarian considerations, "the elderly, women and children and civilians in general" should be guarded against "the perils of war."[31]

The attack on Remedios led by "Che" Guevara began on December 25. As in Placetas, the army had abandoned its advance positions in the town's suburbs and had taken refuge inside the barracks and the city hall. The guerrillas moved through deserted streets without firing a shot and surrounded both positions. At this point the police seem to have decided to fight. From inside the city hall, where they were quartered, came a rain of bullets upon the rebels, who hastily withdrew. There were three assaults within an hour, and all were repelled by the police. The rebels then used Molotov cocktails; as the old building burst into flames, the police emerged, hands above their heads. The army did not follow the police example and surrendered without firing a single shot. Eighty-five rebels had proved victorious over 250 regular troops,[32] and in so doing had gained 150 automatic rifles.

To the north, Camilo Cienfuegos advanced without opposition until he reached the town of Yaguajay. Behind Yaguajay, which linked the area to Santa Clara, the rebels had established control over the towns of Meneses and Mayajigua. Thus, Yaguajay was the last bastion of the army, and it stood in Cienfuegos' path toward Santa Clara. The 250-man army post was commanded by Captain Abon Ly, who had been transferred from Camagüey to Las Villas province.[33] The battle of Yaguajay lasted for a record 11 days, in the most heated encounter of the series of battles preceding the fall of Santa Clara. Captain Ly, a Cuban of Chinese ancestry, fought with a determination and courage unequaled by any other army officer commanding small posts. Practically bombed out, completely encircled, without water or electricity, and with no hope of receiving reinforcements. Captain Ly still refused to surrender.

On December 19, Major Camilo Cienfuegos summoned his general staff and the guerrillas available in the area for the battle of Yaguajay. Cienfuegos' original guerrilla group of 150 men was increased threefold with the arrival of guerrillas from Mayajigua, Zulueta and Meneses. The guerrillas encircled the town, and fire broke out on December 21, with the guerrillas attacking city hall and the police precinct. On December 24 the rebels captured city hall and the police precinct, but were repelled at the hotel and at the electric plant by Captain Ly's troops. Late that day, Major Cienfuegos asked Ly for a truce to attend to the wounded. The encounter began again early the following morning, with Cienfuegos leading an attack against Ly's position. The guerrillas were held off by the troops in hand-to-hand combat. On December 22, Cienfuegos ordered another assault, and Ly's men stood their ground. The fighting continued all day. In the evening Cienfuegos asked Captain Ly to surrender, explaining that his men were totally surrounded, and that no reinforcements would reach Yaguajay. In turn, Ly asked that his men be allowed to leave the town; Cienfuegos refused and battle was resumed.[34] Convinced that the army's 8th Regiment at Santa Clara would send reinforcements to Yaguajay, Captain Ly had decided to hold until news arrived from his superior officers.

On December 26, the guerrillas began to use a homemade tank produced by workers at the Narcisa sugar mill; it was a large tractor encased with iron plates and a .50 caliber machine gun on top.[35] There was another rebel assault during the night of December 27, but the army still maintained its position. The "tank" was damaged and withdrawn from the encounter. On the morning of the 28th, Captain Ly asked for a truce to remove the dead and wounded from inside the small one-floor barracks building. Again, Major Cienfuegos took the opportunity to ask the captain to surrender in view of the fact that there was no sign of reinforcements from Santa Clara and Ly's men had been without food or water for almost four days. Ly explained to Cienfuegos that his duty was to fight until otherwise ordered by his superior officers; since he had received no such orders, he would continue to fight to the last man if necessary.[36]

Fighting continued on December 29. The rebels were once more repulsed by the regular troops; Captain Ly led a group of men out of the barracks, rescued a few rifles left by the rebels, and pushed the guerrillas back 200 yards from the army post. Cienfuegos counterattacked, and Ly fell back into the barracks, but prevented the rebels from approaching the post. That night, Cienfuegos asked for a third truce to remove dead and wounded. Major Cienfuegos told Captain Ly that he was only interested in the small airstrip behind the army post and the army's equipment. The truce ended with no agreement, and fighting continued throughout the night. The following morning, December 30, "Che" Guevara sent a mortar, some ammunition and a bazooka to Cienfuegos.[37] On this eleventh day of Ly's resistance his men could only fire sporadic shots at the guerrillas because they had almost run out of ammunition. They had no medicine to care for the wounded; the men could no longer bear their thirst; and most soldiers were convinced that they would never receive reinforcements. After reviewing the situation, Ly concluded that without reinforcements it was just a matter of time before the guerrillas overpowered his men. That evening, the Captain asked for a ceasefire and told Major Cienfuegos of his decision to surrender.[38] Cienfuegos, who was one of the most gallant of the rebel officers, allowed Ly to remain armed and accepted his honorable surrender. Cienfuegos then continued his delayed advance toward Santa Clara.

Caibarien surrendered before the rebels entered the port. The navy extended its congratulations to Major Cienfuegos and placed its ships at his disposal. The port of Isabela de Sagua declared itself in favor of the rebels, so there was no need to fight. The road between the city of Cienfuegos and Santa Clara had been heavily mined by the rebels of the Second Front of Gutiérrez Menoyo. Cienfuegos city itself was completely surrounded by guerrillas under the command of Major William Morgan of the Second Front. The navy at Cienfuegos also communicated its support to the insurrectionists. Guevara now regrouped his forces. The decisive engagement of the Cuban insurrection was about to begin.

On December 27, Guevara met with his officers to study the plan for the final attack on Santa Clara.[39] The rebel chief pointed out that military results were not as important as the psychological impact of the fall of the city. Guevara further stressed that if the rebels failed in their first attempt to take over the city, precious hours would be lost and Batista might feel more optimistic about a counterattack.

All guerrilla units were to move toward the city, Camilo Cienfuegos from the north, and Guevara and Cubela and Chomón from the south and southwest, respectively. Each column was to arrive at its destination on time, and no excuses would be accepted. Guevara's Column No. 8 would take over the university, where headquarters for the final attack would be located. The university, only eight kilometers from the center of the city, would provide access along the railroad lines. The only obstacles on the way were the Capiro Hills, which loomed between the university and the city. The DR, under Rolando Cubela, would attack Barracks No. 31, another access point into the city.[40] The three assaults were to take place simultaneously.

On December 29, all officers received their orders and the mobilization began. Less than 24 hours later, the battle raged throughout the capital of Las Villas province. At Batista's Camp Columbia in Havana, reports arriving from Santa Clara were alarming. Sergeant Alfredo Armas Somoza reported that "there is fighting around the university. The Military District is not yet under attack. Will keep you informed in the event reinforcements are needed."[41]

As had been planned, Guevara took over the university with little resistance, while the DR attacked Barracks No. 31. Major Cienfuegos was unable to join the operation because he was still engaging the army in Yaguajay. Suddenly an obstacle appeared: Colonel Casillas Lumpuy had sent a train with 350 soldiers to the Capiro Hills under orders to impede Guevara's advance into the city, presumably giving the colonel time to develop a counterattack. During the first two hours after the DR began its attack on Barracks No. 31, with Cienfuegos' guerrillas unable to move out of Yaguajay, Colonel Casillas Lumpuy seems to have become aware of his numerical superiority. Myth had preceded the guerrillas wherever they went, and it was believed that they had thousands of men under arms, when there were no more than 500 at any time during the actual attack on Santa Clara. Colonel Casillas Lumpuy probably felt that he could defeat the guerrillas in open combat and cut their retreat into the countryside.

But the colonel underestimated the organization of Santa Clara's M-26-7 and DR underground organizations. As soon as the first army vehicles left the barracks they were attacked by cells of the DR and the M-26-7 from the University of Las Villas. Bombs and snipers prevented the regular troops from walking freely through the streets. Enrique Oltusky's efforts to create an efficient organization within the city were paying dividends. The soldiers felt themselves surrounded by phantom fighters whom they could not destroy without reducing the entire city to ashes.[42] Time was of the outmost importance. The guerrillas had to take the Capiro Hill by assault as the last remaining obstacle to their entrance into the city. For this reason Guevara asked for volunteers to take the hill immediately and at any cost. The youngest members of Column No. 8 formed a platoon with grenadiers supported by a suicide squad under the command of Gabriel Gil.[43] Following the assault of the grenadiers a wave of about 90 guerrillas would attempt to overrun the army's position. When the grenadiers began their assault it was expected that the army would open fire when the attackers had reached a point a few hundred yards from the top of the hill. But the grenadiers reached the top of the hill without finding any resistance. To their amazement, Batista's forces had fled, and the rebels found only empty trenches. The troops had boarded the train that had brought them to the Capiro Hills, and turned it back to Santa Clara.

The Armored Train

The "armored train" had been Batista's last attempt to reinforce Santa Clara's weakening command. The train's 600 men, equipped with the best possible arms, not only had the main task of repairing all damage caused by the guerrillas, but also, commanded by Colonel Florentino Rosell Leyva, were to fight them. However, Colonel Rosell simply abandoned Las Villas province, the war and the train at the Capiro Hills, and fled the country, even though the train was fully loaded with a large variety of arms and ammunitions. At this point rebel Captain Ramón Pardo Guerra ordered a bulldozer to be taken from the school of agriculture to destroy the tracks. Close by, rebel Lieutenant Roberto Espinosa Puig, with a platoon of 18 guerrillas, guarded the tracks while Captain Pardo accompanied Guevara on an inspection tour of the front lines.

During this tour Guevara and Pardo were informed that rebel Lieutenant Espinosa had attacked the train, capturing 41 prisoners and three of the 18 cars. At about 4:30 PM Captain Pardo asked for time to approach the train and talk to the troops, and the army acquiesced. The guerrilla captain told the troops to surrender, that there was no way out for them, and that their safety would be guaranteed. "Che" Guevara arrived at the scene, approaching the train and telling the troops that "if you decide to continue fighting you'll be responsible for any bloodshed."[44] If the troops did not answer in 15 minutes, the guerrillas would attack. But before that time had elapsed, the army surrendered. The troops were immediately transported by trucks to the port of Caibarién, where they could choose their final destination.

The train, with 401 men and 18 armored cars, was full of arms of all calibers—some still in boxes marked "U.S. Army." It was from this newly acquired arsenal that the rebel army equipped itself for the last push on Santa Clara.[45]

The radio station of Column No. 8 told the people, and Camilo Cienfuegos in particular—who requested arms for his battle in Yaguajay—that over 300 soldiers and officers of the corps of engineers had "refused to fight against the people," and had "patriotically surrendered to save the Fatherland rather than Batista."[46]

In Oriente province, Fidel Castro and the rebel army continued the general offensive with their main objective the takeover of Santiago de Cuba. On December 23 the rebel army attacked the city of Palma Soriano, taking 336 prisoners and capturing 355 arms of various calibers. Columns No. 1 and 3 were rapidly approaching Santiago de Cuba. The same day, Major Hubert Matos' Column No. 9 attacked and defeated the army at Boniato. The Central Highway was controlled by the rebels from Bayamo to Santiago de Cuba and by December 26, an army battalion commanded by Major Leopoldo Hernández Rios was confronting Fidel Castro's attack in Maffo. From December 23rd to the 26th the offensive had cost the rebels 26 dead and over 50 wounded, but the army had sustained 600 casualties. On December 30, Maffo fell to Fidel Castro after 20 days of siege. With the fall of this city, the area between Bayamo and the capital of Oriente had been cleared, and the battle for Santiago de Cuba could begin. Major Hubert Matos' guerrillas had taken over control of the city's refineries while Fidel's men—Column No. 1—approached the Central Highway. Elsewhere, the rebels were also moving against the army in earnest. In Camagüey, Major Víctor Mora, heading Column No. 11, "Ignacio Agramonte," attacked the army in Morón and Chambas, and by December 28 the rebels had control of most of the Central Highway between the capital of Camagüey and the city of Holguín in Oriente province. Also active in Camagüey province was Major Eduardo ("Lalo") Sardiñas, who led Column No. 12, "Simón Bolívar," and who took the town of Jobabo on December 29.[47]

The Fall of Santa Clara

The army had organized its defense of Santa Clara at five points: the Leoncio Vidal Camp, with about 3,000 troops; the police station, with about 1,000 men; the municipal building; the Grand Hotel; and the Palace of Justice, where there were approximately 2,500 men.[48] As the rebels moved close to Santa Clara, the air force arrived. But most pilots refused to bombard the city—although they strafed parts of it—and instead dropped their lethal cargo at sea.

The guerrillas advanced to the Palace of Justice, which was defended by two tanks and machine gun emplacements. Shortly before the attack began, at least two army companies deserted the position. After 30 minutes, the tanks withdrew, leaving the remaining troops alone. It was not too long before they, too, surrendered to the rebel army. The Grand Hotel and the municipal building fell shortly afterwards. Many of the loyal soldiers succeeded in reaching the police station, where they prepared to resist to the last man.

By mid-morning, the only two strongholds remaining in the hands of the army were the Leoncio Vidal Camp and the police station. The fighting concentrated around the latter, where the rebels were stopped. Some police officers advanced on the rebels, forcing them to withdraw to a safer position. Still the fighting continued, with the rebels trying to burn the building, and the police keeping them at bay.

Guevara was informed that Colonel Casillas Lumpuy had been captured while trying to escape.[49] Actually, the colonel had attempted to organize the defense against the rebel offensive, and probably found that the troops' morale was simply impossible to build at that late date. The army had to confront an internal uprising, for the troops did not want to continue fighting.

Meanwhile, men at the police station were still resisting. Colonel Cornelio Rojas, who commanded that position, fought bravely, together with police and army officers and troops. Roberto Rodríguez ("El Vaquerito"), a rebel officer, died leading one assault. Colonel Rojas stood firmly against succeeding waves of attack by the rebels, and forced the guerrillas to fall back to reorganize their forces.

Shortly after noon, Colonel Rojas counterattacked and succeeded in pushing the rebels out of their positions, but then a rebel counterattack forced him to retreat. The house-to-house fighting forced his exhausted troops to return to the police station after they ran short of ammunition. Colonel Rojas issued orders to fight to the last man. The rebels made three more attempts to dislodge the colonel and were repulsed each time. Toward the end, the colonel and his men were surrounded by reinforcements from Guevara, the DR and the urban underground. Even though no help came from the army (the regular troops refused to leave the Leoncio Vidal Camp) Colonel Rojas kept on fighting and was the last man captured, when he ran out of ammunition. Still, he escaped his escort momentarily, joining a group of police officers and trying to regroup other regular troops. He was surrounded again by the rebels, captured, and placed under the custody of a full squad of rebel soldiers. Colonel Rojas was later summarily tried, and sentenced to die before a firing squad. Rojas asked and was granted permission to lead his execution squad, and his last words were, "Muchachos, now you have your Revolution, don't lose it."[50]

Now that the rebel army controlled Santa Clara, Guevara and Rolando Cubela considered attacking the Leoncio Vidal Camp. Without their chief commander, the troops and officer corps would probably be ready to discuss terms with the rebels, and so Guevara sent a committee headed by Antonio Núñez Jiménez (who had joined the insurgents in December 1958) to obtain the army's surrender. Upon the committee's arrival at the main gate of the camp the troops welcomed them with shouts, demanding an immediate end to hostilities, and calling the rebels "brothers." Jiménez relates that when the guerrillas entered, the soldiers approached them and embraced them, and then the troops told the rebels that they had not been paid for almost three months.[51] Representatives of the M-26-7 and the DR guerrillas held a discussion with the army officers in charge. Their demands were simple—unconditional surrender.

Meanwhile the population was in the streets celebrating. They had suffered the bulk of the fighting, for Guevara had entered the city through its most populated area so as to prevent any attacks from army tanks.[52] Firing briefly broke out again from the Grand Hotel, where some of Rolando Masferrer's "tigers" still resisted. They died fighting, asking no mercy, for they knew that none would have been given.

Notes

1. Fulgencio Batista, *Cuba Betrayed* (New York: Vantage Press, 1962), pp. 104–05. Letter from Tabernilla to Batista, dated February 13, 1959.

2. On September 25, Colonel Carrasco was in a group of officers who had been invited to have lunch with Batista at Columbia, in Havana, as a gesture to front-line officers; Carrasco claims that he was prevented from rendering a personal report to Batista on the deteriorating conditions of the army in Oriente province by Marcelo Tabernilla, Jr. Carrasco was to be transferred to Camagüey province—with Battalion No. 10—at the request of Colonel Leopoldo Pérez Cougil, chief of operations in that province, who was returning to Oriente's Sierra Maestra front. Instead, Carrasco was transferred to Maffo and on September 27 fought Almeida's guerrillas was wounded and was taken prisoner of the guerrillas. The army never officially notified Carrasco's family; refused to allow an army surgeon to attend to his wounds after the rebels authorized such a visit to Almeida's camp; and refused to let Carrasco's soldiers attempt to rescue their leader (Nelson Carrasco Artiles, in a letter to the authors dated December 27, 1972, Miami. Florida).

3. Fidel Castro, "The Battle of El Cerro," in Rolando E. Bonachea and Nelson P. Valdés, eds., *Revolutionary Struggle, 1947–1958* (Cambridge: MIT Press, 1972), p. 420. See also Nelson Carrasco Artíles, "97 dias prisionero de los guerrilleros; torturas mentales; mi odisea," *America Libre* (Miami), January 5, 1973, pp. 4–6; January 12, 1973, pp. 2–3; January 19, 1973, p. 5, and the same author in "Mi muerte silenciada, nada se informa a mis familiares y amigos," *América Libre* (Miami), February 1, 1973, pp. 6, 11.

4. Fidel Castro, "In the Face of the Plot by Batista and Yankee Imperialism," *Granma* (Havana), March 18, 1973, pp. 20–21.

5. Fidel Castro, "The Battle of El Cerro," in Bonachea and Valdés, *Revolutionary Struggle*, p. 423. Castro reported that in a period of 36 days (to September 27, 1958) the rebel army defeated 14 battalions, took 400 prisoners, inflicted 800 casualties and captured 500 weapons.

6. Earl T. Smith, *The Fourth Floor* (New York: Random House, 1962), p. 175. See also Mario Lazo, *American Policy Failures in Cuba, Dagger in the Heart!* (New York: Funk and Wagnalls, 1970), pp. 165–66.

7. *Diario de la Marina* (Havana), October 11, 1958, and October 13, 1958. See also *Prensa Libre* (Havana), October 15, 1958.

8. Lazo, *American Policy Failures*, p. 167.

9. Earl T. Smith, *El cuarto piso* (Mexico: Editorial Diana, 1968), p. 158.

10. Smith, *The Fourth Floor*, p. 101, and Lazo, *American Policy Failures*, pp. 167–68.

11. Smith, *El cuarto piso*, p. 158.

12. Fidel Castro, *Ley No. 2*, Comandancia del Ejército Rebelde, Sierra Maestra, October 10, 1958 (mimeo). See also Jules Dubois, *Fidel Castro: Liberator or Dictator?* (Indianapolis: Bobbs-Merrill, 1959), pp. 316–17; also Fidel Castro, "No Election Decree, October 10, 1958," in Bonachea and Valdés, *Revolutionary Struggle*, pp. 426–28.

13. Authors' interview with guerrilla Captain Dionisio Suárez of Column No. 9, "Antonio ('Tony') Guiteras" (January 14, 1973, Union City).

14. Ibid.

15. The results, announced on November 20, were: Ramón Grau San Martin, 75,789; Carlos Márquez Sterling. 95,447; Alberto Salas Amaro, 8,752; and Andrés Rivero Aguero. 428,166, See *El Mundo* (Havana), November 21, 1958, and *Diario de la Marina* (Havana). November 21 and 22, 1958.

16. Smith, *El cuarto piso*, p. 158, says that Batista's violation of his "solemn promise" to the U.S. ambassador to conduct "free elections" was the "last of his big mistakes." What seems to be suggested, within the Cuban context, is that "free elections" meant the "election" of Márquez Sterling in order to attempt a neutralization of the insurrection with Batista out of the country, Even Mario Lazo, *American Policy Failures*, p. 168, noticed that on "election" day, "there were few people on the streets and little traffic."

17. This viewpoint was corroborated in an interview with former secretary of labor Jesús Portocarrero (August, 1961, Miami, Florida).

18. Fidel Castro, "Orders to the Rebel Army," in Bonachea and Valdés. *Revolutionary Struggle*, pp. 437–38.

19. Many of the houses by the road between the town of Cueto and Holguín were burned or shot at indiscriminately by the army; the army also destroyed vehicles along the road while the neighbors fled, terrorized, into the nearby sugar cane fields; the chief of the army in this area was General Jesús Sosa Blanco (Evidence of one of the authors).

20. For the final stage of the insurrection in Oriente province, see the war communiques published by the clandestine newspapers "Surco," "Revolución" and "Sierra Maestra," in "21 partes de guerra," *Días de combate* (Havana: Instituto del Libro, 1970), pp. 259–71; "Cuba 1958: mujeres guerrilleras," *Bohemia* (Havana), July 28, 1967, pp. 15–17; Fidel Castro, "La batalla de Guisa," *Verde Olivo* (Havana), January 22, 1967, pp. 8–11; Roger González Guerrero, "Oriente 1958," *Verde Olivo* (Havana), January 5, 1969, pp. 6–11; "Breve historia gráfica de Cuba: cronologia de los 100 años de lucha (1868–1968)," *Universidad de la Habana*, no. 2 (Havana: October–December, 1968): 245. For the leaders and their guerrilla columns, see *Historia de Cuba* (Havana: Instituto Cubano del Libro, 1971), pp. 231–32. For the regular army's war communiques, see Gervasio G. Ruiz, "La dictadura que cayó derrotada por sus victorias," *Carteles* (Havana), January 4, 1959, pp. 26–28, 134.

21. Guerrero, "Oriente 1958," pp. 6–11; Fidel Castro, "Este es un minuto extraordinario," *Verde Olivo* (Havana), January 5, 1969, p. 8.

22. Ernesto "Che" Guevara, *Reminiscences of the Cuban Revolutionary War* (New York: Monthly Review Press, 1968), p. 32.

23. "Plano de defensa del Regimiento 3 de la Guardia Rural, Leoncio Vidal," *Ché*, p. 222.

24. Batista, *Cuba Betrayed*, p. 88.

25. *Granma* (Havana), October 29, 1967.
26. Interview with guerrilla Captain Francisco Pantoja of Column No. 8, July 2, 1971, Union City, New Jersey.
27. Ernesto "Che" Guevara, "La batalla de Santa Clara," in *Ché*, pp. 135–37; Ernesto "Che" Guevara, "The General Strike and the Battle of Santa Clara," in Guevara, *Reminiscences*, pp. 250–1: Antonio Nuñez Jiménez, *Geografía de Cuba* (Havana, 1962), pp. 502–03, and the same author in "La toma de Santa Clara." *Carteles* (Havana), January 4, 1959, pp. 14–18. As a result of these encounters, Dr. Oscar Fernández Mell was promoted to captain; Lieutenant Roberto Rodríguez, chief of the suicide squad of Column No. 8, was promoted to captain as was Lieutenant Orlando Pantoja Tamayo; Francisco Chacón, Gilberto del Rio and Enrique Acevedo were promoted to lieutenants by "Che" Guevara.
28. Authors' interview with René Romero, treasurer of the DR and a witness to the military gains of the rebel columns (June 10, 15 and 16, 1972, Union City).
29. J. Hernández, "Despacho oficial al Director de Operaciones G-3, Estado Mayor del Ejército, 11:20 AM," December 23, 1958, in *Ché*, p. 244.
30. Guevara, *Reminiscences*, pp. 250–51.
31. J. Hernández, "Despacho oficial al Director de Operaciones G-3, Estado Mayor del Ejército, 17:45 hrs.," in *Ché*, p. 245.
32. Jiménez, *Geografía*, pp. 502–03.
33. Authors' interview with Captain Abon Ly (November 1972, Union City).
34. William Gálvez, "Ragos de la campaña de Camilo en Las Villas," *Bohemia* (Havana), July 23, 1965, pp. 47–50.
35. William Gálvez, "Rasgos del combate de Yaguajay," in *Días de combate*, pp. 357–60.
36. Evidence of Abón Ly to the authors.
37. Gálvez, "Rasgos del combate," pp. 359–60. He also writes that Cienfuegos expected a rebel airplane to bombard Ly's position but that the airplane crashed in Mayajigua's airport.
38. Captain Ly received honorable treatment from Major Cienfuegos; however, following Batista's downfall, Ly was placed under arrest but was not charged with any crimes, whereupon he asked Cienfuegos about the situation; Cienfuegos died in an alleged accident in October 1960, and Ly was kept in prison without trial until 1970, when he was released. Evidence of Abón Ly to the authors.
39. Evidence of guerrilla Captain Francisco Pantoja to the authors (July 2, 1971, Union City).
40. Guevara, *Reminiscences*, p. 251.
41. A. F. Nespral, "Despacho oficial al Oficial de Operaciones, Estado Mayor del Ejército," December 29, 1958, in *Ché*, p. 229.
42. Bernardo Perdomo, "La batalla de Santa Clara," *El Triunfo* (Miami), July 21, 1970, p. 13.
43. Gabriel Gil was a veteran of the Granma expedition. For the assault on the Capiro Hill, see Oscar Fernández Mell, "La batalla de Santa Clara," in *Días de combate*, p. 370.
44. Ramón Pardo Guerra, "El tren blindado," *Días de combate*, pp. 381–87.
45. Ibid.

46. A report on the train's capture from Guevara to Cienfuegos through mobile radio unit appears in "Versión taquigráfica de la trasmisión captada el 30 de diciembre de 1958," in *Días de combate*, p. 230. See also "Reporte de operaciones del 19 al 20 de diciembre": "Reporte de operaciones del 23 al 24 de diciembre": "Reporte de operaciones del 24 al 25 de diciembre"; "Reporte de operaciones del 28 al 29 de diciembre"; "Reporte de operaciones del 30 al 31 de diciembre," in *Días de combate*, pp. 412–27.

47. The guerrillas were led by Vilo Acuña, Raúl Menéndez Tomassevich, Diocles Torralba, Luis Carrera and Universo Sánchez, "La toma de Palma Soriano," *Días de combate*, pp. 249–58. See also Fidel Castro, "La toma de Palma Soriano," *Verde Olivo* (Havana), January 5, 1969, p. 11. Descriptions of these battles were transmitted by various rebel stations (Radio Rebelde de Cruces, Indio Azul, 7 Radio Rebelde, 6BF, Radio Rebelde) and appear in "He aquí algunas trasmisiones de Radio Rebelde y otras plantas durante los dias finales de la guerra revolucionaria," in *Dias de combate*, pp. 390–410.

48. J. Fernández, "Plan 'A' operación 'Iguara,'" in *Ché*, p. 222; "Confidencial: Director de Operaciones G-3," in *Ché*, pp. 225–26; and J. Fernández, "Secreto: Plan alterno 'A.'" in *Días de combate*, pp. 375–80.

49. Colonel Casillas Lumpuy was summarily executed by order of "Che" Guevara; the firing squad was selected from among guerrillas attached to Major Victor Bordón's column. Lieutenant Jorge Villas—adjutant and pilot to Bordón — to one of the authors in January 1959, Havana, Cuba. See Jiménez, *Geografía de Cuba*, p. 503, and *Revolución* (Havana), January 5, 1959, claim that Casillas Lumpuy was shot to death while trying to escape, after being tried and sentenced to death by a revolutionary tribunal. Also see Thomas, *Pursuit of Freedom*, p. 1028.

50. *El Gran Recuento*, a documentary film of the insurrection by the Revolutionary Government of Cuba, exhibited in Cuba during 1959. Colonel Rojas was the uncle of Rolando Masferrer Rojas.

51. Jiménez, "Diario de guerra," in *Geografía*, pp. 282–95.

52. Guevara, *Reminiscences*, p. 251.

14

The Final Decision:
Batista Leaves

As New Year's Eve approached, the reports sent to Batista from Santa Clara grew increasingly ominous. The situation there seemed hopeless, for only a handful of officers still had any will to fight, and defection and insubordination were increasing. According to Batista, "The noise made by the undisciplined personnel and the purposeless shooting was aggravated by . . . interference in communications, caused by the shortwave transmitter that had fallen into the hands of the enemy." This, Batista said, created further confusion in the orders emanating from headquarters.[1]

In the capital, the morale of some of the high-ranking officers showed the impact of the events at Santa Clara. "The signs of make- believe courage were increasing," Batista wrote. "General Tabernilla, Jr., continued to be the barometer of his father, the chief of the Joint Chiefs of Staff." General Tabernilla, Jr., one of the most ardent supporters of Batista's regime, was the first to announce: "If there is nothing else to be done, we had better go, the sooner the better." When Batista asked him not to repeat that phrase, Tabernilla, Jr., answered, "If the President wishes I shall struggle to death, but if there is no more hope . . . we must fly . . . the sooner the better."

Defeatism had been spreading rapidly throughout the ranks and General Tabernilla, Sr., appears to have been one of the most active officers engaged in activities leading to Batista's removal from power. In late-December, Tabernilla requested an interview with U S. Ambassador Earl T. Smith. This was a serious step, since besides Batista the secretary of state had previously been the only official who was permitted to speak with the ambassador. The general, accompanied by his son and by General Chaviano, explained that a solution had to be found immediately if Castro were to be prevented from assuming power. He proposed the formation of a junta that would call on Vice President Rafael Guás Inclán to assume control of the government, backed by the armed forces. Batista would be given safe conduct out of the country. Ambassador Smith replied that he could only discuss a solution with Batista himself. As soon as Tabernilla, Sr., left, Smith cabled Assistant Secretary of

State Roy Rubottom: he informed him of the interview and concluded that it was obvious that the government was about to fall apart.[2]

Actually, since November the U. S. government had been taking urgent steps to remove Batista from power while trying to prevent Fidel Castro from taking over. But Ambassador Smith had not been informed of a plan which had been adopted by the U. S. State Department. Much better informed was Mario Lazo of the Lazo-Cuba law firm in Havana. Lazo was the attorney for several large American companies in Cuba, and he had learned, from a "responsible and confidential source in the United States," that William D. Pawley, the former ambassador to Peru and Brazil and a personal friend of President Eisenhower, was about to be sent as a secret emissary to negotiate with Batista.[3] Pawley would be authorized to offer Batista an opportunity to live with his family in Daytona Beach, Florida, if the dictator would appoint a caretaker government. Lazo also learned that Ambassador Smith would be recalled to Washington to be briefed on the situation in general, but would not be informed about the specific "mission" that Pawley would undertake. Lazo, however, informed Ambassador Smith of everything.[4]

Pawley had several meetings with President Eisenhower, who arranged for him to be thoroughly briefed by State Department officials, including Roy Rubottom, and chief of the Caribbean affairs, William Wieland (who Pawley viewed as "extremely anti-Batista").[5] Meanwhile, Allen Dulles, director of the CIA, was a strong advocate of the "caretaker government" formula, and of stopping Castro from reaching power. Dulles reported to President Eisenhower that if Castro were to take power the Communists would be close behind him, and that everything indicated they would participate in the government.[6] Finally, it was decided—evidently by the President himself—that Pawley should visit Batista as a "private citizen." Ambassador Smith was recalled on December 4, and U. S. "secret diplomacy" began to work.

Upon his arrival in Washington, D.C., Smith met with Under Secretary of State Robert Murphy, Roy Rubottom, Deputy Assistant Secretary for Inter-American Affairs William Snow, and William Wieland. Also attending the meeting was the CIA liaison with the State Department. Murphy notified Ambassador Smith that Batista was to be approached by someone not officially connected with the State Department. The military-civilian junta which Murphy had in mind to succeed Batista include General Cantillo, Colonel José Rego Rubido and General Sosa de Quesada.[7]

William D. Pawley later testified that he had been authorized to offer Batista an opportunity to live at Daytona Beach with his family, that his friends and family would not be molested; that Pawley would make an effort to stop Fidel Castro from coming to power, but that the caretaker government would be composed of Batista's enemies.[8] Pawley's proposal included the promise that the caretaker government would immediately be recognized by the United States and that $10 million in armaments would be made available to the army.

The key aspect of the plan was that Pawley would be authorized to speak to Batista for President Eisenhower. But before Pawley left, Roy Rubottom told him that "there had been a modification: he was not to disclose to Batista that he was speaking on behalf of the President."[9] Thus, Pawley's proposals would fall into the category of suggestions from a private citizen, depriving him of his most persuasive argument: that the proposals were directly approved by the President of the United States.

In Havana, Pawley met with Cuban Foreign Minister Gonzalo Güell, and then with Batista. Batista maintained that he would stay in power until Andrés Rivero Agüero, his "elected" successor, took over from him in February 1959. Pawley returned to Washington, while Ambassador Smith went back to Cuba for a final meeting with Batista.

On December 14, Ambassador Smith received instructions to the effect that it was time to tell Batista to leave.[10] At long last, and for reasons other than condemnation of Batista's brutal regime, the U. S. government was withdrawing its support from the Cuban dictator. Batista was just one in a family of Latin American military dictators who received support from the Eisenhower-Dulles-Nixon trio. Among them were some of the most savage dictators in the history of the area: Marcos Pérez Jiménez of Venezuela; Anastasio Somoza of Nicaragua; Carlos Castillo Armas of Guatemala; and Rafael Leónidas Trujillo of the Dominican Republic, among others. But a popular insurrection, in destroying a regular army, offered a historical lesson to both Latin Americans and North Americans, a lesson that deeply worried the continental gendarmes. Batista was of no further use, and the next problem for the United States was specifically how to frustrate the Cuban insurrection.

On December 17, Ambassador Smith called on Gonzalo Güell for an urgent meeting with Batista.[11] This meeting took place at Batista's residence in Kuquine. Batista described the meeting; "Despite his nice manner Señor Smith could not hide through his smile his deep sorrow. There was not much to talk about."[12] The ambassador told Batista that the U.S. government wished to avert further bloodshed in Cuba, and that it must now withdraw its support from his regime. Batista asked how much time he had, and was told not to delay his departure unduly. Batista then attempted to convince the ambassador that a provisional military junta (without Batista) could preside over a transitional period until such time as the situation would be favorable. Smith reiterated his original orders: Batista had to go, and no such junta was possible.[13] Later, Smith requested that the State Department resume munitions shipments to the army immediately, but he was refused.[14]

Before abandoning power, Batista let Smith know his opinion of the way the United States was treating him after such a long and friendly relationship. Batista told Smith that so-called U.S. "neutrality" was actually a policy against his regime; the U.S. attitude amounted to intervention in the internal affairs of Cuba, and it was actually opening the way to "supporters of communism and enemies of democracy."[15] But the crux of the dilemma rested not on what attitude the United States would assume vis-à-vis the insurrection or Batista. Rather, it was the inability of the regular army to resist the insurrection. Batista or a military junta could be maintained only through direct military intervention on the part of the United States. Against a real insurrection, old methods of secret diplomacy could not succeed.

Far from being ready to fight the rebels, the army chiefs panicked and tried to find ways to become involved with and take advantage of the insurrectionists. On December 23 General Tabernilla, Sr., called a meeting of various high-ranking army officers. Present at that meeting were General Carlos Tabernilla, Jr., General Chaviano, General Rodríguez Avila. General Carlos Robaina, and Colonels Irenaldo García Báez and Florentino Rosell Leyva.[16] This meeting seems to have precipitated plots and counterplots within the army. General Tabernilla, Sr., reviewed the military situation and said that he doubted whether the guerrillas could be held in Las Villas and Oriente provinces. The consensus of the officers was that the army's position was rapidly worsening. General Tabernilla, Sr., discussed the need to contact Fidel Castro and to discuss the feasibility of an understanding. The selection of an officer to represent the army before Fidel Castro was not difficult to make.

General Eulogio Cantillo, the chief of operations in Oriente province, was in close contact with the military situation there. At least once before, during the summer, Cantillo had demonstrated his willingness to negotiate an end to the conflict with Castro. Cantillo had also received various letters from Major José Quevedo—the officer who surrendered at El Jigüe—inviting him to discuss an end to the war with Castro, and one such invitation was repeated on December 18. That letter was hand-delivered to Cantillo by Father Francisco Guzmán, who also offered to arrange a meeting between Cantillo and Castro. Quevedo's letters and others addressed to Cantillo by officers who had joined the rebels (such as Captain Carlos Durán Batista and Captain Victorino Gómez Oquendo[17]) were all submitted through army channels by Cantillo to the general staff in Havana.

On December 24, Cantillo returned to Havana from Oriente province and General Tabernilla, Sr., summoned him immediately. Present at that meeting were Tabernilla, Sr., and General Pedro Rodríguez Avila, who instructed Cantillo on his mission to Fidel Castro. Cantillo was to establish the necessary contacts to see Castro and to ask the leader of the Sierra Maestra if he would accept a coup d'etat and the creation of a military junta. Batista and his cabinet, plus the most notorious of his army and police officers, were to be taken out of the country. The junta would include men like Colonel Ramón Barquín, a political prisoner since the "conspiracy of the pures" on April 4, 1956. General Cantillo was to convey Castro's answer to Tabernilla, Sr., without delay.[18]

General Cantillo contacted Father Guzmán, who arranged for a meeting with Fidel Castro on December 28. Upon his arrival in Santiago de Cuba,

General Cantillo informed Colonel José Rego Rubido and Commodore Manuel Camero about his mission. Then the general took some precautionary measures against a betrayal on the part of General Tabernilla, Sr., and ordered all flights stopped over a large perimeter including the Oriente sugar mill where the meeting was to take place.[19] Cantillo selected Orlando Izquierdo as his personal helicopter pilot, and all military maneuvers were stopped and a ceasefire ordered until the general's return from his meeting with Castro.

The Castro-Cantillo Meeting

General Cantillo was welcomed by Fidel and Raúl Castro, Vilma Espín, Raúl Chibás and José Quevedo. Orlando Izquierdo,[20] the helicopter pilot, and Father Guzmán joined the others as Castro and Cantillo walked away from the group and began their discussion.

Cantillo initiated the conversation, saying that he was under the direct orders of General Tabernilla, Sr., and that his mission was to convey the proposal of the army's general staff to Castro. He explained the proposal and asked if Castro would accept that conclusion to the civil strife. Fidel's answer developed during the following three hours.[21] The guerrilla leader lectured Cantillo on the history of the insurrection, the errors committed by the army during the summer offensive, and described the army's untenable situation in Oriente and Las Villas provinces. Fidel promised to be inflexible with all war criminals; their punishment must serve as a warning to any potential power-grabber. The two men walked while Castro continued with his own analysis of the situation: the alternatives before Batista were simple: surrender now or risk further heavy losses for the army; the generals were mistaken in defending Batista: the troops refused to fight and victory appeared inevitable for the insurrectionists.

Finally, Fidel came to the point: he would never accept a coup d'etat performed only by the army in Havana. However, Fidel explained what type of plan he would be willing to second and under what conditions. His counterproposal consisted of carrying out a joint operation against Batista starting in Santiago de Cuba, not in the capital. The regular army would revolt against the government; the rebel army would join the regular troops and enter Santiago de Cuba; and together they would march on Havana to force Batista's downfall.

The joint operation was to be based upon an essential condition: Batista could not be permitted to escape the country. In order to capture Batista, an armored column would march directly from Oriente to Havana; all tanks were to be delivered to the rebel army; and Fidel himself would lead that armored column with a two-fold purpose: to capture Batista and to maintain law and order in the capital.[22] If accepted, Castro's plan was to be implemented at exactly 3 PM on December 31. The army was to support the revolution unconditionally, back the president appointed by the revolutionary organizations, and accept whatever decisions were made as to new assignments for the military.

General Cantillo listened to Castro's plan with interest. He thought that Fidel's proposal was not too realistic, and he told Castro that "no one could stop Batista from leaving the country [from Camp] Columbia." Also, Cantillo could not promise his support for Fidel's plan without first communicating the results of the interview to the general staff and to General Tabernilla, Sr., in Havana.[23]

Fidel and Raúl Chibás, who had joined the discussion, argued that Cantillo's return to the capital posed a grave danger of having the entire operation foiled at the last minute.[24] Cantillo explained his position, and told Castro that he would return to Santiago de Cuba with an answer. Fidel asked Cantillo to stay in Oriente to prepare the combined revolt of the army and navy.[25] Fidel added that even if his military colleagues refused to go along with the plan, Cantillo should take the initiative and join the insurrection with the regular army in Santiago de Cuba, or else surrender the garrison under Colonel Rego Rubido's command, as well as the forces under Commodore Carnero of the navy. If these forces mutinied, the rebel army would enter the city and fraternize with the troops and with the people. Cantillo refused to stay in Oriente province, saying that he had to go back to Havana and fulfill his duty as an officer by reporting on his mission to General Tabernilla, Sr. On that note, Fidel and Cantillo departed, with the latter promising to get in touch with Castro before the date for the implementation of the plan.[26]

Upon his arrival at Santiago, General Cantillo explained the plan to Colonel Rego Rubido and Commodore Carnero, who agreed to wait for the general's orders to proceed accordingly. Cantillo's plane landed at Columbia military airport on the evening of December 28 and Cantillo was immediately escorted directly to Batista's residence in Kuquine.

Batista and Cantillo Meet

Batista received Cantillo, and without preliminaries the dictator deplored the willingness of his chief of operations to negotiate with Fidel Castro.[27] General Cantillo explained that since his orders had come from General Tabernilla, Sr., he had assumed that Batista himself had ordered the mission. Batista retorted that the meeting, rather than showing flexibility, announced to Castro the army's unwillingness to continue fighting, and thus its defeat. Cantillo asked Batista directly whether or not the dictator had ordered Tabernilla, Sr. to advance that proposal to Castro, and Batista's response was to launch an attack on Tabernilla, Sr. The general, said Batista, was a traitor who had undermined the army's will to fight; the orders given to Cantillo amounted to high treason.[28]

Batista asked Cantillo for a report on the military situation. The chief of operations reported that the rebels were not strong enough to attack the largest cities, or take over Santiago de Cuba, Bayamo, Holguín, or Victoria de las Tunas in Oriente province. Considering that Batista was planning a last-minute effort to stop the insurrection, Cantillo explained that the army could hold for several weeks more and that there were many officers ready to fight even at that point.

At the time of this meeting (December 29) "Che" Guevara's guerrillas had not yet entered Santa Clara in Las Villas province. The general reported to Batista that Camagüey was quiet and that Matanzas province was under the control of his brother, Carlos Cantillo, who reported everything was normal in that area. Further, the air force was intact and the "March 10" Tank Regiment at Columbia was ready for action. General Cantillo suggested that Batista take personal command of the army in operations, charge Tabernilla, Sr., with treason and execute him in front of the troops to reinforce their will to fight. The troops, Cantillo affirmed, would react favorably to Batista's move and their morale could be recovered in time to organize a counterattack.[29]

Batista told Cantillo that it was too late to effect those changes, and asked Cantillo to obey him to the end; Cantillo was not to report to Tabernilla, Sr., the results of the meeting with Castro. Cantillo should cooperate with Batista because Castro would take over power and then eliminate all army officers regardless of their involvement in the last-minute revolt.[30] Batista had to be the planner, not Tabernilla or Castro. Further, Batista went on, if the cities could be held by the army, a solution could be found that would save the military as an institution while stopping the insurrection from reaching power. Cantillo could return to Santiago de Cuba to assume the defense of the city against Castro's attack. If everything appeared to be quiet, Cantillo could come back to Havana on December 31 and report directly to Kuquine. As Cantillo departed, Batista stressed the point that he should return to the capital, unless Castro attacked Santiago before December 31.[31]

Plots and Counterplots

Retrospectively, it appears clear that General Cantillo was trying to use both Castro and Batista for his own plans. Cantillo was involved in more than one plot to overthrow Batista; thus the analysis of what happened becomes more complex as one discovers Cantillo's name in various lists of conspirators who hoped to depose Batista and to block the insurrection's assumption of power.

Cantillo claims that, while in Havana on December 24, he saw three lists of names of people close to Batista who were to accompany the dictator on his flight out of the country. The list had been compiled by General Carlos Tabernilla, Jr. Thus, it is safe to assume that on December 28, General Cantillo knew that Batista was about to flee the country, but he did not mention that detail to Castro. During his meeting with Batista that evening, Cantillo proposed a radical measure to test Batista's willingness to stay in the country—the proposal that he execute Tabernilla and assume personal leadership of his troops—and found that the dictator was not ready to risk staying any longer than necessary in Cuba.

Cantillo's name appeared in the junta proposed by Tabernilla, Sr., to U. S. Ambassador Smith, and even Robert Murphy viewed the general as a candidate for the junta in the event Pawley (the State Department envoy to Batista) convinced the dictator to accept the caretaker government formula. Colonel Florentino Rosell Leyva had also been engaged in a plot against Batista and the insurrectionary forces; the junta proposed by the plotters in that group included Cantillo as the figure to preside over the military after Batista's demise. That specific group also included Colonel José Rego Rubido, Commodore Carnero and General Chaviano, who were to revolt on a given date issued by their leader, Cantillo. Under this plan, Colonel Ramón Barquín was to be released from the Isle of Pines Penitentiary to assume command of Las Villas province in order to stop "Che" Guevara. Once the revolt had been initiated, Colonel Leopoldo Pérez Cougil—chief of Camagüey province—and Colonel Manuel Ugalde Carrillo—chief of the city of Holguín, Oriente province—were to be invited to join, and if they refused there were standing orders to kill the two officers.[32] That plan failed to materialize when Cantillo met Fidel, since Colonel Rosell Leyva panicked and abandoned the country while Batista removed General Chaviano from his post in Las Villas province.

Cantillo apparently told Batista everything but Castro's timing for the joint operation: December 31 at 3 PM. The general returned to Santiago de Cuba on December 30, and stayed until the following day, not establishing contact with Fidel, who thought Cantillo was under arrest in Havana.[33]

In Santiago de Cuba, Cantillo asked Rego Rubido and Carnero to wait until he issued orders from Havana, and then left for the capital just as he had told Batista he would. At this point, Cantillo was the main axis around which all actors evolved: Fidel Castro, Rego Rubido and even Batista himself. It seems highly doubtful that Cantillo did not realize he had the opportunity to seize power without placing himself under Fidel's orders. Cantillo's maneuver would be to take over from Batista, then, as chief of the armed forces, to negotiate with Castro from a far better position. That negotiation would have taken place only if the general realized that the army was unable to withstand the guerrillas' onslaught. However, it was the general opinion of army officers at the time that without Batista in command, with an officer ready, willing and able to unite the army and to instill morale in the troops, the soldiers would react favorably and stop the rebels from gaining further terrain.[34] At any rate, General Cantillo's ability to conspire and to maneuver has been generally underestimated.[35]

The Last Decision

Back in Havana, General Cantillo saw Batista at Kuquine. The chief of operations explained that Santiago was calm, but with the news from Santa Clara, Las Villas province, a decision had to be made soon to facilitate a solution to the crisis. Batista told Cantillo that "to leave [Cuba] any day was acceptable."

He said he would be leaving within a few hours (it was then around 9 PM), shortly after midnight. December 31.

The plan developed by the caudillo was as follows: Cantillo would remain chief of the armed forces, and a civilian junta would be organized with individuals not involved in the government. Article 148 of the Constitution of 1940, mandated that in the event of the president's absence, the vice president would take over. In the absence of the vice president the president of the senate was to be appointed president of the republic. But Batista did not want Vice President Rafael Guás Inclán, nor the president of the senate, Anselmo Alliegro, to stay in Cuba. Since the United States would not recognize a government headed by Andrés Rivero Agüero, "president-elect," Batista wanted Article 149 of the constitution to be applied. The latter stated that in such a situation the senior member of the Supreme Court was to assume the presidency.[36]

Cantillo agreed to follow this plan, asking that he also be appointed chief of the army's Infantry Division at Columbia in order to prepare for the coming hours. Batista approved of the idea, and Cantillo then asked the identity of the senior member of the Supreme Court. Since Batista did not know, Cantillo telephoned Colonel F. Coll, of the army's legal service department, ordering him to bring the magistrate with the highest position in the seniority list to Columbia. Magistrate Carlos de la Torre was unavailable; Carlos Manuel Piedra, next in line, was escorted to the military camp and told to wait in a room close to Cantillo's office. Magistrate Piedra did not know what was going on at that point.[37]

Departure

On New Year's Eve it was customary for Batista to invite the members of his cabinet and his closest friends to his home at Columbia. There, traditionally, he announced a few changes in government policy, plans for the new year, and presented his guests with expensive gift for service rendered.

Batista's last meeting with his collaborators in Cuba has been described by the general as follows: the upstairs living room of the house was full of relatives, military figures, friends and politicians. Batista arrived at 12 on the dot and greeted his wife's friends, spending a few minutes talking with each one. Displaying complete control over his emotions the caudillo made a survey of the situation: there was little that could be done, although some would fight and die if necessary.[38] All military chiefs were summoned to Batista's office for a meeting. Shortly before 2 AM Batista's commanders rendered their final report to a tired but alert caudillo. The chief of the Infantry Division spoke of the exhausted condition of his men and of the officers' inability to urge their troops into combat. The chief of the District of La Cabaña had only the minimum number of troops needed to keep the camp going. The navy was in a better position, although Admiral José Rodríguez Calderón, was not completely sure of his own command. All were of the opinion that "the armed forces had come to the end of a long and bloody road."[39] Yet the generals still hoped that the regime could be maintained for at least two more months, until February, when the presidential transition was supposed to take place. The capital seemed quiet, although the night before the urban underground had destroyed a large munition depot at Cojímar, thus blowing up some of the army's last rockets, and the air force's 100-pound bombs received from England weeks before.[40]

Batista did not delay his departure from the country. He wrote later: "After the disloyalties, surrenders, treacheries, and with only a scrap of the army left, there was only the prospect of a mountain of corpses"[41] naturally including his. Batista therefore decided to leave immediately and told those present of his decision. He instructed everyone to leave for the airfield to board one of the airplanes that would be waiting for them and their wives. Any undue delay would mean they would have to stay behind. Batista delivered his handwritten resignation to Cantillo, and rushed out of the room.[42] Everyone followed hurriedly, locating their wives and summoning servants to bring children over to the airport immediately.

It was a group of panicked people who stood waiting for their names to be called by Tabernilla, Jr., who read from the three lists authorized by the dictator. They who had boasted for so long of their power and of their decision to fight to the end were now pushing and shoving against each other, trying to get on board one of the air transports. General José Eleuterio Pedraza, once the symbol of *machismo*, whose acts against the people dated back to the 1930s was among the first to board a plane. Colonel Esteban Ventura Novo, the most feared police officer of the regime, arrived at the airport just in time to get a seat, not even waiting for his wife to join him. The men who had associated themselves with Batista on March 10, 1952, civilian and military alike, were all there. Others who had collaborated with the regime, were never told by Batista that the dictatorship was all over: Eusebio Mujal Barniol, the secretary general of the CTC; Justo Luis del Pozo, the mayor of Havana and a close friend of Batista; and Rolando Masferrer, among others. Those who knew were punctual, for a delay meant the possibility of having to confront the insurgents. Fearing a reaction on the part of his troops, who were beginning to realize that the caudillo was betraying the army and abandoning the country, Cantillo ordered the "March 10" Tank Division to the airport to protect Batista's escape.[43]

Major General Fulgencio Batista y Zaldívar boarded his plane; and as it roared over Camp Columbia, the scene of his triumphs, a quarter of a century of Cuba's political history closed.

Now What Do We Do, General?

General Cantillo went back to his office and summoned magistrate Piedra to his presence. A septuagenarian, Piedra was told the news of Batista's resignation and that, according to Article 149 of the Constitution of 1940, he was now the president. Cantillo claims that the "president" stared at him and asked, "Now what do we do, General?"[44] Cantillo suggested that they call some civilians to serve as advisors and mentioned Dr. Raúl de Cárdenas, Dr. Gustavo Cuervo Rubio and one of the last survivors of the War of Independence, General Enrique Loynaz del Castillo. Piedra added the names of Dr. Ricardo Núñez Portuondo, Alberto Blanco and Vicente Barnet.

Before dawn on January 1, General Cantillo, "President" Piedra and their advisors met to discuss the situation. All of those present symbolized the passing of an era; and, confronting a desperate situation, the generals and doctors launched into long, rhetorical discourses. While the speakers reminisced about the revolution of 1933, World War II and Batista's regime, Cantillo received reports from the field in Santa Clara, Las Villas province. The "whole structure of the armed forces was falling apart" while the old men discussed irrelevancies.[45]

Some decisions were taken in that meeting, however, and Piedra, apparently developing an enthusiasm for power, wanted to order a ceasefire throughout the territory. General Cantillo opposed the idea; other advisors suggested that Piedra negotiate with Fidel Castro. Meanwhile some members of the press who had filtered into the room looked on. Piedra rejected the proposal to negotiate with Fidel because the magistrate considered Castro an outlaw, and he would not "deal with outlaws."[46] At that point, a discussion developed over what was juridically to be considered an act outside of the law; thus the classification of Castro as an outlaw was challenged. The word "revolution" happened to be mentioned, and the discussion reached a peak, with the doctors attempting to find a conceptual definition of revolution, the rights emanating from a de facto situation, and Cuba's long revolutionary tradition. General Loynaz del Castillo recalled the Constitution of the Republic in Arms, the patriotic behavior of General Maceo and General Máximo Gómez, and the historic right of citizens to fight despotism. Close to his one hundredth birthday, the *mambí* appeared more in accord with the Cuban youth and their right to resist the dictatorship than with the group of civilian "advisors." Since the situation threatened to get out of hand, and since it was already midmorning, Cantillo proposed that the whole group move to the Presidential Palace to install Piedra as president with the acquiescence of the Supreme Court. But the Court refused to legitimate Piedra as the president. Magistrates Julio Garcerán and Enrique Rodríguez Narezo delivered the Court's decision, which was that the situation was not a normal one, but the result of a "victorious revolution which has taken place in the nation's territory for a long period of time. That revolution is the fount of law . . . leaving the revolutionary forces in the position of organizing its own government."[47] Upon learning of the decision, Piedra told Cantillo that he would not serve as president without his fellow magistrates' approval and went home. The civilian "advisors" had no further role to play and also went home. General Cantillo hurried back to Columbia to a rapidly disintegrating army. The soldiers, tired of years of useless efforts and devoid of discipline, refused to obey orders. Some simply drifted out of the camp.

The end had come abruptly, although not as unexpectedly as had the coup d'etat seven years before. The time to flee the country could not be delayed further, and those who had been associated with the regime hurried to reach safety in exile. Major Jesús Blanco and Captain Julio Laurent of the Naval Intelligence Service, notorious for their participation in the aftermath of the Cienfuegos uprising, fled Cuba in "Martha II," the presidential yacht. Others escaped in their own private yachts and planes, or sought asylum in Latin American embassies.[48]

The Underground Acts

Batista's escape surprised the urban underground in Havana. Regardless of how sure of victory every militant was, the strong-man image of Fulgencio Batista y Zaldívar had been imprinted in the minds of young Cubans after almost 25 years of propaganda. Batista, *el hombre*, would not flee as Machado had done in 1933. Most militants were convinced that he would at least put up a last-minute struggle—that in the last moments he would commit suicide rather than suffer the humiliation of defeat and capture by the insurrectionary forces. Thus the urban underground was ready to fight the battle of Havana, but were less prepared to keep law and order in a victorious situation.

The immediate problem was the reaction of General Cantillo and of the army based at Columbia. The underground's priority was to establish a defense perimeter between the cities of Marianao and Havana to confront the tanks if and when they were released by Cantillo to try to establish control of the streets. The underground could not attack Columbia without the support of the guerrillas, but the latter were still in Santa Clara, Las Villas province. All ports, airports, small airstrips and exits were to be closed to prevent the regime's leaders from leaving. Underground planners also had to figure out how to stop mobs from assassinating government officials. As for arms, a system had to be developed in order to stop opportunists, last-minute insurgents, from passing as members of the resistance only to steal and to murder.

Shortly before dawn on January 1—while Cantillo and Piedra met—cars sped through the isolated streets of the capital shouting the news to an amazed population. At first the radio news bulletins were cautious. As if under the effect of a seven-year spell, the broadcasters announced: "There is an important announcement from Camp Columbia. There is something which is developing there, and we don't yet know what."[49] Then there was more music. Under the influence of old habits all radio stations in the capital remained silent, as if the official bureau for censorship were still working. The apparatus of Batista's bureaucracy still curtailed the impulses of the news broadcasters. Shortly before 9 AM radio and television station CMQ, the largest in the country, interrupted Beethoven's Ninth Symphony, and the announcer said simply.

"*Se fué Batista!*-Batista is gone!" Almost as a reflex, thousands went into the streets and marched toward Havana University. The day was just beginning.

Policemen and soldiers fresh from their New Year's celebration were stopped in the streets on their way to the precincts and their arms were taken away. Students from the DR and the M-26-7 posted themselves at various intersections to direct traffic and to ask people to stay home. At noon some policemen began shooting from their cars randomly into the crowds. Diehards were reported entrenched at various buildings throughout the city. During several encounters most of the *batistianos* chose to die fighting rather than surrender. By 1 PM the Principe Castle prison opened its gates to the militants of the DR, and all prisoners—political and common—were released. Before the day was over, all police precincts had surrendered to the underground.

Reports poured into underground headquarters from all over the capital. Lynching mobs marched through the streets on the lookout for former Batista henchmen and police officers. Such mobs were dangerous instruments of chaos, and most of the participants had never cooperated in the struggle against Batista. Some of the mobsters wore black-and-red bracelets with a "26" painted in while. Several people were shot to death in confrontations between mobs and underground patrols of the M-26-7 and the DR.[50]

Radio and television broadcasters did their utmost to incite passions, publicizing stories of crimes and terrible tortures, and showing an endless parade of people narrating the details of the horrendous persecutions which they and their families had suffered. Some reports were true, others were false, and the "victims" were mostly unstable people trying to gain attention; those who did suffer Batista's brutality were not parading in front of the television cameras, but attempting to keep order in the streets and preparing for an expected confrontation with his army. But the result was collective hysteria and a thirst for vengeance.

Perhaps because they now felt twinges of guilt, those who had turned their backs on the pleas of insurgents during seven years of struggle now emerged as the most energetic revolutionaries. Veterans of the underground struggle maintained their serenity in the face of the most brutal killers while *Revolucionarios de última hora* (last-minute revolutionaries) demanded the immediate execution of those who had become prisoners of the urban cadres. Police officers and well-known henchmen began surrendering at underground headquarters for protection against the mobs.

During the afternoon of January 1, various representatives of the underground visited Columbia and told the troops to surrender unconditionally to the insurrectionary forces. They left the military camp with the impression that the troops were totally demoralized, and that General Cantillo's orders were not being obeyed by other officers. Shortly after noon four tanks were ordered to move toward the university; the tanks left the military camp, but midway the troops abandoned the lethal machines and went home.

Before the end of the first day of 1959, the underground had established control of the capital's streets, police precincts and all official buildings. Patrols had been posted close to the headquarters of the navy in Old Havana, close to the bay; snipers had been placed in the tallest buildings around the university and arms were gathered at various undergound headquarters. But the insurrection had not yet attained a complete victory. There were still thousands of well-armed soldiers in Pinar del Rio, Matanzas, and Camagüey provinces. In Havana, La Cabaña Fortress was still under Cantillo's control, as was La Punta Fortress across the Bay of Havana. The course of events would depend mainly upon Fidel Castro and the rebel army. The Cuban people did not know how Castro would react to the Cantillo military junta—which the general was still frantically trying to put together—but urban Fighters continued to accumulate arms and ammunition, and waited for further developments.

Notes

1. Fulgencio Batista, *Cuba Betrayed* (New York: Vantage, 1962), pp. 123–24.
2. Earl T. Smith, *The Fourth Floor* (New York: Random House, 1962), p. 177, and Fulgencio Batista, *Respuesta* (Mexico: Editorial Botas, 1960), p. 132: Batista learned of the visit through "X-4," his personal secret service.
3. Mario Lazo, *American Policy Failures in Cuba, Dagger in the Heart!* (New York: Funk and Wagnalls, 1968), pp. 169–76. See also *Communist Threat to the United States Through the Caribbean*, Hearings before the Subcommittee of the Senate Judiciary Committee to Investigate the Administration of the Internal Security Act and other Internal Security Laws, 86th Congress, 2nd Sess., August 30, 1960, pp. 694–99.
4. Lazo, *American Policy Failures*, p. 169.
5. Report of the Senate Subcommittee on the Judiciary. *The Case of William Wieland* (1962), p. 109.
6. Dwight D. Eisenhower, *The White House Years: Waging Peace* (New York: Doubleday, 1965), p. 521.
7. Smith, *The Fourth Floor*, p. 165.
8. *Communist Threat through the Caribbean*, Hearings, 86th Congress, 2nd Sess., September 2, 8, 1960, p. 10.
9. Lazo, *American Policy Failures*, p. 174.
10. Smith, *The Fourth Floor*, pp. 169–74.
11. Ibid., p. 70.
12. Batista, *Respuesta*, pp. 101–02.
13. Lazo, *American Policy Failures*, p. 176; Smith, *The Fourth Floor*, pp. 173–76; and Batista, *Respuesta*, pp. 101–02.
14. Smith, *The Fourth Floor*, p. 181.
15. Batista, *Respuesta*, p. 130. On December 20, dictator Trujillo of the Dominican Republic, sent an offer to Batista through Colonel Juan A. Estévez Maymir, Cuban military attache to the Dominican Republic, for the landing of three army battalions of the Dominican army in Las Villas province, and three battalions in Oriente province to stop Fidel Castro from reaching power; Batista refused the offer for the singular reason, he said, that he did

not "want to deal with dictators." See José Suárez Nuñez, *El gran culpable* (Caracas: 1963), p. 108.

16. Ibid., p. 119. Batista was told of this meeting by Colonel Irenaldo García Báez, chief of the SIM, and son of the chief of the national police, General Pilar García.

17. Captain Carlos Durán Batista led army Company 92 and surrendered to the rebel army on July 28, 1958. See "Sección en Cuba," *Bohemia*, (Havana), January 11, 1959; Captain Gómez Oquendo, who also surrendered to the rebels, joined the M-26-7; together with Durán Batista and José Quevedo these officers wrote letters to their comrades in arms inviting them to join the rebel army. See *Bohemia*, (Havana), January 18, 1959: "Sección en Cubs," *Bohemía*, (Havana), January 11, 1959; and Batista, *Respuesta*, pp. 125–26. General Cantillo received letters from all three officers inviting him to defect to the rebels (Cantillo to the authors, December 4, 1972, Miami, Florida).

18. Cantillo claims he did not see Batista on December 22, and that Batista did not order him to approach Fidel Castro as stated by Hugh Thomas, *Cuba: The Pursuit of Freedom* (New York: Harper and Row, 1971), p 1022; Cantillo arrived in Havana on December 24, but was not received by Batista until after the meeting with Castro on December 28, 1958 (Authors' interview with Cantillo).

19. Cantillo told the authors that "the situation was so dangerous, so many events going on at the same time, that I took every precautionary measure against any betrayal on the part of the Tabernillas."

20. Letter from Lieutenant Carlos Pina to the authors (February 22, 1973, Maryland).

21. Cantillo to the authors. For a different version, see "Juzgan en Ciudad Libertad al ex-general Eulogio Cantillo," *Diario de la Marina*, (Havana), May 16, 1959, pp. 1, 9b.

22. Fidel Castro, "Discurso en el Parque de Céspedes," *Avance* (Havana), edición extraordinaria, January 4, 1959, pp. 2–5; Luis Conte Agüero, *Los dos rostros de Fidel Castro* (Mexico, 1960); and Thomas, *Cuba, The Pursuit of Freedom*, pp. 1024–25.

23. Cantillo told the authors that Castro did not object to Tabernilla's involvement at this point but that he did object to Cantillo's return to Havana for fear that "you will be placed under arrest and the plan will fail."

24. Authors' interview with Raúl Chibás (December 1972, New York, New York).

25. Castro, "Discurso en el Parque," pp. 2, 5.

26. Evidence to the authors from Cantillo and Chibás in interviews with the authors.

27. Batista, *Respuesta*, p. 128.

28. Cantillo to the authors.

29. Ibid. Batista made only one reference to Tabernilla within the context of this conversation, and that concerned Batista's request that Cantillo not report his conversation with Castro to Tabernilla, Sr. See Batista, *Respuesta*, p. 128.

30. Asked why he thought Cantillo had obeyed Tabernilla, and then, changing position, decided to follow his orders to the end, Batista replied that "in those days of turbulence which not only affected public order, but also the psyches. Cantillo received orders from his immediate superior officer [Tabernilla] which he followed, but once he realized the enormity of his mission,

he decided—again I imagine in hypothesis—to select the path that through me would facilitate a peaceful constitutional transition." Batista's comments were transcribed and delivered to the authors (unsigned) by Enrique Pizzi de Porras, a Cuban political commentator since the 1930s, close to Batista during 1940–44, and 1952–59, who interviewed Batista and asked questions on behalf of the authors to Batista, in Portugal, in 1970. Batista's comments were presented to the authors under the title "Informe como conclusión de coordinación y ajuste de datos obtenidos en conversaciones diversas que conducen coincidentemente a un esclarecimiento."

31. Evidence of Cantillo to the authors. See also Batista, *Respuesta*, p. 129; and *Bohemia* (Havana), January 11, 1959, pp. 17–31.

32. Batista, *Respuesta*, p. 112. Batista quoted a letter sent to him by General Marcelo Tabernilla, dated April 12, 1959, Miami, Florida.

33. Cantillo to the authors.

34. Surprisingly, this opinion was voiced by all high-ranking officers interviewed in the process of writing this book; yet it does not take into account the national military situation at that point, in which the rebel army was advancing on every front, and the regular army refused to continue fighting.

35. Cantillo participated in more than one conspiracy to overthrow Batista. He managed to clear his position with Batista regarding the meeting with Castro on December 28, by claiming he had received orders from his immediate superior officer, while at the same time recommending to Batista that the Tabernillas be summarily executed. Cantillo kept Castro waiting, while he received command of the armed forces from Batista without the use of violence. When all seemed lost, Cantillo attempted to block the insurrection's way to power by releasing Barquín from prison.

36. *Constitución de la República de Cuba* (Havana: Editorial Lex, 1957), pp. 23–25.

37. According to one author, Piedra was present at Batista's resignation. See Thomas, *Cuba: The Pursuit of Freedom*, p. 1026; but Cantillo, who was present at the last meeting told the authors that Piedra did not know what was taking place until after Batista left Cuba.

38. Batista, *Cuba Betrayed*, pp. 138–40.

39. Ibid.

40. *Bohemia* (Havana, January 11, 1959, pp. 17–31.

41. Batista, *Respuesta*, p. 144. In a letter to Colonel Juan A. Estévez Maymir, General Tabernilla, Sr. wrote that Batista's decision to leave so promptly "did not give us time to withdraw our money from the banks . . . neither to be able to save some personal properties." Batista's decision amounted to a betrayal of the military. Similarly, Tabernilla, Sr. wrote to Batista charging him with cowardice and refuting Batista's interpretation of the role of the army officers as published in Batista's *Respuesta*, pp. 17–31. Tabernilla, Sr. stated that Batista's treason had destroyed the regular army, see José Suárez Núñez, *El gran culpable* (Caracas: 1963). pp. 155–63; 168–74.

42. Batista claims that the chiefs asked for his resignation and that he complied at 2:00 AM on January 1, 1959. See Batista, *Respuesta*, pp. 144–45. All evidence indicates that Batista's statement is false. Cantillo told the authors that Batista wrote his resignation in his library at Kuquine while they held their final meeting before moving on to Columbia, during the evening of December 31. The last information appears to be correct, for at the New

Year's Eve reception, and in the midst of the discussions between the chiefs and Batista on the military situation, there was no time to be spent in dictating a formal resignation, and Batista had planned his escape before that meeting. See also, the letter from General Tabernilla, Sr. to Batista, dated August 24, 1960. Riviera Beach, Florida in José Suárez Núñez, *El gran culpable*, pp. 168–74.

43. Cantillo to the authors.
44. Ibid.
45. Ibid.
46. Ibid.
47. Authors' interview with former magistrate, Julio Garcerán, February 12, 1973, Schenectady, New York. For a sequence of the events, see Leovigildo Ruiz, *Diario de una traición* (Miami, 1960), pp. 8–9.
48. *Bohemia* (Havana), March 1, 1959, pp. 36–38.
49. Personal recollections of the authors.
50. Authors' interviews with underground cadre members Julio Aldama Heros, DR (February 2, 1973, New York, New York); and Alberto L. Rubio, M-26-7 (February 2, 1973, New York, New York). Various personal recollections were gathered by the authors from people residing in different neighborhoods in Havana: José Osorio, La Víbora (December 3, 1971, West New York, New Jersey); René Montenegro, Old Havana (December 3, 1971, West New York); María S. Iglesias, El Príncipe (December 10, 1972, West New York); and Francisco Remedios, Vedado (December 19, 1972, West New York).

15

The Perils of
Counterrevolution

Castro Reacts

As soon as he learned of the developments in Havana, Fidel made a dramatic address to the nation. He told the Cuban people that General Cantillo had allowed Batista to flee the country unpunished; a junta had been organized with Cantillo as its figurehead; and the general had refused to surrender the Leoncio Vidal Camp at Santa Clara to the combined M-26-7 and DR guerrillas. The communique announced the possibility of further bloodshed. "Whatever the news from the capital," Castro announced, "our troops must not, under any circumstances, call a halt to military operations."[1] Castro's orders were clear: "Our forces must continue operations on every front against the enemy. Evidently there has been a coup d'etat in the capital. The conditions under which that coup took place are ignored by the rebel army."[2] Castro repeated: "Military operations shall continue without alteration as long as this rebel headquarters does not order otherwise." A ceasefire would not be declared until all military bodies had been placed under the command of the rebel army, and no coup d'etat would be acceptable, for that would mean "taking victory away from the people." After seven years of struggle the victory had to be absolute so that "never again can another March 10 take place in our fatherland. Let no one be confused or mistaken: orders are to remain on the alert."

The rebel leader warned the workers to be prepared for a general revolutionary strike that would be called to counteract attempts at a military coup.[3] Castro ordered all forces to march on Santiago de Cuba and to prepare to attack the city. Meanwhile, Major Víctor Mora was ordered to subdue all cities in Camagüey province, and to close access to the city of Camagüey from Santa Cruz del Sur on the south and Nuevitas on the north. Raúl Castro was ordered to advance on Guantánamo, and Major Belarmino Castilla to threaten Mayarí and to demand the army's surrender. Victoria de las Tunas and Holguín were to be attacked by guerrillas under the command of Major Eduardo Sardiñas and others.

News of the events taking place in Havana reached Santiago de Cuba in the early morning hours of January 1. Santiago was under army control and a battle with the guerrillas appeared inevitable. On the city's outskirts, Major Hubert Matos' Column No. 9, "Antonio 'Tony' Guiteras," continued to advance from the southwest, while the army held its well-entrenched positions.[4] Leading Columns No. 1 and No. 3, and supported by Column No. 10, Castro began moving toward Santiago de Cuba. On the march, he released a communique, a firm and definitive ultimatum: the regular army was to dispose of its arms before 6 PM, or the guerrillas would take the city by assault.[5]

On December 31, Castro had sent a message to Colonel José Rego Rubido, chief of the army in Santiago. In essence, Castro's message said that it appeared that General Cantillo was not going to fulfill his original promise, and that the plans delineated during the Castro-Cantillo meeting on December 28 had been changed at the last minute without the rebel army's knowledge. Things were not clear, and Fidel could wait no longer. If hostilities started anew, then Castro would demand the surrender of the army in Santiago. Evidently there was some confusion, and the messenger asked Rego Rubido for the surrender of Santiago; the colonel answered this demand in a letter, saying: "Arms are not surrendered to an ally, nor are they delivered without honor."[6] If Castro had no confidence in him, all previous agreements would be considered void. If Castro attacked Santiago, the regular army would be obliged to fight.

Fidel's answer was prompt. A most lamentable error had been committed in the wording of the message, probably due to the "excitement with which I talked to the messenger." At this point Castro did not know that Batista would be permitted to leave Cuba, and he was still concerned about the problems of dealing with the caudillo. Castro again told Rego Rubido that whatever was taking place in the capital he could wait no longer, for the rebel army was in danger of losing all the ground it had recently gained. Castro's main goal was that "the revolution fulfill its destiny, I am also worried that because of an unjustified excess of scruples, the military will facilitate the departure of the guilty ones who, with their vast fortunes abroad, will continue to do all possible harm to our country." He assured the colonel that "power does not interest me, nor do I plan to exercise it." He would only "watch, so that all the sacrifices of so many compatriots are not frustrated, regardless of my future destiny." The leader of the insurrection repeated that in the event that hostilities broke out the rebels would demand the city's surrender. But that did not mean that "we want you to surrender without resistance, because I know—even though lacking a reason to fight—that the Cuban military defends its positions and has cost me many lives." More than allies, Castro hoped that the military "will become our *compañeros* . . . and I hope that you, *compañero*, do not misunderstand my words."[7] Colonel Rego Rubido was glad to answer that evidently there had been a mistake in the wording of Castro's original message, and the colonel also felt that it was a shame that the guilty ones flee the country unpunished. "I am one of those who thinks," the colonel wrote, "that it is absolutely necessary to set an example in Cuba for those who take advantage of power and commit all sorts of punishable acts."[8] But after a few hours, Castro was forced to act on his realization that every minute the rebel army stayed out of Santiago de Cuba, the course of the insurrection was still undecided. He issued his ultimatum when he learned of Cantillo's maneuver in Havana; and Colonel Rego Rubido, confronted by Cantillo's fait accompli in the capital, flew by helicopter to see Castro. Fidel asked the colonel for permission to talk to all the army officers and they met at a place called Escande, on the outskirts of the city. After talking to the officers, Fidel was able to enter the city without firing a shot. In turn, Castro appointed Rego Rubido as commander in chief of the revolutionary army, a gesture that pacified the colonel's troops.

That evening at the Céspedes Park, before an emotional audience, Fidel proclaimed the victory of the insurrection. Seated close to him were Dr. Manuel Urrutia and the archbishop of Santiago, Monsignor Enrique Pérez Serantes. Fidel reiterated the designation of Dr. Urrutia as the provisional president of the revolutionary government and assured army officers who had not been involved in crimes against the people that the revolution would be generous.

Fidel summarized the historical significance of the victory, proclaiming that "this time the revolution will truly reach power." It would not be like in 1898, when the United States intervened at the last minute after 30 years of struggle for independence to make themselves "masters of the situation." The victory of the insurrection would lead to a true revolution, and would not permit another Batista to betray the process, as in 1933, by instituting a military dictatorship. The promises made during the long process of the insurrection would be fulfilled, and the people would not be frustrated, like in 1944, when they were "denied power by the grafters." Fidel promised always to speak to the people with loyalty and frankness, declaring that "hatred, that shadow of ambition and tyranny, is now expelled from the republic. Let nobody think that I pretend to exercise any power above the president of the republic."[9]

Castro moved rapidly, an insurrectionist at his best. He was fully aware of the fact that in Havana the military was still trying to block the victory of the insurrection, and had already ordered "Che" Guevara and Camilo Cienfuegos to move on Havana. The situation was still potentially dangerous: if a military junta succeeded in establishing a coalition government with anti-Batista figures, and if the regular army rallied behind that government, the momentum of the insurrection could be lost. The people and the insurgents feared a battle for Havana. Everyone was convinced that if even the few thousand troops who were still encamped at La Cabaña, La Punta and Columbia decided to put up a fight, casualties would reach incalculable heights. With the air force completely untouched, the regular army might still pose a serious threat.

The first rebels to reach the capital were the guerrillas of Eloy Gutiérrez Menoyo, followed by those of the DR who marched into the Presidential Palace and Havana University. The guerrilla columns headed by "Che" Guevara and

Cienfuegos approached Havana while hundreds joined the rebels on their march toward the capital.

Meanwhile, Castro announced that Santiago de Cuba would be the provisional capital of Cuba, proclaimed a revolutionary general strike, and kept himself abreast of the situation in Havana. Dr. Urrutia named the members of his cabinet. They included: Dr. José Miró Cardona as prime minister; Dr. Roberto Agramonte in charge of foreign relations: Dr. Julio Martínez Páez in charge of health; Raúl Cepero Bonilla in commerce; Manuel Fernández in charge of labor; Armando Hart Dávalos conducting matters of education; Enrique Oltusky in charge of communications; Faustino Pérez directing recovery of stolen goods; Manuel Ray Rivero heading public works; Regino Boti in charge of economic matters; and Raúl Chibás, Angel Fernández Rodríguez, Humberto Sorí Marín, Augusto Martínez Sánchez, Elena Mederos, Luis Buch Rodríguez and Gaspar Buch as advisors to the president. Colonel José Rego Rubido was reaffirmed as chief of the army and Major Efigenio Ameijeiras as chief of the national police.[10]

The cabinet was fully controlled by the M-26-7. Miró Cardona, Cepero Bonilla, Boti, Elena Mederos, Angel Fernández and Luis and Gaspar Buch had led the urban branch of the movement, or were active in the civic institutions which were considered a front organization of the M-26-7. Dr. Agramonte and Chibás represented the Ortodoxo group of politicians who followed Fidel's orders throughout the insurrection. Julio Martínez Páez was the chief surgeon of the rebel army, and Humberto Sorí Marín had been in charge of legal matters for the rebel army. Armando Hart, Faustino Pérez, Enrique Oltusky, Manuel Ray and Manuel Fernández had been leaders in the urban branch of the M-26-7, while Augusto Martínez Sánchez served in Raúl Castro's guerrilla front. By and large the cabinet was controlled by the urban branch of the M-26-7, and included mostly middle-class professionals. There were no peasants in the cabinet, no black Cubans and only one woman.

The Mirage of Power

At Columbia, General Eulogio Cantillo confronted the most difficult situation of his life; so serious were the dangers as time went by that the general thought he would not emerge safely from the maneuver in which he had embroiled himself.[11] Following the refusal of the Supreme Court to recognize magistrate Piedra as the provisional president, Cantillo found himself quite alone in the midst of the crisis.

The general's options were limited by two factors: the disposition of the guerrillas to fight, and the revolutionary general strike. The columns of "Che" Guevara and Cienfuegos were two of the most aggressive forces in the rebel army, and, supported by the DR's guerrillas and the urban underground, they certainly posed a serious challenge to the regular troops remaining in Havana. In the event of a battle for the capital all odds appeared to signal the defeat of the regular troops. Their passivity could be seen in their adamant refusal to engage the rebels in Santa Clara, Las Villas province. There was nothing to indicate that at the last minute the troops would be ready to fight a losing battle. The results of any bloody confrontation would fall squarely upon Cantillo's shoulders. Meanwhile, the people answered Castro's call for a general strike with jubilation. The country's paralysis was universal, and nothing indicated that Cantillo's orders to go back to work would be obeyed, or the streets would be cleared of throngs of elated Cubans. All the police precincts had surrendered to the urban fighters who had established advance positions blocking the possible entrances into Havana from Columbia—two bridges and a tunnel. The very possibility of a struggle to death for control of Havana was so discouraging to the regular troops that many started abandoning the perimeters of the military bases, changing into civilian clothes and putting some safe distance between dangerous areas and themselves.

The mirage of power did not last long for Cantillo. The general reasoned that only a military junta led by an officer with certain special qualities could hope to succeed in rallying the armed forces, placating the insurgents and gaining some popular support. That officer should have an anti-Batista background, but he should also be loyal to the idea that the "military was the country's backbone."[12] He should also possess the capacity to instill "leadership and morale among the troops." General Cantillo concluded that only Colonel Ramón Barquín met those qualifications, to which had to be added an important element: Barquín's ambition for power and notoriety. Thus, Cantillo ordered Barquín's release from the Isle of Pines Penitentiary and his immediate return to Columbia.

Upon Colonel Barquín's arrival at Columbia, Cantillo informed him of the situation. He told Barquín that command of the armed forces was his, and suggested that the colonel not arrest any officers, but rather try to unite everyone behind his leadership. That attitude would instill confidence throughout the ranks and the army might then be able to act cohesively before the insurrectionists. The two agreed that the top priority was to stop the revolutionaries from reaching power. Carlos Cantillo, chief of the army in Matanzas province, would assist in stopping the rebels' movement toward Havana, but Barquín had to move very quickly and take full advantage of the next few hours. Cantillo then announced that he was retiring to his personal quarters, while Barquín suggested that Cantillo take a plane out of Cuba immediately for, in the event that everything failed. Castro had already charged him with treason. Cantillo refused, went to bed at 11 PM, and the following morning he was placed under arrest by Colonel Barquín.[13]

Colonel Barquín appointed his own men to key positions in the armed forces: Admiral Andrés González, navy; Major Vicente León León, national police; Colonel Manuel Varela Castro, chief of the army at La Cabaña; Major Enrique Borbonet, chief of infantry division "Alejandro Rodríguez"; Captain

Vicente Villafaña, chief of the air force; Captain Teobaldo Cuervo, medical division: Major José E. Monteagudo, chief of the Fifth District, and Major Clemente Gómez Sucre, chief of the municipal police.[14]

Colonel Barquín attempted to play the role of moderator between the regular army and the insurrectionary forces. His only instrument for nego-tiation was the threat of a last-minute violent confrontation within Havana. In a patronizing statement, the colonel addressed himself to Fidel, "Che" Guevara and Faure Chomón, saying: "We salute the Army of Liberation and we say to Fidel Castro, "Che"and Chomón that we shall not give the order to shoot . . . "The colonel ignored the proclamation of President Urrutia's provi-sional government and, trying to maneuver for a position, invited the rebels to "come to Havana to form a government"; they would then find that "the army was ready to cooperate."[15] As had Cantillo before him, Colonel Ramón Barquín tried to outmaneuver those who had fought long and hard for a true revolution. One of Barquín's gestures toward the rebels was to place Cantillo under arrest, but as Guevara's and Cienfuegos's guerrilla fighters approached the capital, the colonel's enthusiasm diminished considerably.

In the streets of Havana, the urban fighters prepared for a confrontation with Barquín, who at the last moment was trying to save the remnants of the Batista dictatorship from total destruction. The DR ordered its men to move toward the Miramar suburbs and to approach the military airfields from the north. Urban cadres were posted all along the main road linking Columbia with the Almendares River, which separated Havana from Marianao City, the location of the military installation and of Barquín's weakening hopes.

Colonel Barquín was confronted with the same situation which had, in the final analysis, led to his release from prison by Cantillo. If the colonel decided to fight the insurgents with what was left of the army, his defeat would have been assured, and his death inevitable (either on the field of battle or against the execution wall). It was too dramatic a path for Barquín to follow. His best alternative was not to press for any demands, not to repeat his invitation to the rebels to come to Havana to form a government, but rather to act as a well-meaning, prorevolutionary officer who knew when the time had come to step aside.

Camilo Cienfuegos' guerrillas stopped at El Cotorro[16]; from there the rebel chief continued his advance on Columbia supported by OA militants and guerrillas from the DR, about 500 men in all. Camilo ordered about 200 of his fighters together with the DR guerrillas to move towards Columbia by circling the military camp and approaching it from the north.

"Che" Guevara approached La Cabaña Fortress supported by Víctor Bordón's guerrillas and by hundreds of people who joined the rebel forces. When "Che" arrived at La Cabaña, he was welcomed by Colonel Manuel Varela Castro, who delivered the command of the military camp to the rebel leader. La Punta Fortress, across the Bay of Havana, offered no resistance to the rebels, and the building housing the navy's general headquarters was also taken over without resistance. Camilo Cienfuegos' guerrillas entered Columbia amidst the salutes of the regular troops who had no intention of fighting an armed citizenry.

Command of the army in Havana was delivered by Colonel Ramón Barquín to Cienfuegos. The victory of the insurrection was now completely guaranteed, for the last hope of all those who had wanted the overthrow of Batista, but not the victory of the insurrection, had been eliminated. In spite of Barquín's involvement in a conspiracy against Batista in 1956, most officers who favored the survival of the army as the strongest political institution in the country, saw in Barquín a last chance to sustain some power. Also, anti-Batista elements who had collaborated with the Central Intelligence Agency appeared around Barquín during those critical hours in Havana. Justo Carrillo, the leader of a small anti-Batista group called Montecristi, and Andrés Suárez, strong supporters of Barquín as an alternative to Fidel Castro, saw their hopes extinguished with the arrival of Major Camilo Cienfuegos at Columbia.[17]

By January 3, the insurrection had established control over the entire island. Camagüey and Matanzas provinces were under the control of the M-26-7; and Las Villas province under the joint command of the DR and the M-26-7 guerrilla forces, with guerrillas of the Second Front of Escambray occupying various small towns and villages in the province.[18]

In Havana, Major Rolando Cubela issued a demand in the name of the Directorio Revolucionario addressed to the M-26-7. The DR demanded "the participation of the revolutionary organizations which have overthrown the dictatorship" in the provisional government. "It is therefore necessary," Cubela stated, "that the personality of its members and the blood shed by them be fully recognized." The DR "must participate in the organization of the provisional government and in the discussions for a date for general and democratic elections, and in the creation of a technical army."[19]

The DR's demand caused consternation among thousands of people who thought that all conflict had ended with the departure of Batista. Some student militants realized that the M-26-7 controlled the government, and they were elated at the demands, at the same time pressing for more radical resolutions against what they viewed as an abuse of power on the part of Fidel Castro. Others, however, reacted angrily toward Cubela for fear that the people think of the DR as an opportunist organization, and of the militants as being politically ambitious. Such individuals felt that the DR had fought for the overthrow of the dictatorship, not to demand participation in the spoils of power, and that those who wanted to become politically involved should wait until the organization of political parties and the elections.

Armando Hart demanded that drastic action be taken against the student occupants of the Presidential Palace, so that they would leave the building before President Urrutia arrived from Santiago de Cuba on January 5. Camilo

Cienfuegos issued orders to his guerrillas to remain on the alert in the event they were ordered to forcefully remove the men of the DR from the premises of the Presidential Palace. Student militants moved toward the palace to reinforce the position in the event of a confrontation with the M-26-7. Tension increased, and the people of Havana remained confused as the crisis appeared to escalate.

On January 5, Dr. Urrutia arrived in Havana, and went directly to Columbia. "Che" Guevara and Cienfuegos left Havana and went to see Fidel for instructions. Once at Columbia, Dr. Urrutia formed a committee with various members of his cabinet whose task was to parley with Cubela and Chomón at the palace to avert a violent confrontation. The president's committee, including Dr. Roberto Agramonte, José Manuel Gutiérrez and Manuel Ray, met with Cubela and Chomón. The leaders of the DR were promised that the government would include them in any discussions, and that the president and the cabinet fully recognized the revolutionary merits of the organization. The committee asked the two leaders to postpone their differences for a while, because the unity of all revolutionary organizations was essential.[20] Cubela noted that neither Fidel Castro nor the president had consulted with the DR when a provisional government was being organized. He pointed out that the M-26-7 was not the only movement which had carried out insurrectionary activities, but that it had monopolized all power from the start.[21] However, Chomón was willing to accept the committee's arguments, and in the name of the DR agreed to vacate the premises and to welcome Dr. Urrutia as the president of the republic. A few hours later, President Urrutia arrived at the Presidential Palace and was well received by the militants of the DR.[22]

Fidel embarked upon a long march on the Central Highway from Santiago to Havana. This movement was intelligently designed to secure the support of the people at large, and to move into the capital followed by thousands of allies. The long trip also allowed for time to solve the DR problem. Fidel stopped at the house of José Antonio Echeverría's family in Cárdenas, Matanzas province, to ask José Antonio's sister, Lucy, to help placate Cubela and Chomón. Lucy Echeverría agreed to help for the sake of the revolution, and Fidel continued his march toward the capital.[23]

Castro stopped at every junction to address the people who lined the highway to see the leader of the Sierra Maestra. His extraordinary physical stamina served him well, for he talked endlessly, reviewing the events of previous weeks, alerting the people to the fact that Cantillo was a traitor, promising that the insurrection had opened a path for revolution and that the revolution would punish those who were responsible for so many years of suffering, and explaining why it had been necessary to call for a general strike.

Fidel was asked whether the M-26-7 would become a political party now that the insurrection was over. It would, he said, because that was the only possible way to struggle revolutionary and democratically. As a political party,

Left to right: Armando Hart, Manuel Urrutia Lleó and Faustino Pérez with Fidel Castro before boarding a flight to Havana, January 2, 1959 (Reprinted by permission of Yale University Library).

Major Fidel Castro with Major Camilo Cienfuegos (to his left) addressing the Cuban people at the presidential palace, January 8, 1959, Havana (Reprinted by permission of Yale University Library).

the M-26-7 would be a "party that represents the ideals for which we have struggled for over two years in the Sierra Maestra." Regarding his candidacy for the presidency, Fidel said: "I have the problem of the constitutional requirement on age, 32 as opposed to 36 years old, to be president,,, and he did not expect to be the "next president elect in Cuba in the first free elections we hold.[24]" On the march, thousands, including many who carried arms, joined the caravan. In Havana the people awaited Fidel's arrival and followed all events via television, which was to become the most important vehicle of political education in the Cuban revolution.

The Revolution

Finally, Fidel Castro reached Havana on January 8, 1959, a day after the U.S. government had extended diplomatic recognition to the government of President Urrutia. The foreign minister of Cuba, Roberto Agramonte, received the U.S. note, which stated that the government of the United States was pleased to recognize the provisional government of President Urrutia. The note also expressed the "good will of the government and the people of the United States towards the new government and the people of Cuba."[25] Few people, however, paid any attention to the announcement that the United Slates was granting recognition to the revolutionary government. Castro was the main attraction and everything else was anticlimactic.

At that point, Fidel Castro represented a giant among all previous caudillos in Cuba. Ramón Grau San Martín ("El Lider"), Eduardo R. Chibás ("El Adalid") and Batista ("El Hombre") all seemed like clay figurines compared to Fidel. The Sierra Maestra leader represented a continuation of the *mambises* of the wars of independence. The people viewed Fidel as the nation's savior. Fidel's intelligence was compared to that of José Martí, while in physical appearance he was said to be the image of General Antonio Maceo, the great hero of the wars of independence. He had just defeated Batista; thus his *machismo* was beyond challenge. As for his military strategies, Cubans compared Fidel favorably to Simón Bolívar.

Castro was popularly named the "Savior of the Fatherland" and the "Maximum Leader." He was called to lead the nation forward to fulfill Cuba's destiny, and to take the reins of power. Many now began calling the revolution "Fidel's revolution." The believers in *santería* saw in Fidel the reincarnation of both Martí and Maceo, who had been sent save the nation and the people at a time of crisis. The *santeros* placed their special "protections" along the path followed by Fidel.

As Castro, surrounded by guerrillas, entered the capital, emotion reached incalculable heights. Banners and flags hung from almost every building in Havana. The national anthem was heard from loud speakers all along the way, as was the M-26-7 battle hymn. Children dressed in fatigue uniforms and, adorned with red and black bracelets, threw flowers at Castro. Old ladies blessed the leader and prayed for his health. Young women tried to get close to the revolutionary leader to touch him. The guerrillas marched waving to the crowds, their uniforms decorated with religious medals and *santeria* bead collars of various colors, white and red yellow, white, black, and white and blue combinations; some guerrillas also wore red handkerchiefs around their necks.[26]

Castro stopped at the Presidential Palace to pay his respects to Urrutia. He went to the balcony, and addressed the thousands of people who surrounded the building. An ovation that lasted close to 15 minutes welcomed the Maximum Leader. Castro gave a short, but emotional speech. He closed by raising his right hand, and lowering his voice. The multitude quieted. In a dramatic voice he asked Cubans to open a path for him to walk through. He would show the world, he said, how disciplined Cubans were.[27] As he moved toward the palace's exit, the people, as if enchanted, opened a path for the Maximum Leader. They stood on the sidelines as he walked through, saluting his followers. This act impressed everyone who saw the event. For customarily emotional, undisciplined Cubans it was unprecedented.

Fidel marched toward Columbia, where more thousands were awaiting his arrival. Seated behind the speaker's podium were former president Carlos Prío, former Auténtico politicians. Ortodoxos, labor leaders, representatives of the industrial sector and other professionals. Some of them had participated in the second assault on the Presidential Palace. Also seated were veterans of the wars of independence, some of whom still understood what was going on, others who had been brought to the event by members of their families who were using the old men as shields to approach the newly powerful.

In front of the podium opened the wide space where the troops marched on Batista's September 4 anniversary. There were more regular troops than guerrilla fighters in the crowd. Castro stood on the small platform that Batista had used so many times before. Close to him, also on the podium, was Camilo Cienfuegos, whom the Sierra Maestra leader would ask from time to time, "How am I doing Camilo, I am doing all right?" and Camilo would answer, "Yes, Fidel, you are doing all right."

"The revolution," Castro said, "no longer faces a belligerent army." He asked, "Who can now become the worst enemies of the revolution," and answered himself: "The worst enemies of the revolution in the future are we, the revolutionaries." He continued: "I swear before my compatriots that if any of our *compañeros*, or if our movement, or if I could be an obstacle to peace, from this very moment the people can decide about us, and tell us what to do. I am a man who knows when to leave, because I have demonstrated that more than once in my life, and because that is the way I have taught my *compañeros*." To this, the people reacted in unison, demanding that Castro stay.

"Now the republic enters a new phase." he said, "and so does the revolution. And it is not fair, nor just, that the cult of personality and ambition endanger the destiny of the revolution, which is what interests the people most." The cult of personality, the traditional sickness of Cuba's politics and government, the basis for *caudillismo*, the traditional end of the most pure ideals of Latin American revolutions, would never emerge again in Cuba, lest the revolution be frustrated by its own leaders. In order to consolidate the revolution, Castro said that it was necessary that no more blood be spilled. His greatest preoccupation was that no one overseas should be able to say "that there was more blood, more Cuban blood shed, because then this revolution has not been an example."

While the guerrilla leader addressed the nation, several white pigeons, a symbol of peace, were let loose. One of them circled above Castro's head, and gently landed on his shoulder. A silence fell over the multitude. Former Batista soldiers took off their caps, and placed their right hand on their chests, standing at attention. Many fell on their knees in prayer. The believers touched their white and red collars. Castro stood with the white pigeon on his shoulder, the symbol of a new Cuba. Throughout the nation this event caused awe. Very few people doubted that Fidel Castro was, indeed, a man with a mission.

"We can not become dictators," he continued. "We shall never need to use force because we have the people, and because the people shall judge, and because the day the people want, I shall leave."

The revolutionary strike had ended, and the revolutionary government began its difficult tasks. The people returned to their daily routine with new hope, and with deep confidence in the nation's future. A militaristic, corrupt dictatorship had been overthrown. The insurrection had demonstrated that Cubans would not stand calmly before tyranny, that the very force of the insurrection would deter others from betraying the historical process and erecting new and more savage regimes of militarism and terror. No one doubted, on that day, that Cuba was on its way to democratic, urgently needed reforms, to a system under which individual rights were to be fully respected, and economic and social progress would be effected through the efforts of a united and free people.

Notes

1. *Proclama del Ejército Rebelde*, Comandancia General, January 1, 1959, See also *Bohemia* (Havana), January 2, 1969, p. 74.
2. Ibid., p. 1.
3. *Revolución* (Havana), July 26, 1962, p. 8.
4. Authors' interview with guerrilla Captain Dionisio Suárez, of Column No. 9, October 27, 1972, New York, New York.
5. *Revolución* (Havana), July 26, 1962, p. 8.
6. *El Avance* (Havana), edición extraordinaria, January 4, 1959, p. 2. See also *Revolución* (Havana), January 5, 1959, pp. 1, 4.
7. Ibid., p. 2.
8. Ibid., p. 4. On May 29, 1959, 41 lesser participants in the 1952 coup d'etat were tried by a revolutionary court presided over by DR Captain Jaun Nuiry

Sánchez; sentences ranged from 25 to five years in prison. Defendents included, among others: Colonels Ignacio L. Castell and Sixto Guerra Albo, Brigadier Julio S. Gómez, Major Felipe Mirabal, 25 years; Colonel Carlos Cantillo, 20 years; Ernesto de la Fé, 15 years; Lieutenant Colonel Victor Dueñas Robert and Major General Eulogio Cantillo Porras, 10 years. Thirty-one officers were found guilty, and seven not guilty. See "El 10 de marzo en el banquillo," *Bohemia* (Havana), June 17, 1959, pp. 64–98.

9.   *El Avance* (Havana), January 6, 1959, pp. 1, 3–4.

10.   *Prensa Libre* (Havana), January 6, 1959, p. 1.

11.   Authors' interview with General Eulogio Cantillo (December 4, 1972, Miami, Florida).

12.   Ibid.

13.   Ibid. Cantillo, who remains convinced that Barquín could have stopped Castro and saved the situation for the army, told the authors that Barquín had been "guided by hatred and not by reason," and that his (Cantillo's) selection of Barquin had been a bad choice and his most costly mistake.

14.   "Cantillo y Piedra: la fuga de Batista," *Carteles* (Havana), January 4, 1959, pp. 4–12: and *Prensa Libra* (Havana), January 6, 1959, p. 1.

15.   "Cantillo y Piedra," pp. 4–12.

16.   Andrés Suárez, "The Cuban Revolution: The Road to Power, State of the Research," *Latin American Research Review*, 7, no. 3 (Fall 1972); p. 22. Suárez, who was close to Barquín at the time, states that Cienfuegos telephoned Barquín asking and being granted permission to bring his forces into the military camps. Although the source is unimpeachable, that version may be what Barquín told Suárez, since it was the former who talked to Cienfuegos. One of the authors who entered Columbia with Cienfuegos' guerrillas understands that the rebel leader called Barquín to alert him that any bloodshed would be Barquín's responsibility; that he was marching toward Columbia to take over command of the armed forces as ordered by Fidel Castro. Thus, upon arrival, Cienfuegos took over from Barquin without hesitation and in full control of the situation. The poor impression Suárez received upon the arrival of the badly dressed guerrillas was probably the same that caused the regular army to underestimate the fighting capability of the rebel army in the Sierra Maestra.

17.   In early 1958, Justo Carrillo, leader of a small anti-Batista group called Montecristi, saw in Barquín a military counterweight to Fidel Castro; trying to free Barquín from prison, Carrillo went for help to General Darcey, chief of the U.S. delegation on the Cuban-American Defense Board. Carrillo's argument was that if Fidel reached power "the U.S. could not count on the Cuban [regular] Army." See Hugh Thomas, *Cuba: The Pursuit of Freedom* (New York: Harper and Row, 1971), p. 995. Thomas quotes from Justo Carrillo's manuscript, pp. 38–39. Still trying to use Barquín to stop the insurrection from obtaining a clear victory over the regular army, in December 1958, Justo Carrillo and an aide, Andrés Suárez, established contact with the CIA's representatives in Havana and Miami, an agent named Beardsley and Robert Rogers. See Thomas, *Cuba: The Pursuit of Freedom*, p. 1019 quoting from Carrillo's manuscript, p. 44, William H. Carr of the CIA dispatched a man to the Isle of Pines Pentitentiary (December 30) with $100,000 to be offered to the prison commander for Barquín's release. Barquín's release

was not effected on December 30, but on January 1–2, 1959 under General Cantillo's orders (Authors interview with General Eulogio Cantillo). Another individual involved in attempting to release Barquín from prison as early as October 1957, was Rufo Lopéz Fresquet (who later accepted a post in Castro's cabinet in January, 1959): Fresquet travelled to Washington and talked to William Wieland, and Allen Steward of the State Department for support that "only the U.S. could supply." Fresquet failed in his attempt to stop Castro, or to organize a group "to dispute power with Fidel Castro." Later, Fresquet claimed that he had done his best to "alert the U.S. government to the facts. But we had failed." See Rufo Lopéz Fresquet, *My Fourteen Months With Castro* (New York: World, 1966), pp. 33–39.

18. *El Diario* (Havana), January 6, 1959, p. 1.

19. Ibid., p. 1–2.

20. Authors' interviews with Dr. Manuel Urrutia Lleó (January 8, 1973, New York, New York; February 24, 1973, Union City).

21. One of the authors was present when Major Rolando Cubela discussed that meeting at the request of members of the DR in the office of the Federation of University Students, Havana University, January 9, 1959.

22. Urrutia to the authors (January 8, 1973).

23. Authors' interview with Lucy Echeverría (August 27, 1972, San Juan, Puerto Rico).

24. Riné R. Leal, "Habla Fidel Castro: el 26 de julio será un partido politico, *Carteles* (Havana), January 4, 1959, pp. 74–76.

25. U.S. Department of State, *Bulletin*, January 26, 1959, p. 128.

26. Most necklaces were of white and red beads representing *Changó*, the god of war; while yellow necklaces represented *Ochún*, the Virgin of La Caridad; all white necklaces symbolized *Obatalá*, the equivalent to Christ and a bisexual symbol for protection against evil spirits; all black necklaces represented *Babalú-Ayé*: white and blue symbolized *Yemayá* (life); red handkerchiefs around the neck did not mean "communism," but a protection against bad omens and a symbol of *Changó*.

27. A description of Castro's entrance into Havana appears in *Revolución* (Havana), January 9, 1959, and *Prensa Libre* (Havana), January 9, 1959; the text of his speech was published in most Cuban newspapers on January 9–10, 1959. The white pigeons released should not be taken as the symbol of "socialist" peace; actually white pigeons, "cleansed" with red pieces of clothing and released means in *santería* an act for the protection of the leader. For the influence of Afro-Cuban folklore religion throughout the guerrilla forces, see Joel Iglesias, "En la guerra revolucionaria junto al Che," *Verde Olivo* (Havana), October 13, 1968, pp. 39–40.

Appendices

Leadership Positions Held by Militants of the Insurrection in the Cuban Revolutionary Government (1972–1973)*

Major José Abrantes Fernández
(DR urban underground) First Deputy Minister of the Interior and member of the Central Committee of the Cuban Communist Party (CCP).

Major Rogelio Acevedo González
(M-26-7 Escambray Sierra) Politburo delegate in Camagüey, and member of the Central Committee of the CCP.

Oscar Alcalde
(M-26-7) Member of the CCP in Havana.

Major Juan Almeida
(M-26-7 Sierra Maestra) Member of the Politburo, and delegate of the Politburo in Oriente.

Major René Anillo
(DR urban underground) Former second secretary of the CCP in Oriente, and at present First Deputy Minister of the Ministry of Foreign Relations (MINREX).

Major Egvidio Báez Vigo
(M-26-7 Sierra Maestra) Corvette Captain of the Cuban Revolutionary Navy (EMG) and Chief of the EMG General Staff.

Major Federico Bell Lioch
(M-26-7 urban underground) Director of the Techonological Military Institute (ITM).

Major Enrique Borbonet
(Regular Army officer) Deputy Minister of Technical and Professional Education of the Ministry of Revolutionary Armed Forces (MINFAR).

---

* Dead, exiled or imprisoned militants and PSP members are not included.

Captain Thelma Bornot

(M-26-7 Sierra Cristal) Head of the History Section of the Political Department of the Revolutionary Armed Forces (FAR).

Major Manuel Bravo

(M-26-7 Sierra Maestra) Head of the Department of Foreign Relations of the MINFAR

Major Julio Camacho Aguilera

(M-26-7 urban underground) First secretary of the CCP in Pinar del Río, and member of the Central Committee of the CCP.

Major Lino Carreras

(M-26-7 Sierra Cristal) Chief of the Armored Division of the Army of Havana, and member of the Central Committee of the CCP.

Major Zenén Casas Regueiro

(M-26-7 Sierra Cristal) First Deputy Minister of FAR and Chief of the Joint General Chiefs of Staff of the FA R.

Major Julio Casas Regueiro

(M-26-7 Sierra Cristal) Deputy Minister of FAR and Head of Services of FAR.

Baudilio Castellanos

(M-26-7 urban underground) Cuban Ambassador to France.

Major Humberto Castelló

(DR urban underground) First secretary of the CCP in the region of Puerto.

Major Belarmino Castilla Más

(M-26-7 Sierra Cristal) Deputy Prime Minister of the Education. Culture and Science Sector, and member of the Central Committee of the CCP.

Major Fidel Castro Ruz

(M-26-7 Sierra Maestra) Prime Minister of the Revolutionary Government. First Secretary of the CCP and Chairman of the Executive Committee of the Council of Ministers.

Ramón Castro Ruz

Head of the Valle de Picadura Cattle-Breeding Project. Havana province.

Major Raúl Castro Ruz

(M-26-7 Sierra Cristal) Second Secretary of the CCP and Minister of FAR.

Major José N. Causse

(M-26-7 Sierra Maestra) Member of the Chiefs of Staff of the Oriente army.

Captian Carlos Chaín

(M-26-7 Sierra Maestra) Deputy Minister of the MINREX.

Major Joel Chaveco Hernández

(M-26-7 Sierra Cristal) Minister of the Merchant Marine and Ports and member of the Central Committee of the CCP.

Major Faure Chomón

(DR Escambray Sierra) Member of the Secretariat of the CCP and Head of the Transport Sector in Baracoa, Oriente.

Captain Osmany Cienfuegos

(M-26-7 urban underground) President of the Foreign Relations Commission of the Central Committee of the CCP.

Major Ramón Cintra Frías

(M-26-7 Sierra Maestra) Professor of Artillery at the General Antonio Maceo Inter-Arms School, and member of the Central Committee of the CCP.

Major René de los Santos

(M-26-7 urban underground) Member of the Central Committee of the CCP.

Major Sergio del Valle

(M-26-7 Sierra Maestra) Minister of the Interior (MININT), and member of the Politburo.

Captain Taras Domitro

(M-26-7 urban underground) Officer of FAR.

Major Victor Dreke Crúz

(M-26-7 Sierra Cristal) Deputy Minister of FAR and Chief of the Permanent Infantry Divisions in Oriente province and member of the Central Committee of the CCP.

Major Félix Duque

(M-26-7 Sierra Maestra) Head of the Citric Plan in the region of Victoria de Girón.

Vilma Espín

(M-26-7 urban underground) President of the Federation of Cuban Women (FMC), and member of the Central Committee of the CCP.

Arturo Duque Estrada

(M-26-7 urban underground) Member of the CP in Oriente.

Major José R. Fernández Alvarez

(Regular Army) Former Head of the Combat Readiness Department of FAR, and at present First Deputy Minister of Education.

Marcelo Fernández Font

(M-26-7 urban underground) Deputy Minister of Foreign Commerce.

Major Oscar Fernández Mel

(M-26-7 Sierra Maestra) Deputy Chief of the General Joint Chiefs of Staff of FAR, and member of the Central Committee of the CCP.

Major Carlos Figueredo

(DR urban underground) Chief of a Department of the Revolutionary Air Force (DAAFAR) ground troops unit. Pinar del Río province.

David Figueredo

(M-26-7 urban underground) Member of the CP in Oriente.

Major Rigoberto García Fernández

(M-26-7 Sierra Cristal) Deputy Minister of FAR and Chief of the Department of Combat Readiness of FAR.

Major Guillermo García Frias

(M-26-7 Sierra Maestra) Chief of the Western Army, member of the Politburo and Deputy Prime Minister of the Transportation and Communications Sector.

Major Julio García Olivera

(DR urban underground) Chief of the Political Section of the Army of Havana and member of the Central Committee of the CCP.

Major Francisco González

(M-26-7 Sierra Cristal) First Secretary of the CP in the Region of the Second Front "Frank País," Oriente.

Major Pedro Güelmes González

(M-26-7 Sierra Maestra) Chief of Communications of the Joint General Chiefs of Staff.

Major Raúl Guerra Bermejo

(M-26-7 Sierra Cristal) Former Chief of the San Antonio Air Force Base, and at present a delegate of the Agency for Agricultural Development (DAP).

Alfredo Guevara

(M-26-7 urban underground) President of the Cuban Institute of Cinema Arts (ICAIC).

Armando Hart Dávalos

(M-26-7 urban underground) Former Minister of Education and Secretary of Organization. At present, member of the Politburo of the CCP.

Enrique Hart Dávalos

(M-26-7 urban underground) President of the Cuban Supreme Court.

Melba Hernández

(M-26-7 urban underground) Chairman of the Cuban Committee of Solidarity with Vietnam, Cambodia and Laos, and member of the Central Committee of the CCP.

Major Joel Iglesias Leyva

(M-26-7 Escambray Sierra) Member of the Central Committee of the CCP.

Major Omar Iser Mojena

(M-26-7 Sierra Cristal) Member of the Oriente Army Chiefs of Staff, and member of the Central Committee of the CCP.

Major Reyneiro Jiménez

(M-26-7 Sierra Cristal) Member of the Eastern Army Chiefs of Staff, and member of the Central Committee of the CCP.

Major Carlos Lahite

(M-26-7 Sierra Cristal) DAP delegate in Oriente.

Major César Lara Roselló

(M-26-7 Sierra Cristal) Chief of the Independent Army Corps of Camagüey.

Major Arturo Lince

(M-26-7 Sierra Cristal) First secretary of the CP in the Isle of Pines.

Major Antonio E. Lussón

(M-26-7 Sierra Cristal) Minister of Transportation and member of the Centrai Committee of the CCP.

Major José R. Machado Ventura

(M-26-7 Sierra Cristal) First secretary of the CP in Havana, and member of the Central Committee of the CCP.

Major Raúl Menéndez Tomassevich

(M-26-7 Sierra Cristal) Chief of the Oriente Army, and member of the Central Committee of the CCP.

Major Pedro Miret

(M-26-7 urban underground) Minister of Mining, Fuels and Metallurgy, and member of the Central Committee of the CCP.

Major Jesús Montané Oropesa

(M-26-7 urban underground) Minister of Communications, secretary of organization of the CCP Secretariat, and member of the Central Committee of the CCP.

Major Demetrio Montseny

(M-26-7 Sierra Cristal) Chief of a Fronterizo Batallion in Oriente.

Major José A. Naranjo

(M-26-7 urban underground) Minister of the Food Industry, and member of the Central Committee of the CCP.

Major Juan Nuiry

(DR urban underground) Head of the National Center for Agricultural Festivals, Oriente.

Captain Antonio Nuñez Jiménez

(M-26-7 Escambray Sierra) Cuban Ambassador to Perú.

Major Arnaldo Ochoa

(M-26-7 Sierra Maestra) Chief of the Army of Havana, and member of the Central Committee of the CCP.

Major Mario Oliva

(M-26-7 Sierra Cristal) National Head of the Agency for Agricultural Development (DAP), and member of the Central Committee of the CCP.

Major Eduardo B. D. Ordaz

(M-26-7 Sierra Maestra) Director of the Havana Psychiatric Hospital.

Major Ramón Pardo Guerra

(M-26-7 Escambray Sierra) Member of the Political Section of the Army of Havana, and member of the Central Committee of the CCP.

Major Faustino Pérez

(M-26-7 Sierra Maestra) Cuban Ambassador to Bulgaria

Major Antonio Pérez Herrero

(M-26-7 Sierra Cristal) First Deputy Minister of Political Work of the FAR and member of the Politburo of the CCP.

Major Manuel Piñeiro

(M-26-7 Sierra Cristal) Deputy Minister of the Department of Foreign Relations of the MININT, and Head of the General Directorate of Intelligence.

Major José Ponce Díaz

(M-26-7 urban underground) Head of the National Institute of Forestry Development.

José Ramírez

(M-26-7 Sierra Cristal) President of the National Association of Small Farmers, and member of the Central Committee of the CCP.

Major Jorge Risquet

(M-26-7 Sierra Cristal) Minister of Work, and member of the Politburo of the CCP.

Captain Julián Rizzo

(M-26-7 Sierra Cristal) First secretary of the CP in Matanzas province, and member of the Central Committee of the CCP.

Captain Lester Rodríguez

(M-26-7 urban underground) Director of the Automative and Allied Technical Services Center.

Carlos Rafael Rodríguez

(M-26-7 Sierra Maestra) Deputy Prime Minister. Head of the Foreign Agencies Sector, and member of the Secretariat of the CCP.

Major Fernando Ruíz Bravo

(M-26-7 Sierra Cristal) Deputy Minister of FAR, and Head of the Department of Schools and Academies of the MINFAR.

Celia Sánchez Manduley

(M-26-7 Sierra Maestra) Member of the Central Committee of the CCP and secretary of organization to the Council of Ministers.

Major Aldo Santamaría Cuadrado

(M-26-7 Sierra Maestra) Chief of the EMG and member of the Central Committee of the CCP.

Haydée Santamaría Cuadrado

(M-26-7 urban underground) Director of Casa de las Américas, and member of the Central Committee of the CCP.

Major Jorge Serguera

(M-26-7 Sierra Cristal) Director of the Cuban Broadcasting Institute.

Major Diócles Torralba González

(M-26-7 Sierra Cristal) Deputy Prime Minister, Head of the Sugar Industry Sector, and member of the Central Committee of the CCP.

Major Ramiro Valdés Menéndez

(M-26-7 Sierra Maestra) Deputy Prime Minister, Head of the Construction Sector and member of the Central Committee of the CCP.

Captain Fernando Vecino Allegret

(M-26-7 Sierra Maestra) Deputy Minister and Second Chief of the Political Section of FAR.

Appendix 2

Major Events of the Urban Insurrection 1952–1959.

1952

March 10	FEU delegation visits President Prío Socarrás to offer its support against the military coup d'etat.
May 8	FEU holds a mass rally on the anniversary of Antonio "Tony" Fuiteras's death; police surrounds campus.
May 20	Professor Rafael García Bárcena forms the Movimiento Nacionalista Revolucionario (MNR); members include, among others: Mario Llerena, Faustino Pérez, Armando and Enrique Hart, Julián Fernández, Silvino Rodríguez.
August 16	Ortodoxo Youth holds a mass rally at the Colon cemetery in Havana; Fidel Castro and Abel Santamaría distribute the mimeographed paper El Acusador.

1953

January 15	A new statue of Julio Antonio Mella is smeared with paint, and the students hold a mass rally; José Antonio Echeverría delivers a fierce speech, a demonstration follows and Rubén Batista, a student, is seriously wounded by police gunfire.
January 28	José Martí's birthday; students demonstrate with lighted torches; Fidel Castro's men participate in organized form.
February 13	Rubén Batista dies; funeral held at Aula Magna in Havana University with thousands marching in protest against police brutality.
April 5	MNR militants areintercepted on their way to attack the Columbia Military Camp; several are imprisoned and tortured.
June 2	Auténticos and Ortodoxos agree on a common insurrectionary strategy at Montreal, Canada.
July 26	Fidel Castro leads the attack on the Moncda Barracks in Oriente province and a simultaneous attack on the Bayamo barracks takes place. Scores of people are laced under arrest,tortured and assassinated by the Servicio de Inteligencia Regional (SIR).
September 23	Police forces violate university autonomy with violent confrontation between students and General Rafael Salas Cañizares, Chief of the National Police. Protests follow by students in Las Villas and Oriente.

1954

February José Antonio Echeverría assumes the acting presidency of FEU; police raids are held seeking Aureliano Sanchez Arango, leader of the Triple A organization.

March 3-9 The Triple A explodes bombs in Havana, Matanzas, Las Villas, and Camagüey provinces.

March 10 Bombs explode in several locations throughout Havana and Santiago de Cuba, attributed to the Triple A.

March 28 José Antonio Echeverría. Juan Pedro Carbó Serviá, René Anillo, Jorge Valls and Osmel Francis demonstrate during the carnivals in front of the presidential stand; all are placed under arrest.

March 29 Student demonstrations in Havana demanding release of student leaders.

May 1 Student demonstrations in Santiago de Cuba. Anti-Communist slogans are chanted by students in Havana during labor demonstrations.

May 7 FEU sponsors the Third National Congress of Students of Secondary Institutions held in Havana University; student demonstrations, beatings and arrests.

May 8-9 Student protests in Santiago de Cuba demanding release of students in Havana.

June 22 FEU sponsors public action in favor of the Guatemalan Revolution; students organize the "Antonio Maceo" and the "Rubén Batista" brigades to offer their volunteer services to Guatemala.

October 1 Echeverría assumes presidency of FEU.

October 3-28 Echeverría leads FEU demonstration at El Cerro Stadium viewed by thousands: several students are beaten and placed under arrest. Bombs credited to the OA explode in Havana.

November 27- Student demonstrations ending in several students
December being placed under arrest and various police officers wounded by students. Costa Rica is invaded by mercenary forces from Nicaragua; Echeverría. Fructuoso Rodríguez, Rolando Cubela, Carbó Serviá lead a group of FEU leaders to Costa Rica to fight with President José Figueres against the invaders; Echeverría returns with honors from Costa Rica bestowed upon him by the president of that country.

1955

January 28	FEU sponsors massive demonstration in honor of José Martí's birthday; Frank País, and José "Pepito" Tey lead student march in Santiago de Cuba; fighting between students and police officers, several students wounded and arrested.
January 29	Student demonstrations in Havana and Matanzas demanding release of students in Santiago de Cuba. Violent clashes: more students are placed under arrest.
February 13	On the anniversary of Rubén Batista's death, Echeverría leads student demonstration, is savagely beaten and placed under arrest; student protests follow in Santiago de Cuba, Matanzas and Las Villas.
March-April	Student protests; bombs in Havana credited to the Triple A and OA; several anti-Batista militants assassinated by the police.
May 8	FEU sponsors action on the anniversary of Julio Antonio Mella's death: police forces invade campus and violent clash ensues; Echeverría, Fructuoso Rodríguez, Jorge Valls and Carbó Serviá are arrested.
August-September	Directorio Revolucionario (DR) is founded by Echeverría, Jorge Valls, Joe Westbrook Rosales, Rolando Cubelas and others. Bombs explode in several districts in Havana, Matanzas and Las Villas, credited to the OA and Triple A.
September 14	Bombs explode throughout Havana, credited to young militants of the FEAP; Ramón Rodríguez, leader of FEAP, promises to carry the struggle to its end.
November 27	Frank País, Tey and Otto Parellada lead students in Santiago de Cuba. Nationwide protest led by students demanding release of student prisoners in Santiago de Cuba, Echeverría declares a general student strike; all private and public institution suspend classes.
December 2	FEU is led by Echeverría to deliver letter to Cosme de la Torriente and police forces intercept demonstration; violent clash and Echeverría, Jorge Valls, Fructuoso Rodríguez are placed under arrest.
December 3	Police officers are shot to death in Havana by FEAP students; police react and several students are shot to death, others arrested.
December 4	Demonstration led by FEU at El Cerro Stadium; several students beaten and placed under arrest.

December 7	Antonio Maceo's death is honored by large student meeting in Havana; demonstration ends with police forces firing upon the multitude; Carbó Serviá and camilo Cienfuegos are wounded.
December 9-10	Bombs explode in Havana (OA): and in Santiago de Cuba (OA).
December	Frank País' ANR merges with the M-26-7 and the first provincial cell of the movement is created in Oriente province.

1956

February 24	Echeverría publicly announces the organization of the DR. Bombs explode in Matanzas, Las Villas and Camagüey (Triple A).
March 15	Student clashes with the police in Santiago de Cuba, several arrested.
April 19	Attack against the Goicuría Barracks in Matanas province (OA); scores are killed.
August 31	Pact of Mexico between the DR and the M-26-7.
November 27	Student demonstrations change in strategy. Mass demonstration in Havana led by Echeverría ends with violent exchange of gunfire between students and police; several police officers seriously wounded. Bombs explode in several districts throughout the capital (DR).
November 30	Uprising in Santiago de Cuba led by Frank Pais (M-26-7). Frustrated uprisings in Guantánamo, Mayarí and Holguín in Oriente province.
December 2	Granma lands in southern Oriente province.

1957

January 28	Bombs, killings of students and police officers mark Marti's birthday anniversary.
March 13	DR attacks the Presidential Place; Echeverría shot to death; scores of students are shot to death as brutal persecution follows. And the first reinforcements sent by Frank País arrive in Sierra Maestra.
March 14-15	Corpse of Senator Pelayo Cuervo Navarro is found; dozens of students are left dead on busy corners and intersections by the police.
March 20	Five students are found shot to death and hanged by the neck in a Havana suburb.

March 25-26	A bomb destroys a police patrol car killing four officers (DR) in Havana. A hand grenade destroys a patrol car belonging to the palace guard; one guard is wounded.
April 20	Humboldt 7. Joe Westbrook Rosales, Juan Pedro Carbó Serviá, Fructuoso Rodríguez, José Machado are delivered to the Batista police by a traitor and member of the Communist youth.
May 1	Several bombs (DR) kill seven and wound 12 at labor rallies inspired by the CTC.
June 7-8	Bombs and shootings reported in all provinces.
June 30	Josue País is shot to death when attempting to sabotage a *Masferrerista* meeting in Santiago.
July 30	Frank País is shot to death by forces of Colonel José M. Cañizares.
September 5	Cienfuegos uprising (M-26-7, navy).

1958

January 28	Police officers are shot to death at four different locations in Havana; several students are also killed by police forces. A bomb destroys a cafeteria in Matanzas (M-26-7).
February 8	DR expeditions arrive in Nuevitas, northern Camagüey province. Several dozen bombs explode in Havana close to police precincts; several police officers are killed, others wounded (DR).
March 13	Police officers are wounded when bomb explodes at central police headquarters in Havana (DR); an informer working for Colonel Esteban Ventura Novo is shot to death by FEAP students.
April 9	Frustrated general strike; scores of dead insurrectionists in several cities and towns throughout the country. Official terrorism reaches a peak; M-2-67 urban movement almost destroyed in Havana; DR in perilous condition; OA and Triple A urban cadres almost totally destroyed.
April 20	Anniversary of Humboldt 7 is honored through bombings in Havana, Matanzas and Pinar del Río provinces. Four FEAP student militants shot to death by Ventura Novo's agents; several DR militants captured in Pinar delRío and assassinated by Colonel Jacinto Menocal.
May 1	DR hits back with bombs in Havana and Matanzas; police officers are hunted during the night; FEAP is almost destroyed after persecution by Ventura Novo's and Martin Perez's men.

May 2-3	FEAP survivors hit back at police precincts; several students are shot to death, and FEAP suffers further setback. M-26-7 supports diversionary tactics with bombs and shootings against police officers and SIM patrol cars.
May 9	Triple A, OA, DR, M-26-7 and FEU and FEAP militants meet to discuss Batista's assassination; no agreement is reached.
June	Intensive terroristic activities in three western provinces (DR, M-26-7); more militants are captured by police forces and shot to death, their bodies thrown in business sections.
July 26	Potent bombs explode, killing several soldiers and SIM agents in Marianao, Havana (M-26-7).
July 27	Fighting between police. SIM agents and DR and M-26-7 erupts in Havana: several M-26-7 militants are killed, others are captured and later assassinated. Two are hanged by the neck in El Vedado section of Havana.
August 5	Encounter between DR militants and police officers under Colonel Ventura Novo; several people wounded, no insurrectionists arrested.
September 3	Potent bomb explodes close to the Ninth Precinct in El Vedado section of Havana; several people under arrest are immediately shot to death by the police.
September 4	Several police officers are shot to death by M-26-7 and DR militants: bombs explode; hand grenades destroy several police patrol cars; several insurrectionists are shot to death.
September 9	OA militants are killed by police while holding a secret meeting. Bombs explode in public restaurants and theatres (M-26-7 and DR).
October–November	Intensive wave of urban terrorism in all provinces. In Havana, over 100 bombs explode in one night; shootings at police officers and known pro-Batista civilians. Scores of insurrectionists are captured and shot to death by SIM and police forces; operations against shopping centers conducted by insurrectionists to disrupt commerce (DR).
December 5-7	Police raids by Ventura Novo's men in El Vedado section; several insurrectionists are captured and shot to death. Reports from Oriente and Las Villas provinces reach Havana underground to prepare for an all-out struggle in the capital.

December 20-25	Urban terrorism concentrates in civilian figures close to the regime and disruption of public places, DR and M-26-7 conduct coordinated operations against shops, movie theatres, and buses.
December 31	DR/M-26-7 combined operation blow up the army's last shipment of bombs for the air force at Cojimar's arms depot.

1959

January 1	DR forces take over the Ninth Police Precinct; M-26-7 take over the SIM; DR occupies the Fifth Police Precinct in Havana and the Principe Castle releasing political prisoners.Several encounters between former Batista soldiers and police officers and students take place throughout the capital; scores are killed or wounded.
January 2	Columbia Military Camp falls to Camilo Cienfuegos rebel column; La Cabaña fortress to Ernesto "Che" Guevara; the Presidential Palace and Havana University to the Dr. The DR forces also take over most army posts in Pinar del Río province. Last police officers holding fast against the insurrection surrender to combined DR/M-26-7 forces in Havana.

Appendix 3

Guerrilla Actions against the Regular Army, December 2, 1956–December 31, 1958

Date	Type of Action	Place	Province
12-5-56	Combat	Alegría de Pío	Oriente
1-17-57	Attack	La Plata	Oriente
1-22-57	Ambush	Arroyo del Infierno	Oriente
1-30-57	Attack	Loma de Caracas	Oriente
1-28-57	Combat	El Uvero	Oriente
7-26-57	Attack	Estrada Palma Sugar Mill	Oriente
7-29-57	Encounter	Majagua	Oriente
8-1-57	Attack	Minas de Bueycito	Oriente
8-20-57	Combat	Palma Mocha	Oriente
8-30-57	Battle	Hombrito	Oriente
9-17-57	Battle	Pino del Agua	Oriente
9-18-57	Ambush	Pino del Agua	Oriente
11-8-57	Encounter	Pilón	Oriente
11-16-57	Attack	Barracks at Mabay Sugar Mill	Oriente
11-20-57	Encounter	Mota, San Lorenzo, and Gaviro	Oriente
11-29-57	Combat	Mar Verde	Oriente
12-3-57	Encounter	Manzanillo surroundings	Oriente
12-6-57	Attack	Salto	Oriente
12-8-57	Combat	Altos de Conrado	Oriente
12-16-57	Encounter	Niquero surroundings	Oriente
12-22-57	Attack	Veguitas	Oriente
1-15-58	Combat	Veguitas	Oriente
1-16-58	Encounter	Manzanillo, Campechuela and Yara	Oriente
2-7-58	Combat	"La Babosa"	Oriente
2-16-58	Combat	Pino del Agua	Oriente
2-24-58	Attack	Military Post near Nicaro Company	Oriente

2-24-58	Combat	Purial	Oriente
3-12-58	Combat	Miranda Sugar Mill	Oriente
4-28-58	Attack	San Ramon de las Yaguas	Oriente
7-11-58 to	Battle		
7-21-58	Battle	El Jigue	Oriente
7-28-58 to		El Jobal and	
8-1-58		Las Mercedes	Oriente
11-7-58	Liberated Zone	Soledad Sugar Mill	
11-14-58	Liberated Zone	Imias	Oriente
11-30-58	Battle	Guisa	Oriente
12-11-58	Liberated Zone	San Luis	Oriente
12-19-58; 12-21-58; 12-31-58	Battles	Yaguajay, Fomento, Placetas, Sancti-Spiritus, Guinia de Miranda	Las Villas
12-31-58	Battle	Tope de Collantes	Las Villas
12-31-58	Battle	Santa Clara	Las Villas
12-31-58	Liberated Zone	Cienfuegos	Las Villas
1-2-59	Liberated Zone	Havana	Havana

Appendix 4

Population in Selected Cities*

Oriente Province	Population
Santiago de Cuba	163,237
Guantánamo	64,671
Holguín	57,573
Manzanillo	42,252
Palma Soriano	25,421
Victoria de las Tunas	20,431
Banes	20,257
Bayamo	20,178
San Luis	11,110
Sagua de Tanamo	7,604
Niquero	7,204
Antilla	6,481
Mayarí	6,386
Cueto	5,983
Preston	3,827
Nicaro	3,074

Camagüey Province	Population
Camagüey	110,388
Elia	5,447
Jatibonico	4,583
Ciego de Avila	35,178
Florida	21,159
Moron	18,624
Nucvitas	12,390
Vertientes	7,021

Las Villas Province	Population
Santa Clara	77,398
Cienfuegos	57,991
Sancti-Spiritus	37,741
Sagua la Grande	26,187

Placetas	25,226
Caibarién	22,657
Trinidad	16,756
Camajuaní	12,574
Remedios	10,602
Fomento	7,852
Yaguajay	5,191
Santo Domingo	4,728
Manicaragua	3,993

Matanzas Province	**Population**
Matanzas	63,917
Perico	6,041

Havana Province	**Population**
Havana	1,000,000
Marianao	219,278
Guanabacoa	32,400
Regla	26,755
Santa Fé	5,372
Batabanó	5,075
Cojímar	3,775
Nueva Gerona(Isle of Pines)	3,203

Pinar del Río Province	**Population**
Pinar del Río	38,885
Artemisa	17,461
Mariel	4,511
Bahia Honda	3,042

* Figures taken from the Census of 1953: cities over 3,000 inhabitants. The City of Havana was estimated to have approximately 1.5 million inhabitants in 1958.

Appendix 5

Density and Distribution of Population by Province 1953–1958

Province	1958 Population	1953 Population/Density(per km.)	
Pinar del Río	505,000	448,422	33.2
Havana	1,732,000	1,538,803	187.2
Matanzas	446,000	395,780	46.9
Las Villas	1,160,000	1,030,162	48.1
Camagüey	696,000	618,256	23.5
Oriente	2,024,000	1,797,606	49.1
Totals	6,563,000	5,829,029	50.9

Bibliography

General Works

1. Books

Aguilar, Luis E., *Cuba 1933: Prologue to Revolution.* (Ithaca: Cornell University Press, 1972). An analysis of the socio-political-economic process from 1924-35 based upon original research and personal interviews. Emphasis on the period from September 1933 to the Batista, U.S. sponsored counterrevolution of January 1934.

Aguilar, Luis E., *Marxism in Latin America* (New York: Alfred A. Knopf, 1968). Useful compilation of documents portraying the activities of Communist parties in Latin America, with a concise introductory discussion. The book contains six sections; Communist activities in Cuba appear in articles and reports. A good background source.

Azcuy, Aracelio, *Cuba: campo de concentración* (Mexico: Ediciones Humanismo, 1954). The author was a member of the Auténtico party. A strong condemnation of the Batista coup d'etat, with a discussion of its political significance.

Batista, Fulgencio. *Respuesta* (Mexico: Ediciones Botas, 1960). Justifying his political role in Cuba. Batista blames army officers as well as Communist insurrectionists for his downfall. Army conspiracies and strategies are discussed in a disorganized manner, but the book offers interesting insights into the dictatorship.

Batista, Fulgencio, *Sobre la marcha* (Havana: Ediciones Populares, 1955). A speech on the state of the economy, and a message to Congress discussing government and politics since 1952.

Batista, Fulgencio, *Cuba Betrayed* (New York: Vantage Press, 1962), 332 pp. An account of the disintegration of his regime, blaming problems on an international Communist conspiracy.

Batista, Fulgencio, *The Growth and Decline of the Cuban Republic* (New York: Devin-Adair, 1964), 800 pp. Economic and political reasons advanced by Batista to justify his rule in Cuba. A subjective interpretation of the country's economic situation prior to the revolution, from the 1930s to Castro's regime.

Bayo, Alberto, *Mi aporte a la revolución cubana* (Havana: Imprenta del Ejército Rebelde, 1960), Castro's guerrillas in Mexico by the man who trained the Granma expeditionaries and later trained Auténtico insurrectionists.

Bonachea, Rolando E. and Nelson P. Valdés, eds., *Che: Selected Works of Ernesto Guevara* (Cambridge: MIT Press, 1969), One of the most serious compilations of Guevara's works, including an introduction in which Che's background and travels before joining Castro in Mexico, in 1956, are discussed. The book includes the Pedrero Pact (1958): an interview with Jorge Masetti (1958): an interview in the Escambray Mountains, (1958): and letters to Castro and Chomón.

Bonachea, Rolando E. and Nelson P. Valdés, eds., *Revolutionary Struggle, 1947–1958*, 2 vols. (Cambridge: MIT Press, 1972). In the first volume of the selected works of Fidel Castro, the authors present the most complete compilation of Castro's works in the English language. The book is divided into six parts, from Castro's university years to Batista's downfall in 1959. The introduction is a useful summary of the period prior to the 1959 revolution: inner-group rivalries are viewed in terms of competition for the conquest of power. The authors' candid reliance on a pro-Batista source to describe Jose Antonio Echeverría's participation in student politics does not weaken an otherwise detailed description of the "action groups," during the 1940s and 1950s.

Bonsal, Philip W. *Cuba, Castro and the United States* (Pittsburgh: University of Pittsburgh Press, 1971). The author, former U.S. Ambassador to Cuba (1959–61) dedicates the first chapter (Batista Paves the Way for Castro, 1952–1958) to the insurrection, demonstrating certain displeasure toward Batista's terror methods. Vice-President Richard M. Nixon's visit to Cuba in 1955 is viewed by the author as an event that helped create the impression of U.S. support for the Batista dictatorship. Bonsal's perception of the causes of the insurrection appear superficial, and it is with that thrust that the period is analyzed.

Brennan, Ray, *Castro, Cuba and Justice* (New York Doubleday, 1959). The author, a *Chicago Sun-Times* correspondent, offers a journalistic account of Castro's planning and successes against Batista's government from 1953-59, including a vivid description of Batista's terroristic counterinsurgency methods.

Casuso, Teresa, *Cuba and Castro* (New York: Random House, 1961). A former revolutionary during the 1930s, and a highly respected figure of that generation describes her relationship with Fidel Castro's movement in Mexico, in 1956, offering an interesting insight into the preparations for the Granma expedition. Castro's personality, relationship with his men and his interest in meeting Carlos Prío Socarrás are discussed.

Che (Havana: Instituto del Libro, 1969). The single most valuable source of information for the strategies of the regular army during the 1957–58 campaign. A study manual for internal circulation in the armed services, this book is divided into three parts. The first part includes articles of a political-military-ideological nature on the insurrection by Ernesto "Che" Guevara, and a collection of documents and military orders of the regular army. The second part includes "Che's" works on guerrilla warfare and revolution in Latin America. The third part is a compilation of military reports by the rebel and the regular armies from 1956–58.

Conte Agüero, Luis, *Los dos rostros de Fidel Castro* (Mexico: Editorial Jus, 1960). Useful collection of letters written by Fidel Castro to the author during the formative years of the M-26-7, and while in prison in 1954–55. Otherwise quite subjective.

Conte Agüero, Luis, *Fidel Castro, vida y obra* (Havana: Editorial Lex, 1959). A favorable biography of the leader of the revolution from his university years to Batista's downfall, by one of his closest friends.

Debray, Regis, *Revolution in the Revolution?* (New York: Grove Press, Inc., 1967). The controversial essay on the theory of the guerrilla *foco* by a French intellectual who conducted first hand research in Cuba. This is a valuable source of information on certain aspects of guerrilla warfare in Cuba, despite its gross oversimplifications.

de Leon, *Ruben, El origen del mal* (Miami, Florida: Service Offset Printers, Inc., 1964). The author was a well-known revolutionary in the 1930s and offers a first hand account of the "sergeant's revolt" in 1933; the organization of the Auténtico party, and the reasons why that party lost its momentum prior to the Batista coup in 1952.

Dias de combate (Havana: Instituto del Libro. 1970). An excellent compilation of articles by actors of the insurrection, with a large selection of military reports issued by the regular army, and transcripts of rebel radio accounts during the insurrection.

Draper, Theodore, *Castro's Revolution: Myths and Realities* (New York: Praeger, 1962). The author rejects the theory of a peasant revolution, and supports the idea of a middle-class revolution. This is a good background source, despite the fact that it was published when original material was scant.

Dubois, Jules, *Fidel Castro: Rebel, Liberator or Dictator?* (Indianapolis: Bobbs-Merrill, 1959). An account of Castro's early life, entry into politics and insurrectionary activities to 1959. This book contains background information on figures of the insurrection and translation of various documents of the anti-Batista movement.

Elizalde, Leopoldo P. *Defamation* (Mexico: Publicaciones de Defensa Institucional, 1961). The author, who was close to Batista, attempts to prove that no social, political or economic problems existed before Castro. The insurrectionists appear as Communist-controlled and the insurrection as an international conspiracy. This is representative of pro-Batista arguments.

Fernández Retamar, Roberto, ed., *Obra Revolucionaria* (Mexico: Ediciones Era, 1967). A collection of "Che" Guevara's works including most of the guerrilla leader's articles on the insurrection.

Gadea, Hilda, *Ernesto: A Memoir of "Che" Guevara* (New York: Doubleday, 1972). "Che" Guevara's first wife offers many interesting and unknown details about "Che's" life before he joined the Granma expedition in 1956. The author, a former member of the Peruvian Aprista Party, objectively analyzes "Che's" personality traits, and discusses some of the problems he confronted under Castro's bureaucracy after 1959, leading to Bolivia and death in 1967.

García Montes, Jorge and Antonio Avila, *Historia del Partido Comunista de Cuba* (Miami, Florida: Ediciones Universal, 1970). The anti-Communist thrust of the authors limits the value of this book to a chronological order of events, names, dates and places and references to documents.

Goldenberg, Boris, *The Cuban Revolution and Latin America* (New York: Praeger, 1965). The author, a European who lived in Cuba, had some participation in the "action groups," and witnessed the insurrection throughout its development. In discussing the insurrectionary years, he analyzes the factors involved in and leading to violence in Cuba. Emphasis is on the impact of the revolution in Latin America.

Guevara, Ernesto "Che," *Reminiscences of the Cuban Revolutionary War* (New York: Grove Press, 1968). Translated by Victoria Ortiz, this book is a compilation of 32 articles by "Che" on the insurrection from the point of view of the guerrillas. It also includes 26 letters written by "Che" from 1959 to his farewell letter to

Castro in 1965. Articles include descriptions of several battles; guerrilla problems: the rebel's relationship to the peasants, and offers a first hand account of the growth of the guerrilla army.

International Commission of Jurists, *Cuba and the Rule of Law* (Geneva: 1962). A book geared to establish legal violations by the revolutionary government after 1959. Its most valuable part is a concise, comprehensive discussion of the Constitution of 1940, including the dogmatic and organic parts of the constitution, Batista's act of 1952, and amendments to the constitution.

Karol, K.S., *Guerrillas in Power: The Course of the Cuban Revolution* (New York: Hill and Wang, 1970). In its second chapter the author, who had access to original material in Cuba, reviews the limited role of the Communists during the insurrection, questioning the official view that the April 9, 1958 frustrated strike was the sole responsibility of the urban underground. The author posits that it was Fidel Castro's perception of the politico-military situation that led to his decision to order a general strike. A good analysis of the political situation during the years of the insurrection; otherwise the book deals with conditions after 1959.

Kozolchyk, Boris, *The Political Biographies of Three Castro Officials* (Santa Monica, California: RAND Corporation, 1966). Study covers Fabio Grobart, a founder of the Communist party: Raul Roa, a veteran of the 1933 revolution: and Rene Anillo, a member of the DR. Good background data on movements and leaders.

LaCharite, Norman, *Case Studies in Insurgency and Revolutionary Warfare: Cuba, 1953-1959* (Washington, D.C.: SORO, 1963). An analysis of the insurrection and of pertinent socioeconomic factors involved in the period.

Lazo, Mario, *American Policy Failures in Cuba* (New York: Funk and Wagnalls, 1968). The author, one of the most important corporation lawyers in Cuba, offers interesting and original data on U.S.-Cuba relations during the insurrection. The efforts of pro-Batista as well as anti-Batista individuals—who were at the same time anti-in-surrectionary—are discussed in detail: trips to Washington: the plight of U.S. Ambassador Earl T. Smith: diplomatic missions to Cuba: and the author's personal attempts to safeguard American economic and political influence in Cuba.

López-Fresquet, Rufo, *My Fourteen Months with Castro* (New York: World, 1966). Personal account of his experiences by the former secretary of economic affairs in 1959–60. The author, describes his efforts in 1957-58 to stop Fidel Castro from reaching power. and how the State Department was asked for logistical support in releasing Colonel Ramon Barquín from the penitentiary in Cuba: the rest deals with the revolution after 1959.

Matthews, Herbert L. *Fidel Castro* (New York: Simon and Schuster, 1969). The first four chapters present a summary description of the insurrection, from the Moncada attack in 1953 to the Sierra Maestra campaign, including data on Castro's early life. The rest of the book deals with the revolution after 1959.

Matthews, Herbert L. *The Cuban Story* (New York: George Brazillier, 1961). The author discusses the effects of his famous interview with Fidel Castro in early 1957, and then proceeds to praise Castro and himself for having produced what the author believes was the greatest newspaper story of recent times. The book contains valuable insights into the early stages of the insurrection.

Marrero, Leví. *Geografía de Cuba* (New York: Minerva Books, 1966). First published in 1943, in Cuba, this book is a general introduction to the island's geography and economy. All the regions where guerrilla warfare took place in the 1950s are examined: topography, local economy, forest formations, rivers, lagoons and available communications. Includes an extensive number of charts, tables and illustrations.

Martinez Páez, Julio, *Medicos en la Sierra Maestra* (Havana: Ministerio de Salubridad y Asistencia Social, 1959). A brief but important primary source offering information about the rebel army's medical services and field hospitals. The author was the chief of the rebel army's medical corps during the insurrection.

Nelson, Lowry, *Rural Cuba* (Minneapolis: The University of Minnesota Press, 1950). Invaluable source of Cuba's socioeconomic structure prior to the insurrection with research conducted in Cuba.

Nelson, Lowry, *Cuba: The Measure of a Revolution* (Minneapolis: The University of Minnesota Press, 1972). The first four chapters offer a good discussion of the socioeconomic and political events in prerevolutionary Cuba with emphasis on the state of agriculture during the 1950s. The author of *Rural Cuba*, measures the results of the revolution and asks the question "Was the revolution necessary?"

Núñez Jiménez. Antonio. *Geografía ele Cuba* (Havana: Editorial Lex, 1959). An economic geography by an officer of the rebel army, including descriptions of the sites where guerrilla warfare took place, and documents on the summer offensive in 1958. Good background book for the island's domination by U.S.-owned companies.

Pardo Llada, José. *Memorias de la Sierra Maestra* (Havana: Editorial Tierra Nueva, 1960). Personal memoirs of a former Ortodoxo politician who was in Sierra Maestra, but did not participate in any military action. Data about rebel officers; rebel headquarters; ideas and Castro's influence as a leader.

Pavón, Luis, ed., *Dias de combate* (Havana: Instituto del Libro, 1970). One of the most valuable sources of reference for the guerrilla war. A compilation of 30 articles written by guerrilla fighters who offer original descriptions of battles with the regular army, the book is divided into three parts: the campaign in Oriente province; the march on Las Villas province, and the guerrilla campaign in Las Villas province. Includes 21 military reports originally published by the clandestine press in 1958, and heretofore confidential reports by the regular army on the battle of Guisa, Oriente province.

Riera Hernández, Mario. *Cuba Libre 1895-1958* (Miami, Fla.: Colonial Press, 1968). A good source for the organization of the Rural Guards Corps, and the influence of U.S. officials during the first decades of the republic, including interesting data on the revolution of 1933; the "action groups." and political parties to the 1950s.

Rodríguez Morejón, Gerardo, *Fidel Castro, Biografía* (Havana: P. Fernández y Cia., 1959). An introductory letter by Lina Ruz de Castro. Fidel's mother, verifying dates, names and places connected with Fidel's early life makes this biography the best source for Castro's childhood years in Oriente province. The rest of the book deals with the insurrectionary years, and the last chapter offers a detailed account of events in Santiago de Cuba, on January 1, 1959.

Ruíz, Ramón Eduardo. *The Making of a Revolution* (Amherst, Mass.: University of Massachusetts Press, 1968). A good background book discussing the political and social antecedents of the revolution with emphasis on the revolution of 1933: unfortunately no footnotes are offered.

Suchlicki, Jaime, *University Students and Revolution in Cuba, 1920-1968* (Coral Gables, Fla.: University of Miami Press, 1969). The only book dealing with student involvement in Cuba in the English language. Student activities in the 1950s appear in the form of a summarized but accurate account with research conducted on primary sources reinforced by some interviews with former student participants in the events.

Seers, Dudley, ed. *Cuba: The Economic and Social Revolution* (Chapel Hill, N.C.: University of North Carolina Press, 1964). The best source for an analytical discussion of the country's economic and social conditions prior to the 1959 revolution. Andrés Bianchi's essay on the state of the agriculture is the best prerevolutionary background available: Richard Jolly's essay on education offers an in-depth analysis of the prerevolutionary years and the educational situation: and Dudley Seers' discussion on the economic and social background makes this an important source with extensive notes and fresh insights.

Smith, Earl T. *The Fourth Floor: An Account of the Castro Communist Revolution* (New York: Random House, 1962). The author, former U.S. Ambassador to Cuba, 1957-59, holds that U.S. policy was responsible for Castro's rise to power. The book demonstrates the ambassador's intensive efforts to stop the insurrection from overthrowing Batista and his lack of political sophistication. The author's "electoralist" formula for a solution of the crisis in Cuba, provides an interesting insight into the ambassador's perception of the insurrection.

Smith, Robert, ed., *Background to Revolution The Development of Modern Cuba* (New York: Alfred A. Knopf, 1966). Excellent compilation of background essays dealing with ideology, society, economics, and politics by well-known students of the Cuban republic, among others: C.A.M. Hennessy; Jorge Mañach; Herminio Portell Vilá; Federico Gil: Fernando Ortiz: Lowry Nelson and Dudley Seers.

Sociedad de Amigos de la República. *El momento político de Cuba, acuerdos, cartas y discursos* (Havana: Editorial Lex, 1955). Collection of documents, letters and speeches by leaders of the organization seeking an electoral solution to Batista's dictatorship in the mid-1950s. This compilation is important in comparing SAR's position to the line maintained by the insurrectionists.

Suárez Núñez, José. *El gran culpable* (Caracas: 1963). Close to dictator Batista, the author was his personal secretary in 1959-60. In this book. Batista is charged with the sole responsibility for the insurrection's victory: account of frauds and political dealings is discussed by one who participated and later turned against Batista for personal reasons. A good source for grasping the regime's lack of legitimacy, and the immorality of most of the author's colleagues.

Taber, Robert, *M-26. Biography of a Revolution* (New York: Lyle Stuart, 1961). One of the best journalistic accounts of the insurrection at a time when few documents were available. The author interviewed Luis Goicochea, survivor of the palace attack, and offers a vivid description of this action in 1957.

Thomas, Hugh, *Cuba: The Pursuit of Freedom* (New York: Harper and Row, 1971). A massive work covering the history of Cuba from 1762 to the revolution after 1959. Book IV dedicates 19 brief chapters to the 1952-59 period, and the author appears convinced that the intensity of the war was not sufficient to defeat a regular army. The author appears to have relied heavily on unpublished manuscripts of people who were not fully involved in the struggle, but his aristocratic outlook is under control most of the time. This is by far the most complete history of Cuba in any language, and makes an excellent reference source.

13 documentos de la insurrección (Havana: Organización Nacional de Bibliotecas Ambulantes y Populares, 1959). Important documents issued during the insurrection are compiled in this book which also includes brief descriptions of the historical importance of each of the documents included.

Urrutia Lleó, Manuel. *Fidel Castro & Company, Inc.* (New York: Praeger, 1964). A former president of Cuba (1959-60), and one of the most respected figures during the insurrection discusses his role in the struggle. A primary source for the author's historical legal decision on the right to use armed resistance against dictatorship. Most of the book concentrates on his experiences as president of the revolutionary government, and on Fidel Castro's coup d'etat.

26 (Havana: Instituto del Libro, 1970). A comprehensive compilation of articles written by actors of the Moncada attack on July 26, 1953 including three about the attack on the Bayamo military garrison. Includes a description of how the first edition of Castro's *History* will *Absolve Me* was published by the underground press, and two articles by Marta Rojas on Moncada and preparations for the attack.

Ventura Novo, Esteban, *Memorias* (Mexico: Imprenta León M. Sánchez, 1961), The author, Batista's number one henchman in Havana, views himself as a compassionate police officer who was never involved in any acts of violence during the regime. His image as a savage assassin was an asset in the officer's dealings with insurrectionists whom, the author claims, were never mistreated by him. Faure Chomón and Raúl Díaz Arguelles are charged by Ventura with betraing the student leaders at Humboldt 7 on April 20, 1957. This is a very important source to understand the realities of urban fighting in Havana. The author ends by criticizing Batista for abandoning the struggle and for refusing to be generous with his money in the Dominican Republic in 1959.

Zeitlin, Maurice, *Revolutionary Politics and the Cuban Working Class* (New York: Harper Torchbooks, 1970). Good study of Cuban workers after the Castro regime in 1959. A chapter dealing with political generations in Cuba offers an interesting approach to the study of the 1953 generation to which most of the insurrectionist leaders belonged. The author fails to mention the student involvement in the sugar workers' strike in 1955, and failed to conduct in-depth research in the Communists' acts of sabotage against the frustrated general strike on April 9, 1958, or the pro- Batista role of the old Communists and their image during the 1950s.

2. Articles

Acevedo, Rogelio, "La Federal," *Dias de combate* (Havana: Instituto del Libro, 1970), pp. 307–10. The author, an officer in "Che" Guevara's column offers a description of the encounter at La Federal in Camagüey province. Useful information on names of rebel guerrillas.

Ameijeiras, Efigenio, "La batalla de Imías," *Dias de combate*, pp. 211–22, The chief of Column No. 6 describes the battle of Imías leading to the capture of Guantánamo.

Armas Somoza, Alfredo, "Despacho Oficial: Oficial de Guardia, EME," *Che* (Havana: Instituto del Libro, 1969), p. 229. Army sergeant Alfredo Armas Somoza sends an urgent dispatch dated December 28, 1958 to the army general staff. Fighting is reported in the proximities of Las Villas University, close to Santa Clara, and regular army troops are said to expect an attack from "Che" Guevara.

"Batalla de Santa Clara," *Bohemia*, (Havana), December 27, 1963, pp. 75–77. Vivid description of the battle of Santa Clara with "Che" Guevara's strategy and the takeover of surrounding towns and cities.

Cabrera, Luis R., "Baldomero, el montuno que salvo a seis expedicionarios del Granma," *Bohemia*, (Havana), March 22, 1959, pp. 46–47: 128. The experiences of a peasant who kept six Granma expeditionaries from falling into the hands of the army.

Cantillo Porras, Eulogio, "Plan de Operaciones," *Che*, pp. 254–57. General Cantillo's last attempt to encircle Fidel Castro in Sierra Maestra during the summer offensive in 1958. Dated July 26, 1958, this plan calls for leading Castro into a trap by placing regular troops in certain key areas around Las Mercedes while Army Battalion No. 22 attracts Castro into an area favorable to the army.

Castillo, Ramos, Rubén, "Junto al Che en la Sierra," *Bohemia*, (Havana), November 21, 1969, pp. 4-11, 112. Aristides Guerra, courier of "Che" and chief of supplies to his column recalls various incidents and sheds lights on the supply and ammunition trails used by Guevara; includes other details on the relationship between guerrillas and the peasantry.

Castillo Ramos, Rubén, "Sierra Maestra, un periódico escuela," *Bohemia*, (Havana), July 21, 1967, pp. 106–09. This is a historical description of the founding of the "Sierra Maestra" newspaper: its role in the struggle, and some of its news coverage during the insurrection.

Castillo Ramos, Rubén, "Misión a Estrada Palma," *Bohemia*. (Havana), July 14, 1957, pp. 74–75, 92. An interview with Colonel Pedro A. Barreras, chief of operations in Sierra Maestra, in which guerrilla activities and the area are discussed.

Castro Ruz, Fidel, "Statements by Fidel Read over Radio Rebelde on October 25, 1958," *Granma Weekly Review*, (supplement), March 18, 1973, pp. 20–21. Castro learns of an incident at the Nicaro nickel plant involving Raúl Castro's rebels and the regular army. Interpreting it as a maneuver on the part of U.S. Ambassador Earl T. Smith and Batista to provoke U.S. intervention, Castro alerts public opinion to the fact that rebels would fight in the even of intervention.

Castro Ruz, Fidel, "Fidel's First Address over Radio Rebelde, April 15, 1958," *Granma Weekly Review*, (supplement), March 18, 1973, pp. 9–11. Castro vows to fight Batista's regime from the Sierra Maestra, and calls on the people to resist dictatorship.

Castro Ruz, Fidel, "Report on the Tyranny's last Offensive. August 18–19. 1958," *Granma Weekly Review*, (supplement), March 18, 1973, pp. 12–19. Complete military report on the summer offensive.

Castro Ruz, Fidel, "Noticiero Radio Rebelde. Ultima Hora: Maffo," *Dias de combate*, pp. 404–05. Brief battle report on the fall of Maffo, in Oriente, where Castro announced that the road to Santiago de Cuba was left wide open; detailed account of regular army casualties, and captured equipment.

Castro Ruz, Fidel, "Noticiero Radio Rebelde, dia 27 de diciembre de 1958," *Dias de combate*, pp. 395–98. Fidel Castro's broadcast on the progress of the rebel offensive; the fall of Palma Soriano is discussed with a description of the battle.

Castro Ruz, Raúl, "El socialismo llego al Turquino a quedarse para siempre," *Bohemia*, (Havana), September 27, 1963, pp. 36–41. Speech by Raúl Castro reminiscing about the first stage of the guerrilla war: La Plata, El Uvero, organization of the first guerrilla column, and reprisals of the army against the peasantry.

Cervantes Núñez, Gilberto, "La Columna 18," *Dias de Combate,* pp. 33–46. A major in the rebel army reviews the military operations of Raúl Castro's second guerrilla front with emphasis on actions led by Column 18 commanded by Major Felix Pena.

Chomón, Faure, "Cuando el Che llegó al Escambray," *Bohemia,* (Havana), December 10, 1965, pp. 52–56. The leader of the DR after Echeverría's death discusses the arrival of "Che" Guevara to Las Villas province, exchange of letters, and situation in general, leading to the Pact of Pedrero with the M-26-7.

Cintra, Leopoldo, "Relato del comandante Leopoldo Cintra," *Días de Combate,* pp. 228–30. The battle of Guisa as described by a front line fighter. Emphasis on the participation of rebel army officers Rafael Verdecía, Calixto García. Braulio Coroneaux, Luis Pérez and Reinaldo Mora.

Cowley Gallegos, Fermín, "Resúmen de Operaciones Militares efectuadas en cl Regimiento 8 GR," *Che,* pp. 217–21. Detailed military report by Colonel Fermín Cow ley, chief of the 8th Regiment of the Rural Guards Corps on the landing of the Corinthia expeditionaries. The report includes a description of military maneuvers and names, dates, and places connected to the capture of Calixto Sánchez White's group by forces under Captain Eliseo Cardenas Taylor.

Cuza, José L., "Combate del centro industrial de Moa," *Días de Combate,* pp. 113–27, How guerrilla company "D" led by Captain Nino Díaz, carried out Raúl Castro's Order No. 30 to detain American citizens in Moa. a mining town in northern Oriented province. Includes a list of kidnapped American and Canadian citizens.

de Castro y Rojas, Pedro J., "Muy Secreto: Estado de la Unidad," *Che,* pp. 151–52. Confidential report on the state of regular troops in the Sierra Maestra: officers whose performance deserved credit are named, among them lieutenant Armando González Finales.

de Castro y Rojas, Pedro J., "Resúmen de Operaciones," *Che,* pp. 156–65. Addressed to Colonel Francisco Tabernilla, Jr., this is a summary of military operations to November 13, 1957. Attached to this document are three military plans to destroy the rebels, with detailed information on rebel strategy, topographic features and the regular army's conditions.

de Nora, Maria Luz, "El combate de Altos de Conrado," *Bohemia,* (Havana), pp. 100–02. 113. One of the first encounters with the regular army as recalled by "Che" Guevara.

del Río Chaviano, Alberto, "Informe sobre las Operaciones hasta el día de la fecha," *Che.* pp. 153–55. Dated September 28, 1957 this is a report on military operations in Oriente province. General del Río Chaviano wrongly estimates Fidel Castro's rebel troops at 500; Raúl Castro's and "Che" Guevara's at 250 guerrillas. Locations of rebel troops and tactics used by the guerrillas are discussed in detail.

del Sol, Curbelo, "Al Director de Operaciones G-3, EME," *Che,* pp. 147–48. Guerrilla ambush at Pino del Agua is described by Colonel Curbelo del Sol, who placed the number of rebels at about 500.

del Valle, Sergio. "Relato del comandante Sergio del Valle." *Días de Combate,* pp. 275–92. Excerpts from Major del Valle's campaign diary, which describe the march of Camilo Cienfuegos' column from Oriente to Las Villas province.

Díaz Tamayo. Martín. "Estudio de la situación en la Sierra del Escambray." *Che.* pp. 176–78. As interesting military study of the situation around the Escambray

Mountains. Las Villas province sent by General Díaz Tamayo to the "Leoncio Vidal" Military Camp in Santa Clara. Topographic features, military operations and rebel locations are discussed.

Díaz Tamayo. Martín. "Ampliación despacho cifrado." *Che.* pp. 175–76. On June 28. 1958 General Díaz Tamayo reports to the general staff that an informer from the Sierra Maestra has offered the whereabouts of "Che" Guevara'a rebel column: also announces that Faustino Pérez has been replaced by an unidentified insurrectionist in Havana (Manuel Ray).

"El 'Che' en el Escambray," *Bohemia,* (Havana). October 20, 1967. pp. 66–69. This article unveils the rendezvous of "Che's" column with the forces of the DR in the Escambray Mountains.

"El 'Che' en la Revolución Cubana." Bohemia, (Havana). November 24. 1967. pp. 8–9. 113. The significance of "Che" Guevara in the revolution from the inception of guerrilla warfare in the 1950s.

"El Jigüe." *Cuba Internacional* (Havana), July, 1972, pp. 20–21. Brief summary of the significance of the battle of "El Jigüe." where troops under the command of Major José Quevedo surrendered to Fidel Castro during the summer of 1958.

Fernández Mell, Oscar, "La batalla de Santa Clara," *Días de Combate,* pp. 361–80. A good description of the rebel strategy for the battle of Santa Clara by a participant.

Fernández R. J., "Plan A. Operación Iguara," *Díaz de Combate,* pp. 375–79. Dated October 21, 1957 this is the regular army's secret plan for the defense of Santa Clara, Las Villas province. The plan includes five sections with details on personnel, administrative regulations and communications.

Fonseca, Luisa, "La rendición de la fragata Máximo Gómez," *Bohemia,* (Havana), March 15, 1959, pp. 38–39. 141. Description of anti-Batista activities aboard a navy frigate whose officers joined the insurrection at the end.

Fuentes, Fluvio y Aldo Isidrón del Valle, "Che, niñez, adolescencia, juventud," *Bohemia,* (Havana), October 20, 1967, pp. 70–77. Useful background information about Guevara's youth, climaxing with his enrollment in the Granma expedition.

Fuentes, Fluvio y Aldo Isidrón del Valle, "La Invasion," *Bohemia,* (Havana), October 20, 1967, pp. 30–35. 90. Interesting description of the invasion from Oriente to Las Villas province.

García, Calixto, "Si salimos, llegamos; si llegamos, desembarcamos: si desembarcamos, triunfaremos," *Bohemia,* (Havana), November 29, 1963, pp. 44–48. Major Calixto García recounts his experiences during the insurrectionary campaign and Fidel Castro's leadership qualities.

García Frías, Guillermo, "El combate de Paraná," *Días deo Combate,* pp. 193–98. Events leading to the September 28, 1958 battle of Paraná. Sierra Maestra, against the troops commanded by Colonel Nelson Carrasco Artíles.

García, R., "Archivo No. 301-C-958," *Díaz de Combate,* pp. 241–42. Colonel R. García, chief of operations in Bayamo, Oriente province, reports to the general staff the list of arms and equipment lost to the rebels during the month of November 1958.

González, Melquíades, "El combate de Levisa," *Días de Combate,* pp. 179–86. A captain of the rebel army serving under Raúl Castro describes an encounter with regular troops led by Colonel Jesús Sosa Blanco at the entrance to the village of Levisa, northern Oriente province.

Grao, R.L., "NC 3940-958," *Días de Combate,* pp. 242–44. A report to General Francisco Tabernilla. Sr. listing the regular army's casualties during November 26-28, 1958 at the battles of Guisa and Campechuela, with a full report of regular army units engaged in these operations.

Guerra, Orestes. "De El Salto a Jobo Rosado." *Días de Combate,* pp. 293–96. Very useful account of Cienfuegos' westward march from El Salto. Sierra Maestra to Jobo Rosado, Las Villas province. Data establish how the guerrillas were able to penetrate the army's defense lines; the aid offered by the urban M-26-7 in Camagüey, and the guerrillas' meeting with Félix Torres' guerrillas band in Las Villas province.

Guevara, Ernesto "Che," "La batalla de Santa Clara," in *Ernesto "Che" Guevara, Obras; 1957-1967* (Havana: Casa de las Américas, 1970), pp. 399–412. Description of the last battle of the insurrection.

Guevara, Ernesto "Che," "El combate de 'El Uvero," in *Ernesto "Che" Guevara, Obras: 1957-1967* (Havana: Casa de las Américas, 1970), pp. 259–64. One of the first battles of the rebel army discussed by the main guerrilla strategist of the insurrection.

Guevara, Ernesto "Che." "Guerra y población campesina." *Bohemia.* (Havana), November 10, 1967, pp 4-5. Significance of the peasantry in the insurrectionary process.

Guevara, Ernesto "Che." *Relatos del Che,* (Montevideo, Uruguay: Editorial Sandino n.d.). This is a collection of "Che's" articles on the insurrectionary campaign from its first stage to the arrival at Las Villas province.

"Guisa," *Cuba Internacional,* (Havana), July 1972, p. 16, Brief, concise description of the stages of the battle of Guisa.

Gutiérrez, Carlos M., "El 'Che' en lo suyo." *Bohemía,* (Havana), December 15, 1967, pp. 8–10. A candid portrait of the guerrilla leader by a Uruguayan newspaperman who went to Sierra Maestra in February 1958 to inverview "Che" Guevara, Gutiérrez focuses on "Che's" personality, organizational skills and relationship with the guerrillas. Insightful and revealing.

Hernández Vidaurreta, Manuel. "El Gobierno Civil en la Sierra Maestra." *Humanismo* (Mexico), nos. 53-54. (January-April. 1959): 7. 363–68. Brief description of the various administrative divisions of the civil government in the Third Guerrilla Front, commanded by Major Juan Almeida.

Hernández, "Despacho Oficial: Al Director de Operacions G-3. EME," *Che.* p. 209. A colonel reports to the general staff that "Che" Guevara and rebel Major Victor Bordon have attacked small army posts in Las Villas province. There is a description of arms and equipment captured by regular army troops from the rebels in an encounter near Banao.

Herrera, Osvaldo, "Ataque a Bayamo, el ascenso de Camilo," *Días de Combate,* pp. 47–54. Campaign diary focusing on Cienfuegos' attack on the army post at Bayamo in April, 1958.

Ibarra, Jorge, Moreno Fraginals, Manuel and Oscar Pino Santos, "Historiografía y Revolución." *Casa de las Américas* (Havana), nos. 51-52, vol. IX (November 1968-February 1969). pp. 101–05. Useful historiography of the insurrection reviewing the guerrilla process.

Iglesias, Joel, "En la guerra revolucionaria junto al 'Che," *Verde Olivo,* (Havana), October 13, 1958, pp. 37–45, 62. Experiences of a guerrilla fighter who served under "Che" Guevara throughout the insurrection. A candid description of the belief that a malevolent black bird roamed the mountains of Sierra Maestra, and a first-hand account of the battle of Santa Clara.

Larrubia, Paneque M., "Confidencial." *Che*, pp. 225–27, Dates November 23, 1958, this is a study of the military situation in Las Villas province, divided into five sections, including a discussion of army strongholds, lines of defense, and military units operating throughout the province.

Le Sante, Jorge R., "Resultado investigación practicada acción Pino del Agua," *Che*, pp. 149–50. The author was the intelligence officer in charge of investigating events at Pino del Agua; includes a copy of statements made by a former prisoner of the rebel army on treatment received and conditions of the guerrillas.

Lesnik Menéndez, Max, "Por qué se disuelve el II Frente Nacional del Escambray," *Bohemía*. (Havana). March 6, 1960. pp. 56–58, 79. The reasons why the guerrilla organization of Eloy Gutiérrez Menoyo emerged in 1958, including lists of officers in the guerrilla's general staff. The article announces the dissolution of the organization in 1960.

Lesnik Menéndez, Max, "10 de noviembre: Escambray heroico," *Bohemia*. (Havana). November 22, 1959. pp. 46–47, 99–100, Good source for names of officers and battles connected with Gutiérrez Menoyo's guerrilla group in Escambray Mountains. It fails to mention the reasons why they separated themselves from the DR in mid-1958.

Lusson, Antonio E., "El ataque al cuartel de San Ramón de las Yaguas," *Días de Combate*, pp. 56–76, Very useful article describing the guerrillas' contacts with the urban underground, and events related lo Raúl Castro's "Frank País" guerrilla front in northern Oriente province.

Menéndez Tomassevich, Raúl, "El asalto al cuartel de Mayarí Arriba." *Días de Combate*, pp. 145–59. A former M-26-7 underground member who became an officer under Raúl Castro offers information about the linkages between urban-rural guerrillas. Describes an attack on an army post in 1957, Raúl Castro's arrival to Sierra Cristal in 1958, and the attack against the army post at Mayarí Arriba.

Messer Jiménez, Julio, "Versión taquigráfica de la trasmisión captada el 9 de diciembre de 1958," *Che*, pp. 227–28. Transcribed by army lieutenant Messer Jiménez this is a conversation between Camilo Cienfuegos and "Che" Guevara via rebel radio in Las Villas province, in 1958.

Messer Jiménez, Julio, "Versión taquigráfica de la trasmisión captada el I de diciembre de 1958," *Che*, pp. 210–12, Published elsewhere, this is the original army transcript of "Che" Guevara's interview through the rebel radio in Escambray Mountains.

Montero, Aeropajito, "Relato del comandante Aeropajito Montero." *Días de Combate*, pp. 230–36. The author was in charge of the first ambush of the regular army leading to the battle of Guisa. This is a discussion of the role played by advanced guerrilla units and the mortar squads.

Morales, Salvador, "Los primeros días de la guerra." *El Caimán Barbudo*, (Havana), 2 (November 1972): 5-9. Useful account of the first stages of guerrilla war in Cuba.

Núnez Jiménez, Antonio, "Crónica: el tren blindado." *Casa de las Américas*, (Havana), February 1969, pp. 218–22, Deals with the surrender of the train sent by Batista to reinforce the regular army in Santa Clara, a key factor in the rapid downfall of that city in December 1958.

Nespral, A. F., "Al Director de Operaciones G-3, EME," *Che*, p. 229. From Cienfuegos, Las Villas province, the chief of the navy reports fighting in the streets, and an imminent rebel attack.

"Oriente, la capital de la historia," (special issue) *Cuba Internacional*, (Havana), July 1972, pp. 10–23, Contents include: Moncada; struggle in the city: La Plata: El Uvero; Pino del Agua II, and El Jigüe. This issue illustrates the most important battle sustained in the Sierra Maestra. Includes a number of regular army communiques as well as excerpted articles from *El Cubano Libre*.

Pardo Guerra. Ramón. "El tren blindado." *Días de Combate*, pp. 381–87. The author is a guerrilla captain who led the ambush and the attack on the armored train with last minute reinforcements to the regular army.

Pardo Llada, José. "La batalla de Guisa," *Bohemia*, (Havana), February 22, 1959, pp. 48–50, 122–23. A politician who sought refuge in the Sierra Maestra describes the battle of Guisa in Oriente province.

"Principales comandantes del 26 de julio," *Revolución*, (Havana), July 26, 1959. pp. 12–13. A list of the most important majors of the rebel army.

"Radio Rebelde's First Broadcast," *Granma Weekly Review*, (supplement), March 18. 1973, pp. 7–8. The first broadcast of the rebel's cadio station in Sierra Maestra calling for war against Batista and promising to continue the struggle until the dictatorship is defeated.

"Reporte de operaciones del 19 al 20; 20-21; 22-23; 24-25; 28-29; 30-31 de diciembre de 1958," *Días de Combate*, pp. 413–27. Numerous military reports issued by the regular army and dealing with the situation in Las Villas province. Reports include air and land operations and state of the front from the time "Che" Guevara initiated his attacks moving toward Santa Clara to the end of the insurrection.

Reyes Trejo, Alfredo, "Los días que precedieron al desembarco del Granma." *Verde Olivo*. (Havana), November 30, 1966, p. 13. A good account of the situation at the time of the Granma landing and the state of the M-26-7.

Reyes Trejo, Alfredo, "Escenarios de lucha." *Verde Olivo*, (Havana), December 5. 1971, pp. 8–33. Comprehensive account of the guerrillas' military operations based on narratives by various column captains, military documents of the regular army, and excerpts from "Che'" Guevara's *Pasajes de la guerra revolucionaria*.

Reyes, Trejo, Alfredo, "Del Moncada a las Montanas," *Verde Olivo*, (Havana), July 30, 1972, pp. 23–33. The retreat from Moncada, led by Fidel Castro, is described in interviews with people who helped the insurrectionists until the latter's capture by the regular army.

Rivero, Arnaldo, "La disciplina revolucionaria en la Sierra Maestra." *Humanismo*, (Mexico), 7, nos, 53-54, (January-April 1959): 369-372. An article discussing revolutionary discipline in the Sierra Maestra and the code of ethics of the gurerilla fighters.

Robainas Piedra. Luis. "Actuación de la FAEC en Operaciones." *Días de Combate*, pp. 239–40. Dated December 12, 1958. This is a report by General Robainas to headquarters describing the participation of the air force in the battle of Guisa.

Robainas Piedra, Luis, "Radiograma cifrado al Coronel Fermín Cowley Gallego." *Che*, p. 217. Dated May 29. 1957 this coded cable from General Robainas to Colonel Cowley orders the latter to say that expeditionaries were not surprised, but killed in battle.

Rodríguez Avila, Pedro, "Al Jefe de Distrito de la Marina de Guerra." *Che*. p. 141 On December 1. 1956 General Rodriguez Avila, adjutant general of the army, orders the navy to locate a yacht answering to the specifications of Granma.

Rojas, Marta. "Los dias que precedieron al Granma." *Bohemia*, (Havana), December 27, 1959, pp. 10–12, 139–40, Description of preparations for the Granma expedition with names, places, dates and anecdotes.

Sanabria, Nydia, "Dos guerrilleros: Camilo y el 'Che'," *Bohemia*. (Havana), November 3, 1967, pp. 30–35, A biographical comparison of two of the most popular leaders of the guerrillas.

Sanabria, Nydia, "Ernesto 'Che' Guevara, fundador del Cubano Libre." *Bohemia*, (Havana), October 27, 1967. pp. 78–81. The guerrillas' newspaper, *El Cubano Libre*, founded by "Che" Guevara; description of how it was made and distributed and its importance throughout the guerrilla army.

Sanabria, Nydia, "'Che' Guevara, fundador de Radio Rebelde," *Bohemia*. (Havana), October 15, 1967, pp. 48–53. In this second article on "Che's" contributions to the guerrilla campaign. Radio Rebelde is discussed and how "Che" organized the propaganda campaign.

Sanabria, Nydia, "Mujeres guerrilleras en la batalla de Guisa." *Bohemia*. (Havana), November 24, 1967, pp. 50–55. Four narratives by women of their enrollment in the women's battalion "Mariana Grajales" and their participation in the battle of Guisa.

Sanabria, Nydia, "Ramón Paz de minero a comandante heroico." *Bohemia*, (Havana), July 23, 1965, pp. 72-81 Historical description of the insurrectionary activities of Major Ramón Paz from his entry into the rebel army to his death during the summer offensive in 1958. The article includes copies of letters to Paz from Fidel Castro, and military orders issued during the insurrection.

"Sierra Maestra, un hijo de Crescensio," *Bohemia*, (Havana), February 22, 1959, pp. 93, 96–97, Crescencio Pérez's son, Sergio, describes how he saved the Granma survivors, leading them into safety. The first recruit to the rebel army narrates his personal experiences and gives valuable details about the first stage of the guerrilla war.

Suñol Ricardo, Eddy. "De la Sierra Maestra a los llanos del norte de Oriente," *Días de Combate*, pp. 161–78. Valuable account of the guerrilla campaign in the plains of northern Oriente province.

Suñol Ricardo, Eddy and Omar Iser Mojena. "Combate de los Güiros." *Días de Combate*, pp. 199–209, Operations by the guerrillas in the plains of northern Oriente province from October-December 1958 offering information on battles, casualties and equipment captured from the regular army.

Suárez Suquet, Armando, "Plan de defensa Escuadrón 23 GR," *Che*, p. 190. Colonel Suárez Suquet, chief of operations in Camagüey province, orders special preparations for possible rebel attacks on small army posts.

Suárez Suquet, Armando, "Confidencial: Informando Operaciones Segundo Distrito Militar," *Che*, pp. 196–207. The most complete report of how the regular army tried to stop the guerrillas from crossing Camagüey province into Las Villas. Dated October 16. 1958 this report is a detailed description of army ambushes, encounters with the rebels, and tactics employed throughout the province.

Tabernilla, Carlos M., "Confidencial: Operaciones de las FAEC en Zona Uvero." *Che*, pp. 146–47. Dated May 28, 1957 this report deals with the air force's bombardment of the area around El Uvero and other air force operations in the Sierra Maestra.

Tabernilla, Francisco, Jr., "Telefonema al Ayudante General del Ejército." *Che*, p. 141. Coded cable informing the general staff that the air force was unable to locate the Granma as of November 30. 1956.

Tandrón, José C., "Declaración del Testigo Aforado 2do. teniente Aquiles Chinea y Alvarez." *Che*, pp. 144–45. Important document with the statements made by the army officer in charge of the post at Niquero on the Granma landing: there is a full report of operations to December 5. 1956.

Tandrón, José C., "Confidencial: 30 de diciembre de 1956." *Che*, p. 142. Captain Tandrón, chief of Squadron 13 of the Rural Guards, reports on the Granma landing to his superior officers and describes the first hours of pursuit of the expeditionaries.

Ugalde Carrillo, Manuel, "Director de Operaciones G-3. EME," *Che*, p. 173. Urgent message to the general staff by Colonel Ugalde Carrillo, dated February 17, 1958: discusses rebel and army casualties a: Pino del Agua.

Ugalde Carrillo. Manuel. "Organización de las Fuerzas en la Zona de Operaciones de Oriente," *Che*. pp. 251–52, Dated October 22, 1957. This is an analysis of the organization of the regular army in the Sierra Maestra with a complete list of names in the general staff, officers in charge of military units and their respective locations.

"Uvero." *Cuba Internacional.* (Havana), July 1972. p. 15. Description of the battle of El Uvero.

Valdés. Ramiro, "El Ejército Rebelde y la Reforma Agraria," *Humanismo* (Havana), 7, nos. 53-54 (January-April. 1959); 343-82, Discusses the relationship between the guerrillas and the peasantry: school for rebel recruits: rebel discipline: political education of the guerrillas: and significance of revolutionary changes.

Vecino, Fernando, "El combate de El Jobal," *Días de Combate*, pp 129-44 Major René Ramos Latour's assistant describes an important battle, and how Major Ramos Latour died during the summer offensive in 1958.

Vecino, Fernando, "Sierra Maestra "58," *Santiago*, (Santiago de Cuba), Revista de la Universidad de Oriente, no. 4. (September 1971); 32-44. Useful discussion of the guerrilla campaign with candid appraisals of its importance in the overall insurrection.

Governmental Decrees

República de Cuba, *Gaceta Oficial,* edición extraordinaria, (Havana). (March 10, 1952). Fulgencio Batista's first proclamation after the coup d'etat with a prologue and nine articles dissolving Congress; imposing a law of public order; defining the executive power; ordering devolution of unlicensed firearms and proclaiming Batista as chief of state and prime minister.

"Ley Constitucional." *Gaceta Oficial* (Havana) vol. 2, no. 1 (April 4, 1952): 1-7, This decree-law passed by Batista defined the functions of the council of ministers following the coup d'etat.

"Ley Decreto No. 105," *Gaceta Oficial* (Havana) vol. 6, no. 9 (June 4, 1952): 1. Sweeping decree-law regulating elections, number of elected candidates and defining requirements for presidential, congressional and mayoral candidates.

"Ley-Decreto No. 721." *Gaceta Oficial* (Havana) vol, 2, no, 21 (March 7, 1953): 1,3. Passed on February 27, 1953 this decree-law modified articles of the constitution in preparation for the elections of 1954. It also set procedures for granting Batista a leave of absence to be a presidential candidate, and ratified the requirements for president.

"Ley-Decreto No. 1164," *Gaceta Oficial* (Havana) vol. 20, no. 90 (November 6, 1953): 2. Decree-law announced on October 30. 1953 scheduling elections for November 1, 1954.

"Ley-Decreto No. 1163," *Gaceta Oficial* (Havana) vol. 21, no. 90 (November 6, 1953): 2. Batista's order to cancel the constitutional law of April 4. 1952; it dissolves the advisory council and reestablishes the constitution of 1940 once the elections had taken place.

"Ley-Decreto No. 1990." *Gaceta Oficial* (Havana) vol. 2. no. 7 (January 27, 1955): 2. Announcing congressional activities to begin on January 28. 1955 and implementing modifications to other decree-laws.

"Juramento del Presidente." *Gaceta Oficial* (Havana) vol. 20, no. 10 (February 25, 1955) : 3021. Oath of office taken by the Supreme Court on February 24, 1955, the date of Batista's inauguration for a four-year term.

"Decreto Presidencial No. 3230." *Gaceta Oficial* (Havana) vol. 23, no. 17 (December 2, 1956) : 1. In response to the Granma landing in Oriente province. Batista suspends constitutional guarantees for 45 days in the provinces of Oriente, Camagüey, Las Villas and Pinar del Rio, but not in Havana. This decree orders the implementation of the law of public order and gives wide powers to the executive to cope with the situation.

"Resolución del Congreso." *Gaceta Oficial* (Havana) vol. 23, no. 18 (December 5, 1956); 23647, Resolution passed by Congress ratifying previous suspension of constitutional guarantees in all provinces except Havana. This resolution was approved three days after the Granma landing and the same day of the encounter between the regular army and the expeditionaries at Alegría de Pío. Oriente province.

"Decreto Presidencial No. 78." *Gaceta Oficial* (Havana) vol. 1. no. 2 (January 15, 1957): 962, Suspension of constitutional guarantees for 45 days and implementation of the law of security and public order in view of the survival of the guerrillas.

"Decreto Presidencial No. 463," *Gaceta Oficial* (Havana) vol. 5. no. 2 (March 2. 1957): 1. Ratification of suspension of guarantees due to disturbances in the cities.

"Acuerdos adoptados por el Congreso sobre reformas específicas de la Constitución de 1940," *Gaceta Oficial* (Havana) vol. 12, no. 18 (June 20. 1957): 11869, Reforms to the constitution by Congress on October 2, 1956, and June 18, 1957: Senate to be composed of not more than 12 senators per province: sessions to last 60 days. This resolution regulated meetings of the House and Senate centralizing more power under Anselmo Alliegro, president of Congress.

"Decreto Presidencial No. 2111," *Gaceta Oficial,* (Havana) vol. 15, no. 4 (August 1, 1957): 1, Suspends guarantees for another 45 days due to increased protests in the cities and in the countryside.

"Resolución del Congreso." *Gaceta Oficial.* (Havana) vol. 15, no. 80 (August 6, 1957): 15133. Congressional resolution approving Batista's measures to curtail public disorders.

"Decreto Presidencial No. 2513." *Gaceta Oficial.* (Havana) vol. 18, no. 6 (September 14, 1957); 1. Batista again decrees suspension of guarantees including suspension of articles 26-30; 32-33; 36-37 of the constitution of 1940.

"Resolución del Congreso." *Gaceta Oficial,* (Havana) vol. 18, no 20 (September 18, 1957): 18037. Congressional ratification of Batista's suspension of articles of the constitution.

"Decreto Presidencial No. 2940." *Gaceta Oficial,* (Havana) vol. 20, no. 18 (October 30, 1957): 21045. Batista extends the application of the law of public order for another 45-day period.

"Ley No. 2, Estado de Emergencia Nacional." *Gaceta Oficial,* (Havana) vol. 7, no. 15 (April 2. 1958): 1-3. Batista prepares the regime for the revolutionary general strike by declaring a state of national emergency. This law includes 16 articles redefining executive powers, granting immunity to the police and the army for acts against insurrectionists, and suspending the constitution of 1940.

"Decreto Presidencial No. 1214." *Gaceta Oficial,* (Havana) vol. 8. no. 17 (April 26, 1958) : 1, Measures taken by Batista to fortify the armed services.

"Estado de Emergencia Nacional," *Gaceta Oficial,* (Havana) vol. 10, no. 14 (May 26, 1958): 926. Compilation of decree-laws passed by Batista and ratified by Congress on May 15, 1958. There were 21 decree laws passed by Batista during the crisis, granting the dictator extraordinary powers which were used to purge the government of anti-Batista elements; increase appropriations for public works connected with the armed services: redefine legal precepts establishing punitive measures against crimes, thus protecting the police against possible prosecution and purging public schools of proinsurrectionary teachers.

"Decreto Presidencial No. 1788." *Gaceta Oficial,* (Havana) vol. 11, no. 13 (June 9, 1958): 10318. Suspension of constitutional guarantees for 45 days. This suspension was extended on July 24. 1958: September 7. 1958; October 22, 1958; and December 14, 1958.

"Decreto Presidencial No. 140," *Gaceta Oficial* (Havana) vol. 23, no. 14 (December 14, 1958): 1. Batista's last decree suspending constitutional guarantees throughout the country, immediately ratified by Congress.

El Moncada: July 26, 1953

Castro Ruz, Fidel, "El asalto al cuartel Moncada." *Humanismo* (Havana) 7, nos. 53-54 (January-April, 1959): 303-26. Castro's self-defense before the court of Santiago where he was tried and sentenced for his participation and authorship in the attack. Also known as "History Will Absolve Me."

Castro Ruz, Fidel, *Pensamiento politico, económico y social de Fidel Castro* (Havana: Editorial Lex, 1959). Includes Castro's self-defense speech at the Santiago trial, the economic thesis of the M-26-7 drafted by Felipe Pazos and Regino Boti, and three other speeches by Castro in 1959.

Castro Ruz, Raúl, "Fragmentos de un diario," *Vida Universitaria* (Havana) 19, no. 212. (July-August 1968). pp. 34–35. Raúl records his impressions in excerpted passages of the diary he kept at the Isle of Pines penitentiary, noting how perilous the mission seemed to him.

"Ciro Redondo García," *Bohemia* (Havana), November 1. 1963. pp. 72, 82. Concise background information on Ciro Redondo, a member of the Ortodoxo Youth in Artemisa who participated in the Moncada attack and was a member of the Granma expedition.

Enrique, Miguel. "Artemisa en el Moncada." *Lunes de Revolución* (Havana), no. 19, July 26, 1959, pp. 6–8. Useful information on the group of *Artemiseños* from Pinar del Rio province, members of the Ortodoxo Youth, who enrolled for the action of the Moncada. The author gives names, places where they trained and some of the weapons they took along.

26 (Havana: Instituto del Libro, 1971), A collection of articles written by several of the Moneada combatants previously published in *Verde Olivo. Revolución, La Calle* and *Hoy* among others.

García del Cueto, "En casa de Abel: 25 y O," *Bohemia* (Havana), July 24, 1970, pp. 4–9, A general reminiscence of the insurrectionary activities of Abel Santamaría coupled with brief episodes about several of the men who visited his house among them. Fidel. Raúl Gómez García, Pedro Miret and others.

García del Cueto, Mario, "Trazo biográfico de Renato Guitart," *Bohemia* (Havana), July 21, 1967, pp. 4–8. A revealing article about the man who was instrumental in providing Castro with hard information about the interior of the Moncada garrison. Guitart's previous alignment with the OA. his relations with Otto Parellada and Frank País of the ARO group and his friendship with Jose Antonio Echeverría are discussed.

Marín, César, "Renato Guitart: mártir del Moncada." *Lunes de Revolución* (Havana), no. 19 (July 26, 1959): 31-32. Biographical data on Guitart and his decisive contribution to the planning of the Moncada attack as Well as his daring storming of post 3 of the barracks.

Miranda, Jorge Valdés. "Ñico López." *Bohemia* (Havana). December 8, 1967, pp. 34–35, Useful political biography on Ñico López, a member of the Ortodoxo Youth and an ardent militant who was instrumental in recruiting other young Ortodoxos to participate in the Moncada attack.

Naborí, El Indio, "Raúl Gómez García, poeta del '26 de Julio' y de la Generación del 'Centenario.'" *Bohemia* (Havana), July 27, 1962, pp. 16–17, 123, Interesting narrative on Raúl Gómez, a gifted student of philosophy with a vocation for poetry who became the Homer of the Moncada combatants. His experience as editor of several small newspapers was a formidable help for the Moncada group in issuing *El Acu*-sador.

Otero, Lisandro, "Aquel 26 de Julio, entrevista a Haydée Santamaría y Melba Hernández," *Bohemia* (Havana), September 9, 1966, pp. 4–19, An extensive colloquia by the two women who went to the Moncada. Illuminating references on how Fidel Castro joined the *Son los Mismos* group, the attack, the trial and the years of inprisonment.

Partido Unido de la Revolución Socialista Cubana (PURS). *Relatos del asalto al Moncada* Havana: Comisión de Orientación Revolucionaria, 1964. Another set of articles assembled in book form and written by former participants of the Moncada attack. Included are articles by Marta Rojas, all previously published.

Reyes Trejo, Alfredo, "Del Moncada a las montañas." *Verde Olivo* (Havana), July 30, 1972, pp. 24–33, Retracing the route to the Gran Piedra mountain, years after the triumph of the Revolution. Oscar Alcade and Mario Lazo reminisce about the days of persecution following the failure to take the Moncada. Useful in tracing sequences, people and events after the men left Siboney farm.

Rodríguez, Javier, "Los combatientes del Moncada vuelven a la granja Siboney," *Bohemia* (Havana), July 28, 1967, pp. 94–95, Some 41 participants who survived the attack met at Siboney to recount the hours that followed when all had failed. According to this account one of the first ones to arrive at Siboney was Fidel Castro.

Rodríguez Zaldívar, Rodolfo, "Por qué Fidel Castro no fué asesinado al capturarlo el Ejército de Oriente." *Bohemía* (Havana), March 8, 1959, pp. 63, 112. This article shows the significant role played by Lieutenant Pedro M. Sarría in forestalling Castro's end at the hands of Major Andrés R. Chaumont.

Rojas, Marta, "El asalto al Moncada," *Bohemia* (Havana), February 1, 1959, pp. 28–30, 166–67. The first of a series of articles dealing with the genesis of the attack, its organization, numerical strength and strategy.

Rojas, Marta, "Itinerario y balance de un infame crimen," *Bohemia* (Havana), February 8, 1959, pp. 40–44, 138–39, Deals with the sequences of the attack and the wave of repression unleashed by the army when the attackers failed to take over the garrison.

Rojas, Marta, "La causa 37," *Bohemia* (Havana), February 15, 1959, pp. 36–39, 112–17. Devoted to aspects of the trial against the *Moncadistas*, and the various irregularities instigated by the government to keep Fidel Castro out of the witness stand.

Rojas, Marta, "Los testigos del hospital," *Bohemía* (Havana), July 24, 1970, pp. 10–20. Excerpted from the book by the same title, this article records the impressions of several nurses from the Saturnino Lora Hospital who were witnesses of the events.

Rojas, Marta, "Los fundadores de la nueva Cuba," *Bohemia* (Havana), July 27, 1962, pp. 28–32. According to this article, the Moncada group was recruited along cell-like patterns, and only Abel Santamaria and Fidel Castro had control over all the cells. The author reveals that only one car in the first group entered the barracks, the squad that attacked Post 3.

Sánchez Otero, Germán. "El Moncada: inicio de la revolución cubana," *Punto Final* (Santiago de Chile), no. 162, July 18, 1972, pp. 1–15. The author argues that Eduardo R. Chibás' ideas influenced the political activism of the Moncada group. In an attempt to set the ideology of the *Moncadistas*, the author concludes they were Ortodoxos disengaged from the bureaucratic ties of the party and innovative in the use of armed struggle against the army. A very candid, thought-provoking essay.

Santamaría, Haydée, *Haydée habla del Moncada* (Havana: Instituto del Libro, 1967). In a lecture to students of political science at Havana University, Haydée recalls the role of the various leaders of the Moncada attack. She suggests that leadership was first in the hands of her brother Abel, that the Moncada combatants did not know the objective of their mission and that several cars did not participate in the attack while about ten men refused to engage in what they thought was a suicidal action.

Zell, Rosa Hilda, "6 documentos del Moncada," *Bohemia* (Havana), July 27, 1962, pp. 64–69. Included are the "Manifiesto a la Nación" written by Raúl Rómez García and Fidel Castro, two poems by Raúl Gómez García, a legal plea, Castro's letter to the tribunal and the July 26 hymn.

Frank Pais and The M-26-7 Urban Struggle

Ameijeiras, Efigenio, "Esperando el refuerzo," *Revolución* (Havana), April, 1963, pp. 2–3. An account of the guerrillas' military situation from the time of the landing on December 2 to March of 1957, showing the importance of the reinforcements from Santiago de Cuba sent by Frank País.

Cabrera, Luis Rolando, "Doña Rosario, la madre de los hermanos País," *Bohemia* (Havana), August 9, 1959, pp. 6–8, An intimate portrait of the País brothers by their mother. Doña Rosario, who sheds insight into the social and Christian values prevalent in their home. She candidly discusses the different personality traits of her three sons, and Frank's early concern for Cuba's political ills.

Cabrera, Guillermo, "Frank y la lucha clandestina en Santiago." *Revolución* (Havana), July 30, 1966, p. 8, Cabrera, a former newspaperman from *Carteles* new exiled in London (himself from Oriente) traces the main clandestine operations led by Frank País and his M-26-7 men in Santiago.

Castro, Fidel, "Carta a Frank País. July 21, 1957," in Rolando E. Bonachea and Nelson P. Valdés, eds, *Revolutionary Struggle 1947–1958* (Cambridge: MIT Press, 1972), pp. 348–49, and in Regis Debray, *Revolution in the Revolution?* (New York: Grove Press, 1967), pp. 85; 112–13. This is the only letter written by Castro to Frank that has ever been made public. Originally, it appeared in *Granma* (Havana), July 7, 1968, p. 9, but was excerpted for unknown reasons. Other excerpts are in Regis Debray's work. The excerpts discuss Frank País" revamping of the M-26-7 internal structure (Bonachea and Valdés) and Castro's intention to fight a guerrilla war in the mountains (Debray).

Cubillas, Vicente Jr., "Los sucesos del 30 de noviembre de 1956," *Bohemia* (Havana), November 29, 1959, pp. 42–45, 89–90 and December 6, 1959, pp. 48–51, 120–23. This is the most comprehensive account of the Santiago uprising led by Frank País and his group of men. It gives information on contacts between the Santiago group and the Moncada group based in Havana as well as the names of insurrectionists who took part in the action, many of whom ended the war in the Sierra Cristal.

Cubillas, Vicente Jr., "Un 30 de noviembre en Santiago de Cuba," *Bohemia* (Havana). November 27, 1960, pp. 44–47, 72. This article deemphasizes the clandestine activities of the M-26-7 and reveals a substantial appreciation of the role played by the guerrillas in their struggle to survive after the defeat at Alegría de Pío.

Espín, Vilma, "Frank País," in Carlos Franqui, *Cuba el libro de los doce* (Mexico: Ediciones Era, S.A., 1966), pp. 157–68. Vilma's account of Frank Pais' death, her role in the November 30 uprising and initial contacts with Raúl Castro in the Second Front.

Estevanell, Justo Esteban, "Frank, el jefe del levantamiento," *Verde Olivo* (Havana), December 5, 1971, pp. 42–49. A discussion of the military objectives of the uprising of November 30, 3nd the reasons for its failure. The author asserts that this action reflected the supportive role assigned to urban guerrilla warfare.

Infante, Enzo and Devlofeo, Miguel, "José Tey Blancard," *Verde Olivo* (Havana), December 3, 1967, p. 29, A concise account of the FEU leader in Oriente, Pepito Tey, and his role in the clandestine struggle waged alongside Frank País, his closest friend.

Mencia, Mario, "¡ Ahora si se gana la revolución.¡" *Bohemia* (Havana), December 1, 1972, pp. 58–64. A very useful narrative on the origins of the urban struggle in Santiago, particularly the emergence of ARO and its merge into ANR and finally into the M-26-7. Frank País' role is depieted and several participants in. the events are interviewed, among others: María A. Figueroa, Gloria Cuadras and David Figueredo. Included are documents and letters.

Nicot, Carlos and Cubillas, Vicente, Jr., "Relatos inéditos sobre la acción revolu-cionaría del lider Frank País," *Revolución* (Havana), July 30, 1963, p. 2. Useful information on Prank País' plans to draft an economic program for the M-26-7, and the aid he enlisted from a team of professors of Oriente University.

Ortega, Gregorio, "Frank País." *Lunes de Revolución* (Havana), no. 19 (July 26, 1959): 16–17. Rich in dates, biographical data and clandestine actions, Ortega's article depicts Frank País as the architect of the M-26-7 without whom the rural guerrillas would not have been able to survive.

Frank País, "La valerosa acción de Santiago de Cuba," *Pensamiento Critico* (Havana) no. 29 (June 1969): 240–46. A crisp, comprehensive account narrated by País to Carlos Franqui on February 15, 1957 in the offices of the magazine *Carteles* in Havana. It shows the strategic craftmanship of País in organizing the uprising and devising contingency plans in case of failure.

"Frank País," *Bohemia* (Havana), July 23, 1965, pp. 20–24. This article includes biographical data on País, the first supplies sent to the rural guerrillas in December and how País was told to abandon the city struggle lest he die in the hands of the police, something which he refused to do.

"Frank País, en el XV aniversario de su muerte," *Verde Olivo* (Havana), July 30, 1972, pp. 17–18. Several accounts by Taras Domitro (brother of Frank's fiancée América). Agustín Navarrete (clandestine member), and Adela Mourlot (assis-tant director of El Salvador School), on País' political leadership qualities. Useful data on the origins of ARO and the preparations of the November 30 uprising.

"Carta de Frank País a Fidel Castro, July 5, 1957," *Pensamiento Crítico* (Havana), 1968, pp. 40–44. First of a series of letters written to Fidel. This one concerns the opening of the second front in Sierra Cristal, and rebukes Castro for not helping the would-be guerrillas reach their destiny.

"Carta de Frank País a Fidel Castro, July 7, 1957," *Pensamiento Crítico* (Havana) no. 29 (June 1969): 252–57. País' plans for restructuring the M-26-7, his opinions to Fidel on the general revolutionary strike imposed by Fidel on the urban underground to coincide with his landing, and the role assigned to the Sierra Maestra within the new framework.

"Carta de Frank País a Fidel Castro, July 26, 1957," *Pensamiento Crítico* (Havana) no. 29 (June 1969): 258–59. The last known letter by País to Fidel Castro In it he acknowledges receipt of Castro's July 21 letter and confesses he is being sought by Colonel José M. Cañizares. This letter proves Castro discussed the revamp-ing of the movement with País though it is not known what his position was.

"Frank País, en el decimoquinto aniversario de su caída," *Bohemia* (Havana), July 28, 1972, pp. 36–37. A concise account containing excerpted articles writ-ten by País for *El Mentor*, a publication of the National Teachers' School. They illustrate Frank's nationalistic ideas and the Cuba he envisioned.

"Frank País, sus últimos días," *Bohemia* (Havana), July 31, 1970, pp. 5–6. Useful article containing a letter of condolence by País to the family of Carlos A. Díaz, dated June 6, 1957, After reminiscing about the deaths of many friends, he confesses fear that those surviving the struggle will not fulfill their obligations to the people.

Pérez Concepción, Hernán, "Una jornada gloriosa de la juventud cubana," *Revista Universitaria de la Habana* (Havana), (1968), pp. 101–07. A descriptive account of the role played by the M-26-7 urban underground during the November uprising, contacts between the M-26-7 and the OA, the role played by the

FEU of Oriente and Havana, and chronological data on Frank and Fidel's early contacts.

Sarabia, Nydia, ". . . y mi honda es la de David," *Bohemia* (Havana), July 28, 1967, pp. 5–9. Sarabia displays heartening candor in tracing the historical background of Frank País' underground organization before it became fused with the M–26-7. Documented with excerpted letters and conversations of País.

Sarabia, Nydia, "Roberto Lamela, combatiente de la clandestinidad," *Bohemia* (Havana), January 19, 1968, pp. 10–13; 98. Illuminating passages on the early insurrectionary activities of members of the ANR led by Frank País, as well as members of the M-26-7 in Pinar del Río, Lamela was one of these who belonged to the ANR and had a long record of clandestine activities in El Caney, Oriente.

Torres Hernández, Lázaro, "Ambito de Frank País," *Bohemia* (Havana), July 30, 1971, pp. 64–69. Illustrative data on Frank's insurrectionary activities as well as his last known letter to Celia Sánchez on July 28, 1957.

José A. Echeverría and The Palace Attack

"Alocución de José Antonio Echeverría," *Combate* (Havana), supplement, March 13, 1959, p. 15, Unfinished address on Radio Reloj by the DR leader announcing the death of Fulgencio Batista, and calling on the people to join the students at Havana University.

"Ante los recientes sucesos 'una apelación mas,'" *DiaDirectorio de la Marina* (Havana) in *Combate* (Havana), supplement, March 13, 1959, p. 13, This pro-Batista newspaper issues a condemnation of the attack on what it termed "the president's home and the mansion of the Commander in Chief."

Benítez Rojo, Antonio, "Echeverría: a toda prueba," *Cuba Internacional* (Havana), October 1968, pp. 117–21. Candid portrait of Echeverría while a student at Havana University.

"Carta de Mexico," *Vida Universitaria* (Havana), no. 213, (September-December, 1968). pp. 30–31. A pact of unity between the M-26-7 and the DR signed by Fidel Castro and José A. Echeverría on August 31, 1956.

Cherson, Samuel B., "José Antonio Echeverría, héroe y mártir," *Bohemia* (Havana), March 15, 1959, pp. 98–99, 104. Written by the FEU's propaganda secretary, this is a political biography of Echeverría providing information on the major sequences of the students' insurrection.

Chomón, Faure, "Fundamentos tácticos del asalto a Palacio," *Bohemia* (Havana), March 13, 1970, pp. 66–72. Strategy of Palace attack is discussed by one of the leaders as well as the meaning of the "hit at the top" tactic.

Chomón, Faure, "El ataque al Palacio Presidencial," *Combate* (Havana), Supplement, March 13, 1959, pp. 2–6, 8–12. First of Chomón's several articles on the attack written immediately after the victory of the insurrection. Most of the information Chomón provides was obtained from Juan Pedro Carbó Serviá before the latter's death or April 20, 1957.

Cossio, Nicolás, "El ataque a Palacio," *Bohemia* (Havana), March 21, 1969, pp. 34–38. Personal account of Luis Goicochea's participation in the palace attack with ample information on the ensuing battle inside the building.

Cubela Secades, Rolando, "Recuento histórico de la lucha estudiantil universitaria," *Bohemia* (Havana) July 23, 1965, pp. 100–05. A general overview of the student movement's main political and insurrectionary activities by one of the DR leaders and guerrilla chiefs in the Escambray region.

"Declaración Pública de la Federación de Institutos, Escuelas y Academias Privadas de la República," March 1, 1956, mimeo. (authors' copy). A call by the FEAP to secondary students to join the DR and Echeverría in the struggle against Batista. A fiery document by Cuban youth.

Echeverría, José A., "Discurso en el Muelle de Luz," (Havana), November 19, 1955, (authors' tape). Speech before the SAR calling on the political parties to abstain from participating in the coming electoral farse, and for radical changes in the socioeconomic and political structures of the nation.

Echeverría, José A., "Sobre América Latina," *Vida Universitaria* (Havana), 20, no. 214, (January-March 1969), pp. 32–33. Speech delivered before a group of Latin American students on March 9, 1956 at Havana University. A useful document illustrating the internationalist thinking of the DR leader.

Echeverría, José A., "Constitución del D.R.," *Combate* (Havana), Supplement, March 13, 1959, p. 12. Echeverría unveils to the students and the public the creation of the DR, which is to wage a speedy insurrectionary struggle against the dictatorship and in which the university students are to bear the brunt of the actions.

García Olivares, Julio, "La operación Radio Reloj," *Bohemia* (Havana), March 15, 1959, pp. 10–12, 152–53. A participant in the Radio Reloj operation describes details on the strategy, names of combatants and the aftermath of the exit from the radio station.

Guma, José Gabriel, "Joe Westbrook Rosales," *Revolución* (Havana), May 7, 1965, p. 3. An account of Westbrook's political background and insurrectionary activities abounding in references and quoted passages from his writings.

Nuiry, Juan, "Una fecha y un hombre," *Bohemia* (Havana), March 11, 1966, pp. 50–53. Former leader of the DR recalls José A. Echeverría's leadership role in the student movement and the struggle against the dictatorship. Ample information on relevant insurrectionary activities.

Nuiry, Juan, "José Antonio Echeverría, Pensamiento y acción!" *Bohemia* (Havana), March 10, 1967, pp. 74–78. A chronology of José Antonio's activities as leader of the FEU and the DR until his death on March 13, 1957.

Páez, Tubal, "April 20, 1957: 7 Humboldt Street," *Granma Weekly Review* (Havana), April 30, 1972, p. 2. Concise biographical and educational data on the DR members who sought refuge at Humbolt 7 where they were killed by police Colonel Ventura Novo.

Puente Blanco, Jorge, "Preámbulo al trece de marzo," *Bohemia* (Havana), March 5, 1971, p. 89. Author witnessed the impact on the DR and FEU members of the news about the Pact of Mexico. Useful information about the steps taken to discuss the pact.

Rodríguez, Javier, "josé Antonio Echeverría y la clase obrera," *Bohemia* (Havana), March 10, 1967, pp. 52–55. A very informative article on DR labor activities connected with the sugar workers' strike in December 1955, Provided are details as to why the DR abandoned student demonstrations and began using student snipers to attack the police.

Rodríguez, Javier, "Visión de José Antonio Echeverría," *Bohemia* (Havana), March 8, 1968, pp. 50–56. The impressions of interviewed militants of the FEU and the DR who shared many insurrectionary and academic experiences with José

A. Echeverría. There is a section on Echeverría and the Cuban workers and his successful effort to rid the University of Havana of remnants of the action groups

Rodríguez Loeches, Enrique, "El ataque a Palacio según la tiranía," *Bohemia* (Havana), March 14, 1969, pp. 36–39. The first available evidence of Major Antolín Falcón's report to the Emergency Tribunal in Havana regarding the Palace attack. Loeches shows how the dictatorship charged the DR men with belonging to the action groups such as the UIR and the ARG. In addition there are numerous references to Major Falcón's denunciation of the attack against "the president's home."

The Strike: April 9, 1958

Alles Soberón, Agustín, "Los primeros periodistas cubanos en la Sierra Maestra," *Bohemia* (Havana), February 22, 1959, pp. 24–27, 134–37. A team of *Bohemia* newspapermen spent several days in La Plata in early March interviewing guerrilla leaders. Portrays Castro's expectations for a successful strike as well as his role in drafting the manifesto calling the M-26-7 to the revolutionary strike.

Cabrera, Luis Rolando, "Sagua la Grande escribió su nombre en la historia, el nueve de abril," *Bohemia* (Havana), April 5, 1959, pp. 36–38. A description of the main insurrectionary actions earned out by the M–26–7 young militias in Sagua, Las Villas province, the names of the participants and an estimate of those who died.

Castro Ruz, Fidel, "Carta a la Junta Cubana de Liberación, December 14, 1957," in *Che* (Havana Instituto del Libro, 1969), pp. 109–20. After criticizing the maneuvers of the Junta, and disengaging himself from it, Castro publicly discloses that the strategy of the M–26–7 is to rest on a general revolutionary strike to be carried out by the Civic Resistance Movement and National Workers' Front.

Castro Ruz, Fidel, "Manifiesto del Movimiento 26 de Julio al Pueblo," in *Pensamiento Crítico* (Havana) no. 28 (May 1969): 122–27. This manifesto, dated March 12, 1958, essentially committed the M-26-7 urban and rural branches to a general revolutionary strike against Batista's government. The manifesto contains 22 points. It was drafted by Fidel Castro and included the name of Faustino Pérez *pro forma*.

Castro Ruz, Fidel, "Discurso en Sagua la Grande, el 9 de abril de 1968," *Politica Internacional* (Havana) nos. 22–24 (1968): 73–77. Castro analyzes the events surrounding the call to strike and candidly reveals the numerical strength of his guerrillas, his position regarding the possibility of a coup should the strike succeed and the tactical differences between the urban and rural branches of the M-26-7.

Delahoza, Tony, "El régimen democrático estimulará los recursos de que dispone la nación," *Bohemia* (Havana), February 15, 1959, pp. 34, 146. Manuel Ray is interviewed in early 1959 by Delahoza who was in charge of the "Sección en Cuba" of *Bohemia* magazine. A brief resume is included on Ray's activities, revealing his position within the M-26-7 power hierarchy and how after the failure of the strike. Fidel Castro promoted him to the rank of M-26-7 coordinator for the city of Havana, a post previously held by Faustino Pérez.

"El 9 de abril de 1958," *Bohemia* (Havana), April 19, 1959, pp. 58–61, 111–12. The most comprehensive written account of the insurrectionary actions carried out in the city of Havana on the morning of April 9. Listed are the names of M–26–7 militia captains, Strategic objectives, excerpted passages of the May report, interviews with Faustino Pérez and Manuel Ray and an estimate of the dead.

Guevara, Ernesto "Che," "Editorial," in *El Cubano Libre* A.C. I, no. 6, (September 1957) as reprinted in "El Cubano Libre por toda la Sierra," *Cuba Internacional* (Havana) 2, no. 11 (May–June 1970): 112. Editorial written by Che Guevara wherein he calls for the burning of canefields and a general revolutionary strike. Clarifies the conceptual genesis of the strike.

Guevara, Ernesto "Che," "El Partido Marxista-Leninista," in Ernesto "Che" Guevara, *Obra revolucionaria*, (Mexico: Ediciones Era, 1967). pp. 566–68. Guevara contradicts himself and the evidence by stating that the April strike was decreed by the M-26-7 urban branch over and against the opinions of the Sierra Maestra leadership.

Guevara, Ernesto "Che," "Proyecciones sociales del Ejército Rebelde," Guevara, *Obra revolucionaria* pp. 285–87. Guevara analyzes why the April strike failed, attributing it to lack of organization, overestimation of the revolutionary reality and lack of contacts by the M-26-7 with the workers. He argues that the failure of the strike strengthened the M-26-7 by providing it with a sound interpretation of the country's realities.

Guevara, Ernesto "Che," "Notas para el estudio de la ideología de la Revolución Cubana," Guevara, *Obra revolucionaria*, p. 111. Guevara asserts that the numerous victories of the Sierra Maestra guerrillas from January to March 1958 were leading the people to a climax in their revolutionary activities. Based on these impressions. Havana posited the need to carry the struggle throughout the nation by means of a revolutionary general strike.

Guzmán, Arturo, "La acción," *Bohemia* (Havana), March 14, 1969, pp. 32–35. A detailed description of Sergio ("El Curita") González's insurrectionary activities as M-26-7 cadre of action and sabotage in Havana. Sheds light on the action-oriented philosophy of men like Sergio who died a useless death before, during or after the strike.

Hernández, Humberto, "Daniel: un comandante del pueblo," *Lunes de Revolución* (Havana), no. 19 (July 26, 1959): 26–28. Depicts "Daniel's" rise within the ranks of the M-26-7 movement, and his outstanding record of insurrectionary activities under Frank País and as national leader of action and sabotage.

Pérez, Faustino, "Carta de Faustino Pérez a los compañeros y compañeras de Santiago," *Lunes de Revolución* (Havana), no. 19 (July 26, 1959): 29, Pérez reveals that he coveted the position of national chief of action and sabotage but gave in to the Oriente militants who favored "Daniel." Essential in understanding the Sierra Maestra strategy concerning the growing strenth of the M-26-7 in the cities.

Pérez, Faustino, "La sierra y el llano: eslabones de un mismo combate," *Pensamiento Crítico* (Havana), no. 31. (1969): 68–93. Pérez's analysis of how the strike came about, reasons for its failure and his self-criticism concerning errors of interpretation He upholds Che's late theory that contacts with the PSP could have helped, that the scheduled hour should have been at 12 noon and admits that the urban movement misread the revolutionary reality. Originally, his speech was in August 1967.

"La huelga del 9 de abril," *Bohemia* (Havana), April 4, 1968, pp. 52–54. A general account of the strike as it took place in several cities of the nation. Included are the names of many of those who died as well as the reasons for its failure postponement of the scheduled date and secrecy.

Rodríguez, Javier, "9 de abril en Sagua la Grande," *Bohemia* (Havana), April 12, 1968, pp. 70–73. A detailed account of "Plan Sagua," the men who carried it out, the actions and targets chosen to paralyze the cities. This article complements an early one written in 1959.

Torres, Simón and Aronde, Julio, "Debray and the Cuban Experience," in Huberman, Leo and Sweezy, Paul M., *Regis Debray and the Latin American Revolution* (New York: Monthly Review Press, 1968), pp. 44–62. A skillfully argumented criticism of Regis Debray's analyses of armed struggle in Cuba during 1952–58. With subtle dialectical interpretations, the authors challenge Debray's knowledge of the Cuban insurrection, particularly his interpretation of the April 9, 1958 strike.

Second Front "Frank País"

Castro Ruz, Raúl, "Diario de campana, travesía dc la Sierra Maestra al segundo Frente Oriental 'Frank País'," *Lunes de Revolución*, (Havana), July 26, 1959, pp. 33–39; and August 3, 1959, pp. 15–16. Raúl Castro's campaign diary describing the march from Sierra Maestra to Sierra Cristal, in northern Oriente province. Valuable source for creation of the peasants' committees and their structure; groups found upon arrival; decision to leave Sierra Cristal; and the first military operations in the "Frank País" guerrilla front.

"XV Aniversario: II Frente Oriental 'Frank País'," *Verde Olivo*, (Havana), March 11, 1973, pp. 4–9. Excerpted passages of Raúl Castro's diary, and a useful map depicting some of the main military actions he mentions.

"El Segundo Frente Orienta. 'Frank País'," *Bohemia*, (Havana), March 14, 1969, pp. 22–27. This article contains a report signed by Raúl Castro, Belarmino ("Aníbal") Castilla Mas, second in command, and Vilma Espín, M-26-7 delegate of the Dirección Nacional, unveiling the constitution, structure and revolutionary policy of the Second Front in October, 1958.

González Guerrero, Roger, "Ofensiva general del ejército rebelde," *Verde Olivo*, (Havana), December 29, 1968, pp. 4–9. Useful account of the rebel army's general offensive toward the end of 1958 with some of the actions conducted by Raúl Castro's guerrilla forces.

"Graduación en el Segundo Frente 'Frank País'," *Bohemia*, (Havana), September 16, 1966, pp. 68–73. This is a detailed account of the politico–military composition of the 11 Front "Frank País," as well as a useful source for battles, casualties and military equipment.

Lupiañez, José, "Segundo Frente Oriental 'Frank País'," *Verde Olivo*, (Havana), March 9, 1969, pp. 9–10. Valuable source for the activities of the urban underground in connection with the opening of the II Front in northern Oriente province; role of René Ramos Latour, Vilma Espín and others is discussed as well as their visits to the Sierra Maestra mountains.

"March 10, 1958: 'Frank País' Second Front in Oriente," *Granma Weekly Review*, (Havana), March 19, 1972, p. 2, Concise summary of events in the II Front "Frank País."

Martínez Igarza, "30 de noviembre de 1956," *Verde Olivo*, (Havana), December 8, 1968, pp. 2–6. Article describing the events of the Santiago de Cuba uprising with some of the names of people who were later involved in the organization of the II Front "Frank País."

Rojas, Marta R., "Antes dc la retención de los norteamericanos," *Bohemia*, (Havana), June 28, 1959, pp. 50–53, 98–99. This article includes a series of reports by Raúl Castro to Vilma Espín and René Ramos Latour concerning the military conditions throughout the second guerrilla front in Oriente province from May to June 1958, Air force raids and lack of arms are discussed.

Rojas, Marta R., "El Segundo Frente Oriental 'Frank País'; operación antiaérea," *Bohemia*, (Havana), July 5, 1955, pp. 50–51. A discussion of Raúl Castro's military order No. 30 to detain American citizens in protest of United States support of the Batista regime. Valuable source of information for the second guerrilla front.

Sandino Rodríguez, José Q., "Operación captura de 29 infantes de marina de la Base Naval Norteamericana, de Guantánamo," *Bohemia*, (Havana), November 17, 1967, pp. 100–01. How a group of U.S. marines was captured by the rebels of Raúl Castro on their return to the Guantánamo Naval Base in protest of shipment of arms to the Batista regime.

"Segundo Frente Oriental "Frank País," *Verde Olivo*, (Havana), March 12, 1972, np. Brief historical description of the opening of the second guerrilla front from March 1, 1958 to Batista's downfall, Includes a map depicting the areas under the command of various rebel army leaders, with a list of columns and commanders.

"III Frente Oriental 'Santiago de Cuba," *Verde Olivo*, (Havana), March 11, 1973, pp. 10–12. Includes a map of the territory held by Major Juan Almeida's guerrillas differentiating areas of operations from Raúl Castro's guerrilla front; list of attacks carried out from March to December, 1958.

Vázquez Candela, Euclides, "El Segundo Frente Oriental 'Frank País', pequeña república insurgente," *Revolución*, (Havana), March 11, 1963, pp. 1, 8, Valuable source of information about the second front with names, dates and places connected to the campaign from March 10 to December, 1958.

Vázquez Candela, Euclides, "Recuerdos del II Frente, una concentración," *Combatiente*, (órgano del Ejército de Oriente). (Santiago de Cuba), March 15, 1965, pp. 1, 4, Important discussion of the worker's congress held at the II Front "Frank País," with comments about the guerrillas' enthusiasm and dedication.

Vázquez Candela, Euclides, "En el octavo aniversario cronología de la apertura del segundo frente," *Bohemia*, (Havana). March 11, 1966, pp. 36–37. Chronological list of dates and events leading to the organization of the II Front "Frank País."

Zamora, Cristóbal A., "Monte Rus: cuna de la revolución agraria," *Carteles*, (Havana), August 9, 1959, pp. 54–55. Data on the formation of the peasant committees by Raúl Castro, and the influence of the peasantry upon the rebel forces; there is also a discussion of the principles of the agrarian reform applied by Raúl Castro in northern Oriente province.

Camilo Cienfuegos: Northern Las Villas Province

Becalí, Ramón, "Las cartas de Camilo," *Bohemia*, (Havana), October 30, 1970, pp. 14–19. Letters from Cienfuegos to his family written while Cienfuegos was in the United States, Chicago and San Francisco, 1953–1956.

"Biografía de un héroe," *Informaciones de Cuba*, (Mexico), 16, October 1962, pp. 4–5. Biographical sketch of Cienfuegos including the period when he was exile in the United States.

"Breve recuento de la infancia del héroe de Yaguajay," *Bohemia*, (Havana), October 30, 1970, pp. 46–49. Interview with Cienfuegos' parents who offer data about his life and participation in demonstrations from 1954 to his death in 1959.

"Camilo Cienfuegos, trayectoria de un héroe," *Informaciones de Cuba*, (Mexico), November-December 1965), pp. 3–4. Summary of Cienfuegos' biography with excerpts from his campaign diary, comments about the battle of Yaguajay against regular army Captain Abon Ly, and his march on Havana.

Cienfuegos, Camilo, *Nuestro homenaje a Camilo Cienfuegos* (Havana: Municipio de La Habana, 1962). This pamphlet includes Cienfuegos' campaign diary in the form of a letter to Castro, dated October 9, 1958 reporting on the invasion of Las Villas province with detailed descriptions of every incident along the way. It also includes Cienfuegos' speech about Major Hubert Matos, in Camagüey, and his last speech on October 26, 1959.

"Diario de campaña de Camilo Cienfuegos," *Lunes de Revolución*, (Havana, No. 19, July 26, 1959, pp. 33–35. Cienfuegos' campaign diary describing his experiences as a guerrilla leader; the march from Oriente to Las Villas, and his arrival in northern Las Villas province.

Gálvez, William, "Rasgos de la campaña de Camilo Cienfuegos en Las Villas," *Bohemia*, (Havana), July 23, 1965, pp. 44–50. One of the most useful articles on the guerrilla campaign in northern Las Villas province, in 1958, covering the arrival from Oriente province, contacts with other guerrilla groups, sugar workers, command posts, strategists, the battle of Yaguajay, and valuable information about the structure of the guerrilla force and Cienfuegos' organizational capabilities.

Sánchez Pinarea, Antonio, "Días de lucha," *Verde Olivo*, (Havana), October 13, 1968, pp. 28–33. The author, a major in the rebel army, joined the insurrection at age 20; here he recounts his experiences in the Sierra Maestra and as a member of Cienfuegos' invasion column. Includes dates, names and places connected to the guerrilla campaign in northern Oriente province.

Sarusky, Jaime, "Camilo, el guerrillero y el politico," *Bohemia*, (Havana), October 27, 1972, pp. 58–65. One of the most complete articles on Cienfuegos' activities in northern Las Villas province, from his arrival on October 27, 1958 to Batista's downfall. Discusses guerrilla organization, the worker's committees, the congress of sugar workers, and organization of peasant militias. Supported by evidence from William Gálvez, Gerardo Nogueras and Ramón Simanca.

Cienfuegos Uprising: September 5, 1957

"Cienfuegos: símbolo de una barbarie," *Revolución*, September 7, 1957, p. 1. The first description of the uprising by the underground newspaper of the M-26-7.

Cubillas, Vicente, Jr., "Cienfuegos: un pueblo a la vanguardia de la revolución," *Bohemia*, (Havana), September 3, 1965, pp. 31–39. Historical description of the uprising with information about the role of the underground, and linkages between the M-26-7 and naval officers.

Cubillas, Vicente, Jr., "Cienfuegos: la gesta heroica del 5 de septiembre de 1957," *Bohemia*, (Havana), April 5, 1959, pp. 46–50, 87, Account of the battle between the recular army and the insurrectionists, from its inception to the defeat. Includes names of dead insurrectionists from the navy and discusses the impact of the events.

Pavón Tamayo, Roberto, "Cienfuegos, el 5 de septiembre de 1957, Cayo Loco y el levantamiento popular, una gloriosa página en la lucha de liberación," *Bohemia*, (Havana), September 9, 1966, pp. 54–57. Description of events leading to the uprising, role of the M-26-7, and significance of the uprising against Batista.

"San Román, González Brito y José María Pérez: 3 víctimas de la tiranía de Batista," *Bohemia*, (Havana), March 29, 1959, pp. 74–75, 92. How the leaders of the Cienfuegos uprising were captured, tortured and assassinated; the role of Esteban Ventura Novo. Jesús Blanco and Emilio Laurent of the police and navy intelligence respectively. The article includes excerpts from statements made to the revolutionary tribunals by captured navy officers in 1959.

Valdés Miranda, Jorge, "Acción revolucionaria del 5 de septiembre de 1957," *Bohemia*, (Havana), September 2, 1966, p. 74. A former naval officer involved in the organization of the uprising offers brief but valuable insight into the anti-Batista movement in the army and navy.

July 26 th Movement: Genesis and Ideology

Castro Ruz, Fidel, "Manifiesto a la Nación," in Marta Rojas, *Mártires dei Moncada* (Havana: Ediciones R, 1965), pp. 7–16. Letter written on December 12, 1953 to Luis Conte Agüero, a radio commentator and leader of the Ortodoxo Youth. Listed are the six basic laws the *Moncadistas* postulated as their ideological program.

Castro Ruz, Fidel, "Manifiesto No. 1 del 26 de Julio al Pueblo de Cuba," *Pensamiento Crítico* (Havana), no. 21, (1968); 207–20. Fidel unveils the creation of a revolutionary movement under the name of the 26th of July, and calls for immediate general elections in addition to stating a 15-point program of social, economic and political reforms. Written on August 8, 1955.

Castro Ruz, Fidel, "Manifiesto No. 2 del 26 de Julio al Pueblo de Cuba," *Pensamiento Crítico* (Havana), no. 21, (1968); 221–27. Fidel calls on the sympathizers of insurrectionary action to ready the people for the national uprising. He states that the only solution to the Cuban situation is revolution, not elections. Written on December 10, 1955.

Castro Ruz, Fidel, "The 26th of July Movement," in Rolando E. Bonachea and Nelson P. Valdés, eds., *Revolutionary Struggle 1947–1958* (Cambridge: MIT Press, 1972), pp. 310–19. Castro defends the insurrectionary thesis of struggle, analyzes the polarization of the Ortodoxo Party and asserts that the M-26-7 was born of the maze of political contradictions within that party. Written on March 19, 1956.

Castro Ruz, Fidel et. al., "El Manifiesto de la Sierra Maestra," *Bohemia* (Havana), July 28, 1957, pp. 69, 96–97. While supporting the idea of free, democratic and impartial elections, Castro proposes the establishment of a provisional government as well as a minimum program.

Castro Ruz, Fidel, "Carta a la Junta de Liberación Cubana," *Ché* (Havana: Instituto del Libro, 1969), pp. 109–20. Castro withdraws from the Junta asserting that the leadership of the struggle, mainly the M-26-7, is inside Cuba, while demanding for the M-26-7 the prerogatives associated with the armed forces and the police. He insists on the revolutionary general strike as the predominant thesis of the M-26-7, Written on December 14, 1957.

Hart Davalos, Armando, "Justificación de la Revolución y estrategia frente a la dictadura." *Lunes de Revolución* (Havana) no. 19 (July 26, 1959); 40. The author argues the generation of the 1950s differs from previous generations in its application of direct action to overthrow the dictatorship. The insurrectionary strategy of the M-26-7 is based on the revolutionary general strike, and it advocates the establishment of a civilian structure to carry out reforms. Written in November 1956.

"Historia de Bayamo," *Revista de la Universidad de La Habana* (Havana) 33, no. 192 (1968); 50–74. A descriptive account of how the Ortodoxo Youth was absorbed into the incipient insurrectionary movement then known as "Fidelista"; the role played by Frank País in its organization as well as the initiatives undertaken by Pedro Miret. Ñico López and Lester Rodríguez to have País' ANR join the movement.

Llerena, Mario, "The Unsuspected Revolution," manuscript. The best account of the ideological program of the M-26-7 by the serious and talented author of *Nuestra Razón.*

Llerena, Mario, "Manifiesto-Programa del Movimiento 26 de Julio," *Humanismo* (Mexico) 7, no. 52 (November–December, 1958); 9–40. The only cohesive and best thought-out statement of the ideological principles of the M-26-7. Written under the title *Nuestra Razón,* it advocated economic independence, national sovereignty, educational reforms, changes in the political structure, and a search for a distinct culture.

Oltusky, E., Franqui, C., and Hart, A., "Filosofía Revolucionaria," *Lunes de Revolución* (Havana), July 26, 1959, pp. 6–8. Vague in its pronouncements, this manifesto is indicative of the lack of theoretical substance in the initial ideological postulates advanced by some members of the Dirección Nacional of the M-26-7.

Pazos, Felipe and Boti, Regino, "Tesis económica del Movimiento 26 ce Julio," *Lunes de Revolución* (Havana) no. 138 (May 18, 1959); 40–47. The authors analyze the Cuban economy concluding that it is necessary to stimulate its growth, foster agricultural mechanization, increase domestic production and adjust foreign investments to the national interest.

Salado, Minerva, "Esta combatiente," *Vida Universitaria* (Havana) 19, no. 212 (July-Auugust, 1968); 39–40. Concise account of the role played by María A. Figueroa, an Ortodoxo grammar teacher from Santiago, in the formation of the first provincial cell of the M-26-7 in Oriente.

Underground Media

Alma Mater. Founded on April 12, 1952 as the paper of the FEU, this was the vehicle through which students informed the people about the struggle. It advocated a return to constitutional democracy by the violent overthrow of the tyranny. Edited in Havana, Miami and New York in Spanish and English depending on whether Havana University was open or closed. Agustín Tamargo of *Bohemia* magazine collaborated.

Son los Mismos. Founded in May 1952, this mimeographed paper edited by ABEL Santamaría and Raúl Gómez García advocated the ideas of the Ortodoxo Youth and was clearly anti-Batista.

El Acusador. Son los Mismos became *El Acusador* in the month of August, 1952. The name was suggested by Fidel Castro who became its chief ideologist and it chiefly challenged the conceptions of senior Ortodoxo politicians. Anti-Batista in tone and content.

Aldabonazo. Founded on May 15, 1956 as the official paper of the 26th of July, this publication was issued in Havana, and distributed to the provinces. It took its name from Eduardo R. Chibás' last speech. Among the collaborators was Carlos Franqui.

Revolución. Founded toward the end of May 1957 at the suggestion of Frank País, it became the official paper of the M-26-7 when *Aldabonazo* ceased publication in the same month. First issued in Santiago de Cuba, and then moved to Havana, it was the national journal of the M-26-7 concerned with reporting the struggle in the mountains and the cities. Carlos Franqui and Enrique Oltusky collaborated in the editing.

Vanguardia Obrera. Under the auspices of Frank País, the Dirección Nacional of the M-26-7 published *Vanguardia Obrera* as the vehicle of orientation for the working class. It had deep ideological content, publicizing the inequitable conditions of the working class and aggressively exposing the policies of Eusebio Mujal, secretary-general of the CTC.

Resistencia Cívica. Founded in the summer of 1957 under the auspices of Frank País, Armando Hart and others, and concerned with mobilizing professional sectors of the Cuban society who repudiated the regime, Mimeographed.

Sierra Maestra. Official publication of the M-26-7, published in Santiago de Cuba by Frank País, First named *Boletín informativo* and *Ultimas Noticias.* The National Teachers' School, and the University of Oriente served as hiding places for mimeograph and printing machines. Its contents included manifestos, war reports, editorials and propaganda work.

Sierra Maestra. Official publication of the M-26-7 in Exile, founded in 1958, Edited under the auspices of Mario Llerena, it printed important documents, manifestos, reports on the insurrectionary struggle and editorials. Issued in Miami, it reached as far as Peru. Costa Rica, Venezuela, Mexico and the northeastern section of the United States.

13 de Marzo. Official publication of the DR founded in late 1957. Included communiques, war reports, military actions, clandestine work and specific ideological orientations. Published in Havana. Tampa, New York, and finally at the Escambray Sierra.

Mella. Founded in 1944, it was the official paper of Socialist Youth. During the insurrection it was outlawed (after 1954). It criticized Batista chiefly through cartoons and caricatures. Articles were signed with pen-names. Contents ranged from movie reviews and cultural features to international briefs. It was not until the late fall of 1958 that *Mella* showed editorial combativeness against Batista.

Carta Semanal. Official publication of the PSP, reporting on political issues, international briefs stressing life in socialist countries. Like *Mella* the *Carta Semanal* began to combat Batista toward the end of 1958, specifically in the month of December 1958.

El Cubano Libre. Founded in October 1957 by Major Ernesto "Che" Guevara at the Hombrito, Sierra Maestra. A mimeographed paper aimed at editorializing the struggle in the mountains, in preparation for the general revolutionary strike, and offering summary war reports on battles and casualties. It reached the peasants in the Sierra and copies were distributed in Santiago de Cuba. An official publication of the Rebel Army.

Surco. Offical publication of the Rebel Army at the Second Front "Frank País," Founded in September 1958, it exchanged news with *El Cubano Libre.* Mostly, it reported on the progress of the Second Front.

Patria. Official publication of the Rebel Army in Las Villas province. Issued at Caballete de Casa. Escambray Sierra, by Major "Che" Guevara toward December 1958. Che's editorials centered on the economic dependence of Cuba, the Platt Amendment and foreign investments.

Milicianos. Official publication of the M-26-7 militias in Las Villas province edited by Major Ernesto "Che" Guevara in December 1958. Its first editorial, written by Che, states that the struggle of the M-26-7 was founded on the peasantry with the support of the city militias. He also called for subordinating the urban militias to the Rebel army.

Radio Rebelde. Radio Rebelde began functioning in Che's territory at Pata de la Mesa. The mobile station was furnished by the M-26-7 underground and began broadcasting in March 1958. Later, Castro used it in La Plata where it remained throughout the campaign. Other stations were set up at Escambray. It was a formidable vehicle of mass media information and orientation, reaching all of Cuba.

Index

Acción Nacional Revolucionaria, in Oriente, 42, 224

Action groups, origins, and the university, 9, 121

Acuña, Vilo, 104, 107, 276

Agramonte, Roberto, and Ortodoxos, 33, 39, 180; and foreign relations, 354

Alcalde, Oscar, 14, 18, 20

Almeida, Juan, 18, 261, 268, 315; and capture, 20; and Pino del Agua, 107

Ameijeiras, Efigenio, 105, 207; chief of police, 354

Anillo, René, Directorio, founder of, 55, 136

Arbenz, President Jacobo, 75

Arévalo, President Juan José, 194

Arms embargo, 270; arms received, 222; documents about, 221–2; impact of 222–3

Army (regular), and Granma expeditionaries, 96; at Pino del Agua, 106–8; strength in 1957, 105; discipline of, 257–8; conditions in 1958, 274; Corinthia, strategy against, 149–50; communique, 153; and Cienfuegos uprising, 162, fighting during, 163; and the peasants, 100; and Santiago uprising, 91–2; and Sierra Cristal, 150–2; and Sierra Maestra, 105; summer offensive, the peasants and, 255; strength, 258; summer offensive, aftermath, 283–4; positions (1958), 274; command problems, 257–8; ransoms offered by, 112; retreat to Estrada Palma, 259–61; small posts, 104; social composition of, 110–2; blockade in Camagüey, 302; and Santa Clara, strategy, 320; troop distribution, 325–6; conspiracies, within, 336

Auténticos, financial aid (see Carlos Prio), 54; internal problems, 33; Escambray guerrillas and, 204

Barquín, Ramón, 63, 336; conspiracy of the pure, 71; provisional command, 355; staff, 335; yields command, 356–7

Batista, Fulgencio, 13, 87, 275, 281–2, 340, 360; and armored train, 324–5; arms embargo, 222; campaign against Prio, 21; corruption, 35–7; elections and, 33, 34, 35, 316–7; situation, estimate of, 334; final orders to Cantillo, 340–1; firing Chaviano, 321; last supper in Cuba, 341–2; leaves country, 341–2 meeting with Cantillo, 338–9; and palace attack, 128, 129; preparations for strike, 228; promotions, 80, 81; and Santa Clara, 320; public rallies, 141; santeria and, 142; and Smith, 334–5; statement on Moncada, 19; sugar workers' strike, 61, 62; and Tabernilla, 333

Bayo, Alberto, 73; hired by Prio, 149

Betancourt, Ernesto, 269; and arms embargo, 222

Betancourt, Rómulo, 74, 194

Bianchi, Ricardo, 55; and the students, 138

Blanca, Luis, 194, 197, 198, 199

Blanco, Alberto, 198, 199, 200

Bosch, Juan, 74

Bueycito, battle of, 105

Camacho, Aguilera, Julio, 90, 92; and Cienfuegos uprising, 162

Cantillo, Eulogio, 281, 342–3; plan of attack, 256–7; military report, 271–4; strategy, 265; new plan, 273; strategy at Las Mercedes, 277; conspiracies,

339–340; and general staff, 336–7; meeting with Castro, 337–8; problems of command, 345; receives resignation, 342; reports to Batista, 338–9; surrenders command, 355

Carbó Servía, Juan Pedro, 54, 78, 79, 136, 152, 201; Santa Marta y Lindero, 54; Directorio, founder, 55; demonstrations, arrest, 59; hard liner, 55; palace attack, 125; inside the palace, 126, 128; wounded, 132; promoted, 133; death of, 139

Carnero, Manuel, 338, 340

Carrasco Artiles, Nelson, 90, 112, 281; and battle of "La Torcaza," 315

Carrillo, Justo, 183, 357; financial contributions, 73

Castello, Humberto, 53, 125; and palace attack, 121

Castillo Armas, Carlos, 51, 75, 335

Castro Ruz, Fidel, 14, 15, 21, 37–8, 90, 100, 101, 119, 149; birth and education, 9; action groups, 9–13; and Confites expedition, 10–11; in Colombia, death of Caral, marriage, 11; Orfila massacre, 11; and El Acusador, 13; initial group, 14; strength of, 16; briefing on assault, 16; calls for retreat, 18; capture of, 19–21; trial of, 21–5; laws proposed by, 23; complaints against Ortodoxos, 38; released from prison, 39; terrorism and, 40; and the Movimiento de Liberación Radical, 40; leaves Cuba, 42; invited by Echeverría, 54; and exile activities, 69–72; in Mexico, 73; meets Prio, 73; and Guevara, 75; and Pact of Mexico, 76–9; Granma landing, 95; La Plata, attack on, 98–9; Pino del Agua, 104–105; as benefactor of peasantry, 108; as romantic fighter, 110; ransom for, 112; agreement with Communists, 140; condemns palace attack, 141; survival of, 141; dependence upon underground, 153; fails to support País, 155; guerrillas as supportive force, 155, 156; coordinator of military affairs, 157; and Dirección Nacional, 157; and racial discrimination, 178; and Junta de Liberación, 182–3; and the exiles, 189; popularity of, 189; discipline imposed by, 205; complaints against, 205; and

the peasants, 213; and prisoners of war, 214; and elections, 225; and strike, 235; establishes control, 242; provisional government in Sierra Maestra, 254–5; and guerrilla strategy, 259; and machismo, 258; and santería, 260; at Las Mercedes, 275; strategic error by, 278; letter to Cantillo, 281; on army offensive, 284–5, orders to Cienfuegos, 293; letter to Cienfuegos, 303; on Guevara's role, 307; proposes plan to Cantillo, 337–8; calls general strike, 351; demands surrender, 352; moves on Santiago, 352; and presidential candidacy, 360; speech at presidential palace, 361; speech at Camp Columbia, 361

Castro, Raúl, 17; sentenced to imprisonment, 25; ransom for, 112; commissioned as leader, 205; march to the north, 205–6; and Second Front "Frank País," 205–9; and peasants' committees, 206; and intelligence service, 206; and bandits, 207; guerrilla strength (1958), 207–8; support from underground, and military organization, 208; communications network, 209, and air force, 209; and battles at Second Front, 208; and structural organization, 210–4; and budget 211–2; and agrarian bureau, 211; peasant congress, and military orders, 212–3; agricultural workers, and discipline, 214; and the communists, 242; and kidnappings 270; attack on Nicaro, 316; and guerrilla offensive, 318–9

Casuso, Teresa, 73, 76

Chaviano, Luis, 149; and Dominican expedition, 88

Cherson, Samuel B., objections to palace attack, 123, 128, 133, 136

Chibás Eduardo R., Ortodoxo leader, 12, 13, 17, 39, 360; opposition to Machado, 47

Chibás, Raúl. 39; trip to Sierra Maestra, 158, 225; and committee in exile, 255; meeting with Cantillo, 338

Chomón, Faure, student leader, 53; Directorio, founder of, 55; and personality, 55, 79, 92, 93; and Operation Rescue, 120–1; commando group, second in command of 125; arrives at university, 129; attacks Valls, 136;

Directorio, assumes leadership of, 140; rejects Castro's position, 186–9; strategy and activities, 189, 195, 198–9, 200, 204–5; meets Guevara, 304; president's committee and, 358

Cienfuegos, Camilo, revolutionary leader, 98, 107; attack on Pino del Agua, 107; social origins of, 111, 261, 268, 276; and El Salto, 293; breaking army blockade, 300–1; instructions from Castro, 303; organizational capabilities, 304; battle of Yaguajay, 322–3; and Barquin, 356; enters Camp Columbia, 355–6

Cienfuegos uprising, 160; contingency plan of, 161; fighting during the 163; casualties, 165

Committee in Exile, arms from the United States, 221–2; propaganda efforts, 221

Communists, informer for 138; network at university, 140; betrayals, 142; and the Moncada attack, 22; and the general strike, 240–2

Confederación de Trabajadores de Cuba (CTC), 244

Corinthia expedition, objectives of, 149–50; execution of expeditionaries, 152–3

Corpión, Ricardo, student leader, 63, 76, 120

Corzo Izaguirre, in Sierra Maestra, 265, 266, 268, 275

Cowley Gallegos, Fermín, and Corinthia expedition, 150–2

Cubela, Rolando, Directorio, leader of, 55, 79, 136, 195, 198; military leader, 203–4; leads guerrilla attack, 324–327; presents demands, 357

Cuervo Navarro, Pelayo, political leader of Ortodoxos, 12; opposition to Machado, 47; death of, 140, 141, 152

de la Aguilera, José María, bank employees, leader of, 230; and the general strike, 234

de la Torriente, Cosme, see Sociedad de los Amigos de la República

de la Torriente Brau, Pablo, opposition to Machado, 47, 73

del Rio Chaviano, Alberto, 40, 77; communique on Moncada attack, 19, 21, 112, 256, 257; and northern campaign, 284; in Santa Clara, 320

Díaz Balart, Mirta, 11

Direcciones Municipales, 156

Dirección Nacional Obrera, 156

Dirección Provincial Obrera, 156

Directorio Estudiantil Universitario, opposition to Machado, 47

Directorio Revolucionario, 48; founded, 54–6; goals and organization of, 55; ideology, 56–7; and SAR, 56–7; and sugar workers' strike, 60–4; manifesto of, 63; call for insurrection by, 63; statement to Inter-American Press Society, 80; underground strength, 81; underground activities of, 87; and the Santiago uprising, 92–3; estimate of the situation (1957), 119–20; and commando operation, 120; plans for palace attack, 121; and the Autenticos, 123; last meeting for palace attack, 125; headquarters for the, 125; commando groups, 125; inside the palace, 126–31; and retreat, 128–9; in Radio Reloj, 125, 128–9; in university, 131; executive meeting, 133–8; and general elections, 134; and the Communists, rejection of, 138; and the Second Front, 153; and the Tampa Declaration, 180; and Junta de Liberación Cubana, 180; basis for unity, 183–4; insurrectionary strategy, 189; overseas, 193–4; and guerrilla warfare, 195–6; expedition of, 196–8; and Cacahual ambush, 198; strength of guerrillas, 198; "La Diana" combat, 198; Escambray Manifesto, 198–200; and Unidad Educational "Joe Westbrook," 201; and workers' brigades, and peasants, 201–2; guerrilla structure, 201–2; and División Legal, 201; guerrilla encounters, 201; and agricultural cooperatives, 202; strength of (1958), 205; internal conflicts, 205; support to general strike, 232, 233; urban growth of, 286–7; and attack on Fomento, 322; patrols cities, 345

Dulles, John Foster, 226; and arms embargo, 222–3; report to President Eisenhower, 334

Dulles, Allen, director, Central Intelligence Agency, caretaker government formula, 334

Echeverría, José Antonio, childhood, 50; and university, 50–1; and Batista's coup, 51; student leader, 51; in Costa Rica, 51; and FEU elections, 52; and Santa Marta y Lindero, 52–4; and Directorio Revolucionario, 54–6; demonstration, wounded at, 57–60; and sugar workers' strike, 60–4; warning against U.S., 63; and revolution, 63; and student congress, 63; in Perú, Costa Rica and Mexico, 64; visit to Ceylon, 64; and Pact of Mexico, 76–9; and Castro, 120; and testament, 133; death of, 131; death, impact of, 87, 92, 93, 126, 152, 160, 189, 199, 204, 258, 358

Echeverría, Lucy, and Castro, 358

Eisenhower, President Dwight E., and kidnappings, 269

El Uvero, battle of, 104

Escalona, Derminio, 105; and Pino del Agua, 107

Espín, Vilma, and País, death, 166, 212, 226, 307

Estrada Palma, battle of, 104–5

Federation of University Students (FEU), 47; and José Tey, 56–7, 59; and financial support, 180

Federación Nacional Trabajadores Azucareros (FENETA), 61

Federación Obrera Nacional (FON), and general strike, 230, 233–4, 304

Fernández, Marcelo, social origins, 112; and *Nuestra Razón*, 175; appointed national coordinator, 225

Figueredo, Carlos, student militant, 125; and Directorio, 131–2, 194

Figueredo, David, and the Auténticos, 88; and Dominican expedition, 89

Figueres, José, supported by Echeverría, 51, 74, 76, 194, 228

Figueroa, María Antonia, underground militant, 41, 75, 88

Fleites, Armando, student leader, 194–5; and Directorio's guerrillas 198, 204

Fourth Guerrilla Front, 319

Gadea, Hilda, Guevara's wife, 74–5

Gálvez, William, 303; and worker's meeting, 304

Garcerán, Julio, 120, 343

García Lavandero, Eduardo, 136, 198–9, 200; death of, 201

García, Guillermo, 95; and attack on Estrada Palma, 104, 107; social origins, 112; ransom for, 112, 277

García Olivera, Julio, student militant, 92, 120–1, 128, 133, 136, 139

García Bárcena, Rafael, and the MNR, 14–5, 16; and Oriente students, 42

Gardner, Ambassador Arthur, 316

Gómez Wangüemert, Luis, student militant, 53–4, 92; and palace attack, 120.

Gómez García, Raúl, 13; and Moncada manifesto, 17

González, Ignacio, 131–2; and palace attack, 121; fails to support, 128

Granma expedition, 95

Grau San Martín, Ramón, former president, 9; presidential candidate, 33–4, 360

Guás Inclán, Rafael, 333, 341

Guerrillas, initial activities, 98–9; and desertions, 99; executions, the peasants and, 99–100; and aid from cities, 101–3; and growth of, 104; and Pino del Agua, 106–8 and guerrilla laws, 108, mystique of, 110; loyalty of, 110; leadership, social composition of, 110–2; and desertion, 119; and Santiago underground (1957), 153; and Second Front "Frank País," 153; and arms shipments, 228

Guevara de la Serna, Ernesto, 104,105, 107, 108, 205, 208, 235, 323; background of 74–6; and Granma landing, 98, 99, 101, 103; and attack on Bueycito, 104; and guerrilla education, 212; and the peasants, 213; and support to general strike, 225; on advantages of frustrated strike, 242; in Vegas de Jibacoa, 270–1; rescuing Castro, 280; on guerrilla organization, 283–4; promoted, 293; in Camagüey, report on conditions, 294; ambushed, 294; retreat at La Federal, 294–5; aid received, 297; and communications network, 259: crossing Jatibonico, 302–3; and guerrilla's conditions, 303; and Chomón, 304; conflict with Oltusky, 307–10; and Santa Clara, 318, Santa Clara, advance on, 320; attack on Remedios, and Sancti Spiritus, 322; at La Cabaña, 356

Guitart, Renato, role in Moncada, 15–6; and attack on Bayamo, 16–7; and Meeting with Echeverría, 50

Guiteras, Antonio, mentor of Joven Cuba, 17, 47, 49, 110, 199, 258

Gutiérrez Menoyo, Carlos, 10; revolutionary background, 53; and palace attack, 121; commando leader, 122, 125; inside the palace, 126–8; death of, 128

Gutiérrez Menoyo, Eloy, Directorio, chief of action of, 194–5, 198; insurrectionary strategy, 205; and Second Front of Escambray, battles of, 204–5; ideology and discipline, 205; guerrilla actions, 309, 310, 323–4, 353

Hart Dávalos, Armando, and the MNR, 14; social origins, 111; and *Nuestra Razón*, 178; secretary of education, 158, 189, 224, 354, 357

Hernández, Melba, 14, 17; sentenced to prison, 25, 39

Humboldt 7, 138

Ideology (M-26–7), Nuestra Razón, 175; nationalism, 177; and objectives of revolution, 177; and international policy, 177; and the United States, 178; and education, 178

Izquierdo, Orlando, in Sierra Maestra, 280–1, 337

Junta de Liberación Cubana, and united front, 180; objectives of, 181; problems within, 182–3; and electoralism, 181; and arms embargo, 222

Labrandero, Daniel M., revolutionary background, 53; escape and death of, 120–1

La Plata, attack on, 98–9; retreat and casualties, 99, landing at, 265, 267

Lazo, Mario, 317, 334

Lesnik, Max, and Second Front of Escambray, 204

Lima, Primitivo, and aid to Directorio, 132; and executive council, 194

Lucero Moya, Oscar, 42, 154; participation in strike, 229, 230, 231

Ly, Abón, in Camagüey, 294; resistance in Yaguajay, 322–3; and surrender, 323

Llerena, Mario, 41, 73, 100, 100; Nuestra Razón, author of, 175–6; and trip to Mexico, 175; and arms to Batista, 221, 225; and committee in exile, 255

Machado, José, student leader, 78; in Santa Marta, 52; and palace attack, 125, 126; inside the palace, 126; escapes, 128; promoted to executive council, 132–3; in hiding, 138; death of, 139

Márquez Sterling, Carlos, 33; attempt of the life of, 34; political participation, 316–7

Martínez Páez, Julio, chief surgeon of rebel army, 354; secretary of health, 354

Martínez Sánchez, Augusto, and Second Front's legal division, 211, 354

Masferrer, Rolando, as student, founder of MSR, 9; and communists, 10; charges Castro with murder, 11; meeting in Santiago, 154; and general strike, 233, and "tigers," 328, 342

Matos, Hubert, 317–8; and attack on Boniato, 326, 352

Matthews, Herbert, and Castro's guerrillas, 100

May Report, 238–40

Mella, Julio Antonio, student leader, 17; opposition to Machado and communists, 47, 49, 110, 258

Miñoso, Aispurúa, in Sierra Maestra, 277; attack on guerrillas, 278; promoted, 279

Miret, Pedro, 13, 16, 40–1; organization of movement, 42, 276

Miró Cardona, José, 183; and arms embargo, 222: prime minister, 354

Moncada, preparations for, 16–7; capture of survivors, 20

Mora Morales, Menelao, and plan for action, 53; meets Echeverría, 53; receives Auténtico support, 53, 54; and Cayo Confites, 53; as professional, 53; in the Triple A, 53; and the palace attack, 121, 126, 128, 134–5, 152

Mora, Victor, 105, 351, 352

Morgan, William, 198, 204, 324

Movimiento de Liberación Radical, ideology and organization, 40–1

Movimiento Socialista Revolucionario, 121

Movimiento 26 de julio (M-26–7), underground terrorism, 81; strategy for

Santiago uprising, 89; failure to support uprising, 92–3; executive meeting in Sierra Maestra, 100; aid to guerrillas, 103; internal organization, 157; reorganization (1957), 157–8; objectives of, 156; and the labor movement, 156; and the strike committee, 156; and militias, 156; and Cienfuegos uprising, 161–2; and Ortodoxos, 173–4; ideological tenets, 173–4; basis for program, 1733–4; ideological commission, 175; and Tampa Declaration, 180; and Junta de Liberación, 181; strength in Havana (1958), 227; national strength (1958), 228; and arms depots, 229; and Youth Brigade, 230; and urban growth and organization, 286–7

Mujal Barniol, Eusebio, and sugar worker's strike, 61, 62; position of, 244; and Ambassador Smith, 317, 342

Neugart, Fernando, 271; mission to Sierra Maestra, 281–3; proposal to end strife, 282–3; and army conspiracies, 288

Nixon, Richard M., and support of dictators, 355

Nuiry, Juan, student leader, 59, 78, 126; and resistance, 131

Nuestra Razon, 175–8

Oltusky, Enrique, 307; conflict with Guevara, 308; secretary of communications, 354

Organización Auténtica, military training of, 149; background to expedition, 149; and the Dominican army, 149; and involvement in Cienfuegos uprising, 160; and general strike, 232; refusal to support strike, 233; support to guerrillas, 257

Ortodoxos, internal divisions, 33; and elections, 34, 54; and guerrilla training, 104

Pact of Caracas, basis of, 264–5
Pact of Mexico, principles and objectives, 76–9
Pact of Pedrero, 305
País, Agustin, 42, 90
País, Frank Isaac, leader of M-26–7, 15, 41, 189, 208, 224, 230; childhood, 41;

and underground activities, 88; meeting with Castro, 89; effectives at the disposal of, 89; and Santiago uprising, 90–3; and aid to guerrillas, 103; and underground organization, 104; and assessment of underground forces, 119; and the Second Front, 153; arms, conflict over, 153; and organization of guerrilla front, 155–6; on the need to improve organization, 155; on democratic procedures, 155; on reorganization, 156; on workers' organization, 156; on unity of insurrectionary sector, 156; on the executive council, 157; and ideology, 157; and subordination of military to civilian, 158; closely persecuted, 159; death of, 160

País, Josué, 41; death of, 154
Partido Socialista Popular, (also communists), and militants, 287; and revolutionary unions, 305
Pawley, William D,, mission to Cuba, 334; and proposal to Batista, 335
Pazos, Felipe, 100, 101; trip to Sierra Maestra, 158, 181
Pena, Félix, 90, 92, 204, 208
Pérez Cougil, Leopoldo, 77, 302–3, 340
Pérez, Crescencio, 98; rescues Granma survivors, 100; social origins of 111; ransom for, 112
Pérez, Faustino, 158, 200; and the MNR, 14; and return to Havana, 100; social origins of, 111; and letter to Echeverría, 120; fails to support palace attack, 134; and Cienfuegos uprising, 161; as strike coordinator, 224; and contacts with churches, 227; and strike meeting, 229; abandons capital, 236; as secretary of stolen goods, 354
Piedra, Carlos Manuel, escorted to Columbia, 341; provisional president, 342–3; refuses to negotiate, 344
Pino del Agua, battle of, 104–5; second battle of, 106–8
Prío Socarrás, Carlos, 13, 221, 33, 34, 123, 135, 140, 204; and Montreal Pact, 15; as leader of DEU, 47; and Santa Marta, 53; as exile, 72; and financial contributions, 73, 76, 81; strength of expeditionary forces, 88; and agreement with Castro, 89, 90; and the palace attack, 123; and

Corinthia expedition, 149; and Pact of Caracas, 265; and Escambray guerrillas, 304

Providencia, 273, 276

Quevedo Pérez, José, and El Jigüe, 266–8, 336–7

Radio Rebelde, importance of, 258

Ramos Latour, René, 184, 206, 208, 224; as underground leader, 90; promotion of, 154; attack on Miranda sugar mill, 154; and Second Front, 153–4; and summer offensive, 276; death of, 278

Ray, Manuel, 234, 235; underground leader, 184; and general strike, 229; as secretary of public works, 354

Rebel Army, see also guerrillas, social composition of, 110–2; effectives of, 261; proclamation to regular army, 315

Rego Rubido, José, 77; and military junta, 334; informed by Cantillo, 337; in Santiago, 338; and letter to Castro, 352; appointed chief of army, 353

Revolutionary insurrectional Union (UIR), 9

Revolutionary Labor Directorate, 180

Revista de Avance, 47

Rivero, Agüero, Andrés, presidential candidate, 335, 341

Rodríguez, Abelardo, escapes prison, 120; and Operation Rescue, 120; and palace attack, 126

Rodriguez Loeches, Enrique, 53, 126, 133, 138, 198; and palace attack, 121; and resistance, 131; and Directorio, 199

Rodríguez, Fructuoso, 54; in Santa Marta, 52, 78; Directorio, founder of, 55; hardliner, 55; wounded, 58; arrested, 59; and underground activities, 125, 131, 136; arrives at university, 131; assumes Directorio's leadership, 132; death of, 140

Rodríguez Calderón, José, 161; and military· strategy, 274; and situation report, 341

Rodríguez, Lester, 13, 41, 90, 212; as organizer, 42; and Dominican expedition, 88; and Santiago uprising, 90; and Prio, 186–7

Rodríguez, Marcos, informer, 138–9; promoted to party membership, 138

Rodríguez, Silvino, and the MNR, 14; student leader, 59, 121, 263

Rojas, Ursinio, visit to Sierra Maestra, 287; and sugar workers, 304

Rosales, Héctor, student leader, 125, 139, 194

Salado, Marcelo, chief of action, 229; and general strike, 230; death of, 234

Salas Amaro, Alberto, 13; presidential candidate, 316

Salas Cañizares, José Maria, persecution of País, 154; in Santiago, 159, 160

Salas Cañizares, Rafael, 15; death of, 80

Salvador, David, sugar worker's strike, 61; labor leader, 231, 236

Sánchez Arango, Aureliano, leader of Triple A, 13; opposition to Machado, 21, 34, 47; and Triple A, 242, 305

Sánchez Mosquera, Angel, 99, 105, 111, 150, 268, 273, 276–7; in Santo Domingo battle, 261–2; and tactics, 275

Sánchez, Calixto, and palace attack, 121, 122; charged with treason, 134; and Corinthia expedition, 149

Sánchez, Celia, 95, 103, 111

Santamaria Cuadrado, Abel, and *Son los mismos,* 13; early involvement, 14, 15, 17; mission of, 18

Santamaría, Haydée, 39, 226, 255; sentenced to prison, 25; and *Nuestra Razón,* 178

Second Front "Frank Pais," 211

Second Front of Escambray, 205–6; structural organization, 234–40

Smith, Earl T., U.S. Ambassador, 316; and kidnappings, 269; and proposed solution, 316–7; recalled to Washington, 333–4

Sociedad de Amigos de la República, 56, 57; objectives of, 69

Sorí Marín, Humberto, social origins, 111; in Sierra Maestra, 282, 354

Sosa Blanco, Jesús, 112, 210

Sosa, Merob, 105, 112; in summer offensive, 268; fights Guevara, 271

Soto, Jesús, labor leader, 230; abandons fighters, 234

Sotús, Jorge, and underground, 90–1; reinforcements to Castro, 104; and Prio, 183

Strikes, basis for, 224–5; call for, 225; preparations for, 228; and the CTC, 228; and zones of operation, 230; and contingency plans, 231; and sabotage, 231; and objections to, 231–3; and Youth Brigade, 232–3; and bank employees, 233; and the provinces, 235; and aftermath, 235–44

Students, university, opponents of Machado, 47; protests against corruption, 47; generation of 1930, 47; Batista, and, 47–8; stages of resistance, 47–8; groups of, 49–50; and Moncada, 50–1; and student congress, 52; and underground, 52–4; and Directorio, 54–6; and demonstrations, 57–60; and sugar workers, 60–4; and Latin American dictatorships, 63; and the closing of the university, 64; and street action, 87

Suárez Suquet, Armando, in Camagüey, 294; at "La Federal," 294–5; and strategy, 297; and orders issued, 297–8, 302, 303

Sugar worker's congress, (1958), 304

Tabernilla, Francisco, Sr., 19, 87; changes in command, 105, 128–9; on national situation, 315, 316; interviews with Ambassador Smith, 333, 337–8

Tampa Declaration, basis for unity, 179–80

Tey, José, 15; and País, 42; meeting with Echeverría, 50; student demonstration, 59, 90; FEU's president, 59, 91; attack on police headquarters, 92; death of, 92

Torres, Félix, guerrilla force, 303; strength of, 304; Communist guerrillas, 242

Trejo, Rafael, martyr, 47, 49, 258

Triple A, support to guerrillas, 257

Trujillo, Rafael Leónidas, 63, 77, 87; role of, 88–9, 335

Tumbasiete Politcial School, 211; recruits, 212

Ugalde Carrillo, Manuel, 77; chief of operations, 105, 316

Underground, sabotage techniques of, 75; strength of the Santiago, 88; Havana's population and, 94; casualties, 96; in Bayamo, 104; expedition from, 104; blow to the, 153–4; Santiago, terrorism in, 154; terror-counter terror

cycle, 153; individualism of members, 200; challenge to Castro, 239–40; increased terrorism, 254; activities prior to summer offensive, 257; support from Bayamo, 257; growth of, 286; strength of, 287; increased sabotage, 287; support in Santa Clara, 327; and Batista's fall, 344–6; preparation to fight Barquin, 357

Unión Insurreccional Revolucionaria (UIR), 121

University Committee Against Racial Discrimination, 178

University of Havana, symbol of student resistance, 47; closing of, and the upper class, 94

Urdanivia, Tirso, palace attack, 121, 122; charged by Chomón, 136, 137–8, 149, 204

Urrutia Lleó, Manuel, Granma survivors, trial of, 173; presidential candidate, 186; revolutionary government, 255, 353; arrival to Havana, 357; and the DR, 358

Valdés, Ramiro, 14; at Moncada, 17–8; sentenced, 25, 98; and revolutionary justice, 99, 104; social origins of, 111, 261; at La Federal, 294

Valls, Jorge, in Santa Marta and Lindero, 52, 54; founder of the Directorio, 55; influence of, 55; conceptualization of struggle, 60–1; palace attack, 121, 122; charged by Chomón, 136, 137, 204

Varela Castro, Manuel, chief of La Cabaña, 355; yields to Guevara, 356

Varona, Manuel Antonio, 180, 263–4

Ventura Novo, Esteban, and demonstrators, 59, 80, 94, 132, 342

Westbrook Rosales, Joe, and the MNR, 14; Directorio, founder of, 55; student leader, 55; leading demonstration, 58; speech by, 78, 125, 131, 132; manifesto to the nation, 134, 136, 137; meets Marcos Rodríguez, 138; meets survivors, 137; visits Humboldt 7, death of, 139, 152

Wieland, William, 334

Wollam, U.S. Consul Parks, 269

Workers, attitude of, and contributions to underground, 286

CPSIA information can be obtained
at www.ICGtesting.com
Printed in the USA
LVHW04s2334190918
590752LV00011B/56/P